The AMERICAN RECORD

Images of the Nation's Past

The AMERICAN RECORD

Images of the Nation's Past

Volume Two

Edited by
William Graebner
State University of New York, College at Fredonia

Leonard Richards
University of Massachusetts, Amherst

Alfred A. Knopf New York

First Edition
987654321
Copyright © 1982 by Alfred Knopf, Inc.

Library of Congress Cataloging in Publication Data
Main entry under title:

The American record.

1. United States—History—Addresses, essays, lectures. 2. United States—History—Sources. I. Graebner, William. II. Richards, Leonard L. E178.6.A4145   1982   973   81-13748
ISBN 0-394-32216-9 (v. 1)   AACR2
ISBN 0-394-32665-2 (v. 2)

Manufactured in the United States of America

Cover design: Edward Vartanian
Text design: Teresa Harmon
Cover photo: © Elliott Erwitt/Magnum.

Preface

During the past two or three decades, the study of history in the United States has become in many ways more sophisticated and, we think, more interesting. Until the 1950s the dominant tradition among American historians was to regard the historian's domain as one that centered on politics, diplomacy, and war. Now, at the outset of the 1980s, historians are anxious to address new kinds of subjects, and to include whole sections of the population that were neglected in the traditional preoccupation with presidential administrations, legislation, and treaties. Women and children, the poor and the economically marginal, have moved much nearer the center of the historians' stage. And we have become almost as anxious to know how our ancestors dressed, ate, reared their children, made love, and buried their dead as we are to know how they voted in a particular presidential election. The result is a collective version of our national past that is more inclusive, more complicated, and less settled.

At the same time, however, the older version of the national history maintains a powerful hold over our imaginations. We still tend to think about the national past as a succession of "periods" whose basic characteristics remain political, constitutional, and military. Most introductions to American history are still organized around a familiar succession: the founding of the colonies; the American Revolution; the adoption of the Constitution; the Age of Jackson; the Civil War and Reconstruction; the Gilded Age; the Progressive period; the New Deal; and the Cold War.

In this book, we have attempted to bridge the gap between the old history and the new, to graft the excitement of modern approaches to history on an existing framework with which most of us feel comfortable. But where this existing framework was once an end in itself, we have taken it as a beginning, as a kind of grounding for the richness and variety of historical experience. Most of the familiar topics are here, together with a range of materials not found in most introductory texts. We have included essays on the early colonial settlements, the Revolutionary War, the Founding Fathers, imperialism, the Second World War, and the Eisenhower presidency. But, by joining these essays to the primary sources, we have tried to make it possible for teachers and students to see links between the early settlements and European poverty; between the Revolutionary War and the colonial class structure; between the Founding Fathers and the physical layout of the nation's capitol; between imperialism and the founding of the American Boy Scouts; between World War II and patterns of child-rearing; between the Eisenhower presidency and the emergence of rock-'n'-roll.

Throughout, we have attempted to incorporate materials with *texture*: documents that are not only striking, but that can be given more than one interpretation; photographs—many never before published—that invite real examination and discussion; tables and charts that have something new and interesting to contribute; and essays, like Frederick Jackson Turner's on the frontier, or Carl Becker's on the American Revolution, that have stood the test of time.

From the beginning, we realized that our approach to American history would require adjustment for many students and teachers. It was one thing to expect a student to place FDR's first inaugural address in context of New Deal politics, yet quite another to expect that student to do the same with a piece of popular literature from the 1930s. For this reason, we have offered a good deal of guidance. Introductions to primary and secondary materials are designed not just to provide basic background information, but to suggest productive avenues of interpretation. Introductory essays and questions are intended to create a kind of mental chemistry in which students will have enough information to experience the excitement of putting things together, and yet not so much guidance that conclusions become obvious. To the extent that we have succeeded in creating this chemistry, we also issue this *caveat*, especially for students, but also for the comfort of their teachers: for many of the problems posed in this book, there are no obvious and simple solutions. This is a book that teaches the skill of making sense out of one's whole world. That process yields answers only grudgingly, but the answers are all the more worthwhile.

Like every text, this book is a product of the historical profession. In some cases, the work of fellow historians is formally acknowledged and credited. Other scholars may recognize an interpretation, analysis, or idea as a product of their own work. As for putting the book together, R. Jackson Wilson, who supervised the project from start to finish and helped draft some sections of the book, deserves a special thanks. We have also benefitted substantially from the comments of reviewers commissioned by Alfred A. Knopf. The task of securing permissions to publish materials in copyright proved of herculean proportions (for the second volume, particularly); we are grateful to Dianne Bennett and Mary Notaro for helping us with it.

William Graebner
State University of New York, College at Fredonia

Leonard Richards
University of Massachusetts, Amherst

Contents

The
AMERICAN
RECORD

Images of the Nation's Past

CHAPTER 1

Reconstruction

When it was first coined in the crisis months between the election of Lincoln and the beginnings of the Civil War, the term "Reconstruction" meant simply the reunification of the nation. By the time the war ended in 1865, the idea of Reconstruction was more complicated: it now meant more than simple political re-establishment of the Union; it meant reconstructing the South, refashioning its social and economic life to some degree or other. For the freedmen—many only days removed from slavery— Reconstruction would soon come to represent freedom itself. Even in 1865, most Southern blacks realized that in the absence of a thoroughgoing Reconstruction, in which freedmen were recipients of land as well as the right to vote, freedom would mean only a new kind of economic oppression.

Twelve years later, in 1877, many people, North and South, realized that Reconstruction had ended. But by then the term had taken on intense moral meanings. To most white Southerners, it was a term of resentment, the name of a bleak period during which vindictive Yankee politicians had tried to force "black rule" on a "prostrate South." Tried and finally failed, for the South had in the end been "redeemed" by its own leaders. Slavery had ended, but at least white supremacy had been firmly re-established. To perhaps a majority of whites in the North, Reconstruction had over the years become a nuisance, and they were glad to let go of it, to reaffirm the value of the Union, and to let the bitter past die. There were other Northerners, however, who looked back from 1877 to twelve years of moral failure, of lost opportunities to force freedom and equality on an unrepentant South.

There were hundreds of thousands of freedmen who experienced this "moral failure" in very real ways. Instead of farming their own land, they farmed the lands of whites as tenants and sharecroppers.

1

Far from benefiting from meaningful suffrage, most blacks were denied the franchise, and those who continued to exercise it did so in a climate of hostility hardly conducive to political freedom. Nonetheless,it was possible for blacks to look back positively at the Reconstruction experience. The 1866 Civil Rights Act granted the Negro both citizenship and all the civil rights possessed by whites. When the constitutionality of that statute seemed in doubt, Congress made ratification of the 14th Amendment (accomplished in 1868) a precondition for Southern restoration to the Union. In theory, that amendment made the federal government the protector of rights that might be invaded by the states. Under "Radical" reconstruction, carried out by Congress after 1867, hundreds of thousands of Southern blacks voted, and many held high elective office. And in 1875, when whites had re-established their authority throughout most of the region, a new civil rights act "guaranteed" blacks equal rights in theaters, inns, and other public places. If in the end it proved impossible to uphold these laws, for many, the amount and quality of the legislation passed suggested a substantial commitment to the freedman.

Reconstruction—both as a concept and as a period of history—had other faces, too. For many, it gradually became a synonym for corruption. In 1871, George Jones of *The New York Times* began a famous exposé of political corruption in the "Tweed Ring," the political machine of the city "boss," William Marcy Tweed. It quickly became apparent that Tweed and his cohorts had systematically plundered the city. The next year, a second shock came when a number of prominent officials—including several figures close to President Grant—were indicted for peddling their political influence to the Union Pacific Railroad in return for shares in the railroad's construction company, the Crédit Mobilier. Even more shocking, in a way, was the indictment of the nation's leading minister of the Gospel, Henry Ward Beecher, on charges of adultery with Elizabeth Tilton, a wealthy member of his congregation.

But, alongside the awareness of corruption, there was a sense of possibility, a sense that options were open now in ways they had not been before—and might not be again. The Civil War had accelerated a number of tendencies in American life, and it was difficult for most Americans to predict what the outcomes would be. In both the North and the South, loose and decentralized political systems had been forced by the war to accept the centralization of power. Both sides used military conscription. The Confederacy, by 1864, was even forcibly seizing foodstuffs and other supplies for its armies. The North levied the first income tax. And Congress passed a program of legislation designed to promote economic growth. For those Republican leaders who came to be called "Radical," Reconstruction was a chance to use federal power in peacetime to foster the creation of a new kind of society in the South.

On the other hand, there were countervailing tendencies, impulses toward the restoration of local control and voluntary organization. The draft itself had provoked four days of deadly rioting in New York in 1863. In the South, even before the war ended, state and local politicians resisted centralization of power, whether in Washington or Richmond. Whites moved as quickly as they could to establish local control of the "race problem" through "Black Codes" like the Mississippi version included in this chapter.

Reconstruction was more than a chronological period in the history of American politics. It was a field of force in which three very general concerns converged: How should the South be treated? How could corruption be controlled and a tradition of political virtue in which most Americans believed be restored? And how would choices be made between a conflicting pair of values involving, on one side, centralization, efficiency, bureaucracy, and regulation, and, on the other, individuality, localism, and voluntary organization?

MICHAEL LES BENEDICT

Andrew Johnson and the Problem of Reconstruction

As they have done so often, Americans seemed to act out all the issues of Reconstruction by focusing them on the presidency, and making the conflicting images of that office the issue. Had Lincoln survived, the drama might have been played out around him. As it happened, his death brought Andrew Johnson into the White House. And Johnson was a man on whom those who wanted a radical reconstruction of the nation's life could focus their agitations. They called him corrupt and a drunkard. They accused him of a weak response to the South's perfidy (he was, after all, a Tennessean). And he appeared to be a figure from the past that many Americans were ready to leave behind. His heroic ideals were the yeoman farmer and the village artisan, not the industrialist. To him, with his reverence for Andrew Jackson, the idea of government power meant only "monopoly" and "special interests."

The hostility to Johnson, and to what he seemed to represent, had enough momentum to bring about impeachment by the House of Representatives. But in 1868, by a margin of only one vote—and just months before his term would expire, in any case—Johnson survived the crucial trial in the Senate.

In the following essay, historian Michael Les Benedict presents a careful analysis of the beginnings of the conflict between President Johnson and the Republicans in Congress. Benedict's view is that the Republicans were not stampeded by a radical faction, but tried hard to find a compromise position that would satisfy both them and the president. As you read the essay, you may want to think beyond the politics of the situation, to try to see what basic assumptions about politics, government, and Reconstruction lay behind both the congressional Republicans' and the president's positions. If Benedict is correct, if the Republicans were reasonable and cautious, does Johnson become the "radical"? Or should we see him as simply the representative of an older (and stubborn) American order which found its center in localism, limited government, and an agrarian-based individualism? On what grounds, if any, did Johnson deserve to be impeached?

At the heart of the only impeachment of a president of the United States lay the crisis of American Reconstruction after the Civil War. In the dry pages of history books, the reality of that crisis sometimes fades. The danger through which the Union had just passed seems to pale. The Union victory appears foreordained, secure reunion certain. But the generation of Northerners who shed their blood or watched loved ones and friends spill theirs had no such assurance. The danger of national disintegration had been all too real, the sacrifices to prevent it great. When the war ended, loyal Americans faced real traitors, people who had fought gallantly and bitterly to rend the fabric of the nation. To understand the spirit of the Reconstruction crisis, one must grasp the reality of civil war, recognize that the generation of Americans caught up in the web of Reconstruction actually lived, actually confronted a situation, today

Abridged selection from *The Impeachment and Trial of Andrew Johnson* by Michael Les Benedict, reprinted with the permission of W. W. Norton & Company, Inc. Copyright © 1973 by Michael Les Benedict.

totally alien to us, where countrymen killed countrymen, where political power involved more than the simple control of administration. In that charged milieu, political differences inevitably transcended mere questions of policy in which well-spirited, restrained disagreement was possible. In the crisis of Reconstruction the future of the nation hung in the balance.

But with all that depended upon a secure Reconstruction, Americans were singularly ill equipped to cope with the problem effectively. By 1865 most Northerners, especially Republicans, had come to identify security for the Union with tangible, fundamental change in southern society, particularly in black-white relations. Most important, Republicans insisted upon protection for former slaves in their new freedom. Yet these same Northerners, including Republicans, displayed a remarkable reluctance to force these changes on the South through the power of the national government. On the part of those who had adhered to a Jacksonian philosophy of limited government before the war, this hesitation is not surprising. But the reluctance to alter fundamentally the relations between the state and national governments also affected former Whigs. At first many Republicans hoped Southerners themselves would inaugurate the necessary changes voluntarily, but it quickly became apparent that even modest change in southern society (beyond the mere abolition of slavery) would require the national action so many Northerners wanted to avoid. So Republicans in 1865 were faced with an intimidatingly difficult problem, even without further complications. But further complications arose—in the person of the seventeenth president of the United States, Andrew Johnson. If the critical importance of Reconstruction for the security of the nation provided the kindling for the impeachment crisis, it was the torch of Andrew Johnson's personal character that ignited the flame.

Raised in poverty in North Carolina, his father dead, his stepfather unwilling and probably unable to improve the family fortunes, Johnson had acquired no formal schooling. But he was remarkably and overpoweringly ambitious. His life, wrote his old enemy, Oliver P. Temple, "was one intense, unceasing, desperate, upward struggle," and the grinding poverty of his youth appears to have been a torment to him not only because of financial hardship but also because of the constant social humiliation he felt he endured. Johnson was embarrassed by the deficiencies of his education all his life, but he overcame them as much as possible by force of his incredible will. Apprenticed to a tailor at the age of fourteen, he taught himself to read with the aid of the foreman of the shop; he was over twenty when his wife taught him to write. But he never acquired the breadth and suppleness of mind that formal training might have developed. Complex problems frustrated him, and he sought refuge from them in general rules to govern all situations. "There is nothing like starting out on principle," he told a confidant while he was president. "When you start out right with principles clearly defined you can hardly go astray." . . .

. . . Elected mayor of Greeneville, state representative, congressman, governor of Tennessee, and senator, the former tailor's apprentice became the most powerful politician of his state. Allied to the Democratic party, he appealed to its radical wing, espousing its most egalitarian, democratic tenets.

As the only southern senator who had remained loyal to the Union in 1861, Johnson was appointed military governor of Tennessee by Lincoln, who then encouraged the Union-Republican party to make him its candidate for vice-president. When Lincoln died, Andrew Johnson, self-educated poor boy from North Carolina and tailor from Tennessee, became president of the United States.

In politics and government, the rules Johnson applied to difficult questions were those he had developed as a strict-constructionist, economizing, Locofoco Jacksonian Democrat. His Jacksonian devotion to limited government and his tight-fistedness with the people's money were so closely interwoven that they defied separation. Johnson's first term in the Tennessee legislature ended in disastrous defeat because he so rigidly opposed state-supported improvements for his region. In Congress, he waged resolute warfare against appropriations for the Smithsonian Institution, tried to reduce the salaries of government white-collar workers, fought to limit the number of clerks in the House, and voted against increasing pay for soldiers during the Mexican War. He spoke against appropriating money to help famine-stricken Ireland and opposed increases in the size of the standing army. On both constitutional and financial grounds, Johnson even opposed a congressional appropriation to pave the streets of the District of Columbia. Johnson set his direction on any public question by his twin guideposts—opposition to governmental "extravagance" and rigid adherence to his own strict interpretation of the Constitution. "I have, during all of my political life, been guided by certain fixed political principles," he once remarked. "I am guided by them still. They are the principles of the early founders of the Republic, and I cannot certainly go far wrong if I adhere to them, as I intend to." . . .

Lincoln's death elevated Johnson to the presidency at a time of crisis. Immediately, the new president faced the complexities of Reconstruction, and his background and principles led him to set a policy that most Republicans eventually repudiated. In following his program, Johnson would ignore some congressional enactments and violate the spirits of others.

Johnson shared with other border-state Unionists a conception of the "fruits of victory" that differed markedly from that of northern Republicans. Concerned only tangentially, if at all, with the well-being of black Southerners, Johnson took victory to mean the return of the southern white masses to loyalty and the humiliation of the southern aristocracy that had misled them into treason. Inheriting from Lincoln the bare outlines of a Reconstruction policy that seemed to pursue a similar goal, Johnson fixed on a program of amnesty for all Southerners who would swear future loyalty to the Union, with the exception of the southern political and economic elite. Those "aristocrats," the men who had attacked him all his life, and most bitterly when he alone of southern senators remained loyal to the Union, would have to petition him personally for pardon.

Beyond a return to loyalty, Johnson demanded what must have appeared to him—as a Southerner—to be significant concessions. In state constitutional conventions, delegates elected by all whites who had received amnesty would have to amend their constitutions to abolish slavery, ratify the Thirteenth Amendment to the United States Constitution, repudiate all debts contracted by the Confederate governments, and nullify the secession ordinances. Having done that, Southerners could organize elections to establish regular civil governments. To Johnson, the abolition of slavery itself must have seemed a radical step, one that overturned the social and economic system of generations. His later actions indicated that he found it almost inconceivable to require more.

As reports came in of renewed southern loyalty and of mass participation in the state elections held in much of the South in the fall of 1865, and as applications for pardons flooded his offices, the President became more and more convinced of the basic success of his policy. . . .

When the 39th Congress of the United States assembled in December 1865, therefore, Johnson believed the process of restoration nearly over. Apathetic to the desires of northern Republicans to protect blacks in their liberty, he felt no need for further interference in the internal political and economic structure of the southern states.

The Republicans

Historians have had a great deal of trouble in trying to understand the nature of the so-called "Radical Republicans," who opposed Andrew Johnson's Reconstruction policy and ultimately replaced it with one of their own. Until recently, they were believed to represent the opinions of only a minority of Republicans, and historians had difficulty explaining how these "radicals" could exercise enough power to take control of the party from the President or maintain the two-thirds majority required in Congress to pass legislation over presidential vetoes and propose constitutional amendments to the states. In general, historians credited this feat to Johnson's ineptness, the strength of personality of the leading Radicals, and the power of the party "lash" and caucus system in Congress.

But in the past decade scholars have revised their interpretations. It has become apparent that the term "radical" has been poorly defined and that the concept needs reassessment. The denomination "radical Republican" was used by contemporaries during the Civil War to denote those Republicans who favored a more active antislavery policy than that followed by President Lincoln. Even after Lincoln promulgated the Emancipation Proclamation, those differences remained, as "radicals" pressed for a Reconstruction policy that would guarantee the permanence of abolition and minimize the danger of continued Rebel political dominance in the South. But when Andrew Johnson vetoed key legislation in 1866, he broke not with these "radicals" alone but with nearly the entire Republican party, radical and nonradical. Johnson and his primarily Democratic allies called all these Republicans "Radicals" in an attempt to discredit their opponents, and perhaps also because they were too single-minded to recognize the real differences among them. In turn, most Republicans defiantly accepted the appellation. . . .

As the 39th Congress convened in December 1865, most Republicans felt that President Johnson had effectively precluded any fundamental alteration of the structure of southern society by his Reconstruction policy. Most Republicans, radical and nonradical, would have preferred at least the enfranchisement of black Southerners in an effort to enable them to protect their newly won freedom; all of them were unhappy that former Rebels were emerging as the strongest political force in most of the governments created by Johnson's authority. Few of those governments displayed any concern for the protection of black rights, and most of them openly limited blacks to a legally sanctioned second-class citizenship. But the President had committed himself to the restoration of these states, and although many Republicans believed that Johnson had exceeded his authority, usurping the functions of Congress in Reconstruction, they knew that to proceed against his clear wishes meant dividing the party and probably restoring the Democrats to power. Most Republicans simply refused to risk it.

To be sure, some radicals . . . urged fellow Republicans to ignore political expediency and at least impose black suffrage on the southern governments. . . . A few others still openly hoped that Congress would repudiate Johnson's work and reorganize the South as United States territories. But as a whole, Republicans concluded that it was politically impossible to force fundamental change by reordering power within the southern states, even by the rather limited mode of imposing black suffrage. . . . Republicans instead reluctantly decided to offer national protection for the rights of southern loyalists [most of them blacks] against their own state governments. . . .

. . . Careful to consult the President [Senator Lyman] Trumbull told senators that Johnson did not object to this mode of guaranteeing freedmen's liberties. Republicans, confident that a rupture with their president had been avoided, passed the Freedmen's Bureau and Civil Rights bills by overwhelming margins, only two Republicans voting against the first and nine against the second in both houses of Congress.

But Trumbull and the other nonradical Republicans had misplaced their confidence in Johnson. Sharing Republican reluctance to expand permanently the powers of the national government, he did not share their commitment to black rights that made that distasteful expansion appear necessary. Even if he had, it is questionable, given the rigidity of his mind, whether he could have deviated from principles to which he had adhered so firmly. Johnson, a strict-constructionist, economy-minded Jacksonian, judged the two bills by the general principles he had so painstakingly developed decades earlier: the Freedmen's Bureau bill would require a prodigious appropriation, "more than the entire sum expended in any one year under the Administration of the second Adams." Both propositions violated the Constitution, repudiating the proper role of the national government in the federal system. "In all our history," the President wrote of the Civil Rights bill, " . . . no such system as that contemplated by the details of this bill has ever before been proposed or adopted. . . . It is another step, or rather stride, toward centralization and the concentration of all legislative powers in the National Government." Resolutely, he vetoed both measures.

Republicans reacted with frustrated outrage. The President had left them no avenue at all to protect southern loyalists. He had exercised questionable powers in the first place. He had scorned Republican attempts at conciliation. He had misled them as to his intentions, indicating his approval of the legislation he had vetoed. Their denunciations were bitter.

The intensity of the reaction shocked Johnson at first. Painfully, he appeared to hesitate and reconsider. Rumors spread that compromise was possible. For Johnson this must have been a difficult process. His narrow mind was accustomed to acting directly upon general principles; reevaluation was foreign to his nature. He must have suffered anguishing self-doubt. Was his unusual reflectiveness a statesmanlike attempt to discover light to illumine a murky problem of constitutional principle or merely a cowardly flinching from duty in the face of surprisingly strong pressure? "Courage" was Johnson's watchword, and these questions must have troubled him.

When he made his final decision, it came with all the force of that tremendous will: he could not bend his long-held convictions. "Sir," he exploded to his secretary, William A. Moore, "I am right. I know I am right and I am damned if I do not adhere to it." Inflexibly, without doubts, Johnson proceeded to carry out his determination, launching a series of biting attacks upon the party that had elected him, rising to the occasion as if he were still on the hustings in Greeneville, Tennessee. The sizzling personal hostility Johnson always directed against opponents now scorched Republicans as it had southern aristocrats before them. Charging that they had threatened his life, he compared Republicans to the traitors who had fought for the Rebellion. Both the Southerners and the Republicans, who refused to recognize the restoration of his southern governments, were disunionists and deserved equal disapprobation. Indeed, the Republicans had always been as bad as the secessionists: one stood "for destroying the Government to preserve slavery, and the other to break up the Government to destroy slavery." His former political allies were "a common gang of cormorants and blood-suckers, who have been fattening upon the country. . . ."

Such unbounded personal vindictiveness stunned Republicans. Perhaps appropriate on the stump in Tennessee, Johnson's fierce attack humiliated and outraged them. One of the articles of impeachment would charge him with attempting "to excite the odium and resentment of all the good people of the United States against Congress . . . [through his] intemperate, inflammatory, and scandalous harangues," conduct that was "particularly indecent and unbecoming in the Chief Magistrate of the United States. . . ."

Many radicals had hoped that Republicans would adopt more extreme measures when it became clear that it was impossible to conciliate the President with conservative legislation; they were sorely disappointed. With congressional elections pending and Johnson going over to the opposition, most Republicans became even more committed to a fundamentally conservative course. They dared not risk alienating the conservative elements who might follow the President out of the party. In essence, Republicans decided to continue the policy they had evolved in their efforts to satisfy Johnson. They still refused to impose black suffrage or to force change in southern society in other ways. Instead, they persevered in their development of measures to enable the national government to protect citizens' rights. Adhering to the Civil Rights bill and passing a new Freedmen's Bureau bill over a presidential veto, Republicans completed their program by proposing a constitutional amendment* which forbade state action that denied citizens' fundamental rights or subjected them to discriminatory laws. The southern state governments erected under Johnson's authority need only ratify that amendment and repeal their discriminatory laws. Upon doing so, they would be restored to normal relations in the Union.

The manifest conservatism of the Republican program blunted Johnson's appeal to the conservative elements of the Republican party. Wavering Republicans, like Governor Jacob D. Cox of Ohio and the editor of the New York *Evening Post*, William Cullen Bryant, returned to the fold. Johnson's own cabinet split over his determination to form a coalition with Democrats to oppose Republicans in the 1866 congressional elections. Three of the department heads resigned. . . .

The decisions of leading Republican conservatives reflected the decision of Republican voters as a whole. With Republican campaigners emphasizing the moderation of their Reconstruction program, the party's candidates overwhelmingly defeated the opponents put forward by the Democratic-Johnsonian coalition.

In the face of such a decisive repudiation, another man might have acquiesced in the Republicans' policy of restoration. Had Johnson done so, at least some of the southern governments might have accepted Congress's terms and returned to normal federal relations. Tennessee had already followed this course in July 1866. Movements to "accept the situation" as a distasteful necessity developed in Alabama and Virginia, but Johnson aborted them with private and public exhortations to remain firm. As a result, every southern state but Tennessee rejected the amendment. Throughout his term, Johnson would use his prestige and power to stiffen southern resistance to Republican construction. This was merely the first example.

The Reconstruction Act

Republicans gathered in Washington, D.C. for the second session of the 39th Congress in December 1866, just as the southern states, encouraged by

*This became, eventually, the Fourteenth Amendment to the Constitution.—Ed.

the President, one after another rejected the Fourteenth Amendment. Reassured by their campaign victories, they responded to southern intransigence by formulating a new Reconstruction policy, embodied in the Reconstruction Acts of 1867.

Traditionally, historians interpreted this legislation as proof of radical ascendancy in the Republican party in 1867, but once again recent scholarship has challenged established interpretations. In fact, the first Reconstruction Act, which set the new policy, passed only after a long and bitter struggle between radical and nonradical Republicans, and it seriously compromised the radical position.

When Republicans first began discussing how to react to the southern refusal to acquiesce in the conservative Reconstruction policy embodied in the Fourteenth Amendment, radicals hoped to enforce the program of fundamental change for which they had been pressing unsuccessfully for so long. . . .

But instead of cooperating with this program, nonradical Republicans checked its advocates and substituted a new scheme of their own. The Reconstruction Act of 1867 still provided for the restoration of southern states upon their ratification of the Fourteenth Amendment, but added to that condition was a new one—a requirement that Southerners extend the right of suffrage to blacks on the same terms as whites. Until Southerners agreed to meet these conditions for restoration, the rights of southern loyalists, especially blacks, would be protected by the United States Army. . . .

Although this program, especially the black-suffrage requirement, might have seemed outrageously radical to southern whites, to Andrew Johnson, and to later generations of historians, it was in fact no more than most Republicans had been ready to demand in the summer of 1865, before Johnson's policy had become settled and his opposition to imposing impartial suffrage in the South manifest. It certainly did not satisfy the radicals. . . .

The Republican majority had refused to adopt the radicals' alternatives. Instead, they had placed the task of enforcing the Reconstruction Acts in the hands of the Army. And the Constitution recognized Andrew Johnson as commander in chief of the armed forces for as long as he remained in office.

Republicans had proved unwilling to take Reconstruction completely out of the hands of the President. . . . Many of them now believed that Johnson had usurped the rightful legislative powers of Congress by inaugurating his own system of Reconstruction and then denying them any power in the premises. They would not now usurp his powers. They had fulfilled their duty by framing a Reconstruction law. The President would fulfill his by administering it. The government could operate in no other way under the rather rigid concept of separation of powers to which most Americans adhered at mid-century.

It was because so many Republicans could not envision legislative despotism that the impeachment question arose. "[W]e must have laws in which the executive will cooperate, in order to make those laws effective," Banks had insisted. But he had added, "And if, after we . . . have agreed as to what laws are necessary to secure the peace of the country and to maintain the existence of the Government, . . . the President then refuses cooperation, it is our duty to lay aside the question of reconstruction for a time and proceed to a consideration of the position and purposes of the President himself." Because Republicans respected the presidency, they would if necessary remove the President.

The Impeachment Movement

The reluctance of nonradical Republicans to abandon traditional reliance upon the presidency for the enforcement of laws led directly to the impeachment movement. While more conservative Republicans hoped for Johnson's cooperation, radicals shared no such illusions. In their opinion, the President had already demonstrated his capacity for destructiveness. His mild restoration policy had reawakened southern belligerence after Lee's surrender and was responsible for all the suffering that implied for southern loyalists. Republicans laid directly at his feet responsibility for the brutal New Orleans massacre of the summer of 1866, in which the city police killed 40 mainly black Republicans and injured 160 more in dispersing a peaceful convention of doubtful legality. They were equally convinced that the general mood of hostility to Union soldiers and blacks could be traced to the President's lenience.

Moreover, Johnson had already shown his willingness to nullify congressional legislation. Where it suited him, he had ignored the Senate's right to confirm government appointments, disregarded the Test Oath law, and emasculated the Freedmen's Bureau and Confiscation Acts.

Republican congressmen had not passed a Reconstruction law before the Rebel armies laid down their arms, in April and May 1865, but they had passed a series of measures that should have had a great impact on the reorganization of southern political, social, and economic institutions after the war. The "ironclad" test oath, required of all elected and appointed officers in the public service of the United States, effectually barred former Rebels from national office.

Furthermore, a strong start had been made in solving the problem of transition from slave to free labor. The Freedmen's Bureau, funded by the income of abandoned, seized, and confiscated lands, would cooperate with missionary organizations in educating black people, guard freedmen's interests in the unaccustomed process of contracting for wages, and begin the process of distributing land to establish black homesteads.

But within a year of Andrew Johnson's elevation to the presidency, the preliminary Reconstruction program enacted by Congress lay in utter ruin. In pursuing his own policy, Johnson had destroyed it, without violating a law, using only his constitutional powers, as president of the United States. Ignoring the Test Oath Act of Congress, he appointed former Rebels provisional governors in several southern states. . . . The Johnson administration had also ignored the congressional oath requirement in making ordinary appointments to the national civil service in the South. . . .

. . . After the fall of 1865, one of the Freedmen's Bureau's primary functions was to administer the *restoration* of seized and abandoned property to pardoned Rebels. The Freedmen's Bureau held roughly 800,000 acres of land in September 1865. It never gained control of any more. By April 1866, 414,652 acres had been restored to former owners, including almost 15,000 acres that had already been turned over to freedmen.

Bad as the effect of these laws was on the Freedmen's Bureau, the real tragedy lay in their effect on the lives of individual men and women. [Freedmen's Bureau] Commissioner [Oliver Otis] Howard recalled with anguish the meeting at which he informed black men who had been promised ownership of the soil they worked in the Sea Islands that they had to restore the land to their former owners. "Why . . . do you take away our lands?" one of the freedmen had asked. "You take them from us who are true, always true to the Government! You give them to our all-time enemies!" Silently agreeing, Howard could give no answer. . . .

By May 1866, Johnson's interference on behalf of the South had become so blatant that many Republicans feared the President might attempt a *coup d'état*. This apprehension, fanned by Johnson's intemperate language and by the open advocacy of such a course by southern and northern Democratic organs, continued until the impeachment.

A correspondent of the New York *Times* had gauged the sentiment in Congress correctly. . . . "If the President persistently stands in the way . . .; if he fails to execute the laws in their spirit as well as in their letter, if he will forget nothing, if he will learn nothing; if, holding the South in his hand, either by direct advice or personal example he shall encourage them to such resistance to progress as may tend to defeat the public will—in such event . . . the President may, after all, come to be regarded as an 'obstacle' which must be 'deposed.' "

Experiencing Freedom: The Mississippi Black Code, 1865

Passed in 1865 and 1866 in states reconstructed under Johnson's aegis, the so-called Black Codes represented the South's view of how to deal with changed economic and social conditions. The Mississippi code was among the most severe. In December 1865, Johnson referred to the codes as "measures . . . to confer upon freedmen the privileges which are essential to their comfort, protection, and security." For the president, the codes were designed to assist and regulate the difficult transition from slavery to freedom. Many Northerners, however, found in the codes evidence that the South intended to re-establish slavery under another name, and with Radical Reconstruction these laws were largely eliminated.

What were the objects of Mississippi's Black Code? What did white Southerners think of the freedman? Were the codes, as some have argued, a *political* mistake? Could the South have achieved its purposes in some less blatant fashion and perhaps avoided retribution?

1. Civil Rights of Freedmen

Sec. 1. *Be it enacted,* . . . That all freedmen, free negroes, and mulattoes may sue and be sued, implead and be impleaded, in all the courts of law and equity of this State, and may acquire personal property, and choses in action, by descent or purchase, and may dispose of the same, in the same manner and to the same extent that white persons may: *Provided,* That the provisions of this section shall not be so construed as to allow any freedman, free negro, or mulatto to rent or lease any lands or tenements except in incorporated cities or towns . . .

Sec. 3. . . . That all freedmen, free negroes, or mulattoes who do now and have herebefore lived and cohabited together as husband and wife shall be taken and held in law as legally married, and the issue shall be taken and held as legitimate for all purposes; that it shall not be lawful for any freedman, free negro, or mulatto to intermarry with any white person; nor for any white person to intermarry with any freedman, free negro, or mulatto; and any person who shall so intermarry, shall be deemed guilty of felony, and on conviction thereof shall be confined in the State penitentiary for life; and those shall be deemed freedmen, free negroes, and mulattoes who are of pure negro blood, and those descended from a negro to the third generation, inclusive, though one ancestor in each generation may have been a white person.

Sec. 4. . . . That in addition to cases in which freedmen, free negroes, and mulattoes are now by law competent witnesses, freedmen, free negroes, or mulattoes shall be competent in civil cases, when a party or parties to the suit, either plaintiff or plaintiffs, defendant or defendants, and a white person or white persons, is or are the opposing party or parties, plaintiff or plaintiffs, defendant or defendants. They shall also be competent witnesses in all criminal prosecutions where the crime charged is alleged to have been committed by a white person upon or against the person or property of a freedman, free negro, or mulatto: *Provided,* that in all cases said witnesses shall be examined in open court, on the stand; except, however, they may be examined before the grand jury, and shall in all cases be subject to the rules and tests of the common law as to competency and credibility. . . .

Sec. 6. . . . That all contracts for labor made with freedmen, free negroes, and mulattoes for a longer period than one month shall be in writing, and in duplicate, attested and read to said freedman, free negro, or mulatto by a beat, city or county officer, or two disinterested white persons of the county in which

From Black Code of Mississippi, 1865 (*Laws of Mississippi, 1865,* pp. 82–88, 90–91, 93, 165–167).

the labor is to be performed, of which each party shall have one; and said contracts shall be taken and held as entire contracts, and if the laborer shall quit the service of the employer before expiration of his term of service, without good cause, he shall forfeit his wages for that year, up to the time of quitting.

Sec. 7. . . . That every civil officer shall, and every person may arrest and carry back to his or her legal employer any freedman, free negro, or mulatto who shall have quit the service of his or her employer before the expiration of his or her term of service without good cause; and said officer and person shall be entitled to receive for arresting and carrying back every deserting employe aforesaid the sum of five dollars, and ten cents per mile from the place of arrest to the place of delivery; and the same shall be paid by the employer, and held as a set-off for so much against the wages of said deserting employe: *Provided*, that said arrested party, after being so returned, may appeal to a justice of the peace or member of the board of police of the county, who, on notice to the alleged employer, shall try summarily whether said appellant is legally employed by the alleged employer, and has good cause to quit said employer; either party shall have the right of appeal to the county court, pending which the alleged deserter shall be remanded to the alleged employer or otherwise disposed of, as shall be right and just; and the decision of the county court shall be final. . . .

Sec. 9. . . . That if any person shall persuade or attempt to persuade, entice, or cause any freedman, free negro, or mulatto to desert from the legal employment of any person before the expiration of his or her term of service, or shall knowingly employ any such deserting freedman, free negro, or mulatto, or shall knowingly give or sell to any such deserting freedman, free negro, or mulatto, any food, raiment, or other thing, he or she shall be guilty of a misdemeanor, and, upon conviction, shall be fined not less than twenty-five dollars and not more than two hundred dollars and the costs; and if said fine and costs shall not be immediately paid, the court shall sentence said convict to not exceeding two months' imprisonment in the county jail, and he or she shall moreover be liable to the party injured in damages: *Provided*, if any person shall, or shall attempt to, persuade, entice, or cause any freedman, free negro, or mulatto to desert from any legal employment of any person, with the view to employ said freedman, free negro, or mulatto without the limits of this State, such person, on conviction, shall be fined not less than fifty dollars, and not more than five hundred dollars and costs; and if said fine and costs shall not be immediately paid, the court shall sentence said convict to not exceeding six months imprisonment in the county jail. . . .

2. Mississippi Apprentice Law

Sec. 1. . . . That it shall be the duty of all sheriffs, justices of the peace, and other civil officers of the several counties in this State, to report to the probate courts of their respective counties semi-annually, at the January and July terms of said courts, all freedmen, free negroes, and mulattoes, under the age of eighteen, in their respective counties, beats or districts, who are orphans, or whose parent or parents have not the means or who refuse to provide for and support said minors; and thereupon it shall be the duty of said court to apprentice said minors to some competent and suitable person, on such terms as the court may direct, having a particular care to the interest of said minor: *Provided*, that the former owner of said minors shall have the preference when, in the opinion of the court, he or she shall be a suitable person for that purpose.

Sec. 2. . . . That the said court shall be fully satisfied that the person or persons to whom said minor shall be apprenticed shall be a suitable person to have the charge and care of said minor, and fully to protect the interest of said minor. The said court shall require the said master or mistress to execute bond and security, payable to the State of Mississippi, conditioned that he or she shall furnish said minor with sufficient food and clothing; to treat said minor humanely; furnish medical attention in case of sickness; teach, or cause to be taught, him or her to read and write, if under fifteen years old . . .

Sec. 3. . . . That in the management and control of said apprentice, said master or mistress shall have the power to inflict such moderate corporal chastisement as a father or guardian is allowed to inflict on his or her child or ward at common law: *Provided*, that in no case shall cruel or inhuman punishment be inflicted.

Sec. 4. . . . That if any apprentice shall leave the employment of his or her master or mistress, without his or her consent, said master or mistress may pursue and recapture said apprentice, and bring him or her before any justice of the peace of the county, whose duty it shall be to remand said apprentice to the service of his or her master or mistress; and in the event of a refusal on the part of said apprentice so to return, then said justice shall commit said apprentice to the jail of said county, on failure to give bond, to the next term of the county court; and it shall be the duty of said court at the first term thereafter to investigate said case, and if the court shall be of opinion that said apprentice left the employment of his or her master or mistress without good cause, to order him or her to be punished, as provided for the punishment of hired freedmen, as may be from time to time provided for by law for desertion, until he or she shall agree to return to the service of his or her master or mistress: . . . if the court shall believe that said apprentice had good cause to quit his said master or mistress, the court shall discharge said apprentice from said indenture, and also enter a judgment against the master or mistress for not more than one hundred dollars, for the use and benefit of said apprentice. . . .

3. *Mississippi Vagrant Law*

Sec. 1. *Be it enacted*, . . . That all rogues and vagabonds, idle and dissipated persons, beggars, jugglers, or persons practicing unlawful games or plays, runaways, common drunkards, common night-walkers, pilferers, lewd, wanton, or lascivious persons, in speech or behavior, common railers and brawlers, persons who neglect their calling or employment, misspend what they earn, or do not provide for the support of themselves or their families, or dependents, and all other idle and disorderly persons, including all who neglect all lawful business, habitually misspend their time by frequenting houses of ill-fame, gaming-houses, or tippling shops, shall be deemed and considered vagrants, under the provisions of this act, and upon conviction thereof shall be fined not exceeding one hundred dollars, with all accruing costs, and be imprisoned at the discretion of the court, not exceeding ten days.

Sec. 2. . . . That all freedmen, free negroes and mulattoes in this State, over the age of eighteen years, found on the second Monday in January, 1866, or thereafter, with no lawful employment or business, or found unlawfully assembling themselves together, either in the day or night time, and all white persons so assembling themselves with freedmen, free negroes or mulattoes, or usually associating with freedmen, free negroes or mulattoes, on terms of equality, or living in adultery or fornication with a freed woman, free negro or mulatto, shall be deemed vagrants, and on conviction thereof shall be fined in a sum not exceeding, in the case of a freedman, free negro or mulatto, fifty dollars, and a white man two hundred dollars, and imprisoned at the discretion of the court, the free negro not exceeding ten days, and the white man not exceeding six months. . . .

Sec. 7. . . . That if any freedman, free negro, or mulatto shall fail or refuse to pay any tax levied according to the provisions of the sixth section of this act, it shall be *prima facie* evidence of vagrancy, and it shall be the duty of the sheriff to arrest such freedman, free negro, or mulatto or such person refusing or neglecting to pay such tax, and proceed at once to hire for the shortest time such delinquent tax-payer to any one who will pay the said tax, with accruing costs, giving preference to the employer, if there be one. . . .

4. Penal Laws of Mississippi

Sec. 1. *Be it enacted*, . . . That no freedman, free negro or mulatto, not in the military service of the United States government, and not licensed so to do by the board of police of his or her county, shall keep or carry fire-arms of any kind, or any ammunition, dirk or bowie knife, and on conviction therof in the county court shall be punished by fine, not exceeding ten dollars, and pay the costs of such proceedings, and all such arms or ammunition shall be forfeited to the informer; and it shall be the duty of every civil and military officer to arrest any freedman, free negro, or mulatto found with any such arms or ammunition, and cause him or her to be committed to trial in default of bail.

Sec. 2. . . . That any freedman, free negro, or mulatto committing riots, routs, affrays, trespasses, malicious mischief, cruel treatment to animals, seditious speeches, insulting gestures, language, or acts, or assaults on any person, disturbance of the peace, exercising the function of a minister of the Gospel without a license from some regularly organized church, vending spirituous or intoxicating liquors, or committing any other misdemeanor, the punishment of which is not specifically provided for by law, shall, upon conviction thereof in the county court, be fined not less than ten dollars, and not more than one hundred dollars, and may be imprisoned at the discretion of the court, not exceeding thirty days.

Sec. 3. . . . That if any white person shall sell, lend, or give to any freedman, free negro, or mulatto any fire-arms, dirk or bowie knife, or ammunition, or any spirituous or intoxicating liquors, such person or persons so offending, upon conviction thereof in the county court of his or her county, shall be fined not exceeding fifty dollars, and may be imprisoned, at the discretion of the court, not exceeding thirty days. . . .

Sec. 5. . . . That if any freedman, free negro, or mulatto, convicted of any of the misdemeanors provided against in this act, shall fail or refuse for the space of five days, after conviction, to pay the fine and costs imposed, such person shall be hired out by the sheriff or other officer, at public outcry, to any white person who will pay said fine and all costs, and take said convict for the shortest time.

The Postwar Spirit

The village of Fredonia, New York, lies near Lake Erie, halfway between Buffalo, New York, and Erie, Pennsylvania. On an August day in 1867, little more than two years after the surrender of the Confederacy, the town turned out in force for the ceremonial laying of the cornerstone for a new state-supported Normal School, intended primarily as a training institution for public school teachers. Ira Wilson's address on the occasion is a remarkable document, one that reveals a good deal about postwar attitudes toward the nation, progress, civilization, and the place of Americans in the sweep of history. Would one expect similar remarks at a present-day version of the same ceremony? Why or why not?

Fredonia, August 8, 1867

To our Posterity

I address each of you who may chance to read this letter, which may lie imbedded in the rock hundreds of years after the bones of this assemblage shall have mingled with the dust. If history precedes this note and divulges every word it contains, still it may have a valuation based upon *time*!

This day in the presence of *five thousand* persons we celebrate the

From Ira H. Wilson, "To Our Posterity," August 8, 1867, Reed Library Archives, Reed Library, State University College, Fredonia, New York.

laying of the *corner stone* of this Normal School, from which we trust may spring Philosophers, Astronomers, Statesmen and Orators, to ornament the age in which they live.

One man, *Israel Lewis*, 99 years of age, and the oldest of our community, still lives to behold the march of improvement since he felled the first forest tree where this corner stone now takes its permanent foundation. But 70 years ago, the native tribes of this country and the wild beasts of the forests held their carnivals upon this spot of ground which we now dedicate to the promotion of art and science, for the mutual benefit of our selves and our posterity. A thousand years hence the people will be familiar with us and our time, the names of our late Webster and Clay, will be admired by *them*, as Cicero and Demosthenes are by us—and in the belief that this Institution will be productive of great men for other times, we cheerfully donate one hundred thousand dollars to the erection of this Institution of *Education* which is the theme of our ambition and the glory of our age. Truly

Ira H. Wilson

The War and Modernization: Letters from Frederick Law Olmsted

Born in 1822, Frederick Law Olmsted is perhaps best remembered as the landscape architect who designed New York City's Central Park. The first selection dates from Olmsted's tenure with the U.S. Sanitary Commission during the Civil War; the second from the 1870s, when he was commissioned to design the Capitol grounds in Washington, D.C. What does each letter tell us about the Civil War and its impact on American life? What was Olmsted's intent in designing the Capitol grounds? Was his vision reasonable or naive?

The Sanitary Commission

Dear Mother,

Could you not come at your duty somewhat in this way? You want to do something for all the men who have been wounded or sickened in

From the *Private Book* of F. L. Olmsted, January 27, 1863, p. 219, Olmsted Papers, Library of Congress Manuscript Division, Washington D.C., microfilm reel 2.

the cause of the Union and who need aid and you want to do a little more for Connecticut soldiers than for any others. Will all of your society admit that to be a fair statement? If so, then ask how much more. Recollect that from every state contributions are being made for Connecticut soldiers. The Sanitary Commission is distributing at the lowest estimate more than two thousand dollars worth of goods every day. (I think it is over three thousand—we give out over one thousand dollars worth daily on an average from the Washington station alone.) Of this Connecticut soldiers get their full share. There are many soldiers of Connecticut and of all other states who get nothing except through the Sanitary Commission. How much more do you want to give for any Connecticut soldier than for any other: twice—four times—ten times as much? (Say then)

How many Connecticut soldiers does the "Connecticut Relief" or do all of the other channels which you employ, reach in hospitals? Their reports will probably show you. Possibly 1500. The Sanitary Commission visits every week more than 10,000 in hospitals. If then you accept the Sanitary Commission as your only medium of administering to the wants of all the Union soldiers in hospital needing help beyond the Connecticut men and you give to Connecticut Relief the value of $1, for each patient they reach, and you give one tenth of that for each other man not reached by them, that is ten cents, you should send the Sanitary Commission if I am right in my hasty calculation of it 66 times as much as you do the rest. But really the Sanitary reaches a great many Connecticut boys exclusively. Does the Connecticut Relief reach those in hospital in New Orleans or Newberne?

Your affectionate son,
Fred. Law Olmsted

Mrs. John Olmsted

Landscaping the Capitol

Sir:

Before any thing [sic] more is done about the improvement of the public grounds in Washington concerning which you have asked my opinion, the question should be conclusively settled, what shall be the motive of their improvement.

For convenience sake I will consider this question first with reference to the whole body of open ground from the Capitol to Lafayette Square, and afterwards, more especially to that immediately about the Capitol.

Olmsted to Hon. Justin R. Morrill, Chairman, Committee on Public Grounds, January 22, 1874, Olmsted Papers, Library of Congress Manuscript Division, Washington, D.C., microfilm reel 14.

Within or on the borders of the larger ground stand the Capitol, the Executive Mansion and the several buildings occupied by the State, Judiciary, Treasury, and War and Navy Departments, the Agricultural Bureau and the Smithsonian Institution. To these, the National Library and other buildings are expected to be added. . . .

[The existing buildings] represent an investment by the Nation of millions of dollars, made solely with a view of producing certain impressions upon the mind of observers. Had they been judiciously placed and this outlay wisely and competently directed to the purpose in view, no nation in the world would now possess as noble and fitting a capital as the United States. As it is, the effect produced is admitted to be a broken, confused and unsatisfactory one and is unhappily often alluded to as a standing reproach against the system of government which has been able to secure no better adaptation of means to such an end. . . .

In short, the capital of the union manifests nothing so much as disunity. This is not because of the distance between the government buildings simply: were this reduced one half the intervening spaces remaining occupied as at present, the lack of any coordinating purpose would be felt none the less. What is [missing?] is a federal bond. . . . It should be requisite to the end in view that the motive should be absolutely controlling in all parts of the ground and the first obstacle to success would exist in that fact that certain portions of it have already been worked and are held and managed under divers and other authorities each with a different purpose. . . .

I apprehend that the first step necessary to be taken toward a comprehensive improvement would be the most difficult one, that is, to place the control of all these grounds under one body so constituted that it would be likely to pursue a sustained policy year after year and not be led off by regard to special and temporary interests.

Labor and Capital

Thomas Nast drew some of history's most famous cartoons for *Harper's Weekly*. He invented the elephant as the symbol of the Republican party and helped popularize the Democratic donkey. His work on Reconstruction supported the views of "Radical" Republicans such as Thaddeus Stevens and Charles Sumner. As the examples on page 22 demonstrate, Nast was also interested in economic issues. Are Nast's views as revealed here inconsistent? Was it natural for Nast to take a radical position on Reconstruction and yet support industrialization? What are the components of Nast's ideology?

Supplement, March 4, 1871.]   HARPER'S WEEKLY.

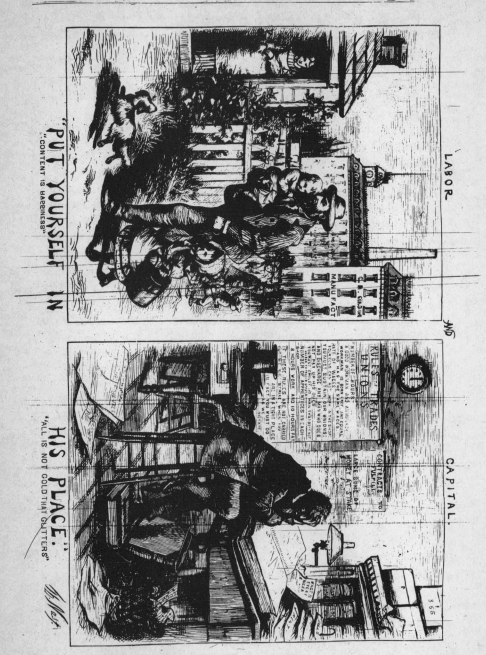

Reproduced from the collection of the Library of Congress.

The Reverend and Reconstruction: The Beecher-Tilton Affair

To the Americans who settled New England in the seventeenth century, religion meant a rigorous and complex theology. Men and women struggled with predestination, the calling, the conversion experience, and other aspects of Calvinist doctrine that affected every part of their lives. Much of the Calvinist tradition remained in 1800. For most Protestants, for example, going to church still had to do with finding out about heaven and hell, salvation and sin. By the time of the Reconstruction, however, much of the rigor had ebbed from Protestantism. Churches were disestablished, separated from the sustenance of the state. Attendance at church became less a time to search one's soul, and more a time for socializing with other members of the congregation and for celebrating the love of God. The clergy lost their influence and prestige. Religion became increasingly sentimental. Ministers more and more tended to the needs of another group of declining influence—women.

Henry Ward Beecher preached the new sentimental religion, and more successfully than most of his colleagues. He regularly drew audiences of more than 2,500 to the services at his Plymouth Congregational Church in Brooklyn, where he presided after 1847. The sequence of events that would nearly destroy Beecher was initiated on a July night in 1870, when Elizabeth Tilton confessed to her husband, Theodore, that she had committed adultery with her pastor, Beecher. It seems that she had gone to Beecher for consolation following the death of a young son and (she would claim) had yielded to his wishes in recompense for the emotional succor he had provided. She yielded for eighteen months.

Theodore Tilton, editor of a leading religious periodical, sued Beecher for damages in Brooklyn's Municipal Court. The ensuing trial was one of those public events which now and then capture the public imagination. Though the evidence against Beecher was clear enough (indeed, he did not deny the affair), a jury was unable to reach a verdict.

In the selection below, Beecher's attorney presents his client to the jury. The result is not so much a defense against the specific charge of adultery as an attempt to describe Beecher in terms that would appeal to an audience concerned with civil war, Reconstruction, and corruption. How does the defense seek to make Beecher attractive to the jury? Of what values is he presumed representative? Why would so many Americans refuse to acknowledge his obvious guilt? In contrast, how does the defense characterize the plaintiff, Theodore Tilton? To what extent does Beecher's attorney succeed in making *Tilton*, rather than Beecher, the source of moral decline?

Opening Address of Mr. Tracy for Defendant

Thirty-Sixth Day, February 24, 1875. Mr. Tracy.—May it please the court—Gentlemen of the Jury: The time having arrived when the defendant is permitted to be heard in his own behalf, my associates have assigned to me the duty of stating his case to this Honorable Court and to you. I am sure, gentlemen, when you consider for whom and in whose presence I speak, you will believe that it is for me an occasion of great personal embarrassment. When I think of the interests involved in this trial and the effects which may follow it, when I contemplate the deep and painful anxiety which it everywhere excites, I am oppressed by the burden of responsibility which the over-kindness of my associates has laid upon me, and would gladly surrender it to other and abler hands. Nothing, indeed, prevents me from sinking beneath the task I have undertaken, but a clear conviction of the absolute innocence of my client, and the assurance of my eminent associates that his case is too strong to be injured by my unskillful advocacy. And moreover, I am assured by the knowledge which comes to me from every quarter, that, in my effort to make his innocence as plain to you and to the world as it has long been to his counsel and his people, I have the universal sympathy of mankind.

The magnitude and importance of the questions here involved can not be over-estimated, for they go down to the very foundations of our social, moral, and religious life. If the effect of your decision in this case could be limited to determining whether the plaintiff has suffered a wrong at the hands of the defendant, for which he is entitled to be compensated in money, this trial would not excite the wide-spread interest which has attached to it from the beginning, and which must follow it to the end. But, gentlemen, I need not remind you how utterly impossible it is to circumscribe its effect within such narrow limits. Either the defendant is to go forth from this court-room vindicated by your verdict, or you and I and all who take part in this day's work are actors in one of the greatest moral tragedies which has ever occupied the stage of human life.

Look at it as we may, it is impossible to separate the defendant from his representative character. Not that I would endorse the remarkable statement of the plaintiff's counsel in his opening that "upon the result of your verdict, to a very large extent, will depend the integrity of the Christian religion." God forbid that the integrity of the Christian religion should depend upon the character or the fortunes of any man, however learned, eloquent, or devout.

From "Opening Address of Mr. Tracy for Defendant," in *Official Report of the Trial of Henry Ward Beecher, With Notes and References by Austin Abbott*, 4 vols. (New York, 1875), Vol. 2, pp. 797–802, 810–811, 946–948.

The Christian religion is founded upon the eternal rock of God's nature and God's decrees. It is from everlasting to everlasting, and will abide when the remotest records of future history shall have faded from the annals of time, and the heavens shall have been "rolled together as a scroll." . . .

The son of one of the most eminent clergymen of the last generation, a member of a large family of which all the men are clergymen and all the women authors of repute—a family, let me say, gentlemen, on whose fair fame the shadow of reproach has never rested hitherto—the defendant early devoted himself to the self-denying pursuit of a minister of the Gospel. For it was no bed of roses in a luxurious abode that he spread for himself; he made no use of a dominant family influence to secure the refinements and privileges of a wealthy city parish. He struck boldly out into the wilds and hardships of the far West. He rode the rough circuit of a home-missionary life. With his own hands he made the fires, swept the floor, and rang the bell in his forest church; with his own hands, assisted only by the faithful wife who stood by him then, and who—to the honor of womanhood—stands by him to-day, he ministered to the necessities of his forest home. When the thunders of his manly eloquence had reached even this distant coast, and the imperative demand of the church had summoned him to a wider sphere of action, he left neither his simplicity nor his independence behind. He has been the same genuine, true-hearted, unaffected man here that he was in the West. In the midst of all the refinements and luxuries of city life, his motto has been that of the great apostle he so much resembles, "I know how to be abased, and I know how to abound." To some who, in the early days, when he was less known than now, undertook to control his utterances by threatening loss of place, he made this memorable reply: "You may unseat me, but you can not control me. I came from the woods, and I can go back to the woods again."

This man so introduced to us, has wrought and taught for near thirty years in our midst. He is no longer a stranger, and no longer a new acquaintance. Genial and unassuming in his manners; inspiring in his speech as new wine; accessible to all, from the gravest citizen to the humblest child—the life he has lived before us has been as warm and fruitful as God's summer, as open and beneficent as His day.

No truth struggling with error has ever failed to find in him a champion; no phase of human sorrow has sought him in vain for sympathy and relief. Nay, as we have too much reason to know, the very excess of his sensibility has at times become to him an element of weakness, and left him for the moment at the mercy of colder and keener men.

And, if this is a fair picture of his private and domestic life, what shall be said of his life and influence as a preacher of the Gospel? Let the immense assemblies that for nearly thirty years—without abatement, without fluctuation—have thronged his chapel, more numerous and enthusiastic to-day than ever before, bear testimony. To this great congregation, presenting an unusual proportion of able and thoughtful men, he has ministered all these years untiringly. That his ministrations have been marked by a rare spirituality, and a wonderful mastery over the various motives of human character and moods of human experience, is universally acknowledged. He has been emphatically a preacher of the people. Living himself in constant communion with the unseen, he has interpreted the mysteries of the soul and given voice to those dim intuitions—those immortal yearnings—which spring in every human breast, but which so few can ever utter. A clergyman of the Congregational Church, he has labored for the aggrandizement of no sect, for the building up of no denomination. His creed is as broad as humanity itself; and his deep, warm heart, instinctively responding to the feeling of all, has enabled him to summon the race to a higher, nobler, and purer life. Though a Protestant, he has ever been able to discern the common Christian faith in all churches bearing the Christian name. Moral integrity, sincere devotion, and an earnest consecration to the common Lord, have always been recognized by him, without reference to the question of his own recognition by those to whom his charity has extended. Every honest soul that labored for the salvation and elevation of mankind, whether minister, priest or monk, or only self-sacrificing layman, has been to him a Christian brother, a minister of God. It is then no wonder that, besides the power of his personal teaching, the demand for his printed sermons should be beyond all precedent. Their weekly issue is read in every town and hamlet throughout this broad land, they are met with in the cabin of the backwoodsman, in the hut of the miner, in the forecastle at sea. Not only this, but they have been translated into every European language. In England alone, as I am informed, their circulation is thrice as large as that in all this country. . . .

But if there are those who are not interested in the minister of the Gospel, I invite them to contemplate the patriot and philanthropist. Espousing the cause of the oppressed, he labored for the emancipation of a race. When the agitation resulted in a conflict of arms, imperiling the Union of the States, his clarion voice was heard everywhere arousing the nation to the holy strife. . . . In that struggle, Henry Ward Beecher won the nation's gratitude and the nation's love. When the fury of the storm had spent its force, when the war was over, and the nation was saved—then the voice which had rung like a trumpet in the strife was the first to plead for forbearance to the vanquished, for a generous condonation of the past, and a permanent peace resting upon universal amnesty. This, gentlemen, is a true and unflattered portrait of the defendant in this case—as a husband, a father, a citizen, a patriot, a philanthropist, a minister, and a man. If it were a statement to be established by testimony, thousands upon thousands of witnesses might crowd this court to confirm its truth; for the name of Henry Ward Beecher has long been the treasure of the nation, as it has been the special pride and glory of this city, famous throughout the world as the scene of his life and labors. . . .

It now becomes my unpleasant duty to invite you, gentlemen, to consider for a moment who and what is Theodore Tilton. The plaintiff in this case presents the most impressive instance that has ever come within my observation, of the remorseless power and the destructive effect of a single absorbing master passion. An all-dominating, selfish egotism is the basis of his character. As a boy, he was bright and ambitious, and his quickness of apprehension and felicity of statement brought him early recognition and praise. Everybody flattered and encouraged him, regarding his self-conceit as something which mature years and the hard experience of life would modify into a reasonable self reliance and an honorable pride. Beginning life as a reporter on the public press, he was brought into contact with great orators and public men, and he early resolved to devote himself to a public career. All his studies turned upon this point—to make himself a graceful and powerful speaker and writer. The art of appearing well and sounding well was the art he sought—a dangerous pursuit for one already strongly predisposed by constitutional vanity to consider life a drama and himself its hero. He began, with unbounded confidence, and cool, calculating pertinacity, to work his way upward. Possessed of a fine address, a lively imagination, fertile fancy and flowing speech, he lacked powers of deep and original thought, and more than these, the sound sense, the discriminating judgment, and the unselfish aims which are the prime elements of a noble manhood. Anxious above all things to shine, he seized every opportunity and advocated every cause which would give him prominence. He adopted the ideas of leading men of the country—Sumner, Phillips, Garrison, and more than any other, of Mr. Beecher, who, as we have seen, was lavish of friendship and aid—and reproduced them in sensational editorials and lectures. The extremists in politics and religion to whom he joined himself, were ready to reward the facility with which he yielded himself to their uses by fostering his conceit; representing him as the successful antagonist of Mr. Beecher—the young David who had overthrown the great Goliath in debate, and the brilliant occupant of the editorial chair of *The Independent*, who had eclipsed the light of his predecessor.

He fell in with gay, fascinating people, who considered themselves free from the conventional restraints of society, and little by little, he slid into their ways of thinking. His unbalanced vanity was not proof against the wine of dangerous theories, when presented by the hand of the flatterer. Surrounded only by those who burned incense to his vanity, he became inflated with success, and fancied himself a monumental genius, a prolific source of wit and wisdom—in a word, the foremost man of his time. Conspicuously destitute alike of logical power and the poise of a nice moral sense, he embraced the wildest views and rushed forward, believing that the world would follow where he led. Some persons of cool heads can speculate on social, political, or religious questions, without losing their balance; but with Theodore Tilton, to calculate the depths of an abyss was to plunge headlong into it. A believer in the Christian faith and a member of an orthodox church, he speculated on the origin of matter and the attributes of God until he became a deist, denying the deity of Christ, and rejecting the Scriptures as a Divine revelation of God's will to man. The husband of a gifted, pure, and loving wife—the father of an interesting family, having, as he describes it, an "ideal home," he speculated on social problems, and was led by the malign influence under which he fell, to denounce the marriage relation as a remnant of effete civilization—a clog and hindrance to the development of the race. His remedy for the evils of marriage was easy divorce, leaving parties as free to dissolve the relation as they were to enter into it. He denies that he is a free lover, but Victoria Woodhull, the apostle of free love, asks for no greater social freedom than this. A leader of men must know how to construct and to preserve, but Theodore Tilton knew only how to unsettle and destroy. The moment he assumed a position of such prominence that he could be studied and criticised, the glaring defects of his character discovered themselves even to those who had hitherto been his dupes. Opposition sprang up in every quarter, and at last he was forced to realize that the foundation which had been reared for him, and on which he had been placed by others more than by himself, was crumbling beneath his feet. The end was near. Theodore Tilton fell—fell from an eminence seldom attained by men of his age—to the very bottom of the abyss the depths of which he had attempted to sound.

From that abyss, he beheld afar off the man who had been his early friend and patron, but whom he had long regarded as his rival and inferior, standing firm and erect, his influence widening and deepening, and his hold on public favor becoming more permanent and secure. A man fed by inordinate vanity can never awake to a sane, reasonable estimate of himself. Failure and disappointment never lead such a man to self-examination, but excite within him only bitterness, rage, and malice. With him, it is never his own folly and impotence that have impeded his advance, but some malevolent power has interfered. In the blindness of his rage, Theodore Tilton persuaded himself that the sole and efficient cause of his overthrow was Beecher; that the one man who had prevented him from reaching the topmost summit of fame was Beecher. But one resource was left to him. If he had not power to rebuild, he still had power to destroy, and Beecher should feel that power. To be eclipsed and neglected was gall and wormwood to his soul. If he could not be famous, he could at least be infamous; and he preferred infamy to oblivion. Mr. Beecher had long been his friend, and the intimate friend of his wife. That friendship he could pervert, and make himself the author, and at the same time the central figure, of the most famous scandal of modern times. If he could not supplant Beecher in the affection of the people, he could scandalize him. If he had made it impossible for any honorable pen to write his own biography, then was it worth any cost to have a line devoted to him in the biography of Henry Ward Beecher? His natural bent towards plots and conspiracies now fully revealed itself, and Beecher was the object of his schemes. Tilton is nothing if not dramatic, and his grand genius for attitudinizing began to be displayed. As in a play, everything was arranged with a view to effect. Facts were of no consequence to him, except as they could be adroitly used to serve the purpose of his pageant. Friends, wife, children—all that other men hold sacred and dear, he was ready to trample down and walk over, to reach the notice and applause for which he would barter his immortal soul. Pure women might abhor and shun him, but one pure woman at least should go to her grave, bearing witness to his power in a blasted life and a broken heart. Here, gentlemen, here speaks the "master passion" of this perverted man. At this very moment, if he could realize the sad truth that he is morally dead, he would still rejoice in the *post mortem* investigation of his character. He would rather be dissected than buried; but we propose, gentlemen, to dissect him first in the interest of truth, and to bury him afterwards in the interest of decency. . . .

But the change in his religious convictions was not the only departure made by Mr. Tilton from opinions he had held before. There followed soon after a very marked alteration in his views respecting the relations of the sexes, and particularly on the subjects of marriage and divorce. Mr. Tilton espoused with zeal the cause of woman's suffrage. He reports himself in *The Golden Age* as having said during the war that, after the abolition of slavery, the next great question which would agitate the public mind would be that of woman's suffrage; and undoubtedly believing that a great social revolution was impending, he aspired to make himself the leader of the movement. But its adherents differed widely among themselves in their views of the marriage relation. Many, perhaps a majority, coincided with all Christian people upon this subject; while others held that marriage was merely a civil contract, and that the parties thereto should be as free to dissolve the tie as they were to accept it. Tilton, with his usual radicalism, embraced the extremest views upon the subject, and soon began to make them a theme of conversation with friends visiting at his house. He did not hesitate to declare before his wife that he had now come to regard the marriage relation very differently from what he once did. To him it was no longer a sacred institution, to be regulated by the Church or State. His most intimate friends of both sexes gradually came to be those who agreed with him upon the subject of marriage. They used to converse much upon the relations of the sexes; the great value of friendships between married men and unmarried women, or between married men and other men's wives; the extent to which such intimacies could be carried and still be innocent; and finally the impossibility of criminality in any relation which love had sanctified. This, I say, gentlemen, we shall show you, was a frequent subject of conversation between Mr. Tilton and his associates visiting at his house. To the advocacy of sentiments so offensive to a pure and devoted wife and mother Mrs. Tilton was compelled to listen day after day, and week after week. This change was, if possible, more repugnant to her than his change in religion. The one she strove against with anguish, with entreaty and with tears; the other she resisted and fought against. She despised the doctrine and its adherents; she forbade her house to the women who advocated it; she remonstrated with her husband against the principles he held and the people with whom he associated, and she denounced with indignation his peculiar friendships with women, which he characterized as "sacred weddings which knew no sex."

She rejected his sophistry, that they were helps to him in his labors, or pillars against which he could lean for support. She perceived with a woman's instinct the end to which such relations would surely bring him. . . .

You will save Brooklyn, already too much disgraced by the existence of such a scandal, from the far greater disgrace of permitting such a man to be destroyed by such instrumentality—an eagle towering in his pride of place, hawked and killed by mousing owls! You will tell the American people that when innocence is assailed by unscrupulous and cunning malice, however successful for a time the assault may seem, it must find its barrier when it reaches an American jury. And you will say to this heartless and ungodly persecution, "Thus far shalt thou come, but no farther—here all the midnight plottings of cruel craft must cease forever." . . .

Gentlemen, do you believe in God? Then you will recognize to-day what the generations to come will so clearly see; what the Day of Revelation will blaze forth in letters of immortal light—the mark of God's approval upon this, His faithful, upright, suffering servant, whom He hath hitherto guided, sustained, illumined, blessed; whom in the hour of tribulation He hath not forsaken; and whom, by all the truth of His eternal promise and all the resources of His Almighty power, He will surely rescue and reward; for "Though hand join in hand, the wicked shall not be unpunished, but the seed of the righteous shall be delivered."

The South Redeemed

The map on page 31 shows the percentages of slave population in different Southern states in 1860. Below is a list of dates showing when the Southern states were brought back into a full relationship with the federal government and thereby "redeemed"—a biased word meaning a return to conservative Southern governments. Is there some relationship between the percentages of slave population and the dates of redemption? If so, what might lie behind such a relationship?

**Date of Establishment of
Conservative Governments**

1869	Virginia
	Tennessee
1870	North Carolina
1871	none
1872	Georgia
1873–74	Arkansas
	Texas
	Alabama
1875	none
1876	Mississippi
	South Carolina
1877	Louisiana
	Florida

Slaves, 1860. Percent of Slaves in Total Population. *From Charles O. Paullin,* Atlas of the Historical Geography of the United States, *Carnegie Institution of Washington and the American Geographical Society of New York (Washington, D.C., 1932), plate 68B. Reprinted by permission.*

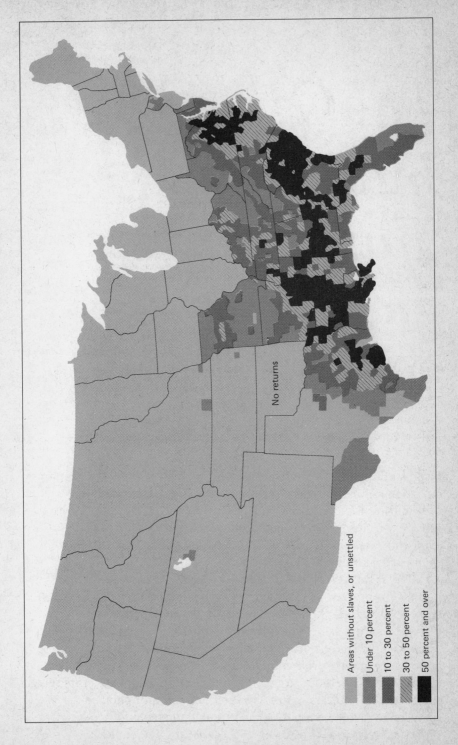

No returns

Areas without slaves, or unsettled

Under 10 percent

10 to 30 percent

30 to 50 percent

50 percent and over

CHAPTER 2

The Gilded Age: Industrial Transformation and the Dream of Order

Nineteenth-century Americans were obsessed with change, progress, development, and growth. And this obsession reached a new kind of peak during the decades after the Civil War. An American who had matured in the 1850s or 1860s could look backward from 1890 or 1900 and remember a lifetime filled with what seemed to be the most astonishing kinds of transformations.

The facts were there to support such memories of change. The population more than doubled between 1870 and 1900. The telegraph, the telephone, the electric light, and the linotype were only a few of the dozens of inventions that made life—and work—remarkably different. In 1850, most workers were artisans, plying their crafts in small shops under employers working beside them on similar tasks. By 1900, larger industrial enterprises were employing thousands of workers; employers seldom had any personal knowledge of their employees; and much of the skill had been removed from the work process. There were new cities, too—six in

1900 with populations of over half a million. The United States leapfrogged over England, France, and Germany to become the leading industrial nation of the world. Steel production increased 2,000 percent between the Civil War and the end of the century. Many firms for the first time faced national and urban markets rather than local and rural ones. This meant new opportunities, more intense competition, and finally the emergence of the big firms that have become the hallmark of the American economy. Change was a whirling, accelerating affair that altered the horizons of experience in every decade.

Above the whirl, a kind of official opinion developed, an orthodox opinion that change was "progress." Presidents and senators, newspaper editors and magazine writers, preachers and book publishers—all the molders of what was coming to be thought of as "public opinion"—voiced a belief that industrialization was creating a better life for the republic. Within this view, industrial growth meant opportunity. Competition meant success. All the inventions created leisure and material comfort. The great new factories meant a sort of democracy of well-being for the workers in them. And, in national terms, industrial growth meant the potential triumph in the world of American principles of freedom and equality.

But the awareness of change also generated problems and anxieties. For the wealthy and the sophisticated, there was the possibility that industrialization might lead to a world of materialism, greed, and speculation, a world with only a thin and false veneer of culture and moral values. This fear was a theme of the book that gave a name to the period, Mark Twain and Charles Dudley Warner's *The Gilded Age*, published in 1873. There was a similar fear that the republican principles of freedom and democracy, which had been proclaimed in a simple, agrarian world, could not survive in an urban and industrial society. And many native Americans doubted that the nation could absorb the huge immigrant work force that industrialization brought to the United States.

But the anxieties were not confined to the wellborn, the rich, and the native-born. The young man or woman moving off a farm in Connecticut into an industrial city had a great deal to fear, too. Would the industrial world be a place of loneliness and isolation, with no family, friends, or neighbors? Those who had worked in shops that were small and relatively easygoing had to worry that the new factories with their unforgiving machines would prove to be intolerable places to work. Immigrants coming into this new and changing world had their own concerns, too. Would their ways and their family ties be able to survive in a new world bent only on an uncertain and formless future?

Everyone, in short, had something to worry about. And worry they did. In this chapter, we will examine some of the ways that Americans tried to meet the exciting and disturbing challenges of an age of economic and cultural revolution.

GEOFFREY BLODGETT

Frederick Law Olmsted: Landscape Architecture as Conservative Reform

Against a background of rapid and profound changes in technology, work, and social structure, Gilded Age politics seem curiously unresponsive. National politics was largely the province of men from small towns and cities, rather than the new industrial centers. The major problems they wrestled with—civil service, the tariff, and the currency— seemed to some contemporaries and to most historians to side-step the central issues of the time. The Pendleton Act of 1883, which took the first steps toward establishing a "merit" system for federal employees based on competitive examination, hardly seems a fitting response to a decade of unrest on the farms, in the cities, and in the factories. Nonetheless, politics has never been so popular nor party loyalties so intense. Voters turned out in record numbers and tended to select a party on the basis of religious background and ethnic heritage.

How, then, did such issues as civil-service reform come to center stage in the Gilded Age? Geoffrey Blodgett's essay contributes to an answer to that question by allowing us to look at the Gilded Age through the eyes of one of its genteel reformers, landscape architect Frederick Law Olmsted. How did Olmsted perceive and interpret his culture? Did he recognize, or dismiss, the new realities of industrialization? Who did Olmsted define as the primary obstacles to reform, and why? What did Olmsted and his like-minded colleagues in reform expect to achieve from park systems, a lower tariff, and civil-service reform?

The coincidence in 1972 of Frederick Law Olmsted's one hundred and fiftieth birthday with a revival of environmentalist concern over the plight of the city won for America's greatest landscape architect a splash of deserved national attention. But some of his celebrants had trouble locating Olmsted as a participant in the history he lived through. Journalists linked him vaguely with Jeffersonian agrarianism, with the New England village green, and in one instance with Edgar Allan Poe. A serious effort was made to tie the young Olmsted of the 1850s to Fourierite utopian socialism and the aging Olmsted of the 1890s to Edward Bellamy's utopian nationalism. One result of all this was a certain historical deracination of the man. His reputation "took off." Lauded for his long vision, Olmsted became a visionary for the 1970s—a planner who shaped the future by transcending his own environment, casting aside its blinders and inhibitions to bring hope and wisdom to the present. "It is against this American," one breathless sesquicentennial enthusiast concluded, "that we must measure the captains who must now guide spaceship Earth."

Historians know Olmsted from his travels through the antebellum South and his work with the U.S. Sanitary Commission in the Civil War as well as his contributions to park design and urban planning. The several facets of his career have merited growing scholarly attention. But Olmsted's experience across the postwar years has yet to be fully understood against the peculiar social and political environment of the Gilded Age.

The purpose of this essay is to fix Olmsted in the group structure of postwar reformers and to appraise the problems he met and the values he wanted to enforce through his professional work. It will try to explain the continuities in Olmsted's social attitudes which spanned his transition from journalism and public administration to the new profession of landscape architecture. These continuities formed the fabric of a profoundly conservative concept of reform. They included a stubborn faith in political and social democracy—provided that democracy remained responsive to the cues of trained and cultivated leadership; a belief that American society urgently needed to fortify itself against the crude and materialistic impulses of popular culture; and a hope that the tensions of a newly urban nation might be moderated by structural arrangements, both political and aesthetic, to foster respect among rival social groups.

Since Olmsted wrote less as he grew older, and what he wrote grew more opaque, his postwar attitudes must be read mostly out of the pattern of friendships, causes, and practical preoccupations which governed his last thirty years of work. Like the careers of his colleagues in conservative reform, his was heavy with both pride and frustration—pride in personal achievement, and frustration at public indifference to his talents and service. One long letter, written in the 1870s to an English-born acquaintance who lived in aristocratic

From Geoffrey Blodgett, "Frederick Law Olmsted: Landscape Architecture as Conservative Reform," *Journal of American History*, 62 (March 1976), 869–889. Reprinted by permission of the Organization of American Historians, copyright holder.

seclusion at Newport, summed up his determination not to be cast aside by popular rebuffs. The American majority had many faults, he confessed. But the worst result of its behavior was the morbid apathy it could inspire among the cultivated few. Olmsted went on to lecture his Newport friend:

> You—your class—perceive your superiority in certain respects to the mass of the people but because they think too well of themselves, are too original, self-sufficient, and too much inclined to recklessly busy themselves in matters with which they have no natural concern, and because they have not made arrangements politically and socially, as in England, with special reference to the convenience with which superior talent, tact and taste may be exercised for the benefit of the community, you assume to yourselves the right to live quiet, scholarly, secluded and selfishly domestic and aesthetic lives.

Olmsted ended with this affirmation:

> The difficulties, annoyances and embarrassments which gentlemen and gentlewomen of any talent have to meet in doing their duty with their talent are certainly very great, and talent is not to be exercised here with the pre-ordained quiet, grace and decorum which may be associated with it in a country of thoroughly well-established and congealed civilization. The greater is the need, however, that it should be exercised courageously, resolutely, and perseveringly.

The decade from 1855 to 1865 had brought Olmsted into friendly contact with others of similar conviction. These included the writer George William Curtis, a Staten Island neighbor whom Olmsted had joined in an abortive publishing venture with *Putnam's Magazine* in 1855; Edwin L. Godkin, whom Olmsted befriended soon after the young Englishman's arrival in New York in 1856; Charles Francis Adams, Jr., the young Boston lawyer who entered into correspondence with Olmsted in 1861; Charles Eliot Norton of Cambridge, an admirer of Olmsted's writings on the South who met him through Curtis in 1862; and the editor Samuel Bowles, of Springfield, Massachusetts, whose friendship with Olmsted dated from 1865. These men formed the core of a gentlemanly cosmopolitan élite which tried hard through the postwar years to impose its will on American political and cultural development. With others of like mind—Henry Adams, Edward Atkinson, Jacob D. Cox, David A. Wells, and Horace White—they launched such ventures as the *Nation* and American Social Science Association, tried to force congressional tariff and civil service reform, helped to start the ill-fated Liberal Republican movement of 1872, and strove thereafter to function as a third force in two-party politics.

The fortunes of this group—an aspiring intellectual élite in a nation which did not want an élite and met its overtures with constant scorn—have been the object of lively scholarly contention. In judging the record of genteel reform, historians have tended until recently to focus on its role in national elective politics and have neglected its strenuous efforts beyond the rim of party strife to build stable institutional props for a nation confronting fast social change. Olmsted's postwar work in landscape architecture, like Godkin's, Bowles' and Curtis' careers in journalism, Henry Adams' career as novelist and historian, Atkinson's and Wells' careers as economic publicists, Cox's career in academic administration, Norton's career as a teacher of fine arts, and Charles Francis Adams' career in railroad regulation, reflected a common urge to focus professional intelligence on goals of social order and cohesion. Olmsted's parks are among the most durable relics of this urge. Their very longevity allows scholars to assess their meaning across an unusually broad perspective against criteria of functional utility and popular acceptance, criteria which were often the nemesis of his colleagues in conservative reform.

Olmsted's connection with the reformist gentry was not a matter of coincidence or chance. He shared their assumptions about the design of a good society, where hierarchy, deference, and skilled leadership might impose tranquility on a contentious, egalitarian people. He disliked the headstrong ideological fanaticism of both abolitionist extremists and evangelical Protestant sectarians in the 1850s—and these attitudes were pervasive among his new friends. With them he also mistrusted the myopic self-interest of freshly rich merchants and entrenched local politicians. Oppressed by the lack of professional standards among lawyers, businessmen, journalists, and publishers, he struggled to translate the private ethics of the gentlemanly amateur into efficient public conduct. The meanders in his own prewar career reflected not only periodic personal aimlessness but a faith in the potential omnicompetence of well-bred men with broad intellectual horizons. The exhilarating sense of public purpose which the Civil War crisis brought to his friends had been matched in Olmsted's case only by the prior task of creating Central Park, a project he eagerly took up after the collapse of *Putnam's Magazine* in the depression of 1857.

By the time the war broke out, the main outlines of Central Park were essentially complete. Olmsted's departure in 1861 to become executive secretary of the U.S. Sanitary Commission hardly ended his ties to the park. It did signal a strong new concern for the politics of national survival. Southern secession, which he called the "dignification of anarchy," stirred him to deep nationalist feelings. Never a believer in laissez-faire, he shared with Curtis, Godkin, and Norton misgivings over the management of the Union war effort. His admiration for "the low, obscure, mysterious strength of the free and unenlightened people" was contingent on a felt need for "large purposes" governed by a "central will and power." While these values endured through the war and beyond, Olmsted was for a long time puzzled how he might help fulfill them.

In the U.S. Sanitary Commission he showed the same combination of managerial talent and impatience toward superiors which marked his career as park superintendent, and by 1863 he had had enough of it. Meanwhile he considered posts as street commissioner in New York and federal commis-

sioner of agriculture in Washington. The alternative of building a private practice in landscape gardening did not seem to promise steady satisfaction. In the
summer of 1863 Olmsted and Godkin laid the first, premature plans for the
Nation, a project to consolidate and elevate the tone of public thought. Two
months later he headed for California to seek success in a hopeless mining
venture. Friends bewailed his departure, certain that his talents were needed
closer to home. While in California he began "a heavy sort of book" about
American civilization which he never finished. A surviving fragment of its
outline shows the tenacity of his concern for adequate political organization in
a ramshackle society of continental scope: "Administration, science of, defective Tendency to trust to laws & machines Neglect executive—incompetency &
recklessness of officials. Diffused responsibility. Short terms. Need of civil
service organization—training, promotion." He planned next to write of hope-
ful symptoms: "How progress to come? Study of wants. Study of modern
requirements, of means to them." Among these, significantly, he listed park
reform and the design of streets.

Meanwhile a career choice still confronted him. Although the barbarous
informality of social relations in California at first put him off, he toyed with
the notion of luring Godkin west to help him start a San Francisco newspaper.
Meanwhile, Godkin joined Curtis in trying to land for Olmsted the director-
ship of the Freedman's Bureau in Washington, and Wells included Olmsted
among potential colleagues on a special postwar revenue commission. Finally
Olmsted decided to come back and join the work of building Brooklyn's Prospect Park. By the summer of 1866 he was happily engrossed in the old tasks.
"[M]y enthusiasm and liking for the work is increasing to an inconvenient
degree," he told Norton, "so that it elbows all other interests out of my mind."
The return to New York had brought him back to the *Nation* as well, and
during the troubled early phase of the journal's management he and Norton
were Godkin's most faithful aides. But writing had gotten difficult for Olmsted.
"I am the slowest and heaviest and sickest dragoon that ever was pushed into
the bogs of literature," he complained in 1867. "A single day's writing knocks
me up for a week." Without quite realizing it, and in a manner that some of his
associates interpreted as retreat, Olmsted had found in landscape architecture
rather than in journalism or administration his life's calling. As it worked out,
the choice would bring him into more intimate practical contact with the problems of urban democracy than any of his collaborators in conservative reform.

His interest in national party politics flagged. The intolerance of congressional Radicals, and their demand for prompt enfranchisement of the freedmen, disillusioned him with Reconstruction. The Radicals, he feared, were
rending the structure and processes of government in a thoughtless, arbitrary
drive for quick results. Moreover, under Radical leadership the Republican
party was filling with "a raft of mercenaries·. . . who don't see beyond their
nose in the real work before us." Increasingly he was persuaded that the "real
work" lay outside party politics. He remained peripherally involved in the

efforts of the cosmopolitan gentry to avert what they regarded as the degeneration of the Republican party and to otherwise shape the course of postwar public life. He was one of the founders of the American Social Science Association (ASSA), whose charter stressed the "responsibilities of the gifted and educated classes toward the weak, the witless, and the ignorant," and delivered one of his major papers on urban parks to a Boston meeting of ASSA in 1870. While he did not count himself a "zealous Free Trader," the intrigue and manipulation swirling around the policy of high protection repelled him; and he shared the desire for tariff reform which Wells, Atkinson, and others pursued within ASSA. He was caught up in the preliminaries to the Liberal Republican movement of 1872 and pulled off the route to the Cincinnati convention only after Horace Greeley moved in on it. His contempt for Greeley as the exemplar of erratic popular journalism and reformist quackery was absolute. When others of like mind tried to undo the Cincinnati fiasco by forming yet another ticket, Olmsted was startled to learn he had been nominated for vice-president by a rump convention of his friends. Angered and embarrassed by this climactic absurdity, he disowned the action and wound up supporting Ulysses S. Grant.

Over the next decade Olmsted stayed clear of reform meetings and joked about "the disorganization of which I am a humble member." For him as for his friends, politics was no longer an opportunity but an ugly problem. Clues to his transformation of attitude cropped up in unexpected contexts. By 1874, when he had begun the project of landscaping Capitol Hill in Washington, his preference for centralized and orderly national governance found expression in a wholly aesthetic perception. To his eye the arrangement of federal buildings in Washington was "broken, confused, and unsatisfactory," and he remarked that the physical appearance of Washington was "often alluded to as a standing reproach against [our] system of government. . . ." "In short, the Capitol of the Union manifests nothing so much as disunity. . . . What is wanting is a federal bond." His old values had survived, but landscape architecture rather than politics was now his method for promoting them.

The one political issue calculated to fire his reform impulse was civil service reform. The Central Park project had engaged him in fierce feuds over patronage; and by the 1870s he had acquired a fund of experience on the subject unmatched among his friends. The chairmanship of Grant's civil service commission was yet another of the posts urged on him after the war. While he shunned the office, his anxiety about the problem was keen. The spoils system, he believed, had produced a new definition of the word "influence," one which turned honest jobseekers into wrecks of demoralized dependence on the favor of party hacks. Washington, he wrote, was the center "of a system between which and its extremities there is a ceaseless flux and reflux of influence." Ironically, the system created a bond between local and national politics which Olmsted—long an advocate of centralized administrative authority—could only repudiate as a symptom of national decay.

The assassination of James A. Garfield in the summer of 1881 revived Olmsted's functional contact with Curtis, Carl Schurz, and other civil service reformers. Writing to Schurz that "the country is at white heat," and ready to be moved on the issue, he joined the Civil Service Reform Association; and his essay, "The Spoils of the Park," was soon being circulated and read as a reform polemic. After the passage of the Pendleton Act, he hoped the movement would swing its attention to the problems of spoils at the city level. Despite a lifelong aversion to the Democratic party, his admiration for Grover Cleveland (who as governor of New York had responded well to the campaign of Olmsted, Norton, and Henry Hobson Richardson to save Niagara Falls) seems to have aligned him with the Mugwump bolters of 1884. But by the mid-1880s the pressures of his professional career precluded further involvement in national politics.

The superb achievements of that career insulated Olmsted from the stigma of genteel failure which dogged his colleagues in conservative reform. Yet his parks may be understood to reflect as accurately as civil service reform or tariff reform or Mugwump journalism a common group desire to counter the headlong popular impulses of the Gilded Age. The urban park, like the well-designed campus or suburb, was in his mind an urgent antidote for the restless habits of the American majority. Because his critique of these habits was so often clothed in an aesthetic rather than political vocabulary, it was less vulnerable to public scorn. He could castigate Andrew D. White, Cornell's president, and Tweed's Peter Sweeny with equal vigor for their shortsighted use of land, and survive with his professional credentials intact. Moreover, the creation of large city park systems was one of the few enterprises of the age around which it proved possible to gather a broad consensus in favor of conscious public planning. Park reform ultimately engaged the support of three important groups—the cosmopolitan gentry, municipal politicians, and businessmen interested in speculative ventures in urbal real estate and transit—which were frequently at each others' throats over other issues confronting the city. Also, Olmsted's parks seemed to offer an attractive remedy for the dangerous problem of discontent among the urban masses. In contrast with other reforms put forward by the gentry, they visibly affected the everyday habits of large numbers of people. By providing pleasant and uplifting outlets in the narrow lives of city-dwellers, they promised a measure of social tranquility.

Yet Olmsted was constantly embittered by the public's failure to understand the purpose of his parks or accept his trained expertise. His attitude on this score was as candidly élitist as that of any political Mugwump. His anger focused on the fate of Central Park and the long quarrel over its meaning and use that ended in Olmsted's ouster from the city's park department in 1878 at the insistence of Tammany's Honest John Kelly. From the outset Olmsted had defined the park primarily as a work of art, and its primary benefits remained in his mind mainly visual and psychic. It would bring relief from the constrictions of Manhattan's expanding street grid (most vividly recalled by Edith

Wharton, who described the city of her childhood as "this little low-studded rectangular New York . . ., this cramped horizontal gridiron of a town without towers, porticoes, fountains or perspectives, hidebound in its deadly uniformity of mean ugliness . . ."). Olmsted wrote at length about the therapeutic value of the urban park in offering escape from the stacked compactions of the commercial city. Frequent release from urban tensions was vital to all urban classes, and Central Park would serve them all. While Olmsted disliked the grandiose park portals proposed by Richard Morris Hunt in the 1860s, the earliest gate names—Merchants', Artisans', Artists', and Scholars'—were consciously intended to symbolize an orderly access to the park by all classes and occupations. (The names of succeeding entries—Women's, Children's, Mariners', Strangers', and so on—pursued this theme.) While in Olmsted's mind the pleasure to be taken from the park was a highly contemplative sort of recreation, he insisted that uncultivated working people could share its subtle refreshment—that rural scenery could impose a calming sense of its own sacredness on the "rough element of the city." As time passed, Olmsted laid increasing stress on the hygienic and sociological benefits of the park. Its open spaces became, in the phrase of the day, the lungs of the city, a resort of cool breezes and cleansing sunlight against the disease-laden miasmic vapors of the inner city. Moreover, the natural simplicity of pastoral landscape would, he hoped, inspire communal feelings among all urban classes, muting resentments over disparities of wealth and fashion. For an untrusting, watchful crowd of urban strangers, the park would restore that "communicativeness" which Olmsted prized as a central American need.

All this was a mighty order for Central Park. Olmsted's insistence on the integrity of the park as a work of art, with all its elements uniting in a single organic design, was doubtless compatible with the several purposes he claimed for it. But more prosaic minds defined its multiple functions in less consistent terms and saw in its vast stretches obvious opportunities to fill empty space with fresh projects on popular demand. Olmsted took grim satisfaction in cataloging the "variety of purposes, vague and variable," urged for the park over the years: parade grounds for military displays, churches, zoos, race tracks, steeplechase, world's fair, concessions for goat, pony and donkey rides, mineral waters, sailboats, merry-go-rounds and roller-coasters, burial grounds for General Grant and other eminent dead, facilities for skating, curling, croquet, archery, tennis, cricket, and baseball, space for private gardening, fireworks displays, balloon ascensions, dog shows, and exhibitions of fat cattle. The list was unending, and the pressures for intrusion relentless.

The combat between the original concept and later amendments has raged down to the present. Defenders of the park have invoked Olmsted's genius as well as his arguments in the cause of preservation. He remains an awesome if embattled authority. Perhaps his most touching lament is found in "The Spoils of the Park," the testimony of a wounded man over his twenty-year fight to save the park from New York's politicians: "Let it be understood what this meant to me—the frustration of purposes to which I had for years given all my heart, to which I had devoted my life; the degradation of works in which my pride was centred; the breaking of promises to the future which had been to me as churchly vows."

One can read "The Spoils of the Park" with entire sympathy for Olmsted's troubles and still detect between its lines a struggle over competing goals which is precisely analagous to the strife, waged across the Gilded Age in other arenas, between the cosmopolitan, professional élitism of the Mugwump gentry and the pluralistic impulses of urban democracy under locally elected leaders. In Olmsted's case much of the problem lay in the inherent ambiguity and novelty of Central Park, the first large public park in the New World. Translating an eighteenth-century, aristocratic, European concept of sculptured pastoral space into the American urban vernacular was no easy feat. Central Park was not only a work of art, a gift of rural beauty for the dreary city, but a massive municipal public works project, and an anticipated center for lively urban recreation. These blurred purposes were built into the city's decision to launch it back in 1857. Conflicting inferences about the park were compounded by contrasting time-spans in men's thoughts about it. The politician habitually construed the park as vacant space to be filled with jobs and structures on a schedule set by the next election, the next audit or appropriation, the next batch of obligations coming due. Whether he was a Tweed man or a Kelly man or a Samuel J. Tilden Democrat, the city official saw the park in relatively short-range terms as a current item on an endless agenda. Olmsted in contrast set his goals for the park well in the future. The long reach of his thought derived in part from his special landscape style, evolved from the English picturesque tradition of Sir Uvedale Price, which aimed for a natural, informal, and untended look to spatial sequences. The appearance of a "finished" Olmsted landscape required decades to mature. The results he wanted lay, in their earliest fulfillment, forty years ahead, when he anticipated that Central Park would lie in the middle of a city population of some two million.

These rival priorities dividing landscape planner from politician sharpened the dispute which pitted Olmsted's personal authority against the pluralistic demands of the city. Landscape architecture was an infant among American professions. Olmsted worried over the complexities of its definition, its lack of popular recognition, and its consequent poverty of sanctions against the sway of democratic "common sense." He was furious about the dilettante image of the profession exploited by his critics, who, he felt, dismissed him as a "silly, heartless, upstart, sophomorical theorist. . . ." The dispute came into focus over issues of labor recruitment, park maintenance, and crime control. Olmsted wanted qualified assistants, trained in their several skills, to guide the work of a diligent labor force, hired at low wages for long hours. Politicians, on the other hand, eyed the labor force in terms of patronage quotas and rewards, tending toward greater indulgence over issues of skills, wages, and hours. Olmsted estimated that the city's park commissioners wasted nine-tenths of their energy on patronage, and he fumed over the large numbers of physical derelicts and deadbeats who wound up on the park rolls. The function of police and maintenance staffs provoked comparable quarrels. Olmsted and his aides wanted to train the keepers' force in the tactics of crowd control to protect the park against "the shock of an untrained public." For politicians the park was municipal space to be policed like the rest of the city against violent, visible, and scandalous crimes. The upshot was that major park thoroughfares were well-guarded while prostitution and petty vandalism thrived in more secluded areas.

Behind all these particular disputes lay a fundamental divergence of attitudes. Olmsted prized the park as an inviolable exemption from the city and as a counterforce against its evils, much as the civil service or tariff reformer idealized his cause as a cure for the corruptions of partisan politics. In contrast the politician, especially in the Tweed era, habitually wove the park into his calculations of local constituents' needs and "projected the city into the park."

Olmsted never satisfactorily reconciled his tranquil, unitary vision of Central Park with the desires of its users. He had special trouble coping with the demands of the active young working-class male. In his writings he repeatedly dwelt on the needs of "town-strained" women, invalid children, busy merchants and their confined wives, and families in search of Sunday relaxation. He offered the park as a surrogate pleasure for city-dwellers who could not escape to the scenic spectacles of mountain and shore favored by the rich. Sharing a widespread conception of the urban lower classes as immobilized by their working environment, he thought of the park as therapy for the plight of trapped and passive people. Like most thoughtful contemporaries of his class, he underestimated the bent for vigorous, organized leisure-time activity among boys and working men, and responded grudgingly to their desire for "manly and blood-tingling recreations," "boisterous fun and rough sports." Eventually, Olmsted built into the design of Riverside Terrace, overlooking the Hudson, certain facilities for these sorts of pastimes, but work on the Riverside project had barely begun when he left the city. Space allocations for such purposes remained for him a curiously difficult concession, symptomatic perhaps of his own rural and gentlemanly upbringing as well as his mistrust of lower-class cultural autonomy.

Lower-class political autonomy was also a problem for Olmsted, as it was for his associates in conservative reform. Over the years he reserved some of his choicest epithets for New York City Irish Democrats and their leaders. Ever since the wartime draft riots his thoughts were scarred by alienation from this breed. Periodically in the struggles over Central Park he and his friends tried to muster the city's social élite against the Democrats in the city hall in support of his positions. But the New York élite of the 1870s was a fragmented scattering of fading Knickerbockers and stylish new rich, lacking both cultural continuity and political cohesion. It was hard to mobilize into a metropolitan civic force against the localism of city politicians.

The Tammany press could afford to dismiss Olmsted's backers as "the Miss Nancies of Central Park art," who "babble in the papers and in Society Circles, about aesthetics and architecture, vistas and landscapes, the quiver of a leaf and the proper blendings of light and shade. . . ." Olmsted's friends, for whom such rhetorical sneers were commonplace, tried hard to avert his dismissal from the park in 1878. But their petition of protest, trailing signatures from prominent merchants, bankers, publishers, journalists, artists, and writers, proved useless against the will of Tammany's Kelly. Four years later Theodore Roosevelt, the young scion of the city's élite serving his political apprenticeship in the state assembly, broached a scheme to lure Olmsted back to Central Park on terms which would give him central executive authority free from local political pressures. The proposal echoed Olmsted's own prescription for sane administration with remarkable fidelity. But by then Olmsted had moved his firm to suburban Boston and washed his hands of further dealings with New York.

Another decade would pass before New York cosmopolitans could score a major victory in defense of Central Park. In 1892 Tammany's George Washington Plunkitt nudged through the state legislature a bill authorizing a race-track speedway along the west side of the park. The reaction was swift: facilities for metropolitan communication, reform mobilization, and "public-interest" lobbying had improved vastly since the 1870s. Led by the City Reform Club (which Roosevelt had organized back in 1882), cosmopolitans mounted a massive publicity campaign against the track, staged a public meeting at Cooper Union, dispatched trainloads of aroused citizens to Albany, and secured repeal within a month. At the Cooper Union rally, a letter from Olmsted had helped fuel the protest. The letter was curiously businesslike and unsentimental, stripped of aesthetic or humanitarian concern. Since the speedtrack was not only immoral but unconstitutional, in his judgment, it would "lessen the security of every man to the enjoyment of his earnings, and tend directly to anarchy." This was Olmsted's last public communication to the city he had served for twenty years.

His work on the Boston park system, to which he gave close attention over the 1880s, is an instructive sequel to his experience in New York. The peculiar topography of Boston combined with its social and political environment to help Olmsted resolve many of the conflicts precipitated over Central Park. He had been in touch with Boston park enthusiasts since his ASSA lecture there in 1870. "Boston is a crooked confused territory," one Bostonian wrote to him; "if we ever get straightened out, it must be in the next or succeeding generations; if we ever have parks, now is the time to secure the lands for the purpose." The incentive for action was the great Back Bay landfill project, which opened up choice new real estate and the promise of suburban development to the west of the city. Gathering taxpayers' support for a park system through this area proved slow work, but just when Olmsted was removed from Central Park, Boston was ready to receive him. Seared by his New York experience, warned about the growing power of Boston's Irish municipal politicians, Olmsted doubted he would fare much better in Boston. "You are dependent on a public which is not only exceedingly ignorant in respect to the concerns with which you are about to deal," he told the chairman of the city's park commission, "but which is always ready to act on superficial views of them with great and dangerous energy." He offered his service as a consultant with careful reserve. By now an established expert in his field, heading a large firm with a national pool of public and private clients, he could insist on administrative arrangements to protect his authority against the political intrusions he expected.

But Boston turned out to be different. The elegant names on the petitions—Martin Brimmer, Henry Winthrop Sargent, Charles R. Codman, Oliver Wendell Holmes, Sr., Richard Henry Dana, Jr., Charles William Eliot, William Endicott, Jr., Leverett Saltonstall—meant far more in the politics of the city than their counterparts in New York. In part because of Boston's slower growth over the century, its upper classes not only enjoyed greater solidarity by family and cultural inheritance, but retained a strong grip on the commercial, professional, and political life of the city. Godkin's remark that "Boston is the only place in America where wealth and the knowledge of how to use it are apt to coincide" seems vindicated by recent systematic analyses of nineteenth-century Brahmin staying power and the strong record of civic responsibility it produced. Olmsted's work in Boston benefited directly from Brahmin patronage. His famous "emerald necklace," winding its way over six miles from the Public Garden across Back Bay and Charlesgate, along the Fenway through Jamaica Pond and the Arnold Arboretum to its climax in Franklin Park, engaged the resources of the city in a remarkable mix of public and private enterprise. The system developed in a pattern of fruitful interaction among wealthy Back Bay and suburban landowners, museums, colleges, and other cultural institutions which migrated to the edges of his park chain. It also enjoyed steady municipal backing.

The caliber of the municipal support startled Olmsted after his bouts with Tammany Hall. His early work on the Fenway—one of the most elaborate technical feats of his career—was barely completed when Boston's first Irish Democratic mayor, Hugh O'Brien, took office in 1885. O'Brien promptly replaced the city's all-Republican park commission with Democrats. The most powerful new member was Patrick Maguire, the rising boss of the city's Democratic party. These ominous events plunged Olmsted into gloom. His fellow landscape architect, Horace Cleveland of Chicago, commiserated with him. "It gave me a sickening sensation to read your account . . .," Cleveland wrote. "It is enough to make the old Bostonians of past generations turn in their graves to think of the city being given over to Irish domination and I cannot but fear that you will suffer discomfort from this last throw of time's whirligig." Olmsted had misjudged both O'Brien and Maguire. O'Brien managed the city's business to the satisfaction of Boston Mugwumps and was soon winning favorable notice in the columns of Godkin's *Nation*. As for Maguire, a tough political professional with substantial real estate interests in suburban Roxbury near the route of Olmsted's park chain, his main political ambition was to bring Boston's Irish Democrats into functional rapport with the party's Yankee élite. His service on the park commission coincided with this aim.

Olmsted's suspicions about the new board were not easily dissolved. "Men less interested in the parks as parks, it would be hard to find," he told Norton. "It will be a study to see how their real interests will be pursued across the Civil Service regulations." By the end of the decade he was ready to confess he had been wrong. Referring to the consequences of the city's "political revolution" of 1885, he acknowledged that his work on the Boston parks had been unimpeded by a single appointment, dismissal, contract, or purchase made for partisan purposes. He knew of no other park department in the country which could match this record. His praise ended with this ultimate accolade: "I do not think that at so early a stage any other park work has come so nearly to be recognized and treated as a work of art." While Boston was hardly free of the turmoil and inefficiencies plaguing urban America, Olmsted's words paid tribute to a singular feature of the city at that time. He had discovered a nineteenth-century political community which had not yet been torn apart by factional strife, class resentment, or ethnic rancor.

There were other satisfactions. The loosely strung, cumulative quality of Olmsted's Boston park system, following topography and residential growth from city to suburb, offered a much less constricted setting for his designs than Central Park. Its development, moreover, coincided with a revolution in the technology of rapid transit—the arrival of the electric trolley—which drew a greatly enlarged and more mobile clientele to his parks. Also by the late 1880s Olmsted was able to respond more flexibly to the growing public taste for active recreation which would change the style of American popular culture in the decade ahead. His rationales for Franklin Park, the last of his three major urban parks, rehearsed the arguments for pastoral tranquility to counteract the oppressions of city life—"excessive nervous tension, over-anxiety, hasteful disposition, impatience, irritability"—and noted that the test of the park would be its value to the wives and mothers of the working class, the class which "shortly in the future [will] lead in the affairs of the city." The broad central space of Franklin Park was designed as a scenic country park. But around this rural core Olmsted introduced some ten other segments—space for boys' athletics, tennis courts and ball diamonds, refreshment pergola, musical ampitheater,·zoo, deer park, nursery, playground (complete with see-saws and goat carriages), and a carriage promenade to be decorated with statues, bird cages, and water jets. One has the sense that Franklin Park was somehow Olmsted's Boston response to the popular pressures on Central Park.

Franklin Park was not expected, however, to bear the whole burden of modern activism. Olmsted wanted no men's athletic teams playing there; he wanted labor agitators and other speechmakers barred from its grounds; he wanted schoolchildren trained in dutiful respect to its peaceful influences; and he repeatedly urged that flat land outside the park be set aside for military musters, fireworks, and balloon ascensions. He specified that other facilities for physical activity be located at scattered sites elsewhere in the city. Most successful of these, in his mind, was the Charlesbank outdoor gymnasium. A letter to the journalist Sylvester Baxter, a chief promoter of his Boston park system, reflects Olmsted's satisfaction at the well-ordered social hierarchy operating at this center. "As far as I can estimate," he wrote, "90% of all those who use it are young men of the 'working class,' factory hands &c. Negroes and Jews in their full proportion. The remaining 10% chiefly clerks, mostly of low degree, about 1% of college men or others coming well dressed and whom you might find at the Athletic Club." The system was working.

In succeeding years, especially during the mayoralty of the young Brahmin Democrat Josiah Quincy, the city would expand its playground and gymnasium program well beyond Olmsted's prescription. And in the early 1890s, under Grover Cleveland's young protégé, Governor William E. Russell of Cambridge, the state created a metropolitan park commission, chaired by Olmsted's old friend Charles Francis Adams, Jr., which supervised a vast elaboration of parkland, boulevards, and beaches through the outer reaches of the city. Two Olmsted disciples, Baxter and the young landscape architect Charles Eliot (son of Harvard's president), were the driving force behind this expansion of Olmsted's Boston work toward the end of the century. As Olmsted's career neared its close, he urged his partners to concentrate their best energies on the completion of the Boston projects. In their potential historical and educational impact they were, he said, "the most important work of our profession now in hand anywhere in the world."

During one of Olmsted's periodic moods of gloomy self-doubt in the early 1880s, his friend Norton told him that he expected too much of the American people if he wanted them to understand him: "You are preaching truths above the comprehension of our generation." Venting his own harsh regard for American culture, Norton added, "You are compelled to throw your pearls before swine, and are fortunate if they do not turn and rend you for not giving them their favorite swill." When Olmsted died in 1903, Norton wrote to Olmsted's son in gentler tones: "Few men have done better service than he, service beneficent not only to his own generation, but to generation after generation in the long future." As it turned out, the years proved kinder to Olmsted's reputation than to his creations.

His major parks, yielding steadily to popular pressures toward redefinition of use and thus of appearance, reached a peak of public acceptance around the time of World War I. Beginning in the 1920s, as the automobile replaced the trolley, exploded the spatial boundaries of the city, and started thinning out the population at its centers, the first small signs of neglect and blight appeared. Americans now took their rural scenery through a car window, and urban carriage boulevards widened into commuter routes, often cutting off parkland from surrounding neighborhoods. A subtle mixture of modern trends—the shift toward commercialized spectator pleasures, the intensified organization of urban play, black and white migration in and out of the city, the relative impoverishment of municipal budgets as the federal welfare state began to deal more directly with individual human needs, the intangible but obvious triumph of city-oriented living styles over rural memories— all diminished the utility and attractions of the large urban park. By the 1960s a much smaller fraction of New Yorkers were using Central Park than a century before, and the desertion of Franklin Park had become a Boston scandal. In the teeth of public indifference, urban planners conferred earnestly to discover safe and vitalizing uses for vacant park space. Twentieth-century sociology and technology had all but overwhelmed Olmsted's planning vision, and the best hope for the survival of his parks seemed to lie in their rediscovery as works of art.

Yet to measure Olmsted's significance by the current condition of his parks would miss the point of his career. He had pioneered a new profession and prodded the idea of the public park well along toward maturity in America. Beyond that, his career forecast the process by which cosmopolitan élites, deprived of grass-roots political power, learned to assert their authority in public life through specific technical expertise in the higher echelons of urban governance. He left reasons for rediscovery beyond his time. As one student of modern urban landscaping put it: "The possibilities of master planning and urban design, by which construction and green space could play a gay and variable counterpoint throughout our communities, are just beginning to make some small impact upon our development thinking, though forecast one hundred years ago by Olmsted." Another specialist added, "We have not shown the ability to design anything much larger than a tot lot which reflects the differences between our way of life and that of Olmsted."

Olmsted's way of life, together with many of the values he shared with the genteel reformers of the Gilded Age, disappeared before the nineteenth century was out. His hopes for a measure of social amelioration through projects in landscape architecture, like the hope of the civil service reformer that democratic politics might be purified by an end to spoils, and the hope of the tariff reformer that freer trade would help solve the riddle of domestic economic strife, depended on an all-but-forgotten social vision. Its believers thought that adequate structures of social and political intercourse could be defined for the popular mass by a cultured élite hovering above, to temper and redress the major public grievances of their day. Few of them ever wholly dropped their faith in gradual human improvement under the stewardship of trained talent. But their chosen tactics of improvement—even Olmsted's—only dimly anticipated the wrenching demands of the century ahead.

For all his artistic genius and brooding concern to enrich the quality of urban life by spatial design, Olmsted shared the programmatic inhibitions of his generation. He and his friends imagined that a commonwealth of free and diverse people, contained in an orderly public environment, governed by a benign and sanitary administrative state, was not only desirable but possible. Idealizing a rather static and formal conception of the social relations which ought to govern the American populace, they underestimated the aggressive thrust of American pluralism. The multiplying dislocations and resentments of social inequality and the bold measures required to order a nation of hostile strangers remained beyond their reckoning. Thus they minimized the need for more direct solutions to the problems accumulating in their lifetime. They saw no virtue in strenuous political manipulation, official coercion of private behavior, or closely managed economic change. Their successors in reform discovered otherwise. Meanwhile Olmsted's parks remained as battered monuments to the imagination of their generation at its best, and also to the constraints of their democratic faith.

ABRAM STEVENS HEWITT

Opening the Brooklyn Bridge

From charter to completion, the Brooklyn Bridge was more than fifteen years in the making, and its opening on May 24, 1883, was a major public event. It was called "The People's Day," and the bridge was presented to "the people."

Major public ceremonies like this one are often important moments of cultural definition in which participants attempt to define where their society has been and what they see as its future. In this case, a structure as seemingly neutral as a bridge from Manhattan to Brooklyn had to be carefully examined for what it had to say about change and the impact of change on the class structure.

That is precisely what Abram Hewitt did when he delivered the keynote address at the opening ceremony. Hewitt was an important Democratic congressman. He had already made a large fortune in iron, steel, railroads, and mining, and in 1886 he would be elected mayor of New York City—partly on the strength of this address. Like most of his audience, he had grown to adulthood in a society entirely different from the one that he now lived in. As persistent a spokesman for change as one is likely to find in the Gilded Age, Hewitt could not preside over the opening of the Brooklyn Bridge without revealing his anxieties and making the bridge into a symbol powerful enough to transcend his doubts.

If we assume that Hewitt's address was a typical Gilded Age statement, what definitions does that term take on? What is Hewitt's attitude toward progress? toward science and technology? In what sense does Hewitt speak for "the people," and in what sense for a narrower constituency?

"What hath God wrought!" were the words of wonder, which ushered into being the magnetic telegraph, the greatest marvel of the many marvelous inventions of the present century. It was the natural impulse of the pious maiden who chose this first message of reverence and awe, to look to the Divine Power as the author of a new gospel. For it was the invisible, and not the visible agency, which addressed itself to her perceptions. Neither the bare poles nor the slender wire, nor the magnetic battery, could suggest an adequate explanation of the extinction of time and space which was manifest to her senses, and she could only say, "What hath God wrought!"

But when we turn from the unsightly telegraph to the graceful structure at whose portal we stand, and when the airy outline of its curves of beauty, pendant between massive towers suggestive of art alone, is contrasted with the over-reaching vault of heaven above and the ever moving flood of waters beneath, the work of omnipotent power, we are irresistibly moved to exclaim, What hath *man* wrought!

Man hath indeed wrought far more than strikes the eye in this daring undertaking, by the general judgment of engineers, without a rival among the wonders of human skill. It is not the work of any one man or any one age. It is the result of the study, of the experience, and of the knowledge of many men in many ages. It is not merely a creation; it is a growth. It stands before us to-day as the sum and epitome of human knowledge; as the very heir of the ages; as the latest glory of centuries of patient observation, profound study and accumulated skill, gained, step by step, in the never-ending struggle of man to subdue the forces of nature to his control and use. . . .

What message, then, of hope and cheer does this achievement convey to those who would fain believe that love travels hand in hand with light along the rugged pathway of time? Have the discoveries of science, the triumphs of art, and the progress of civilization, which have made its accomplishment a possibility and a reality, promoted the welfare of mankind, and raised the great mass of the people to a higher plane of life?

This question can best be answered by comparing the compensation of the labor employed in the building of this bridge, with the earnings of labor upon works of equal magnitude in ages gone by. The money expended for the work of construction proper on the bridge, exclusive of land damages and other outlays, such as interest, not entering into actual cost, is nine million ($9,000,000) dollars. This money has been distributed in numberless channels—for quarrying, for mining, for smelting, for fabricating the metals, for shaping the materials, and erecting the work, employing every kind and form

From Abram Stevens Hewitt, *Address Delivered on the Occasion of the Opening of the New York and Brooklyn Bridge*, May 24th, 1883 (New York: John Polhemus, 1883), pp. 4–5, 7–9, 19–20, 22–24.

of human labor. The wages paid at the bridge itself may be taken as the fair standard of the wages paid for the work done elsewhere. These wages are:

	Average	
Laborers	$1.75	per day
Blacksmiths	3.50 to $4.00	do.
Carpenters	3.00 to 3.50	do.
Masons and stonecutters	3.50 to 4.00	do.
Riggers	2.00 to 2.50	do.
Painters	2.00 to 3.50	do.

Taking all these kinds of labor into account, the wages paid for work on the bridge will thus average $2.50 per day.

Now if this work had been done at the time when the Pyramids were built, with the skill, appliances and tools then in use, and if the money available for its execution had been limited to nine million ($9,000,000) dollars, the laborers employed would have received an average of not more than two cents per day, in money of the same purchasing power as the coin of the present era. In other words, the effect of the discoveries of new methods, tools and laws of force, has been to raise the wages of labor more than an hundred fold, in the interval which has elapsed since the Pyramids were built. I shall not weaken the suggestive force of this statement by any comments upon its astounding evidence of progress, beyond the obvious corollary, that such a state of civilization as gave birth to the Pyramids would now be the signal for universal bloodshed, revolution, and anarchy. I do not under estimate the hardships borne by the labor of our time. . . .

But this is not the only lesson to be drawn from such a comparison. The Pyramids were built by the sacrifices of the living for the dead. They served no useful purpose, except to make odious to future generations the tyranny which degrades humanity to the level of the brute. In this age of the world such a waste of effort would not be tolerated. To-day the expenditures of communities are directed to useful purposes. Except upon works designed for defence in time of war, the wealth of society is now mainly expended in opening channels of communication for the free play of commerce, and the communion of the human race. . . .

. . . Will the Bridge lead, as has been forcibly suggested, and in some quarters hopefully anticipated, to the further union of the two cities under one name and one government? . . .

It is only when we come to consider the problem of governing great masses, that the serious elements of the question present themselves, and must be determined before a satisfactory answer can be given. The tendency of modern civilization is towards the concentration of population in dense masses. This is due to the higher and more diversified life, which can be secured by association and co-operation on a large scale, affording not merely greater comfort and often luxury, but actually distributing the fruits of labor on a more equitable basis than is possible in sparsely settled regions, and among feeble communities. The great improvements of our day in labor-saving machinery, and its application to agriculture, enable the nation to be fed with a less percentage of its total force thus applied, and leave a larger margin of population free to engage in such other pursuits as are best carried on in large cities. . . .

With this rapid growth of urban population, have grown the contemporaneous complaints of corrupt administration and bad municipal government. The outcry may be said to be universal, for it comes from both sides of the Atlantic; and the complaints appear to be in direct proportion to the size of cities. It is obvious, therefore, that the knowledge of the art of local government has not kept pace with the growth of population. . . .

The men who controlled this enterprise at the outset were not all of the best type; some of them, as we have seen, were public jobbers. But they knew that they could not build a bridge, although they had no doubt of their ability to govern a city. They thereupon proceeded to organize the knowledge which existed as to the construction of bridges; and they held the organization thus created responsible for results. Now, we know that it is at least as difficult to govern a city as to build a bridge, and yet, as citizens, we have deliberately allowed the ignorance of the community to be organized for its government, and we then complain that it is a failure. Until we imitate the example of the Ring, and organize the intelligence of the community for its government, our complaint is childish and unreasonable. But we shall be told that there is no analogy between building a bridge and governing a city. Let us examine this objection. A city is made up of infinite interests. They vary from hour to hour, and conflict is the law of their being. Many of the elements of social life are what mathematicians term "variables of the independent order." The problem is, to reconcile these conflicting interests, and variable elements into one organization which shall work without jar, and allow each citizen to pursue his calling, if it be an honest one, in peace and quiet.

Now, turn to the bridge. It looks like a motionless mass of masonry and metal: but, as a matter of fact, it is instinct with motion. There is not a particle of matter in it which is at rest even for the minutest portion of time. It is an aggregation of unstable elements, changing with every change in the temperature, and every movement of the heavenly bodies. The problem was, out of these unstable elements, to produce absolute stability; and it was this problem which the engineers, the organized intelligence, had to solve, or confess to inglorious failure. . . .

Now if our political system were guided by organized intelligence, it would not seek to repress the free play of human interests and emotions, of human hopes and fears, but would make provision for their development and exercise, in accordance with the higher law of liberty and morality. . . .

No, let us rather learn the lesson of the bridge. Instead of attempting to restrict suffrage, let us try to educate the voters; instead of disbanding parties, let each citizen within the party always vote, but never for a man who is unfit to hold office. Thus parties, as well as voters, will be organized on the basis [of] intelligence. . . .

TALIAFERRO P. SHAFFNER

Belonging: The Odd Fellows

Americans could derive only so much inspiration from a bridge, only so much solace from Abram Hewitt's speechmaking. For most people, the stresses of the Gilded Age were expressed and absorbed in more prosaic (but in some ways equally ceremonial) institutions. The most important of these institutions were the churches and the fraternal associations.

At the beginning of the nineteenth century, only a few thousand Americans belonged to fraternal associations. By its end, over six million persons claimed membership in dozens of organizations, and fraternal lodges outnumbered churches in all the large cities.

Odd Fellowship was brought to the United States from England in 1817. Its rituals and symbolic language were controlled through a central national body, the Sovereign Grand Lodge. In 1874, when the following selection was published, the order contained fifteen degrees or levels to which members could aspire, including one for women. The most recent study of the organization finds that membership was concentrated among merchants and tradesmen but included a variety of skilled craftsmen, especially—in the 1870s—railroad workers.

In reading this excerpt, determine what function Odd Fellowship served in late-nineteenth-century America. What was the purpose of the scientific emphasis? Why all the attention to disruptive elements within the lodge? What do you make of these designs (which appear on every page of Shaffner's book)? Were the Odd Fellows largely a social organization? Social for what purpose, and in what context?

One of the staple commodities of Gilded Age culture was the success ethic. According to the prevailing mythology, the ladder to wealth and honor could be climbed by those able and willing to mix hard work, an appropriate moral code, and some measure of luck. The dreams of success that had so powerful an impact on Americans were exemplified in the popular yarns of Horatio Alger, whose first book, *Ragged Dick* (1867), was followed by over one hundred more, all of them eagerly devoured by the reading public. Since not everyone could achieve by the standards which Alger held out, living in the Gilded Age meant finding a way to cope with one's own failures in a world in which success was expected. What might be the relationship between the fraternal association and the success ethic?

From Taliaferro P. Shaffner, *Odd Fellowship Illustrated* in an Address Delivered before the Grand Lodge of the State of Kentucky, by Taliaferro P. Shaffner, Past Grand Representative (New York: Russell Brothers, 1874), pp. 34–36, 114–115, 135–136, 139–145.

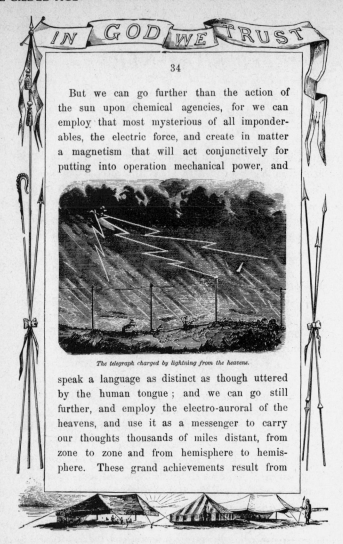

IN GOD WE TRUST

34

But we can go further than the action of the sun upon chemical agencies, for we can employ that most mysterious of all imponderables, the electric force, and create in matter a magnetism that will act conjunctively for putting into operation mechanical power, and

The telegraph charged by lightning from the heavens.

speak a language as distinct as though uttered by the human tongue ; and we can go still further, and employ the electro-auroral of the heavens, and use it as a messenger to carry our thoughts thousands of miles distant, from zone to zone and from hemisphere to hemisphere. These grand achievements result from

the blending together of created elements, thus accomplishing transcendent results from the unison of correlative forces.

I have thus referred to the elements of creation to show you that God has ordained by his law that there shall be a unison of action, that there shall be an association of things, and not one jot or tittle of that law can be changed or modified in the least. The result is produced by the union of forces initiated into existence by Divinity, and coexistent with such initial is the law governing them.

Unison of Man's Purposes

God did not limit the beneficial results to the union of elements or integrals of matter, but he designed the philosophy of association to be indispensable to the condition of man, whom, notwithstanding he created in his own image, he knew required the influence of association to make him subservient to the laws of affinity. Eve was given to man for the purposes of production and association, and for fear that her influence might not accomplish the desired end, God solemnly decreed, by inexorable law, that man should love his fellow man, and that he should do unto others as he would have others do unto him. . . .

Disturbers of Unison

The "harmony" of the lodge for many years has been other than that of the "mug and pipe" kind. It is now confined to a question of sentiment. Men are not always free from passion, and there exist many who are disturbers of the peace and happiness of the lodge meeting. An immaterial question may be under discussion, when up rises some discontented spirit, who cannot rest content if others do not think as he does, and step by step such an one goes on until he works himself into a passion, and, for the time being, becomes a fool, and only needs the clown's apparel to complete his characteristic. We have seen such exhibitions in lodges; and it is only a "show" for a man to lessen his dignity in a sacred place and thus expose his ignorance. Better far that he should learn to curb his temper and employ the force of his mind, because ere long, as surely as water findeth its level by gravitation, he will be forced by circumstances to occupy it. "Man, know thyself," is a good text to study through life.

All zealous Odd Fellows will agree with me that the most unpleasant sight we meet in the lodge meeting is the man with an ungovernable temper. None of us are free from such improprieties, in a greater or less degree, and as we grow older we become ashamed of many such errors in our past career. . . .

Subordination

The welfare of society is dependent upon the complete observance of order, conformably to God's first law. In the organic movements of creation we find that there is precision, and each heavenly body moves in exact limits and time. The planets and the myriads of stars move with conjunctive forces, and the astronomer can determine exactly what time a comet will appear to the people of the earth. This is the result of order—of subordination to superior powers. . . .

And so did God contemplate that animal creation should conform to power, the lesser to the greater, and that power is knowledge—which may be of different gradations, and each perfect or of the highest potential. The artisan can excel by study and the exercise of discriminating judgment; the man of letters can obtain higher recognition just in conformity to the degree of educational and reflective evolvement. In like manner, as creatures of government, we must exercise on the one hand toleration and on the other subordination. The inferior must yield to the superior. But these relative positions may be by consent and subject to limitation; that is to say, the officer, acting as the executive of the conclave, only exercises his superiority when performing his official functions; and in due time and turn, he ceases to be invested with authority, and thus becomes subordinate to his successor. . . .

If we fully comprehend our positions, and know ourselves, as constituents of society we can have order and harmony as glorious in illustration as is exemplified by the gems that ornament the canopy of heaven. On the other hand, if we live in abnegation, and assume to be twins to all mankind, equals at all times and under all conditions, then we will find society disorganized and races existing as wild hordes, and the ploughshare will be turned into scalping knives, tomahawks and arrow heads. . . .

Home and Family

"Lizzie Borden, with an Ax . . ."

Andrew Jackson Borden might well have been an Odd Fellow, at least in the early stages of his career. Born into poverty in 1822—the year of Abram Hewitt's birth—he made his first money as an undertaker. The Dun and Bradstreet reports, below, illuminate Borden's success in his middle years.

In the summer of 1892, Lizzie Borden apparently killed her father, Andrew, and her stepmother. (She was never convicted, but after she died the murder weapon, an ax, was found on the family property.) According to one theory, she committed the crime when her father threatened to rewrite his will and leave all his property to his wife. Guilty or not, she was ostracized by the Fall River, Massachusetts, community for the rest of her life.

From the following documents, develop some possible social explanations for Lizzie's alleged act. Do the floor plan, the credit ratings, and the neighborhood description form a coherent package? Or is something out of whack? To what extent could Lizzie Borden's crime—if she committed it—be a result of stresses produced within her family by the Gilded Age?

Dun and Bradstreet Credit Reports on Andrew Jackson Borden and His Partner

Dec. 8, 1852: "We are well acquainted with both these men and consider them good. They have been in business together some eight years and have always maintained a good reputation. Both have families and appear good for wants."

Materials from Stephen Nissenbaum, "Lizzie Borden and Her World," in Stephen Botein et al. (eds.), *Experiments in Teaching History* (Cambridge, Mass.: Harvard–Danforth Center for Teaching and Learning, 1977), pp. 62–63. Reprinted by permission of the author.

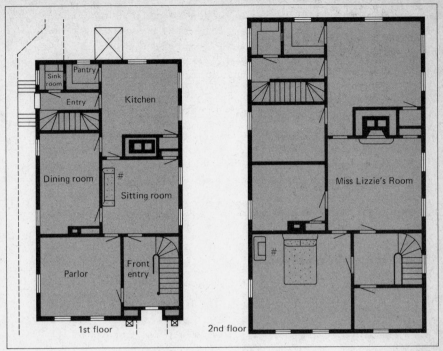

Sink room | Pantry
Entry | Kitchen
Dining room | # | Sitting room
Parlor | Front entry

1st floor

Miss Lizzie's Room

#

2nd floor

# Indicates where bodies were found—Mr. Borden in sitting room and Mrs. Borden upstairs.

Map of the Borden House.

Oct. 13, 1853: "Good for wants."

March 13, 1854: "Young and good businessmen, attentive and industrious, think means sufficient for the business, in good grade and standing here and considered good for their engagements: making money."

Sept. 1, 1854 through July 1, 1855: "Same."

Jan. 1, 1856: "Good for all wants."

July 17, 1856: "Both are rising young men."

Jan. 28, 1863: "Safe and sound."

Aug. 14, 1863: "Doing well and should pay promptly."

Sept. 8, 1866: "Have just bought real estate for $4,000 in good location. Firm among the best."

Feb. 26, 1867: "Getting rich, own $10,000 worth of real estate in the best parts of the city. Sound as a dollar. Doing good business worth $40,000–50,000, good for wants."

Aug. 3, 1867: "Worth at least $60,000."

April 23, 1868: "Good enough they buy for cash."

Oct. 22, 1868: "Doing good business and gaining."

March 6, 1869: "Good enough, worth $75,000 sure and in good credit."

Sept. 10, 1869: "Same."

March 3, 1870: "Good honest and reliable men doing sound business, worth nearly $60,000–70,000, own real estate worth about $50,000, are good and sound."

Sept. 14, 1870: "Doing good business and are good for all wants."
March 8, 1871: "Are safe and reliable, doing a large business, worth
$75,000–100,000, and gaining all the time. Perfectly sound."
March 18, 1872: "Worth $100,000–125,000, sound and substantial."
Sept. 7, 1872: "Means large, doing well, and in excellent standing."

Where the Bordens Lived

Ward 4,B   Second Street

No.	Name	Age	Occupt'n
89	Doughlas, Oscar F.	48	Photographer
89	Paltz, Harold	25	Clerk
89	Young, Frank M.	42	Paver
89	Burton, Austin L.	25	"
89	Robinson, Frank M.	21	"
89	" Alfred	25	"
89	Dowd, Andrew	41	Foreman
89	Welch, Thomas	51	Paver
89	Simmons, Charles	23	Clerk
89	Austin, Anson G.	25	
89	Deloiry, James	21	Laborer
89	Finney, John	50	Peddler
89	Condon, John	36	Machinist
90	Hamilton, Charles	54	Decorator
90	" Elmer	20	"
90	Gormley, John H.	32	Butcher
91	Bowen, Seabury W.	42	Physician
92	Borden, Andrew J.	67	Retired Mer.
93	Miller, Southard H.	80	Carpenter
93	" Franklin H.	43	Artist
96	Kelley, Michael	35	Physician
98	Chace, Nathan	64	Driver
98	" David	29	Clerk
98	" Mark	54	Hostler
100	Lee, Chew	36	Laundryman
100	Sing, Yenk	39	"
104	Hughes Christopher	52	Clergyman
104	O'Keefe, John D.	30	"
104	Sheedy, David F.	27	"
106	Brennan, George H.	27	Editor
110	Kelly, George H.	48	Restauranteur
110	Whitehead, Edward	61	Clerk
110	Barry, Patrick	31	Tailor
110	Creeden, Edward	31	"
110	Rouke, William	30	Clerk
110	Pike, Nathan	55	Stonemason
116	Robinson, John	54	Confectioner
120	Lee, Hop	53	Laundryman
120	Airlie, Gardner	31	Clerk

Victorian Photographs

The following photographs portray the experience of well-to-do Victorian families—families in many respects not unlike that headed by Andrew Jackson Borden. "Bedroom in the Finch House" requires that we ask the meaning of possessions for these late-nineteenth-century elites, and that we try to come up with some reason why the feeling, or tone, of this room is so different from what one would expect to find in its 1980 equivalent.

"Family Gathering Around a Portrait of Its Patriarch" also tells us something about Victorian family life, and especially, of course, about patriarchy (a form of community in which the father is the supreme authority in the family). Was the notion of patriarchy still relevant to the society of the Gilded Age? Might there be some connection between the family relationships suggested here and Lizzie Borden's alleged murder of her father?

Bedroom in the Finch House. *Minnesota Historical Society, St. Paul; photo by T. W. Ingersoll, St. Paul.*

Family Gathering Around a Portrait of Its Patriarch, c. 1890, by Charles Currier. *Library of Congress.*

Adjusting to Industrialization

The following tables deal with two different aspects of adjustment to industrialization. The first—on population of senators' residences— provides some insight into the relationship between economic and political systems during a period of rapid industrial growth. One might normally expect that there would be some clear congruence between our economic and political systems. That is, as industrialists such as those produced in Fall River made their mark on the economic life of the state and nation, political institutions would begin to reflect their growing influence. The table examines this hypothesis for the United States Senate. How rapidly and thoroughly did the Senate respond to the rise of an industrial and urban America?

The second table gives us some data with which to measure the experience of workers under industrialization. It describes the occupational history of 171 common laborers employed in Newburyport, Massachusetts, in 1850. What had happened to them ten, twenty, and thirty years later? Is there a significant amount of occupational and/or geographical mobility in Newburyport? What relationship might exist between worker mobility (or the lack of it) and organizations like the Odd Fellows?

Gilded Age Politics: The U. S. Senate

Population of Senators' Residences Compared with Nation as a Whole

	16th Senate (44)	Nation in 1820	36th Senate (66)	Nation in 1860	56th Senate (89)	Nation in 1900	76th Senate (96)	Nation in 1940
0–2,500	64% (28)	93%	35% (23)	80%	30% (27)	60%	16% (15)	44%
2,500–10,000	23% (10)	3%	36% (24)	5%	17% (15)	8%	19% (18)	9%
10,000–25,000	2% (1)	1%	9% (6)	3%	19% (17)	6%	16% (15)	8%
25,000–50,000	5% (2)	1%	5% (3)	2%	9% (8)	4%	19% (18)	6%
50,000–100,000	2% (1)	1%	5% (3)	1%	8% (7)	4%	8% (8)	6%
Over 100,000	5% (2)	1%	11% (7)	8%	17% (15)	19%	23% (22)	29%

From Ari Hoogenboom, "Industrialism and Political Leadership: A Case Study of the United States Senate," in Frederic Cople Jaher (ed.), *The Age of Industrialism in America: Essays in Social Structure and Cultural Values* (New York: Free Press, 1968), p. 58. Copyright 1968 by the Free Press. Reprinted by permission.

The Working Class

Occupational and Geographical Mobility of Three Groups of Laborers, 1850–1880

Year	Occupational status attained				Rate of persist-ence[a]	Number in sample
	Un-skilled	Semi-skilled	Skilled	Non-manual		
			1850 Census group			
1860	64%	16%	15%	5%	32%	55
1870	36	39	9	15	64	35
1880	57	21	7	14	40	14
			1860 Census group			
1870	74	12	8	5	33	74
1880	69	19	6	6	65	48
			1870 Census group			
1880	79	6	10	5	41	102

[a] This column provides a measure of the geographical mobility of workmen in the sample. The rate of persistence of a group for a particular decade is defined as that proportion of the group recorded on the census at the start of the decade that is still present in the community at the end of the decade. Thus 32 percent of the unskilled laborers of 1850 still lived in Newburyport in 1860; 64 percent of the men in this group as of 1860 still lived in Newburyport in 1870, and so forth.

From Stephan Thernstrom, *Poverty and Progress: Social Mobility in a Nineteenth Century City* (Cambridge, Mass.: Harvard University Press, 1964). This citation from the Atheneum edition (New York, 1970), p. 96. Copyright © 1964 by the President and Fellows of Harvard College. Reprinted by permission.

CHAPTER 3

The City

In 1860 there were only 16 cities in the United States with populations over 50,000, and only 3 cities of more than 250,000. By 1900 the corresponding figures were 78 and 15. In the half-century after 1850, Chicago grew from less than 30,000 to a city of more than a million. For older, Eastern cities, growth meant change in function and structure. Boston, in 1850 a concentrated merchant city of some 200,000 persons, dependent on ocean-going commerce, was by 1900 a sprawling industrial city with a population of over one million.

Entirely new cities arose to meet particular demands of time and place. For George Pullman, of sleeping-car fame, big cities were sordid and disorderly places that spawned crime and violence. He planned and built an entirely new community isolated from disruptive influences where (so he believed) his workers would always be happy (he was mistaken). Western cities also expanded rapidly, usually by virtue of some nearby exploitable resource. Wichita was one of several Kansas towns founded on the cattle trade. Seattle, Washington, was a timber city. Denver had its origins in the 1857 gold rush, but it remained to service the Great Plains much as Chicago did the Midwest.

The new urban residents were often either immigrants from abroad or migrants from the nation's small towns and rural areas. In 1910 perhaps a third of the total urban population were native Americans of rural origin; another one-fourth were foreign-born. Although the nonurban population increased absolutely in each decade before 1950, it diminished relatively. During and after the Civil War, the widespread adoption of a variety of labor-saving devices, including cultivators, reapers, mowers, threshers, and corn planters, allowed fewer and fewer farmers to feed the urban populace. Certain areas such as rural New England showed marked reductions in population. "We cannot all live in cities," wrote Horace Greeley in the 1860s, "yet nearly all seem determined to do so."

The migration into the United States from abroad was, simply put, a major folk migration. There were 4.1 million foreign-born in the United States in 1860, 13.5 million foreign-born in 1910. And to these numbers must be added the children of the foreign-born—15.6 million in 1900, 18.9 million (more than one out of every five Americans) by 1910.

Some cities attracted a disproportionate share of the foreign-born. By 1910, New York City and two older Massachusetts cities, Fall River and Lowell, had more than 40 percent foreign-born. Twelve major cities, including Boston, Chicago, Milwaukee, Detroit, and San Francisco, had between 30 and 40 percent foreign-born. Seventeen other cities, including Seattle, Portland, Omaha, and Oakland, had over 20 percent foreign-born. (Most Southern cities had less than 10 percent.)

After 1880, another change of importance occurred. The national origin of the nation's foreign-born population shifted from the Northern and Western European mix characteristic of previous decades to the Southern and Eastern European, Jewish and Catholic, mix dominant in 1900. In contrast to the earlier immigrants, a larger proportion of the later immigrants concentrated in the ghettoes of Northeastern industrial cities. On New York City's Lower East Side, more than 30,000 people were squeezed into half a dozen city blocks.

Ethnic clustering was nothing new, but the unfamiliar languages, customs, and religious practices of the Italians, Russians, Poles, and Slavs seemed to many observers to be associated with slums, unemployment, delinquency, and disease. The later immigrants were also held responsible for the growth of "alien" ideologies—anarchism and socialism—in large American cities in the last quarter of the century. And there was enough truth in this charge to give it some credence. "Red" Emma Goldman, one of the nation's most active anarchists, was Russian-born. Her friend, Polish-born Alexander Berkman, made an unsuccessful attempt to kill steel magnate Henry Clay Frick during the 1892 Homestead strike. In Chicago, a center of working-class politics, radical political ideas were especially well-represented, and radical leaders were more often than not German-born. Germany, after all, had produced Karl Marx, and Russia the anarchist Mikhail Bakunin. Europe simply had a more well-developed radical tradition than the United States. Many new immigrants had with them some portion of this tradition when they set foot on American shores.

This chapter explores several aspects of late-nineteenth-century urban history. How did urban political structures respond to increased population and to the new immigrants? How and why did urban residential patterns change? Were the cities of 1900 simply larger versions of their ancestors of the 1860s, or did they function in different ways? Most important, we shall be concerned with how the urban experience affected ordinary Americans. Were immigration and ghetto life uprooting and seriously disruptive experiences, or did immigrants easily become attached to new values, customs, and institutions as the old ones were stripped away? How did urban residents perceive their lives in the new cities, and how did they change their behavior based on those perceptions?

Writer Hamlin Garland's perception of the impact of his own mobility may have general relevance. Raised in a stable rural environment, Garland had settled with his family in New York City. Yet he remained uneasy about his decision to live there: "No! I am not *entirely* content. Deep down in my consciousness is a feeling of guilt, a sense of disloyalty to my ancestors, which renders me uneasy. It may be that this is only a survival of the mental habit of my boyhood, a tribute to my father and his self-reliant generation." American cities must have been full of people experiencing similar emotions.

RICHARD SENNETT

Urban Violence: The Union Park Experience

In this essay, sociologist Richard Sennett describes the way the residents of a middle-class Chicago neighborhood responded to an epidemic of violence they thought had overtaken their city. Sennett argues that the residents of Union Park reacted the way they did because of the ways their family structures affected their relationships with the larger urban world around them. As you read the essay, try to think of alternative ways of explaining the conduct of this middle-class neighborhood. Begin with these questions: How were these people to know there *was* a crime wave in Chicago? How can we explain the difference between the way they *perceived* the city and the way it actually was? You may want to consider the possibility that Union Park residents were *not* shadowboxing with a myth after all, but that their ways of life were in real danger from what they chose to call "immigrant anarchists."

. . .This study seeks the hidden connections between two seemingly disparate phenomena in a quiet middle-class neighborhood of Chicago in the late nineteenth century: the family patterns of the people of the community and the peculiar response made by men living there to the eruption of violence in their midst. In imagining how the structure of family life was related to the character of men's reaction to violence, I have tried to recapture some of the subtlety of what it was like to be a middle-class city dweller during this era of rapid urban growth.

In the years 1886 and 1888 an epidemic of violence broke out in this quiet neighborhood of Chicago. The striking feature of this epidemic lay not in the violent events themselves but in the reaction of shopkeepers, store clerks, accountants, and highly skilled laborers to the disorder suddenly rampant among their sedate homes. Their reaction to violence was impassioned to an extent that in retrospect seems unwarranted by events; indeed, it is the contrast between the limited character of the disorder and the sense residents had of being overwhelmingly threatened by anarchy that suggests that the response could have been a product of larger, seemingly unrelated social forces, such as the structure of family life.

The Community Setting

The scene of the disturbance, which I shall name Union Park, was an area centered on the near West Side of Chicago around a rather large park formally landscaped in the early 1850s. Like most of the middle and lower middle-class neighborhoods of American industrial cities in the later nineteenth century, the area was considered so nondescript that it was never given a special name, as were the richer and poorer sections of Chicago. Its people were the forgotten men of that era, neither poor enough to be rebels nor affluent enough to count in the affairs of the city. . . .

During the middle 1880s, it was in modest, cheerless Union Park that a series of unexpected events broke out. A bloody encounter between laborers and police took place on its borders during the Haymarket Riot of 1886, to be followed eighteen months later by a series of highly expert robberies in the community, a crime wave that culminated in the murder of a leading Union Park resident. Union Park reacted by holding a whole class—the poor, and

From Richard Sennett, "Middle-Class Families and Urban Violence: The Experience of a Chicago Community in the Nineteenth Century," in Stephan Thernstrom and Richard Sennett (eds.), *Nineteenth-Century Cities: Essays in the New Urban History* (New Haven: Yale University Press, 1969), pp. 386–388, 397, 399–418. © 1969 by Yale University; all rights reserved. Reprinted by permission.

especially the immigrant poor—responsible for the course of unique and rather narrow events. . . .

The effect of the riot and the train of burglaries and murder was to put the citizens in a frame of mind where only the closure of the community through constant surveillance and patrolling would reassure them. Indeed, the characteristics of their reaction to violence could only lead to such a voluntary isolation: everyone "knew" immediately what was wrong; and what was wrong was overwhelming; it was nothing less than the power of the "foreigner," the outsider who had suddenly become dominant in the city. Isolation, through garrisons and police patrols, was the only solution.

Union Park held onto its middle-class character until the middle of the 1890s; there was no immediate desertion by respectable people of the area in the wake of the violence: where else in a great city, asked one citizen, was it safe to go? Everywhere the same terror was possible.

The contrast between the limited character of civil disturbance and the immediate perception of that disturbance as the harbinger of an unnameable threat coming from a generalized enemy is a theme that binds together much research on urban disorders. . . .

The problem of the Union Park experience was the citizenry's inability to connect the facts seen to the facts as elements of what people knew was a correct interpretation. Expecting "seething passions" to erupt hysterically, the middle-class people of Chicago and their police were somehow immune to the spectacle they should have enjoyed, that of the workers becoming bored with the inflammatory talk of their supposed leaders. The expectations of a seething rabble had somehow to be fulfilled, and so the police themselves took the first step. After the shooting was over, the respectable people of Chicago became in turn inflamed. This blind passion in the name of defending the city from blind passion is the phenomenon that needs to be explained. A similar contradiction occurred in the series of robberies a half year later as well. As in the riot, the facts of the rationality of the enemy and his limited purpose, although acknowledged, were not absorbed; he was felt to be something else, a nameless, elusive terror, all-threatening. And the people reacted with a passion equal to his.

This mystifying condition, familiar now in the voices heard from the "New Right,"* is what I should like to explain, not through a sweeping theory that binds the past to the present, but through a theory that explains this peculiar reaction in terms of strains in the family life of the Union Park people. What I would like to explore—and I certainly do not pretend to prove it—is

---

*The "New Right" has no precise definition. The term is usually used to refer to an intellectual movement of the post–World War II era. The New Right was self-consciously anti-ideological and pragmatic as well as very distrustful of mass movements. Here the term includes late-1960s critics of the civil rights movement.—Ed.

how, in an early industrial city, the fears of the foreign masses by a middle-class group may have reflected something other than the actual state of interaction between bourgeoisie and proletariat. These fears may have reflected instead the impact of family life on the way people like those in Union Park understood their places in the city society.

Studies of overreaction to limited stimuli have centered, for the most part, on the idea of a "frustration-aggression syndrome." This ungainly phrase was given a clear definition in one of the early classic works of American social psychology, *Frustration and Aggression* (1939). The authors wrote that

> aggression is always a consequence of frustration. More specifically . . . the occurrence of aggressive behavior always presupposes the existence of frustration and, contrariwise, the existence of frustration always leads to some form of aggression.

Applied in terms of social class, this frustration-aggression syndrome implies that when a group fails to achieve goals it desires, or when it is unable to maintain a position it covets, it becomes aggressive, and searches out objects on which it can blame its failure. This simple, clear idea [Talcott] Parsons has applied to the formation of the Nazi party in Germany: the fall in status in the 1920s of fixed-income, middle-class groups breeding an aggressive desire to get back at their enemies, without knowing, or really caring, who they were. [Seymour Martin] Lipset has incorporated elements of the same idea in his essay on working-class authoritarianism in the United States after the Second World War. And of course the concept is now used to explain the hostility of lower middle-class whites toward blacks: the whites who have failed to rise high in the economic system they believe in are said to make blacks "aggression objects" of the frustration they themselves have suffered.

If it is true, as this syndrome of frustration-aggression suggests, that in the character one ascribes to one's enemy lies a description of something in one's own experience, the nature of the fear of lower-class foreigners among Union Park families might tell something about the Union Park community itself. The Union Park men, during the time of the riot and robberies, accused their chosen enemies of being, first, lawless anarchists, which was transmuted, secondly, to being pushed by their base passions outside the bounds of acceptable behavior, which resolved itself, finally, to being emotionally out of control. If the poor were reasonable, if they were temperate, ran the argument, these violent things would not have come to pass.

What about the Union Park people themselves, then? Were they masters of themselves? A study I have recently completed on the family patterns of the Union Park people during the decades of the 1870s and '80s may throw some light on the question of stability and purposefulness in their lives: it is the dimension of stability in these family patterns, I believe, that shaped sources of the reaction to violence.

Intensive Family Life

In 1880, on a forty-square-block territory of Union Park, there lived 12,000 individuals in approximately 3,000 family units. These family units were of three kinship types: single-member families, where one person lived alone without any other kin; nuclear families, consisting of a husband, wife, and their unmarried children; and extended families, where to the nuclear unit was added some other relative—a brother or sister of the parents, a member of a third generation, or a son or daughter who was married and lived with his spouse in the parental home. The most common form of the extended family in Union Park was that containing "collateral kin," that is, unmarried relatives of the same generation as the husband or wife.

The dominant form of family life in Union Park was nuclear, for 80% of the population lived in such homes, with 10% of the population living alone in single-member families, and the remaining 10% living in extended family situations. A father and mother living alone with their growing children in an apartment or house was the pervasive household condition. There were few widowed parents living with their children in either nuclear or extended homes, and though the census manuscripts on which my study of the year 1880 is based were inexact at this point, there appeared to be few groups of related families living in separate dwellings but in the same neighborhood.

Is this nuclear-family dominance a special characteristic of middle-class life in this era? At the Joint Center for Urban Studies, I was fortunate in working with other researchers in this field to coordinate census measures of class and family form that could be used comparatively across different studies. Comparison with these other studies, as well as within the limited range of social groups in Union Park, convinces me that this kind of family form was not a middle-class phenomenon. Within Union Park, the 80% dominance of the nuclear families held in lower social strata (of which enough existed to measure and test statistically, since the population as a whole was so large—about 25% of the community fell into a working-class category, excluding the servants in the homes of the other 75%) and throughout the range of middle-class groups. In Lynn Lees' data on an Irish working-class district in London in 1860, it similarly appeared that about 80% of her community's population lived in nuclear family configurations, 10% in single-member families, and 10% in extended families, virtually the same distribution as was found in Chicago's Union Park in 1880.

Again, the *outer* limits on the size of families in Union Park did seem to be the product of a special class condition. Contrary to the stereotype of the sprawling families of the poor, in Union Park the size of poor families was in its contours similar to the size of the wealthier ones: few families were larger than six members, among rich or poor. Similarly, comparison of family sizes in Union Park to the poor Irish of Lynn Lees' study or to the middle-class area of St. Pancras in London reveals the limits on family size in the three areas to have been the same.

Since family studies of nineteenth-century cities are at this date in a primitive stage, the body of future research may show these present examples to be "sports" or explainable by circumstances researchers do not now understand. Yet it does now seem more fruitful to concentrate on the *function* of nuclear families or on the *function* of families of restricted size in middle-class communities in the great cities of the nineteenth century, rather than to try to locate the conditions of peculiarly middle-class life in the *structural* existence of these family types.

What I did find to be true in Union Park was the following: over the course of time internal conditions of family structure and of family size tended to lead to similar family histories. Nuclear families had characteristic histories similar to the experience of smaller families having from two to four kin members in the 1870s and '80s. Extended families, on the other hand, had histories similar to the experience of the minority of families with four to six kin members during these decades. What made this process subtle was that nuclear families did not tend to be smaller, or extended larger. Family size and family kinship structure seemed rather to be independent structures with parallel internal differences in functioning.

Why and how this was so can be understood by assessing the patterns of the generations of the dominant group of nuclear, small-size families during the year 1880. These families were marked, in the relations between husbands and wives, parents and children, by strong patterns of family cohesion. Whether rich or poor, the young men and women from such homes rarely broke away to live on their own until they themselves were ready to marry and found families, an event that usually occurred when the man was in his early thirties. The families of Union Park, observers of the time noted, were extremely self-contained, did little entertaining, and rarely left the home to enjoy even such modest pleasures as a church social or, for the men, a beer at the local tavern. The small family, containing only parents and their immediate children, resisted the diverse influences of either other kin associations or extensive community contacts. This was the mode of family life that dominated Union Park numerically. These families can be called "intensive families," and their life histories contrasted to families of larger size or more complex kinship. The intensive families would seem to epitomize a defined order of stability among the people of Union Park. Yet, Lynn Lees and I have found some functional differences between Chicago and London in families of this general character.

Instability through Separation or Desertion

In most census collections in the United States and Britain, the official tabulations of divorce are very low, because the formal breaking of the marital tie was considered a personal disgrace to both partners. But, as Talcott Parsons has demonstrated, these official figures are misleading, since a great deal of unofficial divorce through separation or desertion occurred, at a higher rate, Parsons thinks, than in our own time. One means of detecting this hidden marital disorder in the census is to locate the individuals who were officially married but living without a spouse in the family. This measurement lets in a certain number of "beachhead migrants," men who have come to the city in advance of their families to establish a job and find a house, but in Union Park such men were less common in this category than spouses who were married, living with their children, but not with their husbands (or wives).

In Union Park the number of families involved in such a break was about 10%. But in London, in the middle-class district of St. Pancras, the incidence of such marital separation was one-half of this, or 5%; in the lower-class Irish district Lynn Lees studied, there were less than a third as many marital separations of this type. In all three communities, of course, the official rate of divorce was nearly zero.

The explanation for this comparatively high incidence of marital break in Union Park is obscure, since there are now so few other comparative measures of family conditions behind the official statistics to use. In terms of these Chicago and London communities themselves perhaps the best thing to be said is the simplest: the higher incidence of marital break occurred in a city whose development was exclusively in the industrial era; the lower incidence of such a break occurred in a city for whom industrial production and large bureaucratic enterprises were but one chapter in a very long history.

Work Mobility and Family Stability

Added to this kind of family instability in the community as a whole, my study of intergenerational mobility in work and residence from 1872 to 1890 revealed a complicated, but highly significant pattern of insecurity in the dominant intensive families when compared to the smaller group of less intensive families.

In the nuclear-family homes and in the smaller families the fathers were stable in their patterns of job holding, as a group, over the course of the eighteen years studied; roughly the same proportions of unskilled, skilled, and white-collar workers of various kinds composed the labor force of these nuclear fathers in 1890 as in 1872. Given the enormous growth of Chicago's industrial production, its banking and financial capital, retail trade volume, as well as the proliferation of the population (100% increase each ten years) and the greatly increasing proportion of white-collar pursuits during this time, such stability in job distribution is truly puzzling. Further, this pattern of job holding among the fathers of intensive families was not shared by the fathers in extended families or fathers of larger families living in Union Park. They were mobile up into exclusively bureaucratic, white-collar pursuits, so that by 1890 virtually none of these fathers worked with their hands. Within the range of white-collar occupations, the extended-family fathers and the large-family fathers gradually concentrated in executive and other lesser management pursuits and decreased their numbers in shopkeeping, toward which, stereotypically, they are supposed to gravitate.

Now the differences between fathers and sons in each of these family groups were even more striking. I found the sons in the dominant family homes to be, unlike their fathers, very unstable in their patterns of job holding, with as much movement down into manual pursuits over the course of the eighteen years as movement up within the white-collar occupations. Following the lead of [P.] Blau and [O. D.] Duncan, we might be tempted to explain this pattern of dispersion simply as regression-toward-the-mean of higher status groups intergenerationally. But the sons of extended and large families did not move in this mixed direction. Rather, they followed in the footsteps of their fathers into good white-collar positions, with almost total elimination of manual labor in their ranks over the course of time. This pattern occurred in small-family sons versus large-family sons and in nuclear-family sons versus extended-family sons. The difference in the groups of sons was especially striking in that the starting distribution of the sons in the occupational work force was virtually the *same*, in the measure of family form and in those of family size. [Stephen] Thernstrom has pointed out in the . . . discussions for this volume that economic aid between generations of workers ought to manifest itself more at the beginning point in the careers of the young rather than when the older generation has retired and the young have become the principal breadwinners. In Union Park, the fact that both extended-family and nuclear-family sons, both large- and small-family sons, began to work in virtually the same pursuits as their fathers, but then became distinctively different in their patterns of achievement, strongly suggests that something *beyond* monetary help was at work in these families to produce divergences in work experience in the city.

The residence patterns of the generations of the intensive and less intensive families also bears on the issues of stability and instability in the lives of the people of Union Park. Up to the time of violence in the Union Park area, the residence patterns of the two kinds of families, in both the parents' and sons' generations, were rather similar. In the wake of the violence it appears that, within the parents' generation, there was significant movement back into the Union Park area, whereas for the half decade preceding the disturbances there was a general movement out to other parts of Chicago. It is in the generation of the sons that differences between the two family groups appeared. In the wake of the violence, the sons of large families and of extended families continued the processes of residential break from Union Park initiated during the early years of the 1880 decade. The sons from intensive families did not; in the years following the violence they stopped migrating beyond the boundaries of the community they had known as children, and instead kept closer to their first homes.

Two Theories of Intensive Family Stability

In my study of Union Park, I tried to explain these differences in work experience and in residence in terms of patterns of family life and child nurturance for bourgeois people in a new, immensely dynamic, disordered city. In so doing, my researches led me into a debate that exists between the work of the sociologist Talcott Parsons and the cultural historian Phillippe Aries. For Parsons has argued that the small nuclear family is an adaptive kinship form to the industrial order; the lack of extensive kin obligations and a wide kin circle in this family type means, Parsons has contended, that the kinship unit does not serve as a binding private world of its own, but rather frees the individual to participate in "universalized" bureaucratic structures that are urban-wide and dynamic. Aries has challenged this theory by amassing a body of historical evidence to show that the extended kinship relationships in large families, at least during the period he studied, were actually less sheltering, more likely to push the individual out into the world where he would have to act like a full man on his own at an early age, than the intense, intimate conditions of the nineteenth-century home. In intensive homes, the young person spent a long time in a state of independence under the protection and guidance of his elders. Consequently, argues Aries, the capacity of the young adult from small nuclear homes to deal with the world about him was blunted, for he passed from a period of total shelter to a state in which he was expected to be entirely competent on his own. Aries' attack has been supported for contemporary American urban communities by a variety of studies, the most notable being those of Eugene Litwak and Marvin Sussman, and it has been supported for English cities by the work of Peter Wilmott and Elizabeth Bott.

The data I have collected on Union Park during the early stages of Chicago's industrial-bureaucratic expansion clearly are in line with the argument made by Aries. The young from homes of small scale or from homes where the structure of the family was nuclear and "privatistic," in Aries' phrase, had an ineptness in the work world, and a rootedness to the place of their childhood not found to the same degree among the more complex, or larger-family situations. (I have no desire to argue the moral virtues of this rootedness to community or failure to "make it" in the city; these simply happened to be the conditions that existed.) But the context of these Union Park families as new urbanites, in a new kind of city form, alters the meaning of stability and shelter leading to instability in the next generation among the intense family households. For it is clear that the nineteenth-century, privatistic, sheltering homes Aries depicts, homes Frank Lloyd Wright describes in his *Autobiography* for his early years in Chicago, homes that observers of the time pointed to as a basic element in the composition of the "dull respectability" of Union Park, could easily have served as a refuge themselves from the confusing, dynamic city that was taking shape all around the confines of Union Park. It indeed seems natural that middle-class people should try to hold onto the status position they had in such a disrupting, growing milieu, make little entrepreneurial ventures outside their established jobs, and withdraw themselves into the comfort and intimacy of their families. Here is the source of that job "freeze" to be seen in the mobility patterns of fathers in intense-family situations; the bourgeois intensive family in this way became a shelter from the work pressures of the industrial city, a place where men tried to institute some control and establish some comforting intimacies in the shape of their lives, while withdrawing to the sidelines as the new opportunities of the city industries opened up. Such an interpretation of these middle-class families complements, on the side of the home, the interpretation Richard Hofstadter has made of the middle classes politically, in the latter part of the nineteenth century. He characterizes them as feeling that the new industrial order was not theirs, but had passed them by and left them powerless. It is this peculiar feeling of social helplessness on the part of the fathers that explains what use they made of their family lives.

Confusion in the Desire for Stability

What makes this complex pattern of family stability–instability significant for wider social orientations are the values about work to be found in the middle classes of this era. For here the idea of seizing opportunities, the idea of instability of job tenure for the sake of rising higher and higher, constituted, as John Cawelti has described it, the commonly agreed-upon notion of how sure success could be achieved at this time among respectable people; in the same way, this chance-taking path was presented, in the Horatio Alger novels and the like, as the road into the middle class itself. One should have been mobile in work, then, for this was the meaning of "opportunity" and "free enterprise," but in fact the overwhelming dislocations of the giant cities seem to have urged many men to retreat into the circle of their own families, to try simply to hold onto what they knew they could perform as tasks to support themselves, in the midst of the upheaval of urban expansion.

This is deduction, to be sure, and perhaps it is characteristic of sociologists dealing with history that they speculate where historians would prefer to remain silent and let the ambiguities stand. Yet the body not only of Union Park data, but the memoirs, fictional portraits, and secondary studies of this period seem to me to indicate that such an internally contradictory response to urbanization among the heads of middle-class families is the means by which the differences in social mobility between kinds of families can be explained. Conditions of privacy and comfort in the home weakened the desire to get ahead in the world, to conquer it; since the fathers of the intensive families were retreating from the confusions of city life, their preparation of their sons for work in Chicago became ambiguous, in that they wanted, surely, success for their sons, yet shielded the young, and did not themselves serve as models of successful adaptation. The result of these ambiguities can be seen directly in the work experience of the sons, when contrasted to the group of sons from families which, by virtue either of family form or size, were more complex or less intense. Overlaid on these family patterns was a relatively high rate of hidden marital breakdown in Union Park—one in every ten homes—while the expectation was, again, that such breakdown must not occur, that it was a disgrace morally.

These contradictions in family process gave rise, I believe, to the characteristics of Union Park's reaction to violence during the years 1886 to 1888.

The Feeling of Threat Generated by the Family Experience

In the older version of the "frustration-aggression" syndrome it was assumed that if a social group failed to achieve a certain goal, it searched for an enemy to punish. But the goals of these middle-class people in Union Park were themselves self-contradictory: they wanted success in the work of the city and yet they didn't want it, given the definition of success at that time as an entrepreneurial grasping of opportunities rather than the fruit of plodding and routine service. The goals for the home were also contradictory: they wanted a stable shelter from the confusion and terror of the city, yet somehow they expected their sons, growing up sheltered, to be able to make it in that city world, and the sons of the dominant family groups seemed unable to do so. Divorce was a disgrace, yet there is evidence that one out of every ten of the neighborhood families were involved in a marital separation or desertion, a voluntary condition as opposed to the involuntary break of widowhood. Thus, because the goals of these middle-class people were bred of an equal desire to escape from and succeed in the city, the possibility of a wholly satisfying pattern of achievement for them was denied. The contradictory nature of the family purpose and products was innately frustrating so that a family impulse in one direction inevitably defeated another image of what was wanted. This meant that the sources of defeat were nameless for the families involved; surely these families were not aware of the web of self-contradictions in which in retrospect they seem to have been enmeshed; they knew only that things never seemed to work out to the end planned, that they suffered defeats in a systematic way. It is this specific kind of frustration that would lead to a sense of being overwhelmed, which, in this community's family system, led easily to a hysterical belief in hidden, unknown threats ready to strike at a man at almost any time.

Feeling of Threat and Perceptions of Violence

What I would like to suggest is that this complex pattern of self-defeat explains the character of the Union Park reaction to violence. For the dread of the unknown that the middle classes projected onto their supposed enemies among the poor expressed exactly the condition of self-instituted defeat that was the central feature of the family system in Union Park. And this dread was overwhelming precisely because men's own contradictory responses to living in such a city were overwhelming. They had defined a set of conditions for their lives that inevitably left them out of control. The fact that there was in Union Park a desire to destroy the "immigrant anarchists" or to garrison the neighborhood against them, as a result of the incidents of violence, was important in that it offered an outlet for personal defeats, not just for anger against lawbreakers. This response to violence refused to center on particular people, but rather followed the "path of hysterical reaction," in Freud's phrase, and centered on an abstract class of evildoers. For the fear of being suddenly overwhelmed from the outside was really a sign that one was in fact in one's own life being continually overwhelmed by the unintended consequences, or "latent consequences" as [Thomas] Merton calls them, of what one did. By blaming the urban poor for their lawlessness, these middle-class people were expressing a passion for retribution that had little to do with riots or thefts. The retribution was rather in the nature of what [Erik] Erikson calls a "cover object" for hostility, an expression of inability to deal with the issues of one's own life, of mobility and stability in the city: the fear in these middle-class people was that if they were to act entrepreneurially in the work world they might be destroyed, yet their desire was to make it big suddenly. The desire to escape to the safety of the simple home of father, mother, and children became, unexpectedly, a crippling shield when the sons went out into the world.

This dilemma, expressed in the terrible fear of attack from the unbridled masses, was also related to the fear of falling into deep poverty that grew up in urban middle-class families of this time. To judge from a wide range of novels in the latter half of the nineteenth century there was a dread among respectable people of suddenly and uncontrollably falling into abject poverty; the Sidwells in Thackeray's *Vanity Fair* plummet from wealth to disorganized penury in a short space of time; Lily Bart's father, in Edith Wharton's *Age of Innocence*, is similarly struck down by the symbol of entrepreneurial chance in the industrial city, the stock market. This feeling of threat from the impersonal, unpredictable workings of the city economy was much like the sense of threat that existed in the Union Park families, because the dangers encountered in both cases were not a person or persons one could grapple with, but an abstract condition, poverty, or family disorder that was unintended, impersonal, and swift to come if the family should once falter. Yet what one *should* do was framed in such a self-contradictory way that it seemed oneself and one's family were always on the edge of survival. In this way, the growth of the new industrial city, with its uncertainties and immense wastes of human poverty not all to be dismissed as personal failures, could surely produce in the minds of middle-class citizens, uneasy about their own class position, living out from the center of town, the feeling that some terrible force from below symbolized by the poor, the foreigner, was about to strike out and destroy them unless they did something drastic.

The demographic reaction among most of the families to the eruption of violence bears out this interpretation of events. With the exception of the upwardly mobile, extended-family sons, most family members did not try to flee the community as a response to the threats of riot and the organized wave of crime. The demographic movement mirrored a renewed feeling of community solidarity in the face of violence, a solidarity created by fear and a common dread of those below. Again, it is significant that the group that did not show this pattern of "sticking out the trouble" is the generation of young family members who lived in more complex family circumstances than the majority, and who achieved, on the whole, greater occupational gains than the majority.

The relations between family life and the perception of violence in this Chicago community could be formed into the following general propositions.

These were middle-class families enormously confused in what they wanted for themselves in the city, considered in terms of their achievements in the society at large and in terms of their emotional needs for shelter and intimacy; their schema of values and life goals was in fact formed around the issues of stability and instability as goals in a self-contradictory way. The result of this inner contradiction was a feeling of frustration, of not really being satisfied, in the activities of family members to achieve *either* patterns of stability or mobility for themselves. The self-defeat involved in this process led these families naturally to feel themselves threatened by overwhelming, nameless forces they could not control, no matter what they did. The outbreak of violence was a catalyst for them, giving them in the figure of the "other," the stranger, the foreigner, a generalized agent of disorder and disruption.

It is this process that explains logically why the people of Union Park so quickly found a communally acceptable villain responsible for violence, despite all the ambiguities perceived in the actual outbreaks of the disorders themselves; this is why the villain so quickly identified was a generalized, nonspecific human force, the embodiment of the unknown, the outside, the foreign. This is why the people of Union Park clung so tenaciously to their interpretation, seemed so willing to be terrorized and distraught.

If the complex processes of family and social mobility in Union Park are of any use in understanding the great fear of disorder among respectable, middle-class urbanites of our own time, their import is surely disturbing. For the nature of the disease that produced this reaction to violence among the industrial middle classes was not simply a matter of "ignorance" or failure to understand the problems of the poor; the fear was the consequence, rather, of structural processes in the lives of the Union Park families themselves. Thus for attitudes of people like the Union Park dwellers to change, and a more tolerant view of those below to be achieved, nothing so simple as more education about poor people, or to put the matter in contemporary terms, more knowledge about Negroes, would have sufficed. The whole fabric of the city, in its impact on staid white-collar workers, would have to have been changed. The complexity and the diversity of the city itself would need to have been stilled for events to take another course. But were the disorder of the city absent, the principal characteristic of the industrial city as we know it would also have been absent. These cities were powerful agents of change, precisely because they replaced the controlled social space of village and farm life with a kind of human settlement too dense and too various to be controlled.

And it comes to mind that the New Right fears of the present time are as deeply endemic to the structure of complex city life as was the violent reaction to violence in Union Park. Perhaps, out of patterns of self-defeat in the modern middle classes, it is bootless to expect right-wing, middle-class repression to abate simply through resolves of goodwill, "education about Negroes," or a change of heart. The experience of these bourgeois people of Chicago one hundred years ago may finally serve to make us a great deal more pessimistic about the chances for reason and tolerance to survive in a complex and pluralistic urban society.

The Physical City

Getting Around in Boston

The first practical system of electrically powered streetcars was installed in Richmond, Virginia, in 1888 and soon many other cities adopted the new technology. The streetcar significantly changed the structure of American cities and, as the cities changed, so did the lives of their inhabitants. The following construction is an attempt to suggest some of the physical changes that took place in the Boston area in the half-century after 1850. How did the street railway change Boston? What groups made special use of it? What purposes do you think they might have had in mind? What basic characteristic did the city have in 1850 that it lacked in 1900, and what impact would the absence of this characteristic have had on Boston area residents?

© 1981 by Bradley H. Clarke.

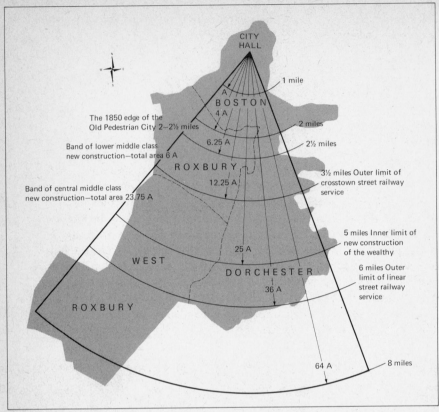

Streetcars and the Growth of Boston. Approximate class building bands of the
Boston area in 1900. A = 357.4 acres. It is the area of a 64-degree segment of a
circle whose radius is one mile, roughly the distance from City Hall to Dover Street.
The other radii are marked in miles from Boston's City Hall, and their area is given
in terms of A. *From Sam B. Warner, Jr.,* Streetcar Suburbs: The Process of Growth in
Boston, 1870–1900 *(Cambridge, Mass.: Harvard University Press, 1962). Copyright ©
1962, 1978 by the President and Fellows of Harvard College.*

The Mind of Frank Lloyd Wright

Frank Lloyd Wright has played an influential role in American
architecture and design since his first independent commission in 1893.
The Prairie House, pictured on page 79 in floor plan and façade, was
perhaps Wright's most important turn-of-the-century contribution.
Introduced in 1901, over sixty Prairie Houses were built in the next
decade, many of them in Chicago and surrounding suburbs. What
characteristics are evident in these designs? What might these houses have
offered the families that occupied them? Does the house seem likely to
have integrated these families more closely with city life, or to have
separated them from it?

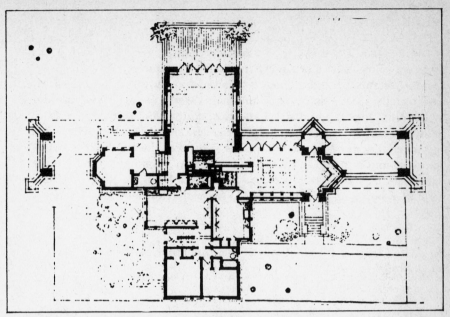

Ward Willitts House Plan. *From Vincent Scully, Jr.,* Frank Lloyd Wright *(New York: Braziller, 1960).*

Frederick C. Robie House, Chicago, Illinois. *Library of Congress, Historic American Buildings Survey, ILL, 16-Chig., 33–2, No. ILL-1005.*

Mobile Americans

Emigration, especially from a foreign country, was a wrenching experience for millions of Americans in the late nineteenth century. Country, friends, neighborhood, and job had to be left behind. Historians have usually argued that urban immigrants were able to survive the shock by huddling together in distinct and close-knit ethnic neighborhoods. The following tables, based on a study of the census for Omaha, Nebraska, a city with large numbers of immigrants (a third of the population in 1880), do not so much challenge this basic conclusion as refine it. What do the figures tell us about patterns of life in Omaha? Do these patterns differ for the native-born and foreign-born? Do the patterns change over time?

Per Cent of Original Samples Living at Same Address in Selected Years, Corrected for Deaths

Sample Area (Tract)	Year 1880–1900								Number in Sample
	1880	1883	1885	1888	1891	1894	1897	1900	
8	100.0	14.9	8.7	3.3	0.9	0.9	0.9	0.5	213
9	100.0	27.2	19.4	9.7	4.2	3.4	3.4	2.1	237
12	100.0	48.3	42.4	24.7	15.0	13.3	12.4	10.6	113
18	100.0	47.8	37.8	18.5	15.9	13.4	8.4	6.7	119
19	100.0	31.5	22.3	13.8	10.0	9.2	8.4	6.9	130
22	100.0	37.0	23.4	13.0	6.8	4.9	3.7	3.7	162
Total 1880 Sample	100.0	31.8	23.1	12.2	7.4	6.4	5.3	4.3	974

Per Cent of Original Samples Living at Same Address in Selected Years, by Nativity

Nativity Group	Year							Number in Sample
	3	5	8	11	14	17	20	
Native 1880	27.3	17.9	9.4	5.5	4.5	3.3	3.1	478
Native 1900	29.5	20.8	14.0	8.7	5.5	3.4	1.5	408
Foreign 1880	35.7	27.7	14.7	9.5	8.1	7.2	5.6	496
Foreign 1900	39.4	27.6	20.2	12.2	8.2	7.0	5.0	323

Source: Sample data.

From Howard P. Chudacoff, *Mobile Americans: Residential and Social Mobility in Omaha, 1880–1920* (New York: Oxford University Press, 1972), tables 1 and 2, pp. 36, 69. Copyright © 1972 by Oxford University Press, Inc. Reprinted by permission.

The Impact of the City: A Photo Essay

By virtue of their size and the new relationships they imposed, American cities of the late nineteeth century required their residents to live and to communicate in ways unknown a few decades before. Many of the adjustments people made—and the institutions they created to facilitate those adjustments—involved either attempts to establish contact where none had existed before or attempts to reduce contact where it was felt to be excessive or inappropriate. Which of the following illustrations fall into each of the two categories? What, for example, is the function of the trademark? Why does it become an important way of marketing goods in the late nineteenth century? Delmonico's was one of New York City's most expensive social clubs. What was its purpose? We know that Americans were extraordinarily mobile in these years. Which of the illustrations bear some relationship to this mobility? The racial stereotype present in the "Excelsior Ginger Ale" photograph suggests the possibility that stereotypes serve a necessary function in an anonymous urban setting. What is that function?

Delmonico's, New York City, 1903. *Library of Congress.*

Excelsior Ginger Ale. *Library of Congress.*

Grand Golf Tournament by Professional Players, 1867. *Library of Congress.*

Opening of the League Baseball Season, the New York Team. *Library of Congress.*

Hebrew Cemetery, New York City. *Library of Congress.*

The Photographer as Reformer: Jacob Riis

Nothing is more embedded in our value structure than the notion that the photograph is objective, a precise rendering of reality ("pictures don't lie"). The photographs of Jacob Riis offer an opportunity to assess this belief, for Riis was reformer as well as photographer. A police reporter for two New York City newspapers, Riis authored an important book about lower-class urban life, *How the Other Half Lives* (1890), founded a settlement house (1901), and was active in the public park and playground movements. What kind of worldview does Riis bring to his work? What does he think of the people clustered at "Bandits' Roost"? Would Riis have argued that the subjects in this photograph were capable of changing their own lives? that their culture was a vital one?

Bandit's Roost, 39½ Mulberry Street, c. 1888. Photograph by Jacob A. Riis. *Jacob A. Riis Collection, Museum of the City of New York.*

CHAPTER 4

New Frontiers and New Problems

The terms "America" and "the West" had always seemed synonymous, from the earliest penetration of the Atlantic coastline down into the nineteenth century. But during the years after the Civil War, a new kind of frontier waited to be conquered by white men and surrendered in bitter defeat by the Indians. Beyond the Mississippi lay a vast expanse of plains, known officially as "the Great American Desert." Further on were the seemingly impenetrable mountains and the real deserts of the Southwest. To most Americans, even as late as the 1850s, this half of the continent appeared to be good for little but a permanent reservation for Indian tribes.

Amazingly, in little over a generation, the trans-Mississippi West was settled. The first transcontinental railroad was opened shortly after the Civil War. It was followed by others, and by a network of lines spreading out into Iowa, Missouri, Texas, and the Dakotas. California became a state on the eve of the Civil War, and by the end of the century the process of state making had filled in almost all the continental map. The last effective Indian resistance was broken in the 1870s and 1880s, when the old policy of war and extermination was replaced with a new form of aggression, called "assimilation." Mining towns sprang from nothing in Nevada, Colorado, and Montana. Texas and Oklahoma became primary cotton-producing states. Cowboys drove Texas longhorns into the new cowtowns of Kansas and Nebraska, where the animals could be loaded onto trains headed for Eastern slaughterhouses. New techniques of dry farming created one of the world's most productive wheat belts in the western half of the Great Plains. In 1890, just twenty-five years after Grant had accepted Lee's surrender, the United States Bureau of the Census officially declared that the frontier had ended forever.

The story was not a simple one of geographical expansion. The settlers of the new West were armed with a new technology that helped explain the remarkable rapidity of their success. The repeating rifle and the Gatling gun subdued the Indians. The railroad took the wheat and cattle east at incredible speeds. Miners used steam power and dynamite to pry gold and silver from the mountains. Farmers— the big ones, at least—had the new mechanical reaper to bring in wheat at a rate that manual labor could not have approached. Californians were tied to the rest of the Union by the railroad and the new telegraph.

Plains farmers also brought with them another kind of weapon, one that helped them overcome an initial reluctance to move onto the hard, unyielding sod of Nebraska and the Dakotas. The weapon was *myth*: the myth that the West was the source of unprecedented opportunity; the myth that climate would respond to the migration of people; the myth that the yeoman farmer—half frontiersman, half man-of-the-soil—could handle anything; the myth that all white people were superior to all Indians.

On the surface, then, the experience was one of triumph—at least for the white society. But there was a dark side to things, too. Myth proved impotent under the harsh realities of plains life and politics. Even dry farming could not overcome periodic droughts, and the droughts came. There was new competition from Russian and Australian wheat, so prices were very unstable. Some railroads gouged the farmers. Worst of all, the new technology proved not to be a blessing at all. The new agriculture was just *too* efficient. By 1890, one farmer could produce and get to market what it had taken eight farmers to produce fifty years before. Together, they produced more food than could be sold. So prices fell and stayed down, and farmers often could not make back the cost of their seed, much less the money to pay interest on their mortgages and on the loans they had made to buy their reapers and plows. Agricultural depression was so severe and frequent that the whole second half of the nineteenth century—except for the war years—was really one long and chronic economic crisis for farmers, not only in the new West, but everywhere.

Farmers sought to redress their grievances through a variety of protest movements, each linked to a particular organization.

Midwestern farmers established the Patrons of Husbandry, better known as the Grange, in the 1860s, partly for social purposes but also to lower the costs of shipment and storage of grain. By the 1890s, farmers in the South, the Great Plains, and the Far West had turned to state and national politics. Through the People's party, or Populists, they sought the aid of the national government in inflating a depressed currency and in regulating the railroads and other trusts. Populist influence peaked in 1896, when William Jennings Bryan was the nominee of both the Democrats and the Populists, but declined after Bryan was defeated for the presidency by Republican William McKinley.

Yet the American West was more than a place where people lived and worked and came to grips with a marketing revolution. It was also a reservoir of images and myths, a mirror of what Americans were and wanted to be. Frederick Jackson Turner triggered an ongoing debate on the meaning of the West in 1893, when he read an essay, "The Significance of the Frontier in American History," to an audience of fellow historians assembled in Chicago. Though Chicago was a city with major industrial and social problems (a strike of Pullman Palace Car Company workers the following year would ultimately shut down most of the Western railroads), Turner read American history as the story of the frontier, a continuously receding area of free land that had placed generations of Americans on the cutting edge between civilization and savagery. This experience had shaped the national character. It had made Americans intensely individualistic, nationalistic, and democratic. When he linked his frontier thesis to the announcement in the 1890 federal census that the frontier had ceased to exist, Turner implied that these values were in danger—his way, perhaps, of sharing his sadness that an era had come to an end.

LAWRENCE GOODWYN

The Cooperative Crusade

Lawrence Goodwyn's study of the Texas alliances in the late 1880s describes the efforts of one group of farmers to wrest control of their economic destinies from bankers, wholesalers, and railroads by forming

cooperatives to purchase supplies, market produce, and provide credit. These efforts ran afoul of established economic interests, culminating, in 1888, in a massive grass-roots campaign to save the financially troubled Texas Exchange. When farmers realized that cooperative efforts could not succeed without parallel changes in the monetary system, they turned to the politics of Populism to secure those changes.

Although the farmers were treated as if they were alien radicals, the solution they offered—the cooperative—was more than familiar to traditional businessmen. One of the most famous ventures in cooperation was spearheaded by financier J. Pierpont Morgan in the summer of 1885, just two years before the Farmers' Alliance undertook to educate its members in the advantages of cooperatives. Aboard his yacht in Jersey City, Morgan welcomed George B. Roberts and Frank Thomson, president and vice-president of the Pennsylvania Railroad, and Chauncey Depew, the president of the New York Central. The two giant roads had long been rivals for the traffic between the East and the Midwest, and recently the rivalry had escalated to the point where it endangered the financial integrity of both lines. The Pennsylvania threatened to compete directly with the New York Central by buying up a parallel but unused route; the New York Central began to construct its own parallel line in Pennsylvania. Morgan had assembled the principals to work out an agreement that later generations would come to know by the name of his craft, the *Corsair*. According to that arrangement, which was oral and informal, the two parties agreed to drop their attempts to establish parallel facilities in the territory normally served by the other.

Established Eastern businessmen shared with their Western agrarian rivals more than a dislike of competition and a reverence for cooperation. They also agreed on debt. When the Populists of the Midwest sought to have their high mortgage rates reevaluated, the "conservative" East called the move "radical." But debt reduction was J. P. Morgan's business. There was nothing much to distinguish the debt reduction that Morgan made possible in his famous railroad reorganizations from the relief that farmers wanted. The farmers were merely asking that a business practice, considered standard procedure in the world of corporate finance, be made available to the American farmer.

Against this background, the central problems posed by the experience of Texas farmers become clear. Can one distinguish between the Corsair agreement (or the cotton trust) and Charles Macune's Texas Exchange? Was the Alliance interested in a radical transformation of American capitalism or only in eliminating its most irrational and destructive characteristics? Were American farmers only businessmen? And if they were, why did some consider them so dangerous?

From Lawrence Goodwyn, *Democratic Promise: The Populist Moment in America* (New York: Oxford University Press, 1976), chapter 5 as edited. © 1976 by Lawrence Goodwyn. Reprinted by permission of the author and Oxford University Press, Inc.

The agrarian revolt cannot be understood outside the framework of the cooperative crusade that was its source. Amidst a national political system in which the mass constituencies of both major parties were fashioned out of the sectional loyalties of the Civil War, the cooperative movement became the recruiting vehicle through which huge numbers of farmers in the South and West were brought into an interest-group institution geared to a new kind of internal "political education." The central educational tool of the Farmers Alliance was the cooperative experiment itself. The massive effort at agrarian self-help, and the opposition it stimulated from furnishing merchants, wholesale houses, cotton buyers, and bankers in the South and from grain elevator companies, railroads, land companies, livestock commission agencies, and bankers in the West, brought home to hundreds of thousands of American farmers new insights into their relationship with the commercial elements of American society. Reduced to its essentials, the cooperative movement recruited the farmers to the Alliance in the period 1887–91, and the resulting cooperative experience radicalized enough of them to make independent political action a potential reality. While other developments were also necessary, those developments, when they materialized, built directly upon the cooperative experience in ways that confirmed its centrality to the evolution of the People's Party. That the chief oracle of cooperation, Charles Macune, consistently opposed Alliance political radicalism and feared the emergence of the third party added a paradoxical dimension to the internal politics of the agrarian revolt.

Irony dogged Charles Macune throughout his years as national spokesman of the Farmers Alliance. The scores of Alliance organizers who fanned out across the South and Midwest in 1887–89 and who sallied north of the Ohio River and across both the Rockies and the Appalachians in 1890–91 had been defined by their previous experience not only as "lecturers," but also as incipient political radicals. Their duties as lecturers carried them to the remotest backwaters of the rural countryside and into the very maw of the crop lien system of the South. Upon the lecturers fell the burden of explaining the function of the suballiance business agent, the county trade committee, and the visionary state exchange that, in the South, might free them all from the furnishing merchant. Upon the same lecturers also fell the burden of explaining the delays, the opposition of merchants, bankers, commission agents, and sundry other functionaries who came to represent "the town clique." Whether in Alabama or South Dakota, a cooperative encountering difficulty constituted an implied rebuke to the Alliance leaders who had praised the idea in the first place. At such a time of difficulty—and it came, eventually, to every Alliance cooperative in every state, from Florida to Oregon—the farmers, so recently brought to a new level of hope by the promise of their movement, looked to the messengers of cooperation both for explanation and guidance. The latter responded in one of two ways. They could blame the difficulties on the farmers, assert that rank and file members did not understand cooperation well enough, and insist that they expected too much, too soon. In the course of this response they could counsel patience and devote much time to thorough explanations of the theory and practice of cooperation. Many Alliance leaders followerd such a course, none with more grace than Macune himself. But the mass program of agrarian cooperation that Macune had visualized also set in motion another and rather different response. In this view, cooperative difficulties were not inherently the fault of the idea itself, nor were they traceable to deficiencies in farmers generally; rather, cooperatives encountered trouble because of the implacable hostility of the financial and commercial world. Alliance leaders holding such views could explain that town merchants selectively cut prices to make the Alliance trade store look bad and that bankers refused to take the notes of the Alliance state exchange because the bank's mercantile clients wanted the exchange to go under. They could add that the Alliance store or warehouse often performed its duty even if it sold not a dollar of goods—if, simply by its presence, it introduced genuine wholesale and retail competition into rural America. Macune was also capable of this analysis, and sometimes with a passion that rivaled the anti-monopoly intensity of spokesmen for the Alliance's left wing. . . .

The cooperative crusade was not the product of individual creativeness; considering the enormous number of farmers eventually involved, it could not have been. . . . The reality that explained this organizational feat rested in the substance of the daily lives of millions of farmers.

In the late nineteenth century a national pattern of emerging banker-debtor relationships and corporation-citizen relationships began to shape the lives of millions of Americans. Throughout the western granary the increasing centralization of economic life fastened upon prairie farmers new modes of degradation that, if not as abjectly humiliating as Southern forms, were scarcely less pervasive.

Of the many ingredients in the new way of life, most easily understood is the simple fact that farm prices continued to fall year after year, decade after decade. The dollar-a-bushel wheat of 1870 brought 80 cents in 1885 and 60 cents in the 1890's. These were official government figures, computed at year's end when prices were measurably higher than those received by the farmer at harvest. . . .

Moreover, the grain that made the nation's bread was a demanding crop; it had to be harvested at breakneck speed each fall before it became too dry and brittle to bind well. The farmer with fifty acres of field grain had to have a $235 binder to cut it. Though he used his binder only five days a year, that time fell in the same five days when his neighbors had to use their own binders. So he went into debt to buy the needed equipment. He made chattel mortgage payments on such machines at rates of annual interest that ranged from 18 to 36 per cent and in currency that appreciated in value every year. Under these circumstance, the steady decline of commodity prices further reduced his margin of economic maneuver.

But this was only a part of the problem facing western agriculturalists. Like most nineteenth-century Americans, farmers were enthusiastic about the arrival of each new railroad that promised to further "open up the country" to new town and new markets. But the farmers' euphoria at the appearance of a new rail line inevitably turned to bitter resentment. Alliance leaders learned the rationalizations of the railroads for their "discriminatory freight rates" while their rural members complained less elegantly of simply being "robbed" and "gypped." Whatever the terminology he employed, the farmer in the West felt that something was wrong with a system that made him pay a bushel of corn in freight costs for every bushel he shipped—especially since the system somehow also made it possible for large elevator companies to transport grain from Chicago all the way to England for less money than it cost a Dakota farmer to send his wheat to the grain mills in near-by Minneapolis. . . .

Underlying the entire new structure of commerce was the national banking system, rooted in the gold standard and dominated by Eastern commercial banks, most prominently, the House of Morgan. The most apparent result of the system was a sharply contracted currency that failed to keep pace with population growth and economic expansion. It produced an annual harvest of steadily diminishing farm prices and a routine condition of "tight" credit that kept interest rates high. . . .

Everywhere the farmer turned, he seemed to be the victim of strange new rules that somehow always worked to the advantage of the biggest business and financial concerns that touched his world. To be efficient, the farmer had to have tools and livestock that cost him forbidding rates of interest. When he sold, he got the price offered by terminal grain elevator companies. To get his produce there, he paid high rates of freight. If he tried to sell to different grain dealers, or elevator companies, or livestock commission agents, he often encountered the practical evidence of secret agreements between agricultural middlemen and trunk line railroads. The Northern Pacific named specific grain terminals to which farmers should ship, the trunk line simply refusing to provide railroad cars for the uncooperative. Pool agreements extended beyond commission houses to include rival railroads so that the rules of competition appeared to have been suspended.

But widespread as suffering was throughout the West, nowhere in America did the burdens of poverty fall more heavily than upon the farm families of the rural South. . . . It was here that the fuel of Populism had come to be stored, waiting to be ignited. While the invisible restraints of a contracted currency affected farmers everywhere, they became unbearable when tied to the crop lien system. The raw mathematics of the situation simply offered farmers no escape from peonage. . . .

The crop lien system had driven millions west in the 1870's; by the late 1880's the system had graduated to new plateaus of exploitation: as every passing year forced additional thousands of Southern farmers into foreclosure and thence into the world of landless tenantry, the furnishing merchants came to acquire title to increasing portions of the Southern countryside. Furnishing men had so many farms, and so many tenants to work them, that it became psychologically convenient to depersonalize the language of agricultural production. Advancing merchants spoke to one another about "running 100 plows this year," a crisp phrase that not only referred to thousands of acres of land but also to hundreds of men, women, and children who lived in peonage. Prosaically, the Tenth Census officially described the lien as "a bond for the payment of a specific amount—usually about $100—given to the storekeeper by the farmer, and pledging the growing crop as collateral security." Ominous acreage and production statistics accounted for the small annual sums of "about $100" that cotton croppers received. The Southern tenant farm of the 1890's averaged seventeen acres, and with an average cotton yield per acre of about one-third of a bale, a five- or six-bale crop was all a family could reasonably expect for its year's labor. Cotton was priced at eight cents a pound, and the $200 gross return allowed the farmer's family roughly $100 credit for the year's living expenses after deductions for fertilizer and other production costs. This sum translated into less than $10.00 per family per month for food, clothing, medicines, and all other essentials. Any tenant showing enough independence to dare to check his merchant's bookkeeping ledger ran the risk of being branded a troublemaker and dispatched from the county by a local deputy sheriff. If he was black—and sometimes if he was white—he could easily find himself exchanging his participation in the crop lien system for a role in the convict lease system. Layers of legal safeguards to protect lien-holders were built into the structure of Southern law. Statutes were so drafted that a tenant "had little chance lawfully to leave his landlord and move elsewhere." If a farmer tried to escape the clutches of his merchant by growing corn and hogs, which would make him less a customer for high-priced pork and meal, he was, in the words of one observer, "notified that reducing his cotton acreage was reducing his line of credit." The universal rule continued to be "no cotton, no credit."

As the degradation of the crop lien spread over the South, middle-class farmers lived in terror of the one bad crop that would put them in the hands of the furnishing merchant. "Never mortgage," children of such families were told, in language they could recall years later; "no matter what happens, don't mortgage . . . and if you haven't cash, don't buy." But regional scholars reported that up to 90 per cent of the farmers in Mississippi, Alabama, and Georgia were living on credit. . . .

It was into this vast domain of silent suffering that the lecturers of the Farmers Alliance deployed in 1887–88. The results were difficult to describe, though a South Carolina Granger made an effort by reporting to his national offices that the Alliance had "swept over our state like a wave." . . . The spark that lit the fuse of agrarian discontent was the message offered by the latest visitors: join the Alliance, build a cooperative, and get free of the credit merchant. A fully organized county Alliance could form its own cotton yard, its own trade committee, and, if need be, its own store. . . .

By 1887 the doctrine was relatively mature, could be delivered with settled confidence, and verified with persuasive stories. It had to be conceded, of course, that one needed to be free of the merchant's crop lien to participate in such Alliance ideas as "bulking" cotton, for only farmers who held title to their own crop could sell it. There were, the lecturers were forced to explain, two stages in the process of economic cooperation—the first designed to redress the power balance with the local merchant in order to get lower prices so the farmer could "pay out," the second focusing on the Alliance selling cooperative that could hold part of the crop off the market at harvest time, when prices were lowest. The farmers of the South thus learned that the Alliance offered two forms of organization—"buying" cooperatives and marketing cooperatives. On whatever level of verbal elegance it was offered them, Southerners learned that the plan of the Farmers Alliance would take a bit of time. But, they could ask themselves, had not the plan worked in Texas?

The message of the lecturers was persuasive because the core of the Alliance program was Macune's central state exchange, which could provide credit at bearable rates for great numbers of moneyless farmers.. The established goal—to change the way most Southerners lived—was one the Grange had never dared to attempt. This, quite simply, explains why the Grange could not reach the farmers and the Alliance could. The larger dream contained in the new and untested Texas plan—the formation of a central state exchange to market the entire state's cotton crop and free everyone from the credit system in one dramatic marketing season—added the final galvanizing ingredient to the formula of hope that was the Farmers Alliance. "It is not an organization" reported one participant happily, "it is a growth."

But the new recruits did not wait idly for the arrival of a statewide marketing system. Across the South, farmers in a dozen states competed with one another in pioneering new varieties of purchasing cooperatives that could be constructed to defeat money-lenders and wholesale and retail merchants. . . . The sheer variety of the efforts "to be a free and independent people" pointed to the fact that the crusade for cooperation took the form of thousands of initiatives within tiny sub-alliances scattered across the South. . . . In one hamlet the Alliance warehouse in one day loaded 150 wagons with fertilizer purchased in bulk at lower prices than Alabama farmers had ever had to pay. Commercial animosity toward such tactics led to violence in Dothan, where merchants, bankers, and warehousemen succeeded in obtaining a $50 tax on the Alliance warehouse. Alliancemen responded by moving their warehouse outside the city limits, whereupon the town council attempted to make the farmers pay for draying their cotton into and out of town. A gunfight resulted, and two men were killed and another wounded. . . .

[Macune] learned . . . that a central exchange in Texas could sell directly to Eastern factories if it possessed sufficient capital to underwrite its contracts properly. He reported this to his Texas colleagues, and the Alliance, after taking competing bids from several cities, selected Dallas as the site for the exchange. The Dallas offer, though it amounted to about $100,000 in cash, deferred rentals, and real estate, was contingent upon a number of specifications that reduced the immediate cash bonus to $3500.

On this shred of capital the "Farmers Alliance Exchange of Texas" opened for business in Dallas in September 1887. The intervening months had confirmed that the uncentralized trade store system could not function effectively within the existing American system. As one student of the Alliance put it, "The local bourgeoisie became very artful in devising and circulating false reports" to complicate life for local Alliance stores. The hostility of merchants increased as the sheer size of the farmer organization dramatized the threat posed by Alliance cooperatives. But even where local Alliancemen became sophisticated enough to cope with false rumors and selective price cutting by merchants, a marginally successful effort merely increased their longing for the statewide marketing cooperative. No sooner had Macune settled into the new exchange in Dallas than he found his directors awash in petitions from suballiances calling for the implementation of some plan so they could "make a crop independent of the merchant."

The Macune system brought the world market into direct competition with local cotton buyers. The exchange charged only twenty-five cents for each bale sold, plus telegraphic expenses. Export buyers were sufficiently impressed; they came to the Texas Exchange. And in one massive transaction, 1500 bales of cotton were selected from samples in Dallas and sold for shipment to England, France, and Germany. The cotton was shipped from twenty-two different stations in Texas.

Impressive as all this activity was as a demonstration of agrarian self-help, the Texas Exchange leadership soon realized it was not nearly enough. . . . The message from the Alliance rank and file was clear: "You said we could get free of the merchant if we joined the Alliance and formed a cooperative. We have done it. Now you do your part." Late in 1887 the directors of the Texas Exchange faced the challenge squarely. The plan they embarked upon was one of the most creative in the annals of American farm organization, and it led directly to the one enduring new political concept of the agrarian revolt, the sub-treasury plan of 1889. At a meeting of its directors, held in Dallas in November 1887, the Texas Exchange advanced an imaginative plan to provide the poorest Alliance members with the credit necessary to enable them to harvest their 1888 crop and sell it themselves through the exchange.

The exchange announced a "joint-note" plan. Each Alliance county business agent was to acquire from each suballiance member who wanted supplies on credit a schedule of his probable individual needs for the coming year, together with a showing of "full financial responsibility" and a pledge of cotton worth at least "three times as much" as the amount of credit requested. The farmers were then to execute a collective joint note for the estimated amount of supplies for all of them. The plan was "cooperation" in the purest sense. The note was to draw interest after May 31 and was to be paid November 15 after the 1888 crop had been harvested. The notes were also to be signed by financially responsible local Alliance farmers who would secure themselves against loss by taking mortgages on the growing crops. The exchange attempted to fortify itself with additional information. Each signer of the joint note was required to specify the number of acres of land he owned, its value, outstanding indebtedness, the number of acres cultivated both in cotton and grain, and the value of his livestock. He also agreed to allow his co-signers to harvest his crop in the event he became incapacitated. Such joint notes from suballiances were then to be screened by the county business agent and the county trade committee before being passed on—along with the collective supply order of all participating suballiance members—to the state exchange in Dallas. . . .

The third part of the plan was, of course, that the exchange would use the notes as collateral to borrow money to purchase the supplies. The supplies were to be shipped on a monthly basis. . . . In addition to making substantial savings in credit costs, farmers might expect much cheaper prices on supplies as a result of the exchange's bulk purchasing power. Finally, by producing a way for farmers to live while they worked their crop the joint-note plan permitted the individual farmer to retain title to his cotton so that he might sell it "independent of the merchant" through the exchange's central selling system. . . .

Macune had meanwhile begun the quest for outside banking capital in March, using the joint notes as collateral. After repeated conferences in Dallas, bankers there refused to advance loans. Macune then went to Houston, Fort Worth, Galveston and New Orleans. In Houston he acquired one loan of $6000 by pledging $20,000 in joint notes as collateral, and some mercantile houses advanced supplies, taking the notes as security, but with few exceptions the answer elsewhere was "no." Macune's regular report to the exchange directors sounded an ominous note:

> The business manager spent the whole of the month of March in trying to negotiate banking arrangements whereby a loan could be affected at a reasonable rate of interest, to provide funds to purchase goods with which to supply the contracts accepted by the committee of acceptance; but all the efforts made were unsuccessful, and tended to produce the conviction that those who controlled the moneyed institutions of the state either did not choose to do business with us, or they feared the ill will of a certain class of business men who considered their interests antagonistic to those of our order and corporation. At any rate, be the causes what they may, the effort to borrow money in a sufficient quantity failed.

The Texas exchange was suddenly in serious trouble. . . .

A confidential circular to the order's leadership in each county added the information that Dallas bankers, wholesale merchants, implement dealers, and manufacturers had "entered into a combination to crush the exchange," that bankers had tried to force the exchange to buy through jobbers and had refused to lend the exchange money "upon any terms of any security," and that they had "kept the mails full and the wires red hot" to prevent the exchange from getting money from Fort Worth, Houston, Galveston, and New Orleans. This final bit of confidential information completed the preparation of the Alliance county leaders for the more than 175 simultaneous county meetings scheduled to act on the exchange crisis. . . .

The farmers came by the hundreds, and in some cases, by the thousands, to almost 200 Texas courthouses on June 9, 1888. . . . Reporters remarked about the "earnestness" of the effort to save the exchange and the "grim determined farmers"who were making pledges of support to some far-off mercantile house. . . . In farmhouses all over Texas women dug into domestic hideaways for the coins that represented a family's investment in the hope of escaping the crop lien. At a mass meeting in southeast Texas frugal German farmers collected $637.70 and one of their number respectfully tendered a five-year lease on some property to the state exchange for use as it saw fit. . . .

Following this remarkable demonstration from the grass roots, Macune announced that results "had exceeded expectations" and that the exchange was on solid footing. But though pledges seemed to have totaled well over $200,000, the central truth of the Texas Alliance was that it represented precisely those it said it did—the agricultural poor. A letter to the *Southern Mercury* earlier in the year portended the outcome of the June 9 effort: "We voted the $2.00 assessment for the exchange, and as soon as we are able, will pay it, [but] we are not able to do so at present." The dignity with which the admission was made, and the willingness of the *Mercury* to eschew proper "promotional" techniques by printing it without comment, is indicative of the commonplace recognition of prevailing poverty among great numbers of those intimately associated with the Alliance movement.

In the light of existing economic conditions in the farming districts, June 9 was indeed a success, but not in the scale of six figures. The Texas Exchange eventually received something over $80,000 from its feverish effort. The farmers' pledges represented their hope for the exchange; their actual contributions measured the reality of their means.

The exchange survived the season, though manifestly it was not well. Credit—the farmer's age-old problem—was the exchange's problem too. In Dallas, during the summer of 1888, Macune put his fertile mind to work on this old truth that had been so forcibly reaffirmed to him. Somehow, the farmer's crop that the advancing merchants took as collateral had to be utilized by the farmer to obtain credit directly. Precisely how this could be done obviously required something less ephemeral than joint notes that bankers would not honor. But what?

The August 1888 convention of the Texas Alliance provided a tentative answer. . . . Macune proposed the creation of a treasury within the exchange to issue its own currency—exchange treasury notes—in payment of up to 90 per cent of the current market value of commodities. Farmers would circulate these notes within the order by using them to purchase their supplies at the Alliance stores. The latter were to be strengthened by having each county Alliance charter a store of $10,000 capital, half paid in by the local farmers and the other half by the central exchange. As outlined by Macune, the plan actually cost the central exchange nothing in capital, for it acquired the use of the $10,000 capital of each of the county Alliances for half that amount—in effect, using the credit of the local stores. The plan, while certainly strengthening the local operation, had as its principal intent the strengthening of the central exchange; indeed, each county Alliance was to be coerced into subscribing for its proportionate per-capita share, based on paid-up membership roles, of the over-all $500,000 capital of the central exchange—on pain of being excluded from the benefits of the treasury note plan. This in turn provided the central exchange with the funds needed to underwrite its half of the capitalization of each county Alliance store. . . .

The plan permitted the farmer to hold his harvested crop off the market until prices rose, rather than having to dump when prices were lowest. It also created a combination of legal money and Alliance treasury notes negotiable at Alliance stores which he could live on in the meantime; thus he could escape the advancing man. As for the cost of his supplies, the plan ensured that the lower retail prices achieved through the first year's operation of the existing exchange would be continued. With a more stable capital base, these accomplishments might even be improved upon.

The treasury note plan attempted to do for farmers what decades of cooperative experiments, including, apparently, the joint-note plan, had failed to do—end the reign of the furnishing merchant by providing the farmer with the non-usurious credit he needed to break the chain of the crop lien. . . .

Alliancemen . . . clearly felt they did not have the immediate means to implement the treasury-note plan. Both Macune and the farmers were forced to acknowledge that the treasury-note plan, however ingenious, was beyond the means of the penniless farmers of Texas. The exchange drew up new by-laws relinquishing, at least for the present, the basic struggle against the credit system: "all purchases made from branch exchanges must be for cash, and notice is hereby given that the books of the exchange are closed against any further debit entries." This was a bitter retreat; it reflected the belief that if the cooperative effort were ever to make a second attempt, the exchange had to be placed on a sound footing. . . .

To farmer advocates who sought to benefit "the whole class," the dynamics of the cooperative movement had also brought a breathtaking new perspective on the larger American society. The discovered truth was a simple one, but its political import was radical: the Alliance cooperative stood little chance of working unless fundamental changes were made in the American monetary system. This understanding was the germ of the Omaha Platform of the People's Party. In August 1888 it materialized in the organization that would carry it to millions of Americans. . . .

These developments set in place the central political definition of Populism and revealed clearly the dynamics that produced the multi-sectional People's Party: the cooperative crusade not only recruited the farmers to the Alliance; opposition to the cooperatives by bankers, wholesalers, and manufacturers generated a climate that was sufficiently radical to permit the acceptance by farmers of the greenback interpretation of the prevailing forms of American finance capitalism. Greenback doctrines thus provided the ideology and the cooperative crusade provided the mass dynamics for the creation of the People's Party. Both reached their peak of intensity in the Texas Alliance in the tumultuous summer of 1888, and the emotional heat from that experience welded radical greenbackism onto the farmers' movement. After 1888, only one step—a rather sizable one—remained to bring to fruition the creation of a multi-sectional radical party—the conversion of the bulk of the national Alliance membership to the greenback doctrines which had become the central political statement of the agrarian movement. Two men, Charles Macune and William Lamb, working toward opposite purposes, were to provide the tactics that produced the mass conversion. . . .

As a decade of Alliance organizing came to an end, cooperation had begun to acquire a record of accomplishment that was both highly visible and highly mixed. . . . The Alliance's most striking achievement involved victory over its announced enemy, a bona fide national "trust." Cotton bagging had traditionally been made from jute, and in 1888 a combine of jute manufacturers suddenly announced that henceforth jute bagging would be raised from seven cents a yard to eleven, twelve and, in some regions, fourteen cents a yard. The action laid a "tribute of some $2,000,000" on the nation's cotton farmers. Alliance leaders in Georgia, Alabama, Mississippi, South Carolina, Louisiana, and Florida reacted with vigor. Evan Jones of Texas, Macune's successor as the order's national president, convened a southwide convention in Birmingham in the spring of 1889 to fashion final plans for a boycott throughout the cotton belt. The state Alliances agreed on common plans for action and entered into arrangements with scores of mills across the South for the manufacture of cotton bagging. Some buyers, particularly in England, complained about the inferior cotton bagging, a problem Florida farmers ingeniously solved by arranging to import cheaper jute bagging from Europe and paying for it with farm produce consigned to the Florida Alliance Exchange. In Georgia, a rising agrarian advocate named Tom Watson helped fortify Alliancemen for the struggle by delineating the larger implications: "It is useless to ask Congress to help us, just as it was folly for our forefathers to ask for relief from the tea tax; and they revolted . . . so should we." He added, with an eye to future struggles, "The Standard of Revolt is up. Let us keep it up and speed it on." Georgia Alliancemen apparently took him at his word. . . .

[In Kansas, an] experiment in multi-state marketing of livestock opened in May 1889 with paid-up capital from farmer members totaling $25,000. The effort proved successful from the start. Within six months the commission company had over $40,000 in profits to distribute to its members. The animosity toward the cooperative among commission companies scarcely promised a serene future, however.

These successes were balanced by a crucial failure. In the late summer of 1889, after twenty months of operation, the Texas Exchange, unable to market its joint notes in banking circles and therefore unable to respond to insistent demands from its creditors, went under. The Texas effort, the first to be chartered, was thus the first to fail. The news sent a wave of anxiety through the entire South: was the Alliance dream unattainable? Were the Texas lecturers wrong? As the Alliance grew, so did the burdens of explaining and proving its program of self-help. With increasing frequency the Alliance founders, driven by the difficulties of cooperation, had to explain to farmers that the opposition to their movement derived from the self-interest of gold-standard financiers who administered and profited by the existing national banking system. Greenback doctrines were thus increasingly marshalled to defend the Macunite dream of large-scale farmer cooperatives. By this process radical monetary theory began to be conveyed to the suballiances by growing numbers of Alliance lecturers. The farmers had joined the Alliance cooperative to escape the crop lien in the South and the chattel mortgage in the West, and the failure of cooperatives, particularly the huge model experiment in Texas, spread deep concern through the ranks of the Farmers Alliance. Wherever a cooperative failed for lack of credit, greenbackism surged like a radical virus through the organizational structure of the agrarian movement. Slowly, the Omaha Platform of the People's Party was germinating.

. . . Macune's belief that cooperation must serve landless tenants and others bound to the crop lien system stamped him as an economic radical, yet he remained firmly traditional on political issues and adamantly opposed to all talk of a third party. In his presidential address, given in Shreveport in 1887, he outlined his political creed:

> Under our system of government, we should not resort to a new political movement to carry out every reform necessary. . . . We have the two great principles and conceptions . . . contended for by John Adams and Thomas Jefferson, as a basis for division into two great political parties; that should suffice. . . . [A]s the agriculturists comprise a large majority of all the voters, they will necessarily comprise a majority in each party . . . but in partisan politics, the members of our order should participate, not as Alliancemen, but as citizens, because politics is for the citizen.

If this homily betrayed a certain innocence, Macune was at the time still experiencing his executive apprenticeship. Indeed, the evolution of his thought toward a more complex analysis of American political institutions constitutes one of the more reliable guides to the dynamics within the Alliance that led to the People's Party. The growing tangle of political beliefs that represented his public position became more apparent the following year in his presidential address in Meridian. On economic issues he was as aggressive as ever: "Ours is no common struggle; upon it depends in a great measure the future prosperity of agriculture and the liberty and independence of those engaged in that pursuit." On political issues he revealed that his opposition to independent political action might emanate from a marked partiality toward the Democratic Party, and that his loyalty might be based on an allegiance to white supremacy. The Alliance was not only a "business organization" and a "nonpartisan" one, it was also "strictly a white man's organization." Macune was able to summarize all of these beliefs in a single sentence: "The people we seek to relieve from the oppression of unjust conditions are the largest and most conservative class of citizens in this country." . . .

Precisely what the Alliance movement was in the process of becoming could scarcely have been predicted by the farmers themselves from the contradictory events of 1888–89. Only one thing was certain: the Alliance was attempting to construct, within the framework of American capitalism, some variety of cooperative commonwealth. Precisely where that would lead was unclear. More than any other Allianceman, Charles Macune had felt the power of the corporate system arrayed alongside the power of a self-help farmer cooperative. He had gone to the bankers and they had replied in the negative. Though his own farmer associates had said "yes," they could not marshall enough resources to defeat the crop lien system. Macune knew that an exchange of considerably reduced scope could be constructed on a sound basis within the means available to organized farmers. One could avoid the credit problem simply by operating cash stores for affluent farmers. But while he was an orthodox, even a reactionary social philosopher, and still a political traditionalist, C. W. Macune was an economic radical. The collapse of the Texas exchange threatened his personal prestige, but he knew the essential problem was not unsound business stewardship, but absence of sufficient capital. The pressure of the multiple experiences that had propelled him to leadership . . . to fame as an organizer and national leader during the Southern expansion, to crisis and potential loss of political power over the exchange, and to constant maneuvering against his driving, exasperating, creative left wing—all, taken together, conjoined to carry Macune to a conception of the uses of democratic government that was beyond the reach of orthodox political theorists of the Gilded Age. Out of his need for personal exoneration, out of his ambition, and out of his exposure to the realities in the daily lives of the nation's farmers, Macune in 1889 came to the sub-treasury plan. Politically, his proposal was a theoretical and psychological breakthrough of considerable implication: he proposed to mobilize the monetary authority of the nation and put it to work in behalf of a sector of its poorest citizens through the creation of a system of currency designed to benefit everyone in the "producing classes," including urban workers.

. . . Through his sub-treasury, Macune proposed to mobilize the currency-issuing power of the government in behalf of the agricultural poor: the federal government would underwrite the cooperatives by issuing greenbacks to provide credit for the farmer's crops, creating the basis of a more flexible national currency in the process; the necessary marketing and purchasing facilities would be achieved through government-owned warehouses, or "sub-treasuries," and through federal sub-treasury certificates paid to the farmer for his produce—credit which would remove furnishing merchants, commercial banks, and chattel mortgage companies from American agriculture. The sub-treasury "certificates" would be government-issued greenbacks, "full legal tender for all debts, public and private," in the words of the Alliance platform. As outlined at St. Louis in 1889, the sub-treasury system was a slight but decisive modification of the treasury-note plan Macune presented to the Texas Alliance the year before. Intellectually, the plan was profoundly innovative. It was to prove far too much for Gilded Age America.

C. D. WILBER

The Great American Desert

Plains settlers like those who supported the Texas Exchange faced a variety of obstacles—a tough, virgin prairie sod that broke their plows, insect pests, harsh winters, a native population already living on the land and using it in entirely different ways, and the general feeling, reinforced for decades, that the area to be settled was inhospitable to agriculture.

C. D. Wilber was one of a breed of bureaucrat-scientists charged with investigating, describing, and evaluating the Western United States. In this selection, published in 1881, Wilber was responding to what he called "the American desert literature, for which there seems to be a demand or craving, especially in eastern circles." According to that literature, lands west of the 100th meridian (i.e., west of a line running through western Kansas and central Nebraska) were arid and unsuitable for agriculture.

For what audience was Wilber writing? Is his appeal rational or emotional? How does he explain the myth of the Great American Desert? Does Wilber's account conform to the information on rainfall and population provided in the maps on pp. 104 and 105?

In the summer of 1869 or 1870, during the first construction of the Kansas Pacific Railway, I saw at a water station in Western Kansas, not far from the Colorado line, on the 102nd meridian, a tall stalk of growing corn. It was doubtless chance sown from a grain car, but regardless of propriety or proper paternity, there it was, a live stalk of corn, like a miniature palm, growing in that desert soil, its broad leaves rustling in the wind with as much assurance of vigorous growth as if in Illinois or Iowa. It had two ears whose silk tips beneath the tall tassel or plume indicated that it would have its career according to the rule, "first the blade, then the ear, then the corn in the ear."

The eastern excursionists on the same train, who had, in terms that denoted more strength than politeness, disposed of the whole region as worthless—an eternal desert, etc., saw in this apparition an argument that kept them silent, especially on the subject of soil and corn raising; but the exciting buffalo hunt doubtless dissipated the impression it should have made. But on the testimony of this living witness I took an appeal from the decision of Fremont and Hazen, preferring to trust my eyes and believe what I saw rather than the hasty and sweeping conclusion of a prejudiced martinet. . . .

From C. D. Wilber, *The Great Valleys and Prairies of Nebraska and the Northwest* (Omaha: Daily Republican Print, 1881), pp. 140, 142–144.

The crop surface on the western border of settlements for 1879, extending north and south through Dakota, Nebraska and Kansas, make a strip or belt ten miles wide and one thousand miles in length. During all the previous years and ages only sparse grass, in tufts or patches, has partially covered the ground, but now the new carpet of green, growing crops, for the first time wholly overspreads and shields the earth from the sun's heat. The earth cannot be heated as before, and is less able to heat the air above it, and the air is, therefore, less able to contain its moisture. This being the fact over the entire area of growing crops, there must result a vast diminution of heat compared with former years. In other words, the crop surface, from sprouting to ripening—a period of four to six months—is a condensing surface, and will cause an increase of rainfall all along the line of farms from north to south, increasing in amount until the average measure of precipitation is reached. Every year will show the work of a large army of pioneer farmers, who, armed with the plow, will overturn and conquer a wide belt of the wild prairie desert, thus preparing the way for a still further advance of rainfall.

In these new States and Territories the experience of farmers proves the following results:

1. The regular increase of precipitation, in periods of years, westward from the Missouri river.
2. The ratio of increase bears a direct ratio to the steady increase of farming and cropping.
3. The relation here stated is that of cause and effect. In other words, rain follows the plow. Across the States of Nebraska and Kansas, from east to west, over 300 miles, the plow has advanced in spite of prophetic starvation. The first settlers, twenty-five years ago, placed the desert limits just west of the Missouri river counties. These being occupied the desert line was established on the Big Blue, seventy miles beyond. But the farmer invaded the Big Blue Valley, and the desert line was established near Kearney, 190 miles west of Omaha. But the irrepressible plow broke the barrier in so many places that the desert-makers fled with their line to the 100th meridian, determined to have and enjoy a desert. But hordes of farmers have gone far beyond and secured farms whose products equal those of Iowa or Illinois.

There being really no reliable line or meridian which can be named as the boundary of our mythical American desert, I do not hesitate to say that it will never be found. There is no desert, neither is there any foundation in fact for the terms "non-farming," "non-irrigable," and "pasturage lands." These flimsy barriers have been interposed by wiseacres, kid-gloved experts and closet-philosophers, but the farmer with his plow tears them asunder, leaving us to remember the experts only as charlatans or quacks.

It has become evident to the people of the Northwestern States that there is a powerful influence working against the present system of distributing and occupying public lands, and we, who know the antipathy that exists on the frontier between the ranchmen and farmers, have no trouble in detecting the main spring of the movement.

The owners of the great herds of cattle are constantly obliged to retreat before the immense army of emigration from the Canadas, the Eastern and Middle States, and especially from Wisconsin, Illinois, Iowa and Minnesota.

Coming with their families and their farming outfit, generally without previous inspection, they become squatters upon any lands not taken at the land office.

As the land laws are impartial, who comes first is first served, and the herd-owner, though a millionaire, as some are, is, much to his disgust, forced further out on the plains.

The reactions that follow are obvious. The ranchmen or herders insist that the country will never raise grain, is only fit for cattle and sheep, is a desert, without water for irrigation, and insufficient rain. It is by nature the herds-man's country, and the national law must be made to coincide. To bring these laws into effect is the animus of the present land movement, and to prepare the way for it is the object of the public land commission sent out by the last Congress. This commission have made their preliminary report, full of desert, as usual. The report to Congress was, of course, a foregone conclusion, and the total expense of it ($10,000) might have been saved, because it could have been gotten up in Washington by the powerful ring, who are determined to force these lands from their present equable distribution in farm sizes, in quarter sections, into large tracts or districts, as may suit the aristocratic tastes of the lords of the herds. They propose an act of Congress enabling persons to lease for herding or grazing purposes, thus remunerating the government for the use of the lands. The prize of this contest is the control of nearly 500,000,000 acres of land in the heart of the republic, which under the present laws will be taken up by farmers.

The Public Land Commission are working, vi et armis, with the wealthy combination of cattle kings, and both present their claims in their report that is proved to be false by every one of the 100,000 new occupants who last year carved his new farm out of these very "non-farming" lands so greatly coveted.

The capitalists, too, have lately been converted to the real value of "Desert America," and by their present investment of scores of millions of dollars, prove the strength and sincerity of their new found faith.

Rainfall and Settlement

There are no simple explanations for American settlement patterns. The price of land and the availability of military protection were important considerations. Some geographers believe that when Americans pulled up roots, they were most likely to move westward, and then only by one state in each generation. The following maps allow an estimate of the impact of a single factor—rainfall—on settlement patterns. To what extent does this one factor explain American patterns of migration, especially in the area west of the Mississippi River?

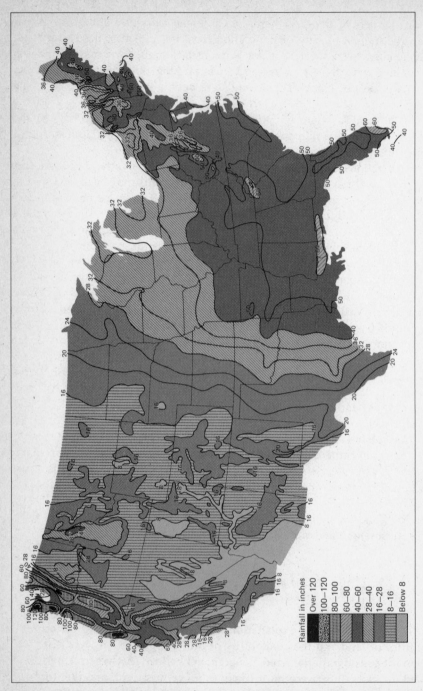

Average Annual Rainfall. *From Charles O. Paullin,* Atlas of the Historical Geography of the United States *(Washington, D.C.: Carnegie Institution of Washington and the American Geographical Society of New York, 1932), plate 5G. Copyright 1932, Carnegie Institution of Washington.*

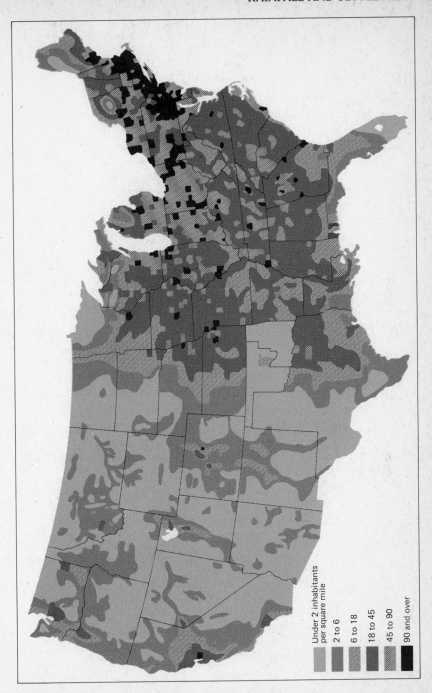

Density of Population, 1890. *From Charles O. Paullin, Atlas of the Historical Geography of the United States (Washington, D.C.: Carnegie Institution of Washington and the American Geographical Society of New York, 1932), plate 78B. Copyright 1932, Carnegie Institution of Washington.*

Victims of Empire

Quanah Parker

It was no easy task to remain a simple yeoman farmer while competing in an international market or struggling with Eastern bankers. And similar pressures fell heavily on the American Indian. This photograph captured Comanche leader Quanah Parker living in two cultures, one Indian and tribal, the other white and commercial.

Comanche leader Quanah Parker with portrait of his mother in the background.
Photograph Archives, Division of Library Resources, Oklahoma Historical Society.

"Civilizing" the Indians

It was inevitable that Quanah Parker would live in two worlds, but the speed with which his life was transformed owed much to a change in Indian policy inaugurated in the early 1880s by President Chester A. Arthur: Indians were no longer to be exterminated or excluded; instead, they were to be "civilized," assimilated into American society.

Indian reaction to the new policy was ambivalent. Sitting Bull—a Sioux leader at the famed Battle of the Little Bighorn—described his feelings for a Senate investigating committee in 1883:

> Whatever you wanted of me I have obeyed. The Great Father sent me word that whatever he had against me in the past had been forgiven and thrown aside, and I have accepted his promises and came in. And he told me not to step aside from the white man's path, and I am doing my best to travel in that path. I sit here and look around me now, and I see my people starving. We want cattle to butcher. That is the way you live, and we want to live the same way. When the Great Father told me to live like his people, I told him to send me six teams of mules, because that is the way the white people make a living. I asked for a horse and buggy for my children; I was advised to follow the ways of the white man, and that is why I asked for those things.

The policy change announced by Arthur was consummated in 1887, with the passage of the Dawes Severalty Act. This legislation legally dissolved the Indian tribes and parceled out Indian lands among tribe members.

How can one account for the shift in Indian policy? What parallels to it can one find in other areas of nineteenth-century politics? What was the purpose of the reservation system? Could Arthur have reasonably expected it to succeed?

Prominent among the matters which challenge the attention of Congress at its present session is the management of our Indian affairs.

While this question has been a cause of trouble and embarrassment from the infancy of the Government, it is but recently that any effort has been made for its solution at once serious, determined, consistent, and promising success.

It has been easier to resort to convenient makeshifts for tiding over temporary difficulties than to grapple with the great permanent problem, and accordingly the easier course has almost invariably been pursued.

It was natural, at a time when the national territory seemed almost illimitable and contained many millions of acres far outside the bounds of civilized settlements, that a policy should have been initiated which more than aught else has been the fruitful source of our Indian complications.

From Chester A. Arthur, *First Annual Message*, December 6, 1881, in James D. Richardson (ed.), *A Compilation of the Messages and Papers of the Presidents*, XI (New York: Bureau of National Affairs, 1897), pp. 4641–4644.

I refer, of course, to the policy of dealing with the various Indian tribes as separate nationalities, of relegating them by treaty stipulations to the occupancy of immense reservations in the West, and of encouraging them to live a savage life, undisturbed by any earnest and well-directed efforts to bring them under the influences of civilization.

The unsatisfactory results which have sprung from this policy are becoming apparent to all.

As the white settlements have crowded the borders of the reservations, the Indians, sometimes contentedly and sometimes against their will, have been transferred to other hunting grounds, from which they have again been dislodged whenever their new-found homes have been desired by the adventurous settlers.

These removals and the frontier collisions by which they have often been preceded have led to frequent and disastrous conflicts between the races.

It is profitless to discuss here which of them has been chiefly responsible for the disturbances whose recital occupies so large a space upon the pages of our history.

We have to deal with the appalling fact that though thousands of lives have been sacrificed and hundreds of millions of dollars expended in the attempt to solve the Indian problem, it has until within the past few years seemed scarcely nearer a solution than it was half a century ago. But the Government has of late been cautiously but steadily feeling its way to the adoption of a policy which has already produced gratifying results, and which, in my judgment, is likely, if Congress and the Executive accord in its support, to relieve us ere long from the difficulties which have hitherto beset us.

For the success of the efforts now making to introduce among the Indians the customs and pursuits of civilized life and gradually to absorb them into the mass of our citizens, sharing their rights and holden to their responsibilities, there is imperative need for legislative action.

My suggestions in that regard will be chiefly such as have been already called to the attention of Congress and have received to some extent its consideration.

First. I recommend the passage of an act making the laws of the various States and Territories applicable to the Indian reservations within their borders and extending the laws of the State of Arkansas to the portion of the Indian Territory not occupied by the Five Civilized Tribes.

The Indian should receive the protection of the law. He should be allowed to maintain in court his rights of person and property. He has repeatedly begged for this privilege. Its exercise would be very valuable to him in his progress toward civilization.

Second. Of even greater importance is a measure which has been frequently recommended by my predecessors in office, and in furtherance of which several bills have been from time to time introduced in both Houses of Congress. The enactment of a general law permitting the allotment in severalty, to such Indians, at least, as desire it, of a reasonable quantity of land secured to them by patent, and for their own protection made inalienable for twenty or twenty-five years, is demanded for their present welfare and their permanent advancement.

In return for such considerate action on the part of the Government, there is reason to believe that the Indians in large numbers would be persuaded to sever their tribal relations and to engage at once in agricultural pursuits. Many of them realize the fact that their hunting days are over and that it is now for their best interests to conform their manner of life to the new order of things. By no greater inducement than the assurance of permanent title to the soil can they be led to engage in the occupation of tilling it.

The well-attested reports of their increasing interest in husbandry justify the hope and belief that the enactment of such a statute as I recommend would be at once attended with gratifying results. A resort to the allotment system would have a direct and powerful influence in dissolving the tribal bond, which is so prominent a feature of savage life, and which tends so strongly to perpetuate it.

Third. I advise a liberal appropriation for the support of Indian schools, because of my confident belief that such a course is consistent with the wisest economy.

Even among the most uncultivated Indian tribes there is reported to be a general and urgent desire on the part of the chiefs and older members for the education of their children. It is unfortunate, in view of this fact, that during the past year the means which have been at the command of the Interior Department for the purpose of Indian instruction have proved to be utterly inadequate.

The success of the schools which are in operation at Hampton, Carlisle, and Forest Grove should not only encourage a more generous provision for the support of those institutions, but should prompt the establishment of others of a similar character.

They are doubtless much more potent for good than the day schools upon the reservation, as the pupils are altogether separated from the surroundings of savage life and brought into constant contact with civilization.

Westward Bound: Images

The journey westward was an experience that real people had. But it was also a popular vehicle for artists and photographers, who tried to capture the reality of that journey while adding to it their own notions about the meaning of the American West. Compare these two versions of the westward movement. Why do you suppose they are so different? Would the artist of "Emigrants Crossing the Plains" have agreed with Frederick Jackson Turner that the frontier was the source of individualism and self-reliance? Or would he have claimed some other quality as the West's peculiar contribution to the national character?

Emigrants Crossing the Plains. Photocopy of engraving by H. B. Hall, Jr., after drawing by F. O. C. Darley. *Library of Congress.*

Westward Bound. *Library of Congress.*

ALFRED TUCKER

A Warm Welcome for the IWW

The frontier was a place where whole societies were created from the ground up, often in a few years. Until the new courts, jails, and police departments could take charge, "law and order" was often an informal matter, provided by individuals or organized groups of vigilantes. Even when regular law-enforcement services were in place, the self-service tradition died hard in the West. We see it all too plainly in the following document, which deals with the treatment of radicals in a city, San Diego, that was far removed in time from the Wild West.

The Industrial Workers of the World (IWW) was founded in 1905. An outgrowth of the Western Federation of Miners, the organization harbored an intense distrust of the state, advocating a society organized into cooperative labor groups. Although the Wobblies (as they were called) had some success in organizing industrial workers in the East, their strength was in the West, among miners, lumbermen, and agricultural workers. The union welcomed workers of any sex, age, race, or skill level.

Between 1909 and 1912, the IWW waged its fight for "free speech"— which to the Wobblies meant the right to present its case against American capitalism directly to working-class crowds on the corners of a city's streets. San Diego was the last of several arenas in which the issue was contested. The following selection describes treatment handed out to some 140 young (half under age 21) Wobblies removed from a train which was transporting them into the city of Los Angeles in early April 1912. In May, anarchist Emma Goldman and her lover, Ben Reitman, were greeted at the San Diego railroad station by a crowd, which included many women, yelling "Give us that anarchist; we will strip her naked; we will tear out her guts." That evening vigilantes abducted Reitman, branded him, forced him to run a gauntlet, kiss the American flag, and sing "The Star Spangled Banner." Reitman was allowed to escape in his underwear "because," Reitman recalled, "the Christian gentlemen thought that I might meet some ladies and shock them." Alfred Tucker was one of those removed from the train. What does his account tell us about why the residents of San Diego, Spokane, and other Western states responded so virulently to the IWW Free Speech movement?

In March, 1912, I was living at Victorville, Calif. The I.W.W. then was engaged in a Free Speech Fight in San Diego for the right to speak on the streets. About the 10th of March I went to Los Angeles to see how the fight was coming out. I found it was lagging and no one willing to go. I met several of the free speech committee from San Diego. They were holding meetings and raising money but did not seem to be able to get any men to go to the fight. I talked with all the members around the hall and I found about a dozen men who said they would go if I would. . . . So we went to work and soon had 27 men ready to go. . . . As I had enough money to take myself I was sent two days ahead of the bunch to see how things were. I took passage on the steamer Governor from San Pedro to San Diego. When I arrived there I found the jails of both city and county were full of free speech fighters; also a large bunch had been sent to Riverside and Orange County jails. A committee of some 2,000 small business men, mostly real estate dealers, had been organized for the purpose of running the fighters out of town. As they had no more room for them in jail, the city authorities had prohibited speaking or selling papers any where in the city. They would grab men and drag them into an automobile, take them outside of the town, give them a clubbing and threaten their lives if they ever came back. . . . Two days later fellow worker Reisick and the 27 men arrived by boat from Los Angeles, and after resting a day we started to sell papers on the streets. We divided up in threes, two going ahead selling papers, while one stayed behind to watch the action of the police and vigilantes. We had sold quite a few papers before they bothered us. Then they commenced taking the papers away from the boys, arresting some and turning them loose, so we soon ran out of papers. They then confiscated the San Diego Herald and the San Francisco Bulletins, and would not allow us to sell any papers that gave a fair report of the fight. The next day, being the 22nd of March, at 2 o'clock P.M. 13 of us went out on the corner of 6th and E. Streets to hold a meeting. We started singing a song entitled Casey Jones, the Scab Engineer. We were immediately surrounded by plain clothes men, some of them police and some vigilantes. They arrested the 13 of us and marched us to the police station. We were placed in the court room and our names taken. We asked what charge was placed against us and they told us we would find out. Then they began picking out men from among us and taking them in to another room where, surrounded by police, they were put through the third degree. In the meantime they brought in the rest of the 27 men. None of us had eaten for 24 hours, but they kept us without food until about midnight. Then they divided us and gave us a very severe lecture, telling us if we ever came back they would bury us on some of their beautiful real estate. Then we were ordered to march and they, I suppose returned to their homes feeling they had done a good job. . . .

After resting a day we went to work to get a large bunch of men to go back to San Diego. About this time 50 men from Fresno joined us and we

From Alfred Tucker to Vincent St. John, September 21, 1914, United States Commission on Industrial Relations Papers, Department of Labor, Record Group 174, National Archives.

recruited the bunch up to 93 men. About half of the bunch were boys under 21 years of age full of courage and enthusiasm, so we started again for San Diego. We walked out of town to a little station and caught a freight train and rode to Fullerton, when we decided to hold meeting and wait until the next night, which we did. Then we caught a train and rode to Santa Ana, where we stopped over another day and held meetings and tried to visit the 30 men we had in jail there from San Diego, but were unable to do so. That night April the 5th at 11:30 P.M. we boarded another train for the south. Train never stopped for 50 miles. It was then about 1 o'clock A.M. The train slowed down and we were between two lines of something like 400 men armed to the teeth with rifles, pistols and clubs of all kinds. The moon was shining dimly through the clouds and I could see pick handles, axe handles, wagon spokes and every kind of a club imaginable swinging from the wrists of all of them while they also had their rifles leveled at us. The train had stopped on a side track in the foot hills, where the only sign of civilization was a cattle corral, where they loaded cattle for shipment. We were ordered to unload and we refused. Then they closed in around the flat car which we were on and began clubbing and knocking and pulling men off by their heels, so inside of a half hour they had us all off the train and then bruised and bleeding we were lined up and marched into the cattle corral, where they made us hold our hands up and march around in the crowd for more than an hour. They searched us for weapons and not even a pocket knife was found. They searched us several times, now and then picking out a man they thought was a leader and giving him an extra beating. Several men were carried out unconscious and I believe there were some killed, for afterwards there were a lot of our men unaccounted for and never have been heard from since. The vigilantes all wore constable badges and a white handkerchief around their left arms. They were all drunk and hollering and cursing the rest of the night. In the morning they took us out four or five at a time and marched us up the track to the county line, which is about a mile from the rest, where we were forced to kiss the flag and then run a gauntlet of 106 men, every one of which was striking at us as hard as they could with their pick axe handles. They broke one man's leg, and every one was beaten black and blue, and was bleeding from a dozen wounds. We walked north a few miles for the rest of the bunch. Some managed to ride back to Los Angeles, but the most of us walked all the way back to the city. My feet were swollen so I could hardly walk for two or three weeks. Several other big bunches of men went to the fight after this, but I was unable to go so this ends my experience in Free Speech Fights up to date. If I ever take part in another it will be with machine guns or aerial bombs.

Yours for a better way of fighting and better results as well as our final emancipation from all slavery and tyranny and the building of the world-wide industrial commonwealth.

[Signed] ALFRED R. TUCKER,
Box 163,
Victorville, Calif.

Opportunity in Wisconsin

In spite of all the problems faced by trappers, farmers, miners, and others who helped push back the frontier, the belief has persisted—to the present day, in fact—that there is more opportunity in the West than in the East, and more in thinly settled regions than in more populated areas. According to historian Frederick Jackson Turner (whose famous essay is excerpted in Chapter 5), equality of opportunity was a special characteristic of frontier regions.

The table on property distribution below was part of an attempt to test Turner's hypothesis by contrasting conditions in Trempealeau County, Wisconsin, which in 1860 was a grain-farming region of very recent settlement, with a section of Vermont which had been settled for nearly a century but which otherwise resembled its Western counterpart. If Turner was right, we would expect property to be more equally distributed on the frontier (Trempealeau County) than in long-settled Vermont.

What conclusions can be drawn from this simple comparison? Was Turner's optimism justified?

Distribution of Total Property Values, Trempealeau and Vermont, 1860 and 1870

1860

| | Trempealeau | | | | Vermont | | | | |
Tenth	Sum of Total Prop. Value	% Grand Total	Cumulative % *	Mean in Tremp.	Sum of Total Prop. Value	% Grand Total	Cumulative % *	Mean in Vt.	Mean of Vermonters in Trempealeau
1	$12,980	1.5	1.5	$223	$39,075	.5	.5	$134	$240
2	20,405	2.4	4.0	352	101,850	1.3	1.8	350	350
3	28,130	3.3	7.3	482	189,850	2.4	4.1	654	552
4	39,530	4.7	11.9	695	317,350	4.0	8.1	1,090	846
5	49,555	5.9	17.8	850	425,750	5.3	13.4	1,463	1,200
6	67,875	8.1	25.9	1,164	592,750	7.4	20.8	2,036	1,250
7	72,875	8.6	34.6	1,250	782,750	9.8	30.6	2,690	1,457
8	96,075	11.4	45.9	1,646	1,047,000	13.1	43.7	3,590	2,311
9	128,725	15.3	61.2	2,288	1,498,000	18.7	62.4	5,140	3,829
10	327,175	38.8	99.9	5,610	3,016,970	37.7	100.0	10,360	15,122
Total	$843,325	100.0		$1,446	$8,011,345	100.0		$2,753	

Total number: 583   Total number: 140

From Merle Curti, *The Making of an American Community: a Case Study of Democracy in a Frontier County* (Stanford, Calif.: Stanford University Press, 1959), p. 78. Reprinted with permission of the publisher.

1870

	Trempealeau				Vermont				
Tenth	Sum of Total Prop. Value	% Grand Total	Cumulative % *	Mean in Tremp.	Sum of Total Prop. Value	% Grand Total	Cumulative % *	Mean in Vt.	Mean of Vermonters in Trempealeau
1	$33,200	.8	.8	$156	$96,275	.7	.7	$308	$297
2	73,150	1.7	2.5	345	194,700	1.3	1.9	620	699
3	94,950	2.3	4.7	454	367,200	2.5	4.4	1,160	1,161
4	162,100	3.8	8.6	775	576,500	3.9	8.3	1,840	1,645
5	244,500	5.8	14.3	1,171	791,500	5.4	13.6	2,536	1,781
6	321,250	7.6	22.0	1,537	1,074,500	7.3	20.7	3,440	2,472
7	403,750	9.6	31.5	1,933	1,441,250	9.7	30.6	4,620	2,978
8	522,250	12.4	44.0	2,500	1,894,000	12.8	43.4	6,070	3,608
9	712,000	16.9	60.7	3,408	2,805,500	19.0	62.4	8,990	4,833
10	1,655,700	39.2	99.9	7,926	5,562,158	37.6	100.0	17,820	8,160
Total	$4,222,900	100.0		$1,989	$14,803,583	100.0		$4,743	
	Total number: 2,123				Total number: 3,121				

*This column is an ongoing addition of numbers in the column to the left. Read it this way: In 1860, the lowest 60% of Trempealeau property holders possessed 25.9% of the county's assessed property.

CHAPTER 5

Empire, Crisis, and Reform

In the last full year of the nineteenth century, Americans suddenly awoke from their preoccupations with domestic life to find themselves with an empire on their hands. In 1895, while very few Americans paid any attention, the subjects of Spain's colony, Cuba, staged an unsuccessful revolution—one more in a series of New World revolutions against European rule that had begun in 1776. But this one failed. The Spanish began a ruthless repression of guerrilla resistance, even herding men, women, and children into concentration camps. The American press took up the Cuban cause in shrill editorials and exaggerated reporting. Before anyone, even those in President McKinley's administration, quite knew what was happening, the American battleship *Maine*, calling at Havana, had been mysteriously sunk, perhaps sabotaged. McKinley asked Congress for a resolution permitting "forcible intervention" in Cuba. An American fleet that Secretary of the Navy Theodore Roosevelt had waiting in the Pacific steamed for Manila Bay in the Philippines to attack Spanish warships there. War was on.

The war lasted only a few weeks, and when it was over the United States "possessed" the Philippines and Puerto Rico, and was faced with the task of governing Cuba for a time under military occupation. The British boasted that the sun never set on their empire. Americans could not yet make the same boast, but they could see from a quick look at the map that the sun never set for *long* on American possessions.

This simple story—of being drawn innocently into "a splendid little war," as John Hay called it, and waking up blinkingly to an unanticipated empire—probably is a fairly accurate summary of the way most Americans experienced the events of 1898 and 1899. But the story misses a lot.

It overlooks, to begin with, the fact that the history of the United States could be written as a history of expansion and conquest. Through exploration, purchase, treaty, and war, the United States had become, in the course of the nineteenth century, a vast nation. And all along there had been plans and dreams to expand even further, down into Mexico and the Caribbean. In this way, the Spanish-American War was a logical outcome to a long history.

The Cuban occupation should also be seen as one of the first of many similar interventions over the next two decades which together helped define the distinctly American version of empire. Carried out with the support of presidents known as reformers and progressives, these ventures added up to a major extension of American influence around the globe. Roosevelt's aid to Panamanian rebels in 1903 made possible American domination of the Canal Zone. Under William Taft, the United States asserted its right to intervene and to supervise the collection of customs receipts in Nicaragua, another nation with a potential canal route. Woodrow Wilson sent American forces into Haiti and the Dominican Republic and, in 1914, seeking to topple the Mexican government, he landed American troops and occupied the coastal city of Veracruz.

On the other hand, this new expansion occurred in a new atmosphere. The 1890s was a decade of deep economic and social crisis. The depression of 1893–1897 was the worst in the nation's history and gave rise to the specter of collapse, as bands of tramps wandered the countryside in numbers large enough to be called "armies." Two of the most violent strikes in American history—one at Homestead in Pennsylvania in 1892, a second at Pullman, Illinois, in 1894—intensified the sense that the country was at a desperate crossroads. For many, particularly for people like Theodore Roosevelt, the war and the chance to be an imperial power were a welcome relief from the brooding sense of decline and collapse the decade had engendered.

In addition, whatever its origins, the new empire appeared to many Americans to be an opportunity, both for commercial and military development and for reform. The connection may seem odd in retrospect but many Americans looked on the chance to govern Cuba or the Philippines as a chance to recover a sense of mission, to bring to "backward" nations government that was honest, efficient, enlightened, and democratic. In the process, such people hoped, the nation might begin to set its own house in order. In fact, the experience of empire may have contributed as much as Populism did to the emergence of the atmosphere of reform that was to give the first decades of the new century their characteristic flavor.

HOWARD GILLETTE, JR.

The Military Occupation of Cuba: Workshop for American Progressivism

In this essay on the military occupation of Cuba, Howard Gillette, Jr., tries to get at the significance of the creation of an American empire in a new way. Instead of asking why Americans got involved in the war with Spain, he asks what they expected of their new empire once they found it on their hands. If Gillette is correct, and if Cuba is typical, what would you say defines the peculiar American *uses* of empire? Is American imperialism in Cuba any different than the kind of empire the United States exercised over the Plains Indians in the 1880s? or that progressive era reformers would extend to children (see the Cleveland play survey in the next chapter)?

The Spanish-American War marked an important turning point in American domestic as well as foreign policy. The intervention on behalf of Cuban independence generated a national sense of mission, not only to uplift the oppressed people of other countries, but also to improve domestic conditions at home. The war and the resulting policy of extraterritorial expansion, according to such a major contributor to progressivism as Herbert Croly "far from hindering the process of domestic amelioration, availed, from the sheer force

From Howard Gillette, Jr., "The Military Occupation of Cuba, 1899–1902: Workshop for American Progressivism," *American Quarterly*, vol. 25 (October 1973), pp. 410–425. *American Quarterly* is published by the University of Pennsylvania. This article is reprinted by permission of the publisher and the author. Copyright 1973, Trustees of the University of Pennsylvania.

of the national aspirations it aroused, to give a tremendous impulse to the work of national reform."

The agents of the occupation in Cuba* brought the prospects of American civilization—good government, education and business efficiency. In this sense the occupation was profoundly conservative, a reflection of already well-established American values and programs. On the other hand Leonard Wood, the second military governor of the island, established an overall pattern of political action which contrasted sharply with previous reform movements of both populists and Mugwumps.† Rejecting both the populist appeal to the masses and the negative Mugwump commitment to laissez-faire and puritan moralism, the Wood administration provided a model of new government powers in the hands of "responsible" leadership. It combined the Mugwump bias for elitism with the belief of populists in government activism. As such it serves as an important, previously neglected, link between old and new reform movements in America. In a real sense the occupation of Cuba served as a workshop for progressivism.

The issues surrounding the early occupation emerged out of the long-term conflict between Mugwump reformers and their opponents. Indeed, John R. Proctor, president of the U.S. Civil Service Commission, could not resist moralizing on Cuba's fate on the occasion of its transfer to American control:

> We do not feel personally responsible for misgovernment in New York or Philadelphia, but every American citizen will feel a personal responsibility for misgovernment in Havana, Santiago, and Manila, and will hold any party to a strict accountability, and any party daring to apply the partisan spoils system to the government of our colonies or dependencies will be hurled from power by the aroused conscience of the American people.

Following as it did the excesses of the Gilded Age, the war inevitably inspired charges from anti-imperialists that it was only the product of greedy business interests wishing to exploit Cuba's natural resources. Such charges made Congress sensitive enough to declare its own good intention through the Teller amendment to the Paris peace treaty: "That the United States hereby

---

*I have chosen to concentrate here on Cuba rather than the other Spanish possessions, because of its central role as the source for the Spanish-American War and Theodore Roosevelt's close connection with the island. The secondary literature on the administration of the Philippines and Puerto Rico suggests that the Cuban reform effort was not atypical for the possessions generally. Cuba should then serve as a proper focus for depicting the ties between the war and emerging progressivism.

†[As the author uses this term, Mugwump refers to the genteel reformers who reached the peak of their influence in the Gilded Age—men like E. L. Godkin of *The Nation* and landscape architect Frederick Law Olmsted (see the selection in this volume). Mugwumps were committed to laissez-faire economics, distrusted the masses, believed in the natural hegemony of an elite, and were expansionists in foreign policy.—*Ed.*]

disclaims any disposition or intention to exercise sovereignty, jurisdiction, or control over [Cuba] except for the pacification therein and asserts its determination, when that is accomplished, to leave the government of the Island to its people." To insure that the new territory would not be subject to economic exploitation, Congress passed the Foraker Amendment to the Army Appropriations bill in February 1899, prohibiting the granting of franchises or concessions in Cuba to American companies during the period of military occupation. President McKinley himself stressed America's good intentions in an effort to distinguish his foreign policy from the prevailing drive among European nations for colonial possessions. The Spanish territories, McKinley claimed in a recurrent theme of his administration, "have come to us in the providence of God, and we must carry the burden, whatever it may be, in the interest of civilization, humanity and liberty."

Cuba's first military governor, John Brooke, a career soldier who made his reputation in the Spanish War by leading invading columns through the virtually bloodless conquest of Puerto Rico, did his best to effect the outlines of good government promised in Washington. He initiated programs to build new schools and to provide basic sanitation facilities for the island. Among his appointees he counted as military governor of Havana William Ludlow, a man who had already established a credible record in the United States as a good government reformer. During his tenure as director of the Water Department in Philadelphia, according to a New York *Times* report, "political heelers who had won sinecures by carrying their wards were discharged and their places filled by efficient men. Political bosses stood aghast at such independence and after trying all kinds of 'influence' and 'pulls' were compelled to leave the Water Department alone as long as Colonel Ludlow remained at its head." Ludlow expressed his confidence in the effectiveness of transporting America's campaign against corruption to the island, claiming in his first annual report in 1900 that, "For the first time, probably in its history, Havana had an honest and efficient government, clean of bribery and speculation, with revenues honestly collected and faithfully and intelligently expended."

But the problems facing Brooke required more than basic services and clean government. The devastation and near anarchy of the island suggested immediately the need for extensive social, economic and political reconstruction. Yet lacking both administrative experience and any philosophical commitment to government activism, Brooke dampened every effort to provide government services whose need he did not find absolutely compelling. At one point he rejected a plan for long-term low-interest loans to destitute farmers, calling the program a kind of paternalism which would destroy the self-respect of the people.

The prospect for more comprehensive reform was discouraged by the lack of direction from Washington. Despite his repeated promise to carry out an American mission in Cuba, President McKinley outlined no general policy for the island. Henry Adams complained in January 1899, that "the government lets everything drift. It professes earnestly its intention to give Cuba its independence, but refuses to take a step toward it, and allows everyone to act for annexation." Fully a year after the military occupation began, McKinley admitted, "Up to this time we have had no policy in regard to Cuba or our relations therewith, for the simple reason that we have had no time to formulate a policy." Under the circumstances Brooke was forced, as he said, to conduct the government by induction.

Without clear direction from Washington, Brooke lapsed into a narrow strain of reform directed at purifying Cuba's social system. Among his first circulars were orders to abolish gambling, to close business houses on Sunday and to prohibit public games and entertainments on Sunday. In perhaps his most misguided effort at reform he ordered in the interest of public safety the confiscation of all machetes on the island, not realizing that the law, if executed faithfully, would ruin the island's sugar business. Brooke's announced restrictions on theaters and dance halls led the Washington *Post* to editorialize: "Our first duty in Cuba is not morals or customs, but the establishment of institutions of law and order . . . if we begin by interference in their private lives, with puritanical compulsion and missionary irritation, the problem of Cuban rehabilitation will be set back twenty years."

The Brooke administration provoked its first serious internal criticism from Leonard Wood, past commander of the Rough Rider brigade Teddy Roosevelt made famous and military governor of the province of Santiago. As a young activist who felt well-tested by the war, Wood bridled at Brooke's timidity. "The condition of the Island is disheartening," he wrote his friend Roosevelt in August 1899. "I tell you absolutely that no single reform has been initiated which amounts to anything to date." Publicly he made no effort to conceal his discontent, telling a New York *Times* reporter, "The Cuban problem can easily be solved. With the right sort of administration everything could be straightened out in six months. Just now there is too much 'tommyrot.' What is needed is a firm and stable military government in the hands of men who would not hesitate to use severe measures should the occasion arise."

Roosevelt took Wood's complaints seriously and launched a campaign to promote him to Brooke's position. Five days after Wood penned his scathing report on Brooke Roosevelt replied: "Your letter makes me both worried and indignant . . . I am going to show it privately and confidentially to [Secretary of War Elihu] Root. I do not know what to say. Root is a thoroughly good fellow and I believe is going to steadily come around to your way of looking at things." As early as July 1 Roosevelt had touted Wood for Military Governor, writing Secretary of State John Hay that he doubted whether "any nation in the world has now or has had within recent time, anyone so nearly approaching the ideal of military administrator of the kind now required in Cuba." Wood, Roosevelt argued, "has a peculiar facility for getting on with the Spaniards and Cubans. They like him, trust him, and down in their hearts are afraid of him." Roosevelt's campaign had its effect, for in December 1899, Wood succeeded to Brooke's position.

Wood accepted his appointment as no ordinary assignment. "He is fur-

ther impressed with the idea he has a mission—is charged with a great reformation," Brooke's retiring chief of staff noted. Such a mission demanded not
just the establishment of civil order as sought by Brooke but reconstruction of
the island as a thriving nation state. Though he showed some sensitivity to
differences between Latin and Anglo-Saxon cultures, Wood could not resist
promoting Americanization of the island—in the administration of justice, the
training of police and general administrative practice—where proven methods
could speed up goals of efficiency and uplift. As he wrote President McKinley
explaining his ultimate objective, "We are going ahead as fast as we can, but
we are dealing with a race that has steadily been going down for a hundred
years and into which we have got to infuse new life, new principles and new
methods of doing things."

Unlike Brooke, Wood established the administrative credibility to effect
the changes he sought. He assiduously avoided imposition of puritanical social
reforms on the Cuban people. "The main thing," he wrote, "is to avoid the
appearance of correcting abuses which do not exist." Instead he emphasized
adoption of "a business-like way of doing things," which he had complained
was missing from the Brooke administration. His interest in corporate administrative efficiency drew sustenance and support from McKinley's new Secretary of War Elihu Root who had left his job as a New York corporate lawyer to
take responsibility both for administering the Spanish possessions and mod-
ernizing the Army along efficient corporate lines. Together they shared the
goals of an emerging social type in America which stressed organization and
efficiency as touchstones of the progress of civilization.

As a start new lines of organization were drawn for the entire administrative system of the island. Wood revamped Brooke's education program, for
example, because it lacked precision. Though Brooke's minister of education
succeeded in building new schools and increasing enrollment, he developed no
institutional controls over the system. With the application of a new approach
fashioned after Ohio law, school administration was divided according to function. A commissioner of education handled all executive matters, including
purchasing supplies and making appointments, while a superintendent of
schools developed educational policy. Together with six provincial commissioners he formed a board of education authorized to determine and introduce
proper methods of teaching in the public schools. Each school district was
granted local autonomy, though individual teachers were held responsible to
central authority through a system of reports. The school board required
teachers to complete reports monthly and yearly. Salaries were withheld for
failure to comply. All teachers were also required to spend the first two sum-
mers of the American occupation in school and pass a certification exam at the
end of their second year. The rigorous system was completely new to Cuba,
where no public school system had previously existed and where teaching
standards had never been defined.

Next to education, Cuban law was the most important object of Wood's
administrative reorganization. In his annual report for 1900, Wood said that no

department was "more in need of thorough and radical reform, rigid inspection, and constant supervision," than the department of justice which "was lacking in efficiency, energy and attention to duty." He complained that the Cuban judiciary and legal body had "surrounded itself with a cobweb of tradition and conservation and adopted a procedure so cumbersome and slow of execution as to render impossible a prompt administration of justice." But he believed progress had been made under his administration. "Incompetent and neglectful individuals have been dismissed, the number of correctional courts has been very greatly increased, the audiencias supplied with necessary material, and very much done to improve the court houses."

Wood also launched a massive program of public works to reconstruct the island's cities. This municipal reform effort started under the crudest conditions. Wood's sanitary engineer in Santiago wrote that when he took office "not a shovel or a broom [was available], and for several days, pieces of oil cans and brushes of trees, and palm branches, were the only implements available." By the close of 1900 chief engineer William Black could report that the streets of the island's major cities were sprinkled and swept nightly. In 1901 Black reported a wide range of services planned for the island, including new sewer systems; modern street pavements; construction of water mains to new buildings; water pollution controls; public parks; construction of new schools and public buildings; a modern slaughterhouse designed after the best Chicago examples and a system of subways for wires for transmission of electricity for light power, telegraph and telephone service.

The Department of Public Works not only provided a wide range of public services, but under Black it reorganized its internal operation to promote efficient conduct of city business. Cuban street cleaners could no longer be haphazard in their work or their dress. Each man was assigned a particular district responsibility and was uniformed smartly in white cotton-duck suits with brown cord trimmings, white metal badges and brown hats. In addition, the department prepared codes for municipal operations, including a list of plumbing specifications that set standard requirements for every class of pipe and fitting.

In order to institutionalize the improved efficiency of municipal departments in particular, Wood urged adoption of a new city charter in Havana. Soon after his promotion, Wood appointed a commission of American and Cuban experts to draw up a model city charter. The commission was given copies of recent American charters, in which the fundamental principles encouraged were "simplicity, effectiveness, responsibility, and the largest measure of autonomy that could with safety be authorized." Following the argument for home rule in the United States, the new charter prevented the central and provincial governments from intervening in municipal affairs, granting the city control of "all matters within its boundary." Specifically city government was held responsible for the comfort and health of the inhabitants, and the security of their persons and property." Significantly the charter provided for regulation of all public utilities at a time when municipal reformers in America were attempting to write the same provision into law. The charter also incorporated an order previously adopted on the island which simplified the tax system by eliminating the ill-defined system of shared responsibility between city and province and making a direct connection between the tax rate and benefits received from city government.

The new city charter pointed the way to the best of American municipal reform. It established the dictum, which would be stated most precisely by Herbert Croly, that government must be efficient and to be efficient its powers must equal its responsibilities. Not only was the city authorized to use broad powers in the public interest, it was held responsible to promote that interest. As such, the charter reflected the general enthusiasm for positive government intervention in public affairs shared by Wood, Root, Roosevelt and Croly. Wood worked to define similar powers of public responsibility at a national level in Cuba through the creation of a railroad commission. He was offended, as he said, that the railroads "have always been able to buy the government and run things about as they saw fit." But much more he felt the state had a responsibility to protect public welfare. "I'm going to insist on state intervention in regulating rates," he wrote President Roosevelt in 1902, "when it is evident that such rates are prejudicial to the public interest."

When the railroads balked at possible state regulation Wood received encouragement from E. H. Moseley, Secretary of the U.S. Interstate Commerce Commission. "The demand of the railroads of Cuba that they should be allowed to control at pleasure, consulting their own interest only, the arteries of the internal commerce of the country is preposterous," he wrote Wood in January 1902. "I'm convinced that the railroad commission, composed of men of high character, is determined to follow the reasonable and correct course, dealing fairly with all, and while having the interest of the State and welfare of the people fully in view, do no act of injustice to the railroads."

The Cuban railroad law enacted a month later incorporated all the major features of the Interstate Commerce Act adopted in the United States in 1887. It forbade railroads to engage in discriminatory practices, required them to publish their rate schedules, prohibited them from entering pooling arrangements to keep rates high and declared that rates should be "reasonable and just." The Cuban law attempted to avoid the major pitfall of its predecessor by holding a ruling valid until revoked by the Supreme Court. Under the American law, where the I.C.C. relied on the Supreme Court for enforcement, fifteen of the first sixteen cases appealed had been decided in favor of the railroads against the commission.

Recent scholarship has revealed how legislation for the I.C.C., though stimulated by agrarian discontent, ultimately reflected the concerns of commercial interests, which wished to rationalize the system for their own profits. Taken out of the American context the Cuban reform represented an ideal in itself divorced from the factions which originally shaped the bill. Significantly, Wood gave it new purpose in protecting middle-class producers and planters for whom, he wrote Root, lower rates would be "a very substantial gain."

Indeed Wood built his program around the establishment of a conservative middle-class ruling elite. He distrusted the Cuban politicians who had gained office in the first elections and who, he said, appeared to be "in a certain sense doctors without patients, lawyers without practice and demagogues living in the subscription of the people and their friends." Planters and producers, on the other hand, appealed to him as "an honest, warm-hearted class of people," who were most appreciative of good order and protection of life and property. Wood often called the planter class conservative in a positive sense, consciously identifying them with the better class of citizens in America who unfortunately, he thought, had bypassed public service. He continued to believe, however, that their success, both political and commercial, was essential to the future of Cuba, for ultimately they would have to provide both the tax revenues to pay for needed services on the island and the leadership to effect those services. Wood underscored his belief in working hard for reciprocal trade agreements:

> The resources on which Cuba must depend for the income necessary to establish a stable government, requiring, as any government does, good schools, good courts, a system of public works, means of communication, hospitals, charities, etc., are those which will be derived from the sale of her two most stable products, and, if we continue to legislate against these, we cannot, with any degree of sincerity, expect the new government to be able to maintain such conditions as constitute stable government.

Ultimately Wood revealed the kind of commitment to conservative political capitalism which Gabriel Kolko has described as characteristic of progressivism. His hope for Cuba lay in a working relationship of responsible businessmen in both countries. He assigned highest priority to sanitation measures, for instance, largely because he believed adequate safeguards against disease were a prerequisite for American investment in the island. Part of his desire to standardize Cuban law derived from reports from American businessmen that the principal reason for the lack of confidence in Cuban investments was the threat of costly time-consuming litigation in native courts. Wood risked criticism from Cuban patriots for limiting popular suffrage because, as he wrote Root, "if it were known to be a fact that we were going to give universal suffrage, it would stop investments and advancement in this island to an extent which would be disastrous in its results."[*]

Wood clearly opposed outright business exploitation, but he could not avoid a bias for conservative middle-class business ideology. In the final year of his administration he worked actively for a stipulation gained in the contro-

---

*Wood to Root, Feb. 23, 1900, Wood Papers. On another occasion he wrote Root, "The people ask me what we mean by a stable government in Cuba. I tell them that when money can be borrowed at a reasonable rate of interest and when capital is willing to invest in the island, a condition of stability will have been reached."

versial Platt Amendment to the Army Appropriations bill which guaranteed the preservation of American commercial interests through the right of intervention. All orders of the military government were granted permanence in Article IV which declared that "all acts of the United States in Cuba during its military occupancy thereof are ratified and validated, and all lawful rights acquired thereunder shall be maintained and protected." Americanization of the island was thus completed, with legal assurance that it would not be quickly or easily overturned.

By every American standard the occupation had been a tremendous success. In guiding Cuba to its independence without succumbing to colonialism, business exploitation or government corruption, Wood rested the worst fears of the Mugwump reformers. Jacob Riis, the New York social reformer, granted the occupation that degree of success, in terms widely adopted by the press at the time:

> Cuba is free, and she thanks President Roosevelt for her freedom. But for his insistence that the nation's honor was bound up in the completion of the work his Rough-Riders began at Las Guasimas and on San Juan hill, a cold conspiracy of business greed would have left her in the lurch, to fall by and by reluctantly into our arms, bankrupt and helpless, while the sneer of the cynics that we were plucking that plum for ourselves would have been justified.

Beyond these essentially negative results, however, the administration provided a positive achievement through government activism which separated Wood and his contemporaries from the Mugwumps. Wood himself stressed this activism, in contrast to Brooke's timid administration, in summarizing his record. He had, as he wrote in 1903, completed work "which called for practically a rewriting of the administrative law of the land, including the law of charities, hospitals and public works, sanitary law, school law, and railway law; meeting and controlling the worst possible sanitary conditions; putting the people to school; writing an electoral law and training the people in the use of it, establishing an entirely new system of accounting and auditing." Not without pride he concluded that the work called for and accomplished "the establishment, in a little over three years, in a Latin military colony, in one of the most unhealthy countries of the world, a republic modeled closely upon the lines of our own great Anglo-Saxon republic."

Our understanding of the special nature of the Wood reform ethic is heightened through a brief analysis of its reception in Cuba. For a country whose economic and social identity lay largely in the countryside, Wood could well have concentrated government expenditures in a program of agricultural reconstruction modeled after methods being instituted in the American South and suggested by Governor James Wilson of Matanzas Province. "I do not consider the future of Cuba depends chiefly upon schools, road-making, improved sanitation or judiciary reform," Wilson said. "The best the United

States can do for Cuba and the Cubans is to give every opportunity for improving the value of the land by putting it to the best uses. In this way capital could do an immense amount of good here as well as get returns." Wood rejected Wilson's plea, resting his hopes for Cuba's future not in small farms but in the cities. He stressed this urban orientation when he wrote Roosevelt in August 1899, "All we want here are good courts, good schools and all the public work we can pay for. Reform of municipal government and a business way of doing things."

Wood's emphasis on urban development ran counter to established Cuban tradition. While his work in Havana drew praise in America, it received a less welcome reception among Cubans. The Havana ayuntamiento (city council) overwhelmingly rejected the charter commission report, although the proposal purportedly incorporated the best features of American law. According to one councilman, the new plan was but one more of the great many fancies which had been thrust on the Cubans by force.

Beyond Wood's urban orientaton lay a bias for government authority which again rankled the Cubans. As governor of Santiago, Wood had gained tremendous popularity by criticizing the centralization of authority in Havana. When Brooke decreed that all customs revenues would be distributed from Havana, Wood took the case for decentralized distribution to Washington and became a hero among Cubans. Wood's act struck a responsive chord with a people who hoped for a substitution of American decentralized administration for the highly centralized Spanish system. The Spanish law of 1878 governing local administration outwardly allowed local autonomy. But a provision making the alcalde (mayor) removable at will placed the executive authority and the towns generally at the mercy of the central government. The Cubans moved toward greater local independence with the Autonomist Constitution of 1897 which stipulated that the ayuntamientos and not the central government made the final selection of alcaldes.

Wood's reputation as champion of Santiago's independence encouraged the Cubans to believe that he would complete the decentralization begun by the Autonomist Constitution. Wood did encourage municipal autonomy. He eliminated many municipalities which had been created during the war solely to act as agents of the Spanish government, making the remaining cities real functioning units with their own taxing and spending power. But with a lack of administrative experience at the local level, cities repeatedly exceeded their budgets, depending on national revenues to remain solvent. Wood's own personal vigor and the fact that he was so insistent on his directives helped sustain all final authority in Havana. As one sensitive observer of America's overseas policy, Leo S. Rowe, said, "The leaders in the work of civic reorganization were determined to put an end to the highly centralized administration of Spanish times, but in actual development of the system the force of tradition has proved stronger than conscious purpose. Although the municipalities enjoy more extensive powers in law, in fact they remain subservient to the central government."

Wood's authoritarian bent must have reflected a military man's desire to get a job done. He recognized, for instance, no restraints in effecting sanitation measures in Santiago. According to President McKinley's special commissioner to the island, Robert Porter, "The doors of houses had to be smashed in; people making sewers of the thoroughfares were publicly horsewhipped in the streets of Santiago; eminently respectable citizens were forcibly brought before the commanding general and sentenced to aid in cleaning the streets they were in the habit of defiling." As A. Hunter Dupree has pointed out, Wood managed to institute his sanitation program in Cuba because island administrators held powers which "would have been entirely unavailable to the President of the United States had the infected city been New Orleans instead of Havana." Wood himself credited his success in Cuba to the wide scope of his power, indicating that if he were to take a role in administering the Philippines "I should like to have a go at the situation with the same authority I have had here. Without such full authority I believe the Islands will be the burial ground of the reputation of those who go there."

Had Wood shared the philosophical restraints of Brooke or other Mugwump leaders of his generation on the limited use of government power he might not have aroused the kind of opposition in Cuba he did. The important factor for the historian of American reform, however, lies in the example Wood held up to his countrymen back home and its reception there, whatever his own motivations for seeking government authority in Cuba. By carefully selecting among existing precedents in the United States those models which allowed the greatest government activism, Wood presented fellow reformers in America with a new spirit of administrative technique and law. His reforms emphasizing administrative efficiency served as a bridge between Root's reorganization of the Army and Gifford Pinchot's program for a professionally managed forest system and later administrative reforms instituted by Theodore Roosevelt as president.

In a general sense Wood's administration, undertaken as it was in the full glare of national publicity, provided a visibility for reform which had been badly lacking in earlier good government movements. The emergence of Roosevelt, Root and Wood from virtual obscurity to national heroes helped dramatize a new spirit of reform and suggested to the public at large the dawn of a new moral leadership for America. "The war with Spain," Secretary of the Navy William H. Moody claimed in a speech in 1902, "disclosed the enormous resources of this country, its wealth, its power, its strength, but it disclosed more. It disclosed the character of our people, and we know that where the Tafts, and the Roots, and the Days, and the Woods, and the Roosevelts came from, there are many more like them to come to the service of the country when their country calls." Wood's heralded decision to turn down a $25,000-a-year street railway presidency offered during his term as military governor set him apart from public figures of the Gilded Age and gave substance to a new leadership ideal, articulated by Roosevelt as early as 1897 when he was still

Assistant Secretary of the Navy that: "The fight well fought, the life honorably lived, the death bravely met—those count far more in building a fine type of temper in a nation than any possible success in the stock-market, than any possible prosperity in commerce or manufactures."

In a more direct sense the philosophical connection between the occupation and emerging progressivism was tied through personal links, the most important of which was Wood's close relationship with Theodore Roosevelt. Among more specialized progressive leaders, Leo Rowe of the University of Pennsylvania recognized immediately the importance of administrative innovation in the Spanish possessions. Though recognized as an expert on municipal reform in America, Rowe found the study of the Spanish possessions irresistible. He wrote not only extensive articles on the administration of Cuba and the Philippines but also a book on the occupation of Puerto Rico, where he served as chairman of the island's code commission. He predicted in March 1899, that the workshop provided by the Spanish possessions would turn America's political philosophy away from limited protection of individual liberties to one of activist intervention for national development. "The readjustment of the country's international relations, which must follow the recent struggle with Spain, will supply the connecting link between economic and political development," he wrote in *The Forum*. "Its influence, however, will extend far beyond these limits. It will modify our political ideas, develop a broader view of the country's relation to the larger affairs of the world, and react upon domestic politics, with the result of raising the level of public life."

In his urban work Rowe reached theoretical conclusions which Wood coincidentally put into pragmatic effect. In 1897 Rowe argued that even though American cities had reached a nadir in the American experience they would have to serve nonetheless as the chief agent of civilization. The reformer's role, then, lay clearly in upgrading the urban environment, precisely the approach Wood took in Cuba. Indeed, Wood's administration both reflected Rowe's philosophy and gave it sustenance through the apparent triumph of urban-oriented programs to give the island the services sought in America through the city beautiful movement, particularly good schools, grand public buildings and clean streets.

On another level the experiments in the Caribbean served to inspire activists among two other major elements of the emerging reform movement, the journalists who would soon become known as muckrakers and the social welfare activists. Robert Bannister cites the tremendous impact the activism of Wood and Roosevelt had on Ray Stannard Baker in converting him from a Mugwump to a progressive. Indeed Baker seems to have absorbed himself the chief principles of Roosevelt's strenuous life, writing in his journal, "A warrior is not made by the battles he avoids but by the battles he fights." Another entry suggests a parallel drive with Roosevelt, Wood and Rowe to take up the challenge of remaking society: "What we must be thankful for is not perfection, not the solution of all our problems; this condition we can never hope to attain—but let us praise God for the struggle! Completeness we can not attain, but where there is restless activity, there is also health and hope. Not beautification, perfection: that is heaven, but turmoil and struggle, progress; that is human life." For the social reformer Jacob Riis, the example of the American occupation was no less inspiring. "How jolly it is to think of you and Roosevelt being both where you are," he wrote Wood in February 1900. "This is a good world anyway, and the pessimists lie like the Dickens."

Despite our recognition today that Wood's specific programs as well as his desire to civilize Cuba generally reflected already established American values, we should not underestimate the impact of the overall reform effort on the United States. For a country in which administrative reform had not yet emerged as a national goal and in which urban reconstruction remained rather a hope than a reality, Wood's achievement must have provided, as Croly said, a tremendous stimulus for domestic reform. The Cuban occupation provided progressives not only with a programmatic cohesion which had been lacking in earlier reform movements but also the kind of favorable national publicity which could give new efforts momentum at home. The success of the occupation, by American standards, underscored the belief that the United States had fulfilled its mandate to lift the Cuban people into the forward stream of Western civilization, and in so doing, it provided for a new generation of progressives faith in man's ability to remake and reform the world around him.

THEODORE ROOSEVELT

Behind the "Big Stick"

Theodore Roosevelt is the physical embodiment of American imperialism. Generations of students have become familiar with an image of Roosevelt, sleeves rolled up, shoveling dirt out of what would become the Panama Canal. The image is important, not simply because of Roosevelt's undeniable role in shaping our Caribbean empire, but because it says so much about *why* Roosevelt thought the nation should be there. In "The Strenuous Life," a famous speech delivered in 1899 and reprinted in part below, Roosevelt expounds on the virtues of striving so strongly identified with his character. Why was Roosevelt so interested in the strenuous life? Were there any indications that not everyone was living it? (Here students may wish to examine the photographs that are part of this chapter.) Why does Roosevelt bring up the Civil War?

It is worth noting that this emphasis on the strenuous life was new.

An earlier generation was more attuned to the lessons of George M. Beard's *American Nervousness: Its Causes and Consequences* (1881). Beard found modern civilization, which he broke down into five elements—the press, the telegraph, the sciences, steam power, and the "mental activity of women"—at the root of the matter. Because the nervous system had not grown sufficiently to compensate for the additional strains imposed by an overspecialized, urban society, nervous disorders had multiplied. Beard counseled Americans to *conserve* their limited supply of nervous energy.

Here are two theories of physical energy, each distinctive and each, apparently, representative of its own time. Why was Roosevelt so fond of the strenuous life when Beard thought it so dangerous? What changes in the late nineteenth century might account for the change?

In speaking to you, men of the greatest city of the West, men of the State which gave to the country Lincoln and Grant, men who preëminently and distinctly embody all that is most American in the American character, I wish to preach, not the doctrine of ignoble ease, but the doctrine of the strenuous life, the life of toil and effort, of labor and strife; to preach that highest form of success which comes, not to the man who desires mere easy peace, but to the man who does not shrink from danger, from hardship, or from bitter toil, and who out of these wins the splendid ultimate triumph.

A life of slothful ease, a life of that peace which springs merely from lack either of desire or of power to strive after great things, is as little worthy of a nation as of an individual. . . . If you are rich and are worth your salt, you will teach your sons that though they may have leisure, it is not to be spent in idleness; for wisely used leisure merely means that those who possess it, being free from the necessity of working for their livelihood, are all the more bound to carry on some kind of non-remunerative work in science, in letters, in art, in exploration, in historical research—work of the type we most need in this country, the successful carrying out of which reflects most honor upon the nation. We do not admire the man of timid peace. We admire the man who embodies victorious effort; the man who never wrongs his neighbor, who is prompt to help a friend, but who has those virile qualities necessary to win in the stern strife of actual life. It is hard to fail, but it is worse never to have tried to succeed. . . . When men fear work or fear righteous war, when women fear motherhood, they tremble on the brink of doom; and well it is that they should vanish from the earth, where they are fit subjects for the scorn of all men and women who are themselves strong and brave and high-minded. . . .

We of this generation do not have to face a task such as that our fathers faced, but we have our tasks, and woe to us if we fail to perform them! We

From Theodore Roosevelt, *The Strenuous Life: Essays and Addresses* (New York: Century, 1901), pp. 1–2, 4–13, 17–18, 20–21. Originally published by S. S. McClure, 1899.

cannot, if we would, play the part of China, and be content to rot by inches in ignoble ease within our borders, taking no interest in what goes on beyond them, sunk in a scrambling commercialism; heedless of the higher life, the life of aspiration, of toil and risk, busying ourselves only with the wants of our bodies for the day, until suddenly we should find, beyond a shadow of question, what China has already found, that in this world the nation that has trained itself to a career of unwarlike and isolated ease is bound, in the end, to go down before other nations which have not lost the manly and adventurous qualities. If we are to be a really great people, we must strive in good faith to play a great part in the world. We cannot avoid meeting great issues. All that we can determine for ourselves is whether we shall meet them well or ill. In 1898 we could not help being brought face to face with the problem of war with Spain. All we could decide was whether we should shrink like cowards from the contest, or enter into it as beseemed a brave and high-spirited people; and, once in, whether failure or success should crown our banners. So it is now. We cannot avoid the responsibilities that confront us in Hawaii, Cuba, Porto Rico, and the Philippines. All we can decide is whether we shall meet them in a way that will redound to the national credit, or whether we shall make of our dealings with these new problems a dark and shameful page in our history. To refuse to deal with them at all merely amounts to dealing with them badly. We have a given problem to solve. If we undertake the solution, there is, of course, always danger that we may not solve it aright; but to refuse to undertake the solution simply renders it certain that we cannot possibly solve it aright. The timid man, the lazy man, the man who distrusts his country, the over-civilized man, who has lost the great fighting, masterful virtues, the ignorant man, and the man of dull mind, whose soul is incapable of feeling the mighty lift that thrills "stern men with empires in their brains"—all these, of course, shrink from seeing the nation undertake its new duties; shrink from seeing us build a navy and an army adequate to our needs; shrink from seeing us do our share of the world's work, by bringing order out of chaos in the great, fair tropic islands from which the valor of our soldiers and sailors has driven the Spanish flag. . . .

No country can long endure if its foundations are not laid deep in the material prosperity which comes from thrift, from business energy and enterprise, from hard, unsparing effort in the fields of industrial activity; but neither was any nation ever yet truly great if it relied upon material prosperity alone. All honor must be paid to the architects of our material prosperity, to the great captains of industry who have built our factories and our railroads, to the strong men who toil for wealth with brain or hand; for great is the debt of the nation to these and their kind. But our debt is yet greater to the men whose highest type is to be found in a statesman like Lincoln, a soldier like Grant. They showed by their lives that they recognized the law of work, the law of strife; they toiled to win a competence for themselves and those dependent upon them; but they recognized that there were yet other and even loftier duties—duties to the nation and duties to the race.

So much for the commercial side. From the standpoint of international honor the argument is even stronger. The guns that thundered off Manila and Santiago left us echoes of glory, but they also left us a legacy of duty. If we drove out a medieval tyranny only to make room for savage anarchy, we had better not have begun the task at all. It is worse than idle to say that we have no duty to perform, and can leave to their fates the islands we have conquered. Such a course would be the course of infamy. It would be followed at once by utter chaos in the wretched islands themselves. Some stronger, manlier power would have to step in and do the work, and we would have shown ourselves weaklings, unable to carry to successful completion the labors that great and high-spirited nations are eager to undertake. . . .

But in the early eighties the attention of the nation became directed to our naval needs. Congress most wisely made a series of appropriations to build up a new navy, and under a succession of able and patriotic secretaries, of both political parties, the navy was gradually built up, until its material became equal to its splendid personnel, with the result that in the summer of 1898 it leaped to its proper place as one of the most brilliant and formidable fighting navies in the entire world. We rightly pay all honor to the men controlling the navy at the time it won these great deeds, honor to Secretary Long and Admiral Dewey, to the captains who handled the ships in action, to the daring lieutenants who braved death in the smaller craft, and to the heads of bureaus at Washington who saw that the ships were so commanded, so armed, so equipped, so well engined, as to insure the best results. But let us also keep ever in mind that all of this would not have availed if it had not been for the wisdom of the men who during the preceding fifteen years had built up the navy. . . .

And, gentlemen, remember the converse, too. Remember that justice has two sides. Be just to those who built up the navy, and, for the sake of the future of the country, keep in mind those who opposed its building up. Read the "Congressional Record." Find out the senators and congressmen who opposed the grants for building the new ships; who opposed the purchase of armor, without which the ships were worthless; who opposed any adequate maintenance for the Navy Department, and strove to cut down the number of men necessary to man our fleets. The men who did these things were one and all working to bring disaster on the country. They have no share in the glory of Manila, in the honor of Santiago. They have no cause to feel proud of the valor of our sea-captains, of the renown of our flag. Their motives may or may not have been good, but their acts were heavily fraught with evil. They did ill for the national honor, and we won in spite of their sinister opposition. . . .

The problems are different for the different islands. Porto Rico is not large enough to stand alone. We must govern it wisely and well, primarily in the interest of its own people. Cuba is, in my judgment, entitled ultimately to settle for itself whether it shall be an independent state or an integral portion of the mightiest of republics. But until order and stable liberty are secured, we must remain in the island to insure them, and infinite tact, judgment, moderation, and courage must be shown by our keeping the island pacified, in relentlessly stamping out brigandage, in protecting all alike, and yet in showing proper recognition to the men who have fought for Cuban liberty. The Philippines offer a yet graver problem. Their population includes half-caste and native Christians, warlike Moslems, and wild pagans. Many of their people are utterly unfit for self-government, and show no signs of becoming fit. Others may in time become fit but at least can only take part in self-government under a wise supervision, at once firm and beneficent. We have driven Spanish tyranny from the island. If we now let it be replaced by savage anarchy, our work has been for harm and not for good. I have scant patience with those who fear to undertake the task of governing the Philippines, and who openly avow that they do fear to undertake it, or that they shrink from it because of the expense and trouble; but I have even scanter patience with those who make a pretense of humanitarianism to hide and cover their timidity, and who cant about "liberty" and the "consent of the governed," in order to excuse themselves for their unwillingness to play the part of men. Their doctrines, if carried out, would make it incumbent upon us to leave the Apaches of Arizona to work out their own salvation, and to decline to interfere in a single Indian reservation. Their doctrines condemn your forefathers and mine for ever having settled in these United States. . . .

I preach to you, then, my countrymen, that our country calls not for the life of ease but for the life of strenuous endeavor. The twentieth century looms before us big with the fate of many nations. If we stand idly by, if we seek merely swollen, slothful ease and ignoble peace, if we shrink from the hard contests where men must win at hazard of their lives and at the risk of all they hold dear, then the bolder and stronger peoples will pass us by, and will win for themselves the domination of the world. Let us therefore boldly face the life of strife, resolute to do our duty well and manfully; resolute to uphold righteousness by deed and by word; resolute to be both honest and brave, to serve high ideals, yet to use practical methods. Above all, let us shrink from no strife, moral or physical, within or without the nation, provided we are certain that the strife is justified, for it is only through strife, through hard and dangerous endeavor, that we shall ultimately win the goal of true national greatness.

Trouble at Home

Late-nineteenth-century America contained large numbers of mobile people, most of them male and most of them poor. Because these people seldom left records and often do not appear in the census, it is not at all clear why they were transient. Some, it seems, were driven from one city to the next by high rates of unemployment. Others were drawn to new locations by opportunities in another community. Still others were attracted by the road itself, or sought to recreate some idealized past experience (the military offered one model—the word "bum" derives from "bummer," coined during the Civil War to describe a soldier off on a private foraging expedition).

Coxey's army, a group of the unemployed heading for Washington, D. C., to protest their condition, was composed in part of people motivated by the economic conditions of 1894. But this only partially explains the phenomenon. What does the photograph reveal about this group? What does the caption—written by photographer/journalist Ray Stannard Baker—indicate about how this group was received as it moved toward the nation's capital?

Coxey's Army, 1894. The commonweal tied up at a toll gate, the town turns out to enjoy the sight. *Library of Congress.*

Hobos Discovered "Riding the Bumpers" of a Freight Train. *Bain Collection, Library of Congress.*

"Every tramp who is not old or infirm should be made to work every day for three months at some central place controlled by the State. I have scared some of them by telling them that, if they do not move on, a complaint will be made in the district court, and then a term at Bridgewater will be the result. The rule in many places, and more especially in country towns, is that the police support that is so much needed is not at hand, unless a good deal of time is spent in the matter. During an experience of nine years as an overseer of the poor in Hadley [Massachusetts], it is a rare case to find one of these knights of the road who will work one hour for the best victuals that any farmer has to give. I asked a strong fellow why he did not go to work, and his answer was, 'I don't know how. I should have to learn.' " —*A.E. Cook, Overseer of Poor, Hadley, Massachusetts, from Massachusetts Association of Relief Officers, 1900, Report on the Best Methods of Dealing with Tramps and Wayfarers (Boston, 1901), Appendix B, pp. 28–32.*

FREDERICK JACKSON TURNER

Running Out of Land: The Turner Hypothesis, 1893

The spectacle of tramps, hoboes, and armies of the unemployed suggested to many Americans that their national experience had turned some sort of critical corner, and that dislocation and confusion might be the way of the future. From another point of view, Roosevelt's fear that his countrymen would fall into a pattern of sloth and ease was an expression of the same concern that a fundamental change was taking place which had to find a new resolution in the strenuous life. To some, the problem was written in history, particularly in the fact that what had once been an expansive frontier society had reached its natural limits. Frederick Jackson Turner, in what was probably the most influential paper ever published by an American historian, "The Significance of the Frontier in American History" (1893), provided the classic statement of this point of view. Can you draw connections between Turner's way of assessing the consequences of the end of the frontier and Roosevelt's Chicago speech? Could Turner's address have been used as a justification for imperialism? Was Cuba in any important sense a "frontier"?

In a recent bulletin of the Superintendent of the Census for 1890 appear these significant words: "Up to and including 1880 the country had a frontier of settlement, but at present the unsettled area has been so broken into by isolated bodies of settlement that there can hardly be said to be a frontier line. In the discussion of its extent, its westward movement, etc., it can not, therefore, any longer have a place in the census reports." This brief official statement marks the closing of a great historic movement. Up to our own day American history has been in a large degree the history of the colonization of the Great West. The existence of an area of free land, its continuous recession,

From Frederick Jackson Turner, "The Significance of the Frontier in American History," American Historical Association, *Annual Report for 1893* (Washington , D.C.: Government Printing Office, 1894), pp. 199–201, 205, 208, 215–217, 219, 220–223, 226–227.

and the advance of American settlement westward, explain American development.

Behind institutions, behind constitutional forms and modifications, lie the vital forces that call these organs into life and shape them to meet changing conditions. The peculiarity of American institutions is, the fact that they have been compelled to adapt themselves to the changes of an expanding people— to the changes involved in crossing a continent, in winning a wilderness, and in developing at each area of this progress out of the primitive economic and political conditions of the frontier into the complexity of city life. Said Calhoun in 1817, "We are great, and rapidly—I was about to say fearfully—growing!" So saying, he touched the distinguishing feature of American life. . . . American development has exhibited not merely advance along a single line, but a return to primitive conditions on a continually advancing frontier line, and a new development for that area. American social development has been continually beginning over again on the frontier. This perennial rebirth, this fluidity of American life, this expansion westward with its new opportunities, its continuous touch with the simplicity of primitive society, furnish the forces dominating American character. The true point of view in the history of this nation is not the Atlantic coast, it is the great West. . . .

The frontier is the line of most rapid and effective Americanization. The wilderness masters the colonist. It finds him a European in dress, industries, tools, modes of travel, and thought. It takes him from the railroad car and puts him in the birch canoe. It strips off the garments of civilization and arrays him in the hunting shirt and the moccasin. It puts him in the log cabin of the Cherokee and Iroquois and runs an Indian palisade around him. Before long he has gone to planting Indian corn and plowing with a sharp stick; he shouts the war cry and takes the scalp in orthodox Indian fashion. In short, at the frontier the environment is at first too strong for the man. He must accept the conditions which it furnishes, or perish, and so he fits himself into the Indian clearings and follows the Indian trails. Little by little he transforms the wilderness, but the outcome is not the old Europe, not simply the development of Germanic germs, any more than the first phenomenon was a case of reversion to the Germanic mark. The fact is, that here is a new product that is American. . . .

By 1880 the settled area had been pushed into northern Michigan, Wisconsin, and Minnesota, along Dakota rivers, and in the Black Hills region, and was ascending the rivers of Kansas and Nebraska. The development of mines in Colorado had drawn isolated frontier settlements into that region, and Montana and Idaho were receiving settlers. The frontier was found in these mining camps and the ranches of the Great Plains. The superintendent of the census for 1890 reports, as previously stated, that the settlements of the West lie so scattered over the region that there can no longer be said to be a frontier line. . . .

The Atlantic frontier was compounded of fisherman, fur-trader, miner, cattle-raiser, and farmer. Excepting the fisherman, each type of industry was on the march toward the West, impelled by an irresistible attraction. Each passed in successive waves across the continent. Stand at Cumberland Gap and watch the procession of civilization, marching single file—the buffalo following the trail to the salt springs, the Indian, the fur-trader and hunter, the cattle-raiser, the pioneer farmer—and the frontier has passed by. Stand at South Pass in the Rockies a century later and see the same procession with wider intervals between. The unequal rate of advance compels us to distinguish the frontier into the trader's frontier, the rancher's frontier, or the miner's frontier, and the farmer's frontier. When the mines and the cow pens were still near the fall line the traders' pack trains were tinkling across the Alleghanies, and the French on the Great Lakes were fortifying their posts, alarmed by the British trader's birch canoe. When the trappers scaled the Rockies, the farmer was still near the mouth of the Missouri. . . .

The frontier promoted the formation of a composite nationality for the American people. The coast was preponderantly English, but the later tides of continental immigration flowed across to the free lands. This was the case from the early colonial days. The Scotch Irish and the Palatine Germans, or "Pennsylvania Dutch," furnished the dominant element in the stock of the colonial frontier. With these peoples were also the freed indented servants, or redemptioners, who at the expiration of their time of service passed to the frontier. . . . Very generally these redemptioners were of non-English stock. In the crucible of the frontier the immigrants were Americanized, liberated, and fused into a mixed race, English in neither nationality or characteristics. The process has gone on from the early days to our own. . . .

The legislation which most developed the powers of the National Government, and played the largest part in its activity, was conditioned on the frontier. . . . The pioneer needed the goods of the coast, and so the grand series of internal improvement and railroad legislation began, with potent nationalizing effects. Over internal improvements occurred great debates, in which grave constitutional questions were discussed. Sectional groupings appear in the votes, profoundly significant for the historian. Loose construction increased as the nation marched westward. But the West was not content with bringing the farm to the factory. Under the lead of Clay—"Harry of the West"—protective tariffs were passed, with the cry of bringing the factory to the farm. The disposition of the public lands was a third important subject of national legislation influenced by the frontier. . . .

It is safe to say that the legislation with regard to land, tariff, and internal improvements—the American system of the nationalizing Whig party—was conditioned on frontier ideas and needs. But it was not merely in legislative action that the frontier worked against the sectionalism of the coast. The economic and social characteristics of the frontier worked against sectionalism. The men of the frontier had closer resemblances to the Middle region than to either of the other sections. Pennsylvania had been the seed-plot of frontier emigration, and, although she passed on her settlers along the Great Valley into the west of Virginia and the Carolinas, yet the industrial society of these

Southern frontiersmen was always more like that of the Middle region than like that of the tide-water portion of the South, which later came to spread its industrial type throughout the South.

The Middle region, entered by New York harbor, was an open door to all Europe. . . . It had a wide mixture of nationalities, a varied society, the mixed town and county system of local government, a varied economic life, many religious sects. In short, it was a region mediating between New England and the South, and the East and the West. It represented that composite nationality which the contemporary United States exhibits, that juxtaposition of non-English groups, occupying a valley or a little settlement, and presenting reflections of the map of Europe in their variety. It was democratic and nonsectional, if not national; "easy, tolerant, and contented;" rooted strongly in material prosperity. It was typical of the modern United States. . . .

But the most important effect of the frontier has been in the promotion of democracy here and in Europe. As has been indicated, the frontier is productive of individualism. Complex society is precipitated by the wilderness into a kind of primitive organization based on the family. The tendency is anti-social. It produces antipathy to control, and particularly to any direct control. The tax-gatherer is viewed as a representative of oppression. . . .

The frontier States that came into the Union in the first quarter of a century of its existence came in with democratic suffrage provisions, and had reactive effects of the highest importance upon the older States whose peoples were being attracted there. An extension of the franchise became essential. It was *western* New York that forced an extension of suffrage in the constitutional convention of that State in 1821. . . .

So long as free land exists, the opportunity for a competency exists, and economic power secures political power. But the democracy born of free land, strong in selfishness and individualism, intolerant of administrative experience and education, and pressing individual liberty beyond its proper bounds, has its dangers as well as its benefits. Individualism in America has allowed a laxity in regard to governmental affairs which has rendered possible the spoils system and all the manifest evils that follow from the lack of a highly developed civic spirit. In this connection may be noted also the influence of frontier conditions in permitting lax business honor, inflated paper currency and wild-cat banking. The colonial and revolutionary frontier was the region whence emanated many of the worst forms of an evil currency. The West in the war of 1812 repeated the phenomenon on the frontier of that day, while the speculation and wild-cat banking of the period of the crisis of 1837 occurred on the new frontier belt of the next tier of States. Thus each one of the periods of lax financial integrity coincides with periods when a new set of frontier communities had arisen, and coincides in area with these successive frontiers, for the most part. The recent Populist agitation is a case in point. Many a State that now declines any connection with the tenets of the Populists, itself adhered to such ideas in an earlier stage of the development of the State. A primitive society can hardly be expected to show the intelligent appreciation of the complexity of business interests in a developed society. . . .

From the conditions of frontier life came intellectual traits of profound importance. The works of travelers along each frontier from colonial days onward describe certain common traits, and these traits have, while softening down, still persisted as survivals in the place of their origin, even when a higher social organization succeeded. The result is that to the frontier the American intellect owes its striking characteristics. That coarseness and strength combined with acuteness and inquisitiveness; that practical, inventive turn of mind, quick to find expedients; that masterful grasp of material things, lacking in the artistic but powerful to effect great ends; that restless, nervous energy; that dominant individualism, working for good and for evil, and withal that buoyancy and exuberance which comes with freedom—these are traits of the frontier, or traits called out elsewhere because of the existence of the frontier. Since the days when the fleet of Columbus sailed into the waters of the New World, America has been another name for opportunity, and the people of the United States have taken their tone from the incessant expansion which has not only been open but has even been forced upon them. He would be a rash prophet who should assert that the expansive character of American life has now entirely ceased. Movement has been its dominant fact, and, unless this training has no effect upon a people, the American energy will continually demand a wider field for its exercise. But never again will such gifts of free land offer themselves. For a moment, at the frontier, the bonds of custom are broken and unrestraint is triumphant. There is not *tabula rasa*. The stubborn American environment is there with its imperious summons to accept its conditions; the inherited ways of doing things are also there; and yet, in spite of environment, and in spite of custom, each frontier did indeed furnish a new field of opportunity, a gate of escape from the bondage of the past; and freshness, and confidence, and scorn of older society, impatience of its restraints and its ideas, and indifference to its lessons, have accompanied the frontier. What the Mediterranean Sea was to the Greeks, breaking the bond of custom, offering new experiences, calling out new institutions and activities, that, and more, the ever retreating frontier has been to the United States directly, and to the nations of Europe more remotely. And now, four centuries from the discovery of America, at the end of a hundred years of life under the Constitution, the frontier has gone, and with its going has closed the first period of American history.

ERNEST THOMPSON SETON

The Boy Scout Handbook, 1910

The dreary prospect of life without the stimulus of the frontier did not inevitably lead to any particular course of action. Imperialism was one

response. Another response, exemplified by the Boy Scouts, found Americans looking inward, recreating the frontier in the midst of the culture that had apparently destroyed it.

Founded in England in 1908, the Boy Scouts was incorporated in the United States in 1910. The English-born Ernest Thompson Seton had established an American precedent with his Woodcraft Indians, organized in 1902.

How do Seton's analyses of man's needs and of the problems of modern life compare with Roosevelt's? Were any of Seton's goals shared by the Americans who controlled Cuba? Why isn't Seton satisfied with nature working its peculiar magic on *individuals*? Why would the *nation* become involved?

Introduction

Every American boy, a hundred years ago, lived either on a farm or in such close touch with farm life that he reaped its benefits. He had all the practical knowledge that comes from country surroundings; that is, he could ride, shoot, skate, run, swim; he was handy with tools; he knew the woods; he was physically strong, self-reliant, resourceful, well-developed in body and brain. In addition to which, he had a good moral training at home. He was respectful to his superiors, obedient to his parents, and altogether the best material of which a nation could be made.

We have lived to see an unfortunate change. Partly through the growth of immense cities, with the consequent specialization of industry, so that each individual has been required to do one small specialty and shut his eyes to everything else, with the resultant perpetual narrowing of the mental horizon.

Partly through the decay of small farming, which would have offset this condition, for each mixed farm was a college of handicraft.

And partly through the stereotyped forms of religion losing their hold, we see a very different type of youth in the country to-day.

It is the exception when we see a boy respectful to his superiors and obedient to his parents. It is the rare exception, now, when we see a boy that is handy with tools and capable of taking care of himself under all circumstances. It is the very, very rare exception when we see a boy whose life is absolutely governed by the safe old moral standards.

The personal interest in athletics has been largely superseded by an interest in spectacular games, which, unfortunately, tend to divide the nation into two groups—the few overworked champions in the arena, and the great crowd content to do nothing but sit on the benches and look on, while indulging their tastes for tobacco and alcohol.

From Ernest Thompson Seton, *Boy Scouts of America: A Handbook of Woodcraft, Scouting, and Lifecraft* (New York: Doubleday, Page, 1910), pp. xi, xii, 2–4, 34–38. Reprinted by permission.

It is this last that is turning so many thoughtful ones against baseball, football, etc. This, it will be seen , is a reproduction of the conditon that ended in the fall of Rome. In her days of growth, every man was a soldier; in the end, a few great gladiators were in the arena, to be watched and applauded by the millions who personally knew nothing at all of fighting or heroism.

Degeneracy is the word.

To combat the system that has turned such a large proportion of our robust, manly, self-reliant boyhood into a lot of flat-chested cigarette-smokers, with shaky nerves and doubtful vitality, I began the Woodcraft movement in America. Without saying as much, it aimed to counteract the evils attendant on arena baseball, football, and racing, by substituting the better, cleaner, saner pursuits of Woodcraft and Scouting. . . .

Nine leading principles are kept in view:

(1) This movement is essentially for *recreation*.
(2) *Camp-life*. Camping is the simple life reduced to actual practice, as well as the culmination of the outdoor life.

Camping has no great popularity to-day, because men have the idea that it is possible only after an expensive journey to the wilderness; and women that it is inconvenient, dirty, and dangerous.

These are errors. They have arisen because camping as an art is not understood. When intelligently followed camp-life must take its place as a cheap and delightful way of living, as well as a mental and physical saviour of those strained and broken by the grind of the over-busy world.

The wilderness affords the ideal camping, but many of the benefits can be got by living in a tent on a town lot, piazza, or even house-top.
(3) *Self-government*. Control from without is a poor thing when you can get control from within. As far as possible, then, we make these camps self-governing. Each full member has a vote in affairs.
(4) *The Magic of the Camp-fire*. What is a camp without a camp-fire?—no camp at all, but a chilly place in a landscape, where some people happen to have some things.

When first the brutal anthropoid stood up and walked erect—was man, the great event was symbolized and marked by the lighting of the first camp-fire.

For millions of years our race has seen in this blessed fire the means and emblem of light, warmth, protection, friendly gathering, council. All the hallow of the ancient thoughts, hearth, fireside, home, is centered in its glow, and the home-tie itself is weakened with the waning of the home-fire. Not in the steam radiator can we find the spell; not in the water coil; not even in the gas-log: they do not reach the heart. Only the ancient sacred fire of wood has power to touch and thrill the chords of primitive remembrance. When men sit together at the camp-fire, they seem to shed all modern form and poise, and hark back to the primitive—to meet as man and man—to show the naked soul. Your camp-fire partner wins your love, or hate, mostly your love; and having camped in peace together, is a lasting bond of union,—however wide your worlds may be apart.

The camp-fire, then, is the focal centre of all primitive brotherhood. We shall not fail to use its magic powers. . . .

(6) *Honors by Standards*. The competitive principle is responsible for much that is evil. We see it rampant in our colleges to-day, where every effort is made to discover and develop a champion, while the great body of students is neglected. That is, the ones who are in need of physical development do not get it, and those who do not need it are over-developed. The result is much unsoundness of many kinds. A great deal of this would be avoided if we strove to bring all the individuals up to a certain standard. In our non-competitive tests the enemies are not *"the other fellows,"* but *time and space*, the forces of Nature. We try *not to down the others*, but *to raise ourselves*. A thorough application of this principle would end many of the evils now demoralizing college athletics. Therefore, all our honors are bestowed according to world-wide standards. (Prizes are not honors.)

(7) *Personal Decoration for Personal Achievements*. The love of glory is the strongest motive in a savage. Civilized man is supposed to find in high principle his master impulse. But those who believe that the men of our race, not to mention boys, are civilized in this highest sense, would be greatly surprised if confronted with figures. Nevertheless, a human weakness may be good material to work with. I face the facts as they are. All have a chance for glory through the standards, and we blazon it forth in personal decorations that all can see, have, and desire.

(8) *A Heroic Ideal*. The boy from ten to fifteen, like the savage, is purely physical in his ideals. I do not know that I ever met a boy that would not rather be John L. Sullivan than Darwin or Tolstoi. Therefore, I accept the fact, and seek to keep in view an ideal that is physical, but also clean, manly, heroic, already familiar, and leading with certainty to higher things.

(9) *Picturesqueness in Everything*. Very great importance should be attached to this. The effect of the picturesque is magical, and all the more subtle and irresistible because it is not on the face of it reasonable. The charm of titles and gay costumes, of the beautiful in ceremony, phrase, dance, and song, are utilized in all ways. . . .

National Deterioration

In the first place we have to recognize that our nation is in need of help, from within, if it is to maintain its position as a leading factor for peace and prosperity among the other nations of the earth.

History shows us, that with scarcely an exception, every great nation, after climbing laboriously to the zenith of its power, has then apparently become exhausted by the effort, and has settled down in a state of repose, relapsing into idleness and into indifference to the fact that other nations were pushing up to destroy it, whether by force of arms or by the more peaceful but equally fatal method of commercial strangulation. In every case the want of some of that energetic patriotism which made the country has caused its ruin; in every case the verdict of history has been, "Death through bad citizenship."

Signs have not been wanting of recent years that all is not right with our citizenship in Britain. Ominous warnings have been heard from many authorities and many sources, in almost every branch of our national life. These have been recently summed up by one of our public men in the following words:—

"The same causes which brought about the fall of the great Roman Empire are working to-day in Great Britain."

The Unemployed

One sign of the disease (which was also one of the signs of decay in Rome before her fall) is the horde of unemployed leading miserable, wasted lives in all parts of the country—the great army of drones in our hive.

It is no longer a mere temporary excrescence, but is a growing tumor pregnant with evil for the nation.

These people, *having never been taught to look after themselves, or to think of the future or their country's good*, allow themselves to become slaves by the persuasive power of a few professional agitators whose living depends on agitating (whether it is needed or not); and blinded by the talk of these men they spurn the hand which provides the money, till they force employers to spend fortunes either in devising machinery that will take their place and will not then go on strike, or in getting in foreign labor, or in removing their business to other countries, leaving the agitators fat, but the mass of their deluded followers unemployed and starving and unable to provide for the crowds of children which they still continue improvidently to bring into the world.

CHAPTER 6

Progressivism: The Age of Reform

Historian Richard Hofstadter gave us the theme for this chapter in 1955 when he published his conclusions about populism and progressivism in a book titled *The Age of Reform*. A quarter-century later, it is not at all clear what this phenomenon called "progressivism" was, or whether its agents, the "progressives," were really very progressive. Hofstadter in fact argued that at the heart of progressivism was a vision of the past, an attempt to restore economic individualism and political democracy, values that had been buried under giant corporations, burgeoning unions, and corrupt political bosses. With the exception of Theodore Roosevelt, who believed that most big business could not and should not be eliminated, progressives, according to Hofstadter, generally tried to disassemble existing institutions. The progressive movement, he wrote, was "the complaint of the unorganized against the consequences of organization."

Others have argued that progressivism was not nostalgic but aggressively future-oriented. According to this view, progressivism cannot be separated from the "organizational revolution" taking place at the turn of the century. Products of that revolution include trade associations, new government agencies, the organized professions, and an increased willingness to use federal as opposed to state and local agencies to achieve economic and social goals. But there are real problems even in placing specific movements within this organizational context. Did new government regulations represent the past or the future? Were they designed to bring change or to preserve the status quo?

The title of Hofstadter's study implies the ability to recognize a reform when we see one, and much of the history of the progressive period has been written from this assumption. But here, too, there are difficulties. When Theodore Roosevelt broke with the Republican party in 1912 and campaigned for the presidency under the banner of the Progressive party (not to be confused with the more general term, progressivism), his Bull Moose platform was a classic summary of social reforms long identified with progressivism—minimum wages for women, prohibition of child labor, the eight-hour workday, and workmen's compensation. For years, however, Roosevelt had been involved with birth control advocate Margaret Sanger and with Stanford University president David Starr Jordan and other luminaries in another "reform" effort, the eugenics movement, which many progressives found unappealing. In a letter written in 1914, Roosevelt described and explained his interest in eugenics: "I wish very much that the wrong people could be prevented entirely from breeding; and when the evil nature of these people is sufficiently flagrant, this should be done. Criminals should be sterilized and feeble-minded persons forbidden to leave offspring behind them. But as yet there is no way possible to devise a system which could prevent all undesirable persons from breeding." For Roosevelt, eugenics deserved the label "reform" every bit as much as the movement to abolish child labor. Others, including historians, have disagreed, and therein lies a central problem with the word "reform."

Nor is the difficulty resolved simply by focusing on what seem to be clearly benign reforms. One of the most popular of progressive period programs was state workmen's compensation legislation, under which injured workers were compensated according to predetermined schedules, rather than by virtue of what they could recover through legal action. By what standards is workmen's compensation "reform"? Is it an example of progressivism? Feminists of the 1960s and 1970s would raise similar, and worthwhile, questions about the many progressive era laws that regulated hours and conditions for working women. In 1910 those laws seemed to be important measures of protection; today they seem obstacles to equality of the sexes. Were those laws, even in 1910, a clear example of social progress?

Still, certain features of progressivism stand out. One need only mention the major regulatory measures of the period to grasp the importance of regulation (a word, it should be emphasized, with no more real content than "reform"). Out of a financial panic in 1907 came the Federal Reserve System, created in 1913 to provide a more flexible currency. Several pieces of railroad legislation, including the Elkins Act (1903) and the Hepburn Act (1906), were designed to limit rebates (unfair price cutting by the carriers) and to give the Interstate Commerce Commission, then two decades old, the authority to fix maximum rates. Congress also provided for federal inspection of meat packers shipping in interstate commerce and created the Federal Trade Commission (1914) to supervise the competitive relations of interstate businesses. State and local governments were also active in the regulatory movement and were the major agencies of change in social justice areas such as hours of labor, child labor, and tenement house reform. The progressive period is also well known for a series of measures designed to change the terms of access to the political system: the direct election of United States senators, direct primaries for the nomination of elective officials, initiative, referendum, and recall.

Aside from the dramatic rise in the use of government as a social tool, the qualities that gave unity to progressivism were attitudinal and ideological. Progressives believed in data. They believed in the possibilities of "scientific" social welfare, supported by research; of market research in selling; and of measuring the abilities of employees through psychological testing. This faith in science was often accompanied by a fear of national moral collapse. It was this kind of thinking that led to the founding of the Boy Scouts of America in 1910 and to Roosevelt's enchantment with eugenics. Finally, progressivism was not, at least on the surface, a matter of class interests, of one group seeking hegemony over another. For progressives, the political system was not a device by which conflicting interests compromised (or failed to compromise) their essential differences; it was a means through which the essential harmony of all interests might be expressed.

WILLIAM GRAEBNER

The Regulatory State: Safety in the Coal Mines

William Graebner's essay describes both the events leading to the creation of the United States Bureau of Mines in 1910 and the early history of that agency. In reading the essay, use the specific phenomenon of coal-mining safety reform to answer these larger questions: What are the central ingredients of the experience, and are they clearly and typically "progressive"? Is the bureau an example of "reform"? Who were the reformers? Why was government employed at all? and why one level of government (e.g., state or federal) rather than another? Why does it seem to make little difference which political party is in office? In the case of mine safety, which factors make a reasonable political response possible, and which militate against it?

In November 1968 an explosion in the "safe" No. 9 mine of the Consolidation Coal Company at Farmington, West Virginia, killed seventy-eight miners and produced a brief but potent public outcry for new federal safety legislation. In December 1907, ten miles from Farmington at Monongah, West Virginia, 361 miners died in an explosion in the "safe" Monongah No. 6 and No. 8 mines of the Fairmont Coal Company. The largest coal-mine disaster in American history, Monongah profoundly illustrated the safety problems characteristic of American industry at the turn of the century, which were most serious in mining and railroading, and it signaled the beginning of a major movement for reform of dangerous conditions in the mines.

Participants in the coal-mining safety movement included miners, mine inspectors, scientists, journalists, and government officials. All played important roles, but the coal-mine operators, more than any other group, defined the response of the Progressive years to the problem of safety in the coal mines and determined the perimeters of state, national, and private action. Wary of state safety legislation, and caught up in an industry with nationally competitive markets, operators looked to the national government and to national action for relief. They campaigned for the establishment and adequate funding

From William Graebner, "The Coal-Mine Operator and Safety: A Study of Business Reform in the Progressive Period," *Labor History*, 14 (Fall 1973), 483–505 (edited). Copyright 1973 by *Labor History*. Reprinted by permission.

of a national Bureau of Mines, cooperated with the Bureau in pursuit of coal-mining safety, and participated in the movement to secure mine-safety legislation.

Competition in the coal industry is not a complete explanation of the complex operator response to the safety problem. Concerned with state as well as national legislation and with safety in his own mining operations, the coal-mine operator was also influenced by workmen's compensation and schedule rating, the size of his operations, his view of the union, and his opinion that miners and mine officials were usually responsible for accidents and disasters. Competition, however, does account for the desire of most operators to nationalize—albeit cautiously—coal-mining safety reform, while at the same time opposing some state safety legislation. This is not to say that operators were inconsistent or disingenuous in their approach to coal-mining safety reform. Businessmen often opposed reform legislation, but they were not merely adversaries of liberal reformers; the coal operators' program was positive, a creative response to industrial conditions. From their business perspective, operators saw that only by transcending the states through national action could safety and competition be made compatible. The coal operator experience is evidence that Progressivism was in part a successful attempt by the business community to use the governmental machinery to achieve its own ends.

State and county coal-mining safety legislation was nothing new to the coal-mine operator, having originated in 1869 and proliferated since then, but the rash of explosions in December 1907 spelled a qualitative difference. William N. Page, chairman of a group of West Virginia operators concerned with the recent disasters, wrote to A. B. Fleming, owner of the Fairmont Coal Company, about the problem of explosions. He was particularly interested, he said, because he felt "fully assured that 'undigested' legislation may follow, which will affect every mine in the state, more or less." Another of Fleming's friends described his fears of "radical legislation," particularly in Ohio where new legislation would be "drastic and burdensome if not almost prohibitive. . . ." In reference to a bill then before the Pennsylvania legislature, Pittsburgh operator Thomas Liggett said: "Public clamor is responsible for this bill. Public clamor crucified the greatest man ever upon earth and public clamor has been wrong ever since." Journals of the coal trade expressed similar sentiments. *Coal Trade Bulletin* saw "on the horizon a cloud of present small proportions labeled 'drastic and unnecessary mining laws,' " and expressed the hope it would be "dispersed by the wind of 'sound judgment'. . . ." According to *Coal*, a "venial press" which had riled up the people and legislative demagogues seeking "popularity and reputation" through authorship of safety legislation should share the responsibility of unnecessary additions to the statutes.

Operators' apprehension about state legislation followed from their analysis of competitive conditions in the industry; they claimed that the nature of coal markets made expensive safety legislation unfair. Indiana operator R. S. Tennant opposed a state shot-firing law on the grounds that it would place Hoosier operators at a competitive disadvantage. Trade journals resisted a

Pennsylvania law, claiming it would "add materially to the cost of production of bituminous coal in the state, and will still further handicap an industry that already suffers too much."

Miners, government officials, and inspectors joined the operators in viewing competitive conditions as critical to the safety problem. "The old idea of a coal baron is a myth," said H. M Wilson of the U.S. Bureau of Mines. The operators were progressive, he added, but "the economic condition of the coal industry is not such as will permit it to pay the recognized expenses of operations." Perhaps the most vocal of those sympathetic to the operators' economic problems was Joseph A. Holmes, who became the first permanent Director of the Bureau in 1910. Holmes saw "wasteful and unsafe mining methods" as concomitant with cutthroat competition and lamented the difficulty, indeed the impossibility, of introducing European safety methods and appliances into the United States because "their cost would exceed the profits of the industry." To his friend Fleming, Holmes wrote sympathetically: "As we all realize, as anxious as the operators in this country are to do everything possible for safety and clean mining, it is impossible for many of them to carry out such plans because of the exceedingly low prices of coal at the mines."

These evaluations were correct. In 1904 there were 4,650 commercial mines in the bituminous industry in the United States; in 1910, 5,818; and in 1920, 8,821. The relatively small investment required to begin operation in coal mining and abundant geographical coal resources operated in conjunction with low ton-mile railroad rates to produce intensive national competition. Moreover, although demand for coal underwent substantial seasonal fluctuations, supply was capable only of easy expansion. Shutting down a coal mine was so expensive that it was often cheaper to continue production at a loss for a length of time. Each period of prosperity in the coal business was followed by great increases in capacity. Low labor costs and cheap freight rates enabled the coals of the Eastern states, particularly those of West Virginia, to enter, for example, the natural coal markets of Illinois and sell at competitive prices. Within local coal-producing regions competition was also severe. With the exception of the Pocahontas field of West Virginia, ownership and operation of bituminous mining was everywhere diffused. Price fixing was futile and profits low in this highly competitive industry. This situation had clear implications for safety. Fearful of losing ground in the competitive struggle, operators opposed state legislation and administrative regulation, made much of the great expense entailed by safety legislation, and were reluctant to undertake experimental mine-safety projects requiring heavy financial commitments. Competitive pressures mitigated the great promise of the Illinois Mining Investigation Commission—a tripartite organization of miners, operators, and public representatives established in 1910 to recommend safety legislation to the legislature—and resulted in non-enforcement of laws whose burdens appeared to be too great for the operators.

Injured or threatened by state legislation, operators turned to national solutions. One expression of this was the movement for uniform legislation, a movement which attempted to define and apply nationwide and industry-wide standards for workmen's compensation and for mine-safety conditions, methods, and appliances. While uniform legislation promised to improve engineering by simplifying statutes, it was more commonly defended for its impact on migratory labor. Mine inspector William E. Holland of Iowa said: "A large portion of the coal-mining fraternity, like the wild ducks, migrate with every change of season. . . . They find a different set of laws in every state and accidents are liable to happen from unfamiliarity with the law in the state to which they have removed. With a uniform code, this condition would be eliminated." That the overriding consideration was economic, however, was made clear by two operators from opposite ends of the central competitive field, both interested in uniform workmen's compensation legislation. Z. Taylor Vinson put the case of the West Virginia operator: "If we should have a workmen's compensation law in West Virginia, and you do not have it in Pennsylvania or Illinois, or other coal producing states, then obviously the coal operators of West Virginia will have to bear that burden alone, and it will be impossible under competitive market conditions to bring about any uniformity unless all the states adopt substantially the same plan, but if it exists in practically the same degree throughout the whole country, then the burden would be borne by all in the first instance and ultimately refunded by the consumer." Operator A. J. Moorshead of Illinois, one of the foremost advocates of uniformity, described Illinois' workmen's compensation act as "a good measure if it were a national one," but burdensome "when it is saddled upon one State and not upon the neighboring states. . . ." A decade of efforts to promote interstate cooperation produced little. Operators were so divided that a degree of cooperation requisite to uniformity proved unachievable. "One state does not," Moorshead had noticed, "in the matter of legislation, care a continental about the others."

Coal-mining safety involved some sophisticated science and technology, and the need for unanimity basic to uniform mine-safety legislation led logically to demands for a federal scientific body capable of supplying the latest scientific information. Congressman George A. Bartlett of Tonopah, Nevada, expressed the feelings of numerous operators, union chiefs, and mine inspectors when, in 1908, he said a proposed Bureau of Mines would "aid and assist in bringing about, by investigation and suggestion, a uniformity of State legislation that will lessen the terrible loss of life incident to mining. . . ." Operators, moreover, were seriously concerned with the inadequacy of scientific knowledge about coal-mine explosions. Because the mines of the Fairmont Coal Company had an almost unsurpassed reputation for safety, this concern reached a peak with the Monongah disaster. Fleming's friends were incredulous. A committee of the West Virginia legislature, charged with investigating the Monongah disaster, saw the explosion as "an illustration of the fact that in our most modern equipped mines, lurks a danger which science has yet to discover," and insisted the state legislature could do nothing until the cause of mine explosions were known. At this time the Technologic Branch of the U.S.

Geological Survey was engaged in limited research into the problem of coal-mine explosions, but the Survey's experts could not tell the operators what had caused the recent explosions. "I am sorry that I cannot," said explosives engineer Clarence Hall. "We do not understand it ourselves."

The controversy focused on whether or not coal dust could, by itself and without the presence of methane gas, explode and propagate an explosion. Operators were divided. Fleming and fellow West Virginia operator Justus Collins took the dust theory seriously, and Fleming was, in fact, privately praised by Holmes for his efforts to prevent dust explosions in his mines in 1909. The Juanita Coal and Coke Company of Bowie, Colorado, warned its employees of the dangers of coal dust and took precautions. Other operators were hostile toward the theory. "Between you and I and the gatepost," wrote William N. Page, "I think our Chief Mine Inspector is a crank on the subject of dust." Coal dust, said Page then, "must necessarily play an important part in all explosions, *when the gas is once ignited*, by adding to the forces involved." A Pennsylvania operator asserted flatly that without a gas explosion "the coal dust is not likely to take fire. Don't see how it can take fire."

It was partly this division and confusion over the facts of mine safety which encouraged operators to go to the federal government. At Holmes's request, Fleming appeared in Washington and testified before the House Committee on Mines and Mining about the urgency of mine-accident investigations. Operators from West Virginia, Pennsylvania, and other states met with officials of the U.S. Geological Survey in Washington, D.C., on January 8, 1908. Those present resolved to support appropriations for research into the causes of mine disasters. "The United States Government," concluded the operators, "should take the necessary steps to determine the causes before any attempt is made to apply legislative remedies. . . ."

While coal-mine operators were influential in securing new funds for Survey investigations of explosions, their goal was a Bureau or Department of Mines. Since its inception in 1897, the American Mining Congress, an organization dominated by Western metal-mining operators, had also had a Bureau or Department as a principal aim. Through the need to take advantage of the great potential of the safety issue, by 1907 the organization had become an advocate of safer mines and made overtures to Eastern coal interests, holding its 1908 annual meeting in Pittsburgh, Pennsylvania. Nonetheless, the Bureau envisioned by the Mining Congress was not a safety but a business organization, intended to broaden markets, to provide facilities for classifying and assaying ore, and to control speculation in the mining industry. The alliance between metal and coal operators was one of convenience.

Though lacking a national organization strictly of their own, coal operators worked hard to secure a Bureau. The bill which eventually became law in 1910 was, in fact, authored by one of the nation's most important coal operators, also Chairman of the House Committee on Mines and Mining, George F. Huff of Pennsylvania. "Colonel Huff," wrote the *United Mine Workers Journal*, "regards the passage of this bill as the crowning effort of his congressional career." Huff could count on vigorous operator lobbying. Numerous coal operators testified before his Committee in 1908. G. W. Traer of the Illinois Coal Operators' Association spoke for a committee of operators which was, he said, "unanimously" in favor of a Bureau of Mines. As in the struggle for appropriations for Technologic Branch, Holmes's strongest ally in his quest for a Bureau of Mines was A. B. Fleming, who worked throughout 1908 and 1909 to secure passage of the Bureau bill. Fleming corresponded regularly with Senator Nathan Scott of West Virginia in a successful effort to secure his support for the Bureau. Holmes provided Fleming with information to use in writing Scott and other members of Congress and invited Fleming to the 1908 House hearings, where the Fairmont operator proved to be one of Holmes's most important witnesses. Before the Committee, Fleming admitted that neither the operators nor the states could afford to carry on the kind of scientific investigations requisite to safe mining conditions.

Operator enthusiasm stopped short of a Bureau with investigatory and regulatory powers. The critical challenge here was provided by Representative John G. McHenry of Benton, Pennsylvania, whose bill proved the only bone of contention in the 1908 hearings. McHenry's bill not only empowered its projected Bureau to investigate the causes and effects of all accidents in coal mines, but also provided for a tax of one cent per ton on all coal mined in the U.S., to be collected from operators to alleviate the suffering of the families of men killed or injured in mine accidents. To assure compliance with the latter provision, it gave the Bureau power to examine the books of any coal company. Congressman William B. Wilson, an acknowledged representative of the miners, attacked the measure, knowing serious consideration of it would jeopardize the campaign for a Bureau by encouraging operator resistance. His fears were justified. "The work of the bureau," said operator Traer, "should not have anything to do with the extension and supervision of practical mining operations." *Coal* expressed a national consensus when it suggested that "all legislation governing mining within the States must originate in the legislative bodies of the respective States." . . .

In its first decade, the Bureau had no regulatory authority. "Hence," said Van H. Manning, the Bureau's second Director, "as the bureau can not forbid nor compel, it recommends and advises. It appeals to reason, not to fear. Its campaign for greater safety is essentially a campaign of education." In its most public and widely-known activity, the Bureau, through its stationary and movable cars and stations, tried to reach miners and operators—to instruct them in the proper techniques and equipment of mine rescue and first aid. Success depended on the reception of operators and miners. Miner hostility to program goals or methods would make progress difficult; operator opposition would limit contact between the federal experts on the cars and the men in the mines because the cars could not go or remain on private property for any reason—education, rescue, or investigation—without permission of the owner. . . .

Between 1910 and 1920 operators came increasingly to view safety as a reform movement which made economic sense, and the basic reason was workmen's compensation. "Compensation undeniably is followed by prevention," wrote John Mitchell. Carter Goodrich, a friend of the miner, added that "Workmen's compensation laws have done something toward 'making props cheaper than men.' ". . . .

If the competitive nature of the industry was the primary determinant of the operator relationship to the safety problem, there were important secondary factors. Hoping to allay worker discontent and to cut off the union movement through various forms of welfare, employers provided housing, medical facilities and services, schools, recreation, and safer working conditions for their employees. Thus company safety work was often part of a larger welfare movement motivated not by selfless humanitarianism but by the desire to beat the unions at their own game. Employee representation plans, such as that established by the Colorado Fuel and Iron Company in 1913, operated across the spectrum of employee welfare, including safety. The anti-union paternalism implicit in much company safety activity was made explicit by one Pennsylvania company official. "When government regulation of Coal Mining had to come in Western Penna.," he said, "we did our best to place it on a parental basis instead of a police basis desired by trade union demogogues [sic]."

United States Steel Corporation, in the forefront of the movement to eliminate unions, also employed the most advanced safety measures and systems in its coal-mining subsidiaries. One contemporary who was close to all phases of the safety movement described the work of U.S. Steel's H.C. Frick Coal and Coke Company in terms which reveal the fruits of paternalism: "Many of this company's precautions against accidents are not prescribed by law, but are subject entirely of the company's own initiation and adoption. It has, in fact, anticipated every legal measure laid down by state or national government for mine safety."

U.S. Steel's interest in safety was also logical because of the Company's size. The larger coal companies, with their superior financial resources and greater overhead, were generally the ones to institute employee representation and other programs of more strictly safety content. Only the larger companies could consider placing telephones in the mines; finance their own scientific investigations of safety problems; send men to Europe to study modern methods of conservation and accident prevention, as the H. C. Frick Company did; or publish costly literature in English and foreign languages. Mine inspectors were united in the belief that the larger companies used more specialized safety methods and more advanced safety materials than did the smaller companies and that they were less likely to evade the mining laws. "The greatest trouble we have," noted a Colorado inspector, "is with the small fellows."

Large or small, most operators accepted an interpretation of the safety problem which emphasized miner ignorance, carelessness, and disobedience as causes of mine accidents. One disaster occurred because miners disobeyed printed regulations; "the failure of any employe [sic] properly to perform his duty or the violation of the safety rules of the mine by a careless worker" caused the Monongah explosion; the Cherry mine fire reached tragic proportions because the men in the underground stable "lost their heads at a critical moment. . . ." *Coal Trade Bulletin* attributed ninety-nine percent of all mine accidents to the "carelessness or wilful negligence" of mine employees, while *Coal's* estimate was a more conservative ninety percent. At the heart of the problem, according to the operator, was the new immigrant. The ordinary miner was careless and reckless, but the recently arrived Italian or Slav was worse. He was ignorant of mining skills and the language; he was of low intelligence; he drank too much; he was unmarried and therefore lacking in the steadying influence of family life; and, as the product of "centuries of governmental and social oppression," he naturally confused American freedom with license.

From this analysis, operators united on education as a solution. "More education along sound lines," one operator journal noted, "will bring better results than a mass of loosely drawn laws." *Coal* claimed that unless miners were educated, "a code of laws as big as the State Capitol will be of no service." Operators hoped inexperienced miners would learn the general principles of coal mining; the basics of safety, first-aid, and rescue; American history; and the English language. ("English First is the greatest asset to Safety First in both government and industry," said one operator.) They strongly supported the educational programs of the Bureau of Mines, the YMCA, night schools, state mining institutes, and mining companies. State university short courses for miners were particularly popular with operators. Accident prevention through education received added impetus from the Americanization movement during these years, with the National Safety Council particularly interested in this facet of industrial safety.

Certification was another solution to the problems of employee inexperience, carelessness, and incompetence. The essential purpose—licensing of miners and mine officials by governmental agency to assure that mine employees were competent in their tasks—was embodied in legislation passed as early as the 1870s. . . .

Operators also emphasized the need for increased discipline, through which careless miners, particularly recent immigrants, would learn to respect the law and the lives of fellow workmen. They commonly placed responsibility on the agents of discipline, the numerous officials—mine managers, firebosses, foremen, and inspectors—standing between management and the miner. A solution to the explosion problem, noted *Coal*, "seems to hinge almost entirely on a more faithful performance of duty by the fire and mine bosses, with a watchful eye on their conduct by the mine managers." Operators also demanded arrest and prosecution of careless or disobedient miners and fired employees who clearly disregarded safety procedures. If for some operators discipline was only a means of denying their own responsibility, for others it was a serious attempt to deal with the real problems posed by careless and disobedient miners. . . .

Coal operators' associations held significant but largely unrealized potential for mine safety. The first associations of importance followed the growth of the United Mine Workers in the central competitive field in the 1890s. In 1916 there were twenty-two local, state, and regional associations—and usually, but not always, they had increased safety as one of their goals. Some, among them the Illinois Coal Operators' Association and the West Virginia Smokeless Coal Operators' Association, pursued political functions in state and national capitals, while others, such as the Coal Mining Institute of America, were concerned only with the technical aspects of safety. . . .

The operator was essentially a businessman, a reformer when business conditions allowed or required it, and an ideologue only in his insistence that the national government remain virtually powerless in matters of safety. Coal-mine operators were not social Progressives; their opposition to state safety legislation makes that label inappropriate. Neither, however, were they only obstacles to the reform process. The operator (conservative) versus laborer and reformer (liberal) configuration is a generally accurate picture in the states before and during the Progressive period. For the national arena, however, its irrelevance is manifest. Here the operators were not followers but leaders, creative participants in coal-mining safety reform.

Operators did not step into this role without prodding from Monongah, the Cherry mine fire in 1909, and countless other disasters. Coal operators faced what they felt to be ill-considered and chaotic state legislation. Federal action on mine safety through the Technologic Branch of the Geological Survey, and then through the Bureau of Mines, offered the possibility, at least, of confining the expected legislative avalanche to those measures that were scientifically defensible. "National progressivism," writes historian Gabriel Kolko, "becomes the defense of business against the democratic ferment that was nascent in the states."

The Bureau was an ideal solution for operators in another sense, too, for it was almost risk free. Without any kind of regulatory authority, the Bureau could function only as an educational and information agency. Operators had no need to fear federal mine-safety legislation or administrative mine-safety regulations emanating from the Bureau. Uniformity of state legislation appealed to operators for similar reasons. Operators were not ready for federal safety legislation. They resented infringements on the police powers of the states and would have viewed federal coal-mine safety legislation as a violation of the Constitution. While operators feared the state legislatures, they were as yet unwilling to recognize any other legislative source of social welfare. For the time being, at least, operators insisted that the locus of power remain in the states and that the inter-related problems of safety and competition be solved through uniform state action or private action.

The national component of the Progressive movement was the logical product of a transformation of the coal industry which began in the 1850s and which, by 1900, had produced an intensely competitive bituminous industry with national coal and labor markets as well as scientific problems which transcended state boundaries. In an effort to bring order to these changes, operators and other groups associated with the industry attempted to organize nationally and, through these organizations, to secure solutions—such as the Bureau and uniformity—which would affect the entire industry. This movement for national solutions succeeded only when extraordinary events overshadowed division and when the goal—a Bureau of Mines, for example—involved no risk for local interests. The movement failed to the extent that operators were divided and unable to transcend local frameworks, and this, unfortunately, was the usual state of the industry.

Lewis Hine, Reformer

Consistent with their passion for data and "facts," the progressives were infatuated with the photograph, especially with its potential as a perfectly objective document.

Lewis Hine was both a progressive and a photographer. Once a teacher in a progressive school in New York City, Hine devoted most of his life to making pictures. Much of his best work was done in the progressive period, and most of his pictures were of the world of work.

Young Coal Miner. Photographed by Lewis Hine. *Library of Congress.*

Many, like this one of a young coal miner, were intended as evidence in the photographer's ongoing battle against child labor.

Hine shared this penchant for social reform with nineteenth-century photographer Jacob Riis, whose "Bandits' Roost" is on p. 84. Is there a difference in how the two photographers approach their subjects? Is one more critical than the other? more objective? How you feel about Riis' subjects? about Hines'?

The Weaker Sex

The progressive penchant for investigation, study, and measurement was also applied to the problem of sex discrimination in employment. One case began in 1917, when a committee of women employed in the government service in Washington, D.C., charged the Department of the Interior with discrimination. The following letter was one of many denials written by Interior bureau chiefs. What does the letter reveal about the pitfalls of the progressive trust in the "expert"?

Department of the Interior United States Geological Survey Washington

Office of the Director

January 31, 1917

Mr. E. J. Ayers,
Chief Clerk,
Department of the Interior.

My dear Mr. Ayers:
In reply to your notation on the copy of the letter from Senator Jones, requesting information as to whether any discrimination against women solely upon the grounds of their sex was made by the Geological Survey:

As you are doubtless aware, much of the work carried on by the Survey requires field ability for which it is necessary to employ men rather than women. In the field branches, therefore, women necessarily are unable to meet the strain attendant upon constant exposure in all kinds of weather and in the strenuous physical exertions that are required of the geologists, topographers, and hydrographic engineers.

From letter of George Otis Smith to E. J. Ayers, January 31, 1917; original in Record Group 48, "Records of the Department of the Interior," Office of the Secretary, Personnel Supervision and Management, 1907–1942, File 15-15-35, National Archives, Washington, D.C.

There are on the rolls of the Survey 417 men, distributed as follows among the different field branches: geologists, 188; topographers, 149; water resources engineers, 74; Alaskan geologists, 15.

In the Division of Engraving and Printing, the work is necessarily of a man's type, requiring the handling of machinery, heavy lifting, dirty work and various trades to which men are especially adapted. The conditions under which much of the engraving and printing work is done is such as to preclude the employment of women. There are 126 men employed in the various nonclerical jobs in the division of Engraving and Printing and no women.

The force of laborers, messengers, mechanics, etc., consists of 130 men and one woman. The character of the work performed is such as to practically preclude the possibility of employing women for the various duties.

From the above enumeration it will be seen that there are 646 positions in which, from the character of the work, the employment of men is necessitated.

Turning to the distinctly clerical jobs, the following table shows the distribution among the sexes of the different clerks:

Branches	Males	Females
Field	28	111
Engraving	3	0
Administrative	53	28
Total	84	139

It should be noted in the above table that the great number of males in the administrative branch is due to the inclusion of all the various administrative officers not attached to the field service, as for instance, the Chief Clerk, the Chief Disbursing Officer, the Chief of the Accounts Division, the Chief of the Executive Division, the Chief of the Division of Distribution, etc. . . .

I think the above tables will clearly show that women are chosen for the clerical positions, in general, in preference to the men at a rate of about two to one and that so far as the Geological Survey is concerned, the spirit, as well as the letter of the law, regarding equal chance to both sexes is lived up to.

Yours very truly,

Director.
[George Otis Smith]

How Progressive Was Progressivism? The Question of Race

The two documents that follow illustrate a major problem in the interpretation of progressivism. Progressives were out to clean up what they thought were problems in American life. This might mean cleaning up slums, or political machines. It might mean cleaning up a confusion of unwise mine-safety regulations, or of corrupt practices in monopolies. For white Southern politicians, however, the ethic of cleaning up could easily be transformed into a program to restrict the suffrage, on the sound "progressive" formula that black voting had led to fraud and corruption. The first document is a typical speech by a Southern politician giving the main line of argument for white supremacy. The second is a pair of tables that show plainly how efficient this "reform" was (in Table 1, keep in mind that the figures refer to percentage *reduction* in voter turnout). What seems to you to be progressive about this phenomenon? Finally, evaluate the hypothesis that Southerners turned to the law to regulate voting for the same reason that businessmen turned to the Federal Trade Commission (or mine operators to the Bureau of Mines) to regulate economic behavior.

White Supremacy by Law

But if we would have white supremacy, we must establish it by law—not by force or fraud. If you teach your boy that it is right to buy a vote, it is an easy step for him to learn to use money to bribe or corrupt officials or trustees of any class. If you teach your boy that it is right to steal votes, it is an easy step for him to believe that it is right to steal whatever he may need or greatly desire. The results of such an influence will enter every branch of society; it will reach your bank cashiers, and affect positions of trust in every department; it will ultimately enter your courts and affect the administration of justice.

I submit it to the intelligent judgment of this Convention that there is no higher duty resting upon us, as citizens and as delegates, than that which requires us to embody in the fundamental law such provisions as will enable us to protect the sanctity of the ballot in every portion of the State.

The justification for whatever manipulation of the ballot that has occurred in this State has been the menace of negro domination. After the war, by force

From a speech by John B. Knox, president of the Alabama Constitutional Convention, in Alabama, *Journal of the Proceedings of the Constitutional Convention*, held in the City of Montgomery, commencing May 21, 1901 (Montgomery, 1901), pp. 12–13.

of Federal bayonets, the negro was placed in control of every branch of our government. Inspired and aided by unscrupulous white men, he wasted money, created debts, increased taxes until it threatened to amount to confiscation of our property. While in power, and within a few years, he increased our State debt from a nominal figure to nearly thirty millions of dollars. The right of revolution is always left to every people. Being prostrated by the effects of the war, and unable to take up arms in their own defense, in some portions of this State, white men, greatly in the minority, it is said, resorted to strategem— used their great intellect to overcome the greater numbers of their black opponents. If so, such a course might be warranted when considered as the right of revolution, and as an act of necessity for self-preservation. But a people cannot always live in a state of revolution. The time comes when, if they would be a free, happy and contented people they must return to a constitutional form of government, where law and order prevail, and where every citizen stands ready to stake his life and his honor to maintain it.

Table 1. Impact of Suffrage Restriction in the South: Proportionate Reduction in Overall Turnout and Estimated Turnout by Race

State	Elections	Overall Turnout	Estimated White Turnout	Estimated Negro Turnout
Alabama	1892–1896 Gov.[a]	19	15	24
Alabama	1900–1904 Pres.	38	19	96
Arkansas	1890–1894 Gov.	39	26	69
Florida	1888–1892 Gov.	61	31	83
Georgia	1876–1880 Pres.	13	3	29
Georgia	1904–1908 Pres.	7	23	−6
Louisiana	1896–1900 Gov.	66	46	93
Mississippi	1888–1892 Pres.	57	34	69
No. Carolina	1896–1904 Pres.	46	23	100[b]
So. Carolina	1880–1884 Pres.	49	43	50
So. Carolina	1892–1896 Pres.	13	17	51
Tennessee	1888–1892 Gov.	19	4	68
Texas	1902–1904 Gov.	32	29	36
Virginia	1900–1904 Pres.	54	48	100[b]

[a] The notation means that the elections compared are the 1892 and 1896 governor's races.
[b] In these two cases, Negro turnout after disfranchisement was estimated to be negative. I then set the percentage reduction at 100%

Adapted from J. Morgan Kousser, *The Shaping of Southern Politics: Suffrage Restriction and the Establishment of the One-Party South, 1880–1910* (New Haven Conn.: Yale University Press, 1974). © 1974 by Yale University. All rights reserved. The footnotes for Table 2 have been added.

Table 2. Chronology of Passage of Major Restrictive Statutes in All Southern States, 1870–1910.

Year	Poll Tax	Regis- tration[a]	Multiple- Box[b]	Secret Ballot[c]	Literacy Test	Property Test	Under- standing Clause[d]	Grand- father Clause[e]
1871	Ga.							
1872								
1873								
1874								
1875	Va.							
1876								
1877	Ga.							
1878								
1879								
1880								
1881	Va. (repealed)							
1882		S.C.	S.C.					
1883								
1884								
1885								
1886								
1887								
1888								
1889	Fla.	Tenn.	Fla.	Tenn.				
1890	Miss. Tenn.			Miss.	Miss.		Miss.	
1891				Ark.				
1892	Ark.							
1893		Ala.		Ala.				
1894		S.C.		Va.				
1895	S.C.				S.C.		S.C.	
1896								
1897		La.		La.				
1898	La.				La.	La.		La.
1899		N.C.	N.C.					
1900	N.C.				N.C.	N.C.		N.C.
1901	Ala.				Ala.	Ala.		Ala.
1902	Va. Tex.				Va.	Va.	Va.	
1903				Tex.				
1904								
1905								
1906								
1907								
1908					Ga.	Ga.	Ga.	Ga.

[a] Allowed the registrar to ask for specific information from potential registrants, including exact date of birth and street address.

[b] Box laws allowed up to eight boxes at the polling station, one for each ballot. Ballots deposited in the wrong box were thrown out.

[c] Until 1888 political parties distributed ballots.

[d] Allowed an illiterate to register if he could understand a section of the state constitution if read to him and explain it satisfactorily.

[e] Allowed for the registration of voters if they had voted in 1867 or if they were descendants of 1867 voters.

Education
and Childhood

Before the Pittsburgh alumni of Princeton University in April 1910, Woodrow Wilson spoke critically of the institution's plans to locate the graduate college on a site one mile from the central campus. For Wilson, the issue was one of social democracy. Separation was "undemocratic" and "un-American"; it would encourage graduate students to feel superior to their undergraduate colleagues.

Wilson's desire to reconcile class differences through a democratic educational process and through education itself was one of the staples of the progressive period. Educational reformers such as John Dewey developed the intellectual rationale for education as a means of recreating a more cohesive community. Social settlement leader Jane Addams (who had worked with Dewey in the 1890s) applied his theories to Chicago's neighborhoods.

Progressive period reformers everywhere were anxious to set education on a new and "scientific" footing. And they were just as concerned with the problem of "wayward" youth. All across the nation, there were studies of how children spent their time. And in institutions for "delinquent" children there was a similar determination to classify in scientific terms the kinds of vices that young people were prey to. Behind the science—and not far behind it, either—was an obvious moralism. The officials who made the studies that follow were just as sure as Wilson or John Knox that they knew what a good life was, and just as certain that *knowledge* was the key to solving the problem. The two photographs from the George Junior Republic speak more clearly than words about the kinds of ideological purposes that lay behind the statistics. What does the Cleveland play census reveal about the people who constructed it? What do you suppose the census takers meant when they recorded the children "doing nothing"? What kind of play did Cleveland reformers wish to see? What typically progressive traits are mirrored in the statistics on juvenile boys? For example, where are boys sent when discharged? What characteristics of youth were found most offensive at the Plainfield school, and why?

Recreation material from George E. Johnson, *Education Through Recreation* (Cleveland, Ohio: The Survey Committee of the Cleveland Foundation, 1916), pp. 48–51. Reprinted by permission.

Crime and Reformation material from U.S. Congress, House, Committee on the Judiciary, *Juvenile Crime and Reformation, Including Stigmata of Degeneration,* Being a Hearing on the Bill (H.R. 16733) to Establish a Laboratory for the Study of the Criminal, Pauper, and Defective Classes, by Arthur MacDonald, 60th Cong. (Washington, D.C., 1908), pp. 115, 107.

Recreation

A Play Census of Cleveland Pupils

A play census, taken June 23, 1913, under the direction of the Chief Medical Inspector and Assistant Superintendent in charge of Physical Education in Cleveland, seemed to show this same lack of relationship between the school and the out-of-school activities of children. The results of this study are shown in Table 7.

Conclusions Drawn From This Census
1. That just at the age (under 15) when play and activity are the fundamental requirements for proper growth and development 41 per cent of the children seen were doing nothing. The boy without play is father to the man without a job.
2. Fifty-one per cent of all the children seen were in the streets, in the midst of all the traffic, dirt, and heat, and in an environment conducive to just the wrong kind of play.

Table 7. What 14,683 Cleveland Children Were Doing on June 23, 1913

		Boys	Girls	Total
Where they were seen	On streets	5,241	2,558	7,799
	In yards	1,583	1,998	3,581
	In vacant lots	686	197	883
	In playgrounds	997	872	1,869
	In alleys	413	138	551
What they were doing	Doing nothing	3,737	2,234	5,961
	Playing	4,601	2,757	7,358
	Working	719	635	1,354
What games they were playing	Baseball	1,448	190	1,638
	Kites	482	49	531
	Sand piles	241	230	471
	Tag	100	53	153
	Jackstones	68	257	325
	Dolls	89	193	282
	Sewing	14	130	144
	Housekeeping	53	191	244
	Horse and wagon	89	24	113
	Bicycle riding	79	13	92
	Minding baby	19	41	60
	Reading	17	35	52
	Roller-skating	18	29	47
	Gardening	13	14	27
	Caddy	6	0	6
	Marbles	2	0	2
	Playing in other ways, mostly just fooling	1,863	1,308	3,171

3. That only six per cent of the children seen were on vacant lots despite the fact that in most of the districts vacant lots were available as play spaces. A place to play does not solve the problem: there must be a play leader.

4. That even though 36 playgrounds were open and 16 of them with apparatus up, only 1869, or 11 per cent, of the children seen within four blocks of a playground were playing on playgrounds. Last Friday 6488 children played on playgrounds.

5. That of the 7358 children reported to have been playing, 3171 were reported to have been playing by doing some of the following things: fighting, teasing, pitching pennies, shooting craps, stealing apples, "roughing a peddler," chasing chickens, tying can to dog, etc., but most of them were reported to have been "just fooling"—not playing anything in particular.

6. We need more and better playgrounds and a better trained leadership.

The Recreational Interests of Cleveland Pupils

That the play interests of children and youth answer to deep-seated needs and are essential for fullest development and education is now so universally admitted that only the mere statement is here necessary. It is also evident that these play interests are the prototypes of the great lines of human interest, endeavor, and achievement represented in adult life and in education work today.

Crime and Reformation

Causes for which Boys Were Committed to Louisville, Kentucky, Industrial School, 1906

	White	Colored	Total
Incorrigibility	72	27	99
Delinquency	43	13	56
Larceny	4	3	7
Petit larceny	13	9	22
Grand Larceny	8	1	9
Burglary	4	3	7
Burglary and larceny	19	3	22
Vagrancy and larceny	1	0	1
Vagrancy	8	2	10
Vagrancy and incorrigibility	3	0	3
Incorrigibility and immorality	1	0	1
Assault	2	1	3
Manslaughter in fourth degree	1	0	1
Felony	1	0	1
Attempted rape	0	1	1
Destruction of property	2	0	2
Obstructing railroad	1	0	1
Disturbing the peace	2	0	2

State School for Boys, South Portland, Maine, 1906. Students were heavily concentrated in the 10–15 age group.

Facts connected with the moral condition of the boys when received

Whole number received	2,615
Have intemperate parents	881
Lost father	816
Lost mother	654
Relatives in prison	335
Step parents	491
Idle	1,658
Much neglected	907
Truants	1,140
Sabbath breakers	992
Untruthful	2,053
Profane	1,908

Disposition of those discharged since opening of the school

Discharged on expiration of sentence	223
Discharged by trustees	731
Indentured to—	
Barber	1
Blacksmith	1
Boarding mistress	1
Boilermaker	1
Cabinetmaker	6
Carpenters	13
Cooper	1
Farmers	287
Harness makers	3
Laborers	9
Lumbermen	3
Machinists	5
Manufacturers	2
Mason	1
Miller	1
Sea captains	5
Shoemakers	14
Tailors	3
Tallow chandler	1
Allowed to leave on trial	1,026
Allowed to enlist	19
Illegally committed	19
Remanded	64
Pardoned	15
Finally escaped	81
Violated trust	49
Died	49
Delivered to courts	24
Returned to masters	4

Nativity of all committed

Foreigners	278
Born in United States	2,295
Nativity not known	41

Demerit Offenses, Indiana Boys' School, Plainfield, 1906

Talk	10
Disobedience	10
Disorder	10
Laziness	10
Vandalism	10
Willful waste	20
Quarreling	50
Dormitory	50
Shielding	50
Profanity	50
Fighting	100
Tobacco or money	100
Falsehood	100
Theft	100
Obscenity	100
Disrespect and impudence	100
Vulgarity	200
Insubordination	200
Planning escape	500
Escape	1,000
Secret vice	1,000
Planning immoral association	1,000
Immoral association	2,000

The George Junior Republic

The George Junior Republic was a progressive era camp for destitute and delinquent youth. It had strong appeal for Theodore Roosevelt, economist John R. Commons, and General Robert Baden-Powell (founder of the Boy Scouts). According to these photos, what was the cause of delinquency among youth? What did the George Junior Republic choose to do about it?

The Court. About 1905, with a citizen judge presiding. *Department of Manuscripts and University Archives, Cornell University, Ithaca, N.Y.*

The Republic Store. About 1910, where citizens exchanged Republic currency for groceries. *Department of Manuscripts and University Archives, Cornell University, Ithaca, N.Y.*

Efficient Producers and Consumers

The Story of Schmidt

Frederick Winslow Taylor is the most famous of America's industrial engineers. Though trained as a lawyer at Harvard, Taylor worked as a machinist and laborer in the 1870s. By studying at night, he obtained a degree in mechanical engineering in 1883. Taylor believed that there was one best way to do every job, and that it was possible to discover that way through detailed observation of the worker and his relationship to the machine. Taylor applied his theories in a variety of establishments, including Bethlehem Steel, and his ideas found wide acceptance in American industry after 1910, along with other instruments of industrial relations such as safety campaigns, pensions, and recreation.

"The Story of Schmidt" reveals Taylor's interest in the organization of work itself. For what purpose does Taylor seek to reorganize it? What is Taylor's relationship to Schmidt? What is the difference in Schmidt's work before and after Taylor applies his skills in scientific management? Is Schmidt likely to earn more money under the new system? Would you call Taylor a progressive? What connection can you discover between Taylor's handling of work and the city of Cleveland's interest in children's play?

The first illustration is that of handling pig iron, and this work is chosen because it is typical of perhaps the crudest and most elementary form of labor which is performed by man. This work is done by men with no other implements than their hands. The pig-iron handler stoops down, picks up a pig weighing about 92 pounds, walks for a few feet or yards and then drops it on

From Frederick Winslow Taylor, *Principles of Scientific Management* (New York: Harper, 1911), specified selections from pp. 40–47, 58–59. Copyright © 1911 by Frederick W. Taylor. Reprinted by permission of Harper & Row, Publishers, Inc.

to the ground or upon a pile. This work is so crude and elementary in its nature that the writer firmly believes that it would be possible to train an intelligent gorilla so as to become a more efficient pig-iron handler than any man can be. Yet it will be shown that the science of handling pig iron is great and amounts to so much that it is impossible for the man who is best suited to this type of work to understand the principles of this science, or even to work in accordance with these principles without the aid of a man better educated than he is. . . .

One of the first pieces of work undertaken by us, when the writer started to introduce scientific management into the Bethlehem Steel Company, was to handle pig iron on task work. The opening of the Spanish War found some 80,000 tons of pig iron placed in small piles in an open field adjoining the works. Prices for pig iron had been so low that it could not be sold at a profit, and it therefore had been stored. With the opening of the Spanish War the price of pig iron rose, and this large accumulation of iron was sold. This gave us a good opportunity to show the workmen, as well as the owners and managers of the works, on a fairly large scale the advantages of task work over the old-fashioned day work and piece work, in doing a very elementary class of work.

The Bethlehem Steel Company had five blast furnaces, the product of which had been handled by a pig-iron gang for many years. This gang, at this time, consisted of about 75 men. They were good, average pig-iron handlers, were under an excellent foreman who himself had been a pig-iron handler, and the work was done, on the whole, about as fast and as cheaply as it was anywhere else at that time.

A railroad switch was run out into the field, right along the edge of the piles of pig iron. An inclined plank was placed against the side of a car, and each man picked up from his pile a pig of iron weighing about 92 pounds, walked up the inclined plank and dropped it on the end of the car.

We found that this gang were loading on the average about 12½ long tons per man per day. We were surprised to find, after studying the matter, that a first-class pig-iron handler ought to handle between 47 and 48 long tons per day, instead of 12½ tons. This task seemed to us so very large that we were obliged to go over our work several times before we were absolutely sure that we were right. Once we were sure, however, that 47 tons was a proper day's work for a first-class pig-iron handler, the task which faced us as managers under the modern scientific plan was clearly before us. It was our duty to see that the 80,000 tons of pig iron was loaded on to the cars at the rate of 47 tons per man per day, in place of 12½ tons, at which rate the work was then being done. And it was further our duty to see that this work was done without any quarrel with the men, and to see that the men were happier and better contented when loading at the new rate of 47 tons than they were when loading at the old rate of 12½ tons.

Our first step was the scientific selection of the workman. In dealing with workmen under this type of management, it is an inflexible rule to talk to and deal with only one man at a time, since each workman has his own special abilities and limitations, and since we are not dealing with men in masses, but are trying to develop each individual man to his highest state of efficiency and prosperity. Our first step was to find the proper workman to begin with. We therefore carefully watched and studied these 75 men for three or four days, at the end of which time we had picked out four men who appeared to be physically able to handle pig iron at the rate of 47 tons per day. A careful study was then made of each of these men. We looked up their history as far back as practicable and thorough inquiries were made as to the character, habits, and the ambition of each of them. Finally we selected one from among the four as the most likely man to start with. He was a little Pennsylvania Dutchman who had been observed to trot back home for a mile or so after his work in the evening about as fresh as he was when he came trotting down to work in the morning. We found that upon wages of $1.15 a day he had succeeded in buying a small plot of ground, and that he was engaged in putting up the walls of a little house for himself in the morning before starting to work and at night after leaving. He also had the reputation of being exceedingly "close," that is, of placing a very high value on a dollar. As one man whom we talked to about him said, "A penny looks about the size of a cart-wheel to him." This man we will call Schmidt.

The task before us, then, narrowed itself down to getting Schmidt to handle 47 tons of pig iron per day and making him glad to do it. This was done as follows. Schmidt was called out from among the gang of pig-iron handlers and talked to somewhat in this way:

"Schmidt, are you a high-priced man?"

"Vell, I don't know vat you mean."

"Oh yes, you do. What I want to know is whether you are a high-priced man or not."

"Vell, I don't know vat you mean."

"Oh, come now, you answer my questions. What I want to find out is whether you are a high-priced man or one of these cheap fellows here. What I want to find out is whether you want to earn $1.85 a day or whether you are satisfied with $1.15, just the same as all those cheap fellows are getting."

"Did I vant $1.85 a day? Vas dot a high-priced man? Vell, yes, I vas a high-priced man."

"Oh, you're aggravating me. Of course you want $1.85 a day—every one wants it! You know perfectly well that that has very little to do with your being a high-priced man. For goodness' sake answer my questions, and don't waste any more of my time. Now come over here. You see that pile of pig iron?"

"Yes."

"You see that car?"

"Yes."

"Well, if you are a high-priced man, you will load that pig iron on that car to-morrow for $1.85. Now do wake up and answer my question. Tell me whether you are a high-priced man or not."

"Vell—did I got $1.85 for loading dot pig iron on dot car to-morrow?"

"Yes, of course you do, and you get $1.85 for loading a pile like that every day right through the year. That is what a high-priced man does, and you know it just as well as I do."

"Vell, dot's all right. I could load dot pig iron on the car to-morrow for $1.85, and I get it every day, don't I?"

"Certainly you do—certainly you do."

"Vell, den, I vas a high-priced man."

"Now, hold on, hold on. You know just as well as I do that a high-priced man has to do exactly as he's told from morning till night. You have seen this man here before, haven't you?"

"No, I never saw him."

"Well, if you are a high-priced man, you will do exactly as this man tells you to-morrow, from morning till night. When he tells you to pick up a pig and walk, you pick it up and you walk, and when he tells you to sit down and rest, you sit down. You do that right straight through the day. And what's more, no back talk. Now a high-priced man does just what he's told to do, and no back talk. Do you understand that? When this man tells you to walk, you walk; when he tells you to sit down, you sit down, and you don't talk back at him. Now you come on to work here to-morrow morning and I'll know before night whether you are really a high-priced man or not."

This seems to be rather rough talk. And indeed it would be if applied to an educated mechanic, or even an intelligent laborer. With a man of the mentally sluggish type of Schmidt it is appropriate and not unkind, since it is effective in fixing his attention on the high wages which he wants and away from what, if it were called to his attention, he probably would consider impossibly hard work.

What would Schmidt's answer be if he were talked to in a manner which is usual under the management of "initiative and incentive"? say, as follows:

"Now, Schmidt, you are a first-class pig-iron handler and know your business well. You have been handling at the rate of 12½ tons per day. I have given considerable study to handling pig iron, and feel sure that you could do a much larger day's work than you have been doing. Now don't you think that if you really tried you could handle 47 tons of pig iron per day, instead of 12½ tons?"

What do you think Schmidt's answer would be to this?

Schmidt started to work, and all day long, and at regular intervals, was told by the man who stood over him with a watch, "Now pick up a pig and walk. Now sit down and rest. Now walk—now rest," etc. He worked when he was told to work, and rested when he was told to rest, and at half-past five in the afternoon had his 47½ tons loaded on the car. And he practically never failed to work at this pace and do the task that was set him during the three years that the writer was at Bethlehem. And throughout this time he averaged a little more than $1.85 per day, whereas before he had never received over $1.15 per day, which was the ruling rate of wages at that time in Bethlehem. That is, he received 60 per cent higher wages than were paid to other men who were not working on task work. One man after another was picked out and trained to handle pig iron at the rate of 47½ tons per day until all of the pig iron was handled at this rate, and the men were receiving 60 per cent more wages than other workmen around them. . . .

To return now to our pig-iron handlers at the Bethlehem Steel Company. If Schmidt had been allowed to attack the pile of 47 tons of pig iron without the guidance or direction of a man who understood the art, or science, of handling pig iron, in his desire to earn his high wages he would probably have tired himself out by 11 or 12 o'clock in the day. He would have kept so steadily at work that his muscles would not have had the proper periods of rest absolutely needed for recuperation, and he would have been completely exhausted early in the day. By having a man, however, who understood this law, stand over him and direct his work, day after day, until he acquired the habit of resting at proper intervals, he was able to work at an even gait all day long without unduly tiring himself.

Now one of the very first requirements for a man who is fit to handle pig iron as a regular occupation is that he shall be so stupid and so phlegmatic that he more nearly resembles in his mental make-up the ox than any other type. The man who is mentally alert and intelligent is for this very reason entirely unsuited to what would, for him, be the grinding monotony of work of this character. Therefore the workman who is best suited to handling pig iron is unable to understand the real science of doing this class of work. He is so stupid that the word "percentage" has no meaning to him, and he must consequently be trained by a man more intelligent than himself into the habit of working in accordance with the laws of this science before he can be successful.

Inspection of a Grocery

This photograph is from the files of the federal Food and Drug Administration, one of the proudest creations of progressive reform. It was originally labeled, "Inspection of a Grocery . . . A Clean, Well-Arranged Grocery Store." What kinds of values are represented here?

Records of the Food and Drug Administration in the National Archives.

CHAPTER 7

The 1920s: From War to Normalcy

The generation that came of age in the 1920s did so in the shadow of World War I. A nation led to expect that the struggle would be morally satisfying—which had boldly announced in song that "the Yanks are coming"—would be reduced to seeking meaning in an unidentifiable soldier, buried in Arlington, Virginia. That a war of such short duration—direct American involvement lasted little more than eighteen months—could have had such an impact may seem surprising. But part of an explanation may be found by examining how Americans experienced the conflict, and what they were led to believe it would achieve.

Several groups experienced the war years as a time of increased opportunity. Blacks, migrating from the South into Chicago, Detroit, New York, and other industrial cities, and women, heretofore denied most jobs open to men, found themselves suddenly employable. The same circumstances allowed organized labor to double its membership in the four years after 1914. Farmers prospered because of rising European demand and, after 1917, from government price guarantees. Soldiers, on the other hand, experienced the typical wartime "tax" on income, and many lost their positions on promotional ladders.

Continued deficit spending fueled the economy during demobilization. In 1919, activity in automobile production and building construction, two industries held back by the war, helped the nation avoid a prolonged postwar tailspin. But economic crisis could only be postponed for so long. By mid-1921, the economy was mired in a serious depression which cut industrial output by some 20 percent. It seems likely that a downturn in the postwar economy, deeply affecting a people which had no history of planning for such events, helped to dissolve the aura of economic progress and personal success which had been part of the war and to inaugurate a decade of conflict between young and old, employer and employee, country and city, religion and science, nation and locality. In the minds of many Americans, depression was inseparably linked to demobilization and the peace settlement.

Unlike World War II, World War I was not an especially popular conflict with Americans. Few German-Americans wanted to see the United States declare war on Germany. Irish-Americans feared United States entry into the war would mean assistance to Britain in her struggle against Irish revolutionaries. Socialists—an influential faction in the 1910s—strongly opposed the American declaration of war, branding it "a crime against the people of the United States." This antiwar stance brought Socialist candidates in the 1917 municipal elections 34 percent of the vote in Chicago and 44 percent in Dayton, Ohio. Hundreds of thousands refused to register or to be inducted into the military.

The war had to be sold, systematically and unabashedly, like any other product. The government's advertising agency was the Committee on Public Information, headed by journalist George Creel. The Creel Committee employed an elaborate publicity apparatus to educate Americans to proper wartime values. In one advertisement, a smiling American soldier clenched a White Owl cigar between his teeth and said:

Did I bayonet my first Hun?
Sure! How did it feel? It *doesn't*
feel! There *he* is. There *you*
are. One of you has got to go.
I preferred to stay.

So when sergeant says,
"Smash 'em, boys"—we do.
And we go them one better
like good old Yankee Doodle
Yanks. For bullets and bayonets are the only kind of lingo
that a Hun can *understand!*   (*Saturday Evening Post*, August 31, 1918; reprinted by permission of General Cigar and Tobacco Co.)

Efforts to eliminate criticism of the war effort took many forms. At Columbia University, a professor who opposed United States entry into the war was summarily dismissed. More than 1,500 persons were arrested under the Espionage Act of 1917 and the Sedition Act of 1918. One was Eugene Debs—in 1912 a candidate for the presidency—who served time in Atlanta Penitentiary for criticizing the war. The Industrial Workers of the World, a radical labor group that was strongest on the West Coast, was viciously harassed. Although the organization took no official position on American involvement and although the IWW was involved in only three of more than five hundred wartime strikes, over one hundred Wobblies were tried in 1918 on charges of sabotage and conspiracy to obstruct the war. On the flimsiest of evidence, a jury found all defendants guilty. Fifteen received prison sentences of twenty years, thirty-three were given ten years, and another thirty-five received five years.

Perhaps fighting a war—especially a war with which large numbers of the population disagreed—required a kind of artificially imposed unity. This would explain the Wobbly trials and the Creel Committee propaganda. But when the fighting stopped—when the Great Crusade was over—a new crusade, called the Red Scare, took the place of wartime coercion of dissidents. When this latest hysteria subsided in the spring of 1920, hundreds of radicals of every persuasion—Socialists, Wobblies, syndicalists, Communists, even ordinary union members—had been arrested, beaten, lynched, tried, or deported.

Just as wartime coercion had yielded to the Red Scare, so was the Red Scare reincarnated in the politics of Warren Harding. Harding was elected president in 1920 with over 60 percent of the popular vote. In May, emphasizing that "too much has been said about Bolshevism in America," he coined the word which would capture his appeal, urging a return to "not heroism, but healing, not nostrums, but normalcy." With "normalcy," Harding and the American people seemed to be rejecting the world which Woodrow Wilson had sought to create—the world in which words replaced concrete realities, in which dreams of world government (the League of Nations) transcended political facts. The Creel Committee had described the war as "a Crusade not merely to re-win the tomb of Christ, but to bring back to earth the rule of right, the peace, goodwill to men and gentleness he taught." When it proved much less than this, Americans beat an emotional retreat to the comfort of Harding's slogans.

The 1920s had powerful currents of individualism, of course. In fact, the decade has been rightly famed for its affection for jazz, for its compulsion for mah-jongg and flagpole sitting, for the flapper, and for the iconoclast H. L. Mencken (for whom every group, even the New England town meeting, was a mob run by demagogues). Harding's "normalcy," however, seemed to center on a program of cultural conformity, and it was to infect the entire decade. The Ku Klux Klan, revived at a Georgia meeting in 1915, grew rapidly in the early 1920s through campaigns against blacks, Catholics, Jews, and immigrants. National prohibition, which required millions to give up deeply ingrained drinking habits or evade the law, was in effect throughout the decade. The first law establishing immigration quotas was passed in 1921; a second measure passed three years later was designed to reduce immigration from Eastern and Southern Europe— the later immigrants discussed in Chapter 3. If "normalcy" is broad enough to encompass these aspects of the 1920s, then perhaps wartime coercion, the Red Scare, and "normalcy" were all variations on a theme—a theme perhaps placed in bold relief by the war, demobilization, and postwar economic crisis, but ultimately one set more deeply in the nation's character and its institutions than any of these events.

STANLEY COBEN

The American Red Scare, 1919-1920

In the following essay, historian Stanley Coben describes and analyzes the causes of the Red Scare of 1919–1920. Like the introduction to this chapter, Coben stresses how important it is to see the Red Scare in the context of larger factors such as American nativism and the cultural shock of the Great War. He also suggests that history might have taken a different turn, and the Red Scare might have been much less intense, had Americans not been rendered vulnerable by high rates of unemployment and inflation. But why, if the real problems were things like inflation and unemployment, did so many Americans respond so irrationally, picking out enemies that were far removed from those real concerns? One might imagine a returning veteran having some difficulty identifying his enemies; but what of A. Mitchell Palmer, Woodrow Wilson's attorney general? Why did Palmer join the hunt? Was he irresponsible? politically motivated perhaps? Or is it possible that he saw the Red Scare as a curious capstone for progressivism and Wilsonian reform? Finally, consider another portion of Coben's explanation: the idea that Americans behaved so aggressively because they needed an "island . . . of security." Nothing sounds more reasonable. But why did they choose to define the *nation* as that island? Why not the family (the choice of Chicagoans in the 1880s; see Chapter 3), or their churches, or their states and regions?

At a victory loan pageant in the District of Columbia on May 6, 1919, a man refused to rise for the playing of "The Star-Spangled Banner." As soon as the national anthem was completed an enraged sailor fired three shots into the unpatriotic spectator's back. When the man fell, the *Washington Post* reported, "the crowd burst into cheering and handclapping." In February of the same year, a jury in Hammond, Indiana, took two minutes to acquit the assassin of an alien who yelled, "To Hell with the United States." Early in 1920, a clothing store salesman in Waterbury, Connecticut, was sentenced to six months in jail for having remarked to a customer that Lenin was "the brainiest," or "one of the brainiest" of the world's political leaders. Dramatic episodes like these, or the better known Centralia Massacre, Palmer Raids, or May Day riots, were not everyday occurrences, even at the height of the Red Scare. But the fanatical one hundred per cent Americanism reflected by the Washington crowd, the Hammond jury, and the Waterbury judge pervaded a large part of our society between early 1919 and mid-1920.

Recently, social scientists have produced illuminating evidence about the causes of eruptions like that of 1919–1920. They have attempted to identify experimentally the individuals most responsive to nativistic appeals, to explain their susceptibility, and to propose general theories of nativistic and related movements. These studies suggest a fuller, more coherent picture of nativistic upheavals and their causes than we now possess, and they provide the framework for this attempt to reinterpret the Red Scare.

Psychological experiments indicate that a great many Americans—at least several million—are always ready to participate in a "red scare." These people permanently hold attitudes which characterized the nativists of 1919–1920: hostility toward certain minority groups, especially radicals and recent immigrants, fanatical patriotism, and a belief that internal enemies seriously threaten national security.

In one of the most comprehensive of these experiments, psychologists Nancy C. Morse and Floyd H. Allport tested seven hypotheses about the causes of prejudice and found that one, national involvement or patriotism, proved to be "by far the most important factor" associated with prejudice.

From Stanley Coben, "A Study in Nativism: The American Red Scare of 1919–1920," *Political Science Quarterly*, vol. 79, no. 1 (March 1964), pp. 52–75. Reprinted with permission.

Other widely held theories about prejudice—status rivalry, frustration-aggression, and scapegoat hypotheses, for example—were found to be of only secondary importance. Summarizing the results of this and a number of other psychological experiments, Gordon W. Allport, a pioneer in the scientific study of prejudice, concluded that in a large proportion of cases the prejudiced person is attempting to defend himself against severe inner turmoil by enforcing order in his external life. Any disturbance in the social *status quo* threatens the precarious psychic equilibrium of this type of individual, who, according to Allport, seeks "an island of institutional safety and security. The nation is the island he selects . . . It has the definiteness he needs."

Allport pointed out that many apprehensive and frustrated people are not especially prejudiced. What is important, he found,

> is the way fear and frustration are handled. The institutionalistic way—especially the nationalistic—seems to be the nub of the matter. What happens is that the prejudiced person defines 'nation' to fit his needs. The nation is first of all a protection (the chief protection) of him as an individual. It is his in-group. He sees no contradiction in ruling out of its beneficent orbit those whom he regards as threatening intruders and enemies (namely, American minorities). What is more, the nation stands for the status quo. It is a conservative agent; within it are all the devices for safe living that he approves. His nationalism is a form of conservatism.

Substantial evidence, then, suggest that millions of Americans are both extraordinarily fearful of social change and prejudiced against those minority groups which they perceive as "threatening intruders." Societal disruption, especially if it can easily be connected with the "intruders," not only will intensify the hostility of highly prejudiced individuals, but also will provoke many others, whose antagonism in more stable times had been mild or incipient, into the extreme group. . . .

According to Anthony F. C. Wallace, who has gone farthest toward constructing a general theory of cult formation, when the disruption has proceeded so far that many members of a society find it difficult or impossible to fulfill their physical and psychological needs, or to relieve severe anxiety through the ordinary culturally approved methods, the society will be susceptible to what Wallace has termed a "revitalization movement." This is a convulsive attempt to change or revivify important cultural beliefs and values, and frequently to eliminate alien influences. Such movements promise and often provide participants with better means of dealing with their changed circumstances, thus reducing their very high level of internal stress. . . .

Dominant as well as conquered peoples, Ralph Linton has pointed out, undergo nativistic movements. Dominant groups, he observed, are sometimes threatened "not only by foreign invasion or domestic revolt but also by the invidious process of assimilation which might, in the long run, destroy their distinctive powers and privileges." Under such circumstances, Linton concluded, "the frustrations which motivate nativistic movements in inferior or dominated groups" are "replaced by anxieties which produce very much the same [nativistic] result" in dominant groups. . . .

The ferocious outbreak of nativism in the United States after World War I was not consciously planned or provoked by any individual or group, although some Americans took advantage of the movement once it started. Rather, the Red Scare, . . . was brought on largely by a number of severe social and economic dislocations which threatened the national equilibrium. The full extent and the shocking effects of these disturbances of 1919 have not yet been adequately described. Runaway prices, a brief but sharp stock market crash and business depression, revolutions throughout Europe, widespread fear of domestic revolt, bomb explosions, and an outpouring of radical literature were distressing enough. These sudden difficulties, moreover, served to exaggerate the disruptive effects already produced by the social and intellectual ravages of the World War and the preceding reform era, and by the arrival, before the war, of millions of new immigrants. This added stress intensified the hostility of Americans strongly antagonistic to minority groups, and brought new converts to blatant nativism from among those who ordinarily were not overtly hostile toward radicals or recent immigrants.

Citizens who joined the crusade for one hundred per cent Americanism sought, primarily, a unifying force which would halt the apparent disintegration of their culture. The movement, they felt, would eliminate those foreign influences which the one hundred per centers believed were the major cause of their anxiety.

Many of the postwar sources of stress were also present during World War I, and the Red Scare, as John Higham has observed, was partly an exaggeration of wartime passions. In 1917–1918 German-Americans served as the object of almost all our nativistic fervor; they were the threatening intruders who refused to become good citizens. "They used America," a patriotic author declared in 1918 of two million German-Americans, "they never loved her. They clung to their old language, their old customs, and cared nothing for ours. . . . As a class they were clannish beyond all other races coming here." Fear of subversion by German agents was almost as extravagant in 1917–1918 as anxiety about "reds" in the postwar period. Attorney General Thomas Watt Gregory reported to a friend in May 1918 that "we not infrequently receive as many as fifteen hundred letters in a single day suggesting disloyalty and the making of investigations.

Opposition to the war by radical groups helped smooth the transition among American nativists from hatred of everything German to fear of radical revolution. The two groups of enemies were associated also for other reasons. High government officials declared after the war that German leaders planned and subsidized the Bolshevik Revolution. When bombs blasted homes and public buildings in nine cities in June 1919, the director of the Justice Department's Bureau of Investigation asserted that the bombers were "connected with Russian bolshevism, aided by Hun money." In November 1919, a year after the armistice, a popular magazine warned of "the Russo-German movement that is now trying to dominate America. . . ."

Even the wartime hostility toward German-Americans, however, is more understandable when seen in the light of recent anthropological and psychological studies. World War I disturbed Americans not only because of the real threat posed by enemy armies and a foreign ideology. For many citizens it had the further effect of shattering an already weakened intellectual tradition. When the European governments decided to fight, they provided shocking evidence that man was not, as most educated members of Western society had believed, a rational creature progressing steadily, if slowly, toward control of his environment. When the great powers declared war in 1914, many Americans as well as many Europeans were stunned. The *New York Times* proclaimed a common theme—European civilization had collapsed: The supposedly advanced nations, declared the *Times*, "have reverted to the condition of savage tribes roaming the forests and falling upon each other in a fury of blood and carnage to achieve the ambitious designs of chieftains clad in skins and drunk with mead." Franz Alexander, director for twenty-five years of the Chicago Institute of Psychoanalysis, recently recalled his response to the outbreak of the World War:

> The first impact of this news is [*sic*] unforgettable. It was the sudden intuitive realization that a chapter of history had ended. . . . Since then, I have discussed this matter with some of my contemporaries and heard about it a great deal in my early postwar psychoanalytic treatments of patients. To my amazement, the others who went through the same events had quite a similar reaction. . . . It was an immediate vivid and prophetic realization that something irrevocable of immense importance had happened in history.

Americans were jolted by new blows to their equilibrium after entering the war. Four million men were drafted away from familiar surroundings and some of them experienced the terrible carnage of trench warfare. Great numbers of women left home to work in war industries or to replace men in other jobs. Negroes flocked to Northern industrial areas by the hundreds of thousands, and their first mass migration from the South created violent racial antagonism in Northern cities.

During the war, also, Americans sanctioned a degree of government control over the economy which deviated sharply from traditional economic individualism. Again, fears aroused before the war were aggravated, for the reform legislation of the Progressive era had tended to increase government intervention, and many citizens were further perturbed by demands that the federal government enforce even higher standards of economic and social morality. By 1919, therefore, some prewar progressives as well as conservatives feared the gradual disappearance of highly valued individual opportunity and responsibility. Their fears were fed by strong postwar calls for continued large-scale government controls—extension of federal operation of railroads and of the Food Administration, for example.

The prime threat to these long-held individualistic values, however, and the most powerful immediate stimulus to the revitalistic response, came from Russia. There the Bolshevik conquerors proclaimed their intention of exporting Marxist ideology. If millions of Americans were disturbed in 1919 by the specter of communism, the underlying reason was not fear of foreign invasion—Russia, after all, was still a backward nation recently badly defeated by German armies. The real threat was the potential spread of communist ideas. These, the one hundred per centers realized with horror, possessed a genuine appeal for reformers and for the economically underprivileged, and if accepted they would complete the transformation of America.

A clear picture of the Bolshevik tyranny was not yet available; therefore, as after the French Revolution, those who feared the newly successful ideology turned to fight the revolutionary ideals. So the *Saturday Evening Post* declared editorially in November 1919 that "History will see our present state of mind as one with that preceding the burning of witches, the children's crusade, the great tulip craze and other examples of softening of the world brain." The *Post* referred not to the Red Scare or the impending Palmer Raids, but to the spread of communist ideology. Its editorial concluded: "The need of the country is not more idealism, but more pragmatism; not communism, but common sense." One of the most powerful patriotic groups, the National Security League, called upon members early in 1919 to "teach 'Americanism.' This means the fighting of Bolshevism . . . by the creation of well defined National Ideals." Members "must preach Americanism and instil the idealism of America's Wars, and that American spirit of service which believes in giving as well as getting." New York attorney, author, and educator Henry Waters Taft warned a Carnegie Hall audience late in 1919 that Americans must battle "a propaganda which is tending to undermine our most cherished social and political institutions and is having the effect of producing widespread unrest among the poor and the ignorant, especially those of foreign birth."

When the war ended Americans also confronted the disturbing possibility, pointed up in 1919 by the struggle over the League of Nations, that Europe's struggles would continue to be their own. These factors combined to make the First World War a traumatic experience for millions of citizens. As Senator James Reed of Missouri observed in August 1919, "This country is still suffering from shell shock. Hardly anyone is in a normal state of mind . . . A great storm has swept over the intellectual world and its ravages and disturbances still exist."

The wartime "shell shock" left many Americans extraordinarily susceptible to psychological stress caused by postwar social and economic turbulence. Most important for the course of the Red Scare, many of these disturbances had their greatest effect on individuals already antagonistic toward minorities. First of all, there was some real evidence of danger to the nation in 1919, and the nation provided the chief emotional support for many Americans who responded easily to charges of an alien radical menace. Violence flared throughout Europe after the war and revolt lifted radicals to power in several Eastern and Central European nations. Combined with the earlier Bolshevik triumph in Russia these revolutions made Americans look more anxiously at radicals here. Domestic radicals encouraged these fears; they became unduly optimistic about their own chances of success and boasted openly of their coming triumph. Scores of new foreign language anarchist and communist journals, most of them written by and for Southern and Eastern European immigrants, commenced publication, and the established radical press became more exuberant. These periodicals never tired of assuring readers in 1919 that "the United States seems to be on the verge of a revolutionary crisis." American newspapers and magazines reprinted selections from radical speeches, pamphlets, and periodicals so their readers could see what dangerous ideas were abroad in the land. Several mysterious bomb explosions and bombing attempts, reported in bold front page headlines in newspapers across the country, frightened the public in 1919. To many citizens these seemed part of an organized campaign of terror carried on by alien radicals intending to bring down the federal government. The great strikes of 1919 and early 1920 aroused similar fears.

Actually American radical organizations in 1919 were disorganized and poverty-stricken. The Communists were inept, almost without contact with American workers and not yet dominated or subsidized by Moscow. The IWW was shorn of its effective leaders, distrusted by labor, and generally declining in influence and power. Violent anarchists were isolated in a handful of tiny, unconnected local organizations. One or two of these anarchist groups probably carried out the "bomb conspiracy" of 1919; but the extent of the "conspiracy" can be judged from the fact that the bombs killed a total of two men during the year, a night watchman and one of the bomb throwers, and seriously wounded one person, a maid in the home of a Georgia senator.

Nevertheless, prophesies of national disaster abounded in 1919, even among high government officials. Secretary of State Robert Lansing confided to his diary that we were in real peril of social revolution. Attorney General A. Mitchell Palmer advised the House Appropriations Committee that "on a certain day, which we have been advised of," radicals would attempt "to rise up and destroy the Government at one fell swoop." Senator Charles Thomas of Colorado warned that "the country is on the verge of a volcanic upheaval." And Senator Miles Poindexter of Washington declared, "There is real danger that the government will fall." A West Virginia wholesaler, with offices throughout the state, informed the Justice Department in October 1919 that "there is hardly a respectable citizen of my acquaintance who does not believe that we are on the verge of armed conflict in this country." William G. McAdoo was told by a trusted friend that "Chicago, which has always been a very liberal minded place, seems to me to have gone mad on the question of the

'Reds.'" Delegates to the Farmers National Congress in November 1919 pledged that farmers would assist the government in meeting the threat of revolution.

The slight evidence of danger from radical organizations aroused such wild fear only because Americans had already encountered other threats to cultural stability. However, the dislocations caused by the war and the menace of communism alone would not have produced such a vehement nativistic response. Other postwar challenges to the social and economic order made the crucial difference.

Of considerable importance was the skyrocketing cost of living. Retail prices more than doubled between 1915 and 1920, and the price rise began gathering momentum in the spring of 1919. During the summer of 1919 the dominant political issue in America was not the League of Nations; not even the "red menace" or the threat of a series of major strikes disturbed the public as much as did the climbing cost of living. The *Washington Post* early in August 1919 called rising prices, "the burning domestic issue. . . ." Democratic National Chairman Homer Cummings, after a trip around the country, told President Woodrow Wilson that more Americans were worried about prices than about any other public issue and that they demanded government action. When Wilson decided to address Congress on the question the Philadelphia *Public Ledger* observed that the administration had "come rather tardily to a realization of what is uppermost in the minds of the American people."

Then the wave of postwar strikes—there were 3,600 of them in 1919 involving over 4,000,000 workers—reached a climax in the fall of 1919. A national steel strike began in September and nationwide coal and rail walkouts were scheduled for November 1. Unions gained in membership and power during the war, and in 1919 labor leaders were under strong pressure to help workers catch up to or go ahead of mounting living costs. Nevertheless, influential government officials attributed the walkouts to radical activities. Early in 1919, Secretary of Labor William B. Wilson declared in a public speech that recent major strikes in Seattle, Butte, Montana, and Lawrence, Massachusetts, had been instituted by the Bolsheviks and the IWW for the sole purpose of bringing about a nationwide revolution in the United States. During the steel strike of early fall, 1919, a Senate investigating committee reported that "behind this strike there is massed a considerable element of I.W.W.'s, anarchists, revolutionists, and Russian soviets. . . ." In April 1920 the head of the Justice Department's General Intelligence Division, J. Edgar Hoover, declared in a public hearing that at least fifty per cent of the influence behind the recent series of strikes was traceable directly to communist agents.

Furthermore, the nation suffered a sharp economic depression in late 1918 and early 1919, caused largely by sudden cancellations of war orders. Returning servicemen found it difficult to obtain jobs during this period, which coincided with the beginning of the Red Scare. The former soldiers had been uprooted from their homes and told that they were engaged in a patriotic crusade. Now they came back to find "reds" criticizing their country and threatening the government with violence, Negroes holding good jobs in the big cities, prices terribly high, and workers who had not served in the armed forces striking for higher wages. A delegate won prolonged applause from the 1919 American Legion Convention when he denounced radical aliens, exclaiming, "Now that the war is over and they are in lucrative positions while our boys haven't a job, we've got to send those scamps to hell." The major part of the mobs which invaded meeting halls of immigrant organizations and broke up radical parades, especially during the first half of 1919, was comprised of men in uniform.

A variety of other circumstances combined to add even more force to the postwar nativistic movement. Long before the new immigrants were seen as potential revolutionists they became the objects of widespread hostility. The peak of immigration from Southern and Eastern Europe occurred in the fifteen years before the war; during that period almost ten million immigrants from those areas entered the country. Before the anxious eyes of members of all classes of Americans, the newcomers crowded the cities and began to disturb the economic and social order. Even without other postwar disturbances a nativistic movement of some strength could have been predicted when the wartime solidarity against the German enemy began to wear off in 1919.

In addition, not only were the European revolutions most successful in Eastern and to a lesser extent in Southern Europe, but aliens from these areas predominated in American radical organizations. At least ninety per cent of the members of the two American Communist parties formed in 1919 were born in Eastern Europe. The anarchist groups whose literature and bombs captured the imagination of the American public in 1919 were composed almost entirely of Italian, Spanish, and Slavic aliens. Justice Department announcements and statements by politicians and the press stressed the predominance of recent immigrants in radical organizations. Smoldering prejudice against new immigrants and identification of these immigrants with European as well as American radical movements, combined with other sources of postwar stress to create one of the most frenzied and one of the most widespread nativistic movements in the nation's history.

The result . . . was called Americanism or one hundred per cent Americanism. Its objective was to end the apparent erosion of American values and the disintegration of American culture. By reaffirming those beliefs, customs, symbols, and traditions felt to be the foundation of our way of life, by enforcing conformity among the population, and by purging the nation of dangerous foreigners, the one hundred per centers expected to heal societal divisions and to tighten defenses against cultural change.

Panegyrics celebrating our history and institutions were delivered regularly in almost every American school, church, and public hall in 1919 and 1920. Many of these fervent addresses went far beyond the usual patriotic declarations. Audiences were usually urged to join a crusade to protect our hallowed institutions. Typical of the more moderate statements was Columbia University President Nicholas Murray Butler's insistence in April 1919 that

"America will be saved, not by those who have only contempt and spite for her founders and her history, but by those who look with respect and reverence upon the great series of happenings extending from the voyage of the May-flower. . . .

What one historian has called "a riot of biographies of American heroes—statesmen, cowboys, and pioneers" appeared in this brief period. Immigrants as well as citizens produced many autobiographical testimonials to the superiority of American institutions. These patriotic tendencies in our literature were as short-lived as the Red Scare, and have been concealed by "debunking" biographies of folk heroes and skeptical autobiographies so common later in the nineteen-twenties. An unusual number of motion pictures about our early history were turned out immediately after the war and the reconstruction of colonial Williamsburg and of Longfellow's Wayside Inn was begun. With great fanfare, Secretary of State Lansing placed the original documents of the Constitution and the Declaration of Independence on display in January 1920, and the State Department distributed movies of this ceremony to almost every town and city in the United States. Organizations like the National Security League, the Association for Constitutional Government, the Sons and Daughters of the American Revolution, the Colonial Dames of America, with the cooperation of the American Bar Association and many state Bar Associations, organized Constitution Day celebrations and distributed huge numbers of pamphlets on the subject throughout the country.

The American flag became a sacred symbol. Legionaires demanded that citizens "Run the Reds out from the land whose flag they sully." Men suspected of radical leanings were forced to kiss the stars and stripes. A Brooklyn truck driver decided in June 1919 that it was unpatriotic to obey a New York City law obliging him to fly a red cloth on lumber which projected from his vehicle. Instead he used as a danger signal a small American flag. A policeman, infuriated at the sight of the stars and stripes flying from a lumber pile, arrested the driver on a charge of disorderly conduct. Despite the Brooklyn patriot's insistence that he meant no offense to the flag, he was reprimanded and fined by the court.

Recent immigrants, especially, were called upon to show evidence of real conversion. Great pressure was brought to bear upon the foreign-born to learn English and to forget their native tongues. As Senator William S. Kenyon of Iowa declared in October 1919, "The time has come to make this a one-language nation." An editorial in the *American Legion Weekly* took a further step and insisted that the one language must be called "American. Why even in Mexico they do not stand for calling the language the Spanish language."

Immigrants were also expected to adopt our customs and to snuff out remnants of Old World cultures. Genteel prewar and wartime movements to speed up assimilation took on a "frightened and feverish aspect." Welcoming members of an Americanization conference called by his department, Secretary of the Interior Franklin K. Lane exclaimed in May 1919, "You have been gathered together as crusaders in a great cause. . . . There is no other question of such importance before the American people as the solidifying and strengthening of true American sentiment." A Harvard University official told the conference that "The Americanization movement . . . gives men a new and holy religion. . . . It challenges each one of us to a renewed consecration and devotion to the welfare of the nation." The National Security League boasted, in 1919, of establishing one thousand study groups to teach teachers how to inculcate "Americanism" in their foreign-born students. A critic of the prevailing mood protested against "one of our best advertised American mottoes, 'One country, one language, one flag,'" which, he complained, had become the basis for a fervent nationwide program.

As the postwar movement for one hundred per cent Americanism gathered momentum, the deportation of alien nonconformists became increasingly its most compelling objective. Asked to suggest a remedy for the nationwide upsurge in radical activity, the Mayor of Gary, Indiana, replied, "Deportation is the answer, deportation of these leaders who talk treason in America and deportation of those who agree with them and work with them." "We must remake America," a popular author averred. "We must purify the source of America's population and keep it pure. . . . We must insist that there shall be an American loyalty, brooking no amendment or qualification." As Higham noted, "In 1919, the clamor of 100 per centers for applying deportation as a purgative arose to an hysterical howl. . . . Through repression and deportation on the one hand and speedy total assimilation on the other, 100 per centers hoped to eradicate discontent and purify the nation."

Politicians quickly sensed the possibilities of the popular frenzy for Americanism. Mayor Ole Hanson of Seattle, Governor Calvin Coolidge of Massachusetts, and General Leonard Wood became the early heroes of the movement. The man in the best political position to take advantage of the popular feeling, however, was Attorney General A. Mitchell Palmer. In 1919, especially after the President's physical collapse, only Palmer had the authority, staff, and money necessary to arrest and deport huge numbers of radical aliens. The most virulent phase of the movement for one hundred per cent Americanism came early in 1920, when Palmer's agents rounded up for deportation over six thousand aliens and prepared to arrest thousands more suspected of membership in radical organizations. Most of these aliens were taken without warrants, many were detained for unjustifiably long periods of time, and some suffered incredible hardships. Almost all, however, were eventually released.

After Palmer decided that he could ride the postwar fears into the presidency, he set out calculatingly to become the symbol of one hundred per cent Americanism. The Palmer raids, his anti-labor activities, and his frequent pious professions of patriotism during the campaign were all part of this effort. Palmer was introduced by a political associate to the Democratic party's annual Jackson Day dinner in January 1920 as "an American whose Americanism cannot be misunderstood." In a speech delivered in Georgia shortly before the primary election (in which Palmer won control of the state's delegation to the

Democratic National Convention), the Attorney General asserted: "I am myself an American and I love to preach my doctrine before undiluted one hundred per cent Americans, because my platform is, in a word, undiluted Americanism and undying loyalty to the republic." The same theme dominated the address made by Palmer's old friend, John H. Bigelow of Hazleton, Pennsylvania, when he placed Palmer's name in nomination at the 1920 National Convention. Proclaimed Bigelow: "No party could survive today that did not write into its platform the magic word 'Americanism.' . . . The Attorney-General of the United States has not merely professed, but he has proved his true Americanism . . . Behind him I see a solid phalanx of true Americanism that knows no divided allegiance."

Unfortunately for political candidates like Palmer and Wood, most of the social and economic disturbances which had activated the movement they sought to lead gradually disappeared during the first half of 1920. The European revolutions were put down; by 1920 communism seemed to have been isolated in Russia. Bombings ceased abruptly after June 1919, and fear of new outrages gradually abated. Prices of food and clothing began to recede during the spring. Labor strife almost vanished from our major industries after a brief railroad walkout in April. Prosperity returned after mid-1919 and by early 1920 business activity and employment levels exceeded their wartime peaks. At the same time, it became clear that the Senate would not pass Wilson's peace treaty and that America was free to turn its back on the responsibilities of world leadership. The problems associated with the new immigrants remained; so did the disillusionment with Europe and with many old intellectual ideals. Nativism did not disappear from the American scene; but the frenzied attempt to revitalize the culture did peter out in 1920. The handful of unintimidated men, especially Assistant Secretary of Labor Louis F. Post, who had used the safeguards provided by American law to protect many victims of the Red Scare, found increasing public support. On the other hand, politicians like Palmer, Wood, and Hanson were left high and dry, proclaiming the need for one hundred per cent Americanism to an audience which no longer urgently cared.

It is ironic that in 1920 the Russian leaders of the Comintern finally took charge of the American Communist movement, provided funds and leadership, and ordered the Communist factions to unite and participate actively in labor organizations and strikes. These facts were reported in the American press. Thus a potentially serious foreign threat to national securtiy appeared just as the Red Scare evaporated, providing a final illustration of the fact that the frenzied one hundred per centers of 1919–1920 were affected less by the "red menace" than by a series of social and economic dislocations.

Although the Red Scare died out in 1920, its effects lingered. Hostility toward immigrants, mobilized in 1919–1920, remained strong enough to force congressional passage of restrictive immigration laws. Some of the die-hard one hundred per centers found a temporary home in the Ku Klux Klan until that organization withered away during the mid-twenties. As its most lasting accomplishments, the movement for one hundred per cent Americanism fostered a spirit of conformity in the country, a satisfaction with the *status quo*, and the equation of reform ideologies with foreign enemies. Revitalization movements have helped many societies adapt successfully to new conditions. The movement associated with the American Red Scare, however, had no such effect. True, it unified the culture against the threats faced in 1919–1920; but the basic problems—a damaged value system, an unrestrained business cycle, a hostile Russia, and communism—were left for future generations of Americans to deal with in their own fashion.

WOODROW WILSON

Making the World Safe for Democracy: Woodrow Wilson Asks for War, 1917

Woodrow Wilson was elected to a second term as president in 1916 on the strength of his assurances that he would not take the nation into the European conflict. Just prior to the election the following letter, written by Wilson for publication, appeared in Western newspapers: "Thank you warmly for your letter of October twenty-third. The reason you give for supporting me touches me very deeply, that you should feel when you see 'the boys and mother' together in your home circle that I have preserved the peace and happiness of the home. Such a feeling on the part of my fellow-citizens is a sufficient reward for everything that I have done."

The American policy toward the European combatants had officially been one of neutrality. In practice, however, this policy favored Britain and France at Germany's expense. Early in 1917, Germany resumed unrestricted submarine warfare against all shipping—belligerent and neutral. In late February, Wilson learned that should the United States and Germany go to war, Germany was prepared to offer American territory in return for Mexican intervention. In March three American merchant vessels were sunk with heavy loss of life, and the tsarist government in Russia fell in the opening stage of the Russian Revolution. The first event provided the president with the "overt act" he required; the second made intervention on the side of Russia seem appropriate.

Five months after his election victory, Wilson delivered this war message to a joint session of Congress. The president moved skillfully from a discussion of German violations of American rights on the seas—a minor threat to the national interest—to a larger, ideological explanation for the war as a struggle against "autocracy" and for "freedom." Is this call for a war of "principles" consistent with Coben's explanation of the Red Scare that erupted only a few years after Wilson's speech? What was Wilson's idea of "normalcy" in world politics?

GENTLEMEN OF THE CONGRESS: I have called the Congress into extraordinary session because there are serious, very serious, choices of policy to be made, and made immediately which it was neither right nor constitutionally permissible that I should assume the responsibility of making.

On the third of February last, I officially laid before you the extraordinary announcement of the Imperial German Government that on and after the first day of February it was its purpose to put aside all restraints of law or of humanity and use its submarines to sink every vessel that sought to approach either the ports of Great Britain and Ireland or the western coast of Europe or any of the ports controlled by the enemies of Germany within the Mediterranean. That had seemed to be the object of the German submarine warfare earlier in the war; but since April of last year the Imperial Government had somewhat restrained the commanders of its undersea craft, in conformity with its promise then given to us that passenger boats should not be sunk, and that due warning would be given to all other vessels which its submarines might seek to destroy, when no resistance was offered or escape attempted, and care taken that their crews were given at least a fair chance to save their lives in their open boats. The precautions taken were meager and haphazard enough, as was proved in distressing instance after instance in the progress of the cruel and unmanly business, but a certain degree of restraint was observed.

The new policy has swept every restriction aside. Vessels of every kind, whatever their flag, their character, their cargo, their destination, their errand, have been ruthlessly sent to the bottom without warning and without thought of help or mercy for those on board—the vessels of friendly neutrals along with those of belligerents. Even hospital ships and ships carrying relief to the sorely bereaved and stricken people of Belgium, though the latter were provided with safe conduct through the proscribed areas by the German Government itself, and were distinguished by unmistakable marks of identity, have been sunk with the same reckless lack of compassion or of principle.

From Woodrow Wilson's request for a declaration of war against Germany, a speech delivered at a Joint Session of Congress, April 2, 1917. From *A Compilation of the Messages and Papers of the Presidents,* XVI (New York: Bureau of National Literature, n.d.), pp. 8226–8233.

I was for a little while unable to believe that such things would in fact be done by any government that had hitherto subscribed to the humane practices of civilized nations. International law had its origin in the attempt to set up some law which would be respected and observed upon the seas, where no nation had right of dominion and where lay the free highways of the world. By painful stage after stage has that law been built up, with meager enough results, indeed, after all was accomplished that could be accomplished, but always with a clear view, at least, of what the heart and conscience of mankind demanded.

This minimum of right the German Government has swept aside under the plea of retaliation and necessity, and because it had no weapons which it could use at sea except these which it is impossible to employ as it is employing them without throwing to the winds all scruples of humanity or of respect for the understandings that were supposed to underlie the intercourse of the world.

I am not now thinking of the loss of property involved, immense and serious as that is, but only of the wanton and wholesale destruction of the lives of non-combatants, men, women and children, engaged in pursuits which have always, even in the darkest period of modern history, been deemed innocent and legitimate. Property can be paid for; the lives of peaceful and innocent people cannot be.

The present German submarine warfare against commerce is a warfare against mankind. It is a war against all nations. American ships have been sunk, American lives taken in ways which it has stirred us very deeply to learn of, but the ships and people of other neutral and friendly nations have been sunk and overwhelmed in the waters in the same way. There has been no discrimination. The challenge is to all mankind. Each nation must decide for itself how it will meet it. The choice we make for ourselves must be made with a moderation of counsel and a temperateness of judgment befitting our character and our motives as a nation.

We must put excited feeling away. Our motive will not be revenge or the victorious assertion of the physical might of the nation, but only the vindication of right, of human right, of which we are only a single champion.

When I addressed the Congress on the 26th of February last, I thought that it would suffice to assert our neutral right with arms; our right to use the sea against unlawful interference; our right to keep our people safe against unlawful violence. But armed neutrality, it now appears, is impracticable. Because submarines are in effect outlaws when used as the German submarines have been used against merchant shipping, it is impossible to defend ships against their attacks as the law of nations has assumed that merchantmen would defend themselves against privateers or cruisers, visible craft giving chase upon the open sea. It is common prudence in such circumstances, grim necessity indeed, to endeavor to destroy them before they have shown their own intention. They must be dealt with upon sight, if dealt with at all.

The German Government denies the right of neutrals to use arms at all within the areas of the sea which it has prescribed, even in the defense of rights which no modern publicist has ever before questioned their right to defend. The intimation is conveyed that the armed guards which we have placed on our merchant ships will be treated as beyond the pale of law and subject to be dealt with as pirates would be. Armed neutrality is ineffectual enough at best; in such circumstances and in the face of such pretensions, it is worse than ineffectual; it is likely only to produce what it was meant to prevent; it is practically certain to draw us into the war without either the rights or the effectiveness of belligerents.

There is one choice we cannot make, we are incapable of making—we will not choose the path of submission and suffer the most sacred rights of our nation and our people to be ignored or violated. The wrongs against which we now array ourselves are no common wrongs; they cut to the very roots of human life.

With a profound sense of the solemn and even tragical character of the step I am taking and of the grave responsibilities which it involves, but in unhesitating obedience to what I deem my constitutional duty, I advise that the Congress declare the recent course of the Imperial German Government to be, in fact, nothing less than war against the Government and people of the United States; that is formally accept the status of belligerent which has been thrust upon it; and that it take immediate steps not only to put the country in a more thorough state of defense, but also to exert all its power and employ all its resources to bring the Government of the German Empire to terms and end the war. . . .

While we do these things, these deeply momentous things, let us be very clear, and make very clear to all the world what our motives and our objects are. My own thought has not been driven from its habitual and normal course by the unhappy events of the last two months, and I do not believe that the thought of the nation has been altered or clouded by them.

I have exactly the same things in mind now that I had in mind when I addressed the Senate on the 22d of January last; the same that I had in mind when I addressed the Congress on the 3d of February and on the 26th of February. Our object now, as then, is to vindicate the principles of peace and justice in the life of the world as against selfish and autocratic power and to set up among the really free and self-governed peoples of the world such a concert of purpose and of action as will henceforth insure the observance of those principles.

Neutrality is no longer feasible or desirable where the peace of the world is involved and the freedom of its peoples, and the menace to that peace and freedom lies in the existence of autocratic governments backed by organized force which is controlled wholly by their will, not by the will of their people. We have seen the last of neutrality in such circumstances.

We are the beginning of an age where it will be insisted that the same standards of conduct and of responsibility for wrong done shall be observed among nations and their governments that are observed among the individual citizens of civilized states.

We have no quarrel with the German people. We have no feeling toward them but one of sympathy and friendship. It was not upon their impulse that their Government acted in entering this war. It was not with their previous knowledge or approval.

It was a war determined upon as wars used to be determined upon in the old, unhappy days when peoples were nowhere consulted by their rulers and wars were provoked and waged in the interest of dynasties or of little groups of ambitious men who were accustomed to use their fellow-men as pawns and tools.

Self-governed nations do not fill their neighbor states with spies or set the course of intrigue to bring about some critical posture of affairs which will give them an opportunity to strike and make conquest. Such designs can be successfully worked out only under cover and where no one has the right to ask questions.

Cunningly contrived plans of deception or aggression, carried, it may be, from generation to generation, can be worked out and kept from the light only within the privacy of courts or behind the carefully guarded confidences of a narrow and privileged class. They are happily impossible where public opinion commands and insists upon full information concerning all the nation's affairs. . . .

We are accepting this challenge of hostile purpose because we know that in such a government, following such methods, we can never have a friend; and that in the presence of its organized power always lying in wait to accomplish we know not what purpose, there can be no assured security for the democratic governments of the world.

We are now about to accept gauge of battle with this natural foe to liberty and shall, if necessary, spend the whole force of the nation to check and nullify its pretensions and end its power. We are glad, now that we see the facts with no veil of false pretense about them, to fight thus for the ultimate peace of the world and for the liberation of its peoples, the German peoples included; for the rights of nations great and small and the privilege of men everywhere to choose their way of life and of obedience. The world must be made safe for democracy. Its peace must be planted upon the tested foundations of political liberty.

We have no selfish ends to serve. We desire no conquest, no dominion. We seek no indemnities for ourselves, no material compensation for the sacrifices we shall freely make. We are but one of the champions of the rights of mankind. We shall be satisfied when those rights have been made as secure as the faith and the freedom of the nations can make them. . . .

It will be all the easier for us to conduct ourselves as belligerents in a high spirit of right and fairness because we act without animus, not in enmity toward a people nor with the desire to bring any injury or disadvantage upon them, but only in armed opposition to an irresponsible Government which has thrown aside all considerations of humanity and of right and is running amuck.

We are, let me say again, the sincere friends of the German people, and shall desire nothing so much as the early re-establishment of intimate relations of mutual advantage between us—however hard it may be for them, for the time being, to believe that this is spoken from our hearts. We have borne with their present Government through all these bitter months because of that friendship—exercising a patience and forbearance which would otherwise have been impossible. We shall, happily, still have an opportunity to prove that friendship in our daily attitude and actions toward the millions of men and women of German birth and native sympathy who live among us and share our life, and we shall be proud to prove it toward all who are in fact loyal to their neighbors and to the Government in the hour of test. They are, most of them, as true and loyal Americans as if they had never known any other fealty or allegiance. They will be prompt to stand with us in rebuking and restraining the few who may be of a different mind and purpose.

If there should be disloyalty, it will be dealt with with a firm hand of stern repression; but if it lifts its head at all, it will lift it only here and there and without countenance, except from a lawless and malignant few.

It is a distressing and oppressive duty, gentlemen of the Congress, which I have performed in thus addressing you. There are, it may be, many months of fiery trial and sacrifice ahead of us. It is a fearful thing to lead this great peaceful people into war, into the most terrible and disastrous of all wars, civilization itself seeming to be in the balance. But the right is more precious than peace, and we shall fight for the things which we have always carried nearest our hearts—for democracy, for the right of those who submit to authority to have a voice in their own governments, for the rights and liberties of small nations, for a universal domination of right by such a concert of free peoples as shall bring peace and safety to all nations and make the world itself at last free. To such a task we can dedicate our lives and our fortunes, everything that we are and everything that we have, with the pride of those who know that the day has come when America is privileged to spend her blood and her might for the principles that gave her birth and happiness and the peace which she has treasured. God helping her, she can do no other.

ERNEST HEMINGWAY

"Soldier's Home"

"Soldier's Home" was among Ernest Hemingway's favorite short stories. First published in 1925, it describes one young man's attempt to put the war, his family, his community, and his own growing up into one coherent framework. The issue was a real one for Hemingway, who at eighteen had left his job as a reporter for the *Kansas City Star* and volunteered for ambulance duty in Europe with the American Red Cross.

The central figure in the story is Harold Krebs, who returns home from a war that has affected him profoundly and personally. He soon discovers, however, that no one wants to hear what he has to say about the war; the prevailing orthodoxy has no room for a perception of army life and Germany very different from that of the Creel Committee.

What is Krebs' reaction to the war? Why does he have such difficulty describing his feelings about the conflict to others? What are the historical roots of that difficulty? Would Krebs have been interested in the League of Nations or Wilson's Fourteen Points? Was Krebs, in his own way, a victim of the Red Scare?

Krebs went to the war from a Methodist college in Kansas. There is a picture which shows him among his fraternity brothers, all of them wearing exactly the same height and style collar. He enlisted in the Marines in 1917 and did not return to the United States until the second division returned from the Rhine in the summer of 1919.

There is a picture which shows him on the Rhine with two German girls and another corporal. Krebs and the corporal look too big for their uniforms. The German girls are not beautiful. The Rhine does not show in the picture.

By the time Krebs returned to his home town in Oklahoma the greeting of heroes was over. He came back much too late. The men from the town who had been drafted had all been welcomed elaborately on their return. There had been a great deal of hysteria. Now the reaction had set in. People seemed to think it was rather ridiculous for Krebs to be getting back so late, years after the war was over.

At first Krebs, who had been at Belleau Wood, Soissons, the Champagne, St. Mihiel and in the Argonne did not want to talk about the war at all. Later he felt the need to talk but no one wanted to hear about it. His town had heard too many atrocity stories to be thrilled by actualities. Krebs found that to be listened to at all he had to lie, and after he had done this twice he, too, had a reaction against the war and against talking about it. A distaste for everything that had happened to him in the war set in because of the lies he had told. All of the times that had been able to make him feel cool and clear inside himself when he thought of them; the times so long back when he had done the one thing, the only thing for a man to do, easily and naturally, when he might have done something else, now lost their cool, valuable quality and then were lost themselves.

His lies were quite unimportant lies and consisted in attributing to himself

From Ernest Hemingway, "Soldier's Home," in Charles Scribner, Jr. (ed.), *The Enduring Hemingway: An Anthology of a Lifetime in Literature* (New York: Scribner, 1974), pp. 61–67. "Soldier's Home" is reprinted with the permission of Charles Scribner's Sons from *In Our Time* by Ernest Hemingway. Copyright 1925 Charles Scribner's Sons.

things other men had seen, done or heard of, and stating as facts certain apocryphal incidents familiar to all soldiers. Even his lies were not sensational at the pool room. His acquaintances, who had heard detailed accounts of German women found chained to machine guns in the Argonne forest and who could not comprehend, or were barred by their patriotism from interest in, any German machine gunners who were not chained, were not thrilled by his stories.

Krebs acquired the nausea in regard to experience that is the result of untruth or exaggeration, and when he occasionally met another man who had really been a soldier and they talked a few minutes in the dressing room at a dance he fell into the easy pose of the old soldier among other soldiers: that he had been badly, sickeningly frightened all the time. In this way he lost everything.

During this time, it was late summer, he was sleeping late in bed, getting up to walk down town to the library to get a book, eating lunch at home, reading on the front porch until he became bored and then walking down through the town to spend the hottest hours of the day in the cool dark of the pool room. He loved to play pool.

In the evening he practised on his clarinet, strolled down town, read and went to bed. He was still a hero to his two young sisters. His mother would have given him breakfast in bed if he had wanted it. She often came in when he was in bed and asked him to tell her about the war, but her attention always wandered. His father was noncommittal.

Before Krebs went away to the war he had never been allowed to drive the family motor car. His father was in the real estate business and always wanted the car to be at his command when he required it to take clients out into the country to show them a piece of farm property. The car always stood outside the First National Bank building where his father had an office on the second floor. Now, after the war, it was still the same car.

Nothing was changed in the town except that the young girls had grown up. But they lived in such a complicated world of already defined alliances and shifting feuds that Krebs did not feel the energy or the courage to break into it. He liked to look at them, though. There were so many good-looking young girls. Most of them had their hair cut short. When he went away only little girls wore their hair like that or girls that were fast. They all wore sweaters and shirt waists with round Dutch collars. It was a pattern. He liked to look at them from the front porch as they walked on the other side of the street. He liked to watch them walking under the shade of the trees. He liked the round Dutch collars above their sweaters. He liked their silk stockings and flat shoes. He liked their bobbed hair and the way they walked.

When he was in town their appeal to him was not very strong. He did not like them when he saw them in the Greek's ice cream parlor. He did not want them themselves really. They were too complicated. There was something else. Vaguely he wanted a girl but he did not want to have to work to get her. He would have liked to have a girl but he did not want to have to spend a long time getting her. He did not want to get into the intrigue and the politics. He did not want to have to do any courting. He did not want to tell any more lies. It wasn't worth it.

He did not want any consequences. He did not want any consequences ever again. He wanted to live along without consequences. Besides he did not really need a girl. The army had taught him that. It was all right to pose as though you had to have a girl. Nearly everybody did that. But it wasn't true. You did not need a girl. That was the funny thing. First a fellow boasted how girls mean nothing to him, that he never thought of them, that they could not touch him. Then a fellow boasted that he could not get along without girls, that he had to have them all the time, that he could not go to sleep without them.

That was all a lie. It was all a lie both ways. You did not need a girl unless you thought about them. He learned that in the army. Then sooner or later you always got one. When you were really ripe for a girl you always got one. You did not have to think about it. Sooner or later it would come. He had learned that in the army.

Now he would have liked a girl if she had come to him and not wanted to talk. But here at home it was all too complicated. He knew he could never get through it all again. It was not worth the trouble. That was the thing about French girls and Germans girls. There was not all this talking. You couldn't talk much and you did not need to talk. It was simple and you were friends. He thought about France and then began to think about Germany. On the whole he had liked Germany better. He did not want to leave Germany. He did not want to come home. Still, he had come home. He sat on the front porch.

He liked the girls that were walking along the other side of the street. He liked the look of them much better than the French girls or the German girls. But the world they were in was not the world he was in. He would like to have one of them. But it was not worth it. They were such a nice pattern. He liked the pattern. It was exciting. But he would not go through all the talking. He did not want one badly enough. He liked to look at them all, though. It was not worth it. Not now when things were getting good again.

He sat there on the porch reading a book on the war. It was a history and he was reading about all the engagements he had been in. It was the most interesting reading he had ever done. He wished there were more maps. He looked forward with a good feeling to reading all the really good histories when they would come out with good detail maps. Now he was really learning about the war. He had been a good soldier. That made a difference.

One morning after he had been home about a month his mother came into his bedroom and sat on the bed. She smoothed her apron.

"I had a talk with your father last night, Harold," she said, "and he is willing for you to take the car out in the evenings."

"Yeah?" said Krebs, who was not fully awake. "Take the car out? Yeah?"

"Yes. Your father has felt for some time that you should be able to take the car out in the evenings whenever you wished but we only talked it over last night."

"I'll bet you made him,"Krebs said.

"No. It was your father's suggestion that we talk the matter over."

"Yeah. I'll bet you made him." Krebs sat up in bed.

"Will you come down to breakfast, Harold?" his mother said.

"As soon as I get my clothes on," Krebs said.

His mother went out of the room and he could hear her frying something downstairs while he washed, shaved and dressed to go down into the dining-room for breakfast. While he was eating breakfast his sister brought in the mail.

"Well, Hare," she said. "You old sleepy-head. What do you ever get up for?"

Krebs looked at her. He liked her. She was his best sister.

"Have you got the paper?" he asked.

She handed him *The Kansas City Star* and he shucked off its brown wrapper and opened it to the sporting page. He folded *The Star* open and propped it against the water pitcher with his cereal dish to steady it, so he could read while he ate.

"Harold," his mother stood in the kitchen doorway, "Harold, please don't muss up the paper. Your father can't read his *Star* if it's been mussed."

"I won't muss it," Krebs said.

His sister sat down at the table and watched him while he read.

"We're playing indoor over at school this afternoon,"she said. "I'm going to pitch."

"Good," said Krebs. "How's the old wing?"

"I can pitch better than lots of the boys. I tell them all you taught me. The other girls aren't much good."

"Yeah?" said Krebs.

"I tell them all you're my beau. Aren't you my beau, Hare?"

"You bet."

"Couldn't your brother really be your beau just because he's your brother?"

"I don't know."

"Sure you know. Couldn't you be my beau. Hare, if I was old enough and if you wanted to?"

"Sure. You're my girl now."

"Am I really your girl?"

"Sure."

"Do you love me?"

"Uh, huh."

"Will you love me always?"

"Sure."

"Will you come over and watch me play indoor?"

"Maybe."

"Aw, Hare, you don't love me. If you loved me, you'd want to come over and watch me play indoor."

Krebs's mother came into the dining-room from the kitchen. She carried a plate with two fried eggs and some crisp bacon on it and a plate of buckwheat cakes.

"You run along, Helen," she said. "I want to talk to Harold."

She put the eggs and bacon down in front of him and brought in a jug of maple syrup for the buckwheat cakes. Then she sat down across the table from Krebs.

"I wish you'd put down the paper a minute, Harold," she said.

Krebs took down the paper and folded it.

"Have you decided what you are going to do yet, Harold?" his mother said, taking off her glasses.

"No," said Krebs.

"Don't you think it's about time?" His mother did not say this in a mean way. She seemed worried.

"I hadn't thought about it," Krebs said.

"God has some work for every one to do," his mother said. "There can be no idle hands in His Kingdom."

"I'm not in His Kingdom," Krebs said.

"We are all of us in His Kingdom."

Krebs felt embarrassed and resentful as always.

"I've worried about you so much, Harold," his mother went on. "I know the temptations you must have been exposed to. I know how weak men are. I know what your own dear grandfather, my own father, told us about the Civil War and I have prayed for you. I pray for you all day long, Harold."

Krebs looked at the bacon fat hardening on his plate.

"Your father is worried, too," his mother went on. "He thinks you have lost your ambition, that you haven't got a definite aim in life. Charley Simmons, who is just your age, has a good job and is going to be married. The boys are all settling down; they're all determined to get somewhere; you can see that boys like Charley Simmons are on their way to being really a credit to the community."

Krebs said nothing.

"Don't look that way, Harold," his mother said. "You know we love you and I want to tell you for you own good how matters stand. Your father does not want to hamper your freedom. He thinks you should be allowed to drive the car. If you want to take some of the nice girls out riding with you, we are only too pleased. We want you to enjoy yourself. But you are going to have to settle down to work, Harold. Your father doesn't care what you start in at. All work is honorable as he says. But you've got to make a start at something. He asked me to speak to you this morning and then you can stop in and see him at his office."

"Is that all?" Krebs said.

"Yes. Don't you love your mother, dear boy?"

"No," Krebs said.

His mother looked at him across the table. Her eyes were shiny. She started crying.

"I don't love anybody," Krebs said.

It wasn't any good. He couldn't tell her, he couldn't make her see it. It was silly to have said it. He had only hurt her. He went over and took hold of her arm. She was crying with her head in her hands.

"I didn't mean it," he said. "I was just angry at something. I didn't mean I didn't love you."

His mother went on crying. Krebs put his arm on her shoulder.

"Can't you believe me, mother?"

His mother shook her head.

"Please, please, mother. Please believe me."

"All right, " his mother said chokily. She looked up at him. "I believe you, Harold."

Krebs kissed her hair. She put her face up to him.

"I'm your mother," she said. "I held you next to my heart when you were a tiny baby."

Krebs felt sick and vaguely nauseated.

"I know, Mummy," he said. "I'll try and be a good boy for you."

"Would you kneel and pray with me, Harold?" his mother asked.

They knelt down beside the dining-room table and Krebs's mother prayed.

"Now, you pray, Harold," she said.

"I can't," Krebs said.

"Try, Harold."

"I can't."

"Do you want me to pray for you?"

"Yes."

So his mother prayed for him and then stood up and Krebs kissed his mother and went out of the house. He had tried so to keep his life from being complicated. Still, none of it had touched him. He had felt sorry for his mother and she had made him lie. He would go to Kansas City and get a job and she would feel all right about it. There would be one more scene maybe before he got away. He would not go down to his father's office. He would miss that one. He wanted his life to go smoothly. It had just gotten going that way. Well, that was all over now, anyway. He would go over to the schoolyard and watch Helen play indoor baseball.

Aspects of Normalcy

The KKK

For several years in the mid-1920s, the Ku Klux Klan was an important feature of American political life. Unlike the Klan of the 1870s, this new version began innocently enough as a fraternal association, and the organization had considerable strength outside the South, in the cities

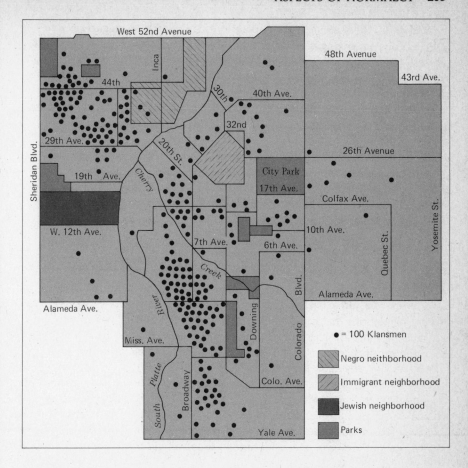

The KKK in Denver. *From Kenneth T. Jackson,* The Ku Klux Klan in the City, 1915–1930 *(New York: Oxford University Press, 1967), p. 225. Copyright © 1967 by Oxford University Press, Inc. Reprinted by permission.*

and countryside of the Midwest and Far West. Its members were often religious fundamentalists who were against immigrants, against sexual immorality, and for prohibition.

What does this map, of Klan strength in Denver, tell us about the Klan?

Public Confession

The atmosphere of the Harding era was normalcy. The message of the Red Scare was conformity. But there was, as always, another side to American life: an insistence on individuality, even eccentricity. One way of resolving the tension was simply to make individual lives, no matter how unique, the stuff of mass-circulation media such as magazines and movies. The following selections from *True-Story Magazine* illustrate the process perfectly. Each individual is supposed to have "inner secrets." But the magazine encourages the revelation of these secrets on the apparent assumption that everyone's "inner" world will be understood and appreciated by a mass audience, that there is no contradiction between the private and the public, between individuality and the "unchangeable principles of life."

The first issue of *True-Story Magazine*, from which the selections are taken, appeared on newsstands in May of 1919, not long before Hemingway's Krebs returned from the Rhineland. Would the magazine have appealed to him? What conditions of life in his hometown might have made the publication important to him?

Why the True-Story Magazine *is "Different"*

The *True-Story Magazine* makes its first appearance with this issue.

Its excuse for existence rests upon the belief that *truth is stranger than fiction*. The stories that it presents will be taken as nearly as possible from the actual experiences of life, and we believe they will be read with keener interest than the products of the imagination, even when coming from inspired pens.

Our only deviation from the rule we have laid down will be in stories of the future. Stories of the past must be controlled by the environments of the age in which they are written, but stories of the future give absolutely free play to the imagination. The author makes his own world. On this account we believe that stories of the future have greater possibilities in the way of interest than stories of the past, and from time to time we will try to present fiction of this sort.

Stories are, to a certain extent, like music. They may inspire or depress. A story of the right sort should leave you with a "wholesome taste." You should feel better for having read it. We hope that our literature will have that effect. We also hope that it will assist in building the right sort of principles, add strength to your character and force and stability to your life purposes.

The writers of most of our stories will be influenced by a high moral purpose. They may wish to teach lessons of great value, but the editors will measure each story by its ability to entertain.

We want to furnish mental recreation of the right sort. We will try to avoid depressing influences. Tragedy may creep into our plots from time to time, and if your emotional instincts are keen, your sympathies for the hero or heroine may carry you through the entire gamut of human feeling—from the depths of misery to the delights of the most glorious human experiences.

The writers of stories that bare the inner secrets of the human heart, as will those that appear in the *True-Story Magazine*, must necessarily remain

From *True-Story Magazine*, (May 1919), 3, 16. Copyright © by The Macfadden Group, Inc. Reprinted by permission.

anonymous. Their real names cannot be published without risk or certainty of unpleasant consequences. But the name of the individual responsible for each and every story will be scrupulously recorded and preserved as a warranty of its truth, as well as of the good faith of the publishers.

We expect the *True-Story Magazine* to be edited, to a large extent, by its readers. Every reader of this publication is invited to send in his life story, or any story that he knows to be true.

We hope our readers will feel themselves a part of our organization; that they will freely criticize what they do not like, or commend what seems to them excellent. We want each reader to consider himself or herself an associate editor of this publication. Send us your thoughts, whatever they may be. If we publish them we will gladly pay our regular rates, or your own price, if you set a price which we consider reasonable.

WHAT DOES LIFE MEAN TO YOU?

By Dr. George Wharton James

Life!

Life Stories!

True Life Stories!

There is nothing that concerns man so much as life—his own life.

What is it for? Why is it?

What is he getting out of it? How can he make the most of it? What *is* the most?

What standard shall he set for himself? Is it any use setting any standard? Is he a Blind Puppet of Fate, or is he the Arbiter of His Own Destinies?

Does he have Free Will, or is he controlled by Blind Forces?

Does he choose for himself, or predestined to certain actions and their natural consequences?

Who can—*who dare*—answer?—except, of course, the ignorant, conceited, fanatic, who assumes to know all the hidden purposes of the Divine Creator?

The ordinary man, however, doesn't know. He is willing to learn. He is receptive to what other men have learned.

Hence, after his own life, there is nothing else on earth so interesting to him as the lives of other men.

What have they discovered of life?

How have they lived? What have they found out of the immutable, unchangeable principles of life?

The value of their testimony depends largely upon their truthfulness.

How many men in all time ever have truthfully told their own stories?

Can a man help being a liar when he talks or writes about himself?

Dare any man ever tell all he has thought in his own inner heart?

Dare you?

Have you ever thought what it means to lay your very soul bare, even your own self, let alone others?

Dare you reveal every thought, motive and act of your life to your fellow men?

Think it out.

Try it.

Let us know the answer.

Defending the Faith

In "Soldier's Home," Krebs' family proves curiously unable to help him. The problem was widespread and of long standing. Over the course of a century, the family had gradually given up its functions—to the state, the school, the amusement parks, and (after 1920) the radio. This process was less advanced in the nation's rural areas, where adults still had vocational skills to pass on to children and where the mass media had not yet penetrated.

The Tennessee evolution controversy developed out of a state law passed in March 1925 forbidding educational institutions supported by public funds from teaching "the theory that denies the story of the divine creation of man as taught in the Bible." A Dayton public school biology teacher, John T. Scopes, brought a test care, which came to trial that July. Clarence Darrow represented Scopes, William Jennings Bryan the state. Because the case was brought to a sudden close by Bryan's appearance as a *defense* witness, the following remarks—which Bryan had intended as a summation of the case—were never orally delivered. They were published posthumously by his wife.

What was it that Bryan was defending? Was he simply an ignorant old man propping up an outmoded fundamentalist religion? Or did he have some genuine understanding of the meaning of the Scopes trial? What connections can you draw between Bryan's address and Coben's explanation of the Red Scare?

May It Please the Court,
and Gentlemen of the Jury:

Let me, in the first place, congratulate our cause that circumstances have committed the trial to a community like this and entrusted the decision to a jury made up largely of the yeomanry of the State. The book in issue in this trial contains on its first page two pictures contrasting the disturbing noises of a great city with the calm serenity of the country. It is a tribute that rural life has fully earned.

From William Jennings Bryan, *The Last Message of William Jennings Bryan*, foreword by Mrs. Bryan (New York: Revell, 1925) pp. 14–17, 39–41. Excerpts from *The Last Message of William Jennings Bryan* by William Jennings Bryan are used by permission of Fleming H. Revell Company who first published this volume in 1925.

I appreciate the sturdy honesty and independence of those who come into daily contact with the earth, who, living, near to nature, worship nature's God, and who, dealing with the myriad mysteries of earth and air, seek to learn from revelation about the Bible's wonder-working God. I admire the stern virtues, and vigilance and the patriotism of the class from which the jury is drawn, and am reminded of the lines of Scotland's immortal bard, which, changed but slightly, would describe your country's confidence in you:

> "O Scotia, my dear, my native soil!
>   For whom my warmest wish to Heav'n is sent,
> Long may thy hardy sons of rustic toil
>   Be blest with health, and peace, and sweet content!
> And oh, may Heav'n their simple lives prevent
>   From luxury's contagion, weak and vile!
> Then, howe'er crowns and coronets be rent,
> A virtuous populace may rise the while,
> And stand, a wall of fire, around their much-loved isle."

Let us now separate the issues from the misrepresentations, intentional or unintentional, that have obscured both the letter and the purpose of the law. This is not an interference with freedom of conscience. A teacher can think as he pleases and worship God as he likes, or refuse to worship God at all. He can believe in the Bible or discard it; he can accept Christ or reject Him. This law places no obligations or restraints upon him. And so with freedom of speech; he can, so long as he acts as an individual, say anything he likes on any subject. This law does not violate any rights guaranteed by any constitution to any individual. It deals with the defendant, not as an individual, but as an employee, an official or public servant, paid by the State, and therefore under instructions from the State.

The right of the State to control the public schools is affirmed in the recent decision in the Oregon case, which declares that the State can direct what shall be taught and also forbid the teaching of anything "manifestly inimical to the public welfare." The above decision goes even farther and declares that the parent not only has the right to guard the religious welfare of the child, but is in duty bound to guard it. That decision fits this case exactly. The State had a right to pass this law, and the law represents the determination of the parents to guard the religious welfare of their children.

The Statute Not Conceived in Bigotry

It need hardly be added that this law did not have its origin in bigotry. It is not trying to force any form of religion on anybody. The majority is not trying to establish a religion or to teach it—it is trying to protect itself from the effort of an insolent minority to force irreligion upon the children under the guise of teaching science. What right has a little irresponsible oligarchy of self-styled "intellectuals" to demand control of the schools of the United States, in which twenty-five millions of children are being educated at an annual expenditure of nearly two billion of dollars?

Christians must, in every State of the Union, build their own colleges in which to teach Christianity; it is only simple justice that atheists, agnostics and unbelievers should build their own colleges if they want to teach their own religious views or attack the religious views of others.

The statute is brief and free from ambiguity. It prohibits the teaching, in the public schools, of "any theory that denies the story of Divine creation as taught in the Bible, and teaches, instead, that man descended from a lower order of animals." The first sentence sets forth the purpose of those who passed the law. They forbid the teaching of any evolutionary theory that disputes the Bible record of man's creation and, to make sure that there shall be no misunderstanding, they place their own interpretations on their language and specifically forbid the teaching of any theory that makes man a descendant of any lower form of life. . . .

"Offending" the Little Ones

Shakespeare regards the robbing one of his good name as much more grave than the stealing of his purse. But we have a higher authority than Shakespeare to invoke in this connection. He who spake as never man spake, thus describes the crimes that are committed against the young. "It is impossible but that offences will come: but woe unto him through whom they come. It were better for him that a millstone were hanged about his neck, and he cast into the sea, than that he should offend one of these little ones."

Christ did not overdraw the picture. Who is able to set a price upon the life of a child—a child into whom a mother has poured her life and for whom a father has labored? What may a noble life mean to the child itself, to the parents, and to the world?

And it must be remembered that we can measure the effect on only that part of life which is spent on earth; we have no way of calculating the effect on that infinite circle of life of which existence here is but a small arc. The soul is immortal and religion deals with the soul; the logical effect of the evolutionary hypothesis is to undermine religion and thus affect the soul. I recently received a list of questions that were to be discussed in a prominent Eastern school for women. The second question in the list read, "Is religion an obsolescent function that should be allowed to atrophy quietly, without arousing the passionate prejudice of outworn superstition?" The real attack of evolution, it will be seen, is not upon orthodox Christianity, or even upon Christianity, but upon religion—the most basic fact in man's existence and the most practical thing in life. . . .

The people of Tennessee have been patient enough; they acted none too soon. How can they expect to protect society, and even the Church, from the deadening influence of agnosticism and atheism if they permit the teachers employed by taxation to poison the minds of the youth with this destructive doctrine? And remember that the law has not heretofore required the writing of the word "poison" on poisonous doctrines. The bodies of our people are so valuable that druggists and physicians must be careful to properly label all poisons; why not be as careful to protect the spiritual life of our people from the poisons that kill the soul?

There is a test that is sometimes used to ascertain whether one suspected of mental infirmity is really insane. He is put into a tank of water and told to dip the tank dry while a stream of water flows into the tank. If he has not sense enough to turn off the stream, he is adjudged insane. Can parents justify themselves if, knowing the effect of belief in evolution, they permit irreligious teachers to inject skepticism and infidelity into the minds of their children?

Conformity and Diversity

Here is a collection of photographs from the 1920s that illustrate some of the themes of conformity and diversity which grew out of the experience of World War I. What elements in the illustrations point in the direction of anxious conformity to rigid social norms? What details seem to lead in the opposite direction, toward resistance, individuality, and diversity? If you were Krebs in Hemingway's story, how would you react to each of the scenes depicted? If you were Bryan? A. Mitchell Palmer?

Styles Change

Original Caption: "Styles Change Every Year But They Always Use Same Brand of Face Cream." Chicago, 1920s. *Library of Congress.*

Coed Taxi Day

An institution with early-nineteenth-century origins, the fraternity by 1900 had become an important factor in college and university life. It experienced its greatest growth in the 1920s. What historical conditions— conditions presumably more compelling in the 1920s than before or since—account for the growth of national fraternities? What did fraternities accomplish for their members?

Original Caption: " 'Co-Ed Taxi Day' at the University of Southern California—An annual custom at the Los Angeles institution finds the Trojan coeds hawking for fares on behalf of the scholarship fund, and woe to the mere male passenger who fails to give a generous tip to his pretty chauffeur—for the benefit of the fund!" *National Archives.*

The Automobile Age

In *Middletown*, a sociological study of Munsey, Indiana, in the 1920s, Robert and Helen Lynd found that the automobile had already become an enormously important piece of technology. Americans related to it with ambivalence. One Munsey woman said, "I'll go without food before I'll see us give up the car." Others felt the automobile contributed to family solidarity (a claim made frequently for television in the 1950s): "We don't spend anything on recreation except for the car. We save every place we can and put the money into the car." All-day Sunday motor trips, on the other hand, were a "threat against the church."

What do the following photos reveal about the function of the automobile in the 1920s? What might Bryan have thought of it?

American Tourist Camp, Henderson, N.C. *Witteman Collection, Library of Congress.*

Tyhee Beach No. 6, Savannah, Georgia. *Library of Congress.*

CHAPTER 8

Herbert Hoover and the Age of the Consumer

Until recently, Herbert Hoover had not been considered much of a president—better than Harding or Coolidge, perhaps, but too rigid and too tradition-bound to respond adequately to what future generations would know as the Great Depression. Lending credence to this view were Hoover's origins in an Iowa farming community in the 1870s, his father a blacksmith, his mother a teacher and ardent prohibitionist. Both parents had died before his ninth birthday, and the young boy was sent to Oregon to be raised by an uncle.

Nonetheless, Hoover became one of Stanford University's first graduates and went on to pursue a world-wide career as a mining engineer—at one point living abroad for eighteen years. During World War I, he chaired the Commission for Relief in Belgium and was United States food administrator, activities that brought Hoover a national reputation as a humanitarian and organizer. As secretary of commerce under two Republican presidents in the 1920s, Hoover encouraged and guided the development of private, voluntary associations among businessmen, farmers, and workers. Coal mining, cotton textiles, and farming—"sick" industries suffering from excessive competition, overproduction, or declining demand—received special assistance in moving toward higher levels of cooperation and planning.

Hoover was typical of a generation obsessed with marketing goods. A nineteenth-century businessman assumed that goods produced would find a consumer. His twentieth-century counterpart, well aware of the closing of the frontier, leaps in productivity, an aging population, and other factors that might make it difficult to sell all that was produced, assumed no such thing. Advertising, public relations, and marketing flowered in the 1920s. As psychologists learned more about human behavior, selling—once a hit-and-miss affair—began to resemble a science. The Nielsen ratings, which many years later would describe audiences for television advertisers, date back to 1923, when a Chicago electrical engineer and market researcher developed informational indexes for food, drugs, and other industries. During the Great War, the Creel Committee had demonstrated that one could market ideas as well as things. Employers found some of these new techniques made for smoother relations with employees. Industrial psychology was born in the 1920s. So was "industrial democracy," so called because it presumably meant worker participation in plant governance.

It was Hoover's misfortune to be president in October 1929, when a dramatic decline in stock prices brought down the house of cards that the American economy had become. Not all of the economic expansion of the 1920s was an illusion, of course. Employers, applying concepts of efficiency worked out in the progressive era by Frederick W. Taylor and his colleagues in scientific management, were able to obtain a larger product from each worker. Automobiles, consumer durables, and construction were rapidly growing areas of the economy. By the mid-1920s, an estimated four million jobs—close to 10 percent of the labor force—had been created directly or indirectly by the automobile. The boom, therefore, was fueled largely by consumer spending, which was itself in part a creature of installment buying and the new sales tactics of modern advertising. In part because prices remained stable, some Americans were earning substantially more in real wages at the end of the decade than at the beginning. Corporate profits increased 62 percent in the six years after 1923.

The 1920s version of prosperity was, in a sense, self-destructive, for it was based on foundations that were being eaten away, year by year, by the same economic characteristics that defined it. The purchasing upon which prosperity depended could not be sustained because the groups most likely to spend their wages on consumer goods—the working and middle classes—did not find their paychecks rising with corporate profits. The fruits of increased productivity went to management rather than labor, into dividends for stockholders rather than wages for the assembly-line worker. In 1910, the richest

30 percent of the population received 56.4 percent of the nation's pretax personal income; the poorest 30 percent received 13.8 percent. In 1921, the corresponding percentages were 61.5 and 9.8, and in the year of the crash, 61.1 and 10. Income went to those most likely to save and least likely to consume. Moreover, the productive efficiency of the economy was itself troubling in that the capacity to produce goods threatened to outrun the population's ability to consume them.

There were other signs that the economy was fundamentally unsound. Despite Hoover's aid, the sick industries of the decade remained unhealthy. The railroads, already a mature industry at the time of the Great War, now faced intense competition from the motor truck and automobile. Total employment in the industry, as in public utilities and manufacturing as a whole, declined or stagnated— one of many indications that the economy was experiencing difficulty in generating jobs for all those who wished to work. Agriculture was perhaps the most troubled area. Farmers who had increased production to meet war needs now found saturated world markets and declining demand. By 1924–1926, almost one farmer in every five was going bankrupt each year. Many farmers—especially tenants— simply packed what few possessions they had and moved to the city. In the first six months of 1922, over 100,000 farm people left lands they had been working in the state of Georgia alone. Those who remained felt their standard of living fall in 1921 and remain depressed throughout the decade.

The "Bull Market" whose precipitous decline would bring this fragile structure crashing down was not special or unique. Indeed, it was part and parcel of a speculative temper which ran deep in a decade marked by the rise and fall of dozens of miniature empires. Florida—the mecca of the new leisured society—was the heart of a real estate mania, fed by advertising. Miami became "the Wonder City"; Fort Lauderdale "the Tropical Wonderland." A Coral Gables developer somehow hired William Jennings Bryan to perch on a raft in a lagoon and expound on the benefits of the Florida climate. Thousands of Americans invested in property they had never seen, at prices which could not be justified. By 1927 the Florida boom had collapsed.

The fate of the stock market held more serious consequences for the nation's economy. In less than two and one-half months in the fall of 1929, *The New York Times* index of industrial stocks fell from 452 to 224. This dramatic decline cut deeply into the spending and investment of the well-to-do, a group of no little importance to the functioning of the economy. Its effects rippled through a corporate structure weakened by holding companies and investment trusts. It severely damaged another prop—the foreign loans which had helped the nation balance its international accounts. And it shattered business confidence, pumped up as it was. The Great Depression had begun.

Hoover, whose election and entire career had been built around progress and prosperity, now had to try to lead the nation for three years into a reality that was very different indeed, a reality of suffering and stagnation, unemployment and insecurity. Schooled in the new world of public relations and advertising, the engineer from Iowa would spend much of the next four years trying to convince Americans that prosperity was "just around the corner."

CRAIG LLOYD

Aggressive Introvert: Herbert Hoover and Public Relations Management

In this essay, historian Craig Lloyd examines the contradictions between the myths that Herbert Hoover brought to his presidency and the realities those myths had to confront. Hoover is treated here as something of a progressive, a modern president who was skilled in the techniques of public relations and advertising and committed to the gospel of efficiency. In fact, in Hoover's mind, these were the means for the perfection of a modern democracy.

But what did Hoover mean by democracy? Did he mean participation by all the people in a political process? If not, what *did* he have in mind? Did Hoover see himself as an "expert"? If so, isn't that self-image antithetical to genuine democracy? In what ways was Hoover's conception of reform and progress different from, or similar to, that of progressive era advocates of change?

Hoover's attraction to the mass media is partially explained in the introduction to this chapter. Like everyone else, he grew up with these strange and potentially very powerful instruments. But readers should also ask whether certain characteristics of his formative years, especially his apparent rootlessness, might also have led Hoover to pioneer in the use of the new forms of communication.

As a progressive, Hoover was intensely concerned with a multitude of problems jeopardizing the stability and well-being of postwar America. Labor unrest, industrial inefficiency, the wildly fluctuating business cycle, the stagnation of American foreign trade, inadequate housing and child health facilities, the menace of alien ideologies—all of these threatened the American social order, required immediate attention, and could not be adequately or safely handled without the expertise of a skilled elite, made up particularly of the engineer, the scientist, the economist, and the businessman. Yet, though Hoover's recognition of this made him a social engineering elitist, he was also a passionate democrat, convinced that American society must be run from the "bottom up." Unlike some "advanced" progressives, he felt that augmented federal powers would only undermine the individual initiative and responsibility that constituted the essence of democracy as well as the mainspring of progress. The big question was how best to bridge the gap between the expert and the citizen. How could one achieve stability in a complex industrial society without sacrificing the democratic right and obligation of participation by all individuals in that society? How could he preserve and respect local institutions while using them in the solution of pressing national problems? For Hoover, when he became secretary of commerce, the answer would be publicity and public relations. Just as these had been used in the CRB [Commission for Relief in Belgium] and Food Administration to bridge the gap between centralized planning and decentralized execution of those plans, so would they now serve as a means for resolving the tension between Hoover's elitism and his commitment to the democratic ethos.

One might note, in fact, that Hoover's high regard for publicity, his belief in the efficacy of mobilizing public opinion to effect large public policies, and his view of the journalist, editor, magazine, and newspaper as "partners" in the work of the policy-maker, all attitudes that he had held as early as his work for the Panama-Pacific Exposition, were also typical progressive attitudes. As several historians have noted, the progressive period placed a high value on popular education and social reform through journalism. Both Theodore Roosevelt and Woodrow Wilson appreciated the uses to which publicity might be put in carrying out social reforms, and both conceived of its deployment via the press

From Craig Lloyd, *Aggressive Introvert: A Study of Herbert Hoover and Public Relations Management, 1912–1932* (Columbus: Ohio State University Press, 1972), pp. 106–109, 111–112, 155–164, 166, 168–170, 174–175. Copyright © 1973 by the Ohio State University Press. All rights reserved.

as part of a process of "educational leadership." Reform journalism, in the words of Rush Welter, was an important "informal device" in the progressive movement's attempt "to find ways of educating the self-governing public to a better understanding of contemporary problems." Or, as Richard Hofstadter has put it:

> To an extraordinary degree the work of the Progressive movement rested upon its journalism. The fundamental critical achievement of American Progressivism was the business of exposure, and journalism was the chief occupational source of its creative writers. It is hardly an exaggeration to say that the Progressive mind was characteristically a journalistic mind, and that its characteristic contribution was that of the socially responsible reporter-reformer. The muckraker was a central figure. Before there could be action, there must be information and exhortation. Grievances had to be given specific objects, and these the muckraker supplied. It was muckraking that brought the diffuse malaise of the public into focus.

Thus, running through much of progressivism was the conviction that educating "the people" through the mass media would enable them to handle social problems without sacrificing democratic ideals. And it was this conviction that Hoover carried into the 1920s and acted upon to a greater extent than any other public official. Through the deployment of his public relations machinery and the utilization of his many press contacts, he became America's foremost public "instructor" in the "new era." . . .

In 1917, as food administrator, he had referred to his work as a process of "constant hammering and teaching," and had seen the propaganda of his "Education Division" as important in instructing the citizenry in proper nutrition as well as food conservation. And in 1920, he commented that "only by propaganda" was the "there any promise of educating the American public . . . in the ideals of democracy." One must note, too, that many of his statements of the 1919–20 period resemble commencement addresses, particularly in their sweeping world-encompassing analyses of the role of the United States in the "new era" of rapid economic change and conflicting ideologies. In them, he explained to his audience the causes of such social phenomena as world conflict, rapid urbanization, and the Communist revolution, interpreted for them the meaning of such phenomena and their relation to developments in the United States, and drew "lessons" with which to guide future policy. Always, as he discussed such matters, Hoover's stance was that of the public lecturer and "educator," never that of the political campaigner. Consequently when he became secretary of commerce, he continued to view his function as that of "an economic interpreter to the American people," as head of "a clearing house [for the] helpful dissemination of ideas," or of "a domestic intelligence department to inform the public as well as the men in trade and commerce." And to aid in this task of "ceaseless public education on the elemental facts," to "insure that the community [acted out of] knowledge rather than in ignorance," he mobilized publicity and gladly accepted the assistance of his many friends in the press. . . .

In his rhetoric and social attitudes, his educational approach to the public, and his assumption that the scholar and the journalist were partners of the governmental executive in the making and promulgation of public policy, Hoover ought to be seen by historians today (as he was by many of his reformer friends and contemporaries) as a post-war survival of progressivism in the executive branch of government. It is true that as the 1920s passed by Hoover's fear of the federal government's actively intervening in the economy deepened. So great was this fear that he came to view federal legislation itself—even simply regulatory legislation—as, at best, inefficient and, at worst, tending to bureaucratic domination by the national state. But his grave concern here was not the product of a probusiness orientation as some have assumed; it was rather a concern that he shared with many progressives, and one that stemmed from his wartime apprehension of what bureaucracy could do to democratic institutions and values. While acclaiming the journalistic exposures and the legislative reforms of the progressive era, he was convinced that the federal government had been sufficiently strengthened to prevent domination by big business. What was needed now was not further legislative solutions but solutions reached through demobilization of the wartime state—solutions dependent upon the "education and voluntary action of our people." The role of government in the "new era" was not to "cure foolishness by legislation" or to "catch an economic force with a policeman" or a "bureau." Rather, it should function to educate, disseminate information, and create cooperation between groups in order to promote the welfare and growth of the whole social and economic order. Nor were such doctrines an excuse for inaction, as they were with some conservatives. Hoover was indefatigable in trying to organize cooperation and make his approach work.

To govern without resorting to legislation, to utilize the expertise of the scientist, economist, and businessman in tandem with the resources of local communities and private institutions, to achieve social and economic stability while preserving democratic institutions and values—these, as Hoover saw it, were the central problems. And one way to solve them was through the mobilization and proper use of publicity. As he had once campaigned in the press for the Panama-Pacific Exposition, for Belgium, and for wartime food conservation, so would he campaign via the mass media of the 1920s for a multitude of domestic social and economic causes designed to advance social progress while forestalling the growth of big government. Thus, his social outlook and political philosophy led to an approach quite similar to the one demanded by the ambivalent, aggressive, yet introverted, nature of his personality. The two, in effect, reinforced and combined with each other. His behind the scenes apolitical administrative posture fused with his negative attitudes toward the role of the state. His personal desire for influence merged with his great concern for social control and guidance. And together, they produced an extraordinary reliance upon publicity as an administrative tool, one that stemmed both from psychological needs and intellectual commitments. It is an index to the depth of bitterness and frustration engendered by the depression that so many independent journalists should fail to recognize this fact and instead ascribe Hoover's use of publicity to an overweening ambition for the presidency. . . .

Hoover came to the White House, he writes in his *Memoirs*, "determined" to "carry forward the reconstruction and development measures in which [he] had participated as Secretary of Commerce," to "initiate reforms in our social and business life," and to "reorient our foreign relations" toward the promotion of "peace and international progress." "Instead of being able to devote [his] four years wholly to these purposes," he laments, he found himself quickly "overtaken by the economic hurricane" and forced to contend with the problem of "economic recovery and employment." What he fails to say, however, is that in dealing with the crucial issues of "recovery and employment," his basic approach was essentially that used for "reconstruction and development" when he had been secretary of commerce. And it was this application of formerly successful methods in the face of a thoroughly changed social and economic situation that, ironically, began to alter Hoover's public image and thus to destroy the rapport that he had enjoyed over so many years with the American people.

In late October, 1929, eight months after Hoover's inauguration, the stock market crashed, causing reverberations throughout the economy. The presidents's response, though virtually identical to his response to the economic recession and unemployment crisis of eight years earlier, was nonetheless unprecedented in the annals of the American presidency. Refusing to accept the fatalism of his secretary of the treasury, Andrew Mellon, who urged that the "natural" downturn of the business cycle be allowed to run its course, Hoover embarked upon a program to resist the deflationary trend and to mitigate its effects; and acting out of a lifetime of habit and years of intensifying conviction, he carried out this program by "stimulating others to action" from behind the scenes. Between November 19 and November 27, 1929, he called leaders from industry and labor to the White House for a series of conferences. At these they pledged themselves to maintain the prevailing wage rate, to hold firmly to current employment levels, and to increase construction activity; and at the termination of each conference, the president issued press releases announcing the agreement reached and forecasting an improvement in business conditions as a result of the meeting. In addition, just as he had done in 1921, he contacted each of the state governors and requested that they combat unemployment by "speeding up" "road, street, [and] public building construction."

Then to coordinate the efforts of the business leaders in carrying out their pledges, Hoover turned to his close friend and former Food Administration subordinate, Julius H. Barnes, now president of the United States Chamber of Commerce. . . .

In early December, 1929, Barnes assembled in Washington his National Business Survey Conference, consisting of "more than 400 'key men,' representing every branch of industry, finance, trade and commerce," and designed to plan the "means of carrying out" the president's "efforts to stimulate and stabilize business." Throughout his career, beginning with his creation of the "British Committee" in his 1913 fight for the Panama-Pacific Exposition, Hoover had used similar "celebrity" conferences and committees. Through them, with the coordination of national newspaper and magazine publicity, he had sought to carry his ideas to the larger constituencies represented by their members, and he planned now to use the NBSC in the same manner. Addressing its opening session, he told the businessmen that they had been invited "to create a temporary organization for the purpose of systematically spreading into industry as a whole the measures which have been taken by some of our leading industries to counteract the effect of the recent panic in the stock market." What the country needed, he argued, was reassurance that the "vast organism of production and distribution" was "fundamentally stable." . . .

As the NBSC pursued its difficult tasks of maintaining wages and stimulating construction in the private sector of the economy, Hoover, in October, 1930, created another voluntary committee, this time to organize relief for the jobless. In purpose and key personnel, the new agency was virtually identical to the Woods committee that Hoover had called into being at the close of the Conference on Unemployment in 1921. Again, Hoover's old friend, Colonel Arthur Woods, was chairman. . . . Instead of Lupton A. Wilkinson, however, Hoover now retained Edward Bernays to handle public relations; and it was Bernays who gave the agency its official title, the President's Emergency Committee for Employment. There was a "Woman's Division," headed by Lillian D. Gillbreth and Alice M. Dickson, the former a Hoover associate in Belgian relief, the latter in his housing and child health concerns. Their agency organized "Spruce Up Your Home" and "Spruce Up Your Garden" campaigns, activities that were quite similar to the "clean up" campaign of 1921.

In spite of all their activity, however, both NBSC and PECE died quietly and unproductively in the late spring of 1931. By that time, the president was at odds with Woods and especially with Bernays, who had become highly critical of the almost total reliance on words without action. As early as December, 1930, both he and Woods had begun pressing for stronger executive action, increased public works, and "a real set of objectives.". . . .

Why did Hoover not respond to such criticism from within and move in the direction of enlarged federal authority and new governmental responsibilities? A part of the explanation appears to lie in the fact that after almost thirty years of orchestrating national publicity and committee activity, this type of administrative approach had become virtually ingrained. In the beginning, to be sure, during his campaigns for the Panama-Pacific Exposition and the CRB, he had regarded it as being purely instrumental. But during the Food Administration years, he had come to view it as more than a matter of practicality or expediency. It became for him the servant of a strongly held political point of view, the way, in other words, to implement the ideal of decentralized authority with its moral virtues of individual initiative and responsibility; and after seven years of successful coordination of public relations and committee work as secretary of commerce, he was apparently convinced that this was the only type of administration consistent with the "American system." Wedded to it now by temperament and political conviction, convinced, moreover, that it had been eminently "constructive" for a quarter of a century, he could do no other than apply it and persist in it as president.

Hoover's faith in his "theory of administration," i.e., centralized decision-making and decentralized execution, had been frequently affirmed in his campaign speeches. . . . As late as July, 1932, in urging the continuation of PECE's successor, the Organization on Unemployment Relief, he remained convinced of the rightness of his old methods:

> This organization is comprised of leading men and women throughout every state in the Union. . . . [It] is the only agency for national coordination and stimulation for the multitude of voluntary efforts. . . . Voluntary effort amongst our people is of far more importance both morally and financially than the direct aid of local or other governmental agencies.

In his addresses of this period, Hoover was fond of saying that if the nation clung to its institutions and ideals during the economic crisis, those institutions and ideals would emerge stronger than ever after the emergency had passed. He had expressed the same sentiment as food administrator during World War I and as secretary of commerce during the unemployment crisis of 1921.

In the economic chaos following the stock market crash, however, the Hoover public relations strategy of "educating the community to its responsibilities," of "stimulating it to action," of "building public confidence," and of relying upon voluntary cooperation could not work. When used before, improvements had seemed to follow, at least as a matter of coincidence if not result. But now they did not, and in a period marked by the growing insolvency of local institutions, palpably falling construction levels and wage rates, and rising unemployment, the administration's continued insistence on local voluntarism and its optimistic evaluations of the situation opened up a wide credibility gap between observable reality and official assessment. Within two years of his inauguration, Hoover's persistent efforts to combat the depression by "assisting others to action" rather than committing the resources of the federal government had begun to cut heavily into the storehouse of public good will that he had accumulated over the years.

A decline in stature, to be sure, would have attended any man confronted with the economic disaster of the early 1930s. But Hoover's fall was especially precipitous, for the public had expected him to meet and overcome the challenge as he had seemed to do so often in the past. Ironically, although his public relations style was actually a manifestation of a "retiring" personality and a "weak" political philosophy, the image that his publicists had created was quite the opposite, They had not, as he had urged, "kept his name out of" administrative publicity. On the contrary, impressed with Hoover as the hardest-working and most devoted public official of the Harding and Coolidge administrations and charmed by his modesty, they had written of him as "America's handyman," a commanding figure who "acted while others talked," and one whose expertise enabled him to act with "facts" in hand on a dozen economic and social problems. During the campaign of 1928, they had been careful to remind the public of his wartime relief work and his handling of the Mississippi flood. Will Irwin, for example, had produced a motion picture, "The Master of Emergencies," from old CRB, ARA, and Mississippi flood film footage. A number of copies of the movie had been distributed across the country for showings by Republican organizations. Through efforts such as these, the image of a "master of emergencies" was deliberately laid upon that of the resourceful "social engineer." . . .

Thus, when Hoover came to the presidency, it was the "practical" component of his 1920 image of "practical idealist" that had been underscored by his publicists. Not projected nearly so much were his more deeply rooted "idealist" tendency and the almost religious intensity with which he valued "individualism" and its political corollaries, "local initiative and responsibility." Some of the phrasing of Hoover's statements of the 1920s had seemed to suggest a strong pragmatic bent to his mind and social outlook. He had said on occasion that *"words without action are the assassins of idealism"* (Hoover's emphasis) or, again, that "wisdom does not so much consist of knowledge of the ultimate, it consists of knowing what to do next." However, these expressions of the "engineering-scientific" side of his personality had always been undercut by his dogmatic faith in "American Individualism" and by the "American system," which constituted for him, in fact, a kind of ultimate truth. Proud of his Quaker church for holding "the most strongly individualistic concept of any of the churches," Hoover had referred to the sentiments expressed in *American Individualism* as his "gospel." His public addresses on "American Individualism" he had referred to as "preaching sermons," and he had urged copies of *American Individualism* on his friends as being "good for their souls." How this absolutist, religious bent of mind had wrestled with, and finally cancelled out, the "pragmatic" tendency is made clear in two short illogical sentences from *American Individualism*: "We cannot ever afford to rest at ease in the comfortable assumption that right ideas always prevail by some virtue of their own. In the long run they do." . . .

Victimized by a false public image that his habitual privateness and concealment had inadvertently helped to prepare, Hoover's rapid fall from public esteem was also facilitated by the notoriously bad relationship that developed between his administration and the Washington press corps. . . . In October, 1931, Washington correspondent Paul Anderson, a Hoover admirer during the 1920s, asserted:

> The relations of Herbert Hoover with the newspapermen whose work brings them in immediate contact with the Presidential office have reached a stage of unpleasantness without parallel during the present century. They are characterized by mutual dislike, unconcealed suspicion, and downright bitterness. This ugly condi-

tion has frequently been reflected in the utterances of the President and the conduct of his aides, and is bound to be reflected in some of the news dispatches,
although to nothing like the extent of its actual existence.

If only partially "reflected in [their] news dispatches," the bitterness of
some correspondents toward the president was fully revealed in their magazine articles and books. They referred to him sarcastically as the "Big,"
"Great," or "Super Administrator," "The Strong Silent Leader," or the "Big
Executive." . . . In reality, it seems, because of his strong self-image as the man
above politics working unselfishly for the commonweal from behind the
scenes, he tended to see the journalists not as "partners," as he sometimes said,
but as subordinates who should do his bidding to help him to serve the public.
He could not and never did appreciate their role as social critics as well as
reporters. And most of the correspondents, apparently admiring Hoover too
much to realize this, had tolerated both his "thin-skin" and the various measures he had taken as secretary of commerce to regulate all news items passing
out of his news-conscious department. This tolerance began to dissipate
quickly after he became president. . . .

Hard-pressed in meeting ever new developments in the economic crisis,
he felt that he could not afford to spend more time with members of the press
corps, nor was he inclined to be more "open" with them. This, he seemed to
think, might engender the spread of confidence-destroying "leaks" or rumors,
thus delaying what was to him the key to economic recovery, the restoration of
"psychological confidence." As we have seen, he had long believed that "psychology" was a key factor in determining levels of economic activity; and now,
just as he had done as secretary of commerce, he tried to build confidence
through the use of optimistic press releases. This time, however, the strategy
was not working, and for this, he tended to blame an uncooperative press
rather than any defect in his approach. To prevent "sabotage" of his efforts, he
retreated into secrecy, conducted his presidential business in unannounced
conferences and over the telephone in the privacy of his office, and became
increasingly guarded in dealing with journalists. Holding fewer and fewer
press conferences as his term ran its course, he was no longer a "grapevine"
for them. Yet all the while, he kept insisting that they should become more
cooperative, that, in particular, they should "express the justified optimism of
American business, industry, and agriculture." To longtime friends in the press
corps, he requested the cancellation of stories and even the suppression of
news, all in the name of "psychological confidence." . . .

In assessing Hoover's calamitous fall from public esteem, then, one must
conclude that, once the stock market crash had occurred, he was as much a
victim of his own behind-the-scenes, public relations style of administration as
he was of the ensuing depression. Having fashioned a publicity-oriented mode
of administrative procedure to fit the unique requirements of his personality
and philosophy, he had risen to the presidency, almost without design, on the
strength of a "grass roots" popularity indirectly produced by his techniques.

Yet, once in the office, he was confronted with problems that called for a quite different approach, one that his temperament, philosophical convictions, and lack of political skills made virtually impossible for him to adopt. Reacting as only personality, philosophy, and past experience would permit, he applied the same techniques and approach that he had used successfully in the past. But this time they failed. In the lonely isolation of the White House, Hoover's lifelong fears of failure became reality; and ironically, the sense of this was heightened by the image of "master of emergencies" and "social engineer" that his public relations style had created for him. Under the warping pressures of a crisis-dominated presidency, moreover, the traits that had moulded this style and so terribly unsuited him for the times—his distaste, in other words, for public exposure, his inability to dramatize his leadership, his dogmatic individualism and antistatism, his sensitivity to criticism—were painfully revealed for all, even his closest friends, to see; and under the new set of circumstances, such characteristics only antagonized the press, confused and frustrated his aides, publicists, and advisers, and made him all the more unpopular. An effective publicizer of causes throughout his career, Hoover thus saw his own presidency become, paradoxically, a public relations disaster and the White House, truly, "a compound hell."

Production and Consumption: A Balancing Act

The New Leisure

Long before the Wall Street crash of October 1929, it was clear to many observers that the economy was not a simple engine of prosperity. Although few predicted a severe upheaval, the disturbing features of the economy—especially technological unemployment and underconsumption—were a regular feature of pre-Depression forums. One such meeting, excerpted below, was held under the auspices of the Taylor Society and took place in New York City on December 7, 1928.

The Taylor Society was founded in 1911 as an informal vehicle for discussing and popularizing the managerial theory of Frederick W. Taylor. Although Taylor's major contribution was to get more output from workers, some of his followers, including the director of this particular forum, H. S. Person, believed that the society should sometimes step back and assess the impact of Taylor's theory of "scientific management" on the general social order.

Forum participants not only discussed economic problems. They also took up a variety of solutions—the five-day workweek and pensions—which would become basic features of the American economy by 1945. And in the background was the possibility that the consumer of the future would be less interested in washing machines and automobiles and more concerned with a new commodity that no one knew much about—leisure.

What does the discussion reveal about the American economy in the mid-1920s? Was there general agreement among participants? Do Person, Smith, and others share Hoover's assumptions and views? Should participants have been pleased, or troubled, by the "new leisure"?

H. S. Person, Managing Director, Taylor Society:

In three separate conversations during the past six months, three different individuals—one a consulting engineer and two industrial executives—have made essentially the same observation to me *a propos* the shorter work-week and shorter work-day. "I am not certain," each said, "we shall not have to approach this problem as but one aspect of a larger problem which includes also technological unemployment, group insurance, old-age pensions, and so on."

The coincidence of these observations . . . stimulated me to become the instrument for laying before a group of students certain specific propositions, in declarative form and without numerous desirable qualifications, for discussion *en* symposium.

The propositions are as follows:

1. The standard length of the unit work period (day or week) should be governed primarily by the maximum amount of work, scientifically determined, that workers can do and thrive under, proper allowance being made for adult education, recreation, and other cultural factors;
2. A substantial portion of the larger social income which results from marked increase in technological efficiency should be handled after the manner of a credit to be drawn upon by workers after middle age, when physical capacity and productivity decrease as a result of age and of inflexibility in adjustment to new technological conditions. . . .

Elliot Dunlap Smith, Professor of Industrial Engineering, Yale University:

The first thing that occurs to me in regard to this foreground of Dr. Person's television is: Who is going to control this income? If we accept his propo-

From H. S. Person, "The Work-Week or the Work-Life?" *Bulletin of the Taylor Society*, 13 (December 1928), pp. 231–232, 234–237, 239, 241. Reprinted by permission of Society for Advancement of Management. All rights reserved.

sition we must say to the working man, "We would like to have you forego a certain amount of either your earned income or your earned leisure, so that you may have it later when you need it most." Naturally the first answer of the man to whom such a statement is made is, "How do I know that I will get what I forego when my time is fulfilled? . . .

The present day job is characterized by two things, among others. It is being speeded up and it is being narrowed down. Through scientific management and careful time study, we have succeeded in packing every moment on the job with its sixty seconds worth of distance run. In the more scientific shops we have made Kipling's poem not merely an ideal, but a necessity for the man on the job. We have taken out of the job the chance to ruminate. If we look at a tradesman of the old school we shall recall how different the situation was before this speeding up occurred. At the same time, in giving out each job we have said, "This shall be done in this way and no other." A worker must work precisely, according to specifications. By these two means we have taken away from the working man the power of full expression of his personality—of his soul, or whatever you prefer to call it—in his work. At the same time, life is demanding more constructive thought from labor, for bit by bit the laboring class has become the governing class in America. They are becoming the governing class politically because they are becoming aware of their dominating numerical power in government. They are sharing in the government of industry either because they have won this share by their own organized efforts, or because more and more employers have realized that they need the guidance of labor in order to manage well. Thus, on the one hand, while the jobs we have prepared for them have made their working experience narrow and dry, society, on the other hand, is requiring of them an ever wider capacity for judgment.

In the light of this change and of the effect of a man's present conduct on his future self, what insurance for old age is most important—insurance for economic competence, or for intellectual and spiritual competence? It seems to me that here is the weakest point of this proposition. Everything a man is doing from birth until at least well on in his life, is making him. After he leaves school, so long as he remains a worker, his greatest chance to develop and express his personality, to bring out those things in him that make him significant, that make him an individual, that make his life worth while, at least to him under present day factory conditions, come from his leisure. But under Dr. Person's proposition, as I have pointed out, I doubt if the potent place of leisure as insurance for intellecutal and spiritual competence throughout life will be given the recognition that it should have. . . .

J. Douglas Brown, Director, Industrial Relations Section, Princeton University (and one of the authors of the Social Security Act of 1935):

There is no better time for a discussion of this problem of industrial pensions than now when the five-day week is being suggested as a necessity, rather than a luxury, for American industry. Dr. Person has stated the problem concisely and judiciously. Should not the work-week be correlated with the work-life? To bring it down to a concrete question—to employers dealing with both the problem of the sale of their product and the employment of labor—is the five-day work-week more necessary at this time than the forty-five year (let us say) work-life? On the one hand, a seeming underconsumption leads to proposals for a shorter work-week, with more consuming time on the part of labor; on the other hand, the moral and practical obligation of employers to superannuated employees and the possibility of state pensions lead to proposals for an extension of industrial pensions.

The need for industrial pensions can be better discussed by either the industrial executive or the social worker. The economist is too easily accused of being impractical or socialistic if he proposes state pensions as the necessary outcome. It behooves one whose special field is the economics of industrial relations rather than the engineering phase of the problem, to retire to the other side of the question. Is a five-day week to the extent it is an *alternative* to industrial pensions—and the huge cost of pensions must be kept in mind—a *necessity* or a *luxury* for American industry? . . .

The five-day week, some believe with Ford, would create more consumption. It will, if the product is one which requires time to enjoy. Scientific forecasting of consumption of motor cars would probably support Ford, and Ford can profitably make the experiment, if others should imitate him. But there is a multitude of products, and among them the most worth while, which do not require a free Saturday to use; better housing, better clothes, better food, better furniture and, above all, those things which are concerned with the shorter work-life rather than a shorter work-week—preliminary education and old age security. With this vast range of wants, does it take a diversion of an additional four hours a week from production to bring consumption of most goods into balance with production? . . .

It may be far fetched to offer another reason why industrial pensions should be preferred to the five-day week, when the latter is proposed as a cure for technological unemployment. In the past our old workers have become dependent on their children. This has meant that the middle-aged generation has been required to support both the generation preceding it and that which followed. Instead of complete training, whether liberal or technical, the new generation has had to go to work early, in many cases, to help meet family expenses. Blind-alley jobs and narrow training have resulted. When industrial changes have taken place these ill trained workers have found it hard to adapt themselves to new work. Is there not some likelihood that industrial pensions and better trained men will give us a type of worker for whom technological unemployment will hold less fear? Perhaps by the time we are profiting by pensions on a wide scale, our industrial enterprisers will have become so scientific in forecasting and so appreciative of the importance of security to the worker that technological unemployment will have disappeared.

Paul U. Kellogg, Editor, *The Survey* (a social-service journal), New York:

For a third thing, we are in a period where there is an altogether new and refreshing appreciation of leisure as an individual and social good, as never before since the days of the industrial revolution. Working people have tasted it. I agree with Professor Smith as to what it may mean to them, and as to the high significance of the American Federation of Labor's coming out for a long week-end rather than a fatter pay envelope. Here we are just on the threshold of something that may be as important as those new discoveries in health and education in freeing vast numbers of people to share in a bigger way in what leisure means to life—what, as they get the hang of it, it may mean in opportunity for thought, in cultural enrichment and in the pursuit of happiness.

The Ford, the movie, the shorter working week and what it holds are realities which can be weighed and wanted by wage earning families. . . . As Dr. Simon Patten pointed out prophetically twenty-five years ago, we have entered an age of social surplus rather than deficit. That may prove the most revolutionary change of all. We no longer face such rigid "either's" and "or's." In the popular distribution of that surplus, who can say that labor cannot and will not choose both a lessening of the week's toil and a lengthening of the life's income? . . .

George Soule, Associate Editor, *The New Republic*, New York:

It may be true, as Mr. Brown pointed out, that in the long run we do not have to be afraid of general overconsumption, but the long run is a very indefinite period. And if our increases of productivity are of such a nature that they apply to goods made in enormous quantities to sell at a fairly low price, and if those are, principally, not the necessities of life, but the luxuries (the things that are constantly being added to the structure of what we superficially call the standard of living) then we are faced with the necessity, if these goods are to be sold, of increasing the real income of the mass of the population as fast as we increase our production of this type of goods. Theoretically, it would be possible to increase production in general, without an increase in real wages, by letting the surplus income go into more and more profits, provided our surplus goods were of the kind which is produced in small quantities and sells for high prices to those with large incomes. But that is not the actual case with American industry. It is of interest to know, in this connection, that in spite of the very rapid increases of productivity, which have continued since 1923, there is no statistical evidence of any appreciable growth of real wages since 1923. The enormous growth of real wages which has been observed, and is usually dated from some time before the war, occurred almost entirely before 1923.

What are we going to do? Are we going to keep on improving efficiency in the narrower sense of the term, finding out how workers can make increasing quantities of things by mass production methods and paying them higher wages if necessary, so that they can absorb these radios, Fords, and so on, *ad infinitum?*

On the Line

The Taylor Society forum and Herbert Hoover's reliance on public relations are evidence of a developing managerial mentality. At the heart of this mentality was the notion that the economy—at least some aspects of it—could be brought under control and "managed." In his own halting way, Hoover tried to manage the national economy. The Taylor Society was involved in planning and managing consumption and leisure. And in the nation's plants and factories, managers probably had more control over the work process in the 1920s than in any decade before or since. Over the past half-century, the work process had been divided into many separate tasks, each performed by an individual. In accordance with Taylor's ideas, knowledge of how the product was made was transferred from labor to management. The skilled worker, who at one time had power and influence because of his understanding of how goods were made, became increasingly rare.

The union movement, which might have stood between the weakened worker and management, found itself attacked from many quarters in the 1920s. Business used the Red Scare to deepen the association of organized labor and radicalism; the courts deprived unions of tools, such as reasonable picketing, essential to successful strikes; and many corporations weakened the ties between workers and legitimate unions through employee stock ownership programs and company-dominated unions.

Still, as the following boardinghouse dialogue indicates, it would be a mistake to think of labor, even unorganized labor, as passively accepting the dictates of employers or the ideology of scientific management. How did workers respond to management's initiatives? What did their efforts have in common with Hoover's efforts to regulate competition in business through associational activities? (See the introduction to this chapter.) Did these workers have some idea that the market for the products they were producing was limited? Were they, in short, aware of the problem of underconsumption and how it was affecting their own lives? Compare the assumptions here to those depicted in the photographs reproduced later in this chapter: to the values that seem implicit in the Lindbergh statue, or in the dancing employees of the Armour plant.

Walter, at the head of the table, was a leader in a group of about fifteen men at the boarding-house. Walter had native wit and a positive way of talking. He assembled automobiles at Plant X. Henry, who sat at his right, was a youngster on assembly work in Plant Y. Mat was the investigator who reported the conversation. He and Henry were exchanging information about their earnings. When Mat stated that he earned 80 cents an hour as a bench assembler at Plant Z, Henry rather proudly announced that he was earning 85 cents an hour. Walter cut into the conversation to say to Henry, "Whenever you earn more than 75 cents an hour working for that outfit you are in danger."

"In danger of what?" Mat demanded.

"Getting your rate cut. Don't let 'em fool you. I know, I've worked for——Company. I was framing boxes with a buddie, and they kept cutting the rate until we had to frame one every 15 minutes and go after our own stock. If we stopped for a drink of water, we got behind. Some fresh guys came in and killed the job. Believe me, nothing like that happens in the bunch where I'm working now. If anybody, new or old, starts to 'put out,' the whole bunch bumps him. We are turning out four cars a day and earning 90 cents an hour. We could earn $2.50 an hour if we 'put out,' but, as it is, our job's one of the best in this town, and we made it so by holding it down."

"Just how do you hold it down?" Mat wanted to know.

"Yesterday they got in a hurry for a job and we put out four and a half cars," Walter explained. "That was $1.12 an hour, but we got a promise from the boss, first, that he would protect us."

"From the foreman or general foreman?"

"There isn't but one and he will keep his promise."

"There is a fellow where I work who is a whole day ahead," Mat stated. "He's got tomorrow's work already stored away under his bench."

"He's a damn fool," said Walter. "He'll get caught at it and all of you will have to work harder for the same money. You should never get more than an hour ahead—any more is dangerous."

"Our group works together and we help each other out," said Henry. "We are ahead."

"Then you are fixing to get a rate-cut, too," was Walter's prompt warning. He turned to the group. "When a worker can go into these plants and earn $35 to $40 a week, he better be satisfied. It used to be that you could earn that much and not work yourself to death; but look what they done to me out where Henry works. The hogs kept coming in and tearing loose at the job until out there now, and most everywhere else in town, you got to go like hell to make out. The only way to protect yourself is *never to let the boss find out what you can put out.*"

"I think I got gypped on my pay last week," Mat complained.

"I don't like the outfit you work for," Walter commented. "They'll gyp you *every* week. And, boy, when they ring in that 'efficiency' business you are sunk. When I worked there, we never knew what we earned until we got our checks. A working man is entitled to know just where he stands every day.

He's got to protect himself. Believe me, we know every minute where I work now just where we stand—we are going to put out four cars a day and *no more.*"

The Lindbergh Phenomenon

Charles Lindbergh's 1927 solo flight across the Atlantic brought an adulation unprecedented in intensity and duration. Not since Andrew Jackson defeated the British at New Orleans in 1814 had a single individual taken on such heroic proportions. In some sense, Lindbergh was a commodity—created by the media, consumed by the public. But it is also safe to say that Americans badly needed a hero in 1927, and that Lindbergh suited them perfectly. What do the photos which follow tell us about what Americans wanted to be, or of what they feared they had become? Why, for example, did one sculptor put Lindbergh in a greasy mechanic's suit? One possibility is that Lindbergh and his plane, the *Spirit of St. Louis*, appealed to people because of what their journey said, in a symbolic way, about work, technology, and the new managerial mentality. To explore this possibility, try to imagine why Lindbergh might have intrigued the boardinghouse workers or the participants in the Taylor forum.

Original Caption: "San Diego, Cal., May 24, 1932—On this field at San Diego, California, now known as Lindbergh Field, the citizens of the city have erected this statue in honor of Col. Charles A. Lindbergh. It was at this field that the "Lone Eagle" first started to learn to fly and the statue depicts him in his old, rough, greasy clothes that made him a familiar figure around the field." *National Archives.*

**Collection of Statuary
Received by Lindbergh,
Thomas Jefferson Memorial
Building, St. Louis, Missouri,
1930.** *National Archives.*

Work and Play

The two photographs that follow show Americans at play. Or are they
at work? Why is it difficult to tell which is which? How have attitudes of
efficiency and productivity, of scientific management, infiltrated the
recreational activities of these individuals?

Original Caption: "Leo
Reisman, musical director of
the Central Park Casino,
discovers that the average
couple covers ten miles in an
evening's dancing. He is
shown here watching William
E. Cook and Ethel Rosevere,
both of whom are wearing a
pedometer on their ankles,
which indicates the ground
covered." 1929. *National
Archives.*

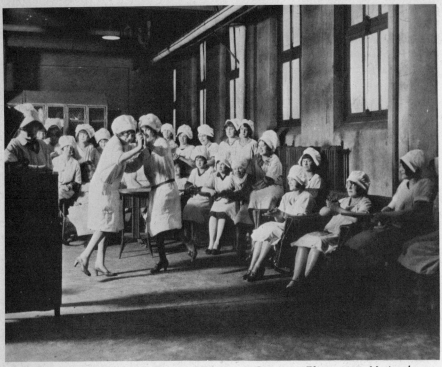

Girls Dancing During Noon Hour at Armour & Company Plant, 1927. *National Archives.*

CHAPTER 9

The Great Depression and the New Deal

The economic decline which followed the stock market crash of October 1929 was unparalleled in the nation's history. Over four million were unemployed in 1930, eight million in 1931, and almost thirteen million, or close to one-fourth of the total civilian labor force, in 1933. Detroit, a city symbolic of the high-flying consumer economy of the 1920s, suffered in proportion to its earlier prosperity. Of the city's 690,000 gainful workers in October 1930, 223,000 were without jobs in March 1931. Because millions of small farmers reacted to falling prices by continuing to produce full crops, agricultural production fell little; farm income, however, was halved in the four years after 1929.

Work for wages was the heart of the economy of the early 1930s, and when it faltered, the effects rippled through every area of American life. In one sixty-day period in Detroit, for example, some fifty thousand homeowners lost the equity in their property—the banks foreclosed on their mortgages and took their homes. Black children went to school without food. Throughout that city, people of all races rummaged through garbage cans in the city's alleys, stole dog biscuits from the pound, and even tried to dig homes in the ground.

Herbert Hoover was not a do-nothing president. His attempts to persuade business to maintain wage rates were moderately successful for more than two years. Through the Agricultural Marketing Act, passed four months prior to the crash, the national government sought to maintain agricultural prices. National expenditures on public works increased. The Reconstruction Finance Corporation lent funds to banks, railroads, building and loan associations, and insurance companies. It saved a number of institutions from bankruptcy.

Perhaps Hoover's greatest failure was his firm opposition to national expenditures for relief. Private charity and city government, the primary agencies of relief, soon proved inadequate. Even in Philadelphia, where philanthropic traditions ran deep, the city's Community Council described its situation in July 1932 as one of "slow starvation and progressive deterioration of family life." Detroit, with its highly developed *public* welfare system, in 1931 debated whether to cut its welfare rolls in half or reduce payments by fifty percent—whether to "feed half the people or half-feed the people."

As people gradually became aware just how deep the crisis went, and as the government under Hoover failed to deal with it, it became obvious that fundamental change of one kind or another might be the only solution. One possible direction of change was dictatorship. The depression was not a domestic crisis only. European nations were just as severely hit as the United States. And there, turning to an authoritarian figure—a Hitler in Germany or a Mussolini in Italy—at least promised to restore order and a sense of purpose. Europe's dictators frightened many Americans. But they also led many to think of strong leadership as a necessary phenomenon of the age, a prerequisite to the restoration of international order and domestic prosperity.

Another possible direction—a threat or a promise, depending on where one stood politically—was revolution. To many, some sort of socialist or communist transformation of the economic and political order seemed the only answer. Early in the decade, the Communist party did make some gains. The party tried to organize unemployed urban workers into "councils," built around neighborhoods, blocks, or even apartment houses. In 1930, these Unemployed Councils managed a series of demonstrations in major cities, drawing crowds ranging from 5,000 to 35,000. Later, after they de-emphasized their talk of immediate revolution, the Communists had some substantial successes within the Congress of Industrial Organizations (CIO), a new and powerful labor union. Large numbers of intellectuals— writers, scientists, teachers, and bureaucrats—also joined the party. The Socialist party, too, began a vigorous program of recruitment and political campaigning, with the very popular Norman Thomas as its presidential candidate.

Into this atmosphere of uncertainty came Franklin Delano Roosevelt. A master at capturing the national mood in his speeches, Roosevelt talked of action, of advance, of what he called a New Deal for the American people.

It was not all talk, of course. Within three months of his inauguration in March 1933, Roosevelt had signed into law a bewildering variety of legislation, much of it designed either to restructure the economy or to bring recovery. In the Emergency Banking Act, Congress gave the president broad discretionary powers over financial transactions. An Economy Act cut government salaries and veterans' pensions in an attempt to balance the federal budget. The Agricultural Adjustment Act granted subsidies to farmers who voluntarily reduced acreage or crops. In an act of boldness not to be repeated, development of the Tennessee River valley was turned over to a public corporation.

Akin to the policy toward agriculture but more comprehensive, the National Industrial Recovery Act (NIRA) attempted to promote recovery by granting businesses the right to cooperate. Each industry wrote its own code of fair competition—setting minimum wages, maximum workweeks, limiting construction of new capacity, even fixing prices by prohibiting sales below cost. In addition, section 7(a) of the NIRA appeared to give workers the right to bargain collectively with employers. (The NIRA is perhaps the best evidence that the New Deal sought to strengthen capitalism rather than replace it with socialism.)

Relief efforts went well beyond those of the Hoover Administration. To absorb the unemployed, Congress created the Civilian Conservation Corps and set up a Public Works Administration to promote construction in the public interest. In 1935, the Works Progress Administration (WPA) was established to coordinate public works. An Emergency Relief Act directed Hoover's Reconstruction Finance Corporation to make relief funds available to the states and signaled the shift away from Hoover's opposition to using federal monies for relief. The Social Security Act of 1935 brought the national government into old-age assistance and insurance and unemployment compensation.

Historians have long debated whether the New Deal had any significant effect on the depression. But of one thing there can be little doubt. Roosevelt did manage to steal the rhetorical thunder from *both* the advocates of dictatorship and the proponents of revolution. And he did so by adopting some of the language of each side. When he presented his legislative program to Congress, he could sound as though he meant to do everything that any European leader could do, asking for "broad Executive power to wage a war against the emergency, as great as the power that would be given to me if we were in fact invaded by a foreign foe." On the other hand, he could sound like a bit of a socialist when the need was there, as when he talked bitterly about the way that "economic royalists" controlled the nation's wealth and had led the people blindly into depression.

Historians have also argued about whether Roosevelt's New Deal "saved" American capitalism, or fundamentally altered it. What he was probably most anxious to save, however, was not the economic system, or even the political structure, but the faith of his constituents *in* the system. The nation did not respond to calls for revolution. The actual power of the Communist party probably declined after Roosevelt's election. On the other hand, those Americans who seemed ready to move toward some kind of dictatorship—with leaders like Senator Huey Long of Louisiana—stood no chance in the long run against Roosevelt's appeal. The "deal" he offered the people may not have been as "new" as he made it sound, but he did convince most of the people that he was in charge of the only game in town.

ARTHUR M. SCHLESINGER, JR.

The Politics of Upheaval

In the following essay, the popular liberal historian Arthur Schlesinger, Jr., discusses the challenge to Roosevelt from "demagogues" on what he thinks of as the political right. As you read, it will be obvious where Schlesinger's sympathies lie. Keep these questions in mind: Why were Americans reluctant to turn to radical solutions? Is Schlesinger disturbed by the ends sought by the "demagogues," or by the means they adopted? Does it seem correct to see Huey Long as in revolt against the "smug and antiquated past" that hung over Louisiana? Can you assess

From Arthur M. Schlesinger, Jr., *The Age of Roosevelt*, 3 vols., vol. 3: *The Politics of Upheaval* (Boston: Houghton Mifflin; Sentry edition, 1966), pp. 15–16, 29–55, 62–64, 66–68, 661–665. Copyright © 1960 by Arthur M. Schlesinger, Jr. Reprinted by permission of Houghton Mifflin Company.

Francis Townsend's program in comparison with similar reform programs discussed earlier in this book? Was Townsend in the mainstream of American life, or outside it? Why were Americans unsuccessful in generating a sustained and cohesive radical response to the most serious depression in the nation's history? Did the system respond so effectively to their needs that radical action seemed inappropriate?

The Rise of the Demagogues

In the half-dozen years before 1935, the American people had been through two profound shocks. The first was the shock of depression, bringing the sudden fear that the national economy could no longer assure its citizens jobs or perhaps even food and shelter. The second was the shock of the New Deal, bringing the sudden hope that the national government offered a magical means of recovery and progress. If the first shock induced a sullen apathy, the second incited a vast discharge of aspiration and energy. The combination of the two shocks—the swift passage from black discouragement to exaggerated optimism—left the people, or at least volatile minorities among them, excited and vulnerable.

The second shock—the impact of the New Deal—terminated the national descent into listlessness and introduced a period of initiative. In the first months this initiative had seemed a presidential monopoly. But soon it began to spread through the country and shoot off in several directions. The people, by uniting their hopes and efforts during the Hundred Days of 1933, regained the energy to fight among themselves in 1934. In the new mood, politics began to recover meaning; the battle of programs and ideas acquired significance once more. Roosevelt, by showing unexpected possibilities in leadership, was exciting others to dream of new leadership (sometimes their own) even more far-reaching and miraculous. The new administration, by restoring a sense of forward motion to American life, was stimulating many Americans to demands which the New Deal itself could not or would not meet.

The reawakening of politics first took place on the right. By the summer of 1934 growing discontent in the business community had led to formation of the American Liberty League, which seemed for a moment the spearhead of conservative opposition to the New Deal. No doubt militance on the right hastened the rise of a corresponding militance on the left. A diffuse and indignant political activism now appeared, compounded of chaotic but passionate yearnings for recognition, salvation, and revenge. If the opposition to the New Deal from the right was, in the main, traditional in its organization and expression, much of that on the left represented something novel in its methods and its purposes.

The left opposition was slower to emerge. Through 1934 Roosevelt and the New Deal had kept the currents of popular discontent from developing significant outlets of their own. Thus the voices of the new unrest played a generally minor role in the congressional elections of the autumn. But with Roosevelt's attack of uncertainty in the months following, the situation began to alter. The apparent vacuum in Washington gave the new political prophets their opportunity. As the President lingered offstage in a seeming paralysis of irresolution, their voices began to sound with increasing confidence. As the President maintained this unwonted silence through the winter and into the spring of 1935, the new clamor began to gain the center of the stage. The rise of the social prophets became the primary political fact of the new year. . . .

No group of Americans, except the Negroes, was harder hit by depression than the aged. There were more old people than ever before: the number of those over sixty had more than doubled since 1900. They were more likely to be sick or disabled than younger people. Where jobs existed, they had far less chance of getting them. In nearly half the states there was no system of old-age pensions; in the rest, pensions averaged around twelve or fifteen dollars a month and were hopelessly inadequate. Nor were these needy old people a rabble of paupers. Depression had brought so-called solid folk into their ranks—men and women who had faithfully worked and saved according to the precepts of the capitalist system and who, in reward for their virtue, had nothing now to keep them in their old age, no savings, no jobs, nothing but relief or charity. Such people were proud and bitter. Their despair was rendered the more poignant by their memories of the America of their youth—a rugged, self-reliant, optimistic land where men always looked ahead to new frontiers.

II

At the same time, this identification with an earlier America gave them a certain incredulity about their present helplessness and thus kept alive the desperate inner conviction that somewhere an answer could be found. So, one morning in the late fall of 1933, Dr. Francis Everett Townsend, an unemployed physician of Long Beach, California, sixty-six years old, looked out his bathroom window while shaving and saw in the alley below, cluttered with rubbish barrels and garbage cans, "three haggard, very old women"—as he later described them—"stooped with great age, bending over the barrels, clawing into the contents." Dr. Townsend had kept his calm through a good deal in the years since the crash. But this indignity to his generation and his country was too much. He broke into a rage of profanity, reminiscent of the days when he had been a doctor in a wide-open town in the Black Hills. He later said, "I let my voice bellow with the wild hatred I had for things as they were." His wife, alarmed, rushed into the room: "Doctor! Oh, you mustn't shout like that! All the neighbors will hear you!" To this, Townsend replied, according to his later recollection, "I want all the neighbors to hear me! I want God Almighty to hear me! I'm going to shout till the whole country hears!"

Francis E. Townsend was ordinarily a gentle man; but a lean intensity occasionally gleamed through his thin face, and he carried from his frontier upbringing a deep belief that America was a land of possibility. He had been born in 1867 in a log cabin on an Illinois farm. Growing up in hard times, he roamed the country west to California, trying his hand at farm labor, mining, homesteading, and schoolteaching. "I came to manhood," he later said, "in the severe depression of the Nineties, so you can see I've had my fill of depression, and that I've reason to hate the word. In the Nineties I was thwarted at every step."

In due course, Townsend decided that he wanted a profession. In 1900, having managed to save up $100, he enrolled in the Omaha Medical College at the age of thirty, the oldest man in his class. For a time he paid his way by selling mail orders to farmers on the sod-house frontier. "This experience in salesmanship stood me in good stead later." Eventually one of his professors lent him the money he needed to finish. The friendly professor, an ardent Socialist, also gave young Townsend the vision that "in a poverty-free world we might see an end to vice and disease." He probably first encouraged Townsend to read Bellamy's *Looking Backward*.

In 1903 Townsend went to a small town on the north slope of the Black Hills. He practiced medicine there for seventeen years until failing health led him to move to Long Beach, California. In Long Beach he kept up practice, but in a desultory way; more of his income came from selling building lots, often for a successful real-estate broker named Robert Earl Clements. Then came the crash, and for a while Townsend caught on as assistant health officer.

The next three years were a shattering experience. Every day needy people, many of them old, crowded the health office. Townsend, treating them in the clinic, visiting them in their homes, saw the depression from the inside— "such distress, pain and horror," he later wrote: "such sobbing loyalties under the worst possible circumstances." He was afflicted particularly by the hopelessness of the old people, their "spiritual panic." When he lost his job with a change in city administration in 1933, he was determined, with all the irrepressible optimism of a man who had grown up on the frontier and read Edward Bellamy, to find the road out. "I suppose I have always been more or less socialistically inclined," he mused in 1959. "I believe we ought to plan as a nation for all the things we need. . . . I suppose that taking care of the people runs against the American grain—against the feeling that everyone ought to hustle for himself. But there comes a time when people can't hustle any more. I believe that we owe a decent living to the older people. After all, they built our country and made it what it is."

III

In September 1933 Dr. Townsend sent a letter to the *Long Beach Press-Telegram*. To solve the problem of unemployment, Townsend said, "it is just as necessary to make some disposal of our surplus workers, as it is to dispose of our surplus wheat or corn." But surplus workers obviously could not be disposed of through slaughter, like surplus hogs. Some means had to be found to

retire them from economic activity. And the natural class to be retired would
be old people. Townsend's proposal was simple. Give everyone over sixty
federal pensions of $150 a month "or more, on condition that they spend the
money as they get it." This program would both pump new purchasing power
into the economy and open up jobs for younger people. The pension system,
Townsend added, could be financed by a national sales tax. . . .

The idea was plainly in the air. Townsend's particular contribution was to
convert the idea into a movement. When his letter set off a mild controversy in
the Long Beach press, Townsend advertised for elderly men and women to
pass around petitions for the pension plan. The ante was quietly upped from
$150 to $200. In two weeks, volunteers had obtained several thousand signatures. Townsend now approached his old real-estate associate [Robert] Clements to help manage the agitation. . . . On January 24, 1934, Townsend and
Clements, along with Townsend's brother, who was a porter in a Los Angeles
hotel, filed the articles of incorporation for a new organization, Old Age Re-
volving Pensions, Ltd.

Clements brought to the movement the hustle of a high-pressure real-
estate promoter. He was thirty-nine years old, a Texan by birth, hard-eyed and
tough, with unusual talents for organization and ballyhoo. Where Townsend
could think of little more to do than circulate petitions and answer mail, Clements perceived the need, as he later put it, of keeping the developing enthusiasm "at a high pitch." In August 1934 he began the formation of local clubs. At
the same time, he started to take over both techniques and organizers from the
Anti-Saloon League (much as the Liberty League was the continuator of the
Association Against the Prohibition Amendment). He found unemployed ministers particularly effective as missionaries for the new faith.

IV

The response was rapid and wistful. For old folks who had lived too long
in the shadows, the promise of $200 a month offered deliverance and dignity.
It told them that the America in which they had grown up, the land of kindliness and faith, was not dead; it meant that their own lives, which they could
not but regard as lives of labor and thrift, would at last have their reward in a
secure old age. In 1934, throughout the West, pathetic old people—mostly
Anglo-Saxon in origin, mostly lower middle class, mostly nonpolitical or Republican—flocked into the Townsend clubs. Some younger people joined
them, hoping to be relieved of the burden of elderly relatives or to benefit by
the new money thrust into circulation. They all listened with rapt attention to
the Townsend orators and obediently sent in their mites to national headquarters.

The atmosphere of the movement was less that of pressure politics than of
the old-time religion. The Townsendites sang hymns and interrupted speakers
with cries of "Amen." Some among them saw in the plan the fulfillment of the
millennial hope. The Townsend ministers were ready to certify authoritatively

that the plan was at least "the God-given way." . . . The Founder himself said that his movement would make "as deep and mighty changes in civilization as did Christianity itself," but "where Christianity numbered its hundreds, in its beginning years, our cause numbered in millions." Once he described the Townsendites as "the instruments through whom the Divine Will proposes to establish on earth the universal brotherhood of man." As the meetings adjourned, the membership sang:

> Onward, Townsend soldiers,
> Marching as to war,
> With the Townsend banner
> Going on before.
> Our devoted leaders
> Bid depression go;
> Join them in the battle,
> Help them fight the foe.

This quasi-religious mood produced an almost hysterical intensity, leading to cruel pressure against nonsigners and to the boycott of merchants who refused to circulate the petitions or put the Doctor's picture in their shop windows. Stanley High, a liberal Methodist minister, wrote Franklin Roosevelt's secretary, Steve Early, about the movement in 1935. "The more I see of it the more I am impressed with its power. It is doing for a certain class of people what—a few years ago—was done by the prohibition movement: giving them a sublimation outlet."

Clements took care that the Townsend organization kept the movement's evangelism under control. The new clubs were permitted no autonomy, and even the organizers had to stick carefully to their scripts. Authority remained firmly in the hands of Townsend and Clements; after all, they were not only apostles of a faith, but owners of an organization. In January 1935 Clements launched the *Townsend National Weekly*; by the end of the year its circulation had leaped to more than 200,000. Patent medicine companies filled its pages with advertisements for bladder tablets, gland stimulators, and the like, headed "How To Live 100 Years" or "Married at 120." Clements saw to it that the ownership of this profitable enterprise was vested, not even in the OARP, but personally in Townsend and himself.

It was Clements whose skill transformed Townsendism from one more crazy California enthusiasm into a crusade. He was quite right to begin, as he did in 1935, billing himself as the Co-Founder.

V

As the Townsend movement grew, the Townsend Plan itself began to take on new dimensions. "The plan is only incidentally a pension plan," Dr. Townsend insisted; "the old people are simply to be used as a means by which prosperity will be restored to all of us." The real objective was nothing less than ending the depression by giving buying power to the masses. "The time has arrived," Townsend said, "when the citizenry must take charge of their government and repudiate the philosophy of want and hunger in a land of wealth and abundance."

Originally, Townsend had meant to finance the plan by a retail sales tax. Then someone pointed out that this would fall most heavily on those least able to pay. In its place Townsend and Clements came up with the idea of a 2 per cent transaction tax, which would hit a commodity, not just at the point of ultimate sale, but every time it changed hands along the way from raw material to finished product. For some reason, this tax, which would have been no more than a multiple sales tax, struck them as more equitable than a retail sales tax—perhaps because they looked to large returns from stock and bond transactions. . . .

The bill was first introduced into the House in January 1935 by John S. McGroarty, an otherwise conservative Democrat who owed his election in the fall of 1934 to Townsend support. McGroarty, who had been chosen poet laureate of California by the state legislature a few years earlier, was himself seventy-two years old. His bill guaranteed a $200 monthly pension to all citizens over sixty on condition that they renounce gainful employment and agree to spend all the pension within the country in thirty days. In April 1935 Mc-Groarty introduced a revised bill which abandoned the flat $200 promise in favor of pensions as large as the reserve fund would permit, but not to exceed $200. (The Townsend leaders approved this, which did not prevent the *Townsend Weekly* from declaring calmly a few months later, "There has never been, nor will be, any compromise on the $200 per month provision in the Townsend demands. All statements to the contrary are false.") The revised bill also added some trivial supplementary taxes and called for an income test.

In the meantime, the Plan was meeting a highly skeptical reaction in most informed circles, liberal or otherwise. Townsend himself guessed that about 8 million men and women would qualify for the Plan, which meant about $1.6 billion disbursed every month. But experts found it hard to believe that, even with a means test, less than 10 million of about 11.5 million people over sixty would qualify. This would mean an annual outlay of $24 billion, about half the national income and twice as much as combined existing federal, local, and state taxes. The Plan, in short, seemed to the unregenerate a system for channeling half the national income to the one-eleventh of the population over sixty.

The Townsendites rejoined that the stimulus to business activity from the forced circulation of the pension money would raise the national income for all and, at the same time, increase the yield from the transactions tax. But opponents questioned whether forced circulation would materially speed up the rate at which money was spent; most Americans, they claimed, were already spending their money the month they received it. And they denounced the transactions tax as regressive and uncollectible. By raising prices, it would reduce purchasing power; it would wipe out profit margins for small business; it would promote economic concentration (since an integrated business would have fewer transactions to be taxed and therefore would be in a better competitive position). In addition, the Plan's provisions for licensing all sellers and for policing the spending of the pension presented vast administrative problems. Provisions for old age might be a good idea—and, indeed, old-age insurance was about to be enacted in the Social Security bill—but the Townsend Plan was fantasy.

None of this impressed the Founder, who prayed, "God deliver us from further guidance by professional economists!" "Every time a 'brain-truster' says this plan is crazy," Townsend told a congressional committee with satisfaction, "a hundred thousand new converts come to our banner. . . . I myself am not a statistician. I am not even an economist, for which fact millions of people have expressed thanks. I am simply a country practitioner of medicine." As Congressman McGroarty put it during the debate in the House of Representatives, "I refuse to talk to college professors. Give me the names of some practical people. [Laughter]." As for the old-age provisions of the Social Security bill, the *Townsend Weekly* denounced them as "outrageous." When Harry Hopkins and Frances Perkins expressed skepticism about the Townsend Plan, the *Weekly* lost all hope in Roosevelt and thereafter scathingly attacked all aspects of the New Deal.

The House approached the Townsend bill in the most gingerly way. No one could afford to be against Mother. . . . Most members of the House, however, were perhaps less concerned with sentimental memories than with the letters and telegrams flooding their offices, the bundles of petitions, the implacable elderly visitors, and the other manifestations of the crusade. When the division finally came, nearly two hundred congressmen bravely absented themselves, and the rest arranged to defeat the proposal without a roll call. According to the Townsend tabulation, 38 Democrats voted for the Plan, 17 Republicans, 3 Progressives, and 2 Farm-Laborites.

The supporters included a number of congressmen better known up to that point as advocates of sales taxes than of old-age pensions. If the pension feature was radical, the tax feature was, after all, profoundly conservative. The Plan thus seemed an all-purpose political weapon, capable of attracting both men of the left eager to dramatize a national need and men of the right eager to find a new basis of popular support.

VI

Townsend's own personality was well designed to put a reassuring face on what seemed at first a radical idea. And the idea, indeed, was all that remained of his youthful utopianism: the splendid dream of Edward Bellamy was dwindling to a huckster's promise of $200 a month for old folks. "One of the great faults of socialism," Townsend told a reporter, "is that it is too vague, people can't get it through their heads. I used to be a Socialist once." There was nothing vague about him now. Nor did he want to risk misunderstanding at a time when the air was full of talk about production-for-use and other such heresies. "We believe," Townsend headquarters declared, "that the profit system is the very main spring of civilized progress." When Upton Sinclair and his End Poverty in California crusade terrified Californian respectability in 1934, Townsend made his position clear. "We don't endorse any socialistic program. The EPIC plan opposes the profit system. The Townsend Plan represents an attempt to make the profit system function." Privately he commented that Sinclair was "our very greatest menace." . . . Roosevelt declined to see him, and the administration had its own social-security program. Stanley High, talking to Townsend in 1935, found him more favorably disposed toward Hoover than toward Roosevelt. . . .

The strain of being a minor prophet was considerable. "Doctor," as his associates called him, was becoming aware of himself as a public figure. He was also becoming aware of the possibilities of his movement. As he wrote Clements in January 1935, "You and I have the world by the tail with a downhill pull on this thing, Earl, if we work it right." As a man with the world by the tail, he could permit himself liberties. His offhand remarks sometimes shocked his disciples. When one brought the rank-and-file of the movement into the conversation, Townsend was reported to have said, "Oh, those old fossils; they don't know what it is all about anyway." Another witness told of complaining to Doctor that Clements had said, "We don't give a damn about the old people"; Doctor responded irritably, "What of it: what of it?"

Clements was infinitely the more cynical of the two. In his frank promoter's way he called the movement "the racket," and when he left in 1936, he took $50,000 for his share in the *Townsend Weekly*. Doctor, on the other hand, let the movement pay no more than his expenses and a salary; there is no evidence that he used it to increase his personal bank account. He had higher rewards. A Townsend state manager once reported the Founder standing before the Lincoln statue in Washington. "Take this man, for example," Doctor said; "just a poor lawyer, no smarter than me and certainly not better educated than me, but just being at the right moment before the people with a plea to save the Nation from slavery . . . and now the world faces a fate worse than slavery and a lowly country doctor comes out of the West to save the world. It might be me sitting up there." . . .

VII

Yet already success was bringing trouble. In the course of 1935 there were stirrings among the rank-and-file—doubts about the rigid centralization of authority, questions about what was happening to the money. For a while Townsend was philosophical. "There are always hell-rumblings in a Townsend organization at all times, I guess," he told Clements. Soon he was taking sterner action against the schismatics, expelling them from the movement, suing them in court, and authorizing editorials in the *Townsend Weekly* which compared himself with Christ and his critics with Judas Iscariot.

Nonetheless, Townsend really believed in his Plan and had the best interests of his movement at heart. In time he felt obliged to recognize the demand from below for a more democratic organization. This brought him into conflict with Clements, who had no intention of relinquishing power. The two men had other differences. Townsend felt that the profits of the *Weekly* should go to the movement; Clements thought they belonged personally to the Founder and the Co-Founder. And on issues Townsend was the more liberal of the two. Where Clements was wedded to the transactions tax, Townsend was willing to listen to criticisms of the tax as regressive and entertain Sheridan Downey's proposal that the pensions be paid for through the issuance of tax-free bonds. Perhaps the most important disagreement, however, had to do with the future of the organization. Clements, impressed by the example of the Anti-Saloon League, wanted the movement to remain a pressure group working within both parties. But by late 1935 Townsend was thinking about organizing a new political party.

Few outside the movement were aware of the strains within. To most, the sudden surge of Townsendism was the striking political phenomenon of 1935. The passage of the Social Security Act could not arrest it; the old-age provisions left millions of old people uncovered, and in any case payments under old-age insurance would not begin till 1942. In August 1935, Stanley High called the Townsend movement "the most vital and fast-moving extra-orthodox movement now under way"; Senator William E. Borah, "the most extraordinary social and political movement in recent years and perhaps in our entire history." "Townsendism," wrote Raymond Moley in December, "is easily the outstanding political sensation as this year ends." "The battle against the Townsend Plan has been lost, I think," reported the economist E. E. Witte, "in pretty nearly every state west of the Mississippi, and the entire Middle-Western area is likewise badly infected."

Much was repellent about the movement—the slick publicity, the autocratic structure, the cynical exploitation of wretchedness and senility, the anti-intellectualism, the economic illiteracy, the greedy emphasis on "$200 a month," the hysteria of the rank-and-file. And the influence of the movement has often been overrated. The Townsend agitation had nothing to do with the initiation of the New Deal social-security policy. Roosevelt established the Committee on Economic Security in June 1934, when the Doctor was unknown outside Long Beach and before there was a Townsend club in existence. Though the threat of the Townsend Plan no doubt speeded the passage of the Social Security bill and assured the inclusion in it of old-age insurance, that bill passed two months before Townsend considered that his own movement "had developed to a size sufficient to justify our calling a national convention."

Yet Townsend and his followers were calling attention in a definitive way to a cruel problem which the American people had too long shoved under the rug. Now the nation could never ignore its old again. And when its chosen issue was not involved, the movement on the whole preserved the old-fashioned kindliness which marked its leader at his best. Though its members were mostly Anglo-Saxon in stock and fundamentalist in faith, Townsend had no truck with racial or religious bigotry. (There were even desegregated Town-send clubs.) He concentrated his own fanaticism and that of his followers on a single goal and for the rest, strove for democracy. Though he himself was wobbled by power, he was not destroyed by it. To the end he kept as best he could the trust reposed in him by millions of elderly people who believed, as he did, that his plan would save them and America. Dr. Townsend had indeed shouted until the whole country heard.

The Messiah of the Rednecks

Louisiana was as natural a breeding place for radicalism as its swamps were for fevers. No state in the Union had been so long misgoverned. The old oligarchy, a dreary alliance of New Orleans businessmen and upstate planners, controlled by the utilities, the railroads, and Standard Oil of Louisiana, had run things without serious challenge almost since Reconstruction. No state had so high a proportion of illiteracy: in 1928, when Huey Long was elected governor, probably one-fifth of the white men on the farms could not read or write. No state treated its children worse: in Louisiana, little boys and girls worked long hours in cane and strawberry fields, in mills and shrimp-packing plants. The system of roads was as run down as the system of schools. And the submerged people of Louisiana had not only been oppressed, they had been bored: no Cole Blease, no Tom Watson, no Heflin nor Bilbo had arisen to make them laugh and hate and to distract them from the drabness of their days. Half a century of pent-up redneck rancor was awaiting release. . . .

Young Huey was the seventh of nine children. He was born in a log house, but it was a comfortable four-room unit, and he was not reared in poverty. Still, he could not escape the drudgery of country life. "From my earliest recollection," he later said, "I hated the farm work. . . . Rising before the sun, we toiled until dark, after which we did nothing except eat supper, listen to the whippoorwills, and go to bed." Only politics and religion—both highly revivalist in style—relieved the tedium. A bright, rather bookish lad, Huey was resolved to be anything but a farmer. He read avidly, particularly romantic history and fiction. . . .

In 1910, when Huey was seventeen, his debating talent won him a schol-arship to Louisiana State University. But he lacked money for books and living expenses; so he put his volubility to other uses and became a traveling sales-man. He sold furniture, soap, groceries, patent medicines for "women's sick-ness" and a vegetable shortening product called Cottolene. . . . In 1912, having strayed as far west as Oklahoma, Long spent a few months at the University of Oklahoma Law School, "the happiest days of my life." When the session ended, he returned to the road. In 1913 he married Rose McConnell, and the next year, with a few hundred dollars of savings and a loan from his brother Julius, he entered Tulane University Law School in New Orleans. Now he applied himself with frenzied determination. Studying from sixteen to twenty hours a day, he completed a three-year law course in eight months. Then he talked the Chief Justice of the state into giving him a special bar examination. In May 1913 he was sworn in as a lawyer. He was twenty-one years old. . . .

And Huey Long meant to help the good people in their consideration. After a careful examination of the state constitution, he found that the post of Railroad Commissioner had no prescribed age limit. In 1918, twenty-five years old, he announced for this office, noisily assailed the big corporations, and won election. During the next nine years on the Railroad Commission and its successor, the Public Service Commission, Huey seized every opportunity to dramatize himself as the champion of the people against the oil companies, the telephone company, the utilities, and the railroads. Nor was this all merely whooping and hollering. His shrewd and persistent attacks put the companies on the defensive and brought rates down.

In 1924 he tried to cash in on this record by running for governor. It was too soon: he was barely thirty-one years old. And he was caught in the cross fire between the Klan and its opponents. Long straddled this issue; despite his poor white sympathies, he did not, like Hugo Black in Alabama, join the Klan.

A few months before the 1928 primaries he again showed up as a candidate, his followers parading under a banner reading (the phrase was adapted from William Jennings Bryan): "EVERY MAN A KING, BUT NO ONE WEARS A CROWN." Huey campaigned furiously around the state, speaking at dusty crossroads and in shaded courthouse squares, his voice raucous and confiding, his arms pumping up and down, his seersucker suit stained with sweat. The poor white farmers—lean, leather-faced, rawboned men, surly and proud—crowded to see him. When he deluged the prominent figures in the community with unsparing personal abuse, they shouted, "Pour it on 'em, Huey! Pour it on 'em!" The oligarchy bewailed his uncouthness, his vituperation, his lack of dignity. "This State's full of sapsucker, hillbilly, and Cajun relations of mine," Long replied, "and there ain't enough dignity in the bunch to keep a chigger still long enough to go brush his hair." And the sapsuckers, the hillbillys, and the Cajuns, the woolhats and the rednecks, laughed and cheered and voted for one of their own. In 1928 they elected Huey Long Governor of Louisiana. He was now thirty-five. . . .

Though Huey would occasionally sell for a price, he could never be relied on to deliver. His essential ambition was not money but power, and he did not want to share the power with anybody else. He proposed now to smash the oligarchy and gain undisputed power for himself. Nor, perhaps, was it just for himself. Huey had not forgotten the poor people of Louisiana. As Governor, he was determined to increase school appropriations, to provide free textbooks, to pave highways and bridge rivers, to build charity hospitals and insane asylums. Long knew where the money was coming from—the big corporations, and especially Standard Oil.

He launched his program with characteristic vigor. When the legislature balked, the Governor appeared personally at the Capitol to cajole, threaten, browbeat, and bribe. He ignored the separation of powers, treated senators and representatives with unconcealed contempt, and bulled through enactments with careless confidence. One opponent shoved a volume before the Governor: "Maybe you've heard of this book. It's the Constitution of the State of Louisiana." "I'm the Constitution around here now," Long replied. . . .

He carried these qualities to Washington—the comic impudence, the gay egotism, the bravado, the mean hatred, the fear. He was a man propelled by a greed for power and a delight in its careless exercise. "The only sincerity there was in him," said Julius Long, "was for himself." He talked broadly about the need for redistributing the wealth, but these were words. When a reporter tried to discover deeper meanings, Long brushed him off: "I haven't any program or any philosophy. I just take things as they come." Yet, for all this, there remained some sense in which his qualities and his ambitions were those of the plain people of his state writ large—the people from the red clay country and the piny woods, from the canebrakes and the bayous, the shrimp fishermen and the moss fishermen, the rednecks and the hillbillies and the Cajuns. Once, standing before the Evangeline Oak, he spoke to the Acadians of southern Louisiana and recalled the legend of Evangeline, weeping for her vanished lover. She was not, Long said, the only Acadian thus to have waited and wept.

> Where are the schools that you have waited for your children to have, that have never come? Where are the roads and the highways that you spent your money to build, that are no nearer now than ever before? Where are the institutions to care for the sick and disabled? Evangeline wept bitter tears in her disappointment. But they lasted only one lifetime. Your tears . . . have lasted for generations.

His conclusion seemed to come from the heart: "Give me the chance to dry the tears of those who still weep here." . . .

At first, Long was—or seemed—enthralled by Roosevelt. "When I was talking to the Governor today," he told a newspaperman in October 1932, "I just felt like the depression was over. That's a fact. I never felt so tickled in my life." After the election, he expressed a constant fear that the new administration might be captured by the reactionaries; but his personal susceptibility to Roosevelt remained undiminished. In January he called on the President-elect at the Mayflower in Washington. "I'm going to talk turkey with Roosevelt," he shouted to reporters, "I am going to ask him, 'Did you mean it or didn't you?' Goddam it, there ain't but one thing that I'm afraid of—and that's the people." He then pounded at the door of Roosevelt's suite, an action he obligingly repeated for the photographers. Half an hour later Huey emerged jubilant. "I come out of this room happy and satisfied," he said. "We've got a great President." Some one asked whether Roosevelt intended to crack down on him. "Crack down on me?" said Long. "He don't want to crack down on me. He told me, 'Huey, you're going to do just as I tell you,' and that is just what I'm agoin' to do." . . .

During the Hundred Days Long's suspicions steadily mounted. He disliked the conservative measures of the first month, such as the Economy Act, strongly supported the inflation drive of April, and in May denounced the administration on the ground that it was dominated by the same old clique of bankers who had controlled Hoover. "Parker Gilbert from Morgan & Company, Leffingwell, Ballantine, Eugene Meyer, every one of them are here— what is the use of hemming and hawing? We know who is running the thing." The National Recovery Act completed his alienation. . . .

X

Long thus built his kingdom—the nearest approach to a totalitarian state the American public had ever seen. And Louisiana was only the beginning. Now that Frank-lin De-La-No Roo-Se-Velt (as he called him, giving unctuous emphasis to each syllable of the hated name) had turned out to be a stooge of the bankers, the Kingfish was out to save all America. . . .

As Long looked at America, he conceived the maldistribution of wealth to be the cause of all social and economic distress. "When one man decides he must have more goods to wear for himself and his family than any other ninety-nine people, then the condition results that instead of one hundred people sharing the things that are on earth for one hundred people, that one man, through his gluttonous greed, takes over ninety-nine parts for himself and leaves one part for the ninety-nine." But one man could not eat the food intended for ninety-nine people, nor wear the clothes, nor live in the houses. And, as the rich grew richer and the poor poorer, the middle class was threatened with extinction. "Where is the middle class today?" Long asked in 1933. "Where is the corner groceryman, about whom President Roosevelt speaks? He is gone or going. Where is the corner druggist? He is gone or going. Where is the banker of moderate means? He is vanishing. . . . The middle class today cannot pay the debts they owe and come out alive. In other words, the middle class is no more." Its only hope of resurrection, Long suggested, was to follow him.

His actual program underwent a succession of versions. The share-the-wealth resolution of 1932 proposed that the government take by taxation all income over $1 million and all inheritances over $5 million. In 1933 he added a capital levy which would reduce all fortunes to somewhere around $3 million. By 1934 he was emphasizing the result more than the method: government would furnish every American family with a "homestead allowance" of at least $5,000 and an annual income of at least $2,000. There were, in addition, fringe benefits. Hours of labor would be limited. Agricultural production and consumption would be balanced through government storage and the control of planting. Everyone over sixty would receive an "adequate" pension (this was first to be $30 a month, but the competition of Dr. Townsend changed that; as Gerald L. K. Smith, the director of Long's movement, explained, "We decided to put in the word 'adequate' and let every man name his own figure. This attracted a lot of Townsendites to us"). Boys and girls of ability would receive a college education at government expense. And no one need worry about money: "taxes off the big fortunes at the top will supply plenty of money without hurting anybody."

Share-the-wealth was, in short, a hillbilly's paradise—$5,000 capital endowment without work, a radio, washing machine, and automobile in every home. It was the Snopeses' dream come true. It had almost no other quality. While Coughlin and Townsend at least went through the motions of economic analysis, Long rested his case on rhetoric and the Scriptures. "I never read a line of Marx or Henry George or any of them economists," he once said. "It's all in the law of God." In 1935 he was still using the same statistics he had used in 1918. He wildly overestimated what the government would gain from confiscation; he underestimated the number of families who would need to have their income jacked up to the $5,000 limit; he ignored the problems involved in redistributing nonmonetary wealth; and he showed little interest in such a mundane issue as economic recovery.

XI

And yet, as economic fantasy, it produced a response. Wealth *was* unfairly distributed. Many of the poor were consumed with envy and rancor. The New Deal seemed awfully complicated and, to some, very far away. Encouraged, the Kingfish decided in January 1934 to convert his aspiration into a crusade. He launched the Share Our Wealth Society and called on Americans everywhere to organize local chapters. "Be prepared for the slurs and snickers of some high ups," he warned. ". . . Be on your guard for some smart aleck tool of the interests to come in and ask questions. . . . To hell with the ridicule of the wise street-corner politician! . . . Who cares what consequences may come following the mandates of the Lord, of the Pilgrims, of Jefferson, Webster and Lincoln? He who falls in this fight falls in the radiance of the future." . . .

XII

At the beginning of 1935, in his forty-second year, Long gave off a sense of destiny. Would there be a third party in 1936? "Sure to be. And I think we will sweep the country." Foreign visitors found him impressive, though unattractive. Rebecca West detected the steely intelligence behind the Mardi Gras mask of his conversation: "He is the most formidable kind of brer fox, the self-abnegating kind that will profess ignorance, who will check his dignity with his hat if he can serve his plans by buffoonery." She said later, "In his vitality and his repulsiveness he was very like Laval." He reminded H. G. Wells of a "Winston Churchill who has never been at Harrow."

Yet the nature of this destiny remained obscure, even to him. All he had was a sense of crisis and opportunity. . . . He often said, with his impish grin, "What this country needs is a dictator." But he also said, "I don't believe in dictatorships, all these Hitlers and Mussolinis. They don't belong in our American life. And Roosevelt is a bigger dictator than any." Then again: "There is no dictatorship in Louisiana. There is a perfect democracy there, and when you have a perfect democracy it is pretty hard to tell it from a dictatorship." . . .

In 1935 some people wondered whether Long was the first serious American fascist. Long himself, when George Sokolsky asked him about it, laughed it off: "Fine. I'm Mussolini and Hitler rolled in one. Mussolini gave them castor oil; I'll give them tabasco, and then they'll like Louisiana." But he was no Hitler or Mussolini. He had no ideological preoccupations; he never said, "When the United States gets fascism it will call it anti-fascism," nor was he likely to think of it in such terms. Read *Mein Kampf*, and one sees a man possessed by a demonic dream which he must follow until he can purge all evil from the world. Read *Every Man a King*, and one finds a folksy and rather conventional chronicle of political success. Read Long's *My First Days in the White House*, ghost-written by a Hearst reporter in 1935, and one has a complacent picture of a painless triumph, with Rockefeller, Mellon and the du Ponts backing President Long in his project of sharing the wealth (the book did have one engaging impudence: in choosing his cabinet, Long appointed as his Secretary of the Navy Franklin D. Roosevelt). Long's political fantasies had no tensions, no conflicts, except of the most banal kind, no heroism or sacrifice, no compelling myths of class or race or nation.

He had no overriding social vision. According to Raymond Daniell, who covered him for the *New York Times*, he did believe in Share Our Wealth "with all his heart"; but it was as a technique of political self-aggrandizement, not as a gospel of social reconstruction. Part traveling salesman, part confidence man, part gang leader, he had at most a crude will toward personal power. He had no doubt about becoming President: the only question was whether it was to be in 1936 or 1940. He told Forrest Davis that he planned to destroy both major parties, organize a single party of his own, and serve four terms. To Daniell he disclosed "the whole scheme by which he hoped to establish himself as the dictator of this country." His hero was Frederick the Great, and he no doubt saw himself as a kind of Frederick the Great from the piney woods. ("He was the greatest son of a bitch who ever lived. 'You can't take Vienna, Your Majesty. The world won't stand for it,' his nitwit ambassadors said. 'The hell I can't,' said old Fred, 'my soldiers will take Vienna and my professors at Heidelberg will explain the reasons why!' Hell, I've got a university down in Louisiana that cost me $15,000,000, that can tell you why I do like I do.")

At bottom, Huey Long resembled, not a Hitler or a Mussolini, but a Latin American dictator, a Vargas or a Perón. Louisiana was in many respects a colonial region, an underdeveloped area; its Creole traditions gave it an almost

Latin American character. Like Vargas and Perón, Long was in revolt against economic colonialism, against the oligarchy, against the smug and antiquated past; like them, he stood in a muddled way for economic modernization and social justice; like them, he was most threatened by his own arrogance and cupidity, his weakness for soft living and his rage for personal power.

OSKAR SCHULZE

Saving the Elderly from Themselves

Traditional politicians found Francis Townsend's grip on older persons threatening. Roosevelt ignored him, the Congress investigated him, and together they sought—unsuccessfully—to undercut the movement with the Social Security Act. At the local level, social workers faced a similar problem. They, too, saw Townsend as irresponsible and dangerous. And they, too, sought to direct older persons to more "appropriate" activities and toward a more "responsible" politics.

One of the pioneers in this kind of social work was Oskar Schulze (pronounced Schult-ze), who emigrated in 1933 from his native Germany, where as a Dresden city councillor and Leipzig mayor he had developed a substantial reputation as an administrator of social-welfare programs. In the late 1930s and early 1940s he worked in Cleveland with private foundations and public-welfare agencies to create the Golden Age Clubs. Success, however, was achieved in Chicago. In this selection, Schulze describes the Chicago project and explains its social importance. What assumptions does Schulze make about old people? Why are they unhappy? What techniques does he apply to treat the problem? Are they legitimate? What does the passage contribute to an understanding of the role of the private foundation (which funded the clubs) in American life?

Although this selection deals only with older persons, students should realize that the same kinds of reasoning, and the same kinds of treatment, could be and were applied to other groups that were considered too militant, or too radical, or too disorderly. Workers were often described in these terms (especially by business, of course), and so were juvenile "delinquents." If one were to apply Schulze's way of looking at things to workers and delinquents, what would be the equivalent of the Townsend clubs? What solutions might one advocate?

Since the beginning of the present year the Olivet Settlement of Chicago has devoted particular attention to aged people past 65. It has been my privilege to participate in this task from its very inception. The longer I engaged in this work the keener my interest grew in it as well as in the manifold problems related to it; gradually I became aware of what a significant problem confronted us, especially in view of the extraordinarily changed composition of the population in the U.S.

To illustrate this latter fact I want to point out briefly the following data: The percentage of the population under 5 years of age has decreased during 1870–1930 from 14.30% to 9.32% and the absolute number of children under 5 years has decreased consistently since 1920. The percentage of old people over 65 years on the contrary amounting in 1870 to only 2.99% and in 1935 to not more than 6% is going to reach 11.6% in 1965 according to the figures given by the Bureau of Census in Washington. In other words: The proportion of children in the total population is becoming smaller, while that of elderly people is constantly increasing.

The sole aim of these lines is to endeavor to enlarge upon a few of the questions arising from the above-mentioned data. Of especial importance is the answer to this question: "What added responsibility devolves upon the profession of social service in general and that of groundwork in particular, in consideration of the fact that in the near future we shall become a nation with so large a population of aged people?"

Viewed from the sheer point of numbers, it is obvious and incontestable that the elderly people are coming to represent a constantly increasing political influence in the state and nation. That this fact has been duly recognized by political parties is apparent in times of elections, when candidates and factions go out of their way to cater to organized groups of elderly people. Experience has demonstrated that it is precisely these men and women in the twilight of their careers who are most susceptible to the blandishments of a clever propaganda.

To corroborate this statement, I should like to cite a very distressing experience which occurred under republican Germany. During the catastrophic inflation of 1923 the middle class lost most of its property and wealth. Virtually all economic and social groups who had possessed some inherited property or who had managed to lay by some savings for old age, by dint of many years of struggle and sacrifice, became suddenly impoverished and had to resort to public relief. The embitterment of these strata of the population, helpless victims of an economical upheaval, was boundless. The tragic plight of these victims was given especially sympathetic consideration in that these so-called

From Oskar Schulze, "A Neglected Age of Social Group Work," address delivered at the Olivet Institute, Chicago, 1940. From the archives of The Benjamin Rose Institute, Cleveland, Ohio. Reprinted by permission.

"Klein-Rentner" (pensioners or people living off a modest revenue) were granted benefits 25% higher than the normal relief allowance. Furthermore they received substantial aid from various bequests and philanthropic foundations. But all this extra assistance beyond normal relief grants did not avail to lessen the bitterness and despair of the ruined middle class. On the contrary their demands became constantly more exacting, so much so that it became impossible to fulfill them. It is, therefore, not to be wondered at that they eagerly hearkened to Hitler's siren call.

It is interesting to recall today the fact that at first the masses of the German workers did not vote for Hitler but largely the so-called "Buerger-lichen", i.e. the middle and higher class. The workers' parties received nearly the same number of votes until the last "normal" election in Germany, but all those who were expropriated in the inflation, succumbed completely to the propaganda of Hitler.

In my work here in Chicago I have observed the same psychology among the old people as in Germany. It is my firm conviction that it is very easy to influence the old people here likewise with clever propaganda. How important this is will be evident when I recall the fact that already in 1930 the percentage of the people of 45 and up was 23 and 10–15 years from now they will constitute more than $\frac{1}{3}$ of the total population. Therefore it will be easier to obtain a majority for proposals like the Townsend plan . . . What dire consequences might flow from such fantastic schemes has been pointed out often enough. But what specific measures can and should be adopted to obviate such a radical swing among these masses? This problem has, unfortunately, thus far received but very meagre attention. . . .

I shall endeavor to demonstrate, through the experiment now in progress at the Olivet Settlement in Chicago, what direction care for the aged might take. Our first step, with the help of an available list of names, was to invite the elderly people living in the neighborhood of the settlement to attend a social gathering one afternoon a week. A large proportion of these people responded, despite the severe winter weather. The settlement arranged for these guests a program consisting of musical numbers, movies, lectures, etc., given on Friday afternoons. On one occasion the children of the settlement kindergarten presented a program of songs and dances. Another time we took them through the settlement and explained to them the various activities of the institution. After the close of the program refreshments were served, followed by all kinds of games, such as Chinese Checkers, Chess, and Cards.

It was found desirable to continue sending them the weekly announcement by postcard, as we realized that the old folks, most of whom received almost no other mail for weeks at a time, took these invitations very seriously.

When we began our work among these oldsters, many of them regarded us with suspicion. Again and again I would hear this query: "What do you want from us?" Even among themselves they were, for a time, extremely reticent and mistrustful. Only gradually did we succeed in making them feel at ease with each other, inducing them to engage in games, and to join in the entertainment and conversation. I then proceeded to make regular visits to their homes. For the most part I was cordially received. In the course of these personal calls I learned almost their entire life's history. And I soon became aware that every one of my elderly friends had an interesting story to relate. To be sure, many of these stories closely parallelled those of their kind in Germany; only it was the Depression rather than inflation, which brought about their impoverishment.

These home visits served the useful purpose of a basis for future efforts, since they contributed toward establishing a feeling of mutual confidence. Naturally, the fact that I was able to speak to many of my clients in their native language, German, helped considerably to "break the ice" and give me "open sesame". Above all these personal interviews helped to give me a clear picture of the conditions and environment in which they lived. . . .

The results of five months of activity in this field are indeed extremely encouraging. We have by now a stable group of about 30 men and women, ranging in age from 65 to 97, and are confident that this number will be measurably augmented next fall through plans now under consideration. As a matter of fact the group as now constituted scarcely bears any resemblance to what it was in its early days. Those who attended the meetings the first few weeks were a shy and distrustful lot, scarcely fitted temperamentally for lively social get-togethers; yet today they have become a happy crowd of old folks, knit together by ties of friendship. At times it almost seems as if they had undergone a metamorphosis. Their former timidity and attitude of suspicion has vanished. They come to us with their problems and seek enlightenment on controversial questions. For example before the recent Primary Elections we were so swamped with their requests for information that we decided to set aside an afternoon for a discussion of this matter. We procured a speaker from a Woman's Club, who explained in detail the workings of the primaries, and answered their numerous questions. The situation that presented itself before the election afforded ample evidence of the devices employed by various politicians and candidates to ingratiate themselves with the older voters, and of how susceptible the latter are to the lure of the demagogue.

At the most recent meeting a committee was elected by the group to take charge of arrangements for future meetings, and to prepare plans for special entertainments. This action is in full accord with my aims to win over the old folks themselves toward a program of active participation in care for the needy aged. I made some headway in this direction when I called upon members of our group to look after certain old folks who had been absent several times from the meetings and were apparently ill. It is my belief that much more can be achieved in the direction of organizing the collaboration of these "oldsters" in aiding one another. In this manner a two-fold goal would be attained. On the one hand we would have at our disposal a valuable auxiliary; and on the other hand the life of these people, who by their own statements have nothing to do, would again become invested with some dignity and meaning through services, however small, rendered their fellowmen and women. . . .

FRANKLIN D. ROOSEVELT

Nothing to Fear but Fear Itself: FDR's First Inaugural, 1933

Franklin D. Roosevelt had soundly defeated Herbert Hoover in November 1932. He had received 57.4 percent of the popular vote to his rival's 39.7 percent. The left, too, seemed to have been badly beaten. Norman Thomas and the Socialists had attracted only 2.2 percent of the electorate, while William Z. Foster's Communist following amounted to less than 1 percent. Although voters had largely remained within the major parties, Roosevelt assumed in his first inaugural address that economic conditions warranted the assumption by the president of extraconstitutional powers. Eleanor Roosevelt found the inauguration "a little terrifying, . . . because when Franklin got to that part of his speech when he said it might become necessary for him to assume powers ordinarily granted to a President in war time, he received his biggest demonstration." Most of the half-million persons who wrote in response to the address felt that Roosevelt had correctly analyzed the situation. "It was the finest thing this side of heaven," wrote one; "Your human feeling for all of us in your address is just wonderful," wrote another.

Does this first inaugural address contain a coherent program or consistent philosophy? Do Roosevelt's proposals in every case go beyond Hoover's actions? What arguments does Roosevelt use to justify his demands for authority beyond that constitutionally granted to the president? Was Roosevelt's "nothing to fear" approach simply another version of Hoover's moral suasion? Did he have anything to say to the old people that Oskar Schulze would discover in Chicago eight years later?

I am certain that my fellow Americans expect that on my induction into the Presidency I will address them with a candor and a decision which the

From U.S. Congress, House, *Inaugural Addresses of the Presidents of the United States: From George Washington 1789 to Lyndon Baines Johnson 1965*, House Document No. 51, 89th Cong., 1 sess. (Washington, D.C.: Government Printing Office, 1965), pp. 235–239.

present situation of our Nation impels. This is preeminently the time to speak the truth, the whole truth, frankly and boldly. Nor need we shrink from honestly facing conditions in our country to-day. This great Nation will endure as it has endured, will revive and will prosper. So, first of all, let me assert my firm belief that the only thing we have to fear is fear itself—nameless, unreasoning, unjustified terror which paralyzes needed efforts to convert retreat into advance. In every dark hour of our national life a leadership of frankness and vigor has met with that understanding and support of the people themselves which is essential to victory. I am convinced that you will again give that support to leadership in these critical days.

In such a spirit on my part and on yours we face our common difficulties. They concern, thank God, only material things. Values have shrunken to fantastic levels; taxes have risen; our ability to pay has fallen; government of all kinds is faced by serious curtailment of income; the means of exchange are frozen in the currents of trade; the withered leaves of industrial enterprise lie on every side; farmers find no markets for their produce; the savings of many years in thousands of families are gone.

More important, a host of unemployed citizens face the grim problem of existence, and an equally great number toil with little return. Only a foolish optimist can deny the dark realities of the moment.

Yet our distress comes from no failure of substance. We are stricken by no plague of locusts. Compared with the perils which our forefathers conquered because they believed and were not afraid, we have still much to be thankful for. Nature still offers her bounty and human efforts have multiplied it. Plenty is at our doorstep, but a generous use of it languishes in the very sight of the supply. Primarily this is because the rulers of the exchange of mankind's goods have failed, through their own stubbornness and their own incompetence, have admitted their failure, and abdicated. Practices of the unscrupulous money changers stand indicted in the court of public opinion, rejected by the hearts and minds of men.

True they have tried, but their efforts have been cast in the pattern of an outworn tradition. Faced by failure of credit they have proposed only the lending of more money. Stripped of the lure of profit by which to induce our people to follow their false leadership, they have resorted to exhortations, pleading tearfully for restored confidence. They know only the rules of a generation of self-seekers. They have no vision, and when there is no vision the people perish.

The money changers have fled from their high seats in the temple of our civilization. We may now restore that temple to the ancient truths. The measure of the restoration lies in the extent to which we apply social values more noble than mere monetary profit.

Happiness lies not in the mere possession of money; it lies in the joy of achievement, in the thrill of creative effort. The joy and moral stimulation of work no longer must be forgotten in the mad chase of evanescent profits.

These dark days will be worth all they cost us if they teach us that our true destiny is not to be ministered unto but to minister to ourselves and to our fellow men.

Recognition of the falsity of material wealth as the standard of success goes hand in hand with the abandonment of the false belief that public office and high political position are to be valued only by the standards of pride of place and personal profit; and there must be an end to a conduct in banking and in business which too often has given to a sacred trust the likeness of callous and selfish wrongdoing. Small wonder that confidence languishes, for it thrives only on honesty, on honor, on the sacredness of obligations, on faithful protection, on unselfish performance; without them it can not live.

Restoration calls, however, not for changes in ethics alone. This Nation asks for action, and action now.

Our greatest primary task is to put people to work. This is no unsolvable problem if we face it wisely and courageously. It can be accomplished in part by direct recruiting by the Government itself, treating the task as we would treat the emergency of a war, but at the same time, through this employment, accomplishing greatly needed projects to stimulate and reorganize the use of our natural resources.

Hand in hand with this we must frankly recognize the overbalance of population in our industrial centers and, by engaging on a national scale in a redistribution, endeavor to provide a better use of the land for those best fitted for the land. The task can be helped by definite efforts to raise the values of agricultural products and with this the power to purchase the output of our cities. It can be helped by preventing realistically the tragedy of the growing loss through foreclosure of our small homes and our farms. It can be helped through insistence that the Federal, State, and local governments act forthwith on the demand that their cost be drastically reduced. It can be helped by the unifying of relief activities which to-day are often scattered, uneconomical, and unequal. It can be helped by national planning for and supervision of all forms of transportation and of communications and other utilities which have a definitely public character. There are many ways in which it can be helped, but it can never be helped merely by talking about it. We must act and act quickly.

Finally, in our progress toward a resumption of work we require two safeguards against a return of the evils of the old order; there must be a strict supervision of all banking and credits and investments; there must be an end to speculation with other people's money, and there must be provisions for an adequate but sound currency.

There are the lines of attack. I shall presently urge upon a new Congress in special session detailed measures for their fulfillment, and I shall seek the immediate assistance of the several States.

Through this program of action we address ourselves to putting our own national house in order and making income balance outgo. Our international trade relations, though vastly important, are in point of time and necessity secondary to the establishment of a sound national economy. I favor as a practical policy the putting of first things first. I shall spare no effort to restore world trade by international economic readjustment, but the emergency at home can not wait on that accomplishment.

The basic thought that guides these specific means of national recovery is not narrowly nationalistic. It is the insistence, as a first consideration, upon the interdependence of the various elements in all parts of the United States—a recognition of the old and permanently important manifestation of the American spirit of the pioneer. It is the way to recovery. It is the immediate way. It is the strongest insurance that the recovery will endure.

In the field of world policy I would dedicate this Nation to the policy of the good neighbor—the neighbor who resolutely respects himself and, because he does so, respects the rights of others—the neighbor who respects his obligations and respects the sanctity of his agreements in and with a world of neighbors.

If I read the temper of our people correctly, we now realize as we have never realized before our interdependence on each other; that we can not merely take but we must give as well; that if we are to go forward, we must move as a trained and loyal army willing to sacrifice for the good of a common discipline, because without such discipline no progress is made, no leadership becomes effective. We are, I know, ready and willing to submit our lives and property to such discipline, because it makes possible a leadership which aims at a larger good. This I propose to offer, pledging that the larger purposes will bind upon us all as a sacred obligation with a unity of duty hitherto evoked only in time of armed strife.

With this pledge taken, I assume unhesitatingly the leadership of this great army of our people dedicated to a disciplined attack upon our common problems.

Action in this image and to this end is feasible under the form of government which we have inherited from our ancestors. Our Constitution is so simple and practical that it is possible always to meet extraordinary needs by changes in emphasis and arrangement without loss of essential form. That is why our constitutional system has proved itself the most superbly enduring political mechanism the modern world has produced. It has met every stress of vast expansion of territory, of foreign wars, of bitter internal strife, of world relations.

It is to be hoped that the normal balance of executive and legislative authority may be wholly adequate to meet the unprecedented task before us. But it may be that an unprecedented demand and need for undelayed action may call for temporary departure from that normal balance of public procedure.

I am prepared under my constitutional duty to recommend the measures that a stricken nation in the midst of a stricken world may require. These measures, or such other measures as the Congress may build out of its experience and wisdom, I shall seek, within my constitutional authority, to bring to speedy adoption.

But in the event that the Congress shall fail to take one of these two courses, and in the event that the national emergency is still critical, I shall not evade the clear course of duty that will then confront me. I shall ask the Congress for the one remaining instrument to meet the crisis—broad Executive power to wage a war against the emergency, as great as the power that would be given to me if we were in fact invaded by a foreign foe.

For the trust reposed in me I will return the courage and the devotion that befit the time. I can do no less.

We face the arduous days that lie before us in the warm courage of national unity; with the clear consciousness of seeking old and precious moral values; with the clean satisfaction that comes from the stern performance of duty by old and young alike. We aim at the assurance of a rounded and permanent national life.

We do not distrust the future of essential democracy. The people of the United States have not failed. In their need they have registered a mandate that they want direct, vigorous action. They have asked for discipline and direction under leadership. They have made me the present instrument of their wishes. In the spirit of the gift I take it.

In this dedication of a Nation we humbly ask the blessing of God. May he protect each and every one of us. May He guide me in the days to come.

RUSSEL BOWKER

Working Under the Blue Eagle

The National Industrial Recovery Act was part of what historians have labeled the "First New Deal"—programs aimed largely at economic relief and recovery. One section of the legislation created a system of industrial self-regulation, under which businesses were to eliminate cutthroat competition and establish conditions of "fair" competition through a system of codes. Each industry was to construct, and to some extent police, its own code. Another section, 7(a), guaranteed labor's right "to organize and bargain collectively through representatives of their own choosing."

Russel Bowker, the New Jersey hosiery worker who wrote the following letter, had read about the NIRA. He knew it was supposed to stabilize the hosiery industry, and he probably assumed this meant something good for him. He wrote Roosevelt at a time when the future of organized labor was not at all clear. Stung by more than a decade of bitter opposition from business and adverse court decisions on picketing and strikes, unions had lost much of their membership. The American Federation of Labor had become increasingly ineffectual, and the CIO would not exist until 1935. Bowker thought the NIRA would help bring a union into his plant.

But once passed, legislation often has a life of its own, and the NIRA hurt Bowker rather than helped him. What had gone wrong? Why was Bowker fired? Historians have usually assumed that it was the assistance of the national government that made possible the dramatic growth in organized labor in the 1930s. Does the letter bring this view into question?

Dear Mr. President:

According to the N.R.A. the workers have a right to join unions and organize. According to the papers recently General [Hugh] Johnson [head of the N.R.A.] said we don't have to strike to get our rights, that the Government would protect us in these rights.

I want to call attention to my case and would like to know what can be done about it.

I am a hosiery knitter and was working for the Swan Hosiery Co., Pleasantville, N.J. until two weeks ago. About three weeks ago one of the organizers of the Amer. Federation of Hosiery Workers, of which I was a former member, called at my home and told me that there was going to be a meeting of the workers in our shop for the purpose of organizing into a union. This meeting was to be held on Saturday, October 14th. On the Friday before the meeting Mr. John Miller, our superintendent came around to each worker and asked them if they were going to the meeting and told them they had better not go because if they did there were going to be "changes" around the shop. When he talked to me he said he would be outside the meeting place with a pencil and paper to take the names of all who attended so he would know what changes to make on Monday morning.

After the meeting there were rumors that all those who went to the meeting would be fired. On the following Friday when I received my pay I called Mr. Miller's attention [to the fact] that I hadn't been paid for a day I put in repairing my machine. He said that was because I had [earned?] more during the rest of the week. I showed him in the Hosiery

From letter of Russel Bowker, Atlantic City, N.J., to Franklin D. Roosevelt, November 8, 1933, in Record Group 9, "Records of the National Recovery Administration," National Archives, Washington, D.C., Consolidated Approved Code Industry File, Box 1815.

Code where I must be paid the minimum wage for each and every hour I worked. He as much as said I knew too much and went back to his office. A few minutes later he called me to his office and showed me twelve (12) stockings which he claimed were bad work and said "you are fired."

This is the first time in 16 years as a knitter that I was fired for any reason.

I worked in the Swan shop over four months and up to this time I had about 3 or 4 stockings which were bad brought back to me. Out of the twelve stockings (Mr. Miller admitted half of them were not my fault) and the other six were made two months previous. I made over 1640 dozen pairs of stockings for this company which is about 39,000 stockings, so you can see that this is not a bad average. Besides I was never warned about bad work.

When I was fired Mr. Miller told one of his workers that he would get the rest who attended the meeting before he was through.

I have made a complaint to the local N.R.A. board and the Union has filed one with the Code Authority for the Hosiery Industry but I am still out of work and wish you would see if something couldn't be done about it.

I think the Government should make the manufacturers, large and small, live up to the N.R.A.

Very Truly Yours
Russel Bowker

DASHIELL HAMMETT

The Detective as Hero

While many responded to the trauma of the Great Depression politically and sought a remedy in Long's "Share-the-Wealth" movement, Townsend's old-age pension plan, the Communist party's Unemployed Councils, or Roosevelt's New Deal, others—often the same people—found a curious kind of comfort and security in a literary form that was rapidly increasing in popularity. The period between the wars was the Golden Age of the detective novel.

Dashiell Hammett's *The Maltese Falcon*, excerpted below, is a classic of the genre. Though written in the late 1920s, the story's fame was a phenomenon of the next decade. Warner Brothers filmed three versions, one in 1931, another in 1936, the third—John Huston's classic, starring Humphrey Bogart—in 1941.

Examine the selection (from the last pages of the novel) from the perspective of Sam Spade, the protagonist and hero. What in Spade—what values, what characteristics of behavior and personality—made him so popular a figure with American readers? What, for example, is so special about Spade's tie to Miles? What alternatives—perhaps represented by the woman in the scene—does Spade reject? Is Spade's appeal in *The Maltese Falcon* similar to Roosevelt's in his inaugural address? Many Americans believed that the Depression required an increased reliance on government. Does the detective, as a social type, speak to that question?

From the selection and from your general knowledge of detective fiction (the Sherlock Holmes books of Arthur Conan Doyle, while mostly written between 1890 and 1920, were widely read in the interwar years), speculate on the reasons for the vogue of the detective story and the rise of the detective as a heroic type.

"You told him he was being shadowed," Spade said confidently. "Miles hadn't many brains, but he wasn't clumsy enough to be spotted the first night."

"I told him, yes. When we went out for a walk that night I pretended to discover Mr. [Miles] Archer following us and pointed him out to Floyd." She sobbed. "But please believe, Sam, that I wouldn't have done it if I had thought Floyd would kill him. I thought he'd be frightened into leaving the city. I didn't for a minute think he'd shoot him like that."

Spade smiled wolfishly with his lips, but not at all with his eyes. He said: "If you thought he wouldn't you were right, angel."

The girl's upraised face held utter astonishment.

Spade said: "Thursby didn't shoot him."

Incredulity joined astonishment in the girl's face.

Spade said: "Miles hadn't many brains, but, Christ! he had too many years' experience as a detective to be caught like that by the man he was shadowing. Up a blind alley with his gun tucked away on his hip and his overcoat buttoned? Not a chance. He was as dumb as any man ought to be, but he wasn't quite that dumb. The only two ways out of the alley could be watched from the edge of Bush Street over the tunnel. You'd told us Thursby

From Dashiell Hammett, *The Maltese Falcon* (New York: Knopf, 1929). Excerpts from the first Modern Library Edition, 1934, pp. 255–256, 259–260, 262–263. Copyright 1929, 1930 by Alfred A. Knopf, Inc. and renewed 1957, 1958 by Dashiell Hammett. Reprinted by permission of Alfred A. Knopf, Inc.

was a bad actor. He couldn't have tricked Miles into the alley like that, and he couldn't have driven him in. He was dumb, but not dumb enough for that."

He ran his tongue over the inside of his lips and smiled affectionately at the girl. He said: "But he'd've gone up there with you, angel, if he was sure nobody else was up there. You were his client, so he would have had no reason for not dropping the shadow on your say-so, and if you caught up with him and asked him to go up there he'd've gone. He was just dumb enough for that. He'd've looked you up and down and licked his lips and gone grinning from ear to ear—and then you could've stood as close to him as you liked in the dark and put a hole through him with the gun you had got from Thursby that evening." . . .

"Miles," Spade said hoarsely, "was a son of a bitch. I found that out the first week we were in business together and I meant to kick him out as soon as the year was up. You didn't do me a damned bit of harm by killing him."

"Then what?"

Spade pulled his hand out of hers. He no longer either smiled or grimaced. His wet yellow face was set hard and deeply lined. His eyes burned madly. He said: "Listen. This isn't a damned bit of good. You'll never understand me, but I'll try once more and then we'll give it up. Listen. When a man's partner is killed he's supposed to do something about it. It doesn't make any difference what you thought of him. He was your partner and you're supposed to do something about it. Then it happens we were in the detective business. Well, when one of your organization gets killed it's bad business to let the killer get away with it. It's bad all around—bad for that one organization, bad for every detective everywhere. Third, I'm a detective and expecting me to run criminals down and then let them go free is like asking a dog to catch a rabbit and let it go. It can be done, all right, and sometimes it is done, but it's not the natural thing. The only way I could have let you go was by letting Gutman and Cairo and the kid go. That's—"

"You're not serious," she said. "You don't expect me to think that these things you're saying are sufficient reason for sending me to the—"

"Wait till I'm through and then you can talk. Fourth, no matter what I wanted to do now it would be absolutely impossible for me to let you go without having myself dragged to the gallows with the others. Next, I've no reason in God's world to think I can trust you and if I did this and got away with it you'd have something on me that you could use whenever you happened to want to. That's five of them. The sixth would be that, since I've also got something on you, I couldn't be sure you wouldn't decide to shoot a hole in *me* some day. Seventh, I don't even like the idea of thinking that there might be one chance in a hundred that you'd played me for a sucker. And eighth—but that's enough. All those on one side. Maybe some of them are unimportant. I won't argue about that. But look at the number of them. Now on the other side we've got what? All we've got is the fact that maybe you love me and maybe I love you." . . .

"And you didn't know then that Gutman was here hunting for you. You didn't suspect that or you wouldn't have shaken your gunman. You knew Gutman was here as soon as you heard Thursby had been shot. Then you knew you needed another protector, so you came back to me. Right?"

"Yes, but—oh, sweetheart!—it wasn't only that. I would have come back to you sooner or later. From the first instant I saw you I knew—"

Spade said tenderly: "You angel! Well, if you get a good break you'll be out of San Quentin in twenty years and you can come back to me then."

She took her cheek away from his, drawing her head far back to stare without comprehension at him.

He was pale. He said tenderly: "I hope to Christ they don't hang you, precious, by that sweet neck." He slid his hands up to caress her thoat.

In an instant she was out of his arms, back against the table, crouching, both hands spread over her throat. Her face was wild-eyed, haggard. Her dry mouth opened and closed. She said in a small parched voice: "You're not—" She could get no other words out.

Spade's face was yellow-white now. His mouth smiled and there were smile-wrinkles around his glittering eyes. His voice was soft, gentle. He said: "I'm going to send you over. The chances are you'll get off with life. That means you'll be out again in twenty years. You're an angel. I'll wait for you." He cleared his throat. "If they hang you I'll always remember you." . . .

She took a long trembling breath. "You've been playing with me? Only pretending you cared—to trap me like this? You didn't—care at all? You didn't—don't—l-love me?"

"I think I do," Spade said. "What of it?" The muscles holding his smile in place stood out like wales. "I'm not Thursby. I'm not Jacobi. I won't play the sap for you." . . .

Caste and Class

One of the paradoxes of the Depression was the persistence with which Americans—many of them, at least—continued to be fascinated by the doings of the rich and the sophisticated. Part of Roosevelt's appeal may have been his "aristocratic" background and manners. The photograph on page 268 is a rather remarkable scene, shot in 1931, which suggests something of the level of public attention that could still be focused on a game like bridge, played in formal dress in an elegant hotel suite in New York. (The fascination may have been the source of irritation, too, the kind of irritation that might have been tapped by a Townsend or a Long.) What similarities does the game of bridge have to the "game" played by detectives? Might Americans have been attracted to these bridge "experts" for the same reason they were drawn to Sam Spade?

Original Caption: "New York City, December 7, 1931—The long-heralded contract bridge pair match between Sidney S. Lenz and Ely Culbertson got under way this evening in the Culbertsons' suite at the Hotel Chatham. The match is intended to test the relative merits of the approach-forcing bidding system favored by Mr. Culbertson and the 1-2-5 system sponsored by Mr. Lenz. Both rivals have agreed to play 150 rubbers. . . . *National Archives.*

On page 269 is a scene from one of Charlie Chaplin's most famous films, *Modern Times*, released in 1936. In it, he played a workingman caught in the factory system, suggested by the fantastic machinery in the background. What game is Chaplin imitating in the scene, and what is the effect of his pose? Can you draw any connection between this photograph and the preceding one showing the bridge match at the Hotel Chatham suite? Had something changed in the five years since 1931? What attitudes toward work and wealth are suggested by Chaplin's manner and dress?

A Scene from "Modern Times" (1936). *National Archives.*

The Movies

Walker Evans of the Farm Security Administration took the 1936 photo of billboards and frame houses in Atlanta, Georgia that appears on page 270. What do you think was Evans' purpose in making this photograph? What did he want to convey to the viewer? On another level, what might the subject of the center billboard, and Carole Lombard's black eye, tell us about how average people survived the Great Depression?

Billboards and Frame Houses, Atlanta, Georgia, March 1936. *Farm Security Administration, Library of Congress.*

Enter the dreamhouse, brothers and sisters, leaving
Your debts asleep, your history at the door:
This is the time for heroes, and this loving
Darkness a fur you can afford.

       (From C. Day Lewis poem, "Newsreel," 1938)

The Civilian Conservation Corps

The legislation creating the Civilian Conservation Corps (CCC) in 1933 authorized the agency to provide work for 250,000 jobless male citizens between the ages of 18 and 25, in soil erosion, reforestation, and similar projects. Enrollees were salaried at $30 per month, a portion of which was sent to dependents.

The CCC became a very popular program, but like other New Deal projects that were unfamiliar, it first had to be sold to the American people. The two photographs which follow, with their original captions, were part of an ongoing public relations effort carried out by the agency. They are visual evidence of what the CCC was designed to achieve (beyond youth employment). Do they, for example, suggest an effort to fundamentally change the nature of American capitalism? From them, we can also take a guess or two at what ordinary Americans thought about the corps and the kinds of doubts they had about becoming a part of this social experiment. Finally, the photographs serve as a bridge to Chapter 10.

Original Caption: "Camp Roosevelt, Edinburg, Virginia, July 22, 1940—*Miscellaneous Activities*: Enrollee Robert Daily of Pittsburgh, Pennsylvania, enjoying a pleasant Saturday evening with his girlfriend, Ruth Copp, at her home near Woodstock, Virginia. Looking to the future, they enjoy examining plans of homes in a late magazine." *National Archives.*

Original Caption: "Company commander and subaltern inspecting barracks. Waterville, Washington camp, Soil Conservation Service, June 1941." *National Archives.*

CHAPTER 10

From a New Deal to a New World War

As the shadows lengthened on the decade of the 1930s and on Franklin Roosevelt's second term, those who had expected the president's New Deal to alter profoundly the conditions of economic and social life must have wondered whether anything of the kind had taken place. Maldistribution of income—so critical in restricting purchasing power and bringing on the crash of 1929—had not been significantly remedied. The "soak-the-rich" Revenue Act of 1935, presumably a response to the challenge of Huey Long and Francis Townsend, did very little to distribute wealth. Of more obvious benefit was the Fair Labor Standards Act of 1938, the major piece of social legislation in the second, or post-1935, New Deal. The act placed a floor under wages and a ceiling on hours, and it prohibited interstate shipment of goods made under "oppressive" conditions of child labor. Unfortunately, the wage and hour provisions of the act left millions of workers uncovered; the minimum wage (40 cents per hour after seven years) failed to provide a reasonable standard of living; and the child-labor sections, like old-age security, had been enacted in part to prevent the participation of a group of workers in a crowded labor market.

No one knew just what to make of two New Deal efforts to restructure the economy—the Robinson-Patman Act, passed in 1936, and a flurry of antitrust activity carried out in the Justice Department. Designed to protect small businesses from the predatory tactics of the new and powerful chain stores, Robinson-Patman had little appeal for a large segment of the liberal community which thought consumers would be best served by allowing the chains free rein in reducing prices. Brain-truster Rexford Tugwell feared that this new posture of opposition to bigness and protection for the exploited meant that the New Deal had rejected genuine planning.

The doubts which many felt about the senile New Deal would have seemed of less consequence had Roosevelt succeeded in reviving the economy. In fact, the opposite happened. Roosevelt's own failure to pursue vigorous deficit spending had in 1937 nipped a feeble recovery in the bud and produced levels of unemployment not seen since 1933. In one year, unemployment increased from 14.3 percent to 19 percent of the labor force. It was war, and the planning for it, which finally brought full employment.

The recession of 1937 also brought a decline in patriotism; in a country whose self-image was bound up with its economic performance, national pride and economic growth were closely linked. The idea of going to war, even against a state as nastily aggressive as Nazi Germany, evoked an ambivalent response. Ninety percent of the population wanted the country to stay out of war; but more than 80 percent wanted the Allies to win it. Certain actions and activities were designed to allow the nation to remain aloof from European concerns. In 1934, the Nye Committee of the Congress sought to insure that economic ties to foreign nations would not, as in 1917, force abandonment of neutrality. In 1940, France was invaded, defeated, and occupied. Yet Roosevelt did not ask for a declaration of war, and Charles Lindbergh emerged as leader of a powerful isolationist group called the America First Committee.

On the other side of the ledger were actions that seemed certain to lead to war. Most of these were taken in the Pacific, where Americans were more likely to see their vital interests at stake. First, Roosevelt encouraged a boycott of Japanese goods with a speech suggesting that the peace could be preserved only through a "quarantine" of aggressors. Then, in September 1940, the president embargoed scrap iron and steel sales to Japan, a move protested as "unfriendly." At home, as Hitler launched the battle of France, a presidential request to Congress for 50,000 planes brought thunderous approval. In an atmosphere beginning to resemble the Hundred Days of 1933, a nation eager to resolve its contradictions and doubts and to end a decade of depression submerged its differences and passed a peacetime conscription act.

The Japanese attack on Pearl Harbor in December 1941 brought a flush of patriotism that temporarily buried any remaining doubts.

Popular economics writer Stuart Chase argued that the two decades since the last war had found Americans living in a fairyland of advertising and consumer goods. "Our job in 1942," he emphasized, "is not to out-talk the enemy. Our job is to outshoot him. We are up against two-ton bombs, fifty-ton tanks and sixteen-inch shells. There is no publicity man in heaven, earth or hell who can tell us how to sell our way through them. We are being drawn back relentlessly to our foundations." A Virginia politician announced that "we needed a Pearl Harbor—a Golgotha—to arouse us from our self-sufficient complacency, to make us rise above greed and hate." Vice President Henry Wallace was one of many who revived Wilsonian idealism. "This is a fight," he wrote in 1943, "between a slave world and a free world. Just as the United States in 1862 could not remain half slave and half free, so in 1942 the world must make its decision for a complete victory one way or the other."

In many ways, the war justified idealism, for it accomplished what the New Deal had not. Organized labor prospered. The name "Rosie the Riveter" described the new American woman who found war-related opportunities in the factories and shipyards. Black people—segregated by New Deal housing programs, injured as tenant farmers by New Deal farm policies, and never singled out as a group worthy of special aid—found skilled jobs in the wartime economy. They also received presidential assistance—in the form of the Fair Employment Practices Committee—in their struggle to end racially discriminatory hiring practices. A growing military budget in 1941 produced the nation's first genuinely progressive income tax legislation. The ever-present threat of a postwar depression allowed liberals to dream, at least, of legislation which would commit the national government to regular support of a full-employment economy. Many, like Tugwell, found in the wartime requirements of efficiency and unity an opportunity to turn from the tyranny of competition to a planned economy.

Yet liberals remained uneasy about the war and its impact on reform. By mid-1943, the conflict had brought an end to the Civilian Conservation Corps, the Justice Department's antitrust program, the Works Projects Administration, and the Home Owners' Loan Corporation. Literary critic Malcolm Cowley suggested another and more serious problem: that the bureaucracy created to implement the New Deal could be easily turned to other uses. "A fascist state," he wrote, "could be instituted here without many changes in government personnel, and some of these changes have been made already."

Others wondered whether a viable democracy could be maintained under conditions of conflict—especially physical conflict with totalitarian states. Must a democracy take on the characteristics of fascism in order to possess its strengths and efficiencies? The problem was not unique to wartime. The nation had faced it in 1939, when Roosevelt sought congressional authorization for a major reorganization of the executive branch. Many thought the legislation would make Roosevelt a "dictator." As a result of such fears, the decade after 1935 found Americans engaged in a delicate balancing act, trying on the one hand to preserve the essence of democratic decision making; on the other, to insure that democratic methods would not interfere with the struggle at hand. Whether this balancing act was a success or a failure is the subject of most of the selections in this chapter.

ROGER DANIELS

Concentration Camps, U.S.A.: Japanese Americans and World War II

The beginning of the war in the Pacific in 1941 confronted millions of Americans—many of them born in Japan or the children of Japanese immigrants—with a curious and tragic problem. What was to be the fate of the Japanese who lived on the Pacific Coast? And if the Japanese-born, the "Issei," were to suffer, would the native-born generation, the Nisei, have the equal protection of the laws guaranteed them by the Constitution and the Fourteenth Amendment? In the following essay, historian Roger Daniels sketches in the background to the decision that was finally made: to "intern" the Japanese, citizen and noncitizen alike, for the "duration" in concentration camps. The episode is one of the most shameful in the history of the United States. As you read Daniels' essay, however, you should try to understand the complex of attitudes, the mixture of Rooseveltian liberalism and simple racism, the complications of bureaucratic machinery, that led to the outcome. In short, it may be instructive to examine this episode as the beginnings of another New Deal "program," unique in its pathos, but still in some ways revealing.

If the attack on Pearl Harbor came as a devastating shock to most Americans, for those of Japanese ancestry it was like a nightmare come true. Throughout the 1930s the Nisei generation dreaded the possiblity of a war between the United States and Japan; although some in both the Japanese and American communities fostered the illusion that the emerging Nisei generation could help bridge the gap between the rival Pacific powers, most Nisei, at least, understood that this was a chimera. As early as 1937 Nisei gloom about the future predominated. One Nisei spoke prophetically about what might happen to Japanese Americans in a Pacific war. Rhetorically he asked his fellow Nisei students at the University of California:

> . . . what are we going to do if war does break out between United States and Japan? . . . In common language we can say "we're sunk." Even if the Nisei wanted to fight for America, what chances? Not a chance! . . . our properties would be confiscated and most likely [we would be] herded into prison camps—perhaps we would be slaughtered on the spot.

As tensions increased, so did Nisei anxieties; and in their anxiety some Nisei tried to accentuate their loyalty and Americanism by disparaging the generation of their fathers. Newspaper editor Togo Tanaka, for example, speaking to a college group in early 1941, insisted that the Nisei must face what he called "the question of loyalty" and assumed that since the Issei were "more or less tumbleweeds with one foot in America and one foot in Japan," real loyalty to America could be found only in his own generation. A Los Angeles Nisei jeweler expressed similar doubts later the same year. After explaining to a Los Angeles *Times* columnist that many if not most of the older generation were pro-Japanese rather than pro-American, he expressed his own generation's fears. "We talk of almost nothing but this great crisis. We don't know what's going to happen. Sometimes we only look for a concentration camp."

While the attention of Japanese Americans was focused on the Pacific, most other Americans gave primary consideration to Europe, where in September 1939 World War II had broken out. Hitler's amazing blitzkrieg against the west in the spring of 1940—which overran, in quick succession, Denmark and Norway and then Holland, Belgium, Luxembourg, and France—caused the United States to accelerate its defense program and institute the first peacetime draft in its history. Stories, now known to be wildly exaggerated, told of so-called fifth column and espionage activities, created much concern about the

From Roger Daniels, *Concentration Camps USA: Japanese Americans and World War II* (New York: Holt, Rinehart and Winston, 1971), pp. 26–29, 31–41, 95–96, 104–105, 157. Copyright © 1971 by Roger Daniels.

loyalty of aliens, particularly German-born aliens, some 40,000 of whom were organized into the overtly pro-Nazi German-American Bund. As a component part of the defense program, Congress passed, in 1940, an Alien Registration Act, which required the registration and fingerprinting of all aliens over four-teen years of age. In addition, as we now know, the Department of Justice, working through the Federal Bureau of Investigation, was compiling a rela-tively modest list of dangerous or subversive aliens—Germans, Italians, and Japanese—who were to be arrested or interned at the outbreak of war with their country. The commendable restraint of the Department of Justice's plans was due, first of all, to the liberal nature of the New Deal. The Attorney General, Francis Biddle, was clearly a civil libertarian, as befitted a former law clerk of Oliver Wendell Holmes, Jr.

Elsewhere in the government however, misgivings about possible fifth column and sabotage activity, particularly by Japanese, were strongly felt. For example, one congressman, John D. Dingell (D-Mich.), wrote the President to suggest that Japanese in the United States and Hawaii be used as hostages to ensure good behavior by Japan. In August 1941, shortly after Japanese assets in the United States were frozen and the Japanese made it difficult for some one hundred Americans to leave Japan, Dingell suggested that as a reprisal the United States should "cause the forceful detention or imprisonment in a con-centration camp of ten thousand alien Japanese in Hawaii. . . . It would be well to remind Japan," he continued, "that there are perhaps one hundred fifty thousand additional alien Japanese in the United States who [can] be held in a reprisal reserve."

And, in the White House itself, concern was evidenced. Franklin Roose-velt, highly distrustful of official reports and always anxious to have indepen-dent checks on the bureaucracy, set up an independent "intelligence" opera-tion, run by John Franklin Carter. Carter, who as the "Unofficial Observer" and "Jay Franklin" had written some of the most brilliant New Deal journalism and would later serve as an adviser to President Harry S Truman and Governor Thomas E. Dewey, used newspapermen and personal friends to make special reports. In early November he received a report on the West Coast Japanese from Curtis B. Munson. His report stressed the loyalty of the overwhelming majority, and he understood that even most of the disloyal Japanese Americans hoped that "by remaining quiet they [could] avoid concentration camps or irresponsible mobs." Munson was, however, "horrified" to observe that

> dams, bridges, harbors, power stations, etc., are wholly unguarded. The harbor of San Pedro [Los Angeles' port] could be razed by fire completely by four men with hand grenades and a little study in one night. Dams could be blown and half of lower California could actually die of thirst. . . . One railway bridge at the exit from the mountains in some cases could tie up three or four main railroads.

Munson felt that despite the loyalty or quiescence of the majority, this situ-ation represented a real threat because "there are still Japanese in the United

States who will tie dynamite around their waist and make a human bomb out of themselves." This imaginary threat apparently worried the President too, for he immediately sent the memo to Secretary of War Henry L. Stimson, specifically calling his attention to Munson's warnings about sabotage. In early December, Army Intelligence drafted a reply (which in the confusion following Pearl Harbor was never sent) arguing, quite correctly as it turned out, that "widespread sabotage by Japanese is not expected . . . identification of dangerous Japanese on the West Coast is reasonably complete." Although neither of these nor other similar proposals and warnings was acted upon before the attack on Pearl Harbor, the mere fact that they were suggested and received consideration in the very highest governmental circles indicates the degree to which Americans were willing to believe almost anything about the Japanese. This belief, in turn, can be understood only if one takes into account the half century of agitation and prophecy about the coming American-Japanese war and the dangers of the United States being overwhelmed by waves of yellow soldiers aided by alien enemies within the gates. . . .

It seems clear that well before the actual coming of war a considerable proportion of the American public had been conditioned not only to the probability of a Pacific war with Japan—that was, after all, a geopolitical fact of twentieth-century civilization—but also to the proposition that this war would involve an invasion of the continental United States in which Japanese residents and secret agents would provide the spearhead of the attack. After war came at Pearl Harbor and for years thereafter many Japanophobes insisted that, to use [H. G.] Wells's phrase, "the Yellow Peril was a peril after all," but this is to misunderstand completely Japan's intentions and capabilities during the Great Pacific War. The Japanese military planners never contemplated an invasion of the Continental United States, and, even had they done so, the logistical problems were obviously beyond Japan's capacity as a nation. But, often in history, what men believe to be true is more important than the truth itself because the mistaken belief becomes a basis for action. These two factors—the long racist and anti-Oriental tradition plus the widely believed "yellow peril" fantasy—when triggered by the traumatic mechanism provided by the attack on Pearl Harbor, were the necessary preconditions for America's concentration camps. But beliefs, even widely held beliefs, are not always translated into action. We must now discover how this particular set of beliefs—the inherent and genetic disloyalty of individual Japanese plus the threat of an imminent Japanese invasion—produced public policy and action, the mass removal and incarceration of the West Coast Japanese Americans.

As is well known, despite decades of propaganda and apprehension about a Pacific war, the reality, the dawn attack at Pearl Harbor on Sunday, December 7, 1941, came as a stunning surprise to most Americans. Throughout the nation the typical reaction was disbelief, followed by a determination to close ranks and avenge a disastrous defeat. Faced with the fact of attack, the American people entered the war with perhaps more unity than has existed before or since. But if a calm determination to get on with the job typified the national mood, the mood of the Pacific Coast was nervous and trigger-happy, if not hysterical. . . .

Day after day, throughout December, January, February, and March, almost the entire Pacific Coast press . . . spewed forth racial venom against all Japanese. The term Jap, of course, was standard usage. Japanese, alien and native-born, were also "Nips," "yellow men," "Mad dogs," and "yellow vermin," to name only a few of the choicer epithets. *Times* columnist Ed Ainsworth cautioned his readers "to be careful to differentiate between races. The Chinese and Koreans both hate the Japs more than we do. . . . Be sure of nationality before you are rude to anybody." (*Life* Magazine soon rang some changes on this theme for a national audience with an article—illustrated by comic strip artist Milton Caniff, creator of *Terry and the Pirates* and, later, *Steve Canyon*—which purported to explain how to tell "Japs" from other Asian nationalities.) The sports pages, too, furnished their share of abuse. Just after a series of murderous and sometimes fatal attacks on Japanese residents by Filipinos, one sports page feature was headlined FILIPINO BOXERS NOTED FOR COURAGE, VALOR.

Newspaper columnists, as always, were quick to suggest what public policy should be. Lee Shippey, a Los Angeles writer who often stressed that *some* Japanese were all right, prophetically suggested a solution to California's Japanese problem. He proposed the establishment of "a number of big, closely guarded, closely watched truck farms on which Japanese-Americans could earn a living and assure us a steady supply of vegetables." If a Nazi had suggested doing this with Poles, Shippey, a liberal, undoubtedly would have called it a slave labor camp. But the palm for *shrecklichkeit* must go to Westbrook Pegler, a major outlet of what Oswald Garrison Villard once called "the sewer system of American journalism." Taking time off from his vendettas with Eleanor Roosevelt and the American labor movement, Pegler proposed, on December 9, that every time the Axis murdered hostages, the United States should retaliate by raising them "100 victims selected out of [our] concentration camps," which Pegler assumed would be set up for subversive Germans and Italians and "alien Japanese."

Examples of newspaper incitement to racial violence appeared daily (some radio commentators were even worse). In addition, during the period that the Japanese Americans were still at large, the press literally abounded with stories, and, above all, headlines, which made the already nervous general public believe that military or paramilitary Japanese activists were all around them. None of these stories had any basis in fact; amazingly, there was not one demonstrable incident of sabotage committed by a Japanese American, alien or native-born, during the entire war. Here are a few representative headlines.

JAP BOAT FLASHES MESSAGE ASHORE

ENEMY PLANES SIGHTED OVER CALIFORNIA COAST

TWO JAPANESE WITH MAPS AND ALIEN LITERATURE SEIZED

JAP AND CAMERA HELD IN BAY CITY

VEGETABLES FOUND FREE OF POISON

CAPS ON JAPANESE TOMATO PLANTS POINT TO AIR BASE

JAPANESE HERE SENT VITAL DATA TO TOKYO

CHINESE ABLE TO SPOT JAP

MAP REVEALS JAP MENACE

NETWORK OF ALIEN FARMS COVERS STRATEGIC DEFENSE AREAS OVER SOUTHLAND

JAPS PLAN COAST ATTACK IN APRIL WARNS CHIEF OF KOREAN SPY BAND

In short, any reading of the wartime Pacific Coast press—or for that matter viewing the wartime movies that still pollute our television channels—shows clearly that, although a distinction was continually being made between "good" and "bad" Germans (a welcome change from World War I), few distinctions were ever made between Japanese. . . .

The Department of Justice, working through the FBI and calling on local law enforcement officials for assistance and detention, began roundups of what it considered "dangerous" enemy aliens. Throughout the nation this initial roundup involved about 3000 persons, half of whom were Japanese. (All but a handful of these lived on the Pacific Coast.) In other words the federal officials responsible for counterespionage thought that some 1500 persons of Japanese ancestry, slightly more than 1 percent of the nation's Japanese population, constituted some kind of threat to the nation. Those arrested, often in the dead of night, were almost universally of the immigrant, or Issei, generation, and thus, no matter how long they had lived here, "enemy aliens" in law. (It must be kept in mind that American law prohibited the naturalization of Asians.) Those arrested were community leaders, since the government, acting as it so often does on the theory of guilt by association, automatically hauled in the officers and leading lights of a number of Japanese organizations and religious groups. Many of these people were surely "rooting" for the Emperor rather than the President and thus technically subversive, but most of them were rather elderly and inoffensive gentlemen and not a threat to anything. This limited internment, however, was a not too discreditable performance for a government security agency, but it must be noted that even at this restrained level the government acted much more harshly, in terms of numbers interned, toward Japanese nationals than toward German nationals (most known members of the German-American Bund were left at liberty), and more harshly toward Germans than to Italians. It should also be noted, however, that more than a few young Nisei leaders applauded this early roundup and contrasted their own loyalty to the presumed disloyalty of many of the leaders of the older generation.

In addition to the selective roundup of enemy aliens, the Justice Department almost immediately announced the sealing off of the Mexican and Canadian borders to "all persons of Japanese ancestry, whether citizen or alien." Thus, by December 8, that branch of the federal government particularly charged with protecting the rights of citizens was willing to single out one ethnic group for invidious treatment. Other national civilian officials discriminated in other ways. Fiorello La Guardia, an outstanding liberal who was for a time director of the Office of Civilian Defense as well as mayor of New York, pointedly omitted mention of the Japanese in two public statements calling for decent treatment for enemy aliens and suggesting that alien Germans and Italians be presumed loyal until proved otherwise. By implication, at least, Japanese were to be presumed disloyal. Seventeen years earlier La Guardia had been one of three congressmen who dared to speak in favor of continuing Japanese immigration, but in December 1941 he could find nothing good to say about any Japanese.

Even more damaging were the mendacious statements of Frank Knox, Roosevelt's Republican Secretary of the Navy. On December 15 Secretary Knox held a press conference in Los Angeles on his return from a quick inspection of the damage at Pearl Harbor. As this was the first detailed report of the damage there, his remarks were front-page news all across the nation. Knox spoke of "treachery" in Hawaii and insisted that much of the disaster was caused by "the most effective fifth column work that's come out of this war, except in Norway." The disaster at Pearl Harbor, as is now generally acknowledged, was caused largely by the unpreparedness and incompetence of the local military commanders, as Knox already knew. (The orders for the relief of Admiral Kimmel were already being drawn up.) But the secretary, who, as we shall see, harbored deep-felt anti-Japanese prejudices, probably did not want the people to lose faith in their Navy, so the Japanese population of Hawaii—and indirectly all Japanese Americans—was made the scapegoat on which to hang the big lie. (Knox, it should be remarked, as a Chicago newspaper publisher in civilian life, had a professional understanding of these matters.)

But the truly crucial role was played by the other service, the United States Army. The key individual, initially, at least, was John L. De Witt, in 1941 a lieutenant general and commander of the Western Defense Command and the 4th Army, both headquartered at San Francisco's Presidio. Despite these warlike titles, De Witt, who was sixty-one years old and would be retired before the war's end, was essentially an administrator in uniform, a staff officer who had specialized in supply and had practically nothing to do with combat during his whole Army career. Even before Pearl Harbor, De Witt had shown himself to be prejudiced against Japanese Americans. In March 1941, for example, he found it necessary to complain to Major General William G. Bryden, the Army's Deputy Chief of Staff, that "a couple of Japs" who had been drafted into the Army were "going around taking pictures." He and Bryden agreed to "just have it happen naturally that Japs are sent to Infantry units," rather than to sensitive headquarters or coast defense installations. De Witt's prejudices, in fact, extended all along the color line. When he discovered that some of the troops being sent to him as reinforcements after Pearl Harbor were Negro, he protested to the Army's chief of classification and assignment that

> you're filling too many colored troops up on the West Coast. . . . there will be a great deal of public reaction out here due to the Jap situation. They feel they've got enough black skinned people around them as it is. Filipinos and Japanese. . . . I'd rather have a white regiment. . . .

Serving under De Witt, in December 1941, as the corps commander in charge of the defense of Southern California, was a real fighting man, the then Major General Joseph W. Stilwell, the famed "Vinegar Joe" of the heartbreaking Burma campaigns. His diary of those days, kept in pencil in a shirt-pocket notebook, gives an accurate and pungent picture of the hysteria and indecisiveness that prevailed at De Witt's headquarters and on the Coast generally.

> *Dec. 8*
> Sunday night "air raid" at San Francisco . . . Fourth Army kind of jittery.
> *Dec. 9*
> . . . Fleet of thirty-four [Japanese] ships between San Francisco and Los Angeles. Later—not authentic.
> *Dec. 11*
> [Phone call from 4th Army] "The main Japanese fleet is 164 miles off San Francisco." I believed it, like a damn fool . . .
> Of course [4th Army] passed the buck on this report. They had it from a "usually reliable source," but they should never have put it out without check.
> *Dec. 13*
> Not content with the above blah, [4th] Army pulled another at ten-thirty today. "Reliable information that attack on Los Angeles is imminent. A general alarm being considered. . . ." What jackass would send a general alarm [which would have meant warning all civilians to leave the area including the workers in the vital Southern California aircraft industry] under the circumstances. The [4th] Army G-2 [Intelligence] is just another amateur, like all the rest of the staff. Rule: the higher the headquarters, the more important is *calm*.

Stilwell's low opinion of General De Witt was apparently shared by others within the Army; shortly after Vinegar Joe's transfer to Washington just before Christmas, he noted that Lieutenant General Lesley J. McNair, Deputy Commander, Army Ground Force, had told him that "De Witt has gone crazy and requires ten refusals before he realizes it is 'No.' " . . .

It was in this panic-ridden, amateurish Western Defense Command atmosphere that some of the most crucial decisions about the evacuation of the Japanese Americans were made. Before examining them, however, it should be made clear that the nearest Japanese aircraft during most of December were attacking Wake Island, more than 5000 miles west of San Francisco, and any major Japanese surface vessels or troops were even farther away. In fact, elements of the Luftwaffe over the North Atlantic were actually closer to California than any Japanese planes. California and the West Coast of the continental United States were in no way seriously threatened by the Japanese military. This finding does not represent just the hindsight of the military historian; the high command of the American army realized it at the time. Official estimates of Japanese capabilities made late in December concluded correctly that a large-scale invasion was beyond the capacity of the Japanese military but that a hit-and-run raid somewhere along the West Coast was possible. . . .

The first proposal by the Army for any kind of mass evacuation of Japanese Americans was brought forward at a De Witt staff conference in San Francisco on the evening of December 10. In the language of a staff memo, the meeting considered "certain questions relative to the problem of apprehension, segregation and detention of Japanese in the San Francisco Bay Area." The initial cause of the meeting seems to have been a report from an unidentified Treasury Department official asserting that 20,000 Japanese in the Bay Area were ready for organized action. Apparently plans for a mass roundup were drawn up locally, and approved by General Benedict, the commander of the area, but the whole thing was squelched by Nat Pieper, head of the San Francisco office of the FBI, who laughed it off as "the wild imaginings" of a former FBI man whom he had fired. The imaginings were pretty wild; the figure of 20,000 slightly exceeded the total number of Japanese men, women, and children in the Bay Area. But wild or not, De Witt's subordinate reported the matter to Washington with the recommendation that "plans be made for large-scale internment." Then on December 19 General De Witt officially recommended "that action be initiated at the earliest practicable date to collect all alien subjects fourteen years of age and over, of enemy nations and remove them" to the interior of the United States and hold them "under restraint after removal" to prevent their surreptitious return. (The age limit was apparently derived from the federal statutes on wartime internment, but those statutes, it should be noted, specified males only.)

De Witt was soon in touch with the Army's Provost Marshal General, Allen W. Gullion, who would prove to be a key figure in the decision to relocate the Japanese Americans. Gullion, the Army's top cop, had previously served as Judge Advocate General, the highest legal office within the Army. He was a service intellectual who had once read a paper to an International Congress of Judicial Experts on the "present state of international law regarding the protection of civilians from the new war technics." But, since at least mid-1940, he had been concerned with the problem of legally exercising military control over civilians in wartime. Shortly after the fall of France, Army Intelligence took the position that fifth column activities had been so successful in the European war in creating an internal as well as an external military front that the military "will actually have to control, through their Provost Marshal Generals, local forces, largely police" and that "the Military would certainly have to provide for the arrest and temporary holding of a large number of suspects," alien and citizen.

Gullion, as Judge Advocate General, gave his official opinion that within the United States, outside any zone of actual combat and where the civil courts were functioning, the "Military . . . does not have any jurisdiction to participate in the arrest and temporary holding of civilians who are citizens of the United States." He did indicate, however, that if federal troops were in actual control (he had martial law in mind), jurisdiction over citizen civilians might be exercised. Although martial law was never declared on the Pacific Coast, Chief of Staff George C. Marshall did declare the region a "Theater of Operations" on December 11. This declaration, which was not made with the Japanese Americans in mind, created the legal fiction that the Coast was a war zone and would provide first the Army and then the courts with an excuse for placing entirely blameless civilian citizens under military control.

By December 22 Provost Marshal General Gullion, like any good bureaucrat, began a campaign to enlarge the scope of his own activities, an activity usually known as empire building. He formally requested the Secretary of War to press for the transfer of responsibility for conduct of the enemy alien program from the Department of Justice to the War Department. This recommendation found no positive response in Stimson's office, and four days later Gullion was on the telephone trying to get General De Witt to recommend a mass roundup of all Japanese, alien and citizen. Gullion told the Western Defense commander that he had just been visited by a representative of the Los Angeles Chamber of Commerce urging that all Japanese in the Los Angeles area be incarcerated. De Witt, who would blow hot and cold, was, on December 26, opposed. He told Gullion that

> I'm very doubtful that it would be common sense procedure to try and intern 117,000 Japanese in this theater. . . . An American citizen, after all, is an American citizen. And while they all may not be loyal, I think we can weed the disloyal out of the loyal and lock them up if necessary.

De Witt was also opposed, on December 26, to military, as opposed to civilian, control over enemy aliens. "It would be better," he told Gullion, if "this thing worked through the civil channels."

While these discussions and speculations were going on all about them, the West Coast Japanese in general and the citizen Nisei in particular were desperately trying to establish their loyalty. Many Japanese communities on the Coast were so demoralized by the coming of war that little collective action was taken, especially in the first weeks after Pearl Harbor. But in Los Angeles, the major mainland center of Japanese population, frantic and often pitiful activity took place. Most of this activity revolved around the Japanese American Citizens League, an organization, by definition, closed to Issei, except for the handful who achieved citizenship because of their service in the United States armed forces during World War I. Immediately following Pearl Harbor the Japanese American Citizens League (JACL) wired the President, affirming their loyalty; the White House had the State Department, the arm of government usually used to communicate with foreigners, coolly respond by letter that "your desire to cooperate has been carefully noted." On December 9 the JACL Anti-Axis Committee decided to take no contribution, in either time or money, from noncitizens, and later, when special travel regulations inhibited the movement of aliens, it decided not to help Issei "in securing travel permits or [giving] information in that regard." In addition, Nisei leaders repeatedly called on one generation to inform on the other.

On the very evening of Pearl Harbor, editor Togo Tanaka went on station KHTR, Los Angeles, and told his fellow Nisei:

> As Americans we now function as counterespionage. Any act or word prejudicial to the United States committed by any Japanese must be warned and reported to the F.B.I., Naval Intelligence, Sheriff's Office, and local police. . . .

Before the end of the week the Los Angeles Nisei had set up a formal Committee on Intelligence and had regular liaison established with the FBI. These patriotic activities never uncovered any real sabotage or espionage, because there was none to uncover. Nor did it provide the protective coloration that the Nisei had hoped it would; race, not loyalty or citizenship, was the criterion for evacuation. It did, however, widen the gap between the generations, and would be a major cause of bitterness and violence after the evacuation took place.

Eight months after Pearl Harbor, on August 7, 1942, all the West Coast Japanese Americans had been rounded up, one way or another, and were either in Wartime Civil Control Administration (WCCA) Assembly Centers or War Relocation Authority (WRA) camps. By November 3 the transfer to WRA was complete; altogether 119,803 men, women, and children were confined behind barbed wire. Almost six thousand new American citizens would be born in the concentration camps and some eleven hundred were sent in from the Hawaiian Islands. The rest—112,704 people—were West Coast Japanese. Of these, almost two-thirds—64.9 percent—were American-born, most of them under 21 and 77.4 percent under 25. Their foreign-born parents presented a quite different demographic profile. More than half of them—57.2 percent—were over 50. The camps, then, were primarily places of confinement for the young and the old, and since young adults of the second generation were, in the main, the first to be released, the unnatural age distribution within these artificial communities became more and more disparate as time went by. . . .

After the [Salt Lake City] conference [in April 1942] WRA policy was clear: the relocation camps would be semipermanent establishments, surrounded with barbed wire and guarded by small detachments of military police. Rather than the large guard force envisioned by Gullion, the military manpower involved would be minimal. At Heart Mountain, Wyoming, for example, the guard contingent for about 10,000 evacuees numbered only 3 officers and 124 enlisted men. Two of the ten eventual concentration camps—Manzanar and Poston—had been selected and construction begun under WCCA—that is, essentially military—auspices. The other eight were selected by the WRA between April and June. All ten sites can only be called godforsaken. They were in places where nobody had lived before and no one has lived since. The Army insisted that all camps be "at a safe distance" from strategic installations, and the WRA decided that, for a number of reasons, the sites should be on federal property. Three of the eight WRA-selected sites— Tule Lake, California; Minidoka, Idaho; and Heart Mountain, Wyoming— were located on undeveloped federal reclamation projects. Gila River, Arizona, like Poston, was on an Indian reservation. Granada (Amache), in southeastern Colorado, was purchased by the Army for the WRA, and Topaz, the central Utah camp, involved some public domain, some tracts that had reverted to local authority for nonpayment of taxes, and several parcels purchased from private individuals. The two Arkansas centers, Jerome and Rohwer, were on lands originally purchased by Rex Tugwell's Farm SecurityAdministration as future subsistence homesteads for low-income southern families. That land originally intended to fulfill the promise of American life for some of its most disadvantaged citizens should, under the stress of war, be used as a place of confinement for other Americans is just one of the smaller ironies of the whole program. . . .

Life in these places was not generally brutal; there were no torture chambers, firing squads, or gas ovens waiting for the evacuated people. The American concentration camps should not be compared, in that sense, to Auschwitz or Vorkuta. They were, in fact, much more like a century-old American institution, the Indian reservation, than like the institutions that flourished in totalitarian Europe. They were, however, places of confinement ringed with barbed wire and armed sentries. Despite WRA propaganda about community control, there was an unbridgeable gap between the Caucasian custodians and their Oriental charges; even the mess halls were segregated by race. Although some of the staff, particularly those in the upper echelons of the WRA, disapproved of the racist policy that brought the camps into being, the majority of the camp personnel, recruited from the local labor force, shared the contempt of the general population for "Japs." . . .

By mid-1944, whatever remote possibilities there had been of a Japanese attack on the West Coast were past. Yet the restrictions remained in force until almost the end of the year. Roosevelt was reelected in November, and by December the Court was ready to hand down *Korematsu*, and more important, *Endo*. After the cases had been argued but before decisions were announced, the easing of exclusion from the West Coast was in the works. I have discovered no evidence that the War Department or the White House knew in advance what the Court would do but, as O. W. Holmes, Jr., used to say, "there is such a thing as presumptive evidence."

Five days before *Endo* made continued confinement for "loyal" citizens unconstitutional, War Secretary Stimson sent a secret message to the White House in which he admitted that "mass exclusion from the West Coast of persons of Japanese ancestry is no longer a matter of military necessity." There had been no military developments that month; if exclusion was unnecessary in mid-December 1944, it had been unnecessary for some time. He did claim that "face saving" raids from Japan were still possible. Then came the real reason:

> The matter is now the subject of litigation in the Federal Courts and in view of the fact that military necessity no longer requires the continuation of mass exclusion it seems unlikely that it can be continued in effect for any considerable period.

The War Secretary speculated that there might be some trouble from whites, but was confident that

> the common sense and good citizenship of the people of the Coast is such that the inauguration of this program will not be marred by serious incidents or disorders.

Just four days after Stimson's secret memorandum and only one day before the Court handed down *Endo*, Major General Henry C. Pratt, who had just taken over Western Defense Command from General Emmons, publicly announced that total exclusion from the West Coast of loyal Japanese American civilians was terminated, effective January 2, 1945.

FRANKLIN D. ROOSEVELT

Attacking the Monopolies

Just three years before the attack on Pearl Harbor, Franklin Roosevelt addressed the following message to Congress. It is a good example— perhaps the best example—of the administration's reformism. In response, Congress created a Temporary National Economic Committee (TNEC). The committee, over the next two years, made a monumental investigation into the concentration of economic wealth and power in the United States, all guided by Roosevelt's dramatic statement that liberty and democracy would not be "safe if the people tolerate the growth of private power to a point where it becomes stronger than their democratic state itself. That, in its essence, is Fascism."

The speech is valuable in part for what it reveals about the economic goals of the New Deal in the late 1930s, and students should begin by examining the speech simply as an expression of one view of what was preventing the revival of the economy. But the speech may be more important for the depth of its concern for "democracy" and "human liberty." For interned Japanese, these words would sound hollow indeed.

What had happened in three years? Had the war somehow suddenly ended the dream of reform? Or might Roosevelt have been pleased that the war had given him new tools with which to fight the old enemy of monopoly power?

To the Congress:

Unhappy events abroad have retaught us two simple truths about the liberty of a democratic people.

The first truth is that the liberty of a democracy is not safe if the people tolerate the growth of private power to a point where it becomes stronger than their democratic state itself. That, in its essence, is Fascism—ownership of Government by an individual, by a group, or by any other controlling private power.

The second truth is that the liberty of a democracy is not safe if its business system does not provide employment and produce and distribute goods in such a way as to sustain an acceptable standard of living.

Both lessons hit home.

Among us today a concentration of private power without equal in history is growing.

This concentration is seriously impairing the economic effectiveness of private enterprise as a way of providing employment for labor and capital and as a way of assuring a more equitable distribution of income and earnings among the people of the nation as a whole. . . .

The statistical history of modern times proves that in times of depression concentration of business speeds up. Bigger business then has larger opportunity to grow still bigger at the expense of smaller competitors who are weakened by financial adversity.

The danger of this centralization in a handful of huge corporations is not reduced or eliminated, as is sometimes urged, by the wide public distribution of their securities. The mere number of security-holders gives little clue to the size of their individual holdings or to their actual ability to have a voice in the management. In fact the concentration of stock ownership of corporations in the hands of a tiny minority of the population matches the concentration of corporate assets.

1929 was a banner year for distribution of stock ownership. But in that year

three-tenths of 1 per cent of our population received 78 per cent of the dividends reported by individuals. This has roughly the same effect as if, out of every 300 persons in our population, one person received 78 cents out of every dollar of

From Franklin D. Roosevelt, "Recommendations to the Congress to Curb Monopolies and the Concentration of Economic Power," April 29, 1938, in Samuel I. Rosenman (ed.), *The Public Papers and Addresses of Franklin D. Roosevelt*, 9 vols., vol. 7: *The Continuing Struggle for Liberalism* (New York: Macmillan, 1941), pp. 305–308, 310, 312–313.

corporate dividends while the other 299 persons divided up the other 22 cents between them.

The effect of this concentration is reflected in the distribution of national income.

A recent study by the National Resources Committee shows that in 1935–36:

> 47 per cent of all American families and single individuals living alone had incomes of less than $1,000 for the year; and at the other end of the ladder a little less than 1 ½ per cent of the nation's families received incomes which in dollars and cents reached the same total as the incomes of the 47 per cent at the bottom.

Furthermore, to drive the point home, the Bureau of Internal Revenue reports that estate tax returns in 1936 show that:

> 33 per cent of the property which was passed by inheritance was found in only 4 per cent of all the reporting estates. (And the figures of concentration would be far more impressive, if we included all the smaller estates which, under the law, do not have to report.)

We believe in a way of living in which political democracy and free private enterprise for profit should serve and protect each other—to ensure a maximum of human liberty not for a few but for all.

It has been well said that "the freest government, if it could exist, would not be long acceptable, if the tendency of the laws were to create a rapid accumulation of property in few hands, and to render the great mass of the population dependent and penniless."

Today many Americans ask the uneasy question: Is the vociferation that our liberties are in danger justified by the facts? . . .

That heavy hand of integrated financial and management control lies upon large and strategic areas of American industry. The small business man is unfortunately being driven into a less and less independent position in American life. You and I must admit that.

Private enterprise is ceasing to be free enterprise and is becoming a cluster of private collectivisms: masking itself as a system of free enterprise after the American model, it is in fact becoming a concealed cartel system after the European model. . . .

Managed industrial prices mean fewer jobs. It is no accident that in industries, like cement and steel, where prices have remained firm in the face of a falling demand, payrolls have shrunk as much as 40 and 50 per cent in recent months. Nor is it mere chance that in most competitive industries where prices adjust themselves quickly to falling demand, payrolls and employment have been far better maintained. By prices we mean, of course, the prices of the finished articles and not the wages paid to workers. . . .

Examination of methods of conducting and controlling private enterprise which keep it from furnishing jobs or income or opportunity for one-third of the population is long overdue on the part of those who sincerely want to preserve the system of private enterprise for profit.

No people, least of all a democratic people, will be content to go without work or to accept some standard of living which obviously and woefully falls short of their capacity to produce. No people, least of all a people with our traditions of personal liberty, will endure the slow erosion of opportunity for the common man, the oppressive sense of helplessness under the domination of a few, which are overshadowing our whole economic life.

A discerning magazine of business has editorially pointed out that big business collectivism in industry compels an ultimate collectivism in government.

The power of a few to manage the economic life of the nation must be diffused among the many or be transferred to the public and its democratically responsible government. If prices are to be managed and administered, if the nation's business is to be allotted by plan and not by competition, that power should not be vested in any private group or cartel, however benevolent its professions profess to be.

Those people, in and out of the halls of government, who encourage the growing restriction of competition either by active efforts or by passive resistance to sincere attempts to change the trend, are shouldering a terrific responsibility. Consciously, or unconsciously, they are working for centralized business and financial control. Consciously or unconsciously, they are therefore either working for control of the government itself by business and finance or the other alternative—a growing concentration of public power in the government to cope with such concentration of private power.

The enforcement of free competition is the least regulation business can expect.

Making America Democratic

Abolishing Sororities

American entry into the world conflict left Thurman Arnold's antitrust campaign in the lurch, but it did not eliminate the social realities which had triggered Roosevelt's animosity to concentrated wealth. The New Deal's opposition to monopoly power was instead reshaped and redirected to suit the needs of a nation at war.

On April 20, 1944, the Stanford University Board of Trustees banned sororities from the campus. The following excerpts are from the report of the board committee appointed fourteen months earlier to study the question. What considerations motivated the board's action? What relationship might have existed between the sorority prohibition and the general social climate associated with World War II (including, for example, the movement of women into the labor market)? What connections might be made between Stanford's action and Roosevelt's antimonopoly address of 1938?

"In recent years the belief has been growing among colleges and universities that they should provide residence halls for women students as an integral part of their educational programs. Stanford now has three large residence units for women and one small unit.

"It is a University requirement that a new undergraduate woman student, unless living with parent or guardian, must live in a University residence from one to four quarters. Also, she is required to continue living in a University residence until she graduates, unless she joins a sorority.

"The sororities at Stanford afford living accommodations for approximately 270 women, in nine houses. Mature women, selected by each sorority, act as house mothers. Through a system of alumnae advising, student self-government, and the program of the national organizations, sororities seek to develop in their members a sense of group loyalty and responsibility. Over the years the sororities have cooperated with the University in its efforts to maintain scholastic standing and to extend the educational process to include student life outside classroom hours."

From the foregoing it is clear that throughout Stanford's history there has been a dual system of responsibility for women's living groups. . . .

In 1933, however, the provision restricting the number of women students was modified. Enrollment increased to 1,050. With no corresponding increase in either the housing capacity or the number of sororities, the numerical relationship between sorority and nonsorority women changed immediately. Under the new conditions, fewer than one in three Stanford women could join a sorority, and by the autumn of 1943 the ratio had risen to one in five.

In the year 1934–35 the issue between women's living groups was again brought to the attention of the administration by the students. Since then sharp differences between sorority and nonsorority women have arisen several times. For example, in 1938 an overwhelming majority of the freshmen at Roble participated in a revolt against the sorority system.

Aside from the changed relationship between sorority and nonsorority women which followed when additional women were admitted to the University, another circumstance inevitably tended to aggravate the condition over the years. The construction of a new Roble Hall in 1918 and Lagunita Court in 1934 provided excellent facilities to intensify the University's own education

From Stanford University, Board of Trustees, Committee on Sororities, *Report*, 1944, printed in *Stanford Observer*, April 1978, p. 3. Reprinted with permission.

policies with respect to women's housing. Fine leadership and strong group loyalty developed among Stanford women in the residence halls. Competition between hall and sorority women became more intense. Again and again, however, hall women who became recognized leaders on the campus finally joined sororities, to the disappointment and chagrin of the other women in the halls.

Following the rushing season of 1943 the 13 sponsors of new undergraduate women in Roble Hall presented a statement to the undergraduate delegates of Pan-Hellenic Council at Stanford which began: The previously recognized faults of the sorority system at Stanford have reached the point where they can be condoned no longer. . . . Six of the 13 sponsors belonged to sororities; 7 were hall women. Two hundred women in the halls subscribed in writing to the statement of the sponsors.

This unanimous and spontaneous action of the sponsors could not be taken as a mere emotional outburst resulting from rushing. Sponsors are chosen for their maturity, qualities of leadership and sense of responsibility. As the result of their experience and observation as sponsors, they had been impelled to place an important question squarely before the interested parties. . . .

Throughout the course of its deliberations the committee has been impressed by the fact that the women students themselves agree upon the existence of serious defects in the sorority system at Stanford.

The existence of residence halls housing 75% of all women students, within a stone's throw of sororities housing only 25%, in itself tends to divide Stanford women into two competitive groups. This division is unmistakable when the rushing period starts. There is an emotional tension which affects prospective pledges and sorority women alike. Parents become involved, as do alumnae and family friends. The women students are so tense and tired that their college work suffers unmistakably. . . .

"At the end of rushing . . . a few of the women who have not been chosen leave Stanford. Some who remain in the halls tend to lose confidence in themselves because they have not been selected to join a sorority. The interests of some of the women change focus. To many, life now centers around the sorority. This has its effect on the former companions who remain in the halls. The division between nonsorority and sorority women then starts. This much the women students themselves freely acknowledge.

"The core of the argument of one group was that the sorority system at Stanford tended to set up artificial distinctions between sorority and nonsorority women. They felt that all too often the basis of selecting pledges was superficial. They believed that the sorority system resulted in an over-emphasis on social life, pointing out that over the years the average of scholarship in the halls was higher than in the sororities. These women felt that the existing system tended to divide Stanford women into those who had been chosen and those who had not. . . . This group felt that no remedy short of discontinuing the sorority system at Stanford would be effective. . . .

"The prosorority group, while acknowledging defects in the present system at Stanford, contended before the committee that these defects could be corrected without sacrificing the sorority system itself. They argued that they had provided advantages to Stanford women that were not obtainable except through sororities. The chief advantages cited were these:

(1) The benefit of small living groups composed of women who have elected to live with each other and who, for the most part, govern themselves.
(2) The influence of the national sororities with their programs of stimulating group responsibility, developing leadership and promoting high standards of scholarship.
(3) The advantages derived from association with sorority sisters in other universities.
(4) The helpful influence and guidance of alumnae. . . ."

The effects of disunity among Stanford women were clearly discernible throughout the fall quarter. "Despite the good intentions and best efforts of both sorority and nonsorority women the conditions with respect to rushing were not measurably improved in the current winter quarter. . . .

"It should be emphasized here that by no means all of the responsibility for existing differences among women students at Stanford can be attributed to the sorority system as such. It is felt that the sorority women have cooperated with the University to the best of their abilities. Their cooperative spirit and loyalty to Stanford are recognized. Early in its deliberations the committee came face to face with the fact that the University's own program in behalf of women students in the halls had contributed to a considerable extent to the existing difficulties.

"Not more than one third of the student's day is spent in the classroom, laboratory, and library. To be fully effective, the cultural and social program of the University must take into account the remainder of the student's day. This important fact, upon which authorities are generally agreed, was recognized by Stanford's founders in the very beginning. It is a residential university not by accident but by design. . . ."

The committee recognizes that this University policy, involving as it does a consistent effort to develop outstanding leadership and group responsibility among Stanford women in the residence halls, inevitably has contributed to the present difficulties and dissatisfaction among women students. Nevertheless it is the belief of the committee that the results of the University's policy amply justify its continuance. Over a long period of years the women in the halls have maintained a better scholastic average than have the sorority women.

It is clear, too, that the supervision and counseling in the halls reflect the policies of the University administration more closely than do those of the sororities. Unless the University modifies or abandons its own housing policy, which we certainly do not advocate, then it is clear to us that regardless of the cooperative spirit of the sororities, additional University residential units will only increase the difficulties which have led to the present situation.

"Similarly, any increase in the number of sororities must inevitably result in decreased occupancy of residence halls unless the number of women admitted to Stanford is increased still further. If additional women were admitted, the numerical balance would again be disturbed. Furthermore, the suggestion that the number of sorority houses be increased has not been acceptable to a majority of the sororities themselves.

"The committee has carefully considered the suggestion that some sorority women should be housed in the residence halls. This proposal is unacceptable to the hall women. The sororities themselves are not agreed upon it. It is the opinion of the committee that such a proposal if put into effect would only intensify present difficulties.

"Our conclusions are:

(1) The dual system of responsibility for the housing and social program now in effect is not in the best interests of the women students at Stanford.
(2) This system has caused serious disunity among Stanford women, impairing the University's ability to meet its imperative obligations and responsibilities in respect of women students.
(3) Remedies heretofore proposed, including changes in rushing rules, will not eliminate the fundamental causes of the disunity.

"Therefore we recommend:

"That the Board of Trustees authorize the president of the University to work out, in cooperation with all interested groups, equitable procedures, including compensation on a fair basis for property rights affected, which will lead to:

(a) Discontinuance of sororities.
(b) Unification of women's housing under University ownership and supervision."

The Common Sense of Doctor Spock

Since 1945, when the first edition of his baby book found its way into the hands of worried mothers, Benjamin Spock has been a figure of cultural importance. During the Vietnam War, Richard Nixon's vice president, Spiro Agnew, and others would see Spock's advice as having corrupted a generation with excessive permissiveness, laying the groundwork (so the argument went) for the riots and demonstrations of the late 1960s.

Like Agnew, most social analysts have been interested in Spock's influence in the decades after 1945. This is perfectly natural and appropriate, but such analyses must take account of one central fact: Spock was a product of the interwar years. He was in medical school in the 1920s, in private practice in the 1930s (when he became a New Deal Democrat), and he wrote *Baby and Child Care* during World War II, while serving as a lieutenant commander in the U.S. Naval Reserve. In short, Spock's work not only *influenced* child-rearing patterns; it also *reflected* the time of its writing and the social and cultural environment of the 1930s and 1940s.

As you read the selection, think of Spock as a reformer, concerned with raising a particular kind of child, one especially suited to the struggle between democracy and fascism. How did Spock, in his role as child-rearing expert, seek to reconcile the need for authority with the requirements of democracy? How did he characterize the small child and seek to influence its development? Against what ideal society did Spock measure his own culture? Can you relate his attitudes to those of the Stanford committee on sororities? or to Roosevelt's concern about the maldistribution of economic and political power in the 1938 speech?

Feeding the Baby

Mothers have sometimes been so scared of the schedule that they did not dare feed a hungry baby one minute early. They have even accepted the idea that a baby would be spoiled if he were fed when he was hungry. What an idea! As if puppies are spoiled by being able to nurse when they are hungry. Why does a baby cry near mealtime? Not to get the better of his mother. He wants some milk. Why does he sleep the next 4 hours? Not because he has learned that his mother is stern. It's because the meal satisfied his system for that long.

It will help you to realize how natural a flexible schedule is if you will stop and think of a mother, far away in an "uncivilized" land, who has never heard of a schedule, or a pediatrician, or a cow. Her baby starts to cry with hunger. This attracts her attention and makes her feel like putting him to breast. He nurses until he is satisfied, then falls asleep. Seeing him peacefully asleep satisfies the mother, too. She puts him down and goes about her work. He

From Benjamin Spock, *The Common Sense Book of Baby and Child Care* (New York: Duell, Sloan and Pearce, 1945), pp. 26, 210–213, 258–259, 329–330. Copyright © 1945, 1946, 1957 by Benjamin Spock, M.D. Reprinted by permission of Simon & Schuster, a Division of Gulf & Western Corporation.

sleeps for several hours until his hunger pains wake him up. As soon as he starts crying again his mother nurses him. The rhythm of the baby's digestive system is what sets the schedule. He never stays unhappy for long. The mother follows her instinct without any hesitation. She doesn't have to bite her nails, waiting for the clock to say it's feeding time. You can see, then, that it doesn't defy the laws of nature to adjust the schedule to the baby. . . .

How to Handle Him

How Do You Make Him Leave Certain Things Alone?   This is the main problem between 1 and 2 years. There will always be a few things which you have to teach him to let alone. There have to be lamps on tables. He mustn't pull them off by their cords or push tables over. He mustn't touch the hot stove, or turn on the gas, or crawl out a window.

You can't stop him by saying no, at least not in the beginning. Even later it depends on your tone of voice and how often you say it. It's not a method to rely on heavily. Don't say "no" in a challenging voice from across the room. This gives him a choice. He says to himself, "Shall I be a mouse and do as she says, or shall I be a man and grab the lamp cord?" Remember that his nature is egging him on to try things and to balk at directions. The chances are he'll keep on approaching the lamp cord with an eye on you to see how angry you get. It's much wiser, the first few times he goes for the lamp, to go over promptly and whisk him to another part of the room. Quickly give him a magazine, an empty cigarette box, anything that is safe and interesting. There's no use tossing him a rattle that he was bored with months ago.

Suppose he goes back to the lamp a few minutes later? Remove him and distract him again, promptly, definitely, cheerfully. It's all right to say "no, no," at the same time that you remove him, adding it to your action, for good measure. Sit down with him for a minute to show him what he can do with the new plaything. If necessary, put the lamp out of reach this time, or even take him out of the room. You are tactfully showing him that you are absolutely sure in your own mind that the lamp is not the thing to play with. You are keeping away from choices, arguments, cross looks, scoldings—which won't do any good but will only get his back up.

You might say, "But he won't learn unless I teach him it's naughty." Oh yes he will. In fact, he can accept the lesson more easily if it's done in this matter-of-fact way. When you waggle a finger at a child from across the room with a disapproving expression and say, "No-o-o," you make it hard for him to give in. And it's no better if you grab him, hold him face to face, and give him a talking-to. You're not giving him a chance to give in gracefully or forget. His only choice is to surrender meekly or to defy you.

I think of a Mrs. T., who complained bitterly that her 16-month-old daughter was "naughty." Just then Suzy toddled into the room, a nice girl with a normal amount of spunk. Instantly Mrs. T. looked disapproving and said, "*Now remember*, don't go near the radio." Suzy hadn't been thinking of the radio at all, but now she had to. She turned and moved slowly toward it. Mrs.

T. gets panicky just as soon as each of her children in turn shows signs of developing into an independent person. She dreads that she won't be able to control them. In her uneasiness she makes an issue when there doesn't need to be any. It's like the person learning to ride a bicycle who sees a rock in the road ahead. He is so nervous about it that he keeps steering right into it.

Take the example next of a baby who is getting close to a hot stove. A mother doesn't sit still and say, "No-o-o," in a disapproving voice. She jumps and gets him out of the way. This is the method that comes naturally if she is really trying to keep him from doing something, and not engaging in a battle of wills.

A mother of a 1 ¾-year-old boy takes him with her every day to the grocery store. But she complains that, instead of walking right along, he wanders up the walk and climbs the front steps of every house they pass on the way. The more she calls to him the more he lingers. When she scolds him, he runs in the opposite direction. She is afraid he is turning into a behavior problem. This baby isn't a behavior problem, though he may be made into one. He's not at an age when he can keep the grocery store in mind. His nature says to him, "Look at that walk to explore! Look at those stairs!" Every time his mother calls to him, it reminds him of his new-felt urge to assert himself. What can the mother do? If she has to get to the store promptly, she can take him in his carriage. But if she's going to use this time for his outing, she should allow four times as long as if she were going alone, and let him make his side trips. If she keeps moving along slowly, he'll want to catch up to her every once in a while.

Here's another tight spot. It's time to go in for lunch, but your small child is digging happily in the dirt. If you say, "Now it's time to go in," in a tone of voice that means, "Now you can't have any more fun," you'll get resistance. But if you say cheerfully, "Let's go climb the stairs," it may give him a desire to go. But suppose he's tired and cranky that day, and nothing that's indoors makes any appeal. He just gets balky right away, disagreeably balky. I'd pick him up casually and carry him indoors, even if he's squealing and kicking like a little pig. You do this in a self-confident way, as if you were saying to him, "I know, you're tired and cross. But when we have to go in, we have to." Don't scold him; it won't make him see the error of his ways. Don't argue with him, because that won't change his mind; you will only get yourself frustrated. A small child who is feeling miserable and making a scene is comforted underneath by sensing that his mother knows what to do without getting angry. . . .

Going to Bed

Keeping Bedtime Happy   There are three or four factors that make a lot of difference between the child who goes to bed willingly and the one who stalls and argues.

Keep bedtime agreeable and happy. Remember that it is delicious and inviting to the tired child, if you don't turn it into an unpleasant duty. Have an air of cheerful certainty about it. Expect him to turn in at the hour you decide as surely as you expect him to breathe. It's good for a child to be able to persuade his mother (or father) to change her mind once in a while about bedtime (Fourth of July, for instance). But bedtime comes too often for regular argument. It usually works best to have the nap come right after lunch, before he has had time to become absorbed in play. The relation between supper and bedtime is usually more complicated because of the bath, the father's coming home.

Until the child is at least 3 or 4, and in any case until he is responsible enough to like to get himself to bed, lead him rather than push him with words. Carry the very small child to bed affectionately. With a 3- or 4-year-old, lead him by the hand, both of you still chatting about what was last on his mind.

Small children are comforted by having a certain amount of ritual about going to bed. For example, the dolly is put in her bed and tucked in. Then the teddy bear is put in the child's bed. Then the child is tucked in and kissed. Then the mother pulls down the shade or puts out the light. Try not to rush going to bed, no matter how much of a hurry you are in. Keep it peaceful. Tell or read a story regularly if you have time. It shouldn't be scary. Most children are helped in going to bed by having a cozy toy animal or doll for company in bed.

Taking Things to Bed   Is there any harm letting a child get used to taking a cozy toy like a woolly animal to bed with him? Definitely not. If a toy gives a sense of comfort and companionship, it's good for him. Human beings are born sociable. In civilizations that are simpler than ours children and grownups too go to sleep curled up together. It's not surprising that a child, particularly an only one, should feel a little lonesome going to sleep in a room by himself. If he can breathe life into a stuffed doll or animal, so much the better. Don't worry if the toy gets dirty or ragged. You can have it washed or cleaned, but don't dispose of it for hygienic reasons. . . .

What a School Is For

Linking School with the World   A school wants its pupils to learn at first-hand about the outside world, about the jobs of the local farmers and business-men and workers, so that they will see the connection between their school-work and real life. It arranges trips to near-by industries, asks people from the outside to come in and talk, encourages classroom discussion. A class that is studying food may have an opportunity, for example, to observe some of the steps in the collecting, pasteurizing, bottling, and delivery of milk, or in the transportation and marketing of vegetables.

High-school and college students have further opportunities to learn about the world by attending summer work camps. A group of students and teachers may work in a factory or in a farming area, discuss together, and come to understand better, the problems of various occupations and industries and how they are solved.

Democracy Builds Discipline   Another thing that a good school wants to teach is democracy, not just as a patriotic motto but as a way of living and getting things done. A good teacher knows that she can't teach democracy out of a book if she's acting like a dictator in person. She encourages her pupils to help decide how they are going to tackle certain projects and the difficulties they later run into, lets them help figure out among themselves which one to do this part of the job and which one that. That's how they learn to appreciate each other. That's how they learn to get things done, not just in school, but in the outside world, too.

Actual experiments have shown that children with a teacher who tells them what to do at every step of the way will do a good job while she is in the room. But when she goes out, a lot of them stop working, start fooling. They figure that lessons are the teacher's responsibility, not theirs, and that now they have a chance to be themselves. But these experiments showed that children who have helped choose and plan their own work and have co-operated with each other in carrying it out, will accomplish almost as much when the teacher is out of the room as in. Why? They know the purpose of the job they are on, and the steps ahead in accomplishing it. They feel that it is their job, not the teacher's. Each one wants to do his share, because he is proud to be a respected member of the group and feels a sense of responsibility to the others.

This is the very highest kind of discipline. This training, this spirit, is what makes the best citizens, the most valuable workers, and even the finest soldiers.

SAMUEL A. STOUFFER

Army Life

The following table and statement are parts of a major study of common soldiers' experiences in World War II. What does the table reveal about the degree to which New Deal reformers' rhetoric about the war had penetrated the popular imagination? Do the two documents suggest anything about the internment of the Japanese? Or does either of them echo the tone of Roosevelt's speech on the concentration of power? Was the war a democratizing experience?

From *The American Soldier: Adjustment During Army Life* by Samuel A. Stouffer et al., vol. 1, *Studies in Social Psychology in World War II*, pp. 370, 436. Copyright 1949 © 1977 by Princeton University Press. Reprinted by permission of Princeton University Press.

Classification of Men's Own Formulations of American War Aims*
(Cross Section of Troops in the United States, July 1943)

Type of formulation		Percentage of men giving each formulation
No response to question		36
One-word, slogan-like concepts		16
(E.g., freedom, peace, democracy, victory)		
Relatively defensive concepts		24
To keep the U.S. the way it is	(11)	
To protect national security and/or existence	(7)	
To prevent dictatorship in the U.S.	(3)	
Just because we were attacked	(3)	
Relatively idealistic concepts		15
To rid the world of the Fascist threat	(7)	
To preserve and extend American blessings to others	(4)	
To make this a better world	(3)	
To help the underdog	(1)	
Cynical attitudes		5
(E.g., capitalists, politics, England is responsible for America's being at war)		
Expression of bewilderment or skepticism		2
Unclassified		2
Total		100
Number of cases		2,125

*The question to which men wrote their replies was: "Different people have different ideas about what the U.S. is fighting for in this war. What is your *own personal opinion* about what the United States is fighting for?"

Statements by Enlisted Men in the Persian Gulf Command

The officers in this command are the most selfish egotistical people I've ever come across. They never think of the men but they get very angry when things do not go right for themselves. A good illustration is the incident where the officers' club was built before the hospital. Another example of the officers' selfishness occurs practically daily in the PX. They are allowed to enter the PX at all hours for the ridiculous reason that it is beneath them to wait their turn to get served. After all, we do belong to the greatest democracy the world has ever known but you would not know it after being stationed in the Persian Gulf Service Command.

When we first came to this camp our barracks was just below the officers' club and we heard that it was built while work was stopped on our hospital.

Well, we had no place to go, no facilities for entertainment, etc., we were practically restricted to the camp. Every place was out of bounds to us while it wasn't to the officers and then at nites we could sit on our bunks in the darkness and hear music, laughter, loud drunken voices coming to us from the officers' club. They were having a good time. Dances every Sat. nite. The colored orchestra was up there a couple nites a week. It didn't help our morale any to see that go on. Then the officers had beer (our canned beer) for several months before we ever got any.

Our roofs on our barracks leaked right through the first rain. The officers immediately had their roof tarred—even tho they had tin under their mud roofing while we had straw. It seems to me that the officers should think of their men first, but instead they think of themselves first and never think of us at all.

Only today I saw an officer with a carton of Luckies, some Fig Newtons, and a new cigarette lighter, all three of which our PX has been out of for days. Pabst beer, supposedly the better of the two kinds available here, is always stocked at the officers PX, and seldom at ours. Because of the time wasted during working hours is the reason for throwing that PX off limits to us. Officers who draw many times more pay are therefore costing the government much more in the time they waste during working hours. And yet, our PX is open to them at any time, and they can barge right up to the counters for immediate service. The officers' mess serves fresh eggs any morning they want them, chicken several times a week, and far greater quantities of fresh fruits and vegetables than we ever see, yet the officers and men are supposed to be rationed equally. If whoever reads this were to talk to every enlisted man in this camp, I think the opinion would be basically the same as mine. We have become bitter at the many injustices imposed on us and don't care who knows.

Trouble on the Home Front

War often serves as a social pressure cooker, and World War II was no exception. The year 1943 brought two major race riots, in Detroit and Harlem, and the "zoot-suit riots," described in the caption for the photo on page 302. How might one account for the hostility sailors felt for the "zooters"? What did it have to do with the war? Could the zoot-suit riots have been caused by the kinds of feelings expressed in the previous document by the Persian Gulf enlistees? Did the Zooters and regular military recruits undergo a similar cultural experience during the war?

Original Caption: "Zoot suiters leave jail to make court appearance. Chains were in fashion, but they wore them on their wrists." *Library of Congress.*

The Zoot suit was assured a place in American history in early June, 1943, when sailors stationed at the Chavez Ravine Naval Base invaded the Mexican section of Los Angeles in search of "zooters" (the costume included flared trousers, a broad felt hat, and a key chain with a pocket knife). "Procedure was standard," according to one description. "Grab a zooter. Take off his pants and frock coat and tear them up or burn them. Trim the 'Argentine ducktail' haircut that goes with the screwey costume." (Quoted in Richard Polenberg, *War and Society: The United States, 1941–1945* [New York: Lippincott, 1972], p. 130.)

End of a Decade

The two photographs that follow were the work of two of the most talented photographers commissioned by the New Deal's Farm Security Administration. What kinds of attitudes seem to lie behind the pictures of home and field? What sort of life do the pictures suggest that the agency was making "secure"? Suppose, for the sake of analysis, that these two scenes represent not any reality, but two faces of a mythic world that the New Deal (and the war) were supposed to preserve and defend. What were the contents of this mythic world? Taken together, do the photographs suggest that the late New Deal was still involved in the creation of innovative programs? or that the New Deal's major efforts at reform had been completed? Does either of the photographs—but Rothstein's particularly—hint at the growing concentration on foreign affairs?

Cutting Hay, Vermont. Photo by Arthur Rothstein for the Farm Security Administration. *Library of Congress.*

FSA Clients at Home, Hidalgo, Texas, 1939. Photo by Russell Lee for the Farm Security Administration. *Library of Congress.*

CHAPTER 11

Cold War and Containment

Some Americans looked to the postwar world for a new birth of
international order and domestic progress, expecting to live, as *Life*
publisher Henry Luce had forecast in 1941, in the "American
Century," and expecting to participate in the great work of
reconstructing the world in the American image. Others expected
only another return to normalcy. What happened was neither.
Instead, there was a new emergency to replace the depression and the
war. This new crisis took shape within months of the surrenders of
1945 and very soon had a name: the cold war. The phrase was used
to describe a state of continued hostility between the United States
and the Soviet Union—a hostility short of war, and therefore "cold,"
but a war nonetheless.

The cold war can be understood neither as a great
misunderstanding nor as a righteous American crusade against
communist aggression and tyranny. The United States and the Soviet
Union had very different ideas about the shape of the postwar world.
The Soviets, who had once again been forced to wage a devastating
campaign on their own soil, wanted immunity from future aggression.
For Joseph Stalin, this meant friendly governments in Eastern Europe
and weak states on his country's other frontiers. The American vision
of the postwar world was inseparably tied to an ideal world economic
order, based on free trade and consistent with its own needs for
security from depression. At Bretton Woods in 1944, the United
States helped create several institutions—including the International
Monetary Fund, the World Bank, and a system of currency
exchange—thought essential to free-flowing trade and investment.
Soviet domination of Eastern Europe had already closed off a

substantial trading area; further "aggression" could seriously restrict markets and access to raw materials.

The cold war came to maturity in a series of crises which took place between 1947 and 1950. In Greece, communist guerrillas threatened to unseat a corrupt, unpopular, and conservative government. Truman couched a request to Congress for funds to provide economic and military assistance to Greece in words that would become known as the Truman Doctrine. "I believe," Truman said, "that it must be the policy of the United States to support free peoples who are resisting attempted subjugation by armed minorities or by outside pressures." The same year, following a communist coup in Czechoslovakia, the United States began a comprehensive aid program for Western Europe. Known as the Marshall Plan, the program was designed to restrict communist influence and preserve American markets by stimulating economic recovery. Both the Marshall Plan and the Truman Doctrine were part of a general policy called "containment." As developed by our Moscow chargé d'affaires, George F. Kennan, in an influential article in the journal *Foreign Affairs*, containment was a policy of resistance. According to Kennan, the Soviets were "impervious to logic of reason," but "highly sensitive to logic of force." Soviet aggression could be effectively countered, but only if it were resisted at every point, and with the threat of physical force.

The administration of Dwight Eisenhower adopted Truman's concept of a bipolar world while reshaping the policy of containment. Perhaps the least bellicose of all postwar presidents, Eisenhower sought to modulate conflict with the Soviets through summit conferences, ended the war in Korea, and managed to avoid direct military intervention in Vietnam. But John Foster Dulles, Eisenhower's able but militant secretary of state, redefined Kennan's containment policy into the more aggressive stance known as "brinkmanship" (defined by Dulles as "the ability to get to the verge without getting into the war"). Another rhetorical escalation, the Dulles doctrine of "massive retaliation," shifted conflict into an arms race and made events like the Soviet launching of the Sputnik satellite in 1957 into traumatic moments of political and military import.

The victory over the Axis and a monopoly of atomic weapons had led Americans to believe that the postwar world could be shaped to suit their needs and desires. Three events made this assumption questionable. Early in 1949, China's incompetent American-supported

Nationalist government withdrew to the island of Formosa, leaving the mainland in the hands of communists under the leadership of Mao Tse-tung. Soon thereafter, Americans learned that the Soviet Union had exploded a nuclear device, ending the American monopoly. And in June 1950, communist North Korea attacked South Korea and began a war that would end in a stalemate more than three years later.

But rather than face their own helplessness in the face of events beyond their control, Americans defended their unrealistic expectations by ferreting out the "real" causes of American weakness. For example: the Soviets had not developed the bomb; they had been given the secrets of atomic energy. Such reasoning led in June 1953 to the death of Julius and Ethel Rosenberg, the first Americans executed specifically for peacetime espionage. Another example: China had not suffered a revolution; State Department representatives, claimed Senator Robert Taft, had "promoted the communist cause in China." Finally, Alger Hiss, convicted of perjury in 1950, served as a scapegoat for the inability of the West to assert control over Eastern Europe as well as a symbol of the New Deal. Scholars still disagree about the actual guilt of the Rosenbergs and Hiss. What is clear is that cold war insecurities made impartial proceedings impossible.

The old dividing lines between questions that were foreign and questions that were domestic dissolved. Internal politics at every level, even down to town and county races, became focused on the question of "communism" and "free enterprise." Almost everything Americans did, from producing washing machines to teaching history, became ideologically tied to the cold war. Government agencies, business, and colleges became concerned with rooting out individuals who had ever displayed any sympathy for the communist movement. And political candidates competed with each other to see who could adopt the most vigorous stance of opposition to the Soviet "threat." The decades after 1945 were as dominated by the cold war as the 1930s had been by the emergency of the depression.

The materials in this chapter are related to both the foreign-policy and the domestic aspects of the cold war. Taken together, they illustrate what amounts to a new consciousness among Americans, a consciousness of their society as an embattled stronghold of "capitalist" or "free enterprise" values, threatened on every side and needing all its energies and resources to stand against its enemies, foreign and domestic.

GEORGE C. HERRING

A Dead-End Alley: War in Indochina, 1950-1954

No single event captures the demise of the idea of an "American Century" quite as well as the Vietnam War. For more than two decades, the United States tried, and failed, to create a Vietnam suitable to its own vision of the postwar world. This failure became most apparent in the 1960s, when the fighting of the war divided Americans into bitter factions. Apologists for John Kennedy believed he would have avoided full-scale involvement. But Kennedy had remarked that a withdrawal from Vietnam would mean collapse in Southeast Asia; and by 1963 he had 15,000 advisors in the country, more than fifteen times Eisenhower's commitment. Lyndon Johnson also believed in the domino theory and defined the Vietnam problem as simple communist aggression, and in 1964 he inaugurated systematic air attacks on North Vietnam. But neither the air war nor an additional half-million American troops were sufficient to bring anything resembling victory. Even before the January 1968 Tet offensive, when Viet Cong and North Vietnamese attacks on major southern cities made clear that the American claim to be winning the war was a sham, many Americans had come to question the war in moral terms. Over 200,000 marched against the war in Washington, D. C., in 1967. When Richard Nixon in 1970 moved ground troops into Cambodia, students closed down many colleges and universities in protest. By 1973, as Nixon withdrew the last of the nation's ground troops, the American Century (as well as the Eisenhower equilibrium—see Chapter 12) was a relic of another era.

What went wrong? The answer to that question lies as much in the seedtime of the cold war as it does in later decades, when defeat and frustration were more apparent. As George Herring makes clear in this essay, early American interest in Vietnam was inseparable from the larger issues of the cold war—the war in Korea, Soviet domination of Eastern Europe, the fall of China. How did American policy makers translate cold war phenomena into a quarter-century of involvement in an obscure nation in the Far East? Was the national interest at stake in Vietnam? Was our failure in Vietnam predictable, even in 1954?

When Ho Chi Minh proclaimed the independence of Vietnam from French rule on September 2, 1945, he borrowed liberally from Thomas Jefferson, opening with the words "We hold these truths to be self-evident. That all men are created equal." During independence celebrations in Hanoi later in the day, American warplanes flew over the city, U.S. Army officers stood on the reviewing stand with Vo Nguyen Giap and other leaders, and a Vietnamese band played the "Star-Spangled Banner." Toward the end of the festivities, Giap spoke warmly of Vietnam's "particularly intimate relations" with the United States, something, he noted, "which it is a pleasant duty to dwell upon." The prominent role played by Americans at the birth of modern Vietnam appears in retrospect one of history's most bitter ironies. Despite the glowing professions of friendship on September 2, the United States acquiesced in the return of France to Vietnam and from 1950 to 1954 actively supported French efforts to suppress Ho's revolution, the first phase of a quarter-century American struggle to control the destiny of Vietnam.

The Vietnamese revolution was in many ways the personal creation of the charismatic patriot Ho Chi Minh. Born in the province of Nghe An, the cradle of Vietnamese revolutionaries, Ho inherited from his mandarin father a sturdy patriotism and an adventurous spirit. Departing Vietnam in 1912 as a cabin boy aboard a merchant steamer, he eventually settled in France with a colony of Vietnamese nationalists, and when the Paris Peace Conference rejected his petition for Vietnamese independence, he joined the French Communist party. Then known as Nguyen Ai Quoc (Nguyen the Patriot), he worked for more than two decades as a party functionary and revolutionary organizer in the Soviet Union, China, Thailand, and Vietnam. In 1930, he organized the Indochinese Communist party and incited a series of revolts which were brutally suppressed by the French. When Hitler conquered France in 1940 and Japan began to move southward into Vietnam, Ho returned to his homeland. A frail and gentle man who radiated warmth and serenity, he was also a master organizer and determined revolutionary who was willing to employ the most cold-blooded methods in the cause to which he dedicated his life. Establishing headquarters in the caves of Pac Bo, by a mountain he named Karl Marx and a river he named Lenin, Ho conceived the strategy and founded the political organization, the Vietminh, that would eventually drive the French from Vietnam.

The Vietminh capitalized on the uniquely favorable circumstances of World War II to establish itself as the voice of Vietnamese nationalism. The Japanese permitted the French colonial authorities to retain nominal power throughout most of the war, but the ease with which Japan had established its position discredited the French in the eyes of the Vietnamese, and the hardships imposed by the Japanese and their French puppets fanned popular dis-

From George C. Herring, *America's Longest War: The United States and Vietnam, 1950–1975* (New York: Wiley, 1979), pp. 1–42 as edited. Copyright © 1979, John Wiley & Sons, Inc. Reprinted by permission of John Wiley & Sons, Inc.

French Indochina.

content. The Vietminh leadership, composed primarily of Communists, adopted a broad nationalist platform, stressing independence and the establishment of "democratic" freedoms. It enticed some rival nationalists into joining it and ruthlessly eliminated some who refused. By the spring of 1945, Ho had mobilized a base of mass support in northern Vietnam, and with the assistance of Giap, a former professor of history, had raised an army of some 5,000 men. When the Japanese deposed the puppet French government in March 1945, the Vietminh, working closely with an American intelligence unit (hence the American presence on September 2), waged an intensive and effective guerrilla war against their new colonial masters. When Japan surrendered in August 1945, the Vietminh quickly stepped into the vacuum, occupying government headquarters in Hanoi and proclaiming the independence of Vietnam.

Independence would not come without a struggle, however, for the French were determined to regain the empire they had ruled for more than half a century. Conscious of their nation's declining position in world affairs, many French politicians felt that France could "only be a great power so long as our flag continues to fly in all the overseas territory." French Indochina, comprising Cambodia, Laos, and the three Vietnamese colonies of Annam, Tonkin, and Cochin China, was among the richest and most prestigious of France's colonial possessions. The Vietminh had been unable to establish a firm power base in southern Vietnam, and with the assistance of British occupation forces, who had been given responsibility for accepting the Japanese surrender south of the seventeenth parallel, the French were able to expel the Vietminh from Saigon and reestablish control over the southern part of the country.

For more than a year, France and the Vietminh attempted to negotiate an agreement, but their goals were irreconcilable. French colonial policy had always stressed assimilation, full French citizenship, rather than independence or dominion status, and France hedged on the Vietminh's demand for immediate self-government and eventual independence. For the Vietminh, unification of their country not only represented fulfillment of the centuries-old dream of Vietnamese nationalists but was also an economic necessity since the south produced the food surplus necessary to sustain the overpopulated, industrial north. The French were determined to keep Cochin China separate from Annam and Tonkin and to maintain absolute control in the southern colony where their economic interests were largest. Negotiations dragged on inconclusively, mutual suspicions increased, and outbreaks of violence became commonplace. The shelling of Haiphong by a French cruiser in November 1946, killing 6,000 civilians, set off a war which in its various phases would last nearly thirty years.

For a time during World War II, the United States actively opposed the return of Indochina to France. Before 1941, Americans had taken little interest in the area, but the Japanese takeover impressed upon them its importance as a source of foodstuffs and raw materials and as a strategic outpost guarding the major water routes of southern Asia. Some U.S. officials perceived the growth of nationalism in Vietnam during the war and feared that a French attempt to regain control of its colony might provoke a long and bloody war, bringing instability to an area of economic and strategic significance. Even if France should succeed, they reasoned, it would restore monopolistic controls which would deny the United States access to raw materials and naval bases. President Franklin D. Roosevelt seems instinctively to have recognized that colonialism was doomed and that the United States must identify with the forces of nationalism in Asia. Moreover, Roosevelt profoundly disliked France and its leader Charles de Gaulle, and regarded the French as "poor colonizers" who had "badly mismanaged" Indochina and exploited its people. Roosevelt therefore advocated placing Indochina under international trusteeship to be prepared for independence. . . .

After Roosevelt's death in April 1945, the United States adopted a policy even more favorable to France. Harry S. Truman did not share his predecessor's personal interest in Indochina or his concern about colonialism. American thinking about the postwar world also underwent a major reorientation in the spring of 1945. Military and civilian strategists perceived that the war had left the Soviet Union the most powerful nation in Europe and Asia, and the subjugation of Eastern Europe raised growing fears that Joseph Stalin had broader, perhaps global, designs. Assigning top priority to the promotion of stable, friendly governments in Western Europe that could stand as bulwarks against Russian expansion, the Truman administration concluded that the United States "had no interest" in "championing schemes of international trusteeship" that would weaken and alienate the "European states whose help we need to balance Soviet power in Europe." France assumed a role of special importance in the new scheme of things, and the State Department insisted that the United States must repair the rift that had opened under Roosevelt by cooperating "wholeheartedly" with France and allaying "her apprehensions that we are going to propose that territory be taken away from her." The Truman administration quickly scrapped what remained of Roosevelt's trusteeship plan and in the summer of 1945 gave de Gaulle firm assurances that it would not stand in the way of the restoration of French sovereignty in Indochina.

The United States viewed the outbreak of war in Indochina with concern. Along with revolutions in Burma, Malaya, and Indonesia, the Vietnamese upheaval underscored the strength and explosiveness of nationalism in Southeast Asia. France's stubborn pursuit of outmoded colonial goals seemed to preclude anything other than a military solution, but the State Department's Far Eastern Office doubted that France had the capacity to subdue the revolution by force and feared that a French defeat would eliminate Western influence from an area of economic and strategic importance. The State Department's Asian experts warned of the dangers of identifying with French colonialism and pressed the administration to use its influence to force France to come to terms with Vietnamese nationalism.

American skepticism about French policy in Asia continued to be outweighed by European concerns, however. In the spring of 1947, the United States formally committed itself to the containment of Soviet expansion in Europe, and throughout the next two years American attention was riveted on France, where economic stagnation and political instability aroused grave fears of a possible Communist takeover. Warned by moderate French politicians that outside interference in colonial matters would play into the hands of the French Communist party, the United States left France to handle the Indochina question in its own way. An "immediate and vital interest" in keeping in power a "friendly government to assist in the furtherance of our aims in Europe," the State Department concluded, must "take precedence over active steps looking toward the realization of our objectives in Indochina."

By early 1947, moreover, the Truman administration had drawn conclusions about Ho's revolution that would determine American policy in Vietnam for the next two decades. On numerous occasions, Ho had openly appealed for American support, even indicating that Indochina would be a "fertile field for American capital and enterprise" and raising the possibility of an American naval base at Camranh Bay. U.S. diplomats in Vietnam insisted that they could find no evidence of direct Soviet contact with the Vietminh, and they stressed that, regardless of his ideology, Ho had established himself as the "symbol of nationalism and the struggle for freedom to the overwhelming majority of the population." But these arguments failed to persuade an administration increasingly obsessed with the Communist menace in Europe. Intelligence reports stressed that Ho had remained loyal to Moscow throughout his career, and the lack of close ties with the Soviet Union simply meant that he was trusted to carry out Stalin's plans without supervision. In the absence of irrefutable evidence to the contrary, the State Department concluded, the United States could not "afford to assume that Ho is anything but Moscow-directed." Unwilling, as Secretary of State George C. Marshall put it, to see "colonial empires and administrations supplanted by philosophies and political organizations emanating from the Kremlin," the administration refused to take any step which might facilitate a "Communist" triumph in Indochina.

As a consequence, during the first three years of the Indochina war, the United States maintained a distinctly pro-French "neutrality." Reluctant to place itself in the awkward position of directly supporting colonialism, the Truman administration rejected French pleas for military aid to be used against the Vietminh. At the same time, however, substantial American funds provided under the Marshall Plan enabled France to use its own resources to prosecute the war in Indochina. Fearful of antagonizing its European ally and of assisting the Vietminh, even indirectly, Washington refused to acknowledge receipt of Ho's appeals for support and declined to use its leverage to end the fighting or bring about a negotiated settlement.

The possibility of a French defeat, along with the Communist victory in China, brought forth in early 1950 a decision to support France in Indochina, the first step toward direct American involvement in Vietnam. The French had launched the war in 1946 confident of victory, but Ho had predicted the nature and eventual outcome of the conflict more accurately. "If ever the tiger [Vietminh] pauses," he said, "the elephant [France] will impale him on his mighty tusks. But the tiger will not pause, and the elephant will die of exhaustion and loss of blood." The Vietminh retreated into the countryside, evading major engagements, mobilizing popular support, and harassing French outposts. France held the major towns and cities, but a series of unsuccessful and costly offensives and relentless hit-and-run raids by Vietminh guerrillas placed a growing strain on French manpower and resources and produced increasing war-weariness at home. The collapse of Chiang Kai-shek's government in China in 1949 and the southward advance of Mao Tse-tung's army raised the ominous possibility of Chinese Communist collaboration with the Vietminh. From late 1949 on, French officials issued increasingly urgent warnings that without direct American military aid they might be compelled to withdraw from Indochina.

The French appeals came at a time when Washington, already gripped by near panic, was frantically reassessing its global Cold War strategy. The fall of China and Russia's successful testing of a nuclear device persuaded many American officials that the Communist threat had assumed even more menacing proportions than that posed by the Axis a decade earlier. Any doubts about the direction of Stalin's foreign policy had long since been waved aside: the Soviet Union, "animated by a new fanatic faith," was determined to "impose its absolute authority on the rest of the world." Recent successes seemed to have spurred the Soviet leadership to a new level of confidence and militancy, and Communist expansion, in the eyes of American policymakers, had already reached a point beyond which it must not be permitted to go. Any further "extension of the area under the domination of the Kremlin," the National Security Council warned, "would raise the possibility that no coalition adequate to confront the Kremlin with greater strength could be assembled." Facing a world divided into two hostile blocs, a precarious balance of power, and the possibility, if not likelihood, of global war, the Truman administration initiated plans to increase American military capabilities, shore up the defense of Western Europe, and extend the containment policy to the Far East.

In the dramatically altered strategic context of 1950, support for France in Indochina was considered essential for the security of Western Europe. Massive expenditures for the war against the Vietminh had retarded France's economic recovery and the attainment of that level of political stability required to fend off the threat of Communism. Certain that Europe was more vulnerable than ever to the Soviet threat, American policymakers in early 1950 began to formulate plans to raise the military forces necessary to defend against the Red Army. Their preliminary proposals required France to contribute sizeable numbers of troops and provided for the rearmament of West Germany, measures the French were likely to resist. The administration thus feared that if it did not respond positively to its ally's appeals for aid in Indochina, France might refuse to cooperate with its strategic design for Western Europe.

American willingness to support France in Indochina also reflected a growing concern about the future of Southeast Asia. The raging conflict in Indochina and insurgencies in Burma, Malaya, and Indonesia all sprang from indigenous roots, but in a seemingly polarized world the mere existence of these revolutions and their leftist orientation persuaded Americans that Southeast Asia was the "target of a coordinated offensive directed by the Kremlin." The European colonial powers and the fragile newly independent governments of the region seemed incapable of subduing the revolutions, and the presence of a hostile China to the north added enormously to the danger.

In the aftermath of the fall of China, American strategists concluded that Southeast Asia was vital to the security of the United States. Should the region be swept by Communism, the National Security Council warned, "we shall have suffered a major political rout the repercussions of which will be felt throughout the world." The loss of an area so large and populous would tip the balance of power against the United States. Recent Communist triumphs had already aroused nervousness in Europe, and another major victory might tempt the Europeans to reach an accommodation with the Soviet Union. The economic consequences could be equally profound. The United States and its European allies would be denied access to important markets. Southeast Asia was the world's largest producer of natural rubber and was an important source of oil, tin, tungsten, and other strategic commodities. Should control of these vital raw materials suddenly change hands, the Soviet bloc would be enormously strengthened at the expense of the West.

American policymakers also feared that the loss of Southeast Asia would irreparably damage the nation's strategic position in the Far East. Control of the off-shore island chain extending from Japan to the Philippines, America's first line of defense in the Pacific, would be endangered. Air and sea routes between Australia and the Middle East and the United States and India could be cut, severely hampering military operations in the event of war. Japan, India, and Australia, those nations where the West retained predominant influence, would be cut off from each other and left vulnerable. The impact on Japan, America's major Far Eastern ally, could be disastrous. Denied access to the raw materials, rice, and markets upon which their economy depended, the Japanese might see no choice but to come to terms with the enemy.

American officials agreed that Indochina, and especially Vietnam, was the key to the defense of Southeast Asia. Soviet recognition of the Vietminh on January 30, 1950, confirmed long-standing beliefs about Ho's allegiance, revealing him, in Secretary of State Dean Acheson's words, in his "true colors as the mortal enemy of native independence in Indochina." It was also interpreted as a "significant and ominous" portent of Stalin's intention to "accelerate the revolutionary process" in Southeast Asia. Ho's well-organized guerrillas had already scored major gains against France, and with increased Soviet and Chinese backing might be able to force a French withdrawal, removing the last military bulwark between China and the rest of Southeast Asia. Indochina was in the "most immediate danger," the State Department concluded, and was therefore "the most strategically important area of Southeast Asia."

Indochina was considered intrinsically important for its raw materials, rice, and naval bases, but it was deemed far more significant for the presumed effect its loss would have on other areas. By early 1950, American policymakers had firmly embraced what would become known as the "domino theory," the belief that the fall of Indochina would bring about in rapid succession the collapse of the other nations of Southeast Asia. Acceptance of this concept reflects the perceived fragility of the region in 1950, as well as the experience of World War II, when Hitler had overrun Western Europe in three months and the Japanese had seized much of Southeast Asia in even less time. First employed to justify aid to Greece in 1947, the idea, once applied to Southeast

Asia, quickly became an article of faith. Americans were certain that if Indochina fell the rest of Southeast Asia would be imperilled. The strategic reassessment of 1950 thus ended American "neutrality" and produced a commitment to furnish France military and economic assistance for the war against the Vietminh. It also established principles that would provide the basis for U.S. policy in Vietnam for years to come and would eventually lead to massive involvement.

The creation of nominally independent governments in Indochina made it easier for the United States to rationalize support of France. Unable to defeat the Vietminh militarily, the French had attempted to undercut it politically by forming native governments in Laos, Cambodia, and Vietnam, the latter headed by the former Emperor of Annam, Bao Dai, and according them the status of "free states" within the French Union. Many U.S. officials were skeptical of the so-called Bao Dai solution, warning that it was only a smoke-screen for continued French domination and had little chance of success. The State Department acknowledged the strength of these arguments, but Bao Dai seemed the only alternative to "Commie domination of Indochina," as Acheson put it, and while American support did not guarantee his success the lack of it seemed likely to ensure his failure. By backing Bao Dai, moreover, the United States would at least avoid the appearance of being an accomplice of French imperialism. In February 1950, the Truman administration formally recognized the Bao Dai government and the free states of Laos and Cambodia and initiated plans to support them with economic and technical assistance.

In retrospect the assumptions upon which American policymakers acted in 1950 appear misguided. The Southeast Asian revolutions were not inspired by Moscow and, although the Soviet Union and China at times sought to control them, their capacity to do so was limited by their lack of military and especially naval power and by the strength of local nationalism. The American assessment of the situation in Vietnam seems to have been well off the mark. Although a dedicated Communist, Ho was no mere tool of the Soviet Union, and while he was willing to accept help from the major Communist powers— indeed he had no choice but to do so—he was not prepared to subordinate Vietnamese independence to them. Vietnam's historic fears of its larger northern neighbor made submission to China especially unlikely. "It is better to sniff French dung for a while than eat China's all our life," Ho once said, graphically expressing a traditional principle of Vietnamese foreign policy. Perhaps most important, regardless of his ideology, Ho by 1950 had captured the standard of Vietnamese nationalism, and by supporting France, even under the guise of the Bao Dai solution, the United States was attaching itself to a losing cause.

American policymakers were not unaware of the pitfalls of intervention in Indochina. Should the United States commit itself to Bao Dai and should he turn out to be a French puppet, a State Department Asian specialist warned, "we must then follow blindly down a dead-end alley, expending our limited resources . . . in a fight that would be hopeless." Some Americans officials even dimly perceived that the United States might get sucked into direct involvement in Vietnam. But the initial commitment seemed limited and the risks seemed smaller than those of inaction. Caught up in a global struggle reminiscent of World War II, with Russia taking Germany's place in Europe and China Japan's place in Asia, U.S. officials were certain that if they did not back France and Bao Dai Southeast Asia might be lost, leaving the more awesome choice of making a "staggering investment" to recover the losses or falling back to a "much contracted" line of defense in the western Pacific.

By the time the United States committed itself to assist France, the Vietminh had gained the military initiative in Indochina. Ho Chi Minh controlled an estimated two-thirds of the countryside, and Vietminh regulars and guerrillas numbered in the hundreds of thousands. The Chinese were furnishing sanctuaries across the border and large stocks of weapons. By early 1950, Giap felt sufficiently confident of his strength to take the offensive for the first time. The French maintained tenuous control in the cities and the major production centers, but at a very high cost, suffering 1,000 casualties per month and in 1949 alone spending 167 million francs on the war. Even in the areas under nominal French control, the Vietminh spread terror after dark, sabotaging power plants and factories, tossing grenades into cafés and theaters, and brutally assassinating French officials. "Anyone with white skin caught outside protected areas after dark is courting horrible death," an American correspondent reported. . . .

Introverted and given to periodic moods of depression, Bao Dai was incapable of rallying popular support, and the reality of French dominance gave him nothing to work with. His government was composed largely of wealthy southern landowners who in no sense were representative of the people. Nationalists of stature refused to support him, and the masses either backed the resistance or remained aloof. Bao Dai's authority scarcely extended beyond the authority of the French army.

The onset of the Korean War in the summer of 1950 complicated an already difficult problem. The Truman administration perceived North Korea's invasion of South Korea as confirmation of its suspicion that the Soviet Union sought to conquer all of Asia, even at the risk of war, and the defense of Indochina assumed even greater importance in American eyes. By the end of the year, however, the United States and France had suffered major reversals. Chinese intervention in Korea forced General Douglas MacArthur into a headlong retreat from the Yalu. In the meantime, Giap had inflicted upon France its "greatest colonial defeat since Montcalm had died at Quebec," trapping an entire army at Cao Bang in northeastern Vietnam and costing the French more than 6,000 troops and enough equipment to stock an entire Vietminh division. Chinese intervention in Korea raised fears of a similar plunge across the border into Vietnam, and American policymakers were increasingly concerned that a growing defeatism in France would raise demands for withdrawal from Indochina.

Against this background of stunning defeat in the Far East, the Truman administration struggled to devise a workable policy for Indochina. With large numbers of American troops committed to Korea and Europe vulnerable to a possible Soviet invasion, the Joint Chiefs of Staff agreed that even should the Chinese invade Indochina the United States could not commit military forces to its defense. France must remain and bear primary responsibility for the war. More certain than ever that Indochina was essential to American security, the administration was forced to rely on military assistance to bolster French defenses. In late 1950, the United States committed more than $133 million for aid to Indochina and ordered immediate delivery of large quantities of arms and ammunition, naval vessels, aircraft, and military vehicles.

Most Americans agreed, however, that military equipment by itself would not be enough. As early as May, Acheson complained that the French seemed "paralyzed, in a state of moving neither forward or backward," and a fact-finding mission dispatched to Indochina *before* the Cao Bang disaster confirmed his fears. American observers reported that the French state of mind was "fatuous, even dangerous," and warned that unless France prosecuted the war with greater determination, made more effective use of native manpower, and moved boldly and generously to win over the Vietnamese, the United States and its ally might be "moving into a debacle which neither of us can afford." The Joint Chiefs of Staff proposed that the United States condition its military aid on French pledges to take drastic measures, including the promise of eventual independence.

The administration approached this question with great caution. Acheson conceded that if the United States supported France's "old-fashioned colonial attitudes," it might "lose out." But the French presence was essential to defend Indochina against Communism, he quickly added, and the United States could not press France to the point where it would say, "All right, take over the damned country. We don't want it." Admitting the inconsistency of American policy, he concluded that the only choice was to encourage the French to remain until the crisis had eased but at the same time persuade them to "play with the nationalist movement and give Bao Dai a chance really to get the nationalists on his side." Rejecting any form of pressure, the administration would go no further than gently urge France to make symbolic concessions and to build a Vietnamese army. The State Department, in the meantime, would hold Bao Dai's "feet to the fire" to get him to assert effective leadership under French tutelage.

To strengthen the governments of Indochina and increase their popular appeal, the United States established a program of economic and technical assistance in 1950 and over the next two years spent more than $50 million on various projects. American experts provided fertilizer and seeds to increase agricultural production, constructed dispensaries, developed malaria-control programs, and distributed food and clothing to refugees. . . .

The Truman policy brought only limited results. Their hopes of victory revived by the prospect of large-scale American assistance, the French in late 1950 appointed the flamboyant Jean de Lattre de Tassigny to command the armed forces in Indochina and instructed him to prosecute the war vigorously. A born crusader and practitioner of what he called *dynamisme*, de Lattre announced upon arriving in Vietnam that he would win the war within fifteen months, and under his inspired leadership French forces repulsed a major Vietminh offensive in the Red River Delta in early 1951. But when de Lattre attempted to follow up his success by attacking Vietminh strongholds just south of Hanoi, France suffered its worst defeat of the war. De Lattre himself would die of cancer in early 1952, and the French military position was more precarious at the time of his death than when he had come to Vietnam.

In other areas as well there was little progress. Desperately short of manpower, the French finally put aside their reluctance to arm the Vietnamese, and de Lattre made determined efforts to create a Vietnamese National Army (VNA). The Vietnamese were understandably reluctant to fight for what they regarded as a French cause, however, and by the end of 1951 the VNA numbered only 38,000 men, far short of its projected strength of 115,000. Responding to American entreaties, the French vaguely promised to "perfect" the independence of the Associated States, but the massive infusion of American supplies and de Lattre's early victories seemed to eliminate any compelling need for real concessions. The French were unwilling to fight for *Vietnamese* independence and never seriously considered the only sort of concession that would have satisfied the aspirations of Vietnamese nationalism. France transferred to the native governments some additional responsibilities, but they remained shadow governments lacking in real authority and in popular support. . . .

Deeply suspicious of American intrusion into their domain, the French expressed open resentment against the aid program and placed numerous obstacles in its ways. De Lattre bitterly complained that there were too many Americans in Vietnam spending too much money, that the American aid program was making France "look like a poor cousin in Vietnamese eyes," and that the Americans were "fanning the flames of extreme nationalism." French officials attempted to block projects which did not contribute directly to the war and encouraged Vietnamese suspicions by warning that American aid contained "hidden traps" to subvert their "independence." Largely as a result of French obstructionism, the aid program touched only a small number of people. American officials conceded that its "beneficial psychological results were largely negated because the United States at the same time was pursuing a program of [military] support to the French." America was looked upon "more as a supporter of colonialism than as a friend of the new nation."

While firmly resisting American influence in Indochina, France demanded larger military assistance and an expanded American commitment. Already facing the threat of a military and political collapse in Indochina, the French grew more concerned when American efforts to negotiate an end to the war in Korea raised the possibility that Chinese troops would be freed for a drive southward. In early 1952, France pressed Washington relentlessly for additional military aid, a collective security arrangement for the defense of Southeast Asia, and a firm commitment to provide American combat forces should Chinese troops cross the border into Vietnam.

Washington was extremely wary of expanding its commitments. The proposal for a collective security arrangement appeared to be a snare to draw the United States more deeply into the conflict, and the Truman administration promptly rejected it. The "line we took," Acheson later recalled, was that "in some places such as Europe and NATO, we had a common responsibility. In other places, one or the other of these nations had to take a leading part." The United States also refused to commit ground forces to Indochina under any circumstances. The administration had initiated a massive rearmamant program, but progress had been slowed by the war in Korea and the National Security Council concluded that the nation faced the "continuing danger of global war, as well as local aggression in a situation of inadequate military strength." The drawn-out, costly stalemate in Korea had produced considerable frustration among the American people and had made abundantly clear the difficulties of fighting a land war in Asia. It would be "futile and a mistake to defend Indochina in Indochina," Acheson observed. We "could not have another Korea, we could not put ground forces into Indochina."

The administration was not prepared to abandon France, however. By early 1952, the domino theory was firmly rooted as a principle of American foreign policy. Policymakers agreed that Southeast Asia must not be permitted to "fall into the hands of the Communists like a ripe plum" and that a continued French presence in Indochina was essential to the defense of that critical region. . . .

America's Indochina policy continued to be a hostage of its policy in Europe, the area to which Truman and Acheson assigned the highest priority. Since 1951, the United States had been pressing for allied approval of the European Defense Community, a plan for the integration of French and German forces into a multinational army originally put forward by France to delay German rearmament. The French repeatedly warned that they could not furnish troops for European defense without generous American support in Indochina, a ploy Acheson accurately described as "blackmail." The European Defense Community had also become a volatile political issue in France, where there was strong nationalistic resistance to surrendering the identity of the French army and to collaborating with a recent, and still despised, enemy. With the question awaiting ratification by the French parliament, Acheson later recalled, no one "seriously advised" that it would be "wise to end, or threaten to end, aid to Indochina unless an American plan of military and political reform was carried out." NSC 124/2, a major policy statement on Indochina of June 1952, would go no further than state that the United States should use its "influence" to "promote positive political, military, economic, and social policies. . . ."

During the last half of 1952, Acheson did make a concerted effort to break through French secretiveness. The Secretary of State bluntly informed French officials in July that since the United States was paying about one-third of the cost of the war it did not seem "unreasonable" to expect some detailed information about its progress. The French did not dissent, Acheson later recalled, but "not much happened as a result." Following a long and heated session of the Council of Foreign Ministers in Paris in December, the French again requested additional military assistance. "At this point tired, hungry and exasperated," Acheson later wrote, "I ran out of patience." He complained forcefully that the United States was "thoroughly dissatisfied" with the information it was getting and warned that this situation "had to be remedied. We must know exactly what the situation was and what we were doing if, as and when we were to take any further step." Acheson's protest revealed the depth of American frustration with more than two years of partnership with France, but it came too late to have any effect. Within less than a month, the Truman administration would leave office, freeing it from further responsibility.

Despite a considerable investment in Indochina, Truman and Acheson left to their successors a problem infinitely more complex and dangerous than the one they had taken on in 1950. What had begun as a localized rebellion against French colonialism had expanded into an international conflict of major proportions. The United States was now bearing more than 40 percent of the cost of the war and had established a stake in its outcome. Chinese aid to the Vietminh had increased from 400 tons per month to more than 3,000, and as many as 4,000 Chinese "volunteers" assisted the Vietminh in various ways. The war had spilled over into neighboring Laos and Thailand where China and the Vietminh backed insurgencies against governments supported by the United States and France. In Vietnam itself, French control had been reduced to enclaves around Hanoi, Haiphong, and Saigon, and a narrow strip along the Cambodian border, and France faced a new and much more ominous type of military threat. "The enemy, once painted as a bomb-throwing terrorist or hill sniper lurking in night ambush," the veteran correspondent Theodore White observed, "has become a modern army, increasingly skillful, armed with artillery, organized into divisional groups." The French had naively hoped that American aid might be a substitute for increased sacrifice on their own part, but they had come to realize that it only required more of them. Fearful of their nation's growing dependence on the United States and aware that victory would require nothing short of an all-out effort, in late 1952 some French political leaders outside the Communist party began for the first time to recommend withdrawal from Indochina. The "real" problem, Acheson warned the incoming administration, was the "French will to carry on the . . .war."

The Republican administration of Dwight D. Eisenhower accepted without modification the principles of Indochina policy bequeathed by the Democrats. Eisenhower and his Secretary of State John Foster Dulles agreed that Ho Chi Minh was an instrument of international Communism and that the fall of Indochina would cause the loss of all of Southeast Asia with disastrous political, economic, and strategic consequences for the United States. In the campaign of 1952, the Republicans had attacked the Democrats for failing to halt the advance of Communism, and they were even more determined than their predecessors to prevent the fall of Indochina. While vowing to wage the Cold War with vigor, Eisenhower and Dulles had also promised cuts in defense spending, and their "New Look" defense policy called for sharp reductions in American ground forces. They were even more reluctant than Truman and Acheson to commit American combat forces to Southeast Asia and agreed that France must remain in Indochina and bear the burden of the conflict.

The changes which Eisenhower and Dulles introduced were changes of mood and tactics rather than of substance. As would happen so often during the long history of American involvement in Vietnam, the new administration came into office confident that new methods or the more persistent application of old ones could turn a deteriorating situation around. The Republicans quickly concluded that the United States and France had made critical errors. The U.S. Army had achieved considerable success training South Korean forces and employing "meatgrinder" tactics in which the Chinese and North Koreans were lured into open engagements and slaughtered by the combined force of ground troops, artillery, and air power. The Joint Chiefs of Staff insisted that France could win the war if it made greater use of Vietnamese forces and adopted an offensive strategy designed to destroy the enemy's regular units. The Joint Chiefs, the State Department, and the White House all agreed, moreover, that France had not done enough to win nationalist support by making timely and genuine political concessions. Eisenhower and Dulles felt that the Truman administration had carelessly squandered the leverage available to it to influence French policy.

The new administration set out zealously to correct the mistakes of its predecessor. Alarmed by growing signs of war-weariness in France, Eisenhower and Dulles gave firm assurances of continued assistance and promised that the nation's "tiredness" would "evaporate in the face of a positive and constructive program." The administration also made clear, however, that continued aid would be conditioned on detailed and specific information about French military operations and plans and on firm French pledges to expand the Vietnamese National Army and to develop a new, aggressive strategy with an explicit timetable for the defeat of the enemy's main forces. Eisenhower himself advised Ambassador Douglas Dillon in Paris to impress upon the French the importance of appointing a *"forceful and inspirational leader,* empowered with the means and authority to win victory," and of making "clear and unequivocal public announcements, repeated as often as may be desireable," that complete independence would be granted "as soon as victory against the Communists had been won."

Under mounting pressure to do something or withdraw from Indochina, the French government responded quickly. In early May 1953, it appointed General Henri Navarre to command French forces in Indochina. Two months later, a new cabinet, headed by Joseph Laniel, promised to "perfect" the independence of the Associated States by turning over responsibilities exercised by France. Shortly after, the French presented for American approval a new strategic concept, the so-called Navarre Plan. Tailored to meet many of the specifications set down earlier by the American Joint Chiefs, the plan called for a vast augmentation of the Vietnamese National Army and for the establishment of a new training program, along with the commitment to Indochina of an additional nine battalions of French regulars. . . . Although dubious of French intentions and capabilities, Washington saw no alternative but to accept the proposal. . . .

Within six months after the United States and France had agreed upon the "end-the-war offensive," the military and political situation in Indochina had drastically deteriorated. Navarre was forced to scrap his ill-fated plan in its initial stages. In the fall of 1953, he began to mobilize his forces for the anticipated offensive in the delta. Recognizing that he must strike a decisive blow before the impact of expanded American aid could be felt, Giap invaded central and southern Laos, intensified guerrilla activity in the delta, and prepared for a major strike into northern Laos. The only response Navarre could devise was to scatter the very forces he had just combined to counter the Vietminh thrusts.

By early 1954, both sides had committed major forces to the remote village of Dienbienphu in the northwest corner of Vietnam. Navarre established a position at the intersection of several major roads near the Laotian border in hopes of cutting off the anticipated invasion and luring Vietminh main units into open battle. In a broad valley surrounded by hills as high as 1,000 feet, he constructed a garrison ringed with barbed wire and bunkers, and hastily dispatched twelve battalions of regulars supported by aircraft and heavy artillery. Giap took the "bait." After a quick strike into Laos, he retraced his steps and encircled the French garrison. Navarre now found 12,000 of his elite forces isolated in a far corner of Vietnam. Although increasingly uncertain that they could hold out against superior Vietminh numbers, in January he decided to remain.

In the meantime, an outburst of Vietnamese nationalism further undercut France's already tenuous political position. When the French opened negotiations to "perfect" Vietnamese independence, non-Communist nationalists, including some of Bao Dai's associates, demanded not only complete independence but also severance of all ties with France. The United States found itself in an awkward predicament. Although it had taken a forthright stand in favor of eventual independence, it feared that the Vietnamese demands would provoke a French withdrawal, and it was certain that the Bao Dai government could not survive by itself. Dulles angrily denounced the "ill-considered" actions of the nationalists and dangled in front of them promises of large-scale American aid if they cooperated. The American Embassy in Saigon pressed the Vietnamese to tone down their demands—"We are the last French colonialists in Indochina," an American diplomat remarked with wry humor. Despite American attempts to mediate, the French and Vietnamese could not reach an agreement on the status of an independent Vietnam.

The political crisis of late 1953, along with an apparent shift in Soviet foreign policy, heightened French tendencies toward a negotiated settlement.

Many French politicians concluded that Vietnamese association with the French Union, if only symbolic, was all that could be salvaged from the war and without this there was no reason to prolong the agony. The leaders who had assumed power in the Kremlin after Stalin's death in February had taken a conciliatory line on a number of major Cold War issues, Indochina included, and the French government hoped that Soviet influence would enable it to secure a favorable settlement. Over Dulles' vigorous opposition, France in early 1954 agreed to place Indochina on the agenda of an East-West conference scheduled to meet in Geneva to consider Far Eastern problems.

Eisenhower and Dulles could only acquiesce. Distrustful of the Soviet overtures and skeptical of the wisdom of the French decision, they were nevertheless unwilling to put the United States in the position of being the only great power to oppose peaceful settlement of a major international crisis. Despite Dulles' threats of an "agonizing reappraisal" of American commitments, moreover, the French still refused to ratify the European Defense Community, and the new Soviet line had complicated the prospect by easing European fears of a Russian attack. Like Acheson before him, Dulles hesitated to press France too hard on Indochina lest it reject the European Defense Community altogether, splitting the Western alliance and playing into the hands of the Russians.

In the spring of 1954, the United States for the first time faced the prospect of direct military intervention in Indochina. As late as mid-March, a special committee appointed by the President to review American policy concluded that the military situation, although dangerous, was not yet critical, and an American observer optimistically reported from Dienbienphu that the French fortress could "withstand any kind of attack the Vietminh are capable of launching." American officials feared, however, that French war-weariness would result in a surrender at Geneva. The special committee recommended that prior to the conference the United States should attempt to discourage defeatist tendencies in France and sl. d use its influence at Geneva to ensure that no agreements were reached. If, despite American efforts, the French accepted a settlement which was unsatisfactory, the United States might have to arrange with the Associated States and other interested nations to continue the war without France.

While Eisenhower and his advisers pondered the long-range possibility of American intervention in Indochina, Giap tightened the noose around Dienbienphu. On March 13, the Vietminh launched an all-out attack and within twenty-four hours had seized hills Gabrielle and Beatrice, the outposts established by France to protect the fortress in the valley below. American and French experts had predicted that it would be impossible to get artillery up to the high ground surrounding the garrison. But the Vietminh formed "human ant-hills," carrying disassembled weapons up piece by piece, then reassembling them and camouflaging them so effectively that they were impervious to artillery and strafing. The heavy Vietminh guns quickly knocked out the airfield, making resupply impossible except by parachute drop and leaving the garrison of 12,000 men isolated and vulnerable.

The spectacular Vietminh success at Diebienphu raised the prospect of immediate American intervention. During a visit to Washington in late March, French Chief of Staff General Paul Ely still estimated a "50-50 chance of success" at Dienbienphu and merely requested the transfer of additional American aircraft to be used by France for attacks on Vietminh lines around the fortress. Ely was deeply concerned about the possibility of Chinese intervention, however, openly inquiring of Dulles how the United States would respond in such a contingency. Much less optimistic about Dienbienphu was Admiral Arthur Radford, Chairman of the Joint Chiefs of Staff, who during the Ely visit began to give serious consideration to a scheme originally devised by French and American officers in Saigon and code-named VULTURE. The plan called for a massive strike by American B-29s and carrier-based aircraft, possibly using tactical atomic weapons, to relieve the siege of Dienbienphu. Although Radford made no commitments, he apparently led Ely to believe that he would push for approval of the plan should the French formally request it.

VULTURE won little support in Washington. Eisenhower briefly toyed with the idea of a "single strike, if it were almost certain this would produce decisive results." "Of course, if we did, we'd have to deny it forever," he quickly added. Dulles was prepared to consider air and naval operations in Indochina, but only as a last resort. Less worried about the immediate threat to Dienbienphu than the long-range threat to Southeast Asia, the Secretary preferred what he called "United Action," the formation of a coalition composed of the United States, Great Britain, France, Australia, New Zealand, and the Associated States, to guarantee the security of Southeast Asia. Such a coalition, by its very existence, might deter Chinese intervention in the Indochina War and Chinese aggression elsewhere in Asia. United Action would help stiffen French resistance to a sellout at Geneva. If military intervention became necessary, it would ensure that the entire burden did not fall upon the United States and would remove the stigma of a war in support of French colonialism.

Dulles and Eisenhower were also unwilling to intervene unless they could extract major concessions from the French. Dulles warned that if the United States intervened its prestige would be "engaged to a point where we would want to have a success. We could not afford a defeat that would have worldwide repercussions." The administration attributed France's failure to its mishandling of the Vietnamese and its refusal to wage the war aggressively; persistent efforts to change French attitudes had been fruitless. Indeed, Ely had only recently rebuffed a proposal to expand the role of the American military advisory group, bitterly complaining about the "invading nature" of the Americans and their "determination to control and operate everything of importance." Dulles and Eisenhower agreed that the United States must not risk its prestige in Indochina until France had made firm commitments to keep its troops there, accelerate the move toward eventual independence, and permit the United States a larger role in training indigenous forces and in formulating military strategy.

Many of Eisenhower's top military advisers raised serious objections to VULTURE. Some questioned whether an air attack could relieve the siege of

Dienbienphu without destroying the fortress itself; others wondered whether intervention, once undertaken, could be kept limited—"One cannot go over Niagara Falls in a barrel only slightly," a Defense Department analyst warned. . . .

Although profoundly skeptical of VULTURE, the administration was sufficiently alarmed by the emerging crisis in Indochina to seek Congressional support for American military intervention. The fall of Dienbienphu seemed certain by early April. Eisenhower and Dulles preferred to act in concert with other nations, but they feared that a defeat at Dienbienphu might produce a French collapse before plans for United Action could be put into effect, leaving American naval and air power as the only means to save Indochina. Sensitive to Truman's fate in Korea, they were unwilling to act without backing from Congress, and Eisenhower instructed Dulles to explore with Congressional leaders the conditions under which the use of American military power might be approved. The purpose of the dramatic meeting at the State Department on April 3 was not, as has often been assumed, to secure approval for VULTURE, but rather was to gain discretionary authority to employ American naval and air forces, with allies if possible, without them if necessary, should the fall of Dienbienphu threaten the loss of all Indochina.

The administration encountered stubborn resistance. Dulles and Radford grimly warned that failure to act decisively might cost the United States all of Southeast Asia and advised that the President should have the power to use naval and air forces "if he felt it necessary in the interest of national security." No one questioned this assessment of the gravity of the situation, but the Congressmen insisted that there must be "no more Koreas, with the United States furnishing 90% of the manpower," and made clear that they would approve nothing until the administration had obtained firm commitments of support from other nations. Dulles persisted, assuring the legislators that the administration had no intention of sending ground troops to Indochina and indicating that he could more easily gain commitments from allies if he could specify what the United States would do. The Congressmen were not swayed by the Secretary's arguments. "Once the flag is committed," they warned, "the use of land forces would surely follow." Sharing the administration's distrust of France, they also insisted that the United States must not go to war in support of colonialism. They would only agree that if "satisfactory commitments" could be secured from Great Britain and other allies to support military intervention, and from France to "internationalize" the war and speed up the move toward independence, a resolution could be obtained authorizing the President to commit American forces to the defense of Indochina. Congressional insistence on prior allied commitments, particularly from Great Britain, eliminated the option of unilateral American intervention and placed major obstacles in the way of United Action. The April 3 session doomed VULTURE. . . .

While the fate of Dienbienphu hung in the balance, the United States frantically promoted United Action. Dulles immediately departed for London and Paris to consult with British and French leaders. Eisenhower penned a long personal letter to Prime Minister Winston Churchill urging British support for a coalition that would be "willing to fight" to check Communist expansion in Southeast Asia. At a much publicized news conference on April 7, the President laid the foundation for possible American intervention. Outlining in simple language the principles that had formed the basis for American policy for four years, he emphasized that Indochina was an important source of tin, tungsten, and rubber, and that having lost China to "Communist dictatorship," the United States "simply can't afford greater losses." More important, he warned, should Indochina fall, the rest of Southeast Asia would "go over very quickly," like a "row of dominoes" when the first one is knocked down, causing much greater losses of raw materials and people, jeopardizing America's strategic position in the Far East, and driving Japan into the Communist camp. "So the possible consequences of the loss," he concluded, "are just incalculable to the free world."

The flurry of American diplomatic activity in April 1954 revealed deep differences between the United States and its allies. The Churchill government was prepared to join a collective security arrangement *after* Geneva, but it was adamantly opposed to immediate intervention in Indochina. Churchill and his Foreign Secretary Anthony Eden did not share the American fear that the loss of all or part of Indochina would bring the fall of Southeast Asia. They were convinced that France retained sufficient influence to salvage a reasonable settlement at Geneva, and they feared that outside military intervention would destroy any hope of a negotiated settlement and perhaps even provoke a war with China. Most important, they had no desire to entangle Britain in a war they felt could not be won.

Dulles' discussion with France were equally unproductive and made clear the widely divergent approaches of the two nations toward the war and the Geneva negotiations. The United States was willing to intervene in Indochina, but only on condition that France resist a negotiated settlement at Geneva, agree to remain in Indochina and fight indefinitely, concede to its ally a greater role in planning strategy and training indigenous forces, and accept Vietnamese demands for complete independence. The French insisted that Vietnam must retain ties with the French Union. They wanted nothing more than an air strike to relieve the siege of Dienbienphu. They opposed internationalization of the war, which would not only threaten their prestige in Indochina but would also remove control from their hands. Dulles may have hoped by offering help to France that he could yet save the European Defense Community, but the French government made clear the EDC would have no chance of approval if France had to commit itself to keep troops in Indochina indefinitely. . . .

. Congressional opposition reinforced the administration's determination to avoid unilateral intervention in support of France. In a speech that won praise from both sides of the aisles, Democratic Senator John F. Kennedy of Massachusetts warned that no amount of military aid could conquer "an enemy of the people which has the support and covert appeal of the people," and that victory could not be attained in Indochina as long as France remained. When a "high administration source," subsequently identified as Vice-President Richard M. Nixon, remarked "off the record" that if United Action failed the United States might have to act alone, the reaction was immediate and strong. Senate Democratic Leader Lyndon Johnson of Texas bitterly denounced the "Nixon war" and opposed "sending American G.I.s into the mud and muck of Indochina on a blood-letting spree to perpetuate colonialism and white man's exploitation in Asia."

Thus, even when France relented a bit, continued British opposition to military intervention settled the fate of United Action. . . . Eisenhower informed Congressional leaders on April 26 that it would be a "tragic error to go in alone as a partner of France" and made clear that the United States would intervene only as part of a "grouping of interested nations." Three days later, the National Security Council formally decided to "hold up for the time any military action in IndoChina until we see how Geneva is coming along."

The American decision sealed Dienbienphu's doom. Without American air power, France had no means of saving the fortress. Subjected to merciless pounding from Vietminh artillery and to a series of human-wave assaults, the hopelessly outmanned defenders finally surrendered on May 7 after fifty-five days of stubborn but futile resistance. The attention of belligerents and interested outside parties immediately shifted to Geneva where the following day the Indochina phase of the conference was set to begin. Buoyed by its victory, the Vietminh confidently savored the prize for which it had been fighting for more than seven years. Its influence in northern Vietnam now reduced to a small pocket around Hanoi, France began preparations to abandon the north and to salvage as much as possible in the area below the sixteenth parallel. The French delegation came to Geneva, Bidault lamented, holding a "two of clubs and a three of diamonds."

The United States was a reluctant participant at Geneva. Negotiation with any Communist nation was anathema, but the presence of Communist China made the conference especially unpalatable. Dulles remained in Geneva only briefly and, in the words of his biographer, conducted himself like a "puritan in a house of ill repute." On one occasion, he remarked that the only way he and Chou En-lai, the top Chinese delegate, would meet was if their cars collided, and when they actually met face-to-face and Chou extended his hand, the Secretary reportedly turned his back. The administration had long feared that the conference would merely provide a fig leaf of respectability for the French surrender of Indochina, and the fall of Dienbienphu increased its concern. After departing Geneva, Dulles instructed the American delegation that it should participate in the conference only as an "interested nation," not as a "belligerent or a principal in the negotiations," and should not endorse an agreement which in any way impaired the territorial integrity of the Associated States. Given the military position of the Vietminh when the conference opened, Dulles was saying that the United States would approve no settlement at all. . . .

[In mid-June, when the Geneva conference was all but over,] the Eisenhower administration adopted a change of policy with momentous long-range implications. Recognizing that the war could not be prolonged without unacceptable risks and that part of Vietnam would probably be lost at Geneva, the administration began to lay plans for the defense of the rest of Indochina and Southeast Asia. Dulles informed Congressional leaders on June 24 that any agreement that emerged from Geneva would be "something we would have to gag about," but he nevertheless expressed optimism that the United States might still be able to "salvage something" in Southeast Asia "free of the taint of French colonialism." The United States would have to take over from France responsibility for defending Laos, Cambodia, and that part of Vietnam beneath the partition line. The first essential was to draw a line which the Communists would not cross and then to "hold this area and fight subversion within it with all the strength we have" by providing economic assistance and building a strong military force. The United States would also have to take the lead in forming a strong regional defense grouping "to keep alive freedom" in Southeast Asia.

Over the next few weeks, Dulles worked relentlessly to get the kind of settlement that would enable the United States to defend Indochina and Southeast Asia after Geneva. He secured British agreement to a set of principles that would constitute an "acceptable" settlement, including the freedom of Laos, Cambodia, and southern Vietnam to maintain "stable, non-communist regimes" and to accept foreign arms and advisers. He applied extreme pressure, even threatening to disassociate the United States entirely from Geneva, until Mendes-France accepted the so-called seven points as the basis for the French bargaining position. Although armed with firm British and French promises, Dulles still approached the last stages of the conference with great caution and with a determination to retain complete freedom of action. The United States should play no more than a passive role in the negotiations, he instructed the head of the American delegation, Walter Bedell Smith. If the agreement lived up to its standards, the administration would issue a unilateral statement of endorsement, but if it fell short the United States would reserve the freedom to "publicly disassociate itself." Under no circumstances would it be a "cosignatory with the Communists," and it would not be placed in a position of guaranteeing the results.

When the conference reconvened, pressures for a settlement had increased significantly. . . . Although the Vietminh's military position gave it strong claim for influence throughout Vietnam, both the Russians and Chinese exerted heavy pressure for a compromise peace. The Soviet Union had only limited interests in Southeast Asia and appears to have pursued a conciliatory line toward France in order to encourage French rejection of the European Defense Community. China sought to enhance its international prestige and to cultivate influence among the neutral nations of South and Southeast Asia by playing the role of peacemaker. Moreover, the Chinese apparently feared that a prolonged war ran serious risks of American intervention, and they may have felt that a partition arrangement would make the Vietminh more susceptible to their influence. For reasons of their own, the Russians and Chinese moderated Vietminh demands and played a crucial role in arranging the settlement.

The Geneva Accords of 1954 reflected these influences. Vietnam was to be partitioned along the seventeenth parallel to permit the regrouping of military forces from both sides. The agreements stressed that the division was to be only temporary and that it should not be "interpreted as constituting a political or territorial boundary." The country was to be reunified by elections scheduled for the summer of 1956 and to be supervised by an international commission composed of Canada, Poland, and India. To insulate Vietnam against a renewal of conflict during the transitional period, the agreements provided that forces should be withdrawn from the respective partition zones within 300 days, and they prohibited the introduction of new forces and equipment and the establishment of foreign military bases. Neither portion of Vietnam was to join a military alliance. The agreements also established cease-fire arrangements for Laos and Cambodia. The two nations' right to self-defense was explicitly recognized, but to assuage Chinese fears of American intervention, they were not to enter military alliances or permit foreign bases on their soil except in cases where their security was clearly threatened.

The Eisenhower administration viewed the Geneva Agreements with mixed feelings. As had been feared, the settlement produced some domestic political backlash; Republican Senate Leader William Knowland denounced it as the "greatest victory the Communists have won in twenty years." The administration itself regarded the loss of northern Vietnam—"the keystone to the arch of Southeast Asia"—with concern. Eisenhower and Dulles realized, as Smith put it, that "diplomacy has rarely been able to gain at the conference table what cannot be held on the battlefield." The administration protected itself against domestic criticism and retained its freedom of action by refusing to associate itself directly with the agreements. In a unilateral statement, Smith simply "took note" of the Geneva Accords and said that the United States would not "disturb them" by the "threat or the use of force."

The administration was not altogether displeased with the results, however. The agreements were better than had been anticipated when the conference opened, and they allowed sufficient latitude to proceed along the lines Dulles had already outlined. Partition was unpalatable, but it gave the United States the opportunity to build up non-Communist forces in southern Vietnam, a challenge Eisenhower and Dulles took up eagerly. The accords placed some limits on outside intervention, to be sure, but the administration did not view them as prohibitive. And some of the provisions seemed advantageous. Eisenhower and Dulles agreed, for example, that if elections were held immediately Ho Chi Minh would be an easy victor. But the two-year delay gave the

United States "fairly good time" to get ready, and Canada's presence on the commission would enable it to "block things."

Eisenhower and Dulles viewed the apparent demise of French colonialism in Southeast Asia with equanimity, if not outright enthusiasm. From the start, the Franco-American partnership in Indochina had been marked by profound mutual suspicion and deep-seated tensions. From 1950 to 1954, the United States had provided France more than $2.6 billion in military aid, but its efforts to influence French policies by friendly persuasion and by attaching strings had failed, and the commitment to France had indeed turned out to be a "dead-end alley." Eisenhower and Dulles attributed France's failure primarily to its attempts to perpetuate colonialism in Indochina, and they were confident that without the problems posed by France the United States could build a viable non-Communist alternative to the Vietminh. "We must work with these people, and then they themselves will soon find out that we are their friends and that they can't live without us," Eisenhower observed. Conceding that the Geneva Accords contained "many features which we did not like" Dulles nevertheless insisted that they included many "good aspects," most important, the "truly independent status" of Laos, Cambodia, and southern Vietnam. The "important thing," he concluded, was "not to mourn the past but to seize the future opportunity to prevent the loss in Northern Vietnam from leading to the extension of communism throughout Southeast Asia and the Southwest Pacific."

The Second Red Scare

Harvard in the McCarthy Era

One consequence of the cold war was what came to be known as "McCarthyism," after Senator Joseph McCarthy, the most flamboyant and aggressive of the politicians whose careers were devoted to "rooting out" communists and communist "sympathizers" in American institutions. Although McCarthy did not create the second Red Scare—the Truman administration warrants this accolade for its federal employee security program—it was the Wisconsin Republican who made anticommunism a crusade. From February 1950, when he charged that the State Department harbored over two hundred communist sympathizers, until December 1954, when his colleagues in the Senate passed a resolution of censure, McCarthy held center stage. Bringing his campaign to television, McCarthy's investigations of the State Department, the United States Information Agency, and the Army convinced many that communism had succeeded in corrupting our basic institutions of communication and defense. They also laid the groundwork for inquiries at all levels of government designed to cleanse American society—its films, libraries, labor unions, and schools, for example—of all vestiges of communist influence.

The following exchange, published in the 1970s, recalls some of the kinds of suspicion, charge, and countercharge that resulted from this domestic phase of the competition with the Soviet Union. The principals are Sigmund Diamond, whose career as an academic had been affected by McCarthyism, and McGeorge Bundy (later influential in the administration of John F. Kennedy), who was part of the administration of Harvard University in the 1950s. There is probably no way to know whether Diamond's or Bundy's version of the events is factually more accurate. What is possible is an understanding of the kinds of concerns and tensions that governed the lives of many Americans who lived through the cold war.

Sigmund Diamond's Account

During the academic year 1953–1954, I was Research Fellow in Entrepreneurial History at Harvard and also, on invitation from Dean McGeorge Bundy, adviser to faculty members from universities throughout the country who had fellowships from the Fund for the Advancement of Education of the Ford Foundation and who chose to spend all or part of their fellowship year at Harvard. In late March or early April, 1954, Mr. Bundy, as Dean of the Faculty of Arts and Sciences, offered me an appointment as Counsellor for Foreign Students and Dean of Special Students, with some teaching in the history department. On April 9, 1954, he sent me the following letter:

Dear Sigmund:
When I talked with you about your appointment for next year, we agreed that you would also do some tutoring in History, and I said I would recommend your appointment as Tutor in the Department of History in addition to the appointments as Counsellor for Foreign Students and Dean of Special Students. However, the Corporation title of "Tutor" was abandoned several years ago, so that your appointment will not include this title. The fact that you will not hold any formal appointment in the Department of History does not in any way affect our understanding that you will do some tutoring in that field, but I wanted to make clear to you the reason why your connection with the Department in a tutoring capacity will not be recognized in your official appointments. If in another year, as I hope may be the case, you are able to do some lecturing in History, we can then add the title of "Lecturer" to your other appointments. But

since the title of "Tutor" no longer exists, there is really no other title which we can now use to show your identification with the Department of History.

Sincerely yours,
McGeorge Bundy

On April 21, 1954, I found the following note on the desk in my office: "Agent Sullivan of the FBI would like to see Mr. Diamond on Wednesday, April 21, at 2:30." At 2:30 PM, Agent Sullivan and another FBI agent entered my office. I wrote the following note on the reverse side of the card informing me of their visit:

2 agents, 4/21/54:—Said had been told by couple people in Boston area, formerly from Baltimore, that I am former member. Would like to talk. Said I didn't feel as if I had anything to say. [They] said if should change my mind, if want to confirm or deny or if want to talk after consulting attorney, to get in touch. Asked if I had any questions—said all was clear.

Four or five days later I received a call from Dean Bundy's secretary telling me to come to his office at once. I did so. Before either of us began to speak he put a disc on a recording machine and recorded the entire conversation that followed. He told me that he had received information that my proposed appointment might be "embarrassing" to Harvard, and he wanted to know if this were true.

I told him about my past beliefs and activities; by then they were a matter of history. I had been a member of the Communist Party; I had joined in 1941 when I was just twenty-one and when the Soviet Union was bearing the main burden of the war against Hitler, and I had walked away several years after World War II—as did how many others?—when both the world and my perceptions of the USSR and of political commitment itself had changed. I had once thought, after leaving the Party, that I could say "Goodbye to all that." Bundy's question showed me I was laboring under an illusion.

For what seemed like several hours (I remember distinctly that he changed the disc on the recording machine at least two or three times) I talked with him about the reasons that had led me to join the Party and then to leave it. At the end of the conversation he said he understood what I had said and that nothing I had said was at variance with the information he had been given. He then asked what I would do if I were asked to discuss the situation with "civic authority" (I am quoting from a copy of a letter I wrote to a friend outside the United States on May 17, 1954, within a few weeks of the event itself), meaning the FBI or a congressional committee. I told him that I would speak fully about myself, but that I would not be an informer against others, that I had no knowledge that others had committed crimes and that, therefore, the only effect of informing upon them would be that they would be fired from their jobs, even those of them who, like me, had long before left the Party.

At that point Bundy told me that to talk only about myself was not good enough, that under those circumstances he would not go through with the appointment that had been agreed upon; but if I were prepared to name the names of those I had known he would put forward my appointment to the Harvard Corporation. He urged this course of action upon me, and suggested that I seek the advice of those members of the faculty who knew me. I've always thought—though of course I cannot prove this—that Bundy expected the members of the Harvard faculty to whom I spoke to urge his course of action upon me. That they did not do so was perhaps one reason he became so angry over my case later on.

None of the Harvard faculty members I talked to—some of them friends, some of them people I'd never met before—urged me to do as Bundy had suggested, that is, to promise that I would name names in return for his presenting the case for my appointment to the Corporation. It was not so much that they disagreed with Bundy's view as that they felt I should make my own decision, that it was not an unworthy one, and that it deserved their support. I made no notes, but I well remember that good man, David Owen, a professor in the history department, saying to me: "Sig, I don't know if I would behave as you are, but I'd like to believe I would. I'll speak to Mac"—and he did, and so did others.

In the second, and final, discussion I had with Bundy, I knew the main question would be whether I would name my former political associates. Once again Dean Bundy recorded the conversation. This time he came to the point at once: Would I cooperate by giving the names to the authorities? I had done some research on one earlier case in which Harvard had not required informing as a condition of continued association with the university, and I called Bundy's attention to it. (I still have the sheet on which I made the notes I took to his office.) In the spring of 1938 Richard Whitney of the New York Stock Exchange was put on trial for committing grand larceny. Two of the witnesses in the case, George Whitney and Thomas W. Lamont, were then and later members of various Harvard governing boards. I pointed out to Bundy that according to *The New York Times* George Whitney felt "no responsibility" to inform the Stock Exchange about Richard Whitney's "criminal actions" (April 20, 1938, p. 33), and replied "Certainly not" to the question: "Did you seek advice of counsel as to what action you should take in view of your brother's improper usage of securities?" (April 21, 1938, p. 3). As to Lamont:

for more than two hours on the witness stand, Mr. Lamont was questioned as to the responsibility he might have felt as a citizen with knowledge of a theft as well as his responsibility to the help of J.P. Morgan and Co. He returned in various forms to the same explanation: That he had not thought so much of the law as of the fact that "my partner, George Whitney" wanted to save his brother. "Would you expect me . . . to say I will help you out, but you must trot down to the DA's office and denounce your brother . . .?" "How about your responsibilities as a citizen?" "I don't know whether you are reading a lecture there . . . I have been in business for many years and I have tried to discharge my duties as a citizen, and in this instance I felt I was discharging all the duties I was conscious of . . . It never occurred to me that I should butt in or that I should denounce Richard Whitney for his terrible mistake." [April 27, 1938, p. 31].

Perhaps, I thought, Bundy would be moved by these facts. Harvard had not required George Whitney and Thomas W. Lamont to break their connection with the university because they had refused to inform against an associate, even when they knew he had broken the law. My own former associates had broken none that I knew of. In retrospect, I suppose, I must have been very naive to think that citing the Whitney case would do anything but enrage Bundy. At the end of the meeting, the last I ever had with Bundy, he repeated what he had said earlier: that under no circumstances would the appointment be made unless I named others besides myself, that he could not guarantee that the Corporation would confirm the appointment even if I were to name the names but that he was prepared to push the matter if I did so, and that President Pusey agreed with his disposition of the case.

By the middle of May a number of faculty members, as a group and individually, had spoken to Bundy about my case. It speaks for the decency of these people and of their desire to spare me and my family the pain of continued disappointment that to this day I do not know of all the meetings they had with Bundy and President Pusey or of all they did to attempt to change their policy. (Some of them are still alive; Professor Lipset* could have asked them.) But I know, for example, that Professor Arthur H. Cole, despairing of getting Bundy to change his mind, asked him if it would be possible for me to work for him personally at the Research Center in Entrepreneurial History, a job which would not need Corporation approval. Dean Bundy answered, "The Corporation is not interested in what you eat for breakfast, Mr. Cole"—while making it clear that Dean Bundy was interested, and unhappy about Cole's idea. I know, too, that David S. Landes, now of Harvard but then an assistant professor at Columbia without tenure, and therefore in a position to be hurt by a powerful university administrator, went to speak to his friend McGeorge Bundy about me. He was told that: 1) my failure to tell him about myself at the time he offered me the appointment revealed a serious flaw in my character; 2) I was now in such emotional turmoil as to be unfit to be a teacher; 3) Harvard had only a limited capital of good will with the public and could not afford to spend it on such cases as mine.

When, on another occasion, Bundy was told that R.H. Tawney and T.S. Ashton of the London School of Economics knew about my case and were disappointed in Harvard's handling of it, he became angry that I was "publicizing" my difficulties while he was trying to handle them quietly. He was told that it was not I who had written to Tawney and Ashton, but members of the

*The Diamond-Bundy exchange began as Diamond's review of *Education and Politics at Harvard*, by Seymour Martin Lipset and David Riesman.—Ed.

Harvard faculty who were inquiring about the possibility of a job for me in England. . . . And so I agreed in early June 1954 to speak to the FBI about myself alone.

I remember two interviews, both of them recorded. At the first, the two FBI agents made it clear that I could not lay down any conditions for the interview. I would have to decide which questions I would not answer, and take responsibility for refusing. When we came to the end of the interview, I was warned that I faced serious danger by my refusal to cooperate fully and that I had better be prepared at the next session to discuss others as well as myself. I talked over what had happened with Professor Cole and with Professor Frederick Merk of the history department. On the morning of the second interview I received a telephone call from Professor Cole saying that he and Professor Merk wanted me to tell the FBI that they would hold themselves available that afternoon and were prepared to come to the FBI office as character witnesses on my behalf. I can still hear Professor Cole, stammering a bit— he was always embarrassed by a display of emotion—saying, "We don't know if it will do any good, but maybe it will ease the tension." When I reported this to the two FBI agents, they replied lightly that it would not be necessary, that they knew how to reach Cole and Merk, and that, besides, there were only a few loose ends left to be tidied up.

I do not, of course, remember all that we talked about in those interviews. But I still have a sheet of paper on which I typed some examples of the "derogatory information" in my FBI dossier about which I was interrogated:

Q. Shortly after your arrival in Detroit in the summer of 1943, did you not attend an Institute on Inter-racial Relations? [I arrived in Detroit, to work in the Education Department of the UAW-CIO, on June 22, 1943, the day the great race riot began. I attended many conferences on inter-racial relations.]

Q. Were you active in the affairs of the American Jewish Congress? [I wrote a few short articles on the history of Jews in the United States for *The Congress Voice*, the publication of the American Jewish Congress in Detroit.]

Q. In the winter of 1946, you were seen at a meeting in the YWCA in Detroit against the poll tax. Were you there? [I was. The meeting was addressed by Mrs. Virginia Durr, of the National Committee to Abolish the Poll Tax, wife of Clifford Durr of the Federal Communications Commission and sister of Mr. Justice Hugo L. Black of the Supreme Court.]

Q. In August 1948 you were seen at a picnic just outside Detroit sponsored by the Michigan edition of the *Daily Worker*. Is that correct? [The picnic had not been sponsored by the *Daily Worker*. It had been sponsored by the Progressive Party, which was supporting the presidential candidacy of Henry A. Wallace, and the two speakers were US Senator Glen Taylor, Wallace's running-mate, and Professor John Ciardi, then of Harvard.]

After my second and final interview with the FBI, I met, late in the afternoon, with President Pusey in his office in Massachusetts Hall. Professor Howe, Professor Helen Cam of the history department, and others had urged Pusey to hear my side of the story, especially since I had shown my willingness to talk to the FBI about myself. Not that Professor Howe expected much to happen as a result of such an interview. I have a copy of a letter I wrote to a friend on June 2, 1954:

> I also have an opportunity to talk to Pusey this Thursday, but I have been warned by Mark Howe not to expect anything to come of that—it seems that he arranged earlier this year for Pusey to meet with [Professor Wendell] Furry, * and, as he put it, never has he seen a colder, more formal, less sympathetic or understanding person than Pusey, despite all his Christian talk.

My talk with Pusey, like my talks with Bundy, was recorded. My recollection is that during the entire meeting, which lasted well over an hour, Pusey interrupted only twice: first to apologize for asking me to stop so that he could change the disc on the recording machine; then to ask me what country my father had been born in. When the meeting was over, he thanked me for having spoken so fully and frankly, and said that I would soon be hearing from him. I never did hear from him, and never saw him again until we met at Rockefeller University in the early 1970s at a conference on the political disruption of universities.

What would Professor Lipset have learned if he had pursued the facts about this "deviant" case? At the very least, some significant questions would have been raised about Harvard during the McCarthy period:

1. How did the Harvard authorities get "derogatory information" about me and others? Was it volunteered by the FBI? Did Harvard request it from the FBI? What was the nature of the relationship between Harvard and the FBI in those years?

2. Did the Harvard administration pass on this information to other universities? In my own case (and I know of at least a few others) I found that, one after another, promising possibilities for jobs collapsed after my experience at Harvard although it never became a matter of public knowledge.

3. How many faculty members were actually fired by Harvard or forced to resign? The cases of faculty members that we know about (like that of Professor Furry, for example) involved those who were also called before congressional committees. Was it Harvard's policy—as is suggested by the example of this "deviant" case—to handle such cases differently from the way in which it handled cases of teachers not called before congressional committees? Was there, in effect, a "public" Harvard policy and a "private" Harvard policy?

4. How many people were refused appointments at Harvard because of "derogatory information" about them? And how many gave such information under the threat of losing prospective jobs?

*Furry, a member of the Harvard physics department, had been an "unfriendly" witness before the Jenner Committee and had been put on probation by Harvard.

5. Were graduate students asked about their political beliefs and associations? I know of one case in which a dean warned a graduate student that he would lose all chance of academic employment if he did not "cooperate fully" with the authorities, but I have no idea how widespread the practice may have been. Until we know that, how can we be sure what Harvard's policy was?

6. What has happened to the recordings that Bundy and Pusey made of their discussions with me and of discussions about me—and possibly about others as well—with members of the faculty? Were they placed in the Harvard archives? Did Bundy and Pusey feel that they were their private possessions and remove them when they left office? Were they made available to the FBI or other investigating agencies? . . .

McGeorge Bundy's Reply

Professor Sigmund Diamond's account (*NYR*, April 28) of his relations with the Harvard administration in the spring of 1954 is seriously misleading. He quite erroneously asserts that his conversations with administrators were recorded, and he pays no attention to the crucial fact that the job at issue was administrative, not academic.

What actually happened is this. Sometime earlier in that year, at a time when none of those concerned had any knowledge of Mr. Diamond's past as a Communist, Professor David Owen, the Chairman of the History Department, told me that the Department was not going to recommend him for an academic appointment. As often happens when a young scholar does not get an academic appointment, Mr. Diamond's friends thought about other possibilities. There was a vacancy on the administrative side, and he seemed highly qualified to fill it. So I offered him appointment as Counsellor for Foreign Students and Dean of Special Studies. He accepted, and I recommended the appointment to the President and Fellows.

I must underline the difference, in the Harvard I knew, between an academic and an administrative appointment. An academic appointment carried all the immunities of academic freedom, and action on such an appointment was the shared responsibility of the faculty, the administrators, and the Governing Boards. Administrative appointments, on the other hand, were made by the Governing Boards on the recommendation of the President and other administrators. Such recommendations were made on the basis of one's judgment that the individual recommended would be highly qualified to carry out specific administrative responsibilities. Sometimes, of course, individuals held dual appointments; a professor might serve also as a dean. In such a case, while the administration might decide for itself whether the person continued as a dean, it must respect the appointment as a professor. But an individual whose central appointment was administrative must be judged on administrative standards—was he or she the right person for the job from the standpoint of the effective conduct of the University's business? The Governing Boards correctly insisted on a sharp distinction between one kind of appointment and the other.

Mr. Diamond's was to be an administrative appointment. The relevant department was not interested in recommending him for an academic appointment. The distinction was fundamental to my handling of his case. It is true that like many young scholars turning for a time to administrative work, Mr. Diamond wanted to go on teaching, and the History Department was glad to have him do some tutoring. I initially thought he could have the title of Tutor, but I found that it no longer existed. But with or without that title, it was an administrative job he was offered and the administrative budget that would have paid his whole salary.

This was the situation on May 3, 1954, when I learned from a colleague that Mr. Diamond might have a past connection with the Communist Party. I no longer remember who told me that, nor whether that colleague told me how the matter had come to his attention.

I asked to see Mr. Diamond and learned from him essentially what he describes in his account—that he had been a Communist from about 1942 to 1950, why he joined and why he left the Party, and that since he knew of no illegal activity by anyone he had known in the Party he was inclined against "naming names" to the FBI, although willing to talk about himself. I reached a prompt decision that he should not be Counsellor for Foreign Students, and on two grounds. I thought it was a bad mistake for him not to have told me of his situation when I offered him the job. I also believed that the Harvard Corporation would not want an ex-Communist with these attitudes in *any* administrative job. Even in cases of academic appointments it had weighed similar behavior negatively in publicly explained decisions a year earlier (before either Mr. Pusey or I was in office).

I told Mr. Diamond of my decision and I wrote to the Corporation withdrawing my recommendation. The decision was based entirely on what Mr. Diamond told me and had failed to tell me earlier. In such cases no information was ever sought from or given to the FBI. I interviewed a number of such individuals in 1954 and 1955, and I never found one who did not seem to me to be doing his best to tell the truth about himself.

I believed that it would be wrong to have in an administrative job a man who had not thought it necessary to tell me he was an ex-Communist when I offered him an appointment which made that fact highly pertinent. In 1954 Harvard was indeed embattled with Senator McCarthy, and precisely because it was engaged in defending its academic freedoms it was under an obligation not to behave foolishly in its administrative appointments. The man in charge of advising foreign students necessarily worked on their behalf with agencies of government. A man in Mr. Diamond's position would certainly have been an unlikely choice for such a job in 1954, and Mr. Diamond undoubtedly knew it. But he needed the job, and so he had not been able to bring himself to tell us of his predicament. The failure was understandable, but it was not one I could ignore.

I explained this position not only to Mr. Diamond but also to every professor who asked me about it at the time; I never heard one who disagreed. Nor did anyone, including Mr. Diamond, ever suggest at the time that the prospect of some tutorial work made the appointment in question anything but administrative. Such a suggestion would have been recognized as nonsensical.

Mr. Diamond is right when he says that his friends tried to find some other solution for him. While none was now ready to urge that he be recommended for any administrative appointment, there was discussion of the possibility of an academic appointment. I remember telling David Owen that I could not support such a proposal. I believed that this question had been decided on its merits earlier in the year, when the History Department did not include Mr. Diamond in its proposed appointments. He held its doctorate, and it knew him well. If it had not proposed him at the usual time, on what ground would it propose him now? It could not be argued that his academic claim was better in May than it had been earlier, and I was sure that this would be the view of the Governing Boards.

The choices Mr. Diamond faced that spring were obviously agonizing. If he had clearly made a mistake in not telling me a relevant fact, he was not so clearly wrong in his choice of candor about himself along with refusal to name other names to the FBI. That position was one that I not only respected but strongly defended in other cases; it was indeed the crucial issue in the crucial case, that of Professor Furry. I was one of those who had helped in persuading Professor Furry to move to that position from his earlier reliance on the Fifth Amendment; it was more dangerous from the standpoint of possible prosecution, but it was morally superior in every way.

So it was no pleasure to be placed where I had to tell Mr. Diamond that if he held to this position he could not have the administrative job of Counsellor for Foreign Students. I think I did tell him that if he changed his position I would try to persuade the Corporation to overlook his earlier failure to tell me of his problem, but I doubt if I pressed him hard to take this course. He faced a decision that honorable ex-Communists were deciding in different ways that spring, and it was much debated in Cambridge. Though I myself believed generally in full disclosure, there were people I respected on both sides of the issue.

The pressures on Mr. Diamond were cruel, and this is where I look for the cause of the most blatant error in his account. He must have come to his interviews with administrators in a state of great stress, and so indeed I remember it. Nothing else could account for his wholly erroneous recollection that Mr. Pusey and I recorded our conversations with him.

Neither Mr. Pusey nor I, either at Harvard or anywhere else, has ever recorded any conversation with anyone, either face-to-face or over the phone. (I suppose some may be surprised today that one could work for five years in the White House on this basis, but it is the simple fact.) It is totally unbelievable that either of us would have made a once-in-a-lifetime exception for Mr. Diamond.

What Mr. Diamond saw on the table behind my desk was what any other visitor saw, a dictating machine. That machine used green discs, but to dictate to them you had to speak directly into the microphone that was attached. If it had any other capability, I would be surprised. What I know is that I never used it for anything but dictation. What Mr. Diamond now remembers simply never happened, either in my office or in Mr. Pusey's. I do not doubt his belief in his memory, but his memory is wholly wrong.

It's not easy to reconstruct these matters across twenty-three years. I have been helped in this case by the kindness of the present Harvard Administration, which gave me access to a long letter that I wrote at the time to Mr. Pusey, reporting my talk with Mr. Diamond and my resulting recommendation. I have relied on that letter in this account, and I have shown it to Mr. Diamond. Its last paragraph shows what I thought then and think now.

> I wish I could recreate for you the impression made upon me by Mr. Diamond in our long interview. I find myself quite able to understand the pressures which led him in the first instance to join the Party. While it seems extraordinary that any man of sense should have stayed a member as long as he did, I believe the explanation of this is to be found in his statement, which I believe, that membership in the Party never dominated his life. I understand and approve the energy and zeal with which Mr. Diamond has tried in recent years to put his past behind him. I think it wholly plain that his record at Harvard is as good, taken by itself, as I have said it was in earlier recommendations to the Corporation. We then come to the question of his failure to let us know that he had a past in the Party at the time when we recommended him for administrative work. He made a serious error, and one which we cannot overlook, but I think it is also clear that pressures which worked upon him as he faced this decision were of a magnitude which not many of us have to face. He knew that what he did was not right, and the fact that he knew this was plain from his eagerness to respond to my first question at the beginning of our interview. But he knew also that this was the best and perhaps the only chance for him to make a record and even a career in our profession. Whatever may be the view of others, Mr. Diamond honestly believes, I think, that there is nothing shameful in his past. Mistakes, yes, but criminal error, no. In concealing his past membership from us, he made a wrong decision, and I think that our own necessary course is clear, but I cannot find much pleasure in the result.

It remains only to remark that as far as I know no one at Harvard ever tried to give Mr. Diamond any trouble in his successful pursuit of an academic career. On the contrary, his friends at Harvard remained steadfast, as indeed he recognizes. In his interest, and obviously with his heartfelt approval, none of them gave any publicity to his situation. I myself, who had to make the decision that he should not be Counsellor for Foreign Students in 1954 never believed that this decision should be held against him for any later academic appointment. I remember that we were glad when Mr. Diamond received such an academic appointment at Columbia a year later, and I regret that his article, at this late date, has required this account of an unhappy incident.

McGeorge Bundy

McCarthyism, Party, and Class

Many historians and political scientists believe that Joseph McCarthy was a kind of working-class hero. They argue that his straightforward, even boorish manner appealed to those who distrusted and disliked the stylish, elite products of the Ivy League colleges, and that his hard anticommunist line found a sympathetic ear among those with too little education to resist its simplistic appeal. The following materials are useful in evaluating the argument. First, make some assumptions about who usually votes Republican, and who Democratic. Then, from the table, draw some conclusions about Joseph McCarthy's base of support. What does the map of Wisconsin—McCarthy's home state—tell us about those who elected him?

Party Sympathies and Voting Records of Those Favorable and Unfavorable to Senator J. McCarthy

Questions
  I. Did you vote for Eisenhower (Republican) or Stevenson (Democratic)?
 II. If the elections for Congress were being held today, which party would you like to see win in this state—the Republican Party or the Democratic Party?
III. (If undecided) As of today, do you lean more to the Republican Party or to the Democratic Party?
IV. In politics, as of today, do you consider yourself a Democrat, Republican, or Independent?

Question	Favorable (%)				Unfavorable (%)			
	I	II	III	IV	I	II	III	IV
Republican	76	53	37	46	49	29	28	24
Democratic	21	29	23	30	49	57	38	58
Undecided	—	17	27	—	—	13	26	—
Other	3	1	13	24	2	1	8	24
	100	100	100	100	100	100	100	100
	(N = 350)	(N = 456)	(N = 77)	(N = 456)	(N = 560)	(N = 693)	(N = 88)	(N = 693)

From Gallup Survey 529 K, April 1954. Material reprinted in Nelson W. Polsby, "Towards an Explanation of McCarthyism," Political Studies, 8 (October 1960), 262. Copyright, The Gallup Poll (American Institute of Public Opinion). Reprinted by permission.

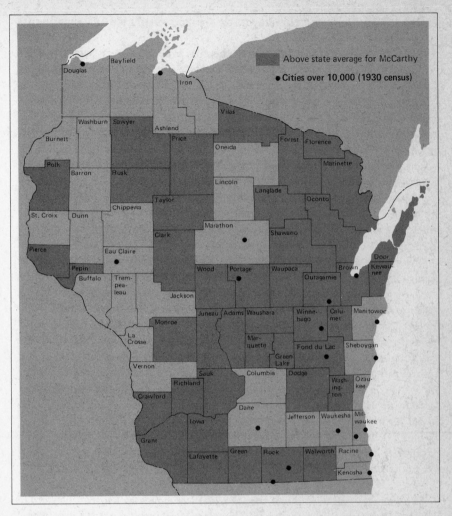

Support in Wisconsin for Senator Joseph McCarthy. *Reprinted by permission of the MIT Press from Michael Paul Rogin,* The Intellectuals and McCarthy: The Radical Specter *(Cambridge, Mass.: MIT Press, 1967), p. 87. Copyright © 1967 by the Massachusetts Institute of Technology.*

The Kitchen Debate, 1959

The "kitchen debate," a 1959 meeting between Soviet Premier Nikita Khrushchev and Vice President Richard Nixon, took place against a backdrop of more than a decade of conflict over the status of Berlin, a city

divided into western and communist sectors and surrounded by communist
East Germany.

The West had no legal claims to the city, whose western sector had
become a capitalist showcase and an embarrassment to the Soviets. In
November 1958, Khrushchev threatened a separate peace with East
Germany—meaning an end to western influence in Berlin—if a
"satisfactory settlement" were not reached within six months. As the
deadline approached, fears grew that Berlin would finally bring a shooting
war. But Khrushchev's deadline passed, and by the time the two leaders
locked horns in the kitchen of the American National Exhibition in
Moscow, it was not guns but butter that held center stage.

Khrushchev had emerged at the top of the Soviet hierarchy following
the death of Joseph Stalin in 1953. His ascendancy presumably signaled a
change in Soviet attitudes, for in 1956 Khrushchev denounced Stalin as a
"distrustful man, sickly and suspicious."

The "kitchen debate" was widely interpreted in the United States as a
moral victory for Nixon, who even at this date was actively campaigning
for the presidency. Whether it was this or not, it was a unique event.
Never before had two national leaders so freely and extemporaneously
explored the relative merits of their respective economic and social
systems. In the process, Nixon and Khrushchev bared national insecurities
and demonstrated how subjects as different as free speech and color
television had become part of the cold war.

Was the "kitchen debate" light entertainment, or did the participants
come to grips with basic differences between the United States and the
Soviet Union? In fact, does the debate reveal difference or suggest
likeness? Why was there so much talk of consumer goods and living
standards? Who was the more effective spokesman? Was Nixon engaged in
a form of verbal containment?

Following is an account of the informal exchanges in Moscow yesterday
between Vice President Richard M. Nixon and Premier Nikita S. Khrushchev.
It was compiled from dispatches of the *New York Times*, the Associated Press,
United Press International and Reuters. . . .

A Trade of Gibes About Trade

On arriving at the gate of the American National Exhibition later in the
morning, Mr. Khrushchev voiced a gibe about the United States ban on the
shipment of strategic goods to the Soviet Union.

Khrushchev: "Americans have lost their ability to trade. Now you have

From "The Two-Worlds: A Day-Long Debate," *New York Times*, July 25, 1959, pp. 1, 3. © 1959 by
The New York Times Company. Reprinted by permission.

grown older and you don't trade the way you used to. You need to be invigorated."

Nixon: "You need to have goods to trade."

The statesmen went on to look at equipment for playing back recordings. Mr. Nixon took a cue from it.

Nixon: "There must be a free exchange of ideas."

Mr. Khrushchev responded with a remark touching on the reporting of his speeches on his recent Polish tour.

Mr. Nixon said he was certain that Mr. Khrushchev's speeches and those of Frol R. Kozlov, a First Deputy Premier, had been fully reported in the West.

Khrushchev (indicating cameras, recording the scene on video tape): "Then what about this tape?" (smiling). "If it is shown in the United States it will be shown in English and I would like a guarantee that there will be a full translation of my remarks."

Mr. Nixon said there would be an English translation of Mr. Khrushchev's remarks and added his hope that all his own remarks in the Soviet Union would be given with full translations in that country.

Khrushchev:"We want to live in peace and friendship with Americans because we are the two most powerful countries, and if we live in friendship then other countries will also live in friendship. But if there is a country that is too war-minded we could pull its ears a little and say: Don't you dare; fighting is not allowed now; this is a period of atomic armament; some foolish one could start a war and then even a wise one couldn't finish the war. Therefore, we are governed by this idea in our policy—internal and foreign. How long has America existed? Three hundreds years?" Nixon: "One hundred and fifty years."

They Will Wave as They Pass U.S.

Khrushchev: "One hundred and fifty years? Well, then, we will say America has been in existence for 150 years and this is the level she has reached. We have existed not quite forty-two years and in another seven years we will be on the same level as America.

"When we catch you up, in passing you by, we will wave to you. Then if you wish we can stop and say: Please follow up. Plainly speaking, if you want capitalism you can live that way. That is your own affair and doesn't concern us. We can still feel sorry for you but since you don't understand us—live as you do understand.

"We are all glad to be here at the exhibition with Vice President Nixon. . . . I think you will be satisfied with your visit and if—I cannot go without saying it—if you would not take such a decision [proclamation by the United States Government of Captive Nations Week, a week of prayer for peoples enslaved by the Soviet Union] which has not been thought out thoroughly, as was approved by Congress, your trip would be excellent. But you have churned the water yourselves—why this was necessary God only knows.

"What happened? What black cat crossed your path and confused you?

But that is your affair, we do not interfere with your problems. [Wrapping his arms about a Soviet workman] Does this man look like a slave laborer? [Waving at others] With men with such spirit how can we lose?"

Exchange of Ideas Urged by Nixon

Nixon (pointing to American workmen): "With men like that we are strong. But these men, Soviet and American, work together well for peace, even as they have worked together in building this exhibition. This is the way it should be.

"Your remarks are in the tradition of what we have come to expect—sweeping and extemporaneous. Later on we will both have an opportunity to speak and consequently I will not comment on the various points that you raised, except to say this—this color television is one of the most advanced developments in communications that we have.

"I can only say that if this competition in which you plan to outstrip us is to do the best for both of our peoples and for peoples everywhere there must be exchange of ideas. After all, you don't know everything—"

Khrushchev: "If I don't know everything, you don't know anything about communism except fear of it."

Nixon: "There are some instances where you may be ahead of us, for example in the development of the thrust of your rockets for the investigation of outer space; there may be some instances in which we are ahead of you—in color television, for instance."

Khrushchev: "No, we are up with you on this, too. We have bested you in one technique and also in the other."

Nixon: "You see, you never concede anything."

Khrushchev:: "I do not give up."

Appearances on TV Are Suggested

Nixon: "Wait till you see the picture. Let's have far more communication and exchange in this very area that we speak of. We should hear you more on our television. You should hear us more on yours."

Khrushchev: "That's a good idea. Let's do it like this. You appear before our people. We will appear before your people. People will see and appreciate this."

Nixon: "There is not a day in the United States when we cannot read what you say. When Kozlov was speaking in California about peace, you were talking here in somewhat different terms. This was reported extensively in the American press. Never make a statement here if you don't want it to be read in the United States. I can promise you every word you say will be translated into English."

Khrushchev: "I doubt it. I want you to give your word that this speech of mine will heard by the American people."

Nixon (shaking hands on it): "By the same token, everything I say will be translated and heard all over the Soviet Union?"

Khrushchev: "That's agreed."

Nixon: "You must not be afraid of ideas."

Khrushchev: "We are telling you not to be afraid of ideas. We have no reason to be afraid. We have already broken free from such a situation."

Nixon: "Well, then, let's have more exchange of them. We are all agreed on that. All right? All right?"

Khrushchev: "Fine. [Aside] Agree to what? All right, I am in agreement. But I want to stress what I am in agreement with. I know that I am dealing with a very good lawyer, I also want to uphold my own miner's flag so that the coal miners can say, 'Our man does not concede.'"

Nixon: "No question about that."

Khrushchev: "You are a lawyer for capitalism and I am a lawyer for communism. Let's compete."

Vice President Protests Filibuster

Nixon: "The way you dominate the conversation you would make a good lawyer yourself. If you were in the United States Senate you would be accused of filibustering."

Nixon (halting Khrushchev at model kitchen in model house): "You had a very nice house in your exhibition in New York. My wife and I saw and enjoyed it very much. I want to show you this kitchen. It is like those of our houses in California."

Khrushchev (after Nixon called attention to a built-in panel-controlled washing machine): "We have such things."

Nixon: "This is the newest model. This is the kind which is built in thousands of units for direct installation in the houses."

He added that Americans were interested in making life easier for their women. Mr. Khrushchev remarked that in the Soviet Union they did not have "the capitalist attitude toward women."

Nixon: "I think that this attitude toward women is universal. What we want to do is make easier the life of our housewives."

He explained that the house could be built for $14,000 and that most veterans had bought houses for between $10,000 and $15,000.

Nixon: "Let me give you an example you can appreciate. Our steel workers, as you know, are on strike. But any steel worker could buy this house. They earn $3 an hour. This house costs about $100 a month to buy on a contract running twenty-five to thirty years."

Khrushchev: "We have steel workers and we have peasants who also can afford to spend $14,000 for a house." He said American houses were built to last only twenty years, so builders could sell new houses at the end of that period. "We build firmly. We build for our children and grandchildren."

Mr. Nixon said he thought American houses would last more than twenty years, but even so, after twenty years many Americans want a new home or a new kitchen, which would be obsolete then. The American system is designed to take advantage of new inventions and new techniques, he said.

Khrushchev: "This theory does not hold water."

He said some things never got out of date—furniture and furnishings, perhaps, but not houses. He said he did not think that what Americans had written about their houses was all strictly accurate.

Gadgetry Derided by Khrushchev

Nixon (pointing to television screen): "We can see here what is happening in other parts of the home."

Khrushchev: "This is probably always out of order."

Nixon: "Da [yes]."

Khrushchev: "Don't you have a machine that puts food into the mouth and pushes it down? Many things you've shown us are interesting but they are not needed in life. They have no useful purpose. They are merely gadgets. We have a saying, if you have bedbugs you have to catch one and pour boiling water into the ear." . . .

Nixon (hearing jazz music): "I don't like jazz music."

Khrushchev: "I don't like it either."

Nixon: "But my girls like it." . . .

Russians Have It Too, Premier Asserts

Khrushchev: "The Americans have created their own image of the Soviet man and think he is as you want him to be. But he is not as you think. You think the Russian people will be dumbfounded to see these things, but the fact is that newly built Russian houses have all this equipment right now. Moreover, all you have to do to get a house is to be born in the Soviet Union. You are entitled to housing. I was born in the Soviet Union. So I have a right to a house. In America if you don't have a dollar—you have the right to choose between sleeping in a house or on the pavement. Yet you say that we are slaves of communism." . . .

Nixon: "To us, diversity, the right to choose, the fact that we have 1,000 builders building 1,000 different houses, is the most important thing. We don't have one decision made at the top by one government official. This is the difference." . . .

U.S. Models Stop the Debate, Briefly

Khrushchev (noting Nixon gazing admiringly at young women modeling bathing suits and sports clothes): "You are for the girls too."

Nixon (indicating a floor sweeper that works by itself and other appliances): "You don't need a wife."

Khrushchev chuckled.

Nixon: "We do not claim to astonish the Russian people. We hope to show our diversity and our right to choose. We do not wish to have decisions made at the top by government officials who say that all homes should be built in the same way. Would it not be better to compete in the relative merits of washing machines than in the strength of rockets? Is this the kind of competition you want?"

Khrushchev: "Yes, that's the kind of competition we want. But your generals say: 'Let's compete in rockets. We are strong and we can beat you.' But in this respect we can also show you something."

Nixon: "To me you are strong and we are strong. In some ways, you are stronger than we are. In others, we are stronger. We are both strong not only from the standpoint of weapons but from the standpoint of will and spirit. Neither should use that strength to put the other in a position where he in effect has an ultimatum. In this day and age that misses the point. With modern weapons it does not make any difference if war comes. We both have had it."

Khrushchev: "For the fourth time I have to say I cannot recognize my friend Mr. Nixon. If all Americans agree with you, then who don't we agree [with]? This is what we want."

Nixon: "Anyone who believes the American Government does not reflect the people is not an accurate observer of the American scene. I hope the Prime Minister understands all the implications of what I have just said. Whether you place either one of the powerful nations or any other in a position so that they have no choice but to accept dictation or fight, then you are playing with the most destructive force in the world.

"This is very important in the present world context. It is very dangerous. When we sit down at a conference table it cannot all be one way. One side cannot put an ultimatum to another. It is impossible. But I shall talk to you about this later."

Premier Insists That's a Threat

Khrushchev: "Who is raising an ultimatum?"

Nixon: "We will discuss that later."

Khrushchev: "If you have raised the question, why not go on with it now while the people are listening? We know something about politics, too. Let your correspondents compare watches and see who is filibustering. You put great emphasis on 'diktat' [dictation]. Our country has never been guided by 'diktat.' 'Diktat' is a foolish policy."

Nixon: "I am talking about it in the international sense."

Khrushchev: "It sounds to me like a threat. We, too, are giants. You want to threaten—we will answer threats with threats."

Nixon: "That's not my point. We will never engage in threats."

Khrushchev: "You wanted indirectly to threaten me. But we have the means to threaten too."

Nixon: "Who wants to threaten?"

Khrushchev: "You are talking about implications. I have not been. We have the means at our disposal. Ours are better than yours. It is you who want to compete, Da Da Da."

Nixon: "We are well aware of that. To me who is best is not material. . . . I see that you want to build a good life. But I don't think that the cause of peace is helped by reminders that you have greater strength than us because that is a threat, too."

Khrushchev: "I was answering your words. You challenged me. Let's argue fairly."

Nixon: "My point was that in today's world it is immaterial which of the two great countries at any particular moment has the advantage. In war these advantages are illusory. Can we agree on that?"

Khrushchev: "Not quite. Let's not beat around the bush."

Nixon: "I like the way he talks."

Peace to Russian Means: End Bases

Khrushchev: "We want to liquidate all bases from foreign lands. Until that happens we will speak different languages. One who is for putting an end to bases on foreign lands is for peace. One who is against it is for war. We have liquidated our bases, reduced our forces and offered to make a peace treaty and eliminate the point of friction in Berlin. Until we settle that question, we will talk different languages."

Nixon: "Do you think it can be settled at Geneva?"

Khrushchev: "If we considered it otherwise, we would not have incurred the expense of sending our foreign minister to Geneva. Gromyko [Foreign Minister Andrei A. Gromyko] is not an idler. He is a very good man."

Nixon: "We have great respect for Mr. Gromyko. Some people say he looks like me. I think he is better looking. I hope it [the Geneva conference] will be successful."

Khrushchev: "It does not depend on us."

Nixon: "It takes two to make an agreement. You cannot have it all your own way."

Khrushchev: "These are questions that have the same aim. To put an end to the vestiges of war, to make a peace treaty with Germany—that is what we want. It is very bad that we quarrel over the question of war and peace."

Nixon: "There is no question but that your people and you want the Government of the United States being for peace—anyone who thinks that it is not for peace is not an accurate observer of America. In order to have peace,

Mr. Prime Minister, even in an argument between friends, there must be sitting down around a round table. There must be discussion. Each side must find areas where it looks at the other's point of view. The world looks to you today with regard to Geneva. I believe it would be a grave mistake and a blow to peace if it were allowed to fail."

Khrushchev: "This is our understanding as well."

Nixon: "So this is something. The present position is stalemate. Ways must be found to discuss it."

Khrushchev: "The two sides must seek ways of agreement."

In the evening, after formal speeches, Mr. Khrushchev and Mr. Nixon, in departing, stopped by a table laden with glasses of wine. Mr. Khrushchev proposed a toast to "elimination of all military bases in foreign lands." Mr. Nixon sidestepped, suggested they drink to peace instead.

A Friendly Toast Set Off New Round

Khrushchev: "We stand for peace and elimination of bases. Those are our words and they do not conflict with our deeds. If you are not willing to eliminate bases then I won't drink this toast."

Nixon: "I don't like this wine."

Khrushchev: "I like this wine but not the policy."

Nixon: "I have always heard that the Prime Minister is a vigorous defender of his policy, not only officially but unofficially."

Khrushchev: "I defend the real policy, which is to assure peace. How can peace be assured when we are surrounded by military bases?"

Nixon: "We will talk about that later. Let's drink to talking—as long as we are talking we are not fighting."

Khrushchev (indicating a waitress): "Let's drink to the ladies."

Nixon: "We can all drink to the ladies."

A waiter: "A hundred years of life to Mr. Khrushchev."

Nixon: "I will drink to that. We may disagree but we want you to be in good health."

Khrushchev: "We accept your hundred years' proposal. But when I reach 99 we will discuss it further—why should we be in haste?"

Nixon: "You mean that in ninety-nine years you will still be in power—no election?"

Mr. Khrushchev drank. Then, leaving, he remarked that usually when foreign guests said good-by they mistakenly used the Russian words for "How do you do."

Khrushchev: "They say just the opposite of what they want to say."

Nixon: "I know a few things and when I see you again I'll know more. At least four words more—about bases."

Khrushchev (bidding farewell): "That's a very difficult thing to learn."

Selling America

The two photographs that follow are idealizations of American life, created by the United States Information Agency, the international propaganda arm of the American government. In a sense, they were weapons in the cold war. As you look at them, try to think of connections between them and the Nixon-Khrushchev "kitchen debate." You may also want to compare them with the two Farm Security Administration photographs in the preceding chapter. What continuities suggest themselves? What differences? According to the first photograph, what apparent relationship exists between technology and domestic bliss and harmony? What idealized notions of youth culture are present in the second photograph? Is there some connection between this photograph and the Nixon/Khrushchev disavowal of jazz in the "kitchen debate"? Between the photograph and the emergence of rock 'n' roll (see Chapter 12)?

Original caption: "Takoma Park, Maryland—In the living room of their home, the A. Jackson Cory family and some friends watch a television program. Some sociologists claim the growing popularity of television will tend to make family life stronger and make the home the center of the family's recreation. 1950." *United States Information Agency photo, National Archives.*

Original Caption: "Washington, D.C.— Brennan Jacques, a typical American teenager, has his own orchestra, the 'Fabulous Esquires,' composed of youngsters aware of what their schoolmates like and do not like in current music. Here, young Jacques plays the piano for a group of young people, who have gathered around him." 1957. *United States Information Agency, National Archives.*

CHAPTER 12

The Eisenhower Equilibrium

Angered by the Soviet Union's European hegemony in the postwar years, many Americans sought to explain communist influence as a product of the Allied decision not to move its armies rapidly toward Berlin in the spring of 1945. General Dwight Eisenhower, who had ultimate responsibility for military operations in the European theater, justified his decision in an account published in 1948. "This future division of Germany," he wrote, "did not influence our military plans for the final conquest of the country. Military plans, I believe, should be devised with the single aim of speeding victory. . . ." While acknowledging that Berlin was a "natural objective," even "politically and psychologically important," Eisenhower had concluded that "it was not the logical or the most desirable objective for the forces of the Western Allies."

The qualities and values that Eisenhower projected here—reason, objectivity, dispassion, the belief that efficiency and politics existed in separate spheres—were characteristics that would lead to his election to the presidency. In 1948 and 1952, politicians of both major parties sought to nominate this man with the "leaping and effortless smile" who promised the electorate a "constitutional presidency," immune from the ideological harangues of European dictators, American demagogues, and New Deal presidents, and a secure economy, immune from major dislocations. In effect, he offered Americans (a certain class of them at least) a "New Equilibrium" to replace the disjointed and unpredictable insecurity of depression and war.

By 1960, it was clear that Eisenhower—and the nation at large—had not sought to gain these ends through any radical departures with the past. The cold war, anticommunism, the welfare state—all

inherited from his Democratic predecessor Harry Truman—were not
so much thrown aside as modulated, or refined, or brought into
balance.

Joseph McCarthy would cease to be a factor after 1954, but
otherwise, anticommunism was almost as much a part of the
Eisenhower years as it was of Truman's. The purges which cleansed
most labor unions of communist influence were completed when Ike
took office, but cold war attitudes permeated the labor movement
throughout the decade. The Committee on Un-American Activities of
the House of Representatives (HUAC) would never know the acclaim
it had mustered in the late 1940s, but each year it received more
money from Congress and continued to function. In 1959, the
Supreme Court refused to declare HUAC in violation of the First
Amendment. New organizations—Robert Welch's John Birch Society
and the Christian Anti-Communist Crusade, for example—emerged
to carry on the struggle against internal subversion. Welch labeled
Eisenhower a "dedicated, conscious agent of the communist
conspiracy."

Those who feared that the first Republican president since
Hoover would grasp the opportunity to dismantle the welfare state
had misunderstood both Eisenhower and the function of government
at mid-century. If only intuitively, Eisenhower knew that what was
left of the New Deal could not be eliminated without risking serious
social and economic disruption. Countercyclical programs like old-age
insurance and unemployment insurance were maintained or
expanded; the Council of Economic Advisers, created in the
Employment Act of 1946 to provide the president with his own
planning staff, remained; spending for military hardware and
interstate highways was expected to create jobs. Republicans did
manage a rollback of New Deal–Fair Deal policies in the areas of
taxation and agriculture.

There was in much of this a pervasive element of acceptance—
acceptance of American institutions as they were, or as Americans
wished they were. The power of the large corporation was accepted,
its influence invited. Many agreed with General Motors president
Charles E. Wilson who during Senate hearings to confirm his
nomination as secretary of defense said, "I thought what was good
for our country was good for General Motors, and vice versa."
Effective government was often conceptualized as the product of big
business, big labor, and big government, each checking and balancing
the others. The antitrust emphasis of the later New Deal was all but
forgotten. Instead, Americans could take comfort in John Galbraith's

theory of countervailing power. Outsiders like Alfred Kinsey who sought only to accurately describe patterns of behavior (in this case, sexual behavior) were treated like revolutionaries.

It followed that a wide variety of social problems—racism, unemployment, poverty, urban life, the cult of domesticity which suffocated women—were ignored, denied, accepted, or left in abeyance to be handled by some future generation. Throughout the 1950s, social commentators affirmed that America's central problems were ones of boredom, affluence, and classlessness. *The Midas Plague*, a science-fiction novel, described a world in which goods were so easily produced and so widely available that consuming had become a personal duty, a social responsibility, and an enormous and endless burden. David Riesman's *The Lonely Crowd*, an influential study published in 1950, argued that the age of scarcity had ended; Americans would henceforth be concerned with leisure, play, and the "art of living." For many analysts of American society, the new conditions of life had eliminated the old conflicts between capital and labor and ushered in the "end of ideology." Economic growth—so the theory went—would increase the size of the total product to be distributed and soon result in a society consisting mainly of white-collar workers.

Beneath this surface of calm equilibrium, there were some currents that disturbed many Americans. Despite a landmark Supreme Court decision ordering the eventual racial integration of public schools in 1954, black Americans remained outside the American system, gathering energies for a spectacular assault on the traditions of prejudice and exploitation. Intellectuals were worried about "conformity," and everyone was concerned about an apparent alienation among many young people, an alienation that expressed itself sometimes frighteningly as juvenile delinquency, sometimes just as a mystifying lack of energetic affirmation, most often in an affinity for a new music called rock 'n' roll. Following the launch of the Soviet satellite Sputnik in 1957, Americans began to ask whether this technological defeat reflected a general withering of national purpose (a theme taken up by Eisenhower's successor, John Kennedy). As the decade wore on, it became obvious, too, that millions of Americans were not participating in the prosperity the administration proclaimed. Eisenhower's farewell address would be silent on most of these issues; but its discussion of the military-industrial complex was perhaps Eisenhower's way of acknowledging that the equilibrium he had tried so hard to preserve—indeed, to create—was fundamentally unstable. If so, the next decade would prove him right.

MARK H. ROSE

Express Highway Politics

Many historians consider the Interstate Highway Act of 1956 to be the most important single piece of legislation to emerge from the Eisenhower presidency. It authorized 41,000 miles of controlled-access, four- to eight-lane roads linking major cities. Total cost of the system was an anticipated $27.5 billion, of which 90 percent was to come from the federal government through taxes on fuels, tires, and commercial vehicles. The national government also agreed to fund half the costs of improvements on existing county, state, and federal highways.

Mark Rose's account of express highway politics raises questions basic to any definition of the political equilibrium to which Eisenhower contributed in the 1950s, and to the place of the Eisenhower equilibrium in post–New Deal American history. The Highway Act might well be interpreted, like concurrent extensions of social security, as an addition to the welfare state and as an affirmation of its principles. Certainly the legislation prescribed a new role for the national government and called for unprecedented domestic expenditures on a single construction project. Yet is it possible to premise a welfare state on the kind of politics which created the interstate system? Whose interests were being served by the project? Who was it designed to benefit? Can you draw any comparisons between the politics which created the interstate system and those which produced the Bureau of Mines in 1910 (mentioned in Chapter 6)? Was the Interstate Highway Act of 1956 a cautious first step toward unifying a segmented society, or should it be interpreted as the product of a culture only temporarily held together in "equilibrium"?

Readers should also speculate on the *impact* of the interstate system, a topic not treated by Rose. What new patterns of life did it encourage? What traditional patterns did it threaten? Was McDonald's (see the photograph later in this chapter) in any sense a product of the interstate system? Was the Shell station?

In highways, then, lies a new national frontier for the pessimist who thinks frontiers have disappeared. It challenges the imagination and spirit of enterprise which always have been the distinctive marks of American life. And even

From Mark H. Rose, *Interstate Express Highway Politics, 1941–1956* (Lawrence, Kansas: Regents Press of Kansas, 1979), edited and abridged. Reprinted by permission of Regents Press of Kansas.

the gloomiest of men admit that America never ignores the challenges of a new frontier, geographical of otherwise.

Paul G. Hoffman, President,
The Studebaker Corporation,
1940

By 1960, a recorded voice promised visitors to General Motor's Futurama exhibit at the 1939 New York World's Fair, fourteen-lane express roads would accommodate "traffic at designated speeds of 50, 75, and 100 miles an hour." Spectators, six hundred at a time, rode around GM's 35, 738 square foot mock-up of future America while the synchronized recording in each chair continued. Automobiles from farm and feeder roads would "join the Motorway at the same speed as cars traveling in the lane they enter," and motorists would be able to "make right and left turns at speeds up to 50 miles per hour." In urban areas, express highways would be "so routed as to displace outmoded business sections and undesirable slum areas." In cities themselves, men would construct buildings of "breath-taking architecture," leaving space for "sunshine, light and air." Great sections of farm land, "drenched in blinding sunlight" according to an observer, were under cultivation and nearly in fruit. Traffic, whether in rural or urban areas, flowed along without delays and without hazards at intersections and railroad crossings. "Who can say what new horizons lie before us . . .," asked the voice on the record, "new horizons in many fields, leading to new benefits for everyone, everywhere." By mid May 1939, only a few weeks after the fair opened, Futurama was the most popular attraction.

Actually, GM's exhibit, if fanciful, contained concepts and plans well-known to engineers, business leaders, urban and regional planners, and highway-minded men. Yet between 1900 and 1939, these planners never managed to construct sufficient highway mileage, to speed-up traffic, to remodel cities and farm areas, or to put everyone to work. . . . During World War II, the framework in which highway enthusiasts shaped policy remained about the same. . . . Enhanced federal funding failed to eliminate the traffic mess. . . .

Beginning around 1948, postwar highway politics included new ideas and different approaches. Increasingly, civil and traffic engineers updated techniques, trying out complicated apparatus and ingenious formulas for analysis of traffic and land use variables. In brief, they tried to understand road design and construction standards required to cope with modern, high speed traffic conditions. Beginning in 1951, leaders of highway groups turned to their traffic surveys and updated notions of highway design with a view toward building upon them toward a restructuring of political relationships, writing new road legislation, and getting traffic under way.

By late 1951, truckers and highway engineers sensed major changes in the dimensions of the traffic tangle. Congestion, National Highway User Conference Director Arthur C. Butler told heads of the conference on October 11, 1951, had . . . "become more costly than we can stand." It was, he thought, a "near crisis."

Political problems—tollway development and competition with rail-roaders—added a special dimension to discussions of traffic tangles. If road users could not agree among themselves about remedies for congestion, Butler claimed, railroaders would take advantage of the squabbling to "promote their own selfish objectives." Federal officials would nationalize the highway system, saddling them with higher taxes. Expanding tollway mileage presented another problem. By 1952, more than 600 toll miles were open and another 1,100 or so under construction. A truck operator, Butler reminded conference heads, "likes the road," but "doesn't like the toll." Toll authorities, according to the opinion of many in highway-related industries, would perpetuate themselves, continuing charges and extending their systems.

For years, leaders of commercial truck operators and organized motorists and state road engineers had lobbied to block tollway schemes, outdistance railroaders, and secure lower taxes. Before 1951, they had concentrated their attention on state and local political bodies, limiting federal level initiatives to biannual pleadings. Often, efforts in Washington and elsewhere had been rit-ualistic. But by 1951, so menacing was the prospect of intervention by bureau-crats and railroaders and so terrible were traffic delays and rising costs and taxes, highway users determined to eliminate obstacles to smooth traffic by remodeling political structures to serve scientific highway development. What was needed, User Conference Director Butler argued, was a program to "get us . . . out of this muddle."

The formal vehicle for this new initiative was Project Adequate Roads (PAR), . . . a national coalition of highway users, manufacturers, public offi-cials, and traffic-research men in the Highway Research Board and Automotive Safety Foundation. While the regular Highway User Conference staff would handle day-to-day operations, the founders of PAR envisioned formation of a series of independent local and state groups. As Butler explained it to members of his board on October 11, 1951, PAR would become a "national committee for highway improvement." . . .

Ultimately, Project Adequate Roads itself was another political move-ment. Leaders of PAR recognized that revising state and federal road legisla-tion would prove simpler if members of their own industry united around common goals. What they undertook, then, was a hard-pushing, nationwide campaign for concentrated, tax-free, federal road building and more efficient highway programming at the local level. At some point, Butler hoped that PAR would act "as the nation's index finger," directing attention to areas of critical highway need. . . .

No sooner had leaders of PAR created an organization than the movement collapsed, more than anything because neither a broad political coalition nor the mumbo-jumbo of scientific road construction could bridge fundamental differences in outlook and self-interest. Late in 1952, state road engineers broke from the PAR movement, largely in an effort to preserve sources of income and bolster their competitive position against tollway officials. . . . While truckers liked the PAR program in principle, it was not sufficiently inviting to overcome fundamental divisions within their own industry. They split on issues according to the transport needs of the region they served, dividing further between fleet owners, large common carriers, and local, single unit operators. . . .

Leaders of the largest trucking industry organizations looked upon federal highway building and industry regulation from still another perspective. Members of this group included Burge N. Seymour of the American Trucking Associations, Roy A. Fruehauf, head of a truck trailer manufacturing firm, and David Beck of the Teamsters Union. These men and the bulk of truck owners differed significantly in the scope of their respective business operations and their assessment of the regulations best suited to commercial needs. As Beck, Seymour, and Fruehauf wrote to President Dwight D. Eisenhower on January 30, 1953, the industry had matured to the point that it required the "guidance and support" of a single federal agency. This new agency would "dedicate itself . . . to the problem of building a road system in this country adequate to serve the needs of motor transport." Although they did not object to local regulation and state road construction, they had concluded that the multitude of state laws "complicated interstate operations." By mid 1953, then, members of the trucking industry had fragmented themselves, and were unwilling to unite around ambitious promotions calculated to eliminate federal participation in their affairs or to return road construction and finance to state officials alone.

The Project Adequate Roads campaign enjoyed no greater impact on federal officials, many of whom had their own pet notions about highway construction matters. Through most of 1953, as a matter of fact, President Eisenhower and his people did not even formulate a highway program. In November, 1953, after nearly ten months in office, Budget Bureau officials awaited a report from Secretary of Commerce Sinclair Weeks on highway funding levels. But the absence of a formal program did not mean that they were not concerned about the relationship between highway building, economic growth, and national transportation development. During the second half of 1953, as the economy sagged following the end of the war in Korea, several of Eisenhower's leading officials viewed road construction as a way of creating useful jobs. Highway and other construction projects, Council of Economic Advisers Chairman Arthur F. Burns wrote to Eisenhower on August 11, 1953, would "provide work for those in need of work and help keep the pump primed." During November and December, 1953, by contrast, top officials in the Department of Commerce prepared plans to charge users of federal transport facilities, air, water, and highway included. User charges, they remained convinced, would assure "that each form of transportation will have the opportunity to compete fairly for the movement of the nation's goods." Fuller use of every type of transport, as the reasoning went, would serve national economic development best.

By 1954, the PAR movement had fragmented into the usual collection of competing factions, arguing and complaining about who paid for roads, who would build them, and who would benefit. Neither truckers and engineers nor politicians had shifted far from older views, themselves the creatures of vastly different experiences and responsibilities. What it came down to was that if PAR members wanted greater attention paid to the Interstate System, they had to finance construction of the sprawling federal highway network. Since they were not prepared to spend more than two cents a gallon, there was not much chance of solving the highway crisis.

Postwar urban highway politics revolved around many of the same issues, though the stakes were immeasurably greater. After World War II, urban businessmen and residents continued to flee to the suburbs, leaving behind declining property values, falling retail sales, and an unsightly collection of decayed buildings and unrented space in the cities. Traffic congestion, since the 1920s a headache for urban leaders, motorists, truckers, and residents alike, composed a particularly critical part of the dilemma. . . .

City planners, as an illustration, focused more or less exclusively on reviving sales and property values in the downtown areas, usually the most congested and run-down section in the older urban centers. . . . Truck operators and truck and automobile manufacturers and professional engineers looked at urban redevelopment plans in different terms. Even before World War II, they had focused on the traffic aspect of urban problems. New highways, in their judgment, were supposed to reduce congestion. "Roads were built for commerce," one of them had argued, and most accepted the idea. . . . That traffic flow was more important than urban affairs in general also governed the thought and decision making of state road engineers. . . .

The initial source of division then, was between truckers and engineers who favored the construction of roads to serve the sources of traffic, and planners and their few allies, men who preferred to construct expressways with a view toward guiding urban growth. The ultimate source of conflict was between those opting for unlimited economic development and others who idealized a process of directed, systematic growth and the imposition of social and economic controls. . . .

American highway building, for whatever purpose, had been stunted at the national level for years. Major roads users had launched strenuous political campaigns, hoping to dislodge farm-market road building from the federal payroll while securing tax-free, expressway construction for themselves. Local road advocates, for their part, wished to charge interstate truckers and motorists with an even greater share of farm highway expenses. Larger questions, concerning the pace and direction of economic development, local autonomy, political independence, and professional judgment, had permeated these debates and fractured highway politics further. Beginning in 1954, President Eisenhower took his turn at trying to loosen traffic and to impose order on the economic and social system.

At an April 12, 1954, meeting in the White House, Eisenhower reorganized government road planning and tried to impress his own views on federal highway programming. Since at least early 1954, Eisenhower had believed that the federal government should boost road spending in order to accommodate traffic. More automobiles, he thought, meant "greater convenience . . ., greater happiness, and greater standards of living." Now, he wanted Sherman Adams, his chief assistant, and Arthur F. Burns, head of the Council of Economic Advisers, to coordinate a search among government officials for methods to accelerate the federal highway building program. Eisenhower himself was seeking a "dramatic" plan to get 50 billion dollars worth of self-liquidating highways under construction." In terms of construction priorities, he thought the federal government ought to devote greater attention to the Interstate system, to roads from airports into downtown areas, and to access roads near defense installations. While he would condone federal loan guarantees, an expanded road program could not be allowed to upset the federal budget.

Soon, several top officials were busy developing plans. Economists and those interested in economic planning evaluated road building formulas in light of long-range business trends. Traffic relief, they thought, was necessary to encourage growth. Sufficient roads for traffic, predicted one economist, would "mean the difference between a prosperous enjoyable economy, and a more restricted, harassed one." At the same time, massive road construction, if timed properly, offered a useful device in their own program for controlling economic swings.

The head of the Public Works Planning Unit in the Council of Economic Advisers, General John H. Bragdon (U. S. Army, Ret.), drew up plans for a more centralized program. He hoped to secure economic adviser Burns' support for a policy of firm, federal direction of highway building. The secretaries of commerce, defense, and the treasury, as he envisioned it, would sit as a board of directors of a National Highway Authority, assuming responsibility for federal road construction and finance. Highway construction was a national obligation, he liked to argue, not something to be divided or left to local governments.

Bragdon and members of his small group defined road policy as part of grander plans for economic improvement and social control. Recent federal highway legislation was "only a start," according to Bragdon. He anticipated greatly increased employment opportunities, especially in the automobile industry, and acceleration of economic growth along new expressways. But all of this development, he added, would serve "as a continuous stabilizing force." Burns saw highway construction in much the same way. Accelerated road building, he believed, was a useful antirecessionary measure and would foster more efficient road transportation. Secretary of the Treasury George M. Humphrey took an even wider view of a road program, stressing not only economic growth but perpetuation of the existing stratification system. Highways, he believed, were a "physical asset," and additional mileage would "create more and more wealth" for Americans. Rather than subdividing the fruits of production, he had told an audience of governors in April, 1954, it was preferable to "make another pie and everybody has a bigger piece."

General Lucius D. Clay—the head of Continental Can Corporation, a friend of Eisenhower since World War II, and the president's choice to prepare new road legislation—was virtually indifferent to proposals sent his way by economists. If tolls were charged on formerly free roads, as many of them urged, Clay predicted "revolution" in several western states. Instead, Clay recommended that the federal and state governments share the cost of Interstate system contruction on a 90–10 basis, dedicating the federal gasoline tax to repayment of bonds over a thirty-year period. . . . On February 22, Eisenhower proclaimed his support for a highway program along lines recommended by General Clay.

Between January and March, 1955, highway users and builders as well as engineers—all men long anxious to get on with the right sort of highway program—endorsed Clay's proposal. By mid 1953, after Project Adequate Roads failed, they had decided to forget tax-free federal highway building and other difficult-to-achieve financing ideals. Governors of states with unusual congestion and high construction expenses looked forward to more help from Washington for costly expressways. Defense Department officers were most interested in completion of a compact, limited access road system within a specified time period. For many business and professional leaders, the Clay plan represented the culmination of more than a decade of promoting express highway construction at the state and federal levels.

As part of an overall effort to win additional endorsements for Clay's program, President Eisenhower himself made several personal appeals. On February 16, he invited Clay to the White House to brief Senators William F. Knowland, H. Styles Bridges, and Eugene D. Millikan, and Congressmen Charles A. Halleck, Joseph W. Martin, and Leslie C. Arends. While Clay sketched his plan, Eisenhower limited his own role to asking leading questions, serving to direct Clay's attention into new areas. But the point of the meeting, insofar as the president was concerned, was to highlight for senior Republicans the urgency of constructing more roads in order to bolster the economy. "With our roads inadequate to handle an expanding industry," he told them, "the result will be inflation and a disrupted economy." Most of the airports built recently were obsolete already, he added, and "we cannot let that happen on our roads."

On February 21, at the urging of Clay, Adams, and other administration leaders, Eisenhower conferred with ranking members of the Senate and House public works committees and roads subcommittees. Never, remarked Senator Dennis Chavez, had the president called all members of a committee to the White House to discuss domestic legislation. Soon, Eisenhower promised them, more than sixty million vehicles will jam our roads, "and we will have to build up our highways to meet that traffic." A ten-year road program, one fashioned along lines prepared by Clay, was "vitally essential for national defense," and would "help the steel and auto spare parts industry." Ultimately, then, an updated road program was "good for America."

If those who stood to enhance their professional skills and reputations or fill their pocketbooks could live with most of Clay's package, others who would benefit little opposed it. A few, especially leaders of the Farm Bureau Federation, wanted the federal government to pay greater attention to farm roads. Others, mostly governors of states lacking traffic, complained about the toll reimbursement feature of the Clay bill. A second highway construction bill, prepared by Representative George H. Fallon of Maryland, promised more aid to build farm roads, but enraged truckers by scheduling graduated taxes on fuel and tires. In July, 1955, nearly 500 truckers went to Washington to complain about the inequity of graduated taxes. By July 27, neither bill appeared acceptable, and by large numbers, members of the House overturned both. Political arm-twisting and complex formulas had failed to soften conflicting views. In 1955, just as earlier, those committed to local and particularized needs had managed to defeat economists and others who were driven by an urge to plan.

Defeat of all road legislation did not soften the opinions of competing highwaymen and political leaders. Beginning in August, 1955, they lobbied for their version of good highway programming, once more debating the virtues of national control of road construction, the merits of toll and free highways, and the proper rate of gasoline taxation. Because of the continuing deadlock, many believed that Congress would again be forced to hold up legislation.

General Bragdon remained the most diligent proponent of toll financing. On July 28, 1955, only one day after House members had rejected any change in road building arrangements, he claimed that toll collections would finance at least 23,000 expressway miles. Provided earnings were transferred from one state to another, Bragdon estimated that about 30,000 miles could be financed from tolls. On September 27, Bragdon outlined his plan in a letter to Sherman Adams. Somehow, he promised political support from those who opposed tolls, and pointed again to "the great savings to the taxpayer." Senator Prescott S. Bush, Representative Jesse P. Wolcott, and others favored toll financing, or so he claimed. Now was the time, then, to "prepare a bill incorporating these factors."

But Bragdon's schemes and proposals did not impress Adams or other top officials and . . . results were only a little better than before. In road politics, there were no secrets. Truckers had made public, usually often, what they expected. At a series of conferences held during the last two weeks of October with members of the Cabinet Committee and their aides, heads of the trucking industry told their story again. Bonds and administration and anything else did not matter, just tax rates. Because the Fallon bill imposed differential rates, especially on tires, they had opposed it. Truckers, a leader of the American

Trucking Associations claimed, "were singled out in the Fallon bill as the whipping boys." Reasonable taxation, as they figured it out, amounted to uniform, one or two cent hikes on gasoline and tires. Without objection, moreover, they would pay another 2 percent excise on new trucks, provided proceeds went straight to highway construction. Tollways were a different matter. Traffic on toll roads moved easier, and truckers liked that well enough, but they opposed schemes encouraging further toll collections or extension of toll networks. As other Americans, truckers preferred low taxes; as their trucking forefathers, they preferred regressive ones.

Word from Eisenhower's administrators ran along different lines, but echoed old claims and notions. Rates, as such, did not matter as long as road construction financed itself; so much the better if they got another handle on economic development. Each man, however, emphasized one or the other. Treasury Secretary Humphrey, always an independent actor on the highway scene, concentrated on insuring self-sufficiency for any road project. He preferred toll financing, but would accept an earmarked user tax if equal to expenses. General Bragdon, by way of contrast, remained anxious to build stabilizers into the economy. On October 18, he pushed members of his Committee on Public Works—another federal interagency group—to prepare long-range construction plans. While such ideas appealed in principle, most on the committee sought immediate plans and fewer regulations, one participant asking if during an economic emergency he "could expect relief from detailed restrictions on contract procedures." Members of the Council of Economic Advisers also focused on linking road expenditures with economic fluctuations. And on November 1, Gabriel Hauge, Eisenhower's personal economic adviser, wrote Secretary of Commerce Sinclair Weeks to ask if his Interstate system plans provided mechanisms for directing the economy. "That was the fundamental purpose of the plan in the initial instance," as he recalled it. All in all, in administration circles, defeat had not dampened enthusiasm for drastic changes in the federal road program.

As men continued to plan for their own version of an upgraded federal road program, most, whether in or out of government, were pessimistic about the chances of anything passing Congress. Prospects appeared dismal, reported long time observers of highway politics. . . .

Beginning late in January, 1956, however, leaders gave ground on a few issues, labeling small concessions as necessary compromises. Following a January 31 meeting with congressional leaders, Eisenhower's aides were told to "yield to Democratic insistence on financing." Senator Harry F. Byrd, chairman of the Finance Committee and critic of the Clay bill, was to "be consulted as to the most desirable procedures for expediting the bill." In the trucking industry, too, leaders spoke of concessions. Between February and April, 1956, in meetings, in industry wide publications, and in correspondence with members of Congress, they announced again their willingness to pay higher taxes. Once rates were fixed at acceptable levels, truckers urged House members to vote for a bill fashioned by Congressmen George Fallon and Hale Boggs.

Actually, few in government or industry had made major concessions;

fewer acted from some spirit of give and take. References to compromise, at least in highway politics, served as functional myth. The fact of the matter was that Boggs and Fallon had written legislation which incorporated long sought goals, asked few significant sacrifices, and managed to sidestep difficult questions.

Basically, the key to success was providing something for everyone without imposing high taxes on truckers. Distribution of funds—at first for farm, urban, and trunk roads, later for Interstate routes—had been a sticky issue since the beginning of the Federal Aid Highway System. Fallon and Boggs handed out record high sums for each, and promised another $25 million yearly for urban as well as rural construction. Urban supporters of Interstate construction came out best. The federal government would pay 90 percent of Interstate expenses, about $25 billion, but distribute the money according to local needs. Since costs in congested urban areas were greatest, they would receive a disproportionate share of funds. In order to finance all this construction, Fallon and Boggs increased automotive taxes. But they largely went along with truckers, asking only for moderate, ungraduated increases. Only Representative Daniel A. Reed's amendment, one imposing a surcharge of $1.50 per thousand pounds on the total weight of trucks heavier than 26,000 pounds, appeared out of line with their willingness to pay.

Delaying action on divisive items was the second factor in the success of the Boggs-Fallon Bill. For years, differences of opinion about toll road repayment and the even more vexing matter of tax equity between big and small truckers, bus operators, and motorists had convulsed road politics. Boggs and Fallon avoided both. Because most agreed that the federal government should pay compensation to states for toll and free roads built already and added to the Interstate system, Boggs and Fallon were able to make that promise. But they delayed a decision on which roads were entitled to a credit pending a study of standards by the secretary of commerce. In turn, Congress would review the results of the secretary's study. No doubt, a lengthy study ordered by Boggs and Fallon of road costs assignable to auto, bus, and truck operators was intended to set aside that question too.

Boggs and Fallon also prescribed industrial and professional standards for highway finance and construction. Since the 1930s, leaders of auto and trucking associations and state road engineers had complained that governments collected more in motor vehicle taxes than they spent for roads. State legislators had crystallized these views into legislation prohibiting expenditure of gasoline tax revenues for non-highway purposes such as schools or mass transit operations. Boggs and Fallon found a place for the antidiversion impulse by creating the Highway Trust Fund. Revenues from taxes on fuels, tires, and new vehicles and Reed's surcharge would go directly into the Trust Fund for road building alone. Finally, Boggs and Fallon allowed advance condemnation of rights of way and limited access design. No longer would engineers and users suffer intolerable delays in acquiring land; no longer would they have to endure the nuisance and hazards of cross traffic.

If the Senate was also going to pass a road bill, as now seemed likely, then nearly every leader of government and industry associated with road transport had something special to include, something equally vital to get dropped. Inclusion of the Davis-Bacon amendment, requiring payment of prevailing wages as determined by the secretary of labor, excited the most controversy. Contractors and state road engineers worked hard to eliminate the amendment. As early as January 19, members of a group of engineers and contractors had declared for local determination of wages, invoking mostly cost arguments. Beginning around March 1 through early June, contractors and chamber of commerce officials joined the struggle against Davis-Bacon, sending letters and petitions to members of Congress. Usually they spoke of efficiency, of lower costs, of states' rights, all symbols, images, and commercial realities celebrated by men in contract road work. In April, administration leaders took up the anti-Davis-Bacon cause, trying to find a way to cut it without angering labor leaders.

By June, 1956, the Senate and House had approved legislation to authorize a vast increase in federal highway spending. . . . On June 25, conferees submitted their report. On the twenty-sixth, members of the Senate approved it, 89–1; members of the House, on the same date, approved it as well, but did not bother recording their vote. On June 29, President Eisenhower signed the bill.

After nearly fifty years of traffic jams and even more of urban decay, after a quarter of a century of fumbling efforts to use road construction to direct economic activity, leading parties had agreed to an accelerated highway building program. Boggs and Fallon had found the key to success. They promised plenty of new roadway for everyone and security for treasury deposits, and had asked truckers to pay only modest tax increases. At the core of this formula was the decision of truckers and leaders of motorist associations, however reluctant, to sponsor the entire federal aid highway program. Once financing was arranged, congressmen were left with the relatively easier task of imposing professional standards on federal road projects and spreading revenues among competitors. . . .

American commitment to automobility—the conviction of most that motor vehicles and fast flowing expressways were good in their own right—also facilitated efforts to find a solution to the legislative tangle. For several decades, motorists had been stalled in traffic jams. Midway through the 1950s, many had determined that highway mileage pure and simple was more important than apportionment and finance formulas. By January, 1956, according to a publicist for the American Automobile Association, motorists wanted "better highways now." President Eisenhower certainly saw things that way too. Initially, he had insisted upon the Clay plan. After losing that battle, however, Eisenhower was ready to sign any bill as long as it included a self-financing feature. In 1956, the president just "wanted the job done."

The Highway Act of 1956 committed the federal government to a massive expenditure of funds. But the act itself left construction in the hands of state officials, imposed standards determined by professional engineers, and promised ever-larger outlays to construct farm, rural-trunk, and urban roads as well as the Interstate system. The federal government, in this scheme, served mainly as a transfer agency for members of business and professional subcultures, each one since 1939 rooted to the local or regional scenes.

JOHN KENNETH GALBRAITH

The Economy in Equilibrium

One of the principal theorists of equilibrium in the 1950s was John Kenneth Galbraith. Galbraith, an economist, was firmly affiliated with the Democratic party, but his analysis of the "new " American economy was quite consistent with the way the Eisenhower administration behaved in matters like the creation of the interstate system. Galbraith's principal idea was that the old "competitive" system had been supplanted by an economy of "countervailing" forces. In a competitive world, as Galbraith described it, producers competed with each other, and so did buyers on their "side" of the market. In the new countervailing system, economic lines of force produced equilibrium *across* the market. Producers did not compete with each other. Instead they combined in an attempt to impose themselves on their customers. The customers, in turn, resisted the imposition. The result was a "self-regulating" economy in which government played the role of a fine-tuning mechanism that corrected momentary imbalances or disorders.

Use Galbraith's presentation as a means of defining the Eisenhower equilibrium. What is the relationship between countervailing power and interstate highway politics? Would Galbraith have been able to place the military-industrial complex (see Eisenhower's speech later in this chapter) within his theory?

The paradox of the unexercised power of the large corporation begins with an important oversight in the underlying economic theory. In the competitive model—the economy of many sellers each with a small share of the total market—the restraint on the private exercise of economic power was provided by other firms on the same side of the market. It was the eagerness of competitors to sell, not the complaints of buyers, that saved the latter from spoliation. It was assumed, no doubt accurately, that the nineteenth-century

From John Kenneth Galbraith, *American Capitalism: The Concept of Countervailing Power* (Boston: Houghton Mifflin, 1956; orig. ed., 1952), pp. 110–112, 114–116, 118–121, 128. Copyright 1952, 1956 by John Kenneth Galbraith. Reprinted by permission of Houghton Mifflin Company.

textile manufacturer who over-charged for his product would promptly lose his market to another manufacturer who did not. If all manufacturers found themselves in a position where they could exploit a strong demand, and mark up their prices accordingly, there would soon be an inflow of new competitors. The resulting increase in supply would bring prices and profits back to normal.

As with the seller who was tempted to use his economic power against the customer, so with the buyer who was tempted to use it against his labor or suppliers. The man who paid less than prevailing wage would lose his labor force to those who paid the worker his full (marginal) contribution to the earnings of the firm. In all cases the incentive to socially desirable behavior was provided by the competitor. It was to the same side of the market—the restraint of sellers by other sellers and of buyers by other buyers, in other words to competition—that economists came to look for the self-regulatory mechanism of the economy.

They also came to look to competition exclusively and in formal theory still do. The notion that there might be another regulatory mechanism in the economy has been almost completely excluded from economic thought. Thus, with the widespread disappearance of competition in its classical form and its replacement by the small group of firms if not in overt, at least in conventional or tacit collusion, it was easy to suppose that since competition had disappeared, all effective restraint on private power had disappeared. Indeed this conclusion was all but inevitable if no search was made for other restraints and so complete was the preoccupation with competition that none was made.

In fact, new restraints on private power did appear to replace competition. They were nurtured by the same process of concentration which impaired or destroyed competition. But they appeared not on the same side of the market but on the opposite side, not with competitors but with customers or suppliers. It will be convenient to have a name for this counterpart of competition and I shall call it *countervailing power.**

To begin with a broad and somewhat too dogmatically stated proposition, private economic power is held in check by the countervailing power of those who are subject to it. The first begets the second. The long trend toward concentration of industrial enterprise in the hands of a relatively few firms has brought into existence not only strong sellers, as economists have supposed, but also strong buyers as they have failed to see. The two develop together, not in precise step but in such manner that there can be no doubt that the one is in response to the other.

The fact that a seller enjoys a measure of monopoly power, and is reaping a measure of monopoly return as a result, means that there is an inducement to

---

*I have been tempted to coin a new word for this which would have the same convenience as the term competition and had I done so my choice would have been "countervailence." However, the phrase "countervailing power" is more descriptive and does not have the raw sound of any newly fabricated word.

those firms from whom he buys or those to whom he sells to develop the power with which they can defend themselves against exploitation. It means also that there is a reward to them, in the form of a share of the gains of their opponents' market power, if they are able to do so. In this way the existence of market power creates an incentive to the organization of another position of power that neutralizes it.

The contention I am here making is a formidable one. It comes to this: Competition which, at least since the time of Adam Smith, has been viewed as the autonomous regulator of economic activity and as the only available regulatory mechanism apart from the state, has, in fact, been superseded. Not entirely, to be sure. I should like to be explicit on this point. Competition still plays a role. There are still important markets where the power of the firm as (say) a seller is checked or circumscribed by those who provide a similar or a substitute product or service. This, in the broadest sense that can be meaningful, is the meaning of competition. The role of the buyer on the other side of such markets is essentially a passive one. It consists in looking for, perhaps asking for, and responding to the best bargain. The active restraint is provided by the competitor who offers, or threatens to offer, a better bargain. However, this is not the only or even the typical restraint on the exercise of economic power. In the typical modern market of few sellers, the active restraint is provided not by competitors but from the other side of the market by strong buyers. Given the convention against price competition, it is the role of the competitor that becomes passive in these markets. . . .

The operation of countervailing power is to be seen with the greatest clarity in the labor market where it is also most fully developed. Because of his comparative immobility, the individual worker has long been highly vulnerable to private economic power. The customer of any particular steel mill, at the turn of the century, could always take himself elsewhere if he felt he was being overcharged. Or he could exercise his sovereign privilege of not buying steel at all. The worker had no comparable freedom if he felt he was being underpaid. Normally he could not move and he had to have work. Not often has the power of one man over another been used more callously than in the American labor market after the rise of the large corporation. As late as the early twenties, the steel industry worked a twelve-hour day and seventy-two-hour week with an incredible twenty-four-hour stint every fortnight when the shift changed.

No such power is exercised today and for the reason that its earlier exercise stimulated the counteraction that brought it to an end. In the ultimate sense it was the power of the steel industry, not the organizing abilities of John L. Lewis and Philip Murray, that brought the United Steel Workers into being. The economic power that the worker faced in the sale of his labor—the competition of many sellers dealing with few buyers—made it necessary that he organize for his own protection. There were rewards to the power of the steel companies in which, when he had successfully developed countervailing power, he could share.

As a general though not invariable rule one finds the strongest unions in the United States where markets are served by strong corporations. And it is not an accident that the large automobile, steel, electrical, rubber, farm-machinery and non-ferrous metal-mining and smelting companies all bargain with powerful unions. Not only has the strength of the corporations in these industries made it necessary for workers to develop the protection of countervailing power; it has provided unions with the opportunity for getting something more as well. If successful they could share in the fruits of the corporation's market power. By contrast there is not a single union of any consequence in American agriculture, the country's closest approach to the competitive model. The reason lies not in the difficulties in organization; these are considerable, but greater difficulties in organization have been overcome. The reason is that the farmer has not possessed any power over his labor force, and at least until recent times has not had any rewards from market power which it was worth the while of a union to seek. As an interesting verification of the point, in the Great Valley of California, the large farmers of that area have had considerable power vis-à-vis their labor force. Almost uniquely in the United States, that region has been marked by persistent attempts at organization by farm workers. . . .

Countervailing power in the retail business is identified with the large and powerful retail enterprises. Its practical manifestation, over the last half-century, has been the rise of the food chains, the variety chains, the mail-order houses (now graduated into chain stores), the department-store chains, and the co-operative buying organizations of the surviving independent department and food stores.

This development was the countervailing response to previously established positions of power. The gains from invading these positions have been considerable and in some instances even spectacular. The rubber tire industry is a fairly commonplace example of oligopoly. Four large firms are dominant in the market. In the thirties, Sears, Roebuck & Co. was able, by exploiting its role as a large and indispensable customer, to procure tires from Goodyear Tire & Rubber Company at a price from twenty-nine to forty per cent lower than the going market. These it resold to thrifty motorists for from a fifth to a quarter less than the same tires carrying the regular Goodyear brand.

As a partial consequence of the failure of the government to recognize the role of countervailing power many hundreds of pages of court records have detailed the exercise of this power by the Great Atlantic & Pacific Tea Company. There is little doubt that this firm, at least in its uninhibited days, used the countervailing power it had developed with considerable artistry. In 1937, a survey by the company indicated that, for an investment of $175,000 it could supply itself with corn flakes. Assuming that it charged itself the price it was then paying to one of the three companies manufacturing this delicacy, it could earn a modest sixty-eight per cent on the outlay. Armed with this information, and the threat to go into the business which its power could readily make effective, it had no difficulty in bringing down the price by approximately ten per cent.* Such gains from the exercise of countervailing power, it will be clear, could only occur where there is an exercise of original market power with which to contend. The A & P could have reaped no comparable gains in buying staple products from the farmer. Committed as he is to the competition of the competitive model, the farmer has no gains to surrender. Provided, as he is, with the opportunity of selling all he produces at the impersonally determined market price, he has not the slightest incentive to make a special price to A & P at least beyond that which might in some circumstances be associated with the simple economies of bulk sale.

The examples of the exercise of countervailing power by Sears, Roebuck and A & P just cited show how this power is deployed in its most dramatic form. The day-to-day exercise of the buyer's power is a good deal less spectacular but also a good deal more significant. At the end of virtually every channel by which consumers' goods reach the public there is, in practice, a layer of powerful buyers. In the food market there are the great food chains; in clothing there are the department stores, the chain department stores and the department store buying organizations; in appliances there are Sears, Roebuck and Montgomery Ward and the department stores; these latter firms are also important outlets for furniture and other house furnishings; the drug and cosmetic manufacturer has to seek part of his market through the large drug chains and the department stores; a vast miscellany of consumers' goods pass to the public through Woolworth's, Kresge's and other variety chains.

The buyers of all these firms deal directly with the manufacturer and there are few of the latter who, in setting prices, do not have to reckon with the attitude and reaction of their powerful customers. The retail buyers have a variety of weapons at their disposal to use against the market power of their suppliers. Their ultimate sanction is to develop their own source of supply as the food chains, Sears, Roebuck and Montgomery Ward have extensively done. They can also concentrate their entire patronage on a single supplier and, in return for a lower price, give him security in his volume and relieve him of selling and advertising costs. This policy has been widely followed and there have also been numerous complaints of the leverage it gives the retailer on his source of supply.

The more commonplace but more important tactic in the exercise of countervailing power consists, merely, in keeping the seller in a state of uncertainty as to the intentions of a buyer who is indispensable to him. The larger of the retail buying organizations place orders around which the production schedules and occasionally the investment of even the largest manufacturers become organized. A shift in this custom imposes prompt and heavy loss. The threat or

*I am indebted to my friend Professor M. A. Adelmen of the Massachusetts Institute of Technology for these details.

even the fear of this sanction is enough to cause the supplier to surrender some or all of the rewards of his market power. He must frequently, in addition, make a partial surrender to less potent buyers if he is not to be more than ever in the power of his large customers. It will be clear that in this operation there are rare opportunities for playing one supplier off against another. . . .

ALFRED C. KINSEY

The Kinsey Report

Within two months of its publication in 1948, *Sexual Behavior in the Human Male*, popularly known as the Kinsey Report, stood in second place on the nonfiction best-seller list. Although Kinsey claimed to be only a "fact finder," to have "never evaluated and analyzed [his] material," the outpouring of protest and concern which greeted the first volume was exceeded only by the reaction to the second, on women, published in 1953. A number of critics, including anthropologist Margaret Mead, lamented Kinsey's apparent disregard for the emotional, interpersonal side of human sexual relationships. Episcopal clergyman William Pittenger found in the Kinsey Report the potential for "the deterioration of personality and the destruction of community." "In order to bring sexuality to its rightful place," he argued, "it must be controlled." Most important, the Kinsey Report forced many Americans to confront a growing discrepancy between the guidance adults were giving the younger generation and the facts of teenage sexuality. At a time when the average advice manual for teenagers spoke disparagingly of petting, Kinsey found sexual intercourse widespread.

The reactions to the Kinsey Report would suggest that Kinsey's conclusions were profoundly disturbing for the postwar equilibrium. And yet it is possible that for many the Kinsey Report was a very comforting document. For Kinsey, certainly, the results connoted not maladjustment but social health. His main concern was to define sexual "normality" in a way that would include almost any sort of sexual life, or lack of it.

Why was Kinsey so widely read? and yet so often criticized? Was the Kinsey Report revolutionary in its implications? Or was Kinsey only doing for sexuality what John Galbraith had accomplished for the discipline of economics?

The possibility of any individual engaging in sexual activity at a rate that is remarkably different from one's own, is one of the most difficult things for even professionally trained persons to understand. Meetings of educators who are discussing sex instruction and policies to be followed in the administration of educational institutions, may bring out extreme differences of opinion which range from recommendations for the teaching of complete abstinence to recommendations for frank acceptance of almost any type of sexual activity. No other subject will start such open dissension in a group, and it is difficult for an observer to comprehend how objective reasoning can lead to such different conclusions among intelligent men and women. If, however, one has the histories of the educators involved, it may be found that there are persons in the group who are not ejaculating more than once or twice a year, while there may be others in the same group who are experiencing orgasm as often as ten or twenty times per week, and regularly. There is, inevitably, some correlation between these rates and the positions which these persons take in a public debate. On both sides of the argument, the extreme individuals may be totally unaware of the possibility of others in the group having histories that are so remote from their own. In the same fashion, we have listened to discussions of juvenile delinquency, of law enforcement, and of recommendations for legislative action on the sex laws, knowing that the policies that ultimately come out of such meetings would reflect the attitudes and sexual experience of the most vocal members of the group, rather than an intelligently thought-out program established on objectively accumulated data.

Even the scientific discussions of sex show little understanding of the range of variation in human behavior. More often the conclusions are limited by the personal experience of the author. Psychologic and psychiatric literature is loaded with terms which evaluate frequencies of sexual outlet. But such designations as infantile, frigid, sexually under-developed, under-active, excessively active, over-developed, over-sexed, hypersexual or sexually over-active, and the attempts to recognize such states as nymphomania and satyriasis as discrete entities, can, in any objective analysis, refer to nothing more than a position on a curve which is continuous. Normal and abnormal, one sometimes suspects, are terms which a particular author employs with reference to his own position on that curve. . . .

The term "abnormal" is applied in medical pathology to conditions which interfere with the physical well-being of a living body. In a social sense, the term might apply to sexual activities which cause social maladjustment. Such an application, however, involves subjective determinations of what is good personal living, or good social adjustment; and these things are not as readily determined as physiologic well-being in an organic body. It is not possible to insist that any departure from the sexual mores, or any participation in socially taboo activities, always, or even usually, involves a neurosis or psychosis, for the case histories abundantly demonstrate that most individuals who engage in

From Alfred C. Kinsey, Wardell B. Pomeroy, and Clyde F. Martin, *Sexual Behavior in the Human Male* (Philadelphia: Saunders, 1948), pp. 199, 201–203, 221–223, 364, 400. Reprinted by permission of the Institute for Sex Research.

taboo activities make satisfactory social adjustments. There are, in actuality, few adult males who are particularly disturbed over their sexual histories. Psychiatrists, clinical psychologists, and others who deal with cases of maladjustment, sometimes come to feel that most people find difficulty in adjusting their sexual lives; but a clinic is no place to secure incidence figures. The incidence of tuberculosis in a tuberculosis sanitarium is no measure of the incidence of tuberculosis in the population as a whole; and the incidence of disturbance over sexual activities, among the persons who come to a clinic, is no measure of the frequency of similar disturbances outside of clinics. The impression that such "sexual irregularities" as "excessive" masturbation, pre-marital intercourse, responsibility for a pre-marital pregnancy, extra-marital intercourse, mouth-genital contacts, homosexual activity, or animal inter-course, always produce psychoses and abnormal personalities is based upon the fact that the persons who do go to professional sources for advice are upset by these things.

It is unwarranted to believe that particular types of sexual behavior are always expressions of psychoses or neuroses. In actuality, they are more often expressions of what is biologically basic in mammalian and anthropoid behav-ior, and of a deliberate disregard for social convention. Many of the socially and intellectually most significant persons in our histories, successful scientists, educators, physicians, clergymen, business men, and persons of high position in governmental affairs, have socially taboo items in their sexual histories, and among them they have accepted nearly the whole range of so-called sexual abnormalities. Among the socially most successful and personally best ad-justed persons who have contributed to the present study, there are some whose rates of outlet are as high as those in any case labelled nymphomania or satyriasis in the literature, or recognized as such in the clinic.

Most of the complications which are observable in sexual histories are the result of society's reactions when it obtains knowledge of an individual's be-havior, or the individual's fear of how society would react if he were discov-ered. In various societies, under various circumstances, and even at various social levels of the population living in a particular town, the sex mores are fundamentally different. The way in which each group reacts to a particular sort of history determines the "normality" or "abnormality" of the individual's behavior—in that particular group. Whatever the moral interpretation, there is no scientific reason for considering particular types of sexual activity as intrin-sically, in their biologic origins, normal or abnormal. Yet scientific classifica-tions have been nearly identical with theologic classifications and with the moral pronouncments of the English common law of the fifteenth century. This, in turn, as far as sex is concerned, was based on the medieval ecclesiastic law which was only a minor variant of the tenets of ancient Greek and Roman cults, and of the Talmudic law. Present-day legal determinations of sexual acts which are acceptable, or "natural," and those which are "contrary to nature" are not based on data obtained from biologists, nor from nature herself. On the contrary, the ancient codes have been accepted by laymen, jurists, and scientists alike as the ultimate sources of moral evaluations, of present-day legal procedure, and of the list of subjects that may go into a textbook of abnormal psychology. In no other field of science have scientists been satisfied to accept the biologic notions of ancient jurists and theologians, or the analyses made by the mystics of two or three thousand years ago. Either the ancient philosophers were remarkably well-trained psychologists, or modern psychologists have contributed little in defining abnormal sexual behavior. . . .

The problem of sexual adjustment for the younger male is one which has become especially aggravated during the last hundred years, and then primarily in England and in America, under an increasing moral suppression which has coincided with an increasing delay in the age of marriage. This has resulted in an intensification of the struggle between the boy's biologic capacity and the sanctions imposed by the older male who, to put it objectively, is no longer hard-pressed to find a legalized source of sexual contact commensurate with his reduced demand for outlet.

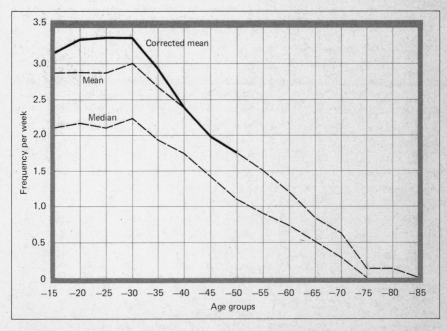

Frequency of Total Outlet in Relation to Age. Based on total population, including single, married, and previously married groups. Broken lines represent raw data; the solid black line represents the mean corrected for the U.S. Census distribution.

The fact that the unmarried male still manages to find an outlet of 3.4 per week demonstrates the failure of the attempt to impose complete abstinence upon him. The sources of this outlet must be a matter of bewilderment to those who have supposed that most males remained continent until marriage. Nocturnal emissions do not provide any considerable portion of the orgasms, in spite of the fact that many persons have wished that to be the case. Masturbation is a more frequent outlet among the upper social level males where, during the last two or three decades, it has been allowed as a not too immoral substitute for pre-marital intercourse; but most of the less-educated 85 per cent of the population still consider masturbation neither moral nor normal. For the mass of the unmarried boys, intercourse still provides the chief sexual activity. This means that the majority of the males in the sexually most potential and most active period of their lives have to accept clandestine or illegal outlets, or become involved in psychologic conflicts in attempting to adjust to reduced outlets. With the data now available, biologists, psychologist, physicians, psychiatrists, and sociologists should be enabled to make better analyses of the problem which has heretofore been imposed on this unmarried male in his middle and late teens, and in his twenties.

Attitudes on Pre-marital Intercourse, at Three Educational Levels

Restraints on Intercourse	Educ. Level	All Ages Cases	%	Adol.–25 Cases	%	26–45 Cases	%	46+ Cases	%
Moral objections	0–8	814	20.8	317	18.9	338	16.2	159	33.9
	9–12	650	25.5	369	22.8	232	28.5		
	13+	3161	61.4	2016	62.5	969	56.6	176	76.2
Fear of public opinion	0–8	775	13.5	300	14.4	322	11.5	153	16.3
	9–12	615	14.3	343	12.0	224	17.0		
	13+	2847	22.8	1756	21.5	918	24.1	173	28.9
Fear of pregnancy	0–8	814	20.4	318	19.2	336	20.6	160	22.5
	9–12	645	17.5	364	18.6	232	15.5		
	13+	3136	27.6	1995	28.0	964	27.5	177	23.7
Fear of venereal disease	0–8	811	28.6	317	27.1	335	29.0	159	30.8
	9–12	641	25.3	361	23.8	231	26.8		
	13+	3143	24.8	2001	25.1	965	23.9	177	25.4
Lack opportunity	0–8	785	34.6	312	36.9	323	33.8	150	32.0
	9–12	627	38.0	358	37.5	225	39.6		
	13+	3104	51.6	1980	51.4	950	55.5	174	33.4
Lack of interest in having more	0–8	327	41.9	155	35.5	117	45.3	55	52.7
	9–12	279	44.5	153	45.1	111	45.9		
	13+	1831	18.8	1041	18.7	688	19.2	102	17.6
Male desires to marry a virgin	0–8	595	43.3	215	40.9	267	38.5	113	59.3
	9–12	523	39.2	309	40.8	176	32.4		
	13+	2972	46.5	1943	50.7	880	36.2	149	41.6

Comparisons of Older and Younger Generations of the College Level: Total Intercourse, and Total Pre-marital Intercourse*

	Accumulative Incidence, Two Generations Educational Level 13+							
	Total Intercourse				Pre-marital Intercourse			
	Older Generation		Younger Generation		Older Generation		Younger Generation	
Age	Cases	% with Exper.	Cases	% with Exper.	Cases	% with Exper.	Cases	% with Exper.
8	382	0.0	2435	0.0	382	0.0	2435	0.0
9	382	0.0	2435	0.0	382	0.0	2435	0.0
10	382	0.0	2435	0.0	382	0.0	2435	0.0
11	382	0.0	2435	0.2	382	0.0	2435	0.3
12	382	0.5	2345	1.1	382	0.5	2435	1.1
13	382	3.7	2435	3.0	382	3.7	2435	3.0
14	382	6.3	2435	5.9	382	6.3	2435	5.9
15	382	9.4	2435	9.5	382	9.4	2435	9.5
16	382	14.9	2434	15.6	382	14.9	2434	15.6
17	382	21.5	2432	23.4	381	21.3	2431	23.4
18	382	27.2	2356	31.5	381	27.0	2353	31.4
19	382	32.5	2192	39.3	380	31.8	2185	39.0
20	382	40.1	1957	46.8	376	38.8	1932	45.4
21	382	44.5	1651	52.4	369	42.5	1611	50.6
22	382	52.4	1290	60.0	363	48.2	1218	55.8
23	382	58.9	1015	64.5	342	52.9	907	58.4
24	382	66.0	770	70.3	320	55.3	647	61.2
25	382	72.8	620	76.5	292	62.0	469	65.9
26	382	79.3	502	80.7	262	63.0	341	66.9
27	382	82.5	392	82.7	214	64.0	218	66.1
28	382	84.8	317	85.5	185	65.9	144	67.4
29	382	87.4	252	86.5	164	67.7	96	66.7
30	382	89.3	191	90.1	142	69.7	60	63.3
31	382	90.8	147	91.2	123	69.1		
32	382	91.9	110	89.1	106	69.8		
33	382	92.1	66	84.8	96	69.8		

*Accumulative incidence data. Pre-marital intercourse based on single males, including intercourse with companions and with prostitutes. Total intercourse based on life span, including pre-marital, marital, extra-marital, and post-marital relations with companions and with prostitutes. Median difference of age between the two generations is 22 years.

The situation is complicated by the fact that the average adolescent girl gets along well enough with a fifth as much sexual activity as the adolescent boy, and the frequency of outlet of the female in her twenties and early thirties is still below that of the average adolescent male. As mothers, as school teachers, and as voting citizens, women are primarily responsible for the care of these boys; and, to a large degree, they are the ones who control moral codes, schedules for sex education, campaigns for law enforcement, and programs for combating what is called juvenile delinquency. It is obviously impossible for a majority of these women to understand the problem that the boy faces in being constantly aroused and regularly involved with his normal biologic reactions.

Rock 'n' Roll: Revolution or Rip-off?

The musical style called "rock 'n' roll" dates from the early 1950s. It is usually considered a sign of revolt, musical evidence that the generational rebellion that would sweep the 1960s was already underway even as Dwight Eisenhower was serving his first term. It was this. But rock 'n' roll was also essentially a white music, and a white music that was developed almost entirely from black musical styles.

The verses below—from the rock 'n' roll classic, "Shake, Rattle and Roll" (1954)—allow us to inquire into the historical meaning of this new music. The verses on the left are from the original version, written by Charles Calhoun and recorded by Joe Turner for the black market. The verses on the right are from the more popular "cover" version by Bill Haley and the Comets. Both versions were hits in 1954.

Why did Haley change the words? What do the new words tell us about the climate in which the Kinsey Report was received? Was rock 'n' roll part of the Eisenhower equilibrium or its antithesis?

"Shake, Rattle and Roll" (1954)

The Charles Calhoun/Joe Turner version

Get out of that bed,
And wash your face and hands. (twice)

Get into the kitchen
Make some noise with the pots and pans.

Well you wear those dresses,
The sun comes shinin' through. (twice)

I can't believe my eyes,
That all of this belongs to you.

I said over the hill,
And way down underneath. (twice)

You make me roll my eyes,
And then you make me grit my teeth.

The Bill Haley version

Get out in that kitchen,
And rattle those pots and pans. (twice)

Roll my breakfast
'Cause I'm a hungry man.

You wear those dresses,
Your hair done up so nice. (twice)

You look so warm,
But your heart is cold as ice.

(the third verse of the Calhoun/Turner version is not part of the Haley version)

Fast Food: McDonald's

Students should examine the McDonald's phenomenon from two perspectives. The first perspective involves Ray Kroc's clientele. Who did he wish to serve and who to exclude? And what did his choice have to do with the Eisenhower equilibrium? The second perspective involves the *employees* at McDonald's. Assume that employment patterns present in McDonald's were increasingly typical of the economy. If so, was it reasonable to conclude that the old blue-collar society was disappearing, and with it many of the stresses of social and economic class? In short, wasn't McDonald's evidence that a classless society was just around the corner?

The first of Ray Kroc's McDonald's opened in the Chicago suburb of Des Plaines, Illinois, in June 1955. *Reproduced courtesy of Golin Communications, Inc.*

"Another judgment I made early in the game," writes Kroc, "was that there would be no pay telephones, no juke boxes, no vending machine of any kind in McDonald's restaurants. Many times operators have been tempted by the side income some of these machines offer, and they have questioned my decision. But I've stood firm. All of those things create unproductive traffic in a store and encourage loitering that can disrupt your customers. This would downgrade the family image we wanted to create for McDonald's." *(Quotation from Ray Kroc, with Robert Anderson,* Grinding It Out: The Making of McDonald's *(New York: Berkley, 1977), p. 84.)*

DWIGHT D. EISENHOWER

The Military-Industrial Complex

When he left office in 1961, Dwight Eisenhower came face-to-face with one great irony of his presidency—that in maintaining conditions of equilibrium in foreign policy and the economy, he had helped create the military-industrial complex, a hydra that threatened to upset the important equilibrium between business and government. In the years since 1940, the federal budget had grown dramatically, the military portion of it even faster. In 1940, military outlays were about 16 percent of the federal expenditures. Two decades later, they had leveled off at about 45 percent. Dozens of the largest American corporations—including General Electric, Raytheon, Ling-Temco-Vought, Kaiser Industries, and Bendix—were dependent on military contracts for more than 40 percent of total sales. Many economic experts believed that military spending could not be significantly reduced without risking a depression.

The complex, such as it was, was less the product simply of increased military expenditures than of the integration of the military with other areas of American life. While theorists of pluralism argued that the military continued to be subordinate to broader, civilian interests, others maintained that these "countervailing" civilians were part of the complex—the professors and scholars at hundreds of universitites and nonprofit research institutions who were dependent on the military for grants; some 2,000 (by 1969) retired military officers who were employed by the leading one hundred defense contractors; politicians from California, Texas, and other states dependent on military contracts.

What was it that Eisenhower found especially disturbing about the military-industrial complex? What did he propose to do about it? Should we be surprised that Eisenhower—a Republican and a five-star general— should have been the first of our presidents to draw attention to the social role of the military?

From Dwight D. Eisenhower, "Farewell Radio and Television Address to the American People, January 17, 1961," *Public Papers of the President of the United States, Dwight D. Eisenhower, 1960–61* (Washington, D.C.: Government Printing Office, 1961), pp. 1035–1040.

My fellow Americans:

Three days from now, after half a century in the service of our country, I shall lay down the responsibilities of office as, in traditional and solemn ceremony, the authority of the Presidency is vested in my successor.

This evening I come to you with a message of leave-taking and farewell, and to share a few final thoughts with you, my countrymen.

Like every other citizen, I wish the new President, and all who will labor with him, Godspeed. I pray that the coming years will be blessed with peace and prosperity for all.

Our people expect their President and the Congress to find essential agreement on issues of great moment, the wise resolution of which will better shape the future of the Nation.

My own relations with the Congress, which began on a remote and tenuous basis when, long ago, a member of the Senate appointed me to West Point, have since ranged to the intimate during the war and immediate post-war period, and, finally, to the mutually interdependent during these past eight years.

In this final relationship, the Congress and the Administration have, on most vital issues, cooperated well, to serve the national good rather than mere partisanship, and so have assured that the business of the Nation should go forward. So, my official relationship with the Congress ends in a feeling, on my part, of gratitude that we have been able to do so much together.

II

We now stand ten years past the midpoint of a century that has witnessed four major wars among great nations. Three of these involved our own country. Despite these holocausts America is today the strongest, the most influential and most productive nation in the world. Understandably proud of this pre-eminence, we yet realize that America's leadership and prestige depend, not merely upon our unmatched material progress, riches and military strength, but on how we use our power in the interests of world peace and human betterment.

III

Throughout America's adventure in free government, our basic purposes have been to keep the peace; to foster progress in human achievement, and to enhance liberty, dignity and integrity among people and among nations. To strive for less would be unworthy of a free and religious people. Any failure traceable to arrogance, or our lack of comprehension or readiness to sacrifice would inflict upon us grievous hurt both at home and abroad.

Progress toward these noble goals is persistently threatened by the conflict now engulfing the world. It commands our whole attention, absorbs our very beings. We face a hostile ideology—global in scope, atheistic in character, ruthless in purpose, and insidious in method. Unhappily the danger it poses promises to be of indefinite duration. To meet it successfully, there is called for, not so much the emotional and transitory sacrifices of crisis, but rather those which enable us to carry forward steadily, surely, and without complaint the burdens of a prolonged and complex struggle—with liberty the stake. Only thus shall we remain, despite every provocation, on our charted course toward permanent peace and human betterment.

Crises there will continue to be. In meeting them, whether foreign or domestic, great or small, there is a recurring temptation to feel that some spectacular and costly action could become the miraculous solution to all current difficulties. A huge increase in newer elements of our defense; development of unrealistic programs to cure every ill in agriculture; a dramatic expansion in basic and applied research—these and many other possibilities, each possibly promising in itself, may be suggested as the only way to the road we wish to travel.

But each proposal must be weighed in the light of a broader consideration: the need to maintain balance in and among national programs—balance between the private and the public economy, balance between cost and hoped for advantage—balance between the clearly necessary and the comfortably desirable; balance between our essential requirements as a nation and the duties imposed by the nation upon the individual; balance between actions of the moment and the national welfare of the future. Good judgment seeks balance and progress; lack of it eventually finds imbalance and frustration.

The record of many decades stands as proof that our people and their government have, in the main, understood these truths and have responded to them well, in the face of stress and threat. But threats, new in kind or degree, constantly arise. I mention two only.

IV

A vital element in keeping the peace is our military establishment. Our arms must be mighty, ready for instant action, so that no potential aggressor may be tempted to risk his own destruction.

Our military organization today bears little relation to that known by any of my predecessors in peacetime, or indeed by the fighting men of World War II or Korea.

Until the latest of our world conflicts, the United States had no armaments industry. American makers of plowshares could, with time and as required, make swords as well. But now we can no longer risk emergency improvisation of national defense; we have been compelled to create a permanent armaments industry of vast proportions. Added to this, three and a half million men and women are directly engaged in the defense establishment. We annually spend on military security more than the net income of all United States corporations.

This conjunction of an immense military establishment and a large arms industry is new in the American experience. The total influence—economic, political, even spiritual—is felt in every city, every State house, every office of the Federal government. We recognize the imperative need for this development. Yet we must not fail to comprehend its grave implications. Our toil, resources and livelihood are all involved; so is the very structure of our society.

In the councils of government, we must guard against the acquisition of unwarranted influence, whether sought or unsought, by the military-industrial complex. The potential for the disastrous rise of misplaced power exists and will persist.

We must never let the weight of this combination endanger our liberties or democratic processes. We should take nothing for granted. Only an alert and knowledgeable citizenry can compel the proper meshing of the huge industrial and military machinery of defense with our peaceful methods and goals, so that security and liberty may prosper together.

Akin to, and largely responsible for the sweeping changes in our industrial-military posture, has been the technological revolution during recent decades.

In this revolution, research has become central; it also becomes more formalized, complex, and costly. A steadily increasing share is conducted for, by, or at the direction of, the Federal government.

Today, the solitary inventor, tinkering in his shop, has been overshadowed by task forces of scientists in laboratories and testing fields. In the same fashion, the free university, historically the fountainhead of free ideas and scientific discovery, has experienced a revolution in the conduct of research. Partly because of the huge costs involved, a government contract becomes virtually a substitute for intellectual curiosity. For every old blackboard there are now hundreds of new electronic computers.

The prospect of domination of the nation's scholars by Federal employment, project allocations, and the power of money is ever present—and is gravely to be regarded.

Yet, in holding scientific research and discovery in respect, as we should, we must also be alert to the equal and opposite danger that public policy could itself become the captive of a scientific-technological elite.

It is the task of statesmanship to mold, to balance, and to integrate these and other forces, new and old, within the principles of our democratic system—ever aiming toward the supreme goals of our free society.

V

Another factor in maintaining balance involves the element of time. As we peer into society's future, we—you and I, and our government—must avoid the impulse to live only for today, plundering, for our own ease and convenience, the precious resources of tomorrow. We cannot mortgage the material assets of our grandchildren without risking the loss also of their political and spiritual heritage. We want democracy to survive for all generations to come, not to become the insolvent phantom of tomorrow.

VI

Down the long lane of the history yet to be written America knows that this world of ours, ever growing smaller, must avoid becoming a community of dreadful fear and hate, and be, instead, a proud confederation of mutual trust and respect.

Such a confederation must be one of equals. The weakest must come to the conference table with the same confidence as do we, protected as we are by our moral, economic, and military strength. That table, though scarred by many past frustrations, cannot be abandoned for the certain agony of the battlefield.

Disarmament, with mutual honor and confidence, is a continuing imperative. Together we must learn how to compose differences, not with arms, but with intellect and decent purpose. Because this need is so sharp and apparent I confess that I lay down my official responsibilities in this field with a definite sense of disappointment. As one who has witnessed the horror and the lingering sadness of war—as one who knows that another war could utterly destroy this civilization which has been so slowly and painfully built over thousands of years—I wish I could say tonight that a lasting peace is in sight.

Happily, I can say that war has been avoided. Steady progress toward our ultimate goal has been made. But, so much remains to be done. As a private citizen, I shall never cease to do what little I can to help the world advance along that road.

VII

So—in this my last good night to you as your President—I thank you for the many opportunities you have given me for public service in war and peace. I trust that in that service you find some things worthy; as for the rest of it, I know you will find ways to improve performance in the future.

You and I—my fellow citizens—need to be strong in our faith that all nations, under God, will reach the goal of peace with justice. May we be ever unswerving in devotion to principle, confident but humble with power, diligent in pursuit of the Nation's great goals.

To all the peoples of the world, I once more give expression to America's prayerful and continuing aspiration:

We pray that peoples of all faiths, all races, all nations, may have their great human needs satisfied; that those now denied opportunity shall come to enjoy it to the full; that all who yearn for freedom may experience its spiritual blessings; that those who have freedom will understand, also, its heavy responsibilities; that all who are insensitive to the needs of others will learn charity; that the scourges of poverty, disease and ignorance will be made to disappear from the earth, and that, in the goodness of time, all peoples will come to live together in a peace guaranteed by the binding force of mutual respect and love.

The Changing Vernacular

Filling Up: 1941, 1960

Important cultural changes are often reflected in our most familiar institutions. The following photographs chronicle a modification in gas station design which presumably reflects more basic changes in the role of the automobile in American life. Were Americans more comfortable with the automobile in 1941 or in 1960? What conflicting needs was the Shell station designed to bring into balance?

Mobilgas Service Station, Washington and Flower streets, Los Angeles, California, **1941.** *Reproduced by permission of Mobil Oil Corporation.*

Two-Bay Ranch-Style Service Station, 1960. *Courtesy, Shell Oil Company.*

The New Suburbia

Levittown, Long Island, named after the builder and pictured below, consisted of 17,500 homes built within 5 and a half years in the 1950s. The community, and others like it, raise questions that go beyond the pent-up war demand for inexpensive housing. According to the dominant school of social thought at the time, the popularity of suburban living reflected the rise of the organization man, willing to live a life of monotony and to subordinate his interests to those of the larger organization. Was this critique necessarily valid? Might the suburbs also be interpreted as America's newest frontier? Why was there so much talk of "mass society" in the Eisenhower era?

UPI

Women in Equilibrium

In the two decades after World War II, growing percentages of American women worked outside the home. Yet this "liberation" was limited. Most women could find work only in factories or in traditionally feminine occupations—as teachers, nurses, secretaries, and telephone operators, for example. And working women were expected to add work outside the home to their duties within it. Even so, this movement of women into the paid labor force produced tensions in the rather rigid social order of the postwar equilibrium. The two documents below reflect the ambivalence of women's position at mid-century. In examining the photograph and the job description, consider how each celebrates the new American woman and yet circumscribes her role.

National Archives, Women's Bureau.

Job Title: Housewife

By Harold W. Jacobson, Job Analyst

National Company, Inc., Malden, Massachusetts

Grade: HIGH

Description:

   Functions in several capacities and offices performing a wide variety of duties semi-routine in nature but where the exercise of independent judgment is required in the application of practices and policies to situations not previously covered:

   Effects the purchase of a wide variety of organic materials for processing, giving special consideration to costs, market conditions, and state of material. Plan, layout, and schedule processing operations, maintaining strict control of flow and inventory to meet schedules. Conduct necessary chemical operations, using various heat treatments as required to transform basic organic materials into completed form for distribution to consumer;

   Maintains budgeting, cost control, and cost accounting systems, operating within a limited financial framework. Strike semi-monthly trial balances to determine relationship between accounts-payable and accounts-receivable and, as required, perform necessary magic to bring accounts into balance;

   Operates and maintains a variety of manually and electrically powered equipment for heating, cooling, stitching, suctioning, cleansing, etc.;

   Performs other miscellaneous duties of a routine nature not specifically mentioned, but where such duties are a normal outgrowth of the job.

Substantiating Data

   Education: This factor appraises the minimum amount of theoretical education required, however attained.

   Broad general knowledge of several specialized fields such as chemistry, mechanical and electrical engineering, marketing, accounting, and fundamentals of human relations.

   Complexity of Duties: This factor appraises the need for initiative, ingenuity, and independent judgment.

   Perform a wide variety of semi-routine duties directed toward the attainment of a general objective: the physiological and psychic welfare of a small social group. Performance requires the use of judgment in devising new methods and modifying or adapting standard practice to meet new conditions.

   Responsibility: This factor appraises the responsibility for equipment, material, process, and health, safety, and work of others.

   Complete responsibility in terms of costs, methods, and personnel for equipment, material, process, etc. Supervise and direct one inept male in the performance of a limited number of routine duties such as: rub, scrub, sweep, brush, mop, polish, etc.

Effort: This factor appraises the mental and/or visual demand required.

High degree of concentration where the volume and nature of work require unusual coordination of hand and eye.

Working Conditions: This factor appraises the surroundings or physical conditions under which the job must be performed. It includes health and accident hazards.

Somewhat disagreeable working conditions due to exposure to dust, dirt, heat, etc. Exposure to accidents where results will probably be minor in nature: cuts, bruises, burns, etc., which, although painful, are not incapacitating in nature. Health hazards negligible. Fatigue factor high.

CHAPTER 13

The Age of Protest: The 1960s

For a time, the decade of the 1960s looked very much like its predecessor. John F. Kennedy, elected by a narrow margin over Richard Nixon in 1960, sought to pump up the nation with rhetoric while practicing a brand of consensus politics designed to avoid overt conflict. The problems of the 1960s, said Kennedy at Yale University's commencement in 1962, presented "subtle challenges, for which technical answers, not political answers, must be provided." Because he believed that basic problems of adequate food, clothing, and employment had been solved through economic growth and the evolution of the welfare state, Kennedy was not the reform activist that many expected him to be. Several of his policies and programs— the commitment to space exploration, the Peace Corps, the rollback of prices in the steel industry—were essentially symbolic gestures. In foreign affairs, Kennedy carried on the cold war in grand fashion— deeper involvement in Vietnam; a CIA-sponsored invasion of Cuba in an attempt to depose Fidel Castro; a blockade to force the Soviets to remove their missiles from Cuba, when less bellicose but less satisfying alternatives were available.

There were signs of change and portents of turmoil in the early years of the decade—the Berkeley Free Speech Movement in 1964, the assassination of John F. Kennedy, the assertive youth culture fostered by the English rock band the Beatles. Yet the Eisenhower equilibrium was not irrevocably shattered until mid-decade. The cause was race. During the 1950s, black efforts to achieve integration had followed, in the main, legal channels. Gradually, though, black leaders like Martin Luther King adopted the tactics of direct action: boycotts, picketing, "sit-ins," and other methods of confrontation. Then, in 1965, a minor summer incident involving police in Watts, a black section of Los Angeles, set off five days of looting and rioting that left thirty-four people dead. Within two years there were over a hundred major urban riots, all centered in black ghettoes in cities like Newark and Detroit. It was in this setting that young black leaders began to question whether integration was an appropriate goal. They began to talk of black power. It was in this setting, too, that two of the most charismatic black leaders, Malcolm X and Martin Luther King, were shot to death.

The urban ghetto riots of the mid-1960s occurred during times of relatively low national rates of unemployment and inflation and within the context of Lyndon Johnson's Great Society—a liberal reform program which included the Voting Rights Act of 1965 and the "war on poverty." While the voting rights legislation had immediate results which went well beyond what the civil rights movement had been able to accomplish in the early 1960s, the war on poverty as well as other Johnson programs were severely limited by a growing backlash against social unrest and the president's own policy of escalation in Vietnam. When Kennedy was killed in late 1963, there were less than 20,000 American personnel in Vietnam; in 1968, there were more than 500,000. For Johnson, each new American commitment was absolutely necessary. Defeat or withdrawal, he believed, would only bring more aggression, new tests of the national and presidential will. Others, however, saw the conflict in Vietnam largely as a civil war and American involvement as an immoral and/or unlawful interference in a domestic dispute.

Protests against the war, centered on the college campuses and utilizing the tactics of the civil rights movement, began in earnest in early 1965 and grew in number and intensity through the decade. Almost every major campus in the United States was torn by rallies, "teach-ins," and riots. One climax of the youth revolt was the massive demonstration—and the violent police response to it— centered on the Democratic National Convention in Chicago in 1968. The "protesters," as they had come to be called, could not prevent the nomination of the party's establishment candidate, Hubert Humphrey, but the event so clouded his candidacy that it almost insured his defeat by Richard Nixon.

Nixon's widening of the Vietnam War in 1970, with an invasion of Cambodia, touched off the last major round of protest on the campuses. On May 4, panicky National Guardsmen, sent to quell a protest at Kent State University in Ohio, killed five students. Ten days later, two black youths were shot by police at Mississippi's Jackson State College.

By the end of the decade, the antiwar and civil rights movements had been joined and fueled by women seeking liberation from confining social roles, and by a new group of environmental and consumer activists who saw that the nation had pursued economic growth at great cost to the quantity and quality of its remaining resources and the health of its citizens. Portions of this counterculture of protest were nonpolitical (Ken Kesey's San Francisco-based Merry Pranksters, for example, painted their faces with Day-Glo and inveigled protesters to "drop acid" and simply turn their backs on the war). But protest movements of the 1960s were by and large committed to making existing political frameworks responsive. Many believed that the Great Society could reconstruct the nation's cities, force corporations to clean up the air and water, provide for genuine equality of opportunity for all races, and even eliminate poverty. Others had faith that Ralph Nader and his "raiders" could mount and sustain a meaningful consumer movement, and that Common Cause, a massive liberal lobby established by former Department of Health, Education, and Welfare secretary John Gardner, would significantly redress the balance in Congress. Not since the 1930s had Americans believed so mightily in the possibilities of change.

ALLEN J. MATUSOW

From Civil Rights to Black Power

In a sense, the Age of Protest began on the first day of December 1955, when Rosa Parks, a black seamstress in Montgomery, Alabama, refused to give up her bus seat to a white man. "I don't really know why I wouldn't move," she said later. "There was no plot or plan at all. I was just tired from shopping. I had my sacks and all, and my feet hurt." President Dwight Eisenhower, announcing that he was for "moderation" and "progress," left Montgomery blacks to their own devices—in this case, a boycott of the city's bus service. Led by local minister Martin Luther King, Jr., Montgomery's blacks went beyond the legal tactics of the National Association for the Advancement of Colored People (NAACP) and the Urban League and forged a powerful combination of nonviolence and civil disobedience.

These methods were put to new ends in the early 1960s, when the Congress of Racial Equality (CORE) sent "freedom riders" into the South to test racial discrimination statutes, and black students from the Student Nonviolent Coordinating Committee (SNCC) organized lunch-counter sit-ins. The illegal nature of much of these activities forced officials at all levels of government to choose between the law and civil rights.

Many, like John Kennedy, were concerned that the civil rights movement was pressing too hard. Kennedy first sought to prevent, and then to co-opt, the famous "March on Washington" in August 1963.

The spirit of militant optimism that characterized black reform efforts in the early 1960s gradually faded, its disappearance coinciding with increased federal intervention in race relations. The Civil Rights Act of 1964 barred racial discrimination in public accommodations like restaurants and hotels, prohibited discrimination in employment, and authorized the attorney general to bring suit over issues of school segregation and denial of voting rights. It had been in effect less than three weeks when blacks in Harlem's ghetto rioted. Predictions of a long, hot summer seemed fulfilled when similar riots broke out in Rochester, N.Y., and Philadelphia.

The Voting Rights Act of 1965, a powerful piece of legislation that allowed a 50 percent increase in black registration in the Deep South a year after its passage, appeared to bring only more frustration.

Johnson administration initiatives in voting rights and in attacking poverty in Northern cities seemed to encourage, rather than reduce, racial conflict. Many black leaders came to believe that the liberal establishment, including the federal government, was the enemy of black people. The Watts riot in August 1965 confirmed that thousands of blacks were unimpressed with the latest in federal efforts; and it made it clear that not all blacks would be confined to the nonviolent tactics of Martin Luther King. Most menacing of all, Watts was evidence that blacks had begun to protest outside the frameworks provided by established civil rights organizations and leaders. And Watts was only the beginning.

After the mid-1960s, more and more young black leaders began to speak of black power, to criticize the eloquent nonviolence of King, and even to speak approvingly of violent black nationalism. In the following essay, Allen J. Matusow examines the very specific origins of the black power revolt. As you read the essay, try to define the relationship between the ideas of Stokely Carmichael and the older traditions of reform you have studied in this book. Was black power a viable approach to the problems facing blacks?

The transformation of black protest in the 1960's from civil rights to black power has seemed in retrospect an inevitable development. When the inherent limitations of the civil rights movement finally became apparent and when the expectations that the movement created met frustration, some kind of militant reaction in the black community seemed certain. However predictable this development may have been, it tells little about the concrete events that led to the abandonment of the civil rights program and to the adoption of a doctrine that is in many ways its opposite. For black power was not plucked whole from impersonal historical forces; nor was its content the only possible expression of rising black militancy. Rather, black power both as a slogan and a doctrine was in large measure the creation of a small group of civil rights workers who in the early 1960's manned the barricades of black protest in the Deep South. The group was called the Student Nonviolent Coordinating Committee (SNCC). Through its spokesman, Stokely Carmichael, SNCC first proclaimed black power and then became its foremost theoretician. Others would offer glosses on black power that differed from SNCC's concept, but because SNCC had contributed so much to the civil rights movement, no other group could speak with so much authority or command a comparable audience. Although SNCC borrowed freely from many sources to fashion black power into a doctrine, the elements of that doctrine were in the main the results of SNCC's own history. An examination of that history reveals not only the roots of black power but also the sad fate of the whole civil rights movement.

Founded in 1960, SNCC was an outgrowth of the historic sit-in movement, which began in Greensboro, North Carolina, on February 1 of that year. Four freshmen from a local Negro college attempted to desegregate the lunch counter at a Woolworth's five and ten store. The example of these four sent shock waves through the black colleges of the South and created overnight a base for a campaign of massive civil disobedience. The new generation of black students seemed suddenly unwilling to wait any longer for emancipation at the hands of the federal courts and in the next months supplied most of the recruits for the nonviolent army of 50,000 that rose spontaneously and integrated public facilities in 140 Southern cities. For the students on the picket lines, the prophet of the sit-in movement was Dr. Martin Luther King, the leader of the successful Montgomery bus boycott of 1955–56. The students found in King's nonviolent philosophy a ready-made ethic, a tactic, and a conviction of righteousness strong enough to sustain them on a sometimes hazardous mission. It was King's organization, the Southern Christian Leadership Conference (SCLC), that first suggested the need for some central direction of the sit-in movement. At the invitation of SCLC's executive secretary,

From Allen J. Matusow, "From Civil Rights to Black Power: The Case of SNCC, 1960–66," in Barton J. Bernstein and Allen J. Matusow (eds.), *Twentieth-Century America: Recent Interpretations* (New York: Harcourt Brace Jovanovich, 1972), pp. 496–519. The essay was first published in this collection; and is reprinted by the permission of Allen J. Matusow.

some 300 activist students from throughout the South met in Raleigh, North Carolina, in April 1960, to discuss their problems. The students agreed to form a coordinating body, which became SNCC, and in May 1960, hired a secretary and opened an office in Atlanta. In October the organization decided to become a permanent one, and 235 delegates approved a founding statement inspired by King's philosophy:

> We affirm the philosophical or religious ideal of nonviolence as the foundation of our purpose, the presupposition of our belief, and the manner of our action. . . . Through nonviolence, courage displaces fear. Love transcends hate. Acceptance dissipates prejudice; hope ends despair. Faith reconciles doubt. Peace dominates war. Mutual regards cancel enmity. Justice for all overwhelms injustice. The redemptive community supersedes immoral social systems.

In truth, the Christian rhetoric of SNCC's founding statement was not appropriate. The author of the statement was James Lawson, a young minister who never actually belonged to SNCC. Most of the students who rallied to the sit-ins in 1960 accepted King's teachings more out of convenience than conviction and respected his courage more than his philosophy. For while King believed that Christian love was an end in itself and that Negro nonviolence would redeem American society, the students preferred to participate in America rather than to transform it. Sociologists who examined the attitudes of protesters in the black colleges found not alienation from American middle-class values but a desire to share fully in middle-class life. . . .

In the beginning, the philosophical inconsistencies of the sit-ins did not trouble SNCC, for it stood at the forefront of a movement whose ultimate triumph seemed not far distant. But within months, as mysteriously as it began, the sit-in movement vanished. By the spring of 1961 the black campuses had lapsed into their customary quiescence, their contribution to the civil rights movement at an end. As for SNCC, since October 1960, the student representatives from each Southern state had been meeting monthly to squander their energies trying to coordinate a movement that was first too amorphous and then suddenly moribund. SNCC's attempts in early 1961 to raise up new hosts of students proved ineffectual, and lacking followers, the organization seemed without a future. Then in May 1961, the Freedom Rides restored a sense of urgency to the civil rights movement and gave SNCC a second life.

On May 14, 1961, members of the Congress of Racial Equality (CORE) began the Freedom Rides to test a Supreme Court decision outlawing segregation in transportation terminals. On May 20, after one of CORE's integrated buses was bombed near Anniston, Alabama, and another was mobbed in Birmingham, CORE decided to call off its rides. But amid sensational publicity, students from Nashville and Atlanta, many associated with SNCC, rushed to Birmingham to continue the journey to New Orleans. After mobs assaulted this second wave of riders, the Federal Government stepped in to protect them, and they were permitted to go as far as Jackson, where local authorities put them in jail for defying segregation ordinances. Throughout the summer of 1961 some 300 citizens from all over America took Freedom Rides that brought them to the jails of Jackson. For SNCC the Freedom Rides provided a temporary outlet for activism and, more important, inspired radical changes in the structure and purpose of the organization.

Perhaps the most important result of the Freedom Rides for SNCC was to focus its attention on the Deep South. Most of the sit-ins had occurred in the cities and larger towns of the Upper South, and the victories there had come with relative ease. Now the magnitude of the task confronting the civil rights movement became clearer. As some in SNCC had already perceived, sit-ins to desegregate public places offered no meaningful benefits to poverty-stricken tenant farmers in, say, Mississippi. In order to mobilize the black communities in the Deep South to fight for their rights, sporadic student demonstrations would be less useful than sustained efforts by full time field workers. In the summer of 1961, as SNCC was beginning to grope toward the concept of community action, the Federal Government stepped in with an attractive suggestion.

Embarrassed by the Freedom Rides, Attorney General Robert F. Kennedy moved to direct the civil rights movement into paths that, in his view, were more constructive. Kennedy suggested that the civil rights organizations jointly sponsor a campaign to register Southern black voters. Such a drive, its proponents argued, would be difficult for even extreme segregationists to oppose and eventually might liberalize the Southern delegation in Congress. When the Justice Department seemed to offer federal protection for registration workers and when white liberals outside the Administration procured foundation money to finance anticipated costs, the civil rights groups agreed to undertake the project. Within SNCC, advocates of direct action fought acceptance of the project, but the issue was compromised and a threatened split was averted. SNCC's decision to mobilize black communities behind efforts to secure political rights decisively changed the character of the organization. It thereafter ceased to be an extracurricular activity of student leaders and became instead the vocation of dedicated young men and women who temporarily abandoned their careers to become full time paid workers (or "field secretaries") in the movement. Moreover, as SNCC workers drifted away form the black campuses and began living among Deep South blacks, they cast aside the middle-class goals that had motivated the sit-ins of 1960 and put on the overalls of the poor. Begun as middle-class protest, SNCC was developing revolutionary potential. . . .

Throughout 1962 and into 1963 SNCC workers endured assaults, offered brave challenges to local power structures, and exhorted local blacks to shake off fear and stand up for freedom. But SNCC scored no breakthroughs to sustain morale, and while its goals remained outwardly unchanged, its mood was turning bitter. To SNCC the hostility of local racists was not nearly so infuriating as the apparent betrayal that it suffered at the hands of the Justice Department. SNCC believed that in 1961 the Kennedy Administration had guaranteed protection to registration workers, but in Mississippi in 1962 and 1963, SNCC's only contact with federal authority consisted of the FBI agents who stood by taking notes while local policemen beat up SNCC members. SNCC and its supporters insisted that existing law empowered the Federal Government to intervene, but the Justice Department contended that it was in fact powerless. SNCC doubted the sincerity of the Government's arguments and became convinced that the Kennedys had broken a solemn promise for political reasons. Thus by 1963 SNCC was already becoming estranged from established authority and suspicious of liberal politicians.

SNCC's growing sense of alienation cut it off even from other civil rights organizations and most importantly from Dr. King, who by 1963 had become a fallen idol for SNCC workers. They believed that King was too willing to compromise, wielded too much power, and too successfully monopolized the funds of the movement. Doubts about King had arisen as early as the Freedom Rides, when students turned to him for advice and leadership and received what they considered only vague sympathy. In fact, after CORE called off the first ride, King privately supported Robert Kennedy's plea for a "cooling-off' period. But much to SNCC's annoyance, when militant voices prevailed and the rides continued, the press gave King all the credit. In Albany, Georgia, in December 1961, after SNCC aroused the black population to pack the local jails for freedom, King came to town, got arrested, monopolized the headlines, and almost stole the leadership of the Albany campaign form SNCC. In SNCC's view, dependence on King's charisma actually weakened the civil rights movement, for it discouraged development of leadership at the grass-roots level. Why, SNCC asked, did King use his huge share of civil rights money to maintain a large staff in Atlanta, and why did he never account for the funds that he so skillfully collected? As King lost influence on SNCC, dissenting attitudes about nonviolence, implicit since 1960, came to be frankly articulated. . . .

During the March on Washington in August 1963, the nation almost caught a glimpse of SNCC's growing anger. John Lewis, the chairman of SNCC and one of the scheduled speakers, threatened to disrupt the harmony of that happy occasion by saying what he really thought. Only with difficulty did moderates persuade Lewis to delete the harshest passages of his address. So the nation did not know that SNCC scorned Kennedy's civil rights bill as "too little and too late." Lewis had intended to ask the 250,000 people gathered at the Lincoln Memorial,

> What is there in this bill to insure the equality of a maid who earns $5 a week in the home of a family whose income is $100,000 a year? . . . This nation is still a place of cheap political leaders who build their careers on immoral compromises and ally themselves with open forms of political, economic, and social exploita- tion. . . . The party of Kennedy is also the party of Eastland. The party of Javits is also the party of Goldwater. Where is our party? . . . We cannot depend on any political party, for the Democrats and the Republicans have betrayed the basic principles of the Declaration of Independence.

In those remarks that he never delivered, Lewis used both the language of Christian protest and images alive with the rage of SNCC field workers. "In the struggle we must seek more than mere civil rights; we must work for the community of love, peace, and true brotherhood." And,

> the time will come when we will not confine our marching to Washington. We will march through the South, through the heart of Dixie, the way Sherman did. We shall pursue our "scorched earth" policy and burn Jim Crow to the ground— nonviolently. We shall fragment the South into a thousand pieces and put them back together in the image of democracy.

The crucial milestone of SNCC's road to radicalism was the Freedom Summer of 1964. Freedom Summer grew out of a remarkable mock election sponsored by SNCC in the autumn of 1963. Because the mass of Mississippi's black population could not legally participate in choosing the state's governor that year, Robert Moses* conceived a freedom election to protest mass disfranchisement and to educate Mississippi's blacks to the mechanics of the political process. COFO [the Council of Federated Organizations] organized a new party called the Mississippi Freedom Democrats, . . . [which] conducted its own poll. Overwhelming the regular party candidates, Aaron Henry, head of the state NAACP and Freedom Democratic nominee for governor, received 70,000 votes, a tremendous protest against the denial of equal political rights. One reason for the success of the project was the presence in the state of 100 Yale and Stanford students, who worked for two weeks with SNCC on the election. SNCC was sufficiently impressed by the student contribution to consider inviting hundreds more to spend an entire summer in Mississippi. Sponsors of this plan hoped not only for workers but for publicity that might at last focus national attention on Mississippi. By the winter of 1963–64, however, rising militancy in SNCC had begun to take on the overtones of black nationalism, and some of the membership resisted the summer project on the grounds that most of the volunteers would be white.

Present from the beginning, by mid-1964 whites made up one-fifth of SNCC's approximately 150 full time field secretaries. Though whites had suffered their fair share of beatings, some blacks in SNCC were expressing doubts about the role of white men in a movement for black freedom. At a staff meeting at Greenville, Mississippi, in November 1963, a debate on the proposed Freedom Summer brought the issue of white-black relations into the open. In his book *SNCC: The New Abolitionists*, Howard Zinn, who attended this meeting, summarizes the views of the militants:

> Four or five of the Negro staff members now urged that the role of whites be limited. For whites to talk to Mississippi Negroes about voter registration, they

---

*[A product of Harlem with an M.A. in philosophy from Harvard, Moses was a legendary figure in SNCC.—Ed.]

said, only reinforced the Southern Negro's tendency to believe that whites were superior. Whites tended to take over leadership roles in the movement, thus preventing Southern Negroes from being trained to lead. Why didn't whites just work in the white Southern community? One man noted that in Africa the new nations were training black Africans to take over all important government positions. Another told of meeting a Black Muslim in Atlanta who warned him that whites were taking over the movement. "I had the feeling inside. I felt what he said was true."

But Fannie Lou Hamer disagreed. Mrs. Hamer had been a time-keeper on a cotton plantation and was one of the local Mississippi blacks whom SNCC discovered and elevated to leadership. Speaking for the majority of the meeting, she said, "If we're trying to break down this barrier of segregation, we can't segregate ourselves." Thus in February 1964, SNCC sent an invitation to Northern college students to spend their summer vacation in Mississippi.

In retrospect, the summer of 1964 was a turning point in the civil rights movement. When the summer began, SNCC was still operating within the framework of liberal America, still committed to integration and equal political rights for all citizens. But by the end of the summer of 1964, the fraying cords that bound SNCC to liberal goals and values finally snapped. In a sense, much of later black power thought was merely a postscript to SNCC's ill-fated summer project.

In June 1964, more than 700 selected students, judged by a staff psychiatrist at MIT to be "an extraordinarily healthy bunch of kids," came to Oxford, Ohio, for two week-long orientation sessions conducted by veteran SNCC workers. The atmosphere in Oxford, tense from the outset, became on June 22 pervaded with gloom. Robert Moses quietly told the volunteers that three workers had gone into Neshoba county in Mississippi the day before and had not been heard from since. One was Michael Schwerner, a CORE staff member; the second was James Chaney, a black SNCC worker from Mississippi; and the third was Andrew Goodman, a student volunteer who had finished his orientation in Ohio a few days before. (In August the bodies of these three were discovered in their shallow graves near Philadelphia, Mississippi.)

The volunteers in Ohio had to face not only their own fear but also unanticipated hostility from the SNCC workers whom they had come to assist. Tensions between black workers and white volunteers seethed under the surface for some days and then finally erupted. One night SNCC showed a film of a grotesque voting registrar turning away black applicants. When the student audience laughed at the scene, six SNCC people walked out, enraged at what they considered an insensitive response. There followed an exchange between the workers and the volunteers, in which the students complained that the staff was distant, uncommunicative, and "looked down on us for not having been through what they had." A SNCC worker replied,

If you get mad at us for walking out, just wait until they break your head in, and see if you don't have something to get mad about. Ask Jimmy Travis over there what he thinks about the project. What does he think about Mississippi? He has six slugs in him, man, and the last one went right through the back of his neck when he was driving a car outside Greenwood. Ask Jesse here—he has been beaten so that we wouldn't recognize him time and time and time and time again. If you don't get scared, pack up and get the hell out of here because we don't need any favors of people who don't know what they are doing here in the first place.

The bitter words seemed to have a cathartic effect, and the meeting culminated in emotional singing. Said one volunteer a bit too optimistically, "The crisis is past, I think."

From one perspective the story of the two months that followed is one of the human spirit triumphant. Though three more people were killed, eighty others were beaten, thirty-five churches were burned, and thirty other buildings bombed, few turned back; black and white together, the civil rights workers in Mississippi worked for racial justice. The student volunteers taught in Freedom Schools, where 3,000 children were given their first glimpse of a world beyond Mississippi. They organized the disfranchised to march on county courthouses to face unyielding registrars. Most importantly, they walked the roads of Mississippi for the Freedom Democratic Party (FDP). Denying the legitimacy of the segregated Democratic party, COFO opened the FDP to members of all races and declared the party's loyalty to Lyndon Johnson. The goal of the FDP in the summer of 1964 was to send a delegation to the Democratic convention in Atlantic City to challenge the credentials of the regular Democrats and cast the state's vote for the party's nominees. . . . The FDP, in which tens of thousands of black Mississippi citizens invested tremendous hopes, was a true grass-roots political movement and the greatest achievement of Freedom Summer.

Although the FDP brought to Atlantic City little more than a sense of moral outrage, it nevertheless managed to transform its challenge of the Mississippi regulars into a major threat to the peace of the national party. Mrs. Hamer helped make this feat possible by her electrifying (and televised) testimony before the credentials committee on how Mississippi policemen had beaten her up for trying to register to vote. As Northern liberals began rallying to the FDP, the managers of the convention sought a compromise that would satisfy the liberals and at the same time keep the bulk of the Southern delegations in the convention. President Johnson favored a proposal to seat all the Mississippi regulars who pledged their loyalty to the party, to deny any voting rights to the FDP delegates, but to permit them to sit on the floor of the convention. In addition, he proposed that at future conventions no state delegations chosen by racially discriminatory procedures would be accredited. But because this compromise denied the FDP's claims of legitimacy, the FDP and many liberals declared it unacceptable and threatened to take their case to the floor of the convention, a prospect that greatly displeased the President. Johnson then sent Senator Hubert Humphrey to Atlantic City to act as his agent in settling the controversy. Unsubstantiated rumors had it that if Humphrey's mission failed, the President would deny the Senator the party's vice-presidential nomination. In close touch with both the White House and the credentials committee, Humphrey proposed altering the original compromise by permitting two FDP delegates to sit in the convention as delegates at large with full voting rights. This was as far as Johnson would go, and at the time it seemed far enough. Though the Mississippi white regulars walked out, no Southern delegations followed them, and, at the same time, most liberals felt that the Administration had made a genuine concession. Black leaders, including Dr. King, pleaded with the FDP to accept Humphrey's compromise. But the FDP denied that the compromise was in any sense a victory. Angered at Humphrey's insistence that he alone choose the two at-large delegates, the FDP announced that it had not come to Atlantic City "begging for crumbs." Mrs. Hamer, by now a minor national celebrity, said of Humphrey's efforts, "It's a token of rights on the back row that we get in Mississippi. We didn't come all this way for that mess again ."

To the general public the FDP appeared to be a band of moral zealots hostile to reasonable compromise and ungrateful for the real concession that the party had offered. The true story was more complicated. Aware that total victory was impossible, the FDP had in fact been quite willing to accept any proposal that recognized its legitimacy. At the beginning of the controversy Oregon's Congresswoman Edith Green offered a compromise that the FDP found entirely acceptable. Mrs. Green proposed that the convention seat every member of both delegations who signed a pledge of loyalty and that Mississippi's vote be divided between the two groups according to the number of seated delegates in each. Since only eleven members of the credentials committee (10 percent of the total) had to sign a minority report to dislodge the Green compromise from committee, the FDP seemed assured that its case would reach the convention floor, where many believed that the Green compromise would prevail over Johnson's original proposal. FDP's hopes for a minority report rested chiefly on Joseph Rauh, a member of the credentials committee, leader of the Democratic party in the District of Columbia, veteran of innumerable liberal crusades, and, happily, adviser and legal counsel of the FDP. But Rauh was also a friend of Hubert Humphrey and an attorney for Humphrey's strong supporter, Walter Reuther. After Humphrey came on the scene with his compromise, Rauh backed away from the minority report.

In his semi-official history of the Mississippi Summer Project, *The Summer That Didn't End*, Len Holt presents the FDP and SNCC interpretation of what happened. Presumably pressured by his powerful friends, Rauh broke a promise to the FDP and would not support the Green compromise. One by one the FDP's other allies on the committee backed away—some to protect jobs, others to keep alive hopes for federal judgeships, and one because he feared the loss of a local antipoverty program. In the end the FDP failed to collect the needed signatures, and there was no minority report. The angry rhetoric that the FDP delegates let loose in Atlantic City was in reality inspired less by Humphrey's compromise than by what the FDP regarded as its betrayal at the hands of the white liberals on the credentials committee. By the end of the Democratic convention SNCC was convinced that membership in the Democratic coalition held little hope for Southern blacks and that, lacking power, they would always be sold out by the liberals. In Atlantic City the phrase "white power structure" took on concrete meaning. Freedom Summer, which began with SNCC fighting for entrance into the American political system, ended with the radical conviction that that system was beyond redemption.

In the end the Freedom Summer Project of 1964 not only destroyed SNCC's faith in the American political system; it also undermined its commitment to integration. Within the project racial tensions between white and black workers were never successfully resolved. Though many white volunteers established warm relationships with the local black families that housed them, healthy communication between students and veteran SNCC workers proved difficult at best. Staff members resented the officious manner of better-educated volunteers and feared that the white students were taking over the movement. "Several times," one volunteer wrote, "I've had to completely re-do press statements or letters written by one of them." Said a SNCC worker, "Look at those fly-by-night freedom fighters bossing everybody around." SNCC people found it hard to respect the efforts of volunteers who they knew would retreat at the end of the summer to their safe middle-class world. One sensitive white female volunteer wrote that SNCC workers "were automatically suspicious of us, the white volunteers; throughout the summer they put us to the test, and few, if any, could pass. . . . It humbled, if not humiliated, one to realize that *finally they will never accept me.*" By the end of the summer a spirit akin to black nationalism was rising inside the SNCC organization. . . .

But the most serious obstacle to healthy race relations inside SNCC was sex, and in this dimension, as really in all others, the villain was neither black worker nor white student, but rather the sad and twisted history of race relations in America. The white girl who came South to help SNCC found herself, according to Dr. Poussaint,* "at the center of an emotionally shattering crossfire of racial tensions that have been nurtured for centuries." In the summer of 1965 a veteran black civil rights worker in SCLC tried to warn white girls of the perils that awaited them in their dealings with black men in the movement:

What you have here is a man who had no possible way of being a man in the society in which he lives, save one. And that's the problem. The only way or place a Negro man has been able to express his manhood is sexually and so you find a tremendous sexual aggressiveness. And I say quite frankly, don't get carried away by it and don't get afraid of it either. I mean, don't think it's because you're so beautiful and so ravishing that this man is so enamoured of you. It's not that at all. He's just trying to find his manhood and he goes especially to the places that have robbed him of it. . . . And so, in a sense, what passes itself as desire is probably a combination of hostility and resentment—because he resents what the society has done to him and he wants to take it out on somebody who symbolizes the establishment of society.

*[Alvin Poussaint, a black psychiatrist close to SNCC.—Ed.]

At the end of the summer a white girl spoke of her experiences:

> Well, I think that the white female should be very well prepared before she comes down here to be bombarded. And she also has to be well prepared to tell them to go to hell and be prepared to have them not give up. . . . I've never met such forward men as I have in Mississippi.

The problem was complicated by the jealousy of black girls toward their white rivals, and by neurotic whites who sought to ease their guilt by permitting blacks to exploit them sexually and financially. On leaving their projects to go home, a few white girls told Poussaint, "I hate Negroes." By the end of the summer of 1965 no one could any longer doubt that the blacks reciprocated the feeling.

The year 1965 was a lost one for SNCC. For the first time since its founding, it was no longer on the frontier of protest, no longer the keeper of the nation's conscience, no longer the driving force of a moral revolution. The civil rights acts of 1964 and 1965 brought the civil rights movement, for which SNCC had suffered so much, to a triumphant conclusion, but SNCC had lost interest in integrated public accommodations and equal political rights. SNCC seemed to be losing its sense of mission and after years of providing heroes for the black protest movement, it now needed a hero of its own. Significantly it chose Malcolm X, the black nationalist who had been assassinated by Muslim rivals in February 1965. Only a few years before, SNCC and Malcolm X had seemed to occupy opposite poles of black protest. Thus while SNCC's John Lewis was toning down his speech at the March on Washington, Malcolm X was saying,

> Who ever heard of angry revolutionists all harmonizing "We Shall Overcome . . . Suum Day . . ." while tripping and swaying along arm-in-arm with the very people they were supposed to be angrily revolting against? Who ever heard of angry revolutionists swinging their bare feet together with their oppressors in lily-pad park pools, with gospels and guitars and "I Have a Dream" speeches?

While policemen were clubbing SNCC workers in Mississippi, Malcolm X was saying, "If someone puts a hand on you, send him to the cemetery." While SNCC was pondering the meaning of Atlantic City, Malcolm X was saying "We *need* a Mau Mau. If they don't want to deal with the Mississippi Freedom Democratic Party, then we'll give them something else to deal with." While black nationalists were still a minority in SNCC, Malcolm X was calling for black control of black politicians in black communities, black ownership of ghetto businesses and black unity "to lift the level of our community, to make our society beautiful so that we will be satisfied in our own social circles and won't be running around here trying to knock our way into a social circle where we're not wanted." This was the language that had made Malcolm X the hero of the urban ghetto, and it was the language appropriate in 1965 to

SNCC's militant mood. In a certain sense Malcolm X was the link that connected SNCC with the black radicalism that was arising in the North.

Unlike SNCC, the ghetto masses never had to disabuse themselves of the colorblind assumptions of the civil rights movement. Trapped permanently in their neighborhoods, the poor blacks of the North have always been painfully conscious of their racial separateness. As Essien-Udom, a historian of black nationalism, has written, blackness "is the stuff of their lives and an omnipresent harsh reality. For this reason the Negro masses are instinctively 'race men.' " But the civil rights movement nevertheless had its consequences in the ghetto. The spectacle of Southern blacks defying their white tormentors apparently inspired among Northern blacks race pride and resurgent outrage at the gap between American ideals and black realities. Thus the civil rights movement had the ironic effect of feeding the nationalist tendency in the ghetto to turn inward, to separate, and to identify the white men outside as the enemy. SNCC's frustrations exploded intellectually in the formulation of black power doctrines, but ghetto rage took the form of riot. . . . Thus in 1965, for different reasons, both the ghetto masses and the members of SNCC were seized by militant anti-white feelings, and it was this congruence of mood that would shortly permit SNCC to appeal to a nation-wide black audience.

After a year on the periphery of the black protest movement, SNCC in 1966 moved again to the forefront. In May 1966, at a time when the organization was apparently disintegrating, 135 staff members (25 of them white) met in Nashville to thrash out their future. Early in the emotional conference, by a vote of 60 to 22, John Lewis, the gentle advocate of nonviolence, retained the chairmanship of SNCC by defeating the challenge of the militant Stokely Carmichael. But as the conference went on, the arguments of the militants began to prevail. When the staff voted to boycott the coming White House conference on civil rights, Lewis announced that he would attend anyway, and the question of the chairmanship was then reopened. This time SNCC workers chose Carmichael as their new leader by a vote of 60 to 12. The conference next issued a statement calling, among other things, for "black Americans to begin building independent political, economic, and cultural institutions that they will control and use as instruments of social change in this country."

A few weeks later the full meaning of Carmichael's election became clear to the whole nation. The occasion was the famous Meredith march through Mississippi in June of 1966. James Meredith, the man who integrated the University of Mississippi in 1962 with the help of the United States Army, embarked on a 200-mile walk from Memphis to Jackson to show the black people of Mississippi that they could walk to the voting booths without fear. On June 6, 28 miles out of Memphis, a white man felled Meredith with buckshot. Erroneously believing that Meredith had been killed, civil rights leaders immediately flew to Mississippi to continue his walk against fear. So it was that arm in arm, Martin Luther King of SCLC, Floyd McKissick of CORE, and Stokely Carmichael of SNCC marched down U.S. Highway 51.

Early efforts of the three leaders to maintain surface unity rapidly broke down. Significantly, the first issue that divided them was the role of white people in the Meredith march. King's workers publicly thanked Northern whites for joining the procession. McKissick also thanked the Northerners but announced that black men must now lead the civil rights movement. And Carmichael mused aloud that maybe the whites should go home. As the column moved onto the back roads and Southern white hostility increased, the leadership of the march failed to agree on how to respond to violence. In Philadelphia, Mississippi, Dr. King conducted a memorial service for Goodman, Chaney, and Schwerner and told a crowd of 300 jeering whites that the murderers of the three men were no doubt "somewhere around me at this moment." Declaring that "I am not afraid of any man," King then delivered a Christian sermon. But after the service was over and local whites got rough, the marchers returned punch for punch.

The real spokesman for the march, it soon developed, was not King but Stokely Carmichael. In one town, after spending a few hours in jail, Carmichael told a crowd, "I ain't going to jail no more. I ain't going to jail no more," and he announced, "Every courthouse in Mississippi ought to be burned down to get rid of the dirt." Carmichael then issued the cry that would make him famous. Five times he shouted "Black Power!" and, the *New York Times* reported, "each time the younger members of the audience shouted back, 'Black Power.'" Informed of this new slogan, Dr. King expressed disapproval, and SCLC workers exhorted crowds to call not for black power but for "freedom now." Nevertheless, by the end of the Meredith march, black power had become a force to reckon with.

At its inception in June, 1966, black power was not a systematic doctrine but a cry of rage. In an article in the *New York Times Magazine,* Dr. Poussaint tried to explain the psychological origin of the anger expressed in the new slogan:

> I remember treating Negro workers after they had been beaten viciously by white toughs or policemen while conducting civil rights demonstrations. I would frequently comment, "You must feel pretty angry getting beaten up like that by those bigots." Often I received a reply such as : "No, I don't hate those white men, I love them because they must really be suffering with all that hatred in their souls. Dr. King says the only way we can win our freedom is through love. Anger and hatred has never solved anything."
> I used to sit there and wonder, "Now, what do they really do with their rage?"

Poussaint reported that after a while these workers vented their mounting rage against each other.

> While they were talking about being nonviolent and "loving" the sheriff that just hit them over the head, they rampaged around the project houses beating up each other. I frequently had to calm Negro civil rights workers with large doses of tranquilizers for what I can describe clinically only as acute attacks of rage.

In time the civil rights workers began to direct their anger against white racists, the Federal Government, and finally white people in the movement. Said Poussaint:

> This rage was at a fever pitch for many months, before it became crystallized in the "Black Power" slogan. The workers who shouted it the loudest were those with the oldest battle scars from the terror, demoralization, and castration which they experienced through continual direct confrontation with Southern white racists. Furthermore, some of the most bellicose chanters of the slogan had been, just a few years before, examples of nonviolent, loving passive resistance in their struggle against white supremacy. These workers appeared to be seeking a sense of inner psychological emancipation from racists through self-assertion and release of aggressive angry feelings.

In the months following the Meredith march, SNCC found itself at the center of a bitter national controversy and spokesman for an enlarged constituency. The anger implicit in the slogan "black power" assured SNCC a following in the ghettos of the North and ended its regional confinement. Through its leader, Stokely Carmichael, SNCC labored through 1966 and into 1967 to give intellectual substance to the black power slogan, seeking especially to frame an analysis that would be relevant to black Americans of all sections. Although his speeches were often inflammatory, Carmichael in his writing attempted serious, even restrained, argument suitable for an educated audience. But the elements of black power were not, in truth, derived from rational reflection but from wretched experience—from the beatings, jailhouses, and abortive crusades that SNCC veterans had endured for six years. SNCC had tried nonviolence and found it psychologically destructive. (The "days of the free head-whipping are over," Carmichael and his collaborator Charles Hamilton wrote. "Black people should and must fight back.") SNCC, for example, had believed in integration and tried it within its own organization, but black and white together had not worked. (Integration, said Carmichael, "is a subterfuge for the maintenance of white supremacy" and "reinforces, among both black and white, the idea that 'white' is automatically better and 'black' is by definition inferior.") SNCC had allied with white liberals in the Democratic party and had come away convinced that it had been betrayed. (In dealing with blacks, Carmichael said, white liberals "perpetuate a paternalistic, colonial relationship.") SNCC had struggled for equal political rights but concluded finally that political inequality was less oppressive than economic exploitation. In 1966 SNCC felt it was necessary to go beyond the assertion of these hard conclusions and to attempt to impose on them systematic form. So it was that after years of activism divorced from ideology, SNCC began to reduce its field work and concentrate on fashioning an intellectual rationale for its new militancy. At a time when the black protest movement was floundering and its future direction was uncertain, SNCC stepped forward to contribute the doctrines of black power, which were really the culmination of its career. No history of SNCC would be complete, therefore, without some consideration of those doctrines.

According to Stokely Carmichael, the black masses suffer from two different but reinforcing forms of oppression: class exploitation and white racism. To illustrate this point, he relies on an analogy apparently inspired by Franz Fanon's *Wretched of the Earth,* a book with considerable influence in black power circles. The black communities of contemporary America, Carmichael says, share many of the characteristics of African colonies under European rule. Thus as Africa once enriched its imperialist masters by exporting valuable raw materials to Europe, so now do the American ghettos "export" their labor for the profit of American capitalists. In both Africa and America, white men own local businesses and use them to drain away any wealth somehow possessed by the subject population. As in Africa, there exists in the ghetto a white power structure that is no abstraction, but is a visible and concrete presence— the white landlords, for instance, who collect rent and ignore needed repairs, the city agencies and school systems that systematically neglect black people, the policemen who abuse black citizens and collect payoffs from white racketeers. By far the most insidious method devised by the white imperialists for perpetuating class exploitation has been the use of race as a badge of inferiority. Colonial masters, says Carmichael, "purposely, maliciously, and with reckless abandon relegated the black man to a subordinated, inferior status in society. . . . White America's School of Slavery and Segregation, like the School of Colonialism, has taught the subject to hate himself and deny his humanity." As the colonies of Africa have done, black Americans must undergo "political modernization," liberate their communities, and achieve self-determination. And like Africa, the ghetto must win the struggle by its own effort.

For Carmichael, liberation begins with eradication of the effects of white racism. To overcome the shame of race bred in them by white men, blacks must develop a cultural identity, rediscover the rich African civilization from which they originally came, and learn from their history that they are a "vibrant, valiant people." Freed of their damaging self-image, they can begin to challenge the capitalist values that have enslaved them as a class. The white middle class, says Carmichael, has fostered esteem for "material aggrandizement," is "without a viable conscience as regards humanity," and constitutes "the backbone of institutional reason in this country." Black men, however, will develop values emphasizing "the dignity of man, not . . . the sanctity of property," "free people," not "free enterprise." "The society we seek to build among black people, then, is not a capitalist one. It is a society in which the spirit of community and humanistic love prevail." To complete the process of liberation, black men will have to purge the ghetto of exploiting institutions and develop structures that conform to their new values.

The reconstruction of the black community, Carmichael contends, should be in the hands of black people in order to "convey the revolutionary idea . . . that black people are able to do things themselves." Among other acts of liberation that they can perform, ghetto blacks should conduct rent strikes against slum landlords and boycotts against the ghetto merchant who refuses to " 'invest' say forty to fifty percent of his net profit in the indigenous community." Governmental structures that have violated the humanity of blacks will have to be either eliminated from the ghetto or made responsive to their black constituency. The school system must be taken from professionals, most of whom have demonstrated "insensitivity to the needs and problems of the black child" and given to black parents, who will control personnel and curriculum. The indifference of the existing political parties to black people necessitates formation of separate (parallel) black organizations, both in the 110 Southern counties with black majorities and in the ghettos of the North. According to Carmichael, it is simply naive to think that poor and powerless blacks have anything in common with the other components of the Democratic coalition. White liberals inevitably fall under the "overpowering influence" of their racist environment, and their demands for civil rights are "doing for blacks." Labor unions accept the existing order and in the case of the AFL, even discriminate against black workers. Black political parties, Carmichael believes, will alone be devoted to real change and will in fact make possible emancipation from dominant American values and power centers.

Carmichael professes to believe that black power is not really a departure from American practice. "Traditionally," he writes, "for each new ethnic group, the route to social and political integration into America's pluralistic society has been through the organization of their own institutions with which to represent their communal needs within the larger society." Once in possession of power, blacks then could reenter the old coalitions for specific goals. But "let any ghetto group contemplating coalition be so tightly organized, so strong, that . . . it is an 'undigestible body' which cannot be absorbed or swallowed up." Given Carmichael's scheme for a radical reconstruction of American society, it is not surprising that the only group that he someday hopes to make his ally is the poor whites. . . .

The true significance of black power lies not in the doctrines into which it evolved but in the historical circumstances that gave it birth. The real message of black power is that after years of struggle to make America an open and just society, an important group of civil rights workers, instructed by the brute facts of its own history, gave up the fight. Black power was a cry of rage directed against white bigots who overcame righteous men by force, a cry of bitterness against white liberals who had only a stunted comprehension of the plight of the black poor, and a cry of frustration against gains that seemed meager when compared to needs. It is possible, however, that even rage can perform a useful function, and if the black power slogan brings about a constructive catharsis and helps rouse the black masses from apathy, then the intellectual shortcomings of black power doctrines may seem of little consequence, and what began as a cry of despair may yet play a creative role in the black protest movement. Therefore, whether the history of SNCC in this decade will be considered triumph or tragedy depends on events yet to occur.

Moon Politics

John Kennedy's was a transition presidency, its focus lying midway between the cold war conservatism of Republican Dwight Eisenhower and the reformist liberalism of Democrat Lyndon Johnson. As a result, perhaps the most striking feature of the Kennedy presidency was the skill with which he tried to adopt the language of "radicalism," but to channel that language into programs of federal action within traditional lines. So charismatic were some of Kennedy's efforts that one historian has described him as "our Hollywood star who was only incidentally our president." In the speech that follows, Kennedy proposed to land an American on the moon before the end of the decade. As you read the speech, think of connections and parallels between it and the doctrines of the civil rights movement.

Following the speech is a drawing made by one of the lunar astronauts, Michael Collins. How does the character of the drawing express Collins' feelings about the meaning of the space program, and how do those feelings differ from or echo Kennedy's remarks? Why is Collins' drawing so freely constructed?

Some scholars believe that most of the events of Kennedy's presidency can be grouped under the phrase "quest for national purpose," which expresses a new-found sense of crisis peculiar to the late 1950s and early 1960s. Is there evidence of such a crisis and of an attempt to define the national purpose in Kennedy's speech or in the Collins drawing? Students familiar with the music of Johnny Horton—"Sink the Bismarck," "North to Alaska," and "Battle of New Orleans"—might speculate on how these songs, popular from 1959 through 1961, relate to this theme of national purpose and to the documents on space flight.

John F. Kennedy: The New Frontier in Space

Mr. Speaker, Mr. Vice President, my co-partners in Government, gentlemen—and ladies:

The Constitution imposes upon me the obligation to "from time to time give to the Congress information on the State of the Union." While this has traditionally been interpreted as an annual affair, this tradition has been broken in extraordinary times.

These are extraordinary times. And we face an extraordinary challenge.

From John F. Kennedy, "Special Message to the Congress on Urgent National Needs, May 25, 1961," *Public Papers of the President of the United States: John F. Kennedy, 1961* (Washington, D.C.: Government Printing Office, 1962), pp. 396–398, 403–405.

Our strength as well as our convictions have imposed upon this nation the role of leader in freedom's cause.

No role in history could be more difficult or more important. We stand for freedom. That is our conviction for ourselves—that is our only commitment to others. No friend, no neutral and no adversary should think otherwise. We are not against any man—or any nation—or any system—except as it is hostile to freedom. Nor am I here to present a new military doctrine, bearing any one name or aimed at any one area. I am here to promote the freedom doctrine.

I   The great battleground for the defense and expansion of freedom today is the whole southern half of the globe—Asia, Latin America, Africa and the Middle East—the lands of the rising peoples. Their revolution is the greatest in human history. They seek an end to injustice, tyranny, and exploitation. More than an end, they seek a beginning.

And theirs is a revolution which we would support regardless of the Cold War, and regardless of which political or economic route they should choose to freedom.

For the adversaries of freedom did not create the revolution; nor did they create the conditions which compel it. But they are seeking to ride the crest of its wave—to capture it for themselves.

Yet their aggression is more often concealed than open. They have fired no missiles; and their troops are seldom seen. They send arms, agitators, aid, technicians and propaganda to every troubled area. But where fighting is required, it is usually done by others—by guerrillas striking at night, by assassins striking alone—assassins who have taken the lives of four thousand civil officers in the last twelve months in Vietnam alone—by subversives and saboteurs and insurrectionists, who in some cases control whole areas inside of independent nations.*

With these formidable weapons, the adversaries of freedom plan to consolidate their territory—to exploit, to control, and finally to destroy the hopes of the world's newest nations; and they have ambition to do it before the end of this decade. It is a contest of will and purpose as well as force and violence—a battle for minds and souls as well as lives and territory. And in that contest, we cannot stand aside.

We stand, as we have always stood from our earliest beginnings, for the independence and equality of all nations. This nation was born of revolution

---

*At this point the following paragraph, which appears in the text as signed and transmitted to the Senate and House of Representatives, was omitted in the reading of the message:

They possess a powerful intercontinental striking force, large forces for conventional war, a well-trained underground in nearly every country, the power to conscript talent and manpower for any purpose, the capacity for quick decisions, a closed society without dissent or free information, and long experience in the techniques of violence and subversion. They make the most of their scientific successes, their economic progress and their pose as a foe of colonialism and friend of popular revolution. They prey on unstable or unpopular governments, unsealed, or unknown boundaries, unfilled hopes, convulsive change, massive poverty, illiteracy, unrest and frustration.

and raised in freedom. And we do not intend to leave an open road for despotism.

There is no single simple policy which meets this challenge. Experience has taught us that no one nation has the power or the wisdom to solve all the problems of the world or manage its revolutionary tides—that extending our commitments does not always increase our security—that any initiative carries with it the risk of a temporary defeat—that nuclear weapons cannot prevent subversion—that no free people can be kept free without will and energy of their own—and that no two nations or situations are exactly alike.

Yet there is much we can do—and must do. The proposals I bring before you are numerous and varied. They arise from the host of special opportunities and dangers which have become increasingly clear in recent months. Taken together, I believe that they can mark another step forward in our effort as a people. I am here to ask the help of this Congress and the nation in approving these necessary measures. . . .

IX. *Space*   Finally, if we are to win the battle that is now going on around the world between freedom and tyranny, the dramatic achievements in space which occurred in recent weeks should have made clear to us all, as did the Sputnik in 1957, the impact of this adventure on the minds of men everywhere, who are attempting to make a determination of which road they should take. Since early in my term, our efforts in space have been under review. With the advice of the Vice President, who is Chairman of the National Space Council, we have examined where we are strong and where we are not, where we may succeed and where we may not. Now it is time to take longer strides—time for a great new American enterprise—time for this nation to take a clearly leading role in space achievement, which in many ways may hold the key to our future on earth.

I believe we possess all the resources and talents necessary. But the facts of the matter are that we have never made the national decisions or marshalled the national resources required for such leadership. We have never specified long-range goals on an urgent time schedule, or managed our resources and our time so as to insure their fulfillment.

Recognizing the head start obtained by the Soviets with their large rocket engines, which gives them many months of lead-time, and recognizing the likelihood that they will exploit this lead for some time to come in still more impressive successes, we nevertheless are required to make new efforts on our own. For while we cannot guarantee that we shall one day be first, we can guarantee that any failure to make this effort will make us last. We take an additional risk by making it in full view of the world, but as shown by the feat of astronaut Shepard, this very risk enhances our stature when we are successful. But this is not merely a race. Space is open to us now; and our eagerness to share its meaning is not governed by the efforts of others. We go into space because whatever mankind must undertake, free men must fully share.

I therefore ask the Congress, above and beyond the increases I have earlier requested for space activities, to provide the funds which are needed to meet the following national goals:

First, I believe that this nation should commit itself to achieving the goal, before this decade is out, of landing a man on the moon and returning him safely to the earth. No single space project in this period will be more impressive to mankind, or more important for the long-range exploration of space; and none will be so difficult or expensive to accomplish. We propose to accelerate the development of the appropriate lunar space craft. We propose to develop alternate liquid and solid fuel boosters, much larger than any now being developed, until certain which is superior. We propose additional funds for other engine development and for unmanned explorations—explorations which are particularly important for one purpose which this nation will never overlook: the survival of the man who first makes this daring flight. But in a very real sense, it will not be one man going to the moon—if we make this judgment affirmatively, it will be an entire nation. For all of us must work to put him there.

Secondly, an additional 23 million dollars, together with 7 million dollars already available, will accelerate development of the Rover nuclear rocket. This gives promise of some day providing a means for even more exciting and ambitious exploration of space, perhaps beyond the moon, perhaps to the very end of the solar system itself.

Third, an additional 50 million dollars will make the most of our present leadership, by accelerating the use of space satellites for world-wide communications.

Fourth, an additional 75 million dollars—of which 53 million dollars is for the Weather Bureau—will help give us at the earliest possible time a satellite system for world-wide weather observation.

Let it be clear—and this is a judgment which the Members of the Congress must finally make—let it be clear that I am asking the Congress and the country to accept a firm commitment to a new course of action—a course which will last for many years and carry very heavy costs: 531 million dollars in fiscal '62—an estimated seven to nine billion dollars additional over the next five years. If we are to go only half way, or reduce our sights in the face of difficulty, in my judgment it would be better not to go at all.

Now this is a choice which this country must make, and I am confident that under the leadership of the Space Committees of the Congress, and the Appropriating Committees, that you will consider the matter carefully.

It is a most important decision that we make as a nation. But all of you have lived through the last four years and have seen the significance of space and the adventures in space, and no one can predict with certainty what the ultimate meaning will be of mastery of space.

I believe we should go to the moon. But I think every citizen of this country as well as the Members of the Congress should consider the matter carefully in making their judgment, to which we have given attention over many weeks and months, because it is a heavy burden, and there is no sense in agreeing or desiring that the United States take an affirmative position in outer space, unless we are prepared to do the work and bear the burdens to make it successful. If we are not, we should decide today and this year.

This decision demands a major national commitment of scientific and technical manpower, materiel and facilities, and the possibility of their diversion from other important activities where they are already thinly spread. It means a degree of dedication, organization and discipline which have not always characterized our research and development efforts. It means we cannot afford undue work stoppages, inflated costs of material or talent, wasteful interagency rivalries, or a high turnover of key personnel.

New objectives and new money cannot solve these problems. They could in fact, aggravate them further—unless every scientist, every engineer, every serviceman, every technician, contractor, and civil servant gives his personal pledge that this nation will move forward, with the full speed of freedom, in the exciting adventure of space. . . .

An Astronaut's Vision

CAST OF CHARACTERS

CSM { Command Module
Service Module
Lunar Module

Neil Armstrong (Commander)
Mike Collins (CM Pilot)
Buzz Aldrin (LM Pilot)

Agena

THIRD STAGE

SECOND STAGE

Columbia

Gemini X

John Young
Mike Collins

Titan II

SATURN V

Eagle

Tranquility Base
July 20-21, 1969

FIRST STAGE

July 18, 1966

M. Collins
-1973-

GEMINI TEN: JULY 18-21, 1966
APOLLO ELEVEN: JULY 16-24, 1969

"Cast of Characters" from Michael Collins, Carrying the Fire: An Astronaut's Journeys *(New York: Farrar, Straus, & Giroux, 1974). Copyright © 1974 by Michael Collins. Reprinted with permission of Farrar, Straus, & Giroux, Inc.*

JAMES KUNEN

The Strawberry Statement

The campus protests of the 1960s owe much to the civil rights movement. Many participants in the Free Speech Movement (FSM) at the University of California's Berkeley campus, where the modern student movement was born in the fall of 1964, were veterans of that summer's Mississippi voter registration drive. The FSM began when campus officials, bowing to outside pressures, attempted to restrict the involvement of Berkeley students in local racial discrimination actions by prohibiting certain on-campus activities. Students responded viscerally, employing tactics—the sit-in and the boycott—learned in tutelage to civil rights.

Until April 1968, when 700 to 1,000 students seized five university buildings, Columbia University had experienced nothing like the troubles at Berkeley, Wisconsin, or Michigan. According to the report of a fact-finding commission, appointed to investigate the disturbances and chaired by Archibald Cox (who in the following decade would take on a similar role in the Watergate affair), "the spark that set off the explosion was an SDS [Students for a Democratic Society] rally," and the issues were Columbia's relationship to the Institute for Defense Analyses and her "racist policies." "But the spark, by itself," continues the Cox report, "seemed feeble; these were familiar issues and demonstrations concerning them had never before aroused widespread indignation, much less challenged peace and reason."

Does Columbia student James Kunen's account of these events contribute to an answer to the dilemma posed by the commission? Why were Columbia students protesting? Answers to these questions take us back to the theme of black power, developed in the mid-1960s by blacks working with white students. On the basis of Kunen's account of his experience at Columbia, were black leaders justified in concluding that middle-class white students were undependable allies? Or that an alliance with students could be harmful to the black cause?

Intro 1

About the Book

My question is a simple one; who am I to write a book? I don't know. I'm just writing it. You're just reading it. Let's not worry about it.

Intro 2

Who Wrote the Book

I wrote the Book.

I should like to point out immediately that just because I happened to be born in 1948, it doesn't mean that what I have to say as a nineteen-year-old is worth any more than what nineteen-year-olds had to say in, to pick a year at random, 1920. To say that youth is what's happening is absurd. It's always been happening. Everyone is nineteen, only at different times. This youth-cult scene is a disservice to everyone. I'm anticipating a severe psychological set-back when I turn twenty, and I don't know what I'm going to do when my youth-fare card runs out. As for this "don't-trust-anyone-over-30" shit, I agree in principle, but I think they ought to drop the zero. . . .

Intro 3

Who We Are

People want to know who we are, and some think they know who we are. Some think we're a bunch of snot-nosed brats. It's difficult to say really who we are. We don't have snot on our noses. What we do have is hopes and fears, or ups and downs, as they are called.

A lot of the time we are very unhappy, and we try to cheer ourselves up by thinking. We think how lucky we are to be able to go to school, to have nice clothes and fine things and to eat well and have money and be healthy. How lucky we are really. But we remain unhappy. Then we attack ourselves for self-pity, and become more unhappy, and still more unhappy over being sad.

We're unhappy because of the war, and because of poverty and the hope-lessness of politics, but also because we sometimes get put down by girls or boys, as the case may be, or feel lonely and alone and lost.

And who we are is people in New York City.

New York is the most exciting city in the world, and also the cruddiest place to be that I can conceive of. The city, where when you see someone on

the subway you know you will never see him again. The city, where the streets
are dead with the movement of people brushing by, like silt in a now-dry
riverbed, stirred by the rush of a dirty wind. The city, where you walk along
on the hard floor of a giant maze with walls much taller than people and full of
them. The city is an island and feels that way; not enough room, very separate.
You have to walk on right-angle routes, can't see where you're going to, only
where you are, can only see a narrow part of sky, and never any stars. It's a
giant maze you have to fight through, like a rat, but unlike the rat you have no
reward awaiting you at the end. There is no end, and you don't know what
you're supposed to be looking for.

And unlike the rat, you are not alone. You are instead lonely. There is
loneliness as can exist only in the midst of numbers and numbers of people
who don't know you, who don't care about you, who won't let you care about
them.

Everywhere you walk you hear a click-clack. The click-clack of your
walking never leaves you, reminding you all the time that you are at the
bottom of a box. The earth is trapped beneath concrete and tar and you are
locked away from it. Nothing grows.

All of this makes us sad. And all of this is at Columbia, is Columbia, for
Columbia is New York. Leaving the school or its city really doesn't help. Once
you live in New York you are locked in the city, and the city is locked in you.

On the beach or in the woods the click-clack follows you, and you carry
pavement beneath your feet. The walls are all around, for you have lived with
people and away from them. You know the story on the world; you see how
far people are. And you feel quite sad.

But sadness is not despair so long as you can get angry. And we have
become angry at Columbia. Not having despaired, we are able to see things
that need to be fought, and we fight. We have fought, we are fighting, we will
fight.

April 1, 1968:   Johnson's Little Drama: Maybe it's an April fool. Or
maybe he'll run as a Republican. (He said he wouldn't seek *his* party's nomination.) Or maybe he won't run because he'll suspend the elections. Or, most
likely, he's playing for a draft, although if he got it people would say oh God
and not vote for him.

I want to do something and know something. Yes, this is really a big thing
in me. Think of all the feelings. I feel sorry for Johnson (that is, I feel sorry for
what was presented on the screen, for what elicited sympathy) and I am hope-
ful for McCarthy and excited and confused and all the while completely alone
in the room here. And worse, just for a second, the feeling that maybe I don't
want the war to end, because then what will I do, then what will I hate?

Thursday, April 4, 1968:   I was going to work for Martin Luther King's
poor people's march, but now he's dead. I suppose there'll be one anyway.
Anyway is the way things always end up going these days.

Then Rudd did the thing at the King Memorial Service. I wasn't there
because we had double crew practice to take advantage of the suspension of

classes. But there was a memorial service on campus, and President Kirk attended, and pious phrases were uttered honoring the memory of what the powerful choose to remember of Dr. King. And Rudd got up, in the middle of the service, and called the memorial service an obscenity, which it was, because, as he explained, while President Kirk was in there "honoring" Dr. King, his university was paying black maids less than they could collect on welfare, and insistently refusing collective bargaining and obstructing unionization of its kitchen workers, not to mention continuing the expansion policies which had in ten years almost completely expunged non-whites from Morningside Heights. Also, President Kirk's university was helping to form imperialist policy and prosecute the imperialist war that Dr. King opposed. President Kirk's little religious service was obscenely hypocritical, it was filthy. Rudd walked out. He was followed by many people. Soon he would be followed by many more.

Cast of Characters

Grayson Kirk—President of Columbia University in the City of New York through August of 1968. An Eastern, scholarly Lyndon Johnson. Reputed to be arbitrary, tyrannical, out of touch with the people of his domain. Not known by students, but disliked all the same. Used to be professor of government a long time ago. Head of Security Section, Division of Political Studies, United States Department of State 1942–43. . . .

Mark Rudd—President Columbia chapter Students for a Democratic Society. Junior in the college. Known to everyone, well known to few (the usual). Hardly revered, but certainly listened to.

Students for a Democratic Society—Just that. Defies more specific definition. Mixed bag. Activist, but often hampered by internal dissension. Maybe four hundred members; no one, least of all SDS, knows exactly. Meetings open, anyway. Influential in student life. Called "pukes" by the jocks.

Students Opposing SDS—Never could get their shit together: Students for a Free Campus, Students for Columbia University, Students for the Defense of Property Rights, Majority Coalition. All powerless because totally disorganized. Called "jocks" by the pukes.

IDA—Institute for Defense Analysis. Consortium of twelve universities doing research for the Pentagon. Columbia secretly, or at least very quietly, affiliated. Total contracts rather meager compared to many of Columbia's other war efforts. Chosen as a symbol for all university involvement with the war machine.

The Gym—An eleven-story private building to be built on public land, Morningside Park, which separates Columbia from Harlem. The community (blacks) could use a certain section of it at certain times, through a certain door (the back). They even were to have a separate little pool to swim in. Sounds all right, but would you let the New York Athletic Club build a building in the middle of Central Park? How about if they'd let you use it once in a while?

The important point was that the community was not consulted, as they had not been consulted with regard to the purchase of one hundred and fifty buildings and the eviction of ten thousand people over the past seven years. The gym served as a symbol for all Columbia expansion. . . .

Columbia used to be called King's College. They changed the name in 1784 because they wanted to be patriotic and *Columbia* means *America*. This week we've been finding out what America means.

Every morning now when I wake up I have to run through the whole thing in my mind. I have to do that because I wake up in a familiar place that isn't what it was. I wake up and I see blue coats and brass buttons all over the campus. ("Brass buttons, blue coat, can't catch a nanny goat" goes the Harlem nursery rhyme.) I start to go off the campus but then remember to turn and walk two blocks uptown to get to the only open gate. There I squeeze through the three-foot "out" opening in the police barricade, and I feel for my wallet to be sure I've got the two I.D.'s necessary to get back into my college. I stare at the cops. They stare back and see a red armband and long hair and they perhaps tap their night sticks on the barricade. They're looking at a radical leftist.

I wasn't always a radical leftist. Although not altogether straight, I'm not a hair person either, and ten days ago I was writing letters to Kokomo, Indiana, for Senator McCarthy; my principal association with the left was that I rowed port on crew. But then I got involved in this movement and one thing led to another. I am not a leader, you understand. But leaders cannot seize and oc- cupy buildings. It takes great numbers of people to do that. I am one of those great numbers. What follows is the chronicle of a single revolutionary digit. . . .

Wednesday, April 24, 5:30 A.M.   Someone just won't stop yelling that we've got to get up, that we're leaving, that the blacks occupying Hamilton with us have asked us to leave. I get up and leave. The column of evicted whites shuffles over to Low Library. A guy in front rams a wooden sign through the security office side doors and about 200 of us rush in. Another 150 hang around outside because the breaking glass was such a bad sound. They become the first "sundial people." Inside we rush up to Kirk's office and some- one breaks the lock. I am not at all enthusiastic about this and suggest that perhaps we ought to break up all the Ming Dynasty art that's on display while we're at it. A kid turns on me and says in a really ugly way that the exit is right over there. I reply that I am staying, but that I am not a sheep and he is.

Rudd calls us all together. He looks very strained. He elicits promises from the *Spectator* reporters in the crowd not to report what he is about to say. Then he says that the blacks told us to leave Hamilton because they do not feel that we are willing to make the sacrifices they are willing to make. He says that they have carbines and grenades and that they're not leaving. I think that's really quite amazing. . . .

At 3:45 I smoke my first cigarette in four months and wonder if Lenin smoked. I don't go to crew. I grab a typewriter and, though preoccupied by its electricness, manage to write:

The time has come to pass the time.

I am not having good times here. I do not know many people who are here, and I have doubts about why they are here. Worse, I have doubts about why I am here. (Note the frequency of the word *here*. The place I am is the salient characteristic of my situation.) It's possible that I'm here to be cool or to meet people or to meet girls (as distinct from people) or to get out of crew or to be arrested. Of course the possibility exists that I am here to precipitate some change at the University. I am willing to accept the latter as true or, rather, I am willing, even anxious, not to think about it any more. If you think too much on the second tier (think about why you are thinking what you think) you can be paralyzed.

I really made the conflicting-imperative scene today. I have never let down the crew before, I think. Let down seven guys. I am one-eighth of the crew. I am one-fiftieth of this demonstration. And I am not even sure that this demonstration is right. But I multiplied these figures by an absolute importance constant. I hate to hamper the hobby of my friends (and maybe screw, *probably* screw, my own future in it), I am sorry about that, but death is being done by this University and I would rather fight it than row a boat.

But then I may, they say, be causing a right-wing reaction and hurting the cause. Certainly it isn't conscionable to hold Dean Coleman captive. But attention is being gotten. Steps will be taken in one direction or another. The polls will fluctuate and the market quiver. Our being here is the cause of an effect. We're trying to make it good; I don't know what else to say or do. That is, I have no further statement to make at this time, gentlemen. . . .

I take my place with seven others at the front barricade. All along the stairs our people are lined up, ready to hole up in the many lockable-from-within rooms on the three floors above me. We sing "We Shall Not Be Moved" and realize that something is ending. The cops arrive. The officer bullhorns us: "On behalf of the Trustees of Columbia University and with the authority vested in me . . ." That's as far as he is able to get, as we answer his question and all others with our commune motto—"Up against the wall, motherfuckers." We can't hold the barricade because the doors open out and the cops simply pull the stuff out. They have to cut through ropes and hoses and it takes them fifteen minutes before they can come through. All the while they're not more than thirty feet from me, but all I can do is watch their green-helmeted heads working. I shine a light in their eyes but Tom tells me not to and he's head of the defense committee so I stop.

At 4:00 A.M. the cops come in. The eight of us sit down on the stairs (which we've made slippery with green soap and water) and lock arms. The big cop says "Don't make it hard for us or you're gonna get hurt." We do not move. We want to make it clear that the police have to step over more than chairs to get our people out. They pull us apart and carry us out, stacking us like cord wood under a tree. The press is here so we are not beaten. As I sit under the tree I can see kids looking down at us from every window in the building. We exchange the "V" sign. The police will have to ax every door to get them out of those offices. They do. Tom Hayden is out now. He yells

"Keep the radio on! Peking will instruct you!" When they have sixty of us out they take us to the paddy wagons at mid-campus. I want to make them carry us, but the consensus is that it's a long, dark walk and we'll be killed if we don't cooperate, so I walk. At the paddy wagons there are at least a thousand people cheering us and chanting "Strike! Strike! Strike!" We are loaded in a wagon and the doors shut. John tells a story about how a cop grabbed the cop that grabbed him and then said "Excuse me." We all laugh raucously to show an indomitable spirit and freak out the cops outside. . . .

Tom Hayden is in Chicago now. As an Outside Agitator, he has a lot of outsides to agitate in. Like the Lone Ranger, he didn't even wave good-bye, but quietly slipped away, taking his silver protest buttons to another beleaguered campus.

Everyone is organizing now—moderates, independent radicals, Liberated Artists, librarians. And the Yippies are trying to sue the University for evicting us from our homes which we owned by virtue of squatters' rights. You can hardly move for the leaflets here. Except at Barnard. The Barnard girls are typing their papers and getting ready to go to Yale for the weekend.

We are on strike, of course. There are "liberation classes" but the scene is essentially no more pencils, no more books.

I saw a cellist math major in Chock Full O' Nuts looking alone. Liberation classes won't help him. He is screwed. Every Revolution leaves a trail of screwed drifting in its wake.

The campus is still locked, although I think you could get in with a Raleigh coupon as an I.D. today. That's our latest issue; a liberated campus should be open. We want free access by June so we can open the summer school under our own aegis.

A particularly thick swatch of air pollution drifted by today and a lot of people thought the gym site was burning. That did not surprise me. Nothing surprises me anymore.

Urban Revolt

Riots in the Cities: A Profile

Severe race riots in Newark, New Jersey, and Detroit in 1967 caused Lyndon Johnson to appoint a National Advisory Commission on Civil Disorders. The commission's report, issued in March of the following year, contained the first reliable information on the participants and nonparticipants in these ghetto revolts. The following tables are adapted from commission data. Who were the rioters?

key:
R rioters
NI noninvolved
A arrestees
CR counter-rioter
p A symbol which represents the probability that a difference this great is a product of chance. The symbol $>$ means is greater than. The symbol $<$ means is less than.

Age Distribution

	Detroit Survey	
Age	R (44)	NI (287)
15–24	61.3%	22.6%
25–35	25.0	15.7
36–50	11.4	32.4
over 50	2.3	29.3
	100.0%	100.0%
	$p < .001$	

Place of Birth

	Detroit Survey		Newark Survey	
Born in riot city	R(43)	NI(285)	R(127)	NI(106)
Yes	59.4%	34.6%	53.5%	22.5%
No	40.6	65.4	46.5	77.5
	100.0%	100.0%	100.0%	100.0%
	$p < .001$		$p < .001$	

From National Advisory Commission on Civil Disorders, *Report* (New York: The New York Times Company and Bantam, 1968), pp. 172, 174, 175. Reprinted by courtesy of The New York Times Company.

Income Level

Annual income	Detroit Survey			Newark Survey	
	R(44)	NI(287)	CR(62)	R(104)	NI(126)
Less than 2,000	13.6%	12.9%	4.8%	4.7%	3.2%
2,000–5,000	25.0	17.4	16.2	27.9	26.2
5,000–7,500	13.6	20.6	22.6	27.9	30.1
7,500–10,000	18.2	13.9	17.7	14.4	11.1
10,000–12,500	2.3	3.8	14.5	1.0	4.0
12,500–15,000	0.0	1.7	1.6	1.0	1.6
More than 15,000	2.3	0.3	3.2	0.0	3.2
No answer	25.0	29.4	19.4	23.1	20.6
	100.0%	100.0%	100.0%	100.0%	100.0%
		p<.50		p<.50	

Employment Status

Currently employed	Detroit Survey*		Newark Survey†	
	R(27)	NI(127)	R(84)	NI(105)
Yes	70.4%	68.5%	70.3%	81.0%
No	29.6	31.5	29.7	19.0
	100.0%	100.0%	100.0%	100.0%
	p<.75		p<.50	

	Detroit Arrest Study	Newark Arrest Records 4 cities‡
Currently Employed	A (496)	A (310)
Yes	78.2%	66.8%
No	21.8	33.2
	100.0%	100.0%

*Males only
†Excludes students
‡Atlanta, Cincinnati, New Brunswick and Tampa (two major, one serious and one minor)

From Montgomery to Watts

Compare and contrast these photographs, representative of a decade of black protest and resistance. What do the photographs tell us about the participants in each decade's protests? about the goals of protest activity? What is the relationship between the activity shown in the Watts photograph and the slogan "black power"?

Walking to Work During the Montgomery Bus Boycott. *Grey Villet, Life Magazine,* © *Time, Inc.*

A decade later, blacks in Watts, a section of Los Angeles, are in the streets with a different purpose—transporting goods taken from ghetto stores. *Wide World Photos.*

CHAPTER 14

Vulnerable Americans: The 1970s

By the late 1970s, it seemed unlikely that the promise of the 1960s would be fulfilled. Of the various "liberation" movements of the previous decade—among women, blacks, homosexuals, older persons, American Indians, Mexican-Americans and other "hyphenates"—only gay rights, women's rights, and the campaign against age discrimination remained vital. Gays, however, found themselves hounded by singer and orange-juice saleswoman Anita Bryant, and after rejections by the Illinois and Virginia legislatures in the spring of 1978, feminists could only wonder if the Equal Rights Amendment would ever gain the last three states needed for passage. Only the elderly, with the Retirement Act of 1978, could claim real legislative gains. Reform may have been stifled by growing concern with economic issues. California voters led a national revolt against high taxes, and President Jimmy Carter, elected in 1976 on a platform of major tax reform, in less than two years found it necessary to abandon his plans and to focus his presidency on the problem of inflation. When, in early 1979, Carter announced substantial cutbacks in federal job programs, there was some speculation that the rollback of FDR's New Deal was finally under way.

At the same time, the president's call for a New Foundation summarized the sense of loss and cynicism that had begun to permeate the national consciousness as early as 1968. In April of that year, Martin Luther King, Jr., was assassinated; two months later, Robert F. Kennedy was killed when he seemed virtually assured of the Democratic presidential nomination. That November, voters chose an issueless Richard Nixon with an undisclosed plan for ending the war in Vietnam over Hubert Humphrey's "politics of joy." The new mood of quiescence was evident the following summer when some 400,000 youths gathered for a peaceful (and nonpolitical) rock concert at Woodstock, New York.

Within months of his inauguration, Nixon launched a secret bombing campaign against enemy forces in Cambodia. The move had far-reaching consequences. First, it reinvigorated, expanded, and made respectable the last stronghold of the radicalism of the 1960s— the antiwar movement. Peace demonstrations in the fall of 1969 drew forty thousand persons in Washington, D. C., sixty-five thousand in New York City, and one hundred thousand in Boston. Second, when news of the bombing of Cambodia reached the public through unofficial channels, the Nixon administration began wiretapping telephones in an effort to plug the information leaks. The series of events that would eventually lead to the Watergate break-in, the cover-up, and the resignation of the president had begun.

Consumed by the need to control, the Nixon administration had by the fall of 1969 embarked on a campaign to isolate and discredit the peace-movement and had brought Jeb Stuart Magruder to Washington to centralize White House public relations. May Day demonstrations against the American invasion of Cambodia in 1970 and the leak of military documents by Pentagon employee Daniel Ellsberg in June 1971 brought increasing pressure on Magruder (who had moved to the Committee for the Reelection of the President [CREEP]) to engage in intelligence-gathering activities. "The basic problem," as Magruder put it, "was that the President and [his chief of staff, H. R.] Haldeman believed that Communist groups were funding the antiwar activists, and when the FBI or the Justice Department's Internal Security Division couldn't find proof of that, Nixon and Haldeman would write off those agencies as inept and want their own investigators who could do the job." Why such paranoia led Magruder and John Mitchell, former attorney general and then CREEP head, to gather information on contenders for the Democratic nomination and on Larry O'Brien, Democratic National Committee chairman, has never been completely clear. But in June 1972, five CREEP operatives were apprehended at the Democratic National Committee headquarters in Washington's Watergate complex. When the president's own tape recordings revealed that he and a number of others in his administration had conspired to conceal information about the break-in, a humiliated Nixon resigned.

Some took Watergate and its results as a sign that American institutions were still healthy—that the hand of justice fell even on those in high places. For most Americans, however, Watergate only confirmed what they had learned from Joe McGinness' *The Selling of the President*, an extraordinarily popular study of Nixon's first victorious campaign: politics was a shuck. In spite of Jimmy Carter's attempt to appeal to the voters as an honest, God-fearing man of the people, the 1976 election set a record for low turnout.

There were other clues to the disappearance of the confident, optimistic spirit of the mid-1960s. Rock music showed signs of *rigor mortis*. Its creative energies produced offshoots that were either cynical and nihilistic, like "punk" rock, or exceptionally rigid, formal, and impersonal, like "disco," the music and dance craze of the late 1970s. Disaster and horror dominated film making. Americans learned in *The Poseidon Adventure*, *Jaws*, and *The Exorcist* that man was virtually helpless before nature, technology, and primitive religious forces.

This sense of ultimate vulnerability was also apparent in the aftermath of the mass suicide and murder of more than 900 Americans at a camp settlement in Jonestown, Guyana. The lesson of Jonestown, wrote Yale professor Harold J. Morowitz, was that the American educational system, in its failure to teach critical thinking and philosophical foundations, had rendered youth vulnerable to irrational movements. But Jimmy Carter's State of the Union address in January 1978 best captured the national self-image. While insisting that the nation was sound in every sense—indeed, "vital" and "dynamic"—Carter's refrain was cautious: "*and so we will remain.*" In concluding his address, Carter joined the late Hubert Humphrey in calling for "reconciliation, rebuilding, and rebirth." Never had a president been so wary of the future.

CAREY WINFREY

Why 900 Died in Guyana

Congressman Leo Ryan arrived in Jonestown, Guyana, in mid-November 1978 on a fact-finding mission. His entourage included several journalists. For Jim Jones, the colony's leader, this intrusion from the

outside spelled the end of his experiment. When Ryan and four others, including three newsmen, were killed as they attempted to board a plane, Jones assembled the members of his community and instructed the town doctor to prepare sufficient cyanide poison for all the residents of Jonestown, including women and children. Within hours, some 900 persons were dead. Some had to be forced to take the poison; most, including Jones, committed suicide.

Though obviously unique in its violent end, Jones' People's Temple was part of a larger historical phenomenon. During the 1960s, traditional organized religion had difficulty accommodating change. The Catholic Church, for example, grappled with demands for liberalized instructions on birth control, an end to priestly celibacy, popularization of the mass, and a strong anti-Vietnam position. Many Americans, particularly youth, withdrew from established religious bodies and gravitated toward more personalized, more responsive religious forms. Some found comfort in the evangelism of Billy Graham and Oral Roberts; others found what they were looking for in smaller, more intense groups—cults and sects. These included the Hare Krishna, whose members shaved heads and sang repetitive songs on city streets; the Moonies (followers of the Reverend Sun Yung Moon); Synanon (featuring intense encounter sessions); and the People's Temple. Parents of the middle-class white youth who formed the nucleus of most of these organizations considered their children brainwashed and often had them "kidnapped" and "reprogrammed." Not all those attracted by the new religious movements were young, however. Nixon aide Charles Colson, deeply involved in the Watergate cover-up, became a born-again Christian.

Jim Jones' life was part of this historical experience. Born in 1931 in a small town east of Indianapolis, Jones was raised a Methodist. As a child, he enjoyed playing the preacher, making sermons, and exercising his powerful personality. In the early 1950s, Jones left the pastorate of a Methodist church and soon opened his first People's Temple in Indianapolis. Troubled by visions of a nuclear holocaust and desperately afraid of contracting cancer, in 1965 he moved the temple to an isolated area of northern California, a site he deemed safe, at least from the bomb. There his influence grew with his fears. When, in 1977, a San Francisco reporter published evidence that Jones had misused temple funds and physically brutalized temple members, Jones packed up his traveling road show and took it to a 27,000-acre leased tract in the jungles of South America.

The following article, by a reporter who covered the Guyanan colony for *The New York Times*, describes something of life in Jonestown and of the people who lived there. What was it that Jones wanted to achieve? Why was he able to attract so many to his vision? What basic feelings did he tap? Does Jonestown demonstrate significant weaknesses in American institutions? Should Americans be concerned about the growing influence of cults in contemporary society? What are some possible solutions?

Why did they die?

Perhaps no explanation will ever satisfy completely. But to review the massacre months later through the eyes of those most deeply involved is to discover a dozen different clues in the deadly dynamics of Guyana, from faith to fear to murder.

We know now through firsthand witnesses that once Jim Jones learned of the Port Kaituma killings of a Congressman, three journalists and a "defector," events moved quickly. Jones called his followers to the main pavilion.

According to reports of a tape recording of the commune's last hour, he began by telling them: "I tried to give you a good life. In spite of all I tried to do, a handful of our people who are alive"—presumably meaning other defectors—"have made our lives impossible." Then, referring to the earlier airstrip killings, he continued: "There's no way to detach ourselves from what's happened today. We are sitting on a powder keg. If we can't live in peace, let's die in peace."

For some—their identities irrevocably intertwined with Jones—his suggestion sufficed. As Odell Rhodes, a survivor who escaped while the killings took place, put it, "Some of these people were with Jim Jones for 10 or 20 years. They wouldn't know what to do with themselves without him." Another voice on the tape: "Dad has brought us this far; my vote is to go with Dad."

Christine Miller, an elderly woman, asked why they couldn't flee instead to Russia. Jones answered calmly that the Russians wouldn't want them now because they had been disgraced by the killings at Port Kaituma. "I want my babies first," he then commanded. "Take my babies and children first."

Stanley Clayton, another eyewitness escapee, testified at the Guyana inquest that many in the commune seemed at first to think it was just another drill. In calling for "babies first," Jones surely knew that mothers duped into killing their children would want to take their own lives.

Clayton testified that, in some cases, "nurses took babies right out of their mothers' arms. The mothers were frozen with shock, scared out of their wits." The nurses then squirted the deadly liquid down the children's throats, sending them into convulsions.

"After you watched your child die," Paula Adams—a Jones follower who survived because she was in Georgetown that Saturday—speculated later, "you'd think, 'What's there to live for. I may as well die.' "

When most of the babies were dead or dying, Clayton testified, "people began realizing this was really taking place."

The crowd grew restive. Jones took another tack. "He kept telling them, 'I love you. I love you. It is nothing but a deep sleep,' " Clayton recalled. " 'It won't hurt you. It's just like closing your eyes and drifting into a deep sleep.' "

Then, Clayton said, Jones stepped into the crowd and began guiding people toward the vat of fruit drink and cyanide. Jones's wife, Marceline, also walked among the followers, embracing them and saying, "I'll see you in the next life."

Jones himself did not believe in reincarnation, but he knew that many of his followers did. "We'll all fall tonight," one communard said, stepping forward for his cup of poison, "but he'll raise us tomorrow."

According to Rhodes, Jones told the group that if they didn't drink the potion, they would be tortured and the men castrated by the Guyanese Army. "Troops will come in here," Rhodes quoted Jones as saying. "They will torture our babies. They will kill everybody. It's better that we die with dignity." The many who shared his paranoia about a C.I.A.-Treasury Department-Guyana Defense Forces conspiracy to destroy the Temple undoubtedly believed him.

Jones "made them feel that in a couple of hours the army was going to be there and take them and put them in concentration camps," Stephan Jones said later. Stephan, the cult leader's natural son, escaped the carnage. As a member of the Jonestown basketball team, he had gone to Georgetown for a game.

To those who felt death inevitable, Jones's repeated entreaties to "die with dignity" would have proved powerfully persuasive, former followers agreed. "If I was down there," said Grace Stoen, "I would say I'd rather go down bravely than be shot in the back. That's the choice they had."

Others may have felt that they had run out of alternatives. Virtual prisoners in a jungle outpost 150 miles from a major airport, lacking money, resources or passports, many must have believed they had come too far, repudiated too much, to turn back.

"In San Francisco, they'd have run," said Willard Gaylin, a psychiatrist who is president of the Institute of Society, Ethics and the Life Sciences. "And once a few ran, it would have changed the whole dynamic and power of the group. But where the hell were they going to run to in Guyana?"

For some, a return to the United States was psychologically out of the question, as Dr. Hardat Sukhdeo, a Guyanese-born cult specialist now working in New Jersey, observed. "They were people in Jonestown," he said of the survivors he interviewed in Georgetown. "For the first time in their lives they were persons." Michael Carter, one of three who escaped with a suitcase containing more than half a million dollars, offered another version of the same thought. "A lot of the people," he said, "had nothing else but the People's Temple and Jonestown."

One more factor in their acquiescence was Jones's call for "revolutionary suicide"; the belief, as Michael Carter reconstructed it, that "we're going to show how a force of so many people can do so much to shape the world." Two who apparently shared this belief were the guards sent to warn (or possibly to kill) the two visiting Temple attorneys, Charles Garry and Mark Lane.

"It's a great moment—we all die," Mr. Garry later reported one of the guards saying. "They had this smile on their faces. They said they were going to die, that it was a pleasure to die for revolutionary suicide, that this is the way it's got to be done as an expression against racism and fascism."

The group need was also critical. For many, the anxiety of being separated from the group—which even at the last moment represented love and security—perhaps outweighed fear of death. Odell Rhodes related that, as he was escaping, he came upon a dormitory full of elderly members. They all said they wanted to join in the suicides. Some asked him to escort them to the pavilion. Others, who could walk, picked themselves up and made their own way.

When 74-year old Hyacinth Thrash awoke the next morning, after sleeping through the holocaust, she panicked. "I thought everybody had run off," she explained after she was rescued. "I started crying and wailing, 'Why did they leave me? Why did they leave me?' "

"It may be a less sick thing," Dr. Gaylin said of suicide, "when it's done as part of the group than when it's done individually, because of the immensity of group pressure on insecure people."

The haste inherent in the event, giving the communards little time to think things over, also helps account for the compliance. "If I was one of the first," Michael Carter admitted, "I think I would have done it willingly. I think as things went on, I would have tried to rebel. I can't imagine no one tried to rebel, [at least] 30 or 40. I know a majority followed him willingly." But, given time, Carter said, "there was definitely a minority in Jonestown of at least 30 people who would have rebelled, with a hundred more in the closet."

Some did rebel. In addition to Rhodes and Clayton, 79-year-old Grover Davis simply walked away from the pavilion and hid in a ditch. "I didn't want to die," he said later.

There is evidence that others also didn't want to die. Mr. Clayton testified that Jones, backed by security guards, pulled some people from their seats and propelled them forcibly toward the vats of poison.

A report by Dr. Leslie Mootoo, the Guyana Government's chief medical examiner, noted that several of the 39 bodies he examined showed punctures "consistent" with injections. He and police estimated that at least 70 persons might have received injections. Mr. Rhodes said he saw some people injected when the poison they took orally failed to kill them.

By one reckoning—counting the 70 "rebels" as murdered, as well as 260 children and five elderly women who may have mistaken the poison for routine medication—perhaps a third of those who died at Jonestown were not suicides at all. But by almost any other reckoning, murder and suicide became so hopelessly intermingled that it was impossible to tell which was which.

The signs were there for some time.

Grace Stoen, one of Jim Jones's closest aides, remembers that, in September 1972, Lester Kinsolving wrote a series of skeptical newspaper articles detailing Jones's claims as faith healer and prophet. "That bad press just freaked Jones out and he got even more paranoid."

A year later, by her recollection, Jones expounded the idea of mass suicide. "We've got to go down in history," she recalls him saying in September

1973. " 'We've got to be in the history books.' And he said, 'Everyone will die, except me of course. I've got to stay back and explain why we did it: for our belief in integration.' "

Two days later, the defection of eight Temple teen-agers ushered in a new era at the Temple. "We hated those eight with such a passion because we knew any day they were going to try bombing us," Neva Sly, a former member recalled recently. "I mean Jim Jones had us totally convinced of this."

The defections, following so rapidly the first mention of "revolutionary suicide," may also have persuaded Jones to set the notion aside—at least temporarily. For it was not until about three years later, according to Mrs. Stoen, that the idea came up again. On New Year's Day, 1976, Jones told about 30 inner-circle followers that he loved them so much he would lift his abstinency rule and allow them each a glass of wine. When all had drunk, he informed them that they would be dead within an hour. Mrs. Stoen says that while she didn't believe him, others did. She recalls Walter Jones, who was attending his first meeting as a member of the Planning Commission, standing up and saying that he just wanted to know "why we're dying. All I've been doing is working on bus engines ever since I got here and I want to know that I'm dying for something more than being a mechanic working on all these buses."

Mrs. Sly, whose husband, Don, threatened Representative Leo J. Ryan with a knife at Jonestown, also believed Jones that evening. She remembers Jones telling the assemblage that the F.B.I. or the C.I.A. was closing in and would kill everyone. "I had so much going through my mind that the 30 minutes was like 20 hours." After a while, Mrs. Sly reported, "Jones smiled and said, 'Well, it was a good lesson. I see you're not dead.' He made it sound like we needed the 30 minutes to do very strong, introspective kind of thinking. We all felt strongly dedicated, proud of ourselves."

Today Mrs. Sly, whose son died at Jonestown, says she had not been afraid of death that evening. After all, she says, Jones "taught that it would be a privilege to die for what you believed in, which is exactly what I would have been doing."

Deborah Layton Blakey has an equally chilling memory of the same evening. She said that Jones took her and a handful of other trusted aides into a room and asked their advice about how to kill off the entire Planning Commission. He suggested sending the group on an airplane trip, she said. Once aloft, "one of us would shoot [the pilot] and the whole plane would go down. And that way he'd have the whole P.C. dead. Then he thought of taking all the buses and running them off the Golden Gate Bridge.

"His big concern," Mrs. Blakey continued, "was that people were starting to leave his church, P.C. people. He got scared and thought the best thing to do was just kill them off."

Those gathered on the Golden Gate Bridge for a Memorial Day service for those who jumped from the landmark, might also have heard intimations of things to come. Jones, an invited speaker, departed from his prepared text to extemporize about the depressing effect a New West magazine article, by San Francisco reporters Marshall Kilduff and Philip Tracy, was having on him and his congregation.

"These past few days," Jones said, "we as a congregation of several thousand have undergone a considerable amount of pressure. It seems that there are elements in society, very wrongfully, who want to use us as an embarrassment to this administration. So I can empathize [with suicide victims].

"This week my son said to me," he continued, " 'For the first time, Dad, I felt like committing suicide . . . Maybe it might cause people to care if I jumped off the bridge while you were speaking.' We worked our way through that, but I think that perhaps we all should identify closely with that kind of personal experience. Because at one time or another we have all felt the alienation and the despair. I think the despair got to me yesterday. If it hadn't been for an Academy Award-winning actress joining our church . . . I think I would have been in a suicidal mood myself today for perhaps the first time in my life." (Jones was mistaken; Jane Fonda, the "Academy Award-winning actress," visited but did not join the People's Temple.)

Less than a year later, in March 1978, Jones would write a letter to United States Senators and Representatives. "We at People's Temple," he said, "have been the subject of harassment by several agencies of the U.S. Government and are rapidly reaching the point at which our patience is exhausted . . . I can say without hesitation that we are devoted to a decision that it is better even to die than to be constantly harassed from one continent to the next."

There are further clues to the tragedy in the life histories of the people themselves.

Long before threats of suicide had appeared in letters to Congressmen, the People's Temple had helped drug addicts break their addictions, offered food and shelter to the destitute, run schools and senior-citizen centers, reformed prostitutes and found jobs for the uneducated. It helped an illiterate black woman become a nurse and a heavy drug-user become a doctor. Although the reality never matched the Temple's stated egalitarian aims, and although some racial friction always existed, blacks and whites worked together in considerable harmony.

Neva Sly remembers that, at her first visit to the Temple in 1967, "a force of love just slapped you in the face." Within a month, she and her husband had moved to Ukiah, Calif., to work full time "for the cause. It was the greatest feeling to me, that I was really giving my all to something."

"When we first joined, it was beautiful, interracial humanitarianism," Jeannie Mills, another defector, recalls. "When you walked into the church, everybody greeted you with hugs. I had never experienced this kind of love before."

"I went into this group to serve mankind by building a tightly knit utopian society which would be a model," said Grace Stoen's husband, Tim, a lawyer who was Jones's most trusted adviser until he defected in April 1977 and became his most hated traitor. "I wanted utopia so damn bad I could die. In fact, I fully expected to die. I really took to heart that verse in Ecclesiastes: 'Whatsoever thy hand findeth to do, do it with thy might.' " Mr. Stoen, then an assistant district attorney, gave the Temple his house, turned over his salary, sold his Porsche sports car, and began buying his suits at the Salvation Army.

At the center of the tragic scene, holding it all together, was Jim Jones—darkly handsome, spellbindingly loquacious and, by the evidence available to most members, committed to the ideals he espoused.

"Jim Jones was warm, friendly, outgoing," recalls Harold Cordell, who joined the "church" at the age of 18 in 1956 and stayed for 20 years. "There were outings for young people. He made young people feel they were part of something. He was meeting the needs of senior citizens. There were programs for the poor. It looked like a good thing. I saw a place I could relate to and feel like I was a part of something. I wanted to feel I was contributing to society. I wanted to do good works."

"Jones was a master mythmaker," adds Stoen. "I've never seen anybody who could weave the tapestry of a utopian dream so beautifully."

But the tapestry never appealed to a broad constituency. In his first four months as a new member, Stoen brought some 35 lawyer friends to hear Jones speak, fully expecting each to be quickly converted, as he had been. To his surprise, not one returned a second time.

Stoen estimates that, in 10 years, somewhere between 50,000 and 100,000 people came to hear Jones speak. But, he says, despite Jones's boasts of 20,000 members, the actual membership never exceeded 3,000.

In the main, the Temple attracted two kinds of people: white, upper-middle-class idealists and uneducated, disenfranchised blacks. The latter out-numbered the former by about 4 to 1; but whites, notably white women, held most of the leadership positions. Jones once referred to his rank-and-file members as "the refuse of America."

"I remember some black mothers would tell you they had seven sons and five were in prison," says Tim Stoen. "Nobody else had ever taken them and looked them in the eye and said, 'I love you,' which Jim would do. When I saw Jim kiss old black ladies on the cheek and their eyes would light up, I would cry, I was so touched."

In the "self-analysis" letters that Jones asked his Jonestown followers to write to him last July, feelings of guilt and worthlessness run rampant.

"Historically, I have been very insecure," wrote Tom Grubbs, the Jonestown high-school principal. "Had a very strong inferiority complex all my life, felt frightfully inadequate. . . . I want to work every damn minute I'm not asleep, largely so I don't have to face my feelings of unworthiness, inadequacy, insecurity."

Agreeing to do whatever the leader asks in exchange for relief from feelings of worthlessness and guilt is a familiar pattern, says Dr. Stanley Cath, a psychiatrist and student of cults at Tufts University. "Anyone in a group like this says, 'My God, if I'm thrown back on myself, and have to put up with what I put up with before. . . .' Then he says of the leader: 'You converted me, you snapped something, you gave me the light and I didn't feel that way anymore. You stopped the pain.'"

The self-analysis letters, rich in avowals of redemption and gratitude, support Dr. Cath's thesis.

"After meeting you I found out that I didn't no anything about love," wrote Odel Blackwell to Jones, "because you are all love. . . . I love you & Mother, and what you say do I will do it, because I no what ever you tell me to do, I can do it if I try."

"Jim Jones was the best friend I ever had," said Bea Orsot Grubbs, a survivor. "When I couldn't pay the rent once, he paid the rent. Nobody else ever did that, including my rich relatives."

Returning to the United States on an airplane two weeks after the massacre, Mrs. Grubbs, 52 years old, tried to explain why the year she spent in Jonestown was "the happiest of my life." "I never had the feeling of being treated different because I was a black woman," she said. "I was respected for my mind and what I could offer people as a whole. We lived in a cooperative community. We shared with each other, caring for people other than yourself. That was very fulfilling."

Last July, Mrs. Grubbs had written to Jones that "I would never betray you, no matter what. . . .I shall not beg for mercy either in the last moment. I shall proudly die for a proud reason." But Mrs. Grubbs was not called upon to put her loyalty to the ultimate test. She was 150 miles away, in Georgetown to keep a dental appointment, during the mass suicides.

As Jim Jones's message of love turned gradually to one of hate and fear, Grace and Tim Stoen, Alfred Cordell, Deborah Layton Blakey, Neva Sly and others grew disillusioned. But because they were committed followers who had entrusted their identities, as well as their financial resources, to his care—who had sacrificed homes, possessions, husbands and wives to their belief in a higher calling—breaking away was a complicated, painful process.

"Once people have made the commitment," Dr. Gaylin observes, "they've invested in the truth of that decision. They become frightened to go back on it. It's terrifying to go back."

"We always blamed ourselves for things that didn't seem right," Neva Sly remembered. "I think we suffered from a lack of confidence."

Jones seemed to have an answer for everything. His end-justifies-the-means philosophy accommodated most doubts. "He had a vision in his mind of a perfect world," Tim Stoen said, that "will come about only when people destroy their own egos from within and replace them with a collective ego. And in order to get people to do that you sometimes have to play tricks. . . . He may have to set you up and embarrass you: Have your spouse attack you in front of everybody so that you can think less of yourself. And after a while, because you think less of yourself, the instinct for self-preservation is more and more destroyed."

Jones dismissed protests against family separations on the grounds that personal alliances diminish concern for the oppressed. He explained his requests for self-incriminating documents as simple tests of loyalty; tests most were willing to take. "Oh, heavens, yes, I'd totally incriminate myself on any-thing," Mrs. Sly remembered. "I was loyal. I was dedicated. I believed. I totally believed in this cause. Why wouldn't I go through a loyalty test?"

Mr. Stoen said he agreed to sign a paper certifying that Jones had fathered his child because "I loved the man and I thought, O.K., his reason for asking me to do so was that if I ever defect from the organization, it would cause me embarrassment."

"You didn't know how to get away," said Grace Stoen. "You didn't know where to go. You didn't know who could help you. You always thought you would be found. And there were always these threats that you would be killed."

"Even though everyone is making good reports and making good fronts," a prophetic communard wrote last July, "we could be sliding downhill to sink." The slide would be rapid.

In the beginning, Jones had little trouble persuading his people to go to Jonestown. As Neva Sly recalls, "To me, my God, it was the greatest privilege in the world to get to go to Guyana. Gee whiz, to be able to work to build paradise! Whooo!"

Tim Stoen also remembers Jonestown with something like fondness. "Everything would run pretty happily when Jim was not around," he says of the three months he spent there in 1977. Deborah Layton Blakey also recalls working in the fields in the summer of 1977 and thinking, "Jonestown would be nice if Jim Jones weren't here."

But Jones was there. He had arrived that June, shortly after delivering his Golden Gate Bridge suicide speech and only days before the New West maga-zine article he so feared was published. He fled San Francisco telling Temple members there that he would be imprisoned for life if he did not do so.

"I came here with no feeling of a future," he later told a Guyanese inter-viewer. "Our movement was dead. If I didn't come here, our movement was finished. We would be destroyed in the U.S.A."

In Jonestown, Jones gained close to total control. He confiscated all pass-ports, and forbade the communards to leave the compound without permis-sion. Beatings, sexual humiliations, solitary confinement—all became com-monplace. By last September, according to testimony of former residents, all mail into and out of Jonestown was censored by a four-member committee. Five armed guards patrolled the commune each night to prevent defections.

But it was as the only source of news in the isolated jungle compound that Jones derived his final power over men's minds. At last he was able to paint a world entirely in hues of his own choosing. For hours on end, and sometimes all night, Jones used the camp loudspeakers to amplify his nightmare vision of a "fascist, racist, imperialist" United States determined to put black people in concentration camps and to destroy Jonestown. Money his followers had spent in the United States, he told them, had financed C.I.A. killings of black babies and of socialists all over the world. He expressed admiration for Charles Man-son and the kidnappers of former Italian Prime Minister Aldo Moro.

Disoriented by the isolation, by low-protein diets and little sleep, the people of Jonestown did not doubt their leader. By September 1977, the communards were starting their days by looking for mercenaries at the jungle's edge and finishing them with self-recriminations. "I feel so guilty," Carrie Langston wrote, "about the money I spent and the food and drinks. I sure didn't know I was helping to murder people."

To commit suicide as an individual, Jones would say, was terrible: You would be reborn into the world of 5,000 years ago and have to live 500 lifetimes just to get back to the 20th century. But a "revolutionary death" put one on a higher plane.

"If I could die," wrote Clifford Geig, expressing a common refrain, "I would like it to be a revolutionary death where I would take some enemies down with me. That would be the final goal of my life."

"I'll be glad to die for Communism," said Maryann Casanova. "I want to help make a world where no one has to be born in a capitalist system."

Eleven-year-old Mark Fields wrote to Jones last July that "if the capitalists came over the hill I'd just drink the potion as fast as I could do it. I wouldn't let the capitalists get me but if they did I'd endure it. I would not say a word. I'd take the pain and when I couldn't stand it anymore I'd pass out."

The attempt by Grace and Tim Stoen to regain custody of their 6-year-old son, know as John-John, hastened the denouement. Jones's rational and irrational fears came into sharp focus. By holding John-John hostage, Jones felt he could keep the Stoens quiet and punish them as well. (Mrs. Stoen says she did not take her son with her when she left the People's Temple in 1976 because she feared for his life. By the time her husband left the Temple, Jones had sent John-John to Guyana.)

In August 1977, the Stoens obtained a ruling from a California judge granting them custody and ordering Jones's appearance in court. By then, both Jones and the boy were in Guyana where—with the help of the affidavit Stoen had signed years before as an act of loyalty—Jones claimed to be the boy's natural father.

In September, Jeffrey Haas, an attorney representing the Stoens, arrived in Guyana. He succeeded in obtaining a bench warrant ordering the child removed from Jonestown. According to Deborah Blakey and Charles Garry, Jones's attorney, the issuance of the bench order led Jones to issue his first threat to destroy the Jonestown commune.

Mrs. Blakey, who was manning the People's Temple radio in San Francisco at the time, remembers that she was told by Jones "to get in touch with [Deputy Prime Minister Ptolemy] Reid, who was in the United States; to call him and tell him that unless something was done in Guyana, they'd have 1,100 people dead in Jonestown. They were all in a big circle. Jones said: 'O.K., listen, my people are with me.' You could hear them all saying 'Yeah!' in the background. You could hear them all the way to San Francisco.' "

"He freaked out," recalls Charles Garry, who spoke to Jones by telephone at the time. "He said, 'This child cannot go because he'll be ruined.' He said, 'We are all so solid that if something happens to any one of us, it's happening to all of us.' "

The Guyanese did not enforce the order for the child's removal, and Jones called off his suicide threat. Later he assured Garry that it had simply been a ploy.

But according to Mrs. Blakey, who came to Jonestown three months afterward, Jones issued similar threats on two other occasions when he felt threatened and under attack: once when Guyanese officials asked that the People's Temple doctor, Laurence E. Schacht, take his internship in a Georgetown hospital and again when the Guyanese asked to place a Guyanese teacher in the Jonestown school.

"If things didn't sound exactly the way he wanted them to be," Mrs. Blakey said, "he'd call for a 'black night' "—a term Jones converted to "white night" because he considered whites, not blacks, the enemy.

"One time, it was 3 or 4 in the morning," she said. "People had to jump out of their bunks, grab their kids and run up to the main pavilion. They took a head count. You'd give your name to this woman and the guards would go search the cabins. You stayed there 12 hours, maybe 20. He'd discuss how the mercenaries were coming. He'd throw out maybe five variables and ask what you'd rather do: Go to Africa and help the people there fight imperialism? Go to Russia? Go to Cuba? Somebody would say, 'No, no, let's stay here and fight it out to the death.' You never knew if you were going to live through it or not."

On one such night, according to Mrs. Blakey, after telling the group that the situation was hopeless, Jones told everyone to line up. They were all given small glasses containing a red liquid and told it was poison; they would be dead in 45 minutes. After the time had passed, Jones informed them that they had been through a loyalty test. Now he knew that the communards would do as they were told.

Mrs. Blakey says she had drunk the liquid that night because "the whole pavilion was surrounded by guards. You also knew that if it was not the real thing and you said, 'No,' and lived through it, you'd have your butt kicked severely. After a while, after you continually had these 'white nights,' after you'd seen your best friends beaten up and you were estranged from your family, after a while you just wanted to be dead."

Stephan Jones, the surviving son, says he spoke out against a mass suicide during a "white night" last May. "They're going to say we're fanatics," he told the group. "It's not going to be understood. But I got shut up. I got booed down by everybody."

He reports that his mother, Marceline Jones, also argued with Jones against a mass suicide, but only in private. "Mother would say, 'You can't kill 914 people. There are going to be people [left] alive, brain-damaged. It's going to be a horrible scene.' " But his father always countered that the only alternative was torture.

By all indications, Jones was deteriorating physically as well as mentally. Three months before the mass suicides, he asked Carlton B. Goodlett, a San Francisco physician, to come to Jonestown to examine him. Jones was a diabetic who had run a 103-degree fever for a month before the examination, Dr.

Goodlett said, adding that he suspected a rare, often fatal, but treatable fungal disease (progressive coccidioidomycosis). Jones promised the physician that he would enter the hospital after Representative Ryan's visit. Others, including Odell Rhodes, who knew the signs, said Jones was an amphetamine addict.

"I told myself I was looking at a man in decay," a reporter traveling with Ryan later recounted. At one point, he said, Jones babbled almost incoherently. "Threat of extinction! I wish I wasn't born at times. I understand love and hate. They are very close. . . . I do not believe in violence. I hate power. I hate money. All I want is peace. I'm not worried about my image. If we could just stop it, stop this fighting. But if we don't, I don't know what's going to happen to 1,200 lives here."

In a matter of hours, the world found out.

The Politics of Mandatory Retirement

In a decade that was characterized by legislative niggardliness, older persons achieved what some have called a "Magna Carta." The Retirement Act of 1978 made it illegal for most public and private employers to require the retirement of employees before age 70; and it prohibited mandatory retirement at any age for employees of the federal government. Some have interpreted this legislation as a "liberal" triumph—a kind of 1970s version of the 1960s civil rights legislation, for example. Others believe that the Retirement Act would not have become law had it not been for the economic crisis of the late 1970s. According to the latter view, the nation's declining economic fortunes could be reversed only if productivity were increased; and that meant doing away with rigid bureaucratic rules and regulations (including mandatory retirement) that limited individual efficiency.

The following documents, including excerpts from testimony given before congressional committees, should help explain this sudden act of generosity. What is the Schulz chart, "The Incidence of Mandatory Retirement," supposed to demonstrate? Does the Labor Department deal successfully with the employment impact of the legislation? On what grounds does big business (represented here by Jankowski of CBS) defend the institution of mandatory retirement? What does the Carter administration expect to gain from the elimination of mandatory retirement?

Statement of Donald E. Elisburg, Assistant Secretary for Employment Standards, Department of Labor, Accompanied by Carin Ann Clauss, Solicitor of Labor

Mr. ELISBURG. . . .As you know, human rights are a vital concern of this administration. When Secretary Marshall appeared before the Senate Human Resources Committee last January, after he had been nominated to be Secretary of Labor, he expressed his high priority on combating discrimination against people for any reason unrelated to their qualifications.

The Department of Labor is very much concerned about conditions in employment which result in the denial to individuals of the right to be considered on the basis of their ability to do the job. To stifle individual ability and productivity is to establish nonproductive economic and employment policies. It obviously costs society less when individuals are working than when they are not. In addition, when they are working they contribute to the production of goods and services.

Denial of equal employment opportunity flows from stereotypes and prejudices against one group or another. Ironically, these prejudices are in the nature of self-fulfilling prophecies because the overall denial of opportunity pushes whole segments of our society into the very status of second-class citizenship which the stereotypes presume. We must continually strive to dispel the myths which hinder individual accomplishment and waste human resources.

Senator [Jacob] JAVITS [Republican, New York]. . . .Now, to ask just a few questions. What about the issue of allegedly increasing unemployment if older workers are entitled to remain in the work force; will older workers deny opportunities for new entrants, or reentrants; what is the view of the Department?

Mr. ELISBURG. . . .I would like to ask our Solicitor, Carin Clauss, to respond to that.

Miss CLAUSS.: Senator, we have made some estimates, and these will be finalized, of course, in our report after the recess. But based on studies done by the Social Security Administration on how many people who are retired at 65 would like to continue working, we estimate—assuming that people will continue to work in the same percentage at 70 as they do at 65—that at most this will result in one tenth of 1 percent increase in the number of women in the work force.

Senator JAVITS. Number of women?

Miss CLAUSS. That is right and a two-tenths of 1 percent increase in the number of men in the work force, which comes out to something like 175,000

From U.S. Congress, Senate, Committee on Human Resources, Subcommittee on Labor, *Age Discrimination in Employment Amendments of 1977: Hearings on S. 1784,* To Amend the Age Discrimination in Employment Act of 1967 . . ., 95th Cong., 1st sess., July 26 and 27, 1977 (Washington, D. C., 1977), pp. 65–66, 70–71, 124–125, 129.

to 200,000 people. Now, I might point out that since November 1976, there has been an increase in the Nation's work force of 3 million, the number of new jobs that have been created. Since the administration came into office in January there has been an increase in public employment from 310,000 to 400,000—almost an increase of 100,000. In our summer youth program there has been an increase of close to 200,000; and the Youth Employment Act which has just recently passed with the help of this committee would increase jobs for young people, young adults, by 250,000 or 300,000. So, we do feel the administration has a number of proposals which will address the employment problems without necessitating excluding people of any one group to make room for others. . . .

Statement of Bert Seidman, Director of the Department of Social Security, AFL–CIO.

. . .It should be recognized that prohibition of mandatory retirement is no panacea and would do little to resolve the problems of most older workers. The legislation will benefit a small number of people who want to work beyond age 65 but do nothing to resolve the more serious problems faced by most older people. An effective full employment policy is the most important contribution that could be made toward the resolution of these problems.

It is difficult to expand job opportunities for older workers when the job market is tight for all. Such efforts will work only in a favorable economic framework, for older workers cannot be placed in jobs if those jobs do not exist. Economic growth and expansion, not abolition of mandatory retirement, are the key factors in keeping more older workers in the labor force.

In short, the greatest advance that could be made toward broader opportunities for employment of older workers would be a full employment economy. A program designed to provide jobs for older workers at the expense of other workers is not a satisfactory program. But neither should we attempt to relieve unemployment problems by excluding older people from the labor market. The burden of unemployment should not be borne by any single group. What is needed are jobs for all who want and need them—and that means older workers along with everyone else. . . .

Mandatory retirement at specified ages may or may not be wise social policy. But it is still practiced in all facets of economic life—business, government, pension plans, and collective bargaining. It may be unjust to force retirement on those who are healthy and want to continue working. It may be equally unjust to lay off younger workers with families to support and retain at work elderly workers who are eligible for social security benefits, a good private pension, and health care. Such hard choices are best handled through collective bargaining which can be tailored to and flexible enough to meet the myriad issues that are involved in such situations.

There is one special problem we wish to bring to your attention. We are confident that the members of this subcommittee will agree with us that voluntary organizations such as trade unions should have the right to determine the qualifications of their own elected officers, including any lower or upper age limitations. Therefore, we urge that if legislation is recommended barring mandatory retirement before a specified age, it should specifically exempt elected officers of trade unions. . . .

Senator JAVITS. Mr. Seidman, I must say that I find it extremely difficult to follow the argument you make that an antidiscrimination statute which is designed to protect the minority should have a collective bargaining exception. Now, if we are going to let collective bargaining wipe out the right of the minority, then we ourselves are supporting discrimination. In short, you say, the older worker should give way to the younger worker. That is true any time. You can do that when you are 45, 55, 65, or 75, and if that is the criterion, I must say I find it extremely difficult to follow how you justify an antidiscrimination statute against race or creed, but not against age. All we are dealing with is one of the shibboleths of our time. Somebody said 65. They probably should never have said it. How long do you keep your job? What kind of a person are you? How can you perform? . . .

Statement of Gene F. Jankowski, Vice-President, Administration, CBS, Inc.

Mr. JANKOWSKI. . . .Before [1960], as I mentioned in my testimony earlier on, there was no mandatory retirement policy [at CBS], but people went from year to year. The recent 1960 policy was put in when we discovered that people who were not competent enough to complete their job, and there were such people, wound up in constant squabbles which led us to put in a policy requiring everyone to plan on retiring at 65. We felt it was fair, despite the disadvantages. It was fair to all employees. They could plan better for their retirement, make better plans earlier on.

I would also like to point out that as far as CBS is concerned, of the 24,000 employees that we have in the United States, last year, we had age 65 reached by only 83 of those people. Only 83 retired last year.

Mr. [Congressman Claude] PEPPER. Who retired at 65?

Mr. JANKOWSKI. Yes, sir.

Mr. PEPPER. That was a question that was directed to Mr. Morris. If there are relatively so few, why maintain that discriminatory policy? You could certainly sift out the ones that should be permitted to remain in employment and those who shouldn't out of 83 people. You have to let people go from time to time for certain reasons, I suppose. I imagine you could find a way of determining when people should be requested to retire or when they shouldn't be.

From U.S., Congress, House, Select Committee on Aging, *Retirement Age Policies: Hearings before the Select Committee on Aging*, 95th Cong., 1st sess., March 16 and 17, 1977, 2 pts. (Washington, D. C., 1977), 1: 35–36.

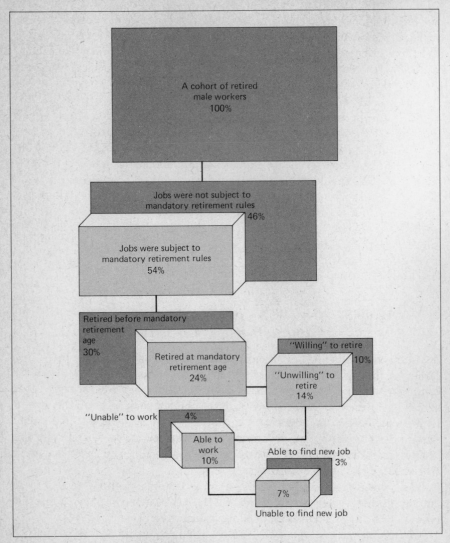

The Incidence of Mandatory Retirement. *From J. Schulz, "The Economics of Mandatory Retirement," Industrial Gerontology (Winter 1974), 5. Reprinted from Industrial Gerontology, Vol. I, No. 1, Winter, 1974, published © The National Council on the Aging, Inc.*

Mr. JANKOWSKI. I would like to point out, Mr. Chairman, that we do have exceptions. We do have people who stay over 65. We have some craftsmen, for example, in the Steinway Piano Co. who, because of the particular skills——

Mr. PEPPER. If you have exceptions, why have the rule? You are a very prestigious company and your retirement policy has influence upon many other companies in the country.

What this committee is concerned about is that what was an arbitrary retirement policy has gained general acceptance in government as well as industry; namely, when a person reaches a particular age, sometimes one age and sometimes another, but at some maximum arbitrarily imposed, a person is not given a chance to prove that he is an exception. Ordinarily, most of the plans are mandatory. If you have actually a program under which you do allow certain individuals ready, willing, and able to work to stay on, what particular criteria do you use when you examine one of the exceptions?

Mr. JANKOWSKI.   Capability for functioning.

Mr. PEPPER.   If you allow that rule to permit the exception, why don't you let that become the rule?

Mr. JANKOWSKI.   The advantages to the employee outweigh the disadvantages.

Mr. PEPPER.   You are not his keeper. You are not the one to tell him what is best for him, are you? Isn't that a decision that he should make?

Mr. JANKOWSKI.   As I stated earlier, Mr. Chairman, I don't think that the age of 65 is ideal. We are continually looking for ways to improve the whole retirement system. That, by the way, is one of the reasons why Holt, Rinehart, and Winston is having this conference next month. We think that many of the problems are more deep-seated than just a mandatory retirement age. The problem really involves the whole sociology of our country.

We Haven't Come a Long Way, and Don't Call Me Baby

A Rally in Washington, D.C., November 1971. The women's protest movement was one of several that successfully bridged the gap between the 1960s and 1970s. What conclusions can you draw from this photograph about the woman's movement—its strengths and its weaknesses? *Photo by Dennis Brack from Black Star.*

A Cultural Mirror

Most of the funds for the National Gallery's East Building were donated by Paul and Bunny Mellon, who on the last day of May 1978 served as hosts to donors, sponsors, and art world figures honoring the architect, I. M. Pei. At one point in the proceedings, someone said to Pei, "You have something here very classical, very noble, but not tyrannical or ponderous." "Thanks," Pei replied. "I didn't want it to be a Lincoln Memorial. Nor a Reichstag." Henry Mitchell, reporting the event for the *Washington Post*, wrote: "What a difference a little glory makes. For the first time, many thought, the city has a building that does not so much interpret this century as give stature to it. Our daily lives—the snafu of airports, the botch of subways, the abrasion of petty concerns—all this is transformed. The building tells every citizen of the town that theirs is no mean city, and their lives are no mean lives, but fit for a fabric of astonishing richness and grace."

Interior View of the East Building, National Gallery, Washington, D.C. Designed by I. M. Pei, the building was opened in 1978. *National Gallery.*

**Exterior View of the East Building,
National Gallery, Washington, D.C.**
National Gallery.

Close Encounters

Released in 1977, *Star Wars* was perhaps the most important media event of the entire decade. The largest total audience in the nation's history saw this George Lucas film in which Luke Skywalker, Princess Leia, and a ragtag collection of space creatures prevent absolute evil (Darth Vader) from establishing dominance over the universe. It was soon followed by another film that became almost as popular. In *Close Encounters of the Third Kind*, the protagonists are irresistibly drawn to the Devil's Tower in the Rocky Mountains, where they witness the awe-inspiring landing of a brilliantly illuminated spacecraft (see photograph). Why were Americans so attracted to such films? Did *Star Wars* and *Close Encounters* invoke similar, or different, feelings?

Richard Nixon:
A Self-Portrait

From humble origins, Richard Nixon fashioned a career that spanned, and in many ways defined, a quarter-century of American political history. He made a name for himself on the House Un-American Activities Committee in the 1940s, then went on to the Senate and, in 1952, to the vice presidency (after averting the loss of the nomination with the famous Checkers speech). Two major defeats—at the hands of John Kennedy in 1960 and over the California governorship in 1962—did not deter this aggressive man, who was proud of his ability to respond to crises. In 1968, he achieved his goal and won the presidency.

If Richard Nixon was the apotheosis of the self-made man, living evidence of the vitality of the American dream, his resignation over Watergate had implications which transcended one man and one presidency.

Nixon made the following statement before leaving the White House on August 9, 1974. How did the president handle the trauma of this event?

How did he define his Watergate crimes and the nightmare that was happening to him?

Members of the Cabinet, members of the White House Staff, all of our friends here:
I think the record should show that this is one of those spontaneous things that we always arrange whenever the President comes in to speak, and it will be so reported in the press, and we don't mind, because they have to call it as they see it.

But on our part, believe me, it is spontaneous.

You are here to say goodby to us, and we don't have a good word for it in English—the best is *au revoir*. We will see you again.

I just met with the members of the White House staff, you know, those who serve here in the White House day in and day out, and I asked them to do what I ask all of you to do to the extent that you can and, of course, are requested to do so: to serve our next President as you have served me and previous Presidents—because many of you have been here for many years—with devotion and dedication, because this office, great as it is, can only be as great as the men and women who work for and with the President.

This house, for example—I was thinking of it as we walked down this hall, and I was comparing it to some of the great houses of the world that I have been in. This isn't the biggest house. Many, and most, in even smaller countries, are much bigger. This isn't the finest house. Many in Europe, particularly, and in China, Asia, have paintings of great, great value, things that we just don't have here and, probably, will never have until we are 1,000 years old or older.

But this is the best house. It is the best house, because it has something far more important than numbers of people who serve, far more important than numbers of rooms or how big it is, far more important than numbers of magnificent pieces of art.

This house has a great heart, and that heart comes from those who serve. I was rather sorry they didn't come down. We said goodby to them upstairs. But they are really great. And I recall after so many times I have made speeches, and some of them pretty tough, yet, I always come back, or after a hard day—and my days usually have run rather long—I would always get a lift from them, because I might be a little down but they always smiled. . . .

I am proud of this Cabinet. I am proud of all the members who have served in our Cabinet. I am proud of our sub-Cabinet. I am proud of our White House Staff. As I pointed out last night, sure, we have done some things wrong in this Administration, and the top man always takes the responsibility, and I have never ducked it. But I want to say one thing: We can be proud of it—5 ½ years. No man or no woman came into this Administration and left it with more of this world's goods than when he came in. No man or no woman ever

From Richard Nixon, "Remarks on Departure from the White House, August 9, 1974," *Public Papers of the President of the United States, Richard Nixon, January 1 to August 9, 1974* (Washington, D.C.: Government Printing Office, 1975), pp. 630–632).

profited at the public expense or the public till. That tells something about you.

Mistakes, yes. But for personal gain, never. You did what you believed in. Sometimes right, sometimes wrong. And I only wish that I were a wealthy man—at the present time, I have got to find a way to pay my taxes—[laughter]—and if I were, I would like to recompense you for the sacrifices that all of you have made to serve in government.

But you are getting something in government—and I want you to tell this to your children, and I hope the Nation's children will hear it, too—something in government service that is far more important than money. It is a cause bigger than yourself. It is the cause of making this the greatest nation in the world, the leader of the world, because without our leadership, the world will know nothing but war, possibly starvation or worse, in the years ahead. With our leadership it will know peace, it will know plenty.

We have been generous, and we will be more generous in the future as we are able to. But most important, we must be strong here, strong in our hearts, strong in our souls, strong in our belief, and strong in our willingness to sacrifice, as you have been willing to sacrifice, in a pecuniary way, to serve in government.

There is something else I would like for you to tell your young people. You know, people often come in and say, "What will I tell my kids?" They look at government and say, sort of a rugged life, and they see the mistakes that are made. They get the impression that everybody is here for the purpose of feathering his nest. That is why I made this earlier point—not in this Administration, not one single man or woman.

And I say to them, there are many fine careers. This country needs good farmers, good businessmen, good plumbers, good carpenters.

I remember my old man. I think that they would have called him sort of a little man, common man. He didn't consider himself that way. You know what he was? He was a streetcar motorman first, and then he was a farmer, and then he had a lemon ranch. It was the poorest lemon ranch in California, I can assure you. He sold it before they found oil on it. [Laughter] And then he was a grocer. But he was a great man, because he did his job, and every job counts up to the hilt, regardless of what happens.

Nobody will ever write a book, probably, about my mother. Well, I guess all of you would say this about your mother—my mother was a saint. And I think of her, two boys dying of tuberculosis, nursing four others in order that she could take care of my older brother for 3 years in Arizona, and seeing each of them die, and when they died, it was like one of her own.

Yes, she will have no books written about her. But she was a saint.

Now, however, we look to the future. I had a little quote in the speech last night from T.R. As you know, I kind of like to read books. I am not educated, but I do read books—[laughter]—and the T.R. quote was a pretty good one.

Here is another one I found as I was reading, my last night in the White House, and this quote is about a young man. He was a young lawyer in New York. He had married a beautiful girl, and they had a lovely daughter, and then suddenly she died, and this is what he wrote. This was in his diary.

He said, "She was beautiful in face and form and lovelier still in spirit. As a flower she grew and as a fair young flower she died. Her life had been always in the sunshine. There had never come to her a single great sorrow. None ever knew her who did not love and revere her for her bright and sunny temper and her saintly unselfishness. Fair, pure and joyous as a maiden, loving, tender and happy as a young wife. When she had just become a mother, when her life seemed to be just begun and when the years seemed so bright before her, then by a strange and terrible fate death came to her. And when my heart's dearest died, the light went from my life forever."

That was T.R. in his twenties. He thought the light had gone from his life forever—but he went on. And he not only became President but, as an ex-President, he served his country, always in the arena, tempestuous, strong, sometimes wrong, sometimes right, but he was a man.

And as I leave, let me say, that is an example I think all of us should remember. We think sometimes when things happen that don't go the right way; we think that when you don't pass the bar exam the first time—I happened to, but I was just lucky; I mean, my writing was so poor the bar examiner said, "We have just got to let the guy through." We think that when someone dear to us dies, we think that when we lose an election, we think that when we suffer a defeat that all is ended. We think, as T.R. said, that the light had left his life forever.

Not true. It is only a beginning, always. The young must know it; the old must know it. It must always sustain us, because the greatness comes not when things go always good for you, but the greatness comes and you are really tested, when you take some knocks, some disappointments, when sadness comes, because only if you have been in the deepest valley can you ever know how magnificent it is to be on the highest mountain.

And so I say to you on this occasion, as we leave, we leave proud of the people who have stood by us and worked for us and served this country.

We want you to be proud of what you have done. We want you to continue to serve in government, if that is your wish. Always give your best, never get discouraged, never be petty; always remember, others may hate you, but those who hate you don't win unless you hate them, and then you destroy yourself.

And so, we leave with high hopes, in good spirit, and with deep humility, and with very much gratefulness in our hearts. I can only say to each and every one of you, we come from many faiths, we pray perhaps to different gods—but really the same God in a sense—but I want to say for each and every one of you, not only will we always remember you, not only will we always be grateful to you but always you will be in our hearts and you will be in our prayers.

Thank you very much.*

---

*NOTE: The President spoke at 9:36 A.M. in the East Room at the White House. His remarks were broadcast live on nationwide radio and television.

About the Editors

WILLIAM GRAEBNER is Professor of History at the State University of New York at Fredonia. He received his B.A. from Stanford University in 1965 and his M.A. and Ph.D. from the University of Illinois in 1966 and 1970. Professor Graebner received the Frederick Jackson Turner Award from the Organization of American Historians for *Coal-Mining Safety in the Progressive Period: The Political Economy of Reform*. Another book, *A History of Retirement: The Meaning and Function of an American Institution, 1885–1978*, was published in 1980. He is currently working on a history of democratic social engineering in twentieth-century America.

LEONARD RICHARDS is Professor of History at the University of Massachusetts at Amherst. Currently chairman of the Department of History, he was awarded the 1970 Beveridge Prize by the American Historical Association for his book, *"Gentlemen of Property and Standing": Anti-Abolition Mobs in Jacksonian America*. He is also the author of *The Advent of American Democracy*. Professor Richards is now writing a book on John Quincy Adams and antislavery politics, and is planning another book on the social history of industrial New England.

A Note on the Type

The text of this book was set in Elegante, a CRT version of the type face Palatino, a type face designed by the noted German typographer Hermann Zapf. Named after Giovanbattista Palatino, a writing master of Renaissance Italy, Palatino was the first of Zapf's type faces to be introduced to America. The first designs for the face were made in 1948, and the fonts for the complete face were issued between 1950 and 1952. Like all Zapf-designed type faces, Palatino is beautifully balanced and exceedingly readable.

Composed by Lehigh-Rocappi, provided by Random House, Inc.
Printed and bound by R.R. Donnelley.